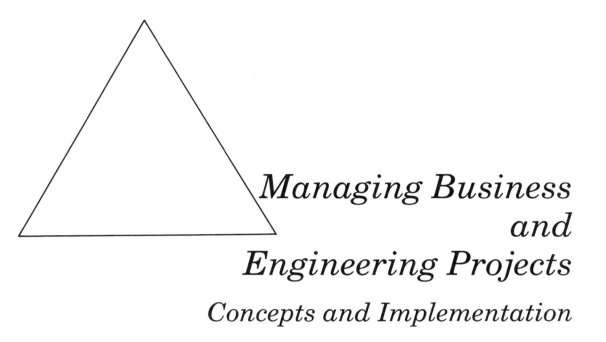

Managing Business and Engineering Projects

Concepts and Implementation

JOHN M. NICHOLAS

Loyola University of Chicago

Prentice Hall, Upper Saddle River, New Jersey 07458

Library of Congress Cataloging-in-Publication Data

Nicholas, John M.
  Managing business and engineering projects: concepts and
implementation/John M. Nicholas.
      p.   cm.
  Includes bibliographical references.
  ISBN 0-13-551854-7
  1. Industrial project management.   I. Title.
HD69.P75N53 1990
658.4'04--dc20   89-37577
                                                  CIP

Editorial/production supervision and
  interior design: *bookworks*
Cover design: *Bruce Kenselaar*
Manufacturing Buyer: *Laura Crossland*
Cover photo created by designer Steven
  Kuhn at ACCM Studios, Englewood, NJ.

© 1990 by Prentice-Hall, Inc.
A Simon & Schuster Company
Upper Saddle River, New Jersey 07458

Printed in the United States of America

10   9   8   7

ISBN 0-13-551854-7

Prentice-Hall International (UK) Limited, *London*
Prentice-Hall of Australia Pty. Limited, *Sydney*
Prentice-Hall Canada Inc., *Toronto*
Prentice-Hall Hispanoamericana, S.A., *Mexico*
Prentice-Hall of India Private Limited, *New Delhi*
Prentice-Hall of Japan, Inc., *Tokyo*
Simon & Schuster Asia Pte. Ltd., *Singapore*
Editora Prentice-Hall do Brasil, Ltda., *Rio de Janeiro*

To Sharry, Julia, Joshua, and Abigail

Contents

SECTION IV SYSTEMS AND PROCEDURES

CONTENTS

CONTENTS

Preface

This book is in response to a growing need for better project management. Modern technology and competitive environments are becoming increasingly more "chaotic." New and unique problems continuously arise calling for innovative, creative, and relevant solutions; domestic and international markets are rapidly expanding, and with them a heightened awareness of "quality" issues and the need for greater responsiveness to customer wants and needs. In fiercely competitive situations and faced with limited resources, managers search for ways to solve problems and satisfy needs within tight scheduling and budgetary constraints. As solutions to social and technological problems become more complex, there is greater need for teamwork and the combined expertise of multiple disciplines. In recent years, awareness about and increased emphasis toward satisfying customer requirements, and the role of innovation, quality, and teamwork in gaining competitive advantage have been driven home by growing competition from overseas.

Much of the influence of modern technology and competitive environments directly impacts on the conduct of projects—whether they are projects to develop products and equipment that effectively compete in domestic and international markets, projects to implement technology that satisfies increasing demands for energy, housing, transportation, communication, scientific knowledge, and recreation, or projects to find solutions to pressing world problems such as pollution and hunger. Of course, the conduct of projects, and that they may be *effective*, argues for better management of projects—being able to bring together people and groups with diverse knowledge and skills to develop and implement solutions that fulfill customer and societal needs within limitations of capital, time, and scarce resources.

Associated with the need for better project management is the growing need to *train* managers in project management. In the past, and still today, project managers were largely those who had demonstrated some exceptional competence, though not necessarily in a management capacity. If you were a good architect, engineer, systems analyst, or accountant, eventually you would be promoted to project manager; then, presumably, you would pick up management skills somewhere along the way. The flaw in this should be evident because project management calls for a broad range of skills—managerial, leadership, and interpersonal skills—much different from skills associated with the technology of the particular project. Also, there is no compelling reason to presume that the project environment alone will provide the opportunity for someone to pick up the "right" management skills.

As a text and handbook, this book is about the right project management skills. It is for university students—advanced undergraduates and graduates—but it is also for practicing managers in business and engineering. As the title says, this book is about "concepts *and* implementation," so the topics in it are meant to be applied. It covers the big picture about project management—origins, applications, and philosophy—and the nitty-gritty, how-to steps. It describes the usual project management topics of PERT/CPM, scheduling, budgeting, and control, but it emphasizes the human side of project management too.

Why a book on managing business *and* engineering projects? The title is intended to draw the attention of two audiences, either of which might ignore a more narrow title. In my experience, most engineers (and other technical specialists like architects, systems analysts, chemists, etc.) have little or no management training. This book, which includes many technical project examples, provides somewhat broad exposure to relevant business concepts and management specifics to help this audience get started in project management.

This book is also intended for audiences involved in all those other product-development, marketing, and related projects that people think of as "business projects." It makes frequent reference to business projects and provides examples. Just as engineering and technical students seldom get management training as part of their formal education, so business students seldom get training about technical endeavors. For business students, this book not only gives them an idea of how "business" projects are conducted, but also what happens in engineering and other kinds of technical projects.

In a sense, most technical projects *are* business projects too, since they involve making numerous business related decisions. Still, complex engineering/development efforts involve aspects and stages different from non-engineering projects. In this book a general scheme called the Systems Development Cycle is employed to describe all projects and show their commonalities as well as differences.

This book is the outgrowth of more than a decade of teaching project management at Loyola University of Chicago, preceded by my several years of experience in both "engineering projects"—including design and flight test work in the aircraft industry, and "business projects" such as productivity improvement programs and information systems development in banking. During my work experience, I developed not only an appreciation for the technical side of project management—systems and procedures for planning, scheduling, budgeting, and control, but also for the organizational and human side too. I saw the benefits of good communication, trust, and teamwork on project outcomes, as well as the costs of conflict and emotional stress. The most successful projects were usually those in which trust, communication, and teamwork flourished, regardless of the formal planning and control systems in place. This book largely reflects these personal experiences and learnings. Of course, the book considers much more that my own efforts or personal experiences. To cover topics in a more general sense I also relied on the works of many other authors.

ACKNOWLEDGMENTS

Like most projects, writing this book involved the effort of numerous individuals and organizations, and to them I want to extend an acknowledgement. First I want to thank Cary Morgen and Louis Schwartzman—my research assistants, and Drs. Harold Dyck and Enrique Venta—my friends and colleagues, for their review, suggestions, and criticisms. Seven individuals served as reviewers for early drafts and provided dozens of helpful suggestions; these include: Richard Discenza, University of Colorado at Colorado Springs; Richard E. Gunther, California State University at Northridge; William N. Ledbetter, Auburn University; David A. Lopez, University of Washington; John Schank, George Mason University; Charles W.N. Thompson, Northwestern University; and Burton Dean, San Jose State University.

I am grateful to all of them; however, one in particular stands out, Charlie Thompson: he helped to shape this book in many ways, and much of his philosophy and teachings are reflected here. Also, I want to thank Gustave J. Rath of Northwestern University for his (unknown to him) many contributions to this book. A few other people also deserve mention and thanks: Sharon Tylus, Debbie Gillespie, Elaine Strnad, and Paul Flugel for assisting with seeming countless revisions, and Joan Schwartz of SRA, Inc. for a kind favor.

The following software companies were gracious in giving permission for carte blanche use of materials: Breakthrough Software Division of Symantec Corporation, Metier Management Systems, Inc., Microsoft Corporation, Primavera Systems, Inc., and Project Software & Development, Inc.

I am also indebted to the School of Business Administration at Loyola University of Chicago and the James A. Kemper Foundation for providing financial support, and particularly to Drs. Donald Meyer and Samuel Ramenofsky for other kinds of assistance that made it possible for me to pursue this "project."

Sharry, my wife, also gets special thanks. She read the entire text and provided numerous helpful suggestions, mostly to reduce the amount of "techno-jargon" I used. If this book is even slightly more readable, it is largely because of her.

There are many other colleagues, students, and friends, too numerous to mention, who gave me support and encouragement, and to them I say thank you. Despite the helpful intentions of many and my own best efforts, there are still likely to be mistakes or omissions; I had final say, so for these I accept full responsibility.

John M. Nicholas

chapter 1

INTRODUCTION

project (praj' ekt, ikt) n. a proposal of something to be done; plan; scheme 2. an organized undertaking; specif., *a*) a special unit of work, research, etc., as in school, a laboratory, etc., *b*) an extensive public undertaking, as in conservation, construction, etc.

Webster's New World Dictionary

1.1 IN THE BEGINNING...

Sometime around the third millennium B.C., workers on the Great Pyramid of Cheops set the last stone in place. Certainly they must have felt jubilant for this event represented a major milestone in one of mankind's grandest undertakings. Although much of their technology is still a mystery, the enormity and quality of the finished product remains a marvel. Despite the lack of sophisticated machinery, the ancient Egyptians were able to raise and fit some 2,300,000 stone blocks, weighing 2 to 70 tons apiece, into a structure the height of a modern 40-story building. Each facing stone was set against the next with an accuracy of .04 inch, and the base, which covers 13 acres, deviates less than one inch from level (Figure 1–1).[1]

Equally as staggering was the number of workers involved. To quarry the stones and transport them down the Nile, about 100,000 laborers were levied. In addition, about 40,000 skilled masons and attendants were employed in preparing and laying the blocks and erecting or dismantling the ramps. Public works were essential to keep this population employed and fed, and it is estimated that no less than 150,000 women and children had to be housed and fed also.[2]

Figure 1–1.   The Great Pyramid of Cheops, an early (circa 2500 B.C.) large-scale project.

But just as mind boggling was the managerial ability of the Egyptians—the planning, organizing, and controlling that were exercised throughout the 20-year duration of the project. Francis Barber, a 19th century American naval attaché and pyramid scholar, concluded that:

> it must have taken the organizational capacity of a genius to plan all the work, to lay it out, to provide for emergencies and accidents, to see that the men in the quarries, on the boats and sleds, and in the mason's and smithies shops were all continuously and usefully employed, that the means of transportation was ample,…that the water supply was ample,…and that the sick reliefs were on hand.[3]

Building the Great Pyramid is what we today would call a large-scale project. But even it was not the first large-scale project; throughout the earliest historic records there is abundant evidence of massive human works and of the managerial planning and control needed to accomplish them. The Bible describes projects which required orchestration of thousands of people and the transport and utilization of enormous quantities of materials. Worthy of note are the managerial and leadership accomplishments of Moses. The scriptural account of the exodus of the Hebrews from the bondage of the Egyptians gives some perspective on the preparation, organization, and execution of this tremendous undertaking. Supposedly, Moses did a magnificent job of personnel selection, training, organization, and delegation of authority.[4] The famed ruler Solomon, among other accomplishments, was the "manager" of numerous great construction projects. He transformed the battered ruins of many ancient cities and crude shanty towns into powerful fortifications. With his wealth and the help of Phoenician artisans, Solomon built the Temple in Jerusalem. Seven years went into the construction of the Temple, after which Solomon built a palace for himself that took 13 more years to complete. He employed a work force of 30 thousand Israelites to fell trees and import timber from the forests of Lebanon.[5] That was almost 3,000 years ago.

With later civilizations, most notably the Greeks and Romans, the number of activities requiring extensive planning and organizing escalated. These societies undertook extensive municipal and government works programs such as street paving, water supply, and sewers. To facilitate their military campaigns and commercial interests, the Romans constructed networks of highways and roads throughout Europe, Asia Minor, Palestine, and northern Africa so that all roads would "lead to Rome." The civilizations of Renaissance Europe and the Far East undertook river engineering, construction of canals, dams, locks, and port and harbor facilities. With the spread of modern religions, construction of churches, temples, monasteries, mosques, and massive urban cathedrals was added to the list of projects. The remains of aqueducts, bridges, temples, palaces, fortifications, and other large structures throughout the Mediterranean and China testify to the ancients' occupation with large-scale projects.

With the advent of industrialization and electricity, the projects of mankind took on increasing complexity. Projects for the construction of railroads, electrical and hydroelectrical power facilities, subways, and factories became commonplace. In recent times, research and applications of atomic energy, computers, communications, missile defense systems, and transportation have spurred different, more complex kinds of project activity.

As long as mankind does things, there will be projects. Many projects of the future will be similar to those in the past. Others will be vastly different either in terms of increased scale of effort or more advanced technology. Representative of the latter are two projects that are currently underway, the trans-English Channel tunnel and the NASA space station. Each will require tremendous resources and take at least a decade to complete. The space station (Figure 1–2) will require new technologies, many of which have yet to be developed.

1.2 WHAT IS A PROJECT?

From these few examples, it is clear that mankind has been involved in project activities for a long time. But why are these works considered "projects" while other human activities, such as planting and harvesting a crop, stocking a warehouse, issuing payroll checks, or manufacturing a product, are not?

What *is* a project? This is a question we will cover in much detail later. Just for an introduction though, some characteristics will be listed that warrant classifying an activity as a project. They center on the purpose, complexity, uniqueness, unfamiliarity, stake, impermanence, and life cycle of the activity:[6]

1. A project involves a single, definable purpose, end product or result, usually specified in terms of cost, schedule, and performance requirements.

Figure 1–2.   The NASA space station, a large-scale project of the future. (Photo courtesy of NASA)

2. Projects cut across organizational lines since they need to utilize skills and talents from multiple professions and organizations. Project complexity often arises from the complexity of advanced technology which relies on task interdependencies, and may introduce new and unique problems.

3. Every project is unique in that it requires doing something different than was done previously. Even in "routine" projects such as home construction, variables such as terrain, access, zoning laws, labor market, public services and local utilities make each project different. A project is a one time activity, never to be exactly repeated again.

4. Given that a project differs from what was previously done, it also involves unfamiliarity. It may encompass new technology and, for the organization undertaking the project, possess significant elements of uncertainty and risk. So the organization usually has something at stake when doing a project. The activity may call for special effort because failure would jeopardize the organization or its goals.

5. Projects are temporary activities. An ad hoc organization of personnel, material, and facilities is assembled to accomplish a goal, usually within a scheduled time frame; once the goal is achieved, the organization is disbanded or reconfigured to begin work on a new goal.

6. Finally, a project is the *process* of working to achieve a goal; during the process, projects pass through several distinct phases, called the *project life cycle*. The tasks, people, organizations, and other resources change as the project moves from one phase to the next.

The organization structure and resource expenditure slowly build with each succeeding phase, peak, and then decline as the project nears completion.

The examples described earlier are for familiar kinds of projects such as construction (pyramid), research (atomic energy), or some combination (space station). Yet other, more commonplace endeavors are also projects. Weddings, remodeling a home, and moving to another house are certainly projects for the families involved. Company audits, major litigations, corporate relocations and mergers are also projects, as are new product development and system implementation efforts. Military campaigns also meet the criteria of projects; they are temporary, unique efforts directed toward a specific goal. The Normandy Invasion, June 6, 1944, is a good (perhaps the ultimate) example:

> The technical ingenuity and organizational skill that made the landings possible was staggering. The invasion armada included nearly 5000 ships of all descriptions protected by another 900 warships. The plan called for landing 150,000 troops and 1500 tanks on the Normandy coast *in the first 48 hours.* There were large-scale air operations with bombers, gliders, paratroopers, and fighter support. There was PLUTO, the Pipe Line Under the Ocean, to bring the flood of petroleum that the armies would need. And there was Mulberry Harbor. Since the French ports were not large enough to handle the traffic anticipated to follow the invasion (12000 tons of stores and 2500 vehicles *per day*), the idea evolved to tow two monstrous breakwaters and floating quays (Mulberries) across the English Channel, each making a complete port the size of Dover.[7]

Most artistic endeavors are projects. Composing a song or symphony, writing a novel, or making a sculpture are one-person projects. The unusual (and somewhat controversial) works of the artist Christo—draping portions of the Grand Canyon, several islands in Biscayne Bay, and 1,000,000 square feet of Australian coastline with colored plastic—are projects too, but bigger. So is the making of motion pictures, whether they are home movies or the releases of major production studios. Some large artistic projects have also involved the skills of many engineers and builders: Mount Rushmore, the Eiffel Tower, and the Statue of Liberty (discussed later) are examples.

Many efforts at saving human life and recovering from man-made or natural disasters become projects. Three examples are the massive cleanup following the Soviet nuclear accident at Chernobyl, and the rescue and salvage operations following disastrous earthquakes in Mexico City and Soviet Armenia.

Figure 1–3 shows generalized project endeavors and some examples of well-known projects (Apollo, Panama Canal, ...). Notice the diversity in the kinds of efforts. The figure shows about where projects fall with respect to the degree of complexity and uncertainty involved. Complexity is roughly measured by magnitude of the effort, number of groups and organizations that need to be coordinated, and diversity in skills or expertise needed to accomplish the work. Time and resource commitments tend to increase with complexity.

Uncertainty is measured roughly by the difficulty in predicting the final outcome in terms of the dimensions of *time, cost,* and *technical performance.* In most projects there is some uncertainty in one or two dimensions, at least in the initial stages of planning (e.g.,

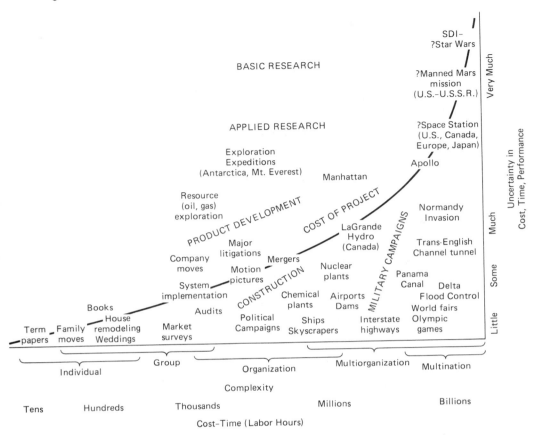

Figure 1–3.   A typology of projects.

weddings and world fairs). The most complex projects have uncertainty in all three (e.g., the space station).

Generally, the more often something is done, the less uncertainty there is to doing it. This is simply because people learn by doing and so improve their efforts—the "learning curve" concept. Projects that are very similar to previous others and about which there is abundant knowledge have lower uncertainty. These are found in the lower portion of Figure 1–3 (e.g., weddings, highways, dams, system implementation). As manned missions to Mars become frequent, they too will move down the uncertainty scale.

The cost curve indicates that the expense of projects increases roughly in proportion to both complexity and uncertainty. Cost, represented in terms of time or economic value, is at the level of tens or hundreds of labor hours for projects with low complexity and uncertainty, but increases to millions and billions of hours for projects with the greatest complexity and uncertainty.

When the uncertainty of a project drops to nearly zero, and when it is repeated a large number of times, then the effort is usually no longer considered a project. For example, building a skyscraper is definitely a project, but mass construction of prefabricated homes more closely resembles an assembly line than a project. Admiral Byrd's exploratory flight to the South Pole was a project, but modern daily supply flights to Antarctic bases are not. When (far in the future) tourists begin taking chartered excursions to Mars, trips there will no longer be considered projects either. They will just be ordinary scheduled operations.

In all cases, projects involve organizations which, after target goals have been accomplished, go on to do something else (construction companies) or are disbanded (Admiral Byrd's crew, the Mars exploration team). In contrast, repetitive, high certainty activities (prefabricated housing, supply flights and tourist trips to Antarctica or Mars) are performed by permanent organizations which do the same thing over and over, with little change in operations other than rescheduling. That projects differ greatly from repetitive efforts requires that they be managed differently.

1.3 PROJECT MANAGEMENT: THE NEED

Although mankind has been involved in projects since the beginning of recorded history, obviously the nature of projects and the environment have changed. Modern projects are subject to greater technical complexity and require greater diversity of skills. Managers are faced with the problem of putting together and directing large temporary organizations while being subjected to constrained resources, limited time schedules, and environmental uncertainty. To cope with new, more complex kinds of activities and greater uncertainty, new forms of project organization and new practices of management have evolved.

Two examples of modern, complex activities that required new management practices and organization are the Manhattan Project to develop the first atomic bomb and the Apollo Space Program to put a man on the moon. Compared to earlier undertakings, projects such as these were not only unparalleled in terms of technical difficulty and organizational complexity, but also in terms of the strict requirements circumscribing them. In ancient times, project "requirements" were more flexible. If the Pharaohs needed more workers, then more slaves or more of the general population was conscripted. If funding ran out during construction of a Renaissance cathedral, the work was stopped until more money could be raised from the congregation (indeed, this is one reason many cathedrals took decades to complete). If a king ran out of money while building a palace, he simply raised taxes. In other cases where additional money could not be raised, more workers could not be found, or the project could not be delayed, then the scale of effort or the quality of workmanship was simply reduced to accommodate the constraints. There are many projects of which nothing remains simply because the work was shoddy and could not withstand the rigors of time.

In projects like Manhattan and Apollo, requirements are not so flexible. First, both projects were subject to severe time constraints. Manhattan, undertaken during World War II, required that the atomic bomb be developed in the shortest time possible, preferably ahead of the Nazis; Apollo, undertaken in the early 1960s, had to be finished by 1970 to fulfill President Kennedy's goal of landing a man on the moon and returning him safely to earth "before the decade is out." For the sake of secrecy, the Manhattan Project restricted the informed personnel to a relative few. Both projects involved advanced research and development and explored new areas of science and engineering. In neither case could technical performance requirements be compromised to compensate for limitations in time, funding, or other resources; to do so would increase the risk to undertakings that were already very risky.

Another more typical example of an activity which needed new management practices is Company Alpha's development of "Product X." This hypothetical example is representative of the kind of new product development effort that companies everywhere must do to remain competitive, indeed, to survive. All products have a limited life; either improved products replace them or the purpose they serve is eliminated. In the past, Company Alpha had relied upon trial and error to come up with new products: in essence, whatever worked was used again; whatever failed was discarded. In recent years, one of Company Alpha's divisions had begun to lose market share to competitors. Even though the division had had several innovative concepts on the drawing board, it lost out because it was too slow to move them into the marketplace. Alpha was now considering development of Product X, a promising, but radically new idea. To translate it from concept to product would require the involvement of engineers and technicians from several Alpha divisions. Extensive marketing analysis would be needed to establish how best to introduce it. As is typical in product development, time was of the essence. Before approving the budget, Company Alpha management wanted assurances that Product X could be introduced early enough to put it well ahead of the competition. It was apparent that the division would need a more efficient means to manage development and marketing of the product.

Complex efforts such as these defy traditional management approaches for planning, organization, and control. The three examples above are representative of activities that require modern methods of project management and organization to fulfill difficult technological or market-related performance goals in spite of severe limitations on time and resources.

As a distinct area of management practice, project management is still a new idea, and its methods are still unknown to many experienced managers. Only 30 years ago, its usage was restricted largely to the defense, aerospace, and construction industries. Today, project management is being applied in a wide variety of industries and organizations, although its application still lags far behind its potential. Originally developed and applied in large-scale, complex technological projects such as Apollo, project management techniques are applicable to any project-type activities, regardless of size or technology. Modern project management would have been as useful to early Egyptian and Renaissance builders as it is now to present day contractors, engineers, and systems specialists.

1.4 RESPONSE TO A CHANGING ENVIRONMENT

Project management arose in response to the need for a managerial approach which could deal with the problems and take advantage of the opportunities of modern society. Three salient characteristics distinguish modern society from earlier periods of history: interdependency, complexity, and rapid, radical change. The challenges and problems of modern society involve risk and uncertainty arising from numerous interacting forces and variables, rapidly changing technology, rising costs, increasing competition, frequent resource shortages, numerous interest groups and their opposing views about the best course of action.[8]

Project management is a departure from the management of simpler ongoing, repeated operations where the market and technology tend to be more predictable, where there is greater certainty about anticipated outcomes, and where fewer parties or organizations are involved. Situations which are more predictable, less risky, and more stable can be efficiently handled by "mechanistic" organizational forms and management procedures. These forms tend to rely on centralized decision making and strict adherence to hierarchical authority. When adaptability and rapid response to change are called for, such as in volatile technological or market environments, more "organic" forms of organization and management are required. These forms accommodate the need for high-level technical and managerial competence, and considerably expand the latitude and degree of decentralization in decision making.

1.5 SYSTEMS APPROACH TO MANAGEMENT

Solutions to problems imposed by the demands of rapid change and technological complexity must themselves be somewhat complex and adaptive to change.[9] In response to these demands, new management approaches under the guise of the "systems approach" have come into use. They apply the concepts of general systems theory and systems analysis to the task of management. More will be said about this in Chapters 3 and 4. The systems approach to management recognizes that organizations exist in a universe of forces and are comprised of interrelated units, the goals and effects of which must be coordinated and integrated for the benefit of the organization. Project management is a systems oriented approach to management because it considers the project as a system of interrelated tasks and work units operating in an influential environment. It seeks to unify the planning and work efforts of numerous organizational units to efficiently accomplish, with minimal tradeoff, the multiple goals of a project.

1.6 THREE GOALS

Virtually every project has a three-dimensional goal: to accomplish the work in accordance with *budget*, *schedule*, and *performance requirements*. The budget dimension is the specified or allowable cost for the project; it is the target cost of the work to be done. The schedule dimension includes the time period over which the work will be done and the target date for when it will be completed. The performance dimension specifies what is to be done to reach the end-item or final result. It includes required features of the final product or service, technological specifications, and quality and quantity measures. As shown in Figure 1–4, the purpose of project management is to direct the project to a target that satisfies all three goals.[10]   Taken together, all three represent a contract to deliver a certain something, by a certain date, for a certain cost.

Unfortunately, technological complexity, changing markets, and uncontrollable environmental forces complicate what can be considered as "certain." The three goals are interrelated and must be addressed simultaneously; exclusive emphasis on any one is likely to detract from the others. In trying to meet time schedules and performance requirements, costs may be forced to increase; conversely, in trying to contain costs, work quality may erode, schedules may slip, and performance degrade. In earlier times, one or two of the goals were simply allowed to vary so that the "most fixed" one could be met. Most modern projects, as the Manhattan, Apollo, and Alpha Company examples show, do not have this luxury; time, cost and performance have to be given equal emphasis. Project management has evolved as an efficient way to maintain focus on all three project goals and to control the necessary tradeoffs among them. As a systems approach, project management integrates resources and puts emphasis on the "wholeness" of project goals.

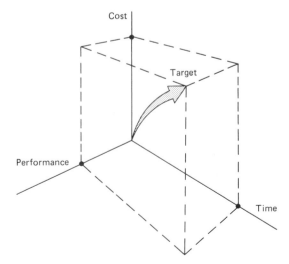

Figure 1–4. Three dimensions of project goals. (Adapted from Milton Rosenau, *Successful Project Management* (Belmont, Ca.: Lifetime Learning Publications, 1981), 16.)

1.7 PROJECT MANAGEMENT: THE PERSON, THE TEAM, THE SYSTEM

Three key features distinguish project management from earlier, traditional forms of management: the project manager, the project team, and the project management system.

The Project Manager

Perhaps the most important element of project management is the project manager, a person whose single, overriding responsibility is to *integrate* the work efforts of participating functional support areas to achieve project goals. In turbulent, complex environments it is becoming increasingly difficult for organizations like Company Alpha to relate facts about technology, production methods, costs, and markets. There are too many crucial decisions to be processed effectively through traditional organizational hierarchies. In most organizations, work proceeds along functional lines and the response to change is exceedingly slow. In the role of project manager, the organization has one person who is accountable for the project and is totally dedicated to achieving its goals. The project manager coordinates efforts across the various involved functional areas and integrates the planning and control of costs, schedules, and work tasks.[11]

The Project Team

Project management is the bringing together of individuals and groups to form a single, cohesive team working toward a common goal. This is because, perhaps more than any other human endeavor, project work is teamwork. It is accomplished by a group of people, often from different functional areas and organizations, who participate wherever and whenever they are needed. Depending on resource requirements of the project, the size and composition of the team may fluctuate, and the team may disband after the project is completed.

The Project Management System

To perform effectively, the project manager and the project team must have available and utilize a "project management system." The project management system comprises organization structure, information processing, and practices and procedures that permit integration of the "vertical" and "horizontal" elements of project organizations. As shown in Figure 1–5, vertical elements include the breakdown of all tasks in the project; horizontal elements include the functional units and departments involved in the project.

The project management system provides for *integrative planning and control.* According to Archibald, integrative planning and control refers to

the pulling together of all important elements of information related to (1) the products or results of the project, (2) the time, and (3) the cost, in funds, manpower, or other key resources. Further, this information must be pulled together for all (or as many as practical) phases of

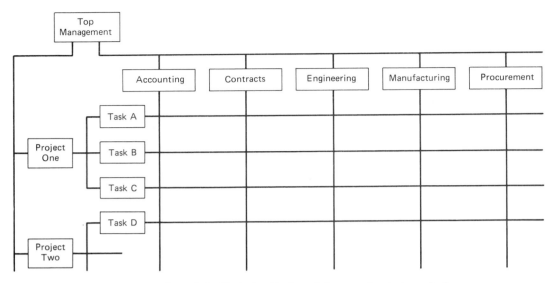

Figure 1–5. Vertical and horizontal elements of project organization.

the project. Finally, integrated planning and control requires continual revision of future plans, comparison of actual results with plans, and projection of total time and cost *at completion* through interrelated evaluation of all elements of information.[12]

As projects move from one phase to the next, resource requirements (labor, facilities, capital, etc.) and organizational responsibilities shift. The project management system provides the means for (1) identification of tasks, (2) identification of resource requirements and costs, (3) establishing priorities, (4) planning and updating schedules, (5) monitoring and controlling end item quality and performance, and (6) measuring project performance.[13]

1.8 ABOUT THIS BOOK

Philosophy and Objectives

Although it has at its foundation traditional management theory and practice, in many ways project management represents a significant departure. A history of the theory and practice of project management would show that its roots touch many disciplines, including management science, systems theory, accounting, operations management, organizational design, law, and applied behavioral science. What has evolved, and will continue to evolve, is a philosophy, approach, and set of practices, the *sum total* of which comprise project management.

As a philosophy and an approach, project management is more sophisticated and complex than traditional management of repetitive activities. Many managers fail to understand this, believing that application of techniques alone, such as "PERT/CPM" or "matrix management" (both explained later) make for successful project management (and successful projects). There is some support for this belief in the literature, much of which focuses rather narrowly on certain methods and procedures of project management.

C. P. Snow wrote an essay entitled "Two Cultures" about the cultural gap that separates scientists from the rest of society. He wrote of the conflict of ideas, the problems of communication, and the lack of understanding between scientists and other intellectuals.[14] Managers and management scholars also tend to see the world from either of two perspectives: some see the world in "hard," quantitative terms, others in "soft," or behavioral terms. The management scientists tend to view projects in terms of economic variables; their approach is to structure problems mathematically and to follow some prescribed set of procedures to arrive at a solution. The behaviorists view problems in terms of human behavior, skills, attitudes, and systems of organization; their solutions are to be found by modifying individual attitudes and behavior, and by altering the processes and structure of groups and organizations. Much of the literature on project management, including texts, is weighted in favor of one or the other of these perspectives, most often that of the management scientists.

The intent of this book is to give a comprehensive, balanced view, one which emphasizes both the behavioral and quantitative sides of project management. The philosophy of this book is that for managers to "do" project management, they must gain familiarity with five aspects of it: systems philosophy, systems development process, human organization and behavior, methods and procedures, and management systems. All five aspects are essential to project management, and neglect or unbalanced attention to some may render the others ineffective. Correspondingly, the objectives of this book are to:

1. Identify and discuss the systems philosophy which guides project management theory and practice.
2. Describe the logical sequence of stages in the life of a project.
3. Describe organizational, managerial, and human behavioral issues relevant to projects.
4. Describe methods and procedures for defining, planning, scheduling, controlling, and organizing project activities.
5. Describe the management information systems necessary for integrated project planning and control.

The techniques of management science are important tools in project management, but individual and group skills, the right attitudes, and teamwork are essential for these tools to be effective. Within the five objectives, both quantitative and behavioral sides of project management are addressed.

This book is intended for "general" project managers. It is comprehensive in the sense that it provides an understanding of project management concepts and techniques widely recognized and of application to virtually any industry or project situation. It is not the intent of this book to dwell on particular methodologies and techniques used only in specific industries or organizations. This would be a difficult task since many industries—construction, defense, computers, social work, and so on—have modified "traditional" project management practices or adopted other approaches to satisfy their unique project needs. Many of these methodologies and techniques are described in texts devoted to construction, product management, research management, and so on.

Just as many of the project management practices described in this book were developed in certain industries—to be later recognized and adopted for general use—there are probably many valuable practices currently in use that most of us are ignorant about. These remain to be "exposed" and to appear in textbooks like this in the future.

The Study Project

A good way to learn about project management is to actually participate in it or, failing that, be a witness to it. At the end of most chapters in this book are two kinds of questions: the first are the usual chapter review questions, the second are called "Questions About the Study Project." The latter are intended to be applied to a particular project of the reader's choosing. This will be called the "study project." The purpose of these questions is to help the reader relate concepts from each chapter to practice and reality.

The study project questions should be used in the following ways:

For readers who are currently working in projects as either managers or project team members, the questions can be related to their current work. The questions serve both to increase readers' awareness of key issues surrounding the project as well as to guide managers in the organization and conduct of project management.

For readers who are currently full- or part-time students, the questions can be applied either to (1) student projects in which they are currently involved (e.g., group research projects) or (2) outside projects which they are permitted to observe. Many business firms and government agencies are willing to let student groups interview them and collect information about projects. Though secondhand, this is nonetheless an excellent way to learn about project management practice (and malpractice).

Organization of This Book

Beyond this introductory chapter, the book is divided into four main sections. The first section is devoted to the basic concepts of project management. This section describes systems concepts, systems methodologies, and the systems approach—the philosophy that underlies project management. Also covered are the origins and concepts of project management, situations where it is needed, and examples of applications. The second section describes the logical process in the creation and life of a system. Commonly called the Systems Development Cycle, it is a sequence of phases through which all man-made systems move from birth to death. The cycle is described in terms of its called the Systems Development Cycle, it is a sequence of phases through which all man-made systems move from birth to death. The cycle is described in terms of its relation to projects and project management. The third section is devoted to project organizations, teams, and the people in projects. It covers structural aspects of project organizations, roles and responsibilities of project managers and team members, styles of leadership appropriate for project managers, and methods for managing teamwork, conflict, and emotional stress. The fourth section is devoted to methods and procedures for planning, scheduling, cost estimating, budgeting, resource allocation, controlling, and terminating a project. The topics of resource planning, computerization of projects, and project evaluation are also covered. Throughout this section, reference is made to the management and information systems needed to integrate planning and work activities.

Thus, the five stated objectives of this book are roughly divided among the chapters in this way:

1. Basic concepts and systems philosophy: Chapters 2, 3, and 4.
2. Systems development and project life cycles: Chapters 5 and 6.
3. Organization, management, and human behavior: Chapters 7 through 10.
4. Methods and procedures for planning and control: Chapters 11 through 17.
5. Management and information systems: Chapter 16 and portions of Chapters 11 through 15.

Chapter 18 discusses project success and failure, and ties together the tenets of the book.

The Appendix expands upon three subjects mentioned throughout the book: systems engineering (Appendix A), contracts (Appendix B), and the project plan (Appendix C). All readers should look at Appendices B and C after they have read Chapter 5 and refer to them again whenever they are mentioned in the book. Readers who are, or expect to be, involved in engineering of large-scale, system integration projects should study Appendix A after they have read Chapter 4.

CHAPTER REVIEW QUESTIONS

1. Look at newspapers, magazines, or television for examples of items that pertain to projects. Surprisingly, a great number of newsworthy topics relate to the status of current or future projects, or to the outcome of past projects. Prepare a list of these topics.
2. Prepare a list of activities that are not projects. What distinguishes them from project activities? Which activities are difficult to classify one way or the other?
3. Because this is an introductory chapter, not very much has been said about why projects must be managed differently, and what constitutes project management—the subject of this book. Now is a good time to speculate about these: Why do you think that projects need to be managed

STUDY PROJECT ASSIGNMENT

Select a project to investigate. You should select a "real" project, that is, a project that has a real purpose and is not contrived just so you can investigate it. It can be a current project or one already completed. It can be a project on which you are currently working. Whatever, it must be a project for which you can readily get information.

If you are not currently involved in a project as a team member, than you must find one that you have permission to study (collect data and interview people, etc.) as an "outsider." The project should include a project team (a minimum of, say, five people) with a project leader, and have at least a two or three month duration. The project should also have specific goals in terms of, for example, a target completion date, a budget limit, as well as a specified end-item result or product.

It is also a good idea, if you decide to study a project as an outsider, to do it *in* a team with three to six people and a project leader (i.e., use a team to perform the study). This, in essence, becomes *your project team*—a team organized for the purpose of studying a project. You can then readily apply many of the planning, organizing, team building, and other procedures discussed throughout the book to see how they work. This "hands-on" experience with your own team, combined with what you learn from the project you are studying, will give you a fairly accurate picture about problems encountered and management techniques used in real-life project management.

ENDNOTES

1. Peter Tompkins, *Secrets of the Great Pyramids* (New York: Harper and Row, 1976), 233–234; Rene Poirier, *The Fifteen Wonders of the World* (New York: Random House, 1961), 54–67.

2. Ibid., 227–228.

3. Francis Barber, *The Mechanical Triumphs of the Ancient Egyptians* (London: Tribner, 1900), as described by Tompkins, ibid., 233.

4. Claude S. George, *The History of Management Thought* (Englewood Cliffs, N.J.: Prentice-Hall, 1968), 11.

5. Chaim Potok, *Wanderings* (New York: Fawcett Crest, 1978), 154–162.

6. See Russell D. Archibald, *Managing High-Technology Projects* (New York: Wiley, 1976), 19; Jack R. Meredith and Samuel Mantel, *Project Management: A Managerial Approach* (New York: Wiley, 1985), 4–5; Daniel D. Roman, *Managing Projects: A Systems Approach* (New York: Elsevier, 1986), 2–10; John M. Stewart, "Making Project Management Work," *Business Horizons*, Vol. 8, No. 3, (Fall 1965), 54–68.

7. See John Terraine, *The Mighty Continent* (London: BBC, 1974), 241–242.

8. D.I. Cleland and W.R. King, *Systems Analysis and Project Management*, 3rd ed. (New York: McGraw-Hill, 1983), 5–6.

9. Ibid., 4.

10. See Meredith and Mantel, *Project Management*, 3; and Milton D. Rosenau, *Successful Project Management* (Belmont, Ca.: Lifetime Learning, 1981), 15–19.

11. Harold Kerzner, *Project Management: A Systems Approach to Planning, Organizing, and Controlling* (New York: Van Nostrand Reinhold, 1979), 6.

12. Archibald, *Managing High-Technology Projects*, 6–7.

13. Kerzner, *Project Management*, 7.

14. C. P. Snow, *The Two Cultures and a Second Look* (Cambridge, England: Cambridge University Press, 1969).

Section I

PHILOSOPHY AND CONCEPTS

The three chapters in this section describe the philosophy and concepts that differentiate project management from traditional, non-project management. Project management is an application of what has been called the systems approach to planning and operating organizations. This section introduces features associated with project management, and describes the principles, terminology, and methodology of the systems approach. It is the foundation part of the book and sets the stage for the more detailed coverage in later sections.

Chapters in this section:

Chapter Two. What is Project Management?

Chapter Three. Systems and Organizations

Chapter Four. Systems Methodologies

chapter 2

WHAT IS PROJECT MANAGEMENT?

The projects mentioned in Chapter One—the Great Pyramids of Egypt, the Manhattan Project, the space station, and the development of Product X—all have something in common with each other and with every other undertaking of human organizations: they all require, in a word, *management*. Certainly the resources, work tasks, and goals of these projects vary greatly, yet without management none of them could happen. Project management is a special kind of management. This chapter contrasts project and nonproject management and looks at the variety of ways and places where project management is used. It also serves as an introduction to the concepts and topics of later chapters.

2.1 FUNCTIONS AND VIEWPOINTS OF MANAGEMENT[1]

The role of management is to integrate resources and tasks to achieve organizational goals. Although the specific responsibilities of managers vary greatly, all managers—whether they are corporate presidents, agency directors, line managers, school administrators, movie producers, or project managers—have this same role.

Management Functions

The activities of a manager can be classified into the five functions identified in Figure 2–1. First, the manager decides what has to be done; this is the *planning* function. It involves setting organizational goals and establishing means for achieving them consistent with available resources and forces in the environment.

Second, the manager decides how the work will be accomplished; this is the *organizing* function. In this function, the manager (1) hires, trains, and assembles people into a system of authority, responsibility, and accountability relationships; (2) acquires and allocates

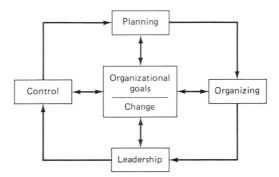

FIGURE 2–1. The functions of management.

facilities, materials, capital, and other resources; and (3) creates an organization structure that includes policies, procedures, reporting patterns, and communication channels.

Third, the manager directs and motivates people to attain objectives; this is the *leadership* function. In this function, the manager focuses on workers, groups, and their relationships to influence work performance and behavior.

Fourth, the manager evaluates performance with respect to standards of efficiency and effectiveness, and takes necessary corrective action; this is the *control* function. For effective control the manager relies upon an information system to collect data and report progress with respect to costs, schedules, and specifications.

All four functions are performed to accomplish organizational goals. This implies a fifth function: the assessment of the other functions to determine where *change* is needed. The change function recognizes that organizations are open systems (discussed in Chapter 3) and that goals and activities have to be adapted to changing forces in the internal and external environment.

On a day by day basis, managers rarely perform the functions in Figure 2–1 in strict sequence. Although planning should precede the others, there is always need to organize activities, direct people, and evaluate work, regardless of sequence. Managers constantly face change, which means that plans, activities, performance standards, and leadership styles must change too. Managers oversee a variety of jobs simultaneously, and for each one they must be able to exercise any of the functions at a given time.

Different managers' jobs carry varying responsibilities depending on the functional area and managerial level of the job. Some managers devote most of their time to planning and organizing, others to controlling, and others to directing and motivating.

In short, no process or set of prescriptive management functions seems to apply equally well in all cases. Managers must be adaptive to the situation. This is the modern *contingency viewpoint* of management.

Viewpoints of Management[2]

The current viewpoint about how to manage organizations is but the latest in an evolving series of management propositions and methodologies. The earliest, called the *classical* viewpoint, originated at the turn of the century. This held that there was one *best way* to manage and a corresponding set of universal bureaucratic and scientific management principles applied to all situations. The classical viewpoint established formal principles for planning, organizing, leading, and controlling. In theory, the principles are useful for outlining the kinds of things managers should do. The drawback is that they presume much more order and rationality than actually exist in organizations and provide poor guidance about how managers should practice these principles in different situations.

Next, starting in the 1930s, came the *behavioral* viewpoint in which the emphasis was shifted from jobs to the human and social aspects of organizations. One of the early proponents of this viewpoint, Elton Mayo, introduced the concept of "social man"—the worker who is motivated by social needs and relationships with others, and is responsive to work group norms and pressures.[3] The contribution of this viewpoint is that it highlighted the importance of leadership style, group dynamics, and social environment, concepts never acknowledged by the classical theorists. But the behaviorists, like their classical counterparts, tended to look at management rather narrowly. Human and organization behavior are much more complex than they presumed, and many behaviorist theories about relationships concerning satisfaction, morale, and productivity are too simplistic to be of practical use. In the end, managers still have to rely on their own best judgment.

During World War II came the third viewpoint, the *systems approach*. Whereas the first two viewpoints sought to simplify management through concepts that would fit all situations, the systems viewpoint faced up to complexity and differing causal relationships. Simply, it stated that before the manager can prescribe action, she must first understand the system and its relationship with the environment. Rather than give a new set of rote prescriptions about how to manage, the approach suggested ways to understand the elements and dynamics of a situation, and some models to help clarify problems and identify courses of action. But even the models of the systems approach were not a panacea. They could not, in the end, always be relied upon to tell the manager what to do because they could not adequately represent "non-quantifiable" elements, such as human motivations, emotions, and values. Even the systems viewpoint must eventually be supplemented by the judgment of the manager. The systems viewpoint is discussed further in the next two chapters.

All three viewpoints represent different perspectives, all make valuable contributions to management theory and practice, and all have limitations. The current *contingency* viewpoint recognizes that none of them alone can guide a manager in all aspects of the job in every situation. The current viewpoint, which includes ideas like situational leadership[4] and the contingency approach to management,[5] stresses that all three views can be applied independently or in some combination, *depending upon the confronting situation.*

The contingency viewpoint suggests that for management practice to be effective, it must be consistent with the requirements of the environment, the tasks to be performed, and the people who perform them. A manager should be familiar with the concepts of the three earlier viewpoints, be able to understand and diagnose each confronting situation, and then choose the mix of procedures, leadership styles, and management functions most appropriate. The contingency viewpoint does not provide prescriptions about what works in all situations, but rather suggestions about what tends to work best in specific cases.

2.2 PROJECT VIEWPOINT VERSUS TRADITIONAL MANAGEMENT

The practice of project management pays attention to goal-oriented systems, environment, subsystems, and relationships; this is what makes project management a "systems approach" to management. Nonetheless, project management also relies heavily upon elements of the classical and behavioral viewpoints. It is, in fact, a good example of the contingency approach because it is a management philosophy and methodology oriented toward effective accomplishment of just one type of undertaking—projects.

Characteristics of Projects

Almost universally, the traditional organization has been structured as a pyramidal hierarchy with vertical superior-subordinate relationships and departmentation along functional, product, or geographic boundaries. Authority flows down from the highest level to the lowest level, and formal communication is similarly directed downward along the chain-of-command. The functional units are highly specialized and tend to operate independently. Although these traditional, functional organizations become very efficient in what they do and are often well-suited for work in stable environments (i.e., turning out large quantities of a uniform product in an unchanging market), they tend to be rigid and, thus, unsuitable for the unstable and dynamic environments that characterize project situations. We will elaborate on this in Chapter 7.

A project was defined in Chapter 1 as:[6]

1. Involving a single, definable purpose, end-item (product or result)—specified in terms of cost, schedule, and performance requirements. Purpose and end-item change from project to project.

2. Utilizing skills and talents from multiple professions and organizations. A project often involves advanced technology and relies on task interdependencies which may introduce new and unique problems. Tasks and skill requirements change from project to project.

3. Being unique: it requires doing things differently than before. A project is a one of a kind activity, never to be exactly repeated again.

4. Being somewhat unfamiliar. It may encompass new technology and possess significant elements of uncertainty and risk. Failure of the project might jeopardize the organization or its goals.

5. A temporary activity. It is undertaken to accomplish a goal within a given period of time; once the goal is achieved, the project ceases to exist.

6. The *process* of working to achieve a goal. During the process, a project passes through several distinct phases; tasks, people, organizations, and resources change as the project moves from one phase to the next.

The characteristics which distinguish projects make it necessary to employ a kind of management suitable just for them. Thus the emergence of project management.

Characteristics of Project Management

Application of principles from the classical, behavioral, and systems viewpoints to the unique requirements of projects has led to a new set of concepts, the "project viewpoint." This viewpoint has evolved to include new management roles, techniques, and organizational forms. It embodies the following characteristics:[7]

1. A single person, the project manager, heads the project organization and operates independently of the normal chain-of-command. This organization reflects the cross-functional, goal-oriented, temporary nature of the project.

2. The project manager is the single focal point for bringing together all efforts toward a single project objective.

3. Since each project requires a variety of skills and resources, the actual work might be performed by many functional areas.

4. The project manager and the project team are responsible for integrating people from different functional disciplines who are working on the project.

5. The project manager negotiates directly with functional managers for support. Functional managers are responsible for individual work tasks and personnel within the project, while the project manager is responsible for integrating and overseeing the start and completion of activities.

6. The project focuses on delivering a particular product or service at a certain time and cost, and to the satisfaction of technical requirements. In contrast, functional units must maintain an ongoing pool of resources to support organizational goals. As a result, conflict may exist between the project and functional managers over the time and talent to be allotted to a project.

7. A project might have two chains-of-command—one vertical and functional, one horizontal and project—and people might report to both the project manager and a functional manager. (There are, of course, problems with this. These are discussed in Chapter 7.)

8. Decision making, accountability, outcomes, and rewards are shared among members of the project team and supporting functional units.

9. Though the project organization is temporary, the functional units from which it is formed are permanent. When a project ends, the project organization is disbanded and people return to their functional units or are reassigned to new projects.

10. Projects can originate at different places in the organization. Product development and related projects tend to emerge from marketing, whereas technological applications originate in R&D, and so on.

11. Project management sets into motion numerous other support functions such as personnel evaluation, accounting, and information systems.

Since projects involve the efforts of different units from within and outside the organization, reliance upon the vertical chain-of-command for authority and communication is too time-consuming and causes frequent disruption and delay of work. To get the job done efficiently, managers and workers in different units and at different levels need to associate directly with each other. Even in traditional organizations, the formal lines of communication and authority are frequently bypassed by *informal* lines which cut through red tape and expedite work. In project organizations, the virtue of these informal lines is recognized and formalized through the creation of a *horizontal hierarchy* to augment the vertical hierarchy. This hybrid organizational form enables personnel in different work units to be formed into highly integrated project groups.

Traditional organizations have rigid, unchanging structures. They work well in environments where there is little change, but because they are rigid, they cannot quickly adjust to change. Given the temporary nature of projects, an organization that works on a stream of projects must be flexible so it can alter structure and resources to meet the shifting requirements of different projects.

Managers in traditional organizations tend to be specialized and have responsibility for a single functional unit or department. This works well for optimizing the efficiency of individual departments, but when projects need the support of many departments there is no one accountable or responsible for the project's goals. In the role of project manager, a single person is given project responsibility and is held accountable for the project. This emphasis on project goals versus functional goals is a major feature distinguishing project and functional management roles.

Project managers often depend upon people who are not "under" them but who are "assigned" to them from other parts of the organization as needed. Thus, the task of project managers is more complicated and diverse then other types of management. Project managers must use diplomacy, worker participation, and conflict resolution skills to be effective leaders.

Example: Project Management in Construction

Construction projects are always in the news, often because of problems owing to cost overruns or schedule slippages. Although many factors are blamed, such as labor unions, materials shortages, or inflation, the real cause is frequently poor management and lack of control. The manager of construction projects is usually either the architect or the contractor. This works on small, less complex jobs, but on big construction jobs it is a bad arrangement since architects and contractors each represent the interests of separate "functional areas." When things go wrong and arguments arise, both tend to be self- serving; there is no one who is impartial and can reconcile differences between them. A better arrangement is when the developer or the building owner appoints an independent construction project manager, leaving architects to design and contractors to build. This is shown in Figure 2–2. Notice the project manager's central position in the organization.

This position enables her to monitor and coordinate all design and building tasks in accordance with the developer's goals. The project manager ensures that the architect's designs are within the developer's cost allowances and building requirements, and that the contractor's work is executed according to contract specifications and at a fair price. The

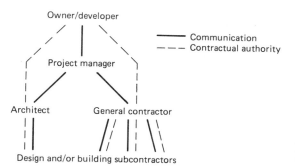

FIGURE 2–2. The project manager in a construction project.

construction project manager is involved throughout the project life cycle: she oversees preliminary architectural design, does the subcontracting, and controls site work according to design specification, time, cost, and the safety of the workers.

Several more examples of projects and project managers are described near the end of this chapter.

2.3 EVOLUTION OF PROJECT MANAGEMENT

History

No one individual or industry can be credited with the idea of project management. It is often associated with the early missile and space programs of the 1960s, but clearly its origins go back much earlier. Elements of project management probably first appeared in the major construction works of antiquity, such as the Pyramids, the Roman aqueducts, and the Great Wall of China. Later, these techniques were improved and modified for usage on other forms of construction projects, such as shipbuilding. The commonality among construction works is that they all require special organizations, labor, facilities, and material resources, just for the purpose of doing one job.

Traditional, nonproject management practices work well for management of high volume, standardized products, but they are often inefficient on large nonstandard items such as specialized machinery and tools. Starting in the early 20th century, industrial managers found that techniques used in construction could also be used for planning and controlling these large-scale, non-construction "product development" jobs. At the same time, improved techniques for planning were being developed. During World War I, a new production scheduling and monitoring tool called the *Gantt chart* was introduced (examples are in Chapter 11); about 30 years later, the first network-type display for describing industrial processes, called a *process flow diagram,* was developed (see, for example, Figure 6–3 on page 116). Both are widely used today.

By the 1950s, the size and complexity of many projects had increased so much that even these techniques proved inadequate. In particular, large-scale weapons systems projects—aircraft, missiles, naval vessels—were becoming so complex that they defied all existing methods to logically plan and control them. Repeatedly these projects ran into enormous cost and schedule overruns. To grapple with the problem, two new network-based planning and control methods were developed, one by the Navy in 1958 called *PERT*, the other by DuPont Corporation in 1957, called *CPM*. Both methods (described later in Chapters 12 and 13) were originated exclusively for planning, scheduling, and controlling large projects having numerous interrelated work activities. A decade later, these methods were combined with computer simulation in a method called *GERT* to permit more realistic analysis of schedules.

By the mid-1950s, the wide-scale development and installation of computerized data processing systems provided increased capability for handling the immense amount of information necessary to manage large-scale projects. Network methods were refined to integrate project cost accounting with project scheduling. These techniques came into widespread usage in the 1960s when the federal government mandated the use of network scheduling/costing methods, called *PERT/COST*, first with Department of Defense and NASA contracts, then later with other large-scale efforts such as nuclear power plants. These methods enabled cost tracking to be integrated with project schedules.

Throughout the 1960s additional methods emerged to help project planners. Some enabled managers to specify the type and quantity of resources needed for each activity in a project, and to plan for and allocate resources among several projects simultaneously. Although the concept was around for over a decade, it not was until the 1970s that planning and costing based upon the *earned value* concept came into widespread usage. This concept led to performance measurement systems which kept track of not only funds expended, but the percentage of work completed, too. This led to more reliable forecasting of what a project would cost at completion and when it would be completed.

The last three decades have witnessed the increased computerization of project management. Initially, project planning and tracking systems were available only for large mainframe computers, then later only for mini's. Most of these systems required investments of $10,000's—$100,000's. The size of the cost and of the organizations needed to operate the systems precluded their usage in all but the largest projects. This all changed in the 1980s with the appearance of the microcomputer. Today a large variety of quality project management software programs are available to expand the planning and control capabilities of managers even for the tiniest projects. Relatively low cost software, between $100 and $2000, makes it possible to apply modern techniques for scheduling, costing, resource planning, performance analysis, and forecasting to virtually all small and medium-sized projects. Some of this software is described in Chapter 16.

Associated with the development of project planning and control methods was the evolution of project organizational forms and the role of project manager. Project management as a distinct organizational form of structure did not come into being until World War II. In the urgency to develop and deliver sophisticated weapons (such as the atomic bomb) and organize massive task forces (such as the Normandy Invasion), pure project forms of organization evolved. In 1961, IBM became one of the first companies to formally use the project manager role in commercial industry; there, project managers (called "systems managers") were given broad responsibility across functional lines to oversee development and installation of computer models.

Types of Project Managers

In 1962, in one of the first discussions of how project management evolved, Davis identified four types of project management organization.[8] He noted that organizations tend to evolve from one type to the next as they become more sophisticated and their problems become more complex. Although the correspondence is not exact, Davis' classification can be used to introduce the four types of project managers:

The first are *project expeditors*—individuals who speed up work and are the project center of communication to the general manager. Their purpose is to achieve *unity of communications*. They are not really managers but rather serve as translators of technical concepts into business concepts of costs, schedules, and markets. Because their role is limited to funneling information to executives and making suggestions, the expeditor role is restricted to smaller projects with low risk and less at stake.

The second type act as staff leaders and *project coordinators*. Their purpose is to achieve *unity of control* over project activities. They have authority to control project matters and disbursement of funds from the budget, but still have no actual line authority over workers. Their authority is derived primarily through their association with upper level executives. The construction project manager in Figure 2–2, for example, would be in this position if he coordinated the work but still needed the approval of the developer for major decisions such as contracting or reallocation of funds.

The third type perform the full range of management functions. They serve the same purpose as the first two, but additionally, have authority to plan, motivate, direct, and control project work. Their purpose is to achieve *unity of direction*. They are called *matrix managers* because the people they direct are located administratively in other, functional departments and the resulting crisscross pattern of vertical-functional and horizontal-project reporting relationships create what is called a *matrix organization*. The manager of a construction project who is employed by the same company that is both designing and constructing the building is such a manager. She must rely upon managers in the architectural and construction departments for the assignment of personnel to her project. These personnel report to the project manager only in regard to the project and for as long as they are needed on the project; otherwise, they report to their respective department managers. The same personnel may also be working on other projects and reporting to other matrix project managers.

The last type, *pure project managers*, direct *pure project* organizations of people who report directly to them. Their purpose is to achieve *unity of command*. These managers are primarily integrators and generalists rather than technical specialists. They must balance technical factors with schedules, costs, resources, and human factors. In the course of a project, they actively deal with top management, functional managers, vendors, customers, and subcontractors. The manager of a large construction project, for example, whom the developer has hired and delegated the power to make *major* decisions (such as letting contracts for architects and builders, or cancelling them) has this role.

Although the last two types are most in keeping with the project management concept in this book, the other two are just as widely found. All four will be discussed further in later chapters.

2.4 WHERE IS PROJECT MANAGEMENT APPROPRIATE?[9]

Project management originated in construction and aerospace because the environments and kinds of activities in those industries demands flexible and imaginative forms of management. But what about other industries and other environments? Certainly there must be many applications of project management beyond the familiar ones cited. This section identifies conditions and situations where it is more appropriate (or essential) to use a project-type organization instead of a traditional, functional organization.

Project management can be applied to any ad-hoc undertaking. As Figure 1–3 in Chapter 1 showed, "ad hoc undertaking" includes a broad range of activities, such as writing a term paper, remodeling a kitchen, or constructing a theme park like Walt Disney's Epcot in Florida. Some of these undertakings are more appropriate for project management than others. Generally, there are two conditions suggesting when project management should be used: first, the more unfamiliar or unique the undertaking, the greater the need for project management to insure nothing gets overlooked; second, the more numerous, interdisciplinary, and interdependent the activities in the undertaking, the greater the need for a project manager to insure everything is coordinated, integrated, and completed.

Frequently, customers such as the U.S. government request or require project management because they believe it offers better cost, schedule, and quality control and they prefer having one person, the project manager, to deal with. In most cases, however, the contractor has the option to decide when to use project management. In some cases, project management is *inappropriate* simply because the effort to implement it would exceed the effort of the undertaking itself.

Cleland and King suggest five general criteria to help decide when to use project management techniques and organization:[10]

1. Magnitude of the Effort

When a job requires substantially more resources (people, capital, equipment, etc.) than are normally employed by a department or organization, project management techniques may be necessary. Undertakings such as facilities relocations, merging two corporations, or developing and placing a new product on the market are examples. Even when the job lies primarily in the realm of one functional area, the task of coordinating its work with other functional areas might be overwhelming. For example, a corporate computer installation might seem to fall within the single functional area of data processing, yet during the course of the project, there will be a continuous meshing of policies, procedures, and resources of all departments affected by the installation. Hundreds of people may be involved, and the required coordination and integration might be more than any one area can tackle.

2. Unfamiliarity

By definition, a project is something different from the ordinary and routine. A project always requires that different things be done, that the same things be done differently, or both. For example, minor changes in products, such as annual automobile design changes, can usually be accomplished without setting up a project team. Modernizing a plant, on the other hand, calls for non-routine efforts such as revising the facilities layout, modifying the assembly line, replacing equipment, retraining employees, and altering policies and work procedures. Project management would be needed to bring all of the functional areas together for this one-of-a-kind undertaking.

3. Changing Environment

Many organizations exist in environments that are rapidly changing. So-called "high-tech" industries like computers, electronics, pharmaceuticals, and communications are examples. The environment of these industries is characterized by high innovation, rapid product changes, and shifting markets and consumer behavior. Other industries, such as chemicals, biotechnology, and aerospace, though less volatile, also have highly competitive and dynamic environments. Changing environments present new opportunities that organizations must move swiftly to capture. To survive and succeed, organizations must be creative, innovative, flexible, and capable of rapid response. Project management provides the flexibility and diversity needed to deal with changing goals and new opportunities.

4. Interrelatedness

Functional areas are sometimes self-serving and work at cross purposes. When a joint effort is required, project management builds lateral relationships between areas to expedite work and reconcile the conflicts inherent in multifunctional undertakings. The project manager links together and coordinates the efforts of areas within the parent organization, as well as the efforts of outside subcontractors, vendors, and customers.

5. Reputation of the Organization

The stake of the undertaking may determine the need for project management. If failure to satisfactorily complete the project will result in financial ruin, loss of market share, a damaged reputation, or loss of future contracts, there is a strong case for project management. Project management cannot guarantee that any of these will not happen (and sometimes they will happen, anyway) but it does provide better planning and control to improve the odds. The likelihood for successfully completing any activity is increased when a single competent individual is assigned responsibility for overseeing it. The project manager, with the assistance of a technical support group, can do much to reduce the problems inherent in large, complex undertakings.

The obverse of all of this is that the more familiar the undertaking, the more stable the environment, the less unique and more standardized the end-item, and the lower the stake in any one particular output, the less the need for project management. Production of standardized industrial and agricultural outputs, for example, is generally much more efficiently managed by continuous or lot size planning and control procedures than by project management. This is because for standardized, repetitive operations, there is greater certainty in the process and outcome, and standardized means of production are well-suited. In projects where outcomes are more unique the process must be tailored to fit each one.

It should be noted that, at some time, all organizations use project approaches. Even in stable repetitive industries, small informal projects, by a few individuals, are always in progress: new machines are installed, old ones are repaired; the office is remodeled; the cafeteria is relocated. It is only when larger or more special undertakings arise, such as company mergers, major equipment installations, or a company move that a more formalized project group is formed.

Example: Renovating the Statue of Liberty[11]

Ninety-five years after the Statue of Liberty was presented to the American people, its skin and interior structure had become so badly corroded that it was judged structurally unsound. To oversee a national fund raising campaign and restoration of the statue and other buildings on Ellis Island, the U.S. Department of Interior established a foundation.

Many firms pooled their talents for the renovation of the statue. The job involved highly specialized skills, such as erection of scaffolding, construction of a new torch, building of windows for the crown, and replacement of the interior framework, all of which tend to be found in smaller firms. As a result, the work was accomplished by a legion of over 50 small businesses, with many workers who were immigrants or descendants of immigrants whom the statue welcomed to America. Very little of the renovation work qualified as "standard."

There were myriad notable features about the job. The scaffolding surrounding the statue never touched it at any point. Constructed of hundreds of thousands of pieces of aluminum, it qualified for the *Guiness Book of World Records* as the largest free-standing scaffolding ever built. To renovate the statue's interior, 1,699 five-foot bars were painstakingly fashioned from 35,000 pounds of stainless steel, then individually installed. Around the crown 25 windows were replaced. Each was handcrafted and had to be treated as a project unto itself. To fashion an entirely new touch, French artisans practiced an ancient copper shaping technique. The project was truly a marriage of art and engineering.

The 30 month, $31 million renovation effort involved thousands of tasks performed by hundreds of people. Most of the tasks were nonroutine and interrelated, and all had to be completed within a tight budget and schedule—certainly the trappings of a situation requiring project management. Indeed, project management was employed and the project was a success. (The company responsible for managing the renovation is discussed in Chapter 9.)

2.5 THE DIFFERENT FORMS OF PROJECT MANAGEMENT

Most projects involve relatively high degrees of technical, marketing, or manufacturing complexity, have high innovative or technical risk, and require significant contribution from several separate organizations—internal, external, functional, or otherwise.[12] But the actual form a project organization takes varies considerably, depending upon the nature of the project, the organization, and the environment.

Project management has been called by different names, including systems management, task force management, team management, ad hoc management, matrix management, program management, and others. Regardless of name, all share two features: (1) a *project team* or project organization, created uniquely for the purpose of achieving a specific goal, and (2) a single person—the *project manager*—who is assigned responsibility for seeing that the goal is accomplished. Beyond these, features differ depending on the application.

The following sections highlight differences among the major forms of project management. In the first section, the term "basic" project management refers to what is meant when we just say "project management"; i.e., the most commonly understood concept of project management. The others are project management variants or forms of management that are similar to project management.

Basic Project Management

The most common project approach places the project manager and functional managers at the same level and reporting to the same person. The project manager is given formal authority to plan, direct, organize, and control the project from start to finish. The project manager may work directly with any level of the organization in any functional area to accomplish project goals. She reports to the general manager and keeps him apprised of project status. Although sometimes the project manager has authority to demand resources such as personnel and facilities, more often she negotiates with functional managers for assignment of resources.

Basic project management is implemented in two widely used forms—pure project and matrix. In pure project management a complete, self-contained organization is created with all the necessary functional elements within. Resources are inherent and do not have to be borrowed. In matrix management, the organization is created by using elements allocated from permanent functional units. The project must time share resources with other concurrent projects and with the functional areas from which they borrow. These two will be described further in Chapter 7 on project organizations.

Although mostly found in construction and high-technology, the potential for project management extends to smaller, non-technical activities as well. " Hard" technology is not a prerequisite for using project management, and efforts based on "soft" technology—the arts and social sciences—can just as readily benefit. Adams, Barndt, and Martin cite these examples where basic project management has yet to be applied:[13]

- HEW performs much of its social work on the basis of grants allocated through state and local agencies to provide specific services. Associated with each grant are time, cost, and performance requirements; clearly these are project efforts, yet there is little use of project management techniques within HEW.

- When a large advertising firm conducts an advertising campaign it utilizes the support of marketing research, accounting, graphics, sales, and other units. Several projects are usually underway in different stages of their life cycles at any given time. There is much similarity between these operations and project management (and program management, mentioned next).

- A good deal of work performed in education development can be considered project work. Much of this work is funded by grants with target goals and cost and time constraints. The efforts of many educators and researchers must be coordinated—a task for which project management is ideally suited.

Program Management

The term program management is often used interchangeably with project management because of the similarity between programs and projects: (1) both are output-oriented, that is, defined in terms of goals or objectives about what must be accomplished; (2) both emphasize the time period over which goals or objectives are to be pursued; and (3) both require plans and budgets to be developed for accomplishing specific goals (and not vice versa as in many traditional operations). In short, both work toward a target specified in terms of a desired product or service output, a date of accomplishment, and a related budget.

For this book, programs and projects have technical differences. A program extends over a longer time horizon—five or more years—and consists of several parallel or sequential work efforts that are coordinated toward program goals. The time scale for projects tends to be shorter, and projects are often the individual "work efforts" of a program. For example, an Urban Development program may include several shorter term projects such as housing rehab, job and skill training, and small business consulting -assistance; a planetary exploration program may include projects for unmanned probes to Mars and Phobos, followed by a manned mission to Mars. (Actually, these projects might grow to become so large that they themselves would have to be set up as full-scale programs, such as the Lunar Apollo Program. The Manhattan Project was really a "program.")

Another distinction is that projects are oriented to producing and delivering a product or service, after which the project is dissolved. Though project contracts specify the end-item, cost, and delivery date, the operation of the end-item is someone else's responsibility. Contractors may be concerned about the quality of their products, but they are usually not responsible for maintaining them afterwards. Once the product or service is "out the door," it is up to program management to ensure that it is integrated with other outputs and remains operational for as long as needed. For example, several contractors might produce and deliver a satellite and its booster rocket, but it becomes someone else's responsibility to launch the rocket and satellite, and then monitor and operate the satellite once in orbit. Program management must arrange for launch support, ongoing satellite monitoring, and so on, so that overall program goals can be achieved.

Most of the concepts and approaches to project management also apply to the management of programs, though some have to be modified to deal with the larger magnitude of programs. For instance, many programs last too long for any one person to be held accountable from start to finish. Thus, the concept of project manager must be modified to include training and replacement to ensure that the role of *program manager* is occupied throughout the program's life cycle. Also, since programs are composed of teams from various projects, a program structure must be created to coordinate them. This structure is similar to (and overlays) the project structure. Contrast the structure of the typical weapons system development program shown in Figure 2–3 with the project management structure shown in Figure 1–5 in Chapter 1.

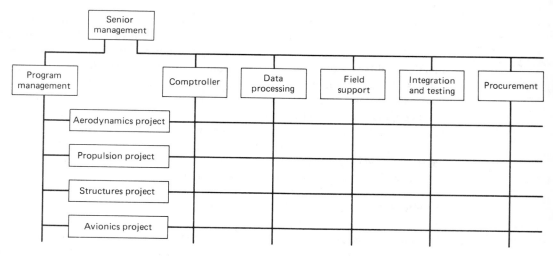

FIGURE 2–3.   Typical aircraft weapons system development program.

New Venture Management

Project management resembles a type of management used in consumer-oriented firms for generating new products or markets, particularly when the product is not well-defined. This is termed *new venture management*. A new venture management team is a team specially created to find new products or markets that fit the organization's specialized skills, capabilities, and resources. Once an idea is defined, the team may go on to design and develop the product, then determine the means for producing, marketing, and distributing it.

There are many similarities between project management groups and venture groups. For example, venture groups:[14]

- Focus on a single unifying goal.

- Are multidisciplinary, with skilled experts and managers from various functional areas working together under a single head.

- Are action-oriented and dedicated to change.

- Are temporary. Once a venture group has completed its charge, members go back to their original departments or to another venture group, or form a new division responsible for the newly developed product or line. The group may become a new division or split off from the parent organization to form a new company.

Product Management

When a single person is given the authority to oversee all aspects of a product's production scheduling, inventory, distribution, and sales, the term *product management* is used. The product manager coordinates and expedites efforts of manufacturing, distribution, and sales to ensure uninterrupted flow of the product from its production to its delivery to the customer. Like the project manager, the product manager communicates directly with all levels and functions within and outside the organization. He coordinates the diverse objectives of various functional units so that the total effort is directed at the accomplishment of product goals. The product manager is active in managing conflicts and resolving problems that would degrade manufacturing capability, forestall distribution, alter price, hinder sales, or in any way affect financing, production, and marketing of his product.

For products with long life cycles, the product manager role is filled on a rotating basis. New and outgoing product managers work briefly together for a period of on-the-job training and apprenticeship to insure smooth transition.

Ad Hoc Committees and Task Forces

For many projects, especially small or short duration ones, a temporary team is created wherever it is needed, usually within a functional department or as a separate organizational arm. These teams, called *task forces* or *interdepartmental committees*, are ad hoc committees with one person specified as project leader. (Toffler terms this phenomenon "ad-hocracy.")[15] Both leaders and members are selected by (and the leader reports directly to) whomever the project is for—a functional manager, vice-president, or CEO. Leaders are responsible for expediting and coordinating efforts and may have authority to direct tasks to certain individuals or units, or to contract work out. Usually though, they have little formal authority over the members of the team. Often, members of the team are not relieved of their other responsibilities, so they must divide their efforts between the committee and their "usual" work.

The variety of projects undertaken by ad hoc committees and task forces is unlimited. They include special purpose assignments such as:

Reorganizations

Mergers, acquisitions, or divestitures

Special studies, surveys, or evaluations

Major audits

Efficiency, modernization, and cost reduction efforts

Geographic or marketing expansions

Relocation of facilities or change in facility layout

Management and organization development programs

New equipment or procedures installation

The special commission assigned by President Reagan for the purpose of studying the space shuttle *Challenger* disaster is an example of an ad hoc committee. The commission, formed just after the shuttle explosion in January 1986, conducted an investigation and presented its findings and recommendations to the president four months later.

2.6 PROJECT ENVIRONMENTS[16]

Projects and project management vary depending on the environment. The four environments of projects as classified by Daniel Roman are: commercial/for profit, nonprofit, government, and military. All of the project forms described above are found in the commercial environment, and product and venture management are found almost exclusively there. Program management, however, is most widely used in government and the military. As Roman describes it, there are significant differences in project management practice in these environments:

Commercial/For Profit Project Management

In commercial projects, the end-item is a clearly defined product or service, often customized or one of a kind to satisfy a customer or an internal requirement. The motivation and success criteria in commercial projects are heavily profit-oriented. The project manager usually guides the project through its entire life cycle, coordinating efforts of the project team with functional areas, subcontractors, and vendors. The project manager maintains close contact with the customer and keeps top management informed of progress toward project and profit objectives.

Once the project is completed, the group is dissolved and the project manager is out of a job. Thus, project managers are constantly working to "perpetuate their existence" through seeking out additional projects and preparing proposals. New projects are sought in extensions from existing work or in applications of technology developed in other projects.

Government and Nonprofit Project Management

Government and nonprofit projects differ from commercial activities in several ways. First, there is no profit incentive in government and nonprofit work, and economic factors are of less importance in project management. Project managers in these environments are frequently reassigned during projects, which is problematic for administrative continuity. Particularly for government work, continuity of projects depends heavily upon political considerations since funding is legislatively appropriated.

Second, most projects focus on evaluation or testing of products or services since virtually all budgeted funds are spent on procurement of products and services developed by commercial vendors. Since design and development work is performed by contractors, the project manager's role is largely administrative. He has little control over technical matters, though he is responsible for checking on the contractors' progress. Project managers may oversee and coordinate multiple, related projects that are components of a larger system; i.e., they are program managers.

Military Project Management

Like government projects, most military projects involve testing and evaluating hardware developed by contractors. Evaluation is often based on the "weapons systems" approach whereby each project is part of a larger systems program and hardware is evaluated for its contribution to the mission of the overall system. The major criteria for evaluating projects are technical and political; costs are of lesser importance and profit is not a consideration. Project managers are military officers. Since their tour of duty is limited, officers typically do not oversee a project for its full life cycle. Thus the military must train, transfer, or promote people with the administrative and technical competence to carry on the job.

Civilians are often employed to provide technical support and managerial continuity. This arrangement is a source of strife since civilians are not subject to the same rotation of assignments and are often paid more, despite their formal "subordinate" status to military project managers.

Many organizations exist in multiple project environments (such as government/military *and* commercial) and utilize a variety of management forms—project, program, matrix, task force and committee. Following are true examples of projects in industry, the service sector, and the government.

2.7 PROJECT MANAGEMENT IN INDUSTRY

The following four cases show typical applications of project management in three industrial settings: product development, manufacturing, and construction. They are intended to portray the diversity in scope and size of typical project management situations in industry.

Product Management: The Development of Product X[17]

Company Alpha, described in Chapter 1, is a firm whose future depends on its ability to continuously develop and market new products. Company Alpha specializes in food and drink additives, but it is representative of all kinds of firms in industries such as pharmaceuticals, food products, biotechnology, home and commercial appliances, computer and entertainment electronics, communications, and numerous others that continuously need new ideas to survive in changing, highly competitive environments.

Company Alpha was concerned about maintaining market share for all of its products, but especially for "Product N," its mainstay that accounts for the majority of its profits. It was known that other companies were developing substitutes for Product N, which would possibly be less expensive. To beat the competition, Company Alpha had to develop its own, improved substitute, "Product X."

To facilitate the product development process, the company created a department called, appropriately, the New Product Development Department. The department's charter includes searching out new business and developing long range plans for the company, but essentially it is a "project office" responsible for managing and coordinating ongoing, future, and external development projects so that successful ideas can be conceived and quickly brought to market. The department has three directors of Product Development. These are the project managers. Each one is responsible for managing certain kinds of projects or portions of projects, such as "exploration and development," or "technology-related new business," or "new product commercialization." Each director typically manages more than one product. The role of the directors is to facilitate, coordinate, and monitor the efforts of the various departments—Research and Development, Applications Engineering, Marketing, Manufacturing, and Legal—related to particular products.

For each new product concept a project team is created with representatives from the various functional departments. The director works with the team on a weekly or daily basis to assess the project's progress and requirements. The director is active in all phases of the project and has the final word over its direction, but it is the functional managers who make decisions about what is done, and how, based on guidelines from upper management.

It is the duty of the director to know the status of the project at all times and convey this to upper management. Problems or delays are reported to upper management so that decisions can be made quickly to minimize losses. Projects showing severe problems or signs of failure are cancelled so resources can be allocated to projects showing more promise.

For the development of Product X, the following tasks had to be completed: R&D had to develop a prototype of the product and prepare specifications; Applications Engineering had to define where and in what ways the product can be used; Marketing had to define the commercial market and determine how to establish a position in it (including packaging, brand name, advertising and sales strategies); Manufacturing had to develop a new, patentable process for making the product to prevent competitors from copying it; Finance had to determine initial costing of the product, perform forecasts for profit/loss, and note changes to policies for large-scale production and marketing of the product; and Legal had to obtain regulatory approval and perform patent research.

Many of the tasks had to be performed in parallel. Frequent meetings were held by the project team to review status and plan for next steps. All costs and time spent on the project were recorded and accumulated by the director. On a quarterly basis the director submitted a report to upper management which was used to determine Product X's priority in relation to other projects.

The director for Product X had been involved in the project from its initiation. She worked with R&D scientists and marketing experts to determine the feasibility of the project and she was active in convincing upper management to approve it. She had worked with scientists and managers to prepare project plans and schedules. When additional or new equipment, instruments, or raw materials were needed, she wrote requests for funds. When additional personnel were needed, she wrote personnel requests and justified them to upper management. Besides issuing monthly and quarterly progress reports, she scheduled and planned all project review meetings. In one sense, the director is a "matrix manager" because she manages people from different departments on a given project, even though the people still report to their functional managers for technical direction. In another sense, the director is a "team coordinator" since she has authority to plan, schedule, and budget project matters but not to directly command the members of the team.

R&D Project Management: LogiCircuit Corporation[18]

Mr. Wilcox is the manager of the Solid State Engineering Department (SSE) of LogiCircuit Corporation. SSE is the firm's R&D support group and receives requests for projects from managers in every area of the corporation. One of Mr. Wilcox's responsibilities is to decide which requests are most urgent. In cases where the speed of completing a project is critical, he does not need to submit the usual cost/benefit analysis to his superiors before starting. Such was the case of a request from a manufacturing division that was experiencing severe quality problems with the production of printed circuit boards. They requested a circuit tester be developed to examine the presence and quality of thousands of components in each board. From the request it was clear that a solution was needed quickly.

As with every project, Mr. Wilcox began by estimating the project's total cost. Two engineers "roughed out" a list of components and prepared estimates of how long it would take to do the development work. Mr. Wilcox then prepared cost estimates based upon the component parts list using standard, off-the-shelf prices, and the cost of an outside contractor to provide expertise that SSE did not possess. As in most projects, the greatest single expense was for direct labor hours. Mr. Wilcox estimated that the project would take five months to complete.

Once SSE and the requesting division agreed to a definition of the problem, project cost, and duration, Mr. Wilcox sent requests for assistance to outside contractors. Often in high-technology industries, portions of a project require expertise which is too costly to maintain in-house and must be contracted out. In the circuit tester project, Harmon-Darwood Corp. was contracted to provide computer programming assistance.

A project team was organized by Mr. Wilcox with members from SSE, Harmon-Darwood, and the manufacturing division. As project manager, Mr. Wilcox would oversee the project and coordinate the efforts of SSE with Harmon-Darwood and manufacturing.

All specifications for the tester unit were provided by manufacturing. The project plan called for building six testing units. Once the final design was completed and the initial unit was assembled and tested, the remaining five would be assembled.

Because of the close cooperation and involvement of manufacturing with SSE and Harmon-Darwood during development, few problems were encountered during installation of the units at the plant. Harmon-Darwood trained the operating personnel on the use of the testers and Mr. Wilcox personally spent two weeks at the plant supervising the units' installation. Afterwards, SSE monitored the operation of the units for malfunctions and mistakes. Once it was agreed that the units were working according to plan, the project was formally terminated by Mr. Wilcox. By this time he had transferred his personnel to other assignments.

This project is similar to many R&D projects in that to produce the end-item, the tester units, the company had no prior examples upon which to base estimates of project time and costs. Every R&D project is unique and has to be estimated, planned, and organized from scratch. Although the tester project was accomplished close to its estimated budget and target completion date, it is not unusual for R&D projects to extend months or years beyond original estimates.

Managing an Ad Hoc Project: R.L. Zept Company[19]

The R.L. Zept Company manufactures motorized carts and forklift trucks. Its management was facing two problems: (1) production volume had grown to where its existing three-story plant and warehouse were inadequate; (2) they wanted to add an entirely new product to their existing line, called the "Mohac." They decided to undertake an "expansion project" to build a new facility next to the existing plant which could be used both to increase production capacity and to manufacture the Mohac.

The company president called a staff meeting with members from sales, finance, manufacturing, engineering, and accounting for the purpose of generating ideas about the initiation and execution of the proposed expansion project. At the meeting numerous considerations were raised and summarized into a list outlining the major tasks of the project. They included:

- Facilities: Review existing facilities for obsolescence and replacement value; evaluate equipment needed for expansion, competitive equipment prices, trends in equipment development, and advanced manufacturing techniques; determine the relationship between equipment needs and facilities planning.
- Product development: Review the Mohac concept and prepare a development plan for building prototype models, obtaining production materials, and setting up for production.
- Standardization: Revise existing product lines with a standard configuration on which accessories can be added.
- Simplification: Eliminate components and different kinds of parts from existing lines to improve production ease and reduce inventory investment.
- Labor: Determine the effect of product changes on kinds of labor needed; review shifts from semiskilled to skilled labor; investigate replacing labor with automated equipment.
- Purchasing: Analyze characteristics of suppliers for ability to give good quality, fair prices, and prompt delivery.
- Training: Evaluate labor and supervisory training programs; consider wage scales, quality of product and line management, and employee relations.
- Systems Planning: Engineer and integrate components and subassemblies for overall design; review information flow necessary for successful company operation.
- Inventories: Determine levels necessary to meet policy goals and service goals; establish ways to reduce and maintain required inventory level.

Some of the tasks had to be started immediately to determine if the project was feasible, so the president immediately appointed a project manager to coordinate the activities on the list. The first step was a study and product survey, after which management concluded that the expansion was necessary and the new product development feasible. The project manager then prepared a six year plan encompassing the facility expansion and simultaneous development of the new product, with first shipments scheduled for midway in the sixth year.

The case illustrates an undertaking which clearly mandates project management. The scope and magnitude of the effort defined by the list of tasks was unprecedented for the company. Most of the tasks were interrelated, and many required long lead times. Given the complexity, risks, scope, and time involved, it was necessary to appoint one person—a project manager—to plan and coordinate the effort, and to give her authority to direct it after it began.

Although this is a somewhat large project, it is representative of all sizes and kinds of "ad hoc" projects—activities which have not been done before, but which suddenly become important to organizational goals and where the means must be found to accomplished them.

Project Management in Small Projects: Delamir Roofing Company

Delamir Roofing Company is in the business of installing and redoing roofs for factories and businesses. It performs work and maintains industrial contracts throughout the United States. Like other businesses associated with the construction industry, Delamir considers each job a project and uses project management organization and techniques to meet work goals.

A project manager is assigned overall responsibility for every job. When a request for work is received from a potential customer, the project manager examines the blueprints to determine what materials and how much labor time will be needed. (This is called "prepping the job.") He then prepares a budget and drafts a short proposal. After a contract is acquired, the project manager goes to the site ahead of the rest of the crew to set up arrangements and accommodations so work can begin. The project manager has discretion in selecting a work crew, depending on how many workers are needed and who is available. After work begins, he is responsible not only for supervision of work and delivery of supplies, but for maintaining budget records and reporting progress to the home office. He performs the final inspection with the customer and signs off when the job is completed.

In this example, use of two key elements of project management—a project team and project manager—ensures that the size and skills of the crew fit the requirements of the job, and that one person has overall responsibility to see that the job is done well.

2.8 PROJECT MANAGEMENT IN THE SERVICE SECTOR[20]

Project management is no longer just a tool for industry. It is a form of management which is employed in a broad range of services, including banking, consulting, and accounting. The major difference between project management in industry and the services is that the output of services is not necessarily a tangible product. In the following examples from two "Big Eight" accounting firms—fictitiously called CPAone and CPAtwo, project management is used to plan and control auditing and management consultation projects.

Improving Auditing Efficiency at CPAone

The auditing division at CPAone generates financial statements to meet generally accepted accounting principles. In larger audits, the size of the task and the range of problems require the involvement of several people. In the audit of a national corporation, for example, numerous auditors with diverse specialties are required to investigate all aspects of the operation in various geographic areas. Given the number of people and the variety in skills, expertise, and personalities involved, a project manager is needed to oversee and conduct the audit efficiently. Thus, every audit begins by assigning the client to a partner, usually someone who is familiar with the client's business. The partner becomes the "project director" of the audit and is responsible for writing proposals, staffing the audit, delegating tasks, scheduling, and budgeting.

The project director begins by studying the client's income statement, balance sheet, and other financial statements. If the client has a bad financial reputation, the project director can make the decision for CPAone to refuse to do the audit. If the client is accepted, the director prepares a proposal outlining the general approach for conducting the audit, the completion date, and the cost estimate.

In determining the general approach for conducting the audit, the project director considers the size of the company and the number of departments. Auditors are then assigned on a department by department basis. The audit team is a pure project team, created anew for every audit with people having the skills best suited to the needs of the audit. Generally, each audit has one or two staff accountants, one or two senior accountants, and the project director. Before the proposal is even accepted, the director specifies who will be performing each task and the completion dates. Cost estimates are based on estimated labor hours multiplied by employees' hourly wages.

During the audit the project director must ensure that all work strictly adheres to the Book of Auditing Standards and is completed on schedule. Each week the client and project director meet to review progress. When problems cannot be solved immediately, the director may call in people from CPAone's tax or consulting divisions. When the team has trouble interpreting financial statements, the project director may request that the client's own personnel be involved.

Follow-up service is provided after the audit is completed. The project director sees to it that the client is represented if the IRS requests an examination.

Management Consulting at CPAtwo

Another member of the Big Eight, CPAtwo, uses project management in its Management Consulting Division (MCD). The primary work of MCD is analytical studies of financial, marketing, and information processing operations. Projects are classified into seven areas: business planning, profit improvement, contract management, systems planning, data security, executive management, and human resources. Project management is used in all of these, though specific methods vary depending on the area.

In the systems planning area, for example, projects focus on determining the most efficient way for a firm to achieve objectives. Systems analysis methodology (described in Chapter 4) is applied to determine alternative systems, define system characteristics, evaluate potential benefits, and assign priorities for implementation. A typical project begins by first reviewing the client's present system. If anything is found lacking, a proposal is written summarizing the findings and suggesting options for a new system. If the proposal is accepted, MCD management determines who will be working on the project, when it should be completed, and the cost. A partner or senior manager is assigned as project leader based on his familiarity with the client or the kind of problem. From then on, the project leader has complete responsibility. He selects people from MCD who will be on the project team. MCD regularly updates records of its employees to help project leaders in selecting people best qualified for a given project. The project leader then makes up schedules and determines costs based upon employee hourly rates and hours needed to complete the job.

When the division has sufficient internal expertise to do an analysis, a pure project organization of MCD personnel is formed; when it does not, a matrix form of project organization is used with other divisions supplying people with the necessary skills. While these people are working on MCD projects they continue to do other work in their home divisions. The project leader plans, coordinates, schedules, and budgets project work, directs the team in project matters, and keeps MCD management informed of progress—much the same role as the project directors in CPAone, Alpha Company, and R.L. Zept.

2.9 PROJECT AND PROGRAM MANAGEMENT IN GOVERNMENT: NASA[21]

The following discussion of NASA illustrates how program management and project management are performed in large-scale joint government/commercial undertakings.

NASA was created in 1958 by absorbing the National Advisory Committee on Aeronautics (NACA). NACA had had a long, successful history of working intimately with researchers in universities, industry, and the military. To permit NASA to satisfy the expectations of Congress and the public, it was necessary for the headquarters to take on greater control and direction at NASA than it had at NACA. Still, there remained a determination to continue a partnershipstyle of operation whereby NASA and industry worked closely together on technical problems, but where technical initiative and technical decisions were left to NASA field installations.

NASA Organization

NASA organization includes (1) top management, (2) functional support for top management, (3) program offices for developing and controlling major programs, and (4) field installations which conduct the programs and their components (on-site, at universities, or at contractors). In 1987, NASA was divided into five operating areas, or offices: the Office for Space Flight (OSF), Space Science and Applications (OSSA), Aeronautics and Space Technology (OAST), Space Station (OSS), and Space Operations (OSO). NASA's organization is shown in Figure 2–4.

Each office is responsible for development, justification, and management of *programs*—activities which support broad NASA goals. Offices are assigned field installations which report to them for general management. Each field installation has the responsibility to carry out permanent activities in its specific area, but, still, it also carries out projects or tasks under the direction of other offices besides its own. For example, though Ames, Langley, and Lewis Centers report to OAST, all make substantial contributions to projects in the OSF (Office of Space Flight).

All four kinds of project manager described earlier—expediting, coordinating, matrix, and pure project—are found at NASA, but the latter two are the most common. The matrix is preferred for its efficient use of talent and flexibility. Employees are assigned to the project

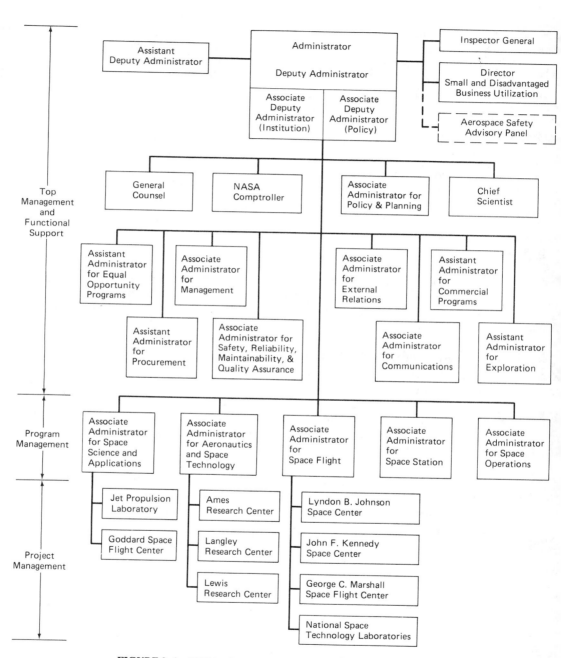

FIGURE 2–4.   NASA program and organization chart, 1987.

but remain on the payrolls of their parent organization and are subject to its merit reviews and promotions. Most even stay in the offices of the parent organization. For the largest projects, however, the pure project form is used. It permits better control, quicker location of responsibility, quicker reaction from the project team, and simpler communication patterns. (Despite these advantages, the matrix and pure project forms do cause problems. These are discussed in Chapter 7.)

In a typical (non-NASA) government project, the agency prepares specifications for a program, lets a contract, then depends upon the contractor for results. NASA uses a different approach; they feel that no single company has all of the capability to execute a large space project. Although NASA relies upon industry to build, integrate, and test-flight hardware, it relies upon its own considerable in-house management and technical competence to monitor and work with contractors. Since NASA projects call for a diversity of technical and managerial competency, project management uses the philosophy of "participative responsibility" (discussed in Chapter 9)—an integration of technical and managerial competence in industry, academia, and NASA laboratories. Irrespective of location, NASA brings in experts from its own field installations, from universities, and from other government laboratories to assist contractors in tackling difficult problems. This participative team approach avoids the delays caused by working across boundaries which separate government, commercial, and military organizations. The concept utilizes teamwork, central control, and decentralized execution, but respects the semiautonomous status of NASA's field installations.

Program and Project Manager Roles

NASA defines a *program* as a series of undertakings which, over several years, is designed to accomplish broad scientific or technical goals in NASA's long-range plan. Responsibility for programs is assigned by NASA headquarters. A *project* is an undertaking within a program with a scheduled beginning and end. It normally involves design, construction, or operation of specific hardware items and necessary support.

NASA uses a dual system of responsibility. Perhaps the single greatest contributor to a project's success is the person upon whom final responsibility rests, the *project manager*. She is the official at a field installation responsible for executing the project within the guidelines and controls of NASA headquarters and the field installation. She is responsible for day to day supervision, execution, and completion of projects, whether conducted by NASA, contractors, or university scientists. Although most of the workers on a project are outside of the administrative authority of the project manager, they do take directions *on project matters* from the project manager.

The project manager has a counterpart in Washington, the *program manager*, who represents the headquarters' interests. The program manager is the senior NASA staff official responsible for developing and administering the headquarters' guidelines and controls with respect to a given project. He must fight the battles for resource allocation within headquarters, monitor project execution, work with organizations interested in participating in the project, relate the project to NASA's broader goals, and testify to, or justify authorizations from Congress and the President. On large projects, the program manager might oversee just one project. The success of the project depends on these two people, the project and program manager, and on the quality of their relationship.

During the 1960s, NASA was as an outstanding example of a government/commercial project organization that worked. In the 1970s and 80s it faced severe budgetary cutbacks and resource constraints that reduced its ability to meet increasingly ambitious goals. Many of NASA's controls were eliminated and its standards were allowed to erode. The *Challenger* disaster is a tragic example of what can happen when project managers are not given adequate authority and information to maintain control over their projects.[22]

2.10 SUMMARY

In this chapter we addressed "What is project management?" by describing the characteristics that distinguish projects, project environments, and project managers from nonproject forms of activities and managers. All managers "manage" tasks and resources: they translate organizational goals into specific objectives, prepare plans about the tasks and resources needed to achieve objectives, organize the resources, and direct, evaluate, and control work tasks and resources to insure that objectives are met.

The contingency approach to management recognizes that there can be no prescribed set of functions and organizations appropriate to all situations and goals. Effective managers need to be familiar with classical, behavioral, and systems viewpoints of management. To be able to apply these concepts and choose the most appropriate course of action, they must first understand and diagnose each confronting situation. Project management is a systems/contingency approach to organization and management; it applies elements of classical and behavioral management and uses organizational forms and management roles best suited to the unique environment of projects.

The most important role in project management is that of the project manager. This person functions to unify project-related planning, communications, control, and direction to achieve project goals. The project manager is an integrator-generalist who ties together the efforts of functional areas, suppliers, and subcontractors, and keeps top management and the customer apprised of project progress. Project management comprises the organizations, systems, and procedures that enable the project manager to perform this function.

Project management applies to any temporary, goal-oriented activity, but it becomes more essential as the magnitude, unfamiliarity, and stake of the undertaking increase. Organizations in rapidly changing environments especially need project management.

Project management takes on a variety of forms: larger efforts typically utilize pure project, matrix, and program management forms; smaller efforts are handled by ad hoc committees and task forces. The venture and product management forms used in consumer-oriented firms are similar to project management. Project management is applied in much the same way in commercial, nonprofit, government, and military projects, with variation to account for differences in the environments.

The purpose of this chapter was to discuss features that distinguish project management, situations where it is used, the variety of forms it takes, and some of its common applications. Project management takes an "open systems" view of organizations; it has been called a "systems approach" to management. The next two chapters describe what that means and discuss the systems philosophy and methodologies that underlie a large part of project management theory and practice.

CHAPTER REVIEW QUESTIONS

1. Describe the five functions of management. Are any of these not performed by managers? How do you think each of these functions comes into play in the course of a project?

2. Describe the classical and behavioral viewpoints of management and how they differ from the systems approach. The classical and behavioral viewpoints were originated decades ago. Are they still of use today? (For a better idea of how the viewpoints differ and how the contingency approach is applied in general practice, refer to management references such as those cited in endnotes 1, 2, 4 and 5.)

3. Explain what distinguishes the contingency approach to management from the other three viewpoints.

4. List the main characteristics of "projects." How do these features distinguish projects from other, nonproject activities?

5. What are the characteristics of "project management?" Contrast these to functional and other types of nonproject management.

6. What makes project management more suitable to project environments than traditional management and organization?

7. Where did project management methods and organization originate? What happened during the 20th century that made project management necessary?

8. What are the four types of project management roles? Describe the responsibilities and authority of managers in each role. Are all four roles ever used in the same organization?

9. What are the five criteria that Cleland and King suggest for determining when to use project management? From these, describe briefly how a manager should know when project management is appropriate for the task.

10. When is project management clearly not appropriate? List some "project-type" activities where you think project management should *not* be used. Describe some organizations or kinds of work where you think both project and nonproject types of management are appropriate.

11. Briefly compare and contrast the following forms of project management: pure project, matrix, program, new venture, product, and ad hoc committee/task force. Give at least one illustration of an organization where each one is used.

12. What are some of the problems of being a project leader in commercial, government, and military projects? Where do organizations in these environments get project leaders?

13. In the industry, service sector, and NASA examples in this chapter, what common characteristics of the environment, the project goals, and the project tasks make project management appropriate (or necessary)? Also, what seem to be the common characteristics of the roles and responsibilities of the project managers in these examples? What are the differences?

14. Now that you know a little about projects and project management (with still a long way to go), list some government and private organizations where you think project management might be useful. You might want to check to see if, in fact, they *are* using project management.

QUESTIONS ABOUT THE STUDY PROJECT

1. In the project you are studying, what characteristics of the company, project goals, tasks, or necessary expertise make the use of project management appropriate or inappropriate? Consider the size, complexity, risk, and other criteria in answering this.
2. How does the project you are studying fit the definition of a project?
3. What kind of project management is used—program, product, matrix, pure, or other? Explain. Is it called "project management" or something else?
4. What kind of role does the project manager have—an expeditor, coordinator, pure project, or matrix manager? Explain. What is his or her title?

ENDNOTES

1. Adopted from Andrew Szilagyi, *Management and Performance*, 2nd ed. (Glenview, IL: Scott, Foresman, 1984), 7–10, 16–20, 29–32.
2. For a comprehensive review of this topic, see Don Hellriegel and John Slocum, *Management*, 4th ed. (Reading, MA.: Addison-Wesley, 1986), 25–64.
3. One of the earliest discussions of this viewpoint appeared in F.J. Roethlisberger and W.J. Dickson, *Management and the Worker* (Boston: Harvard University Press, 1939).
4. See, for example, Paul Hersey and Ken Blanchard, *Management of Organizational Behavior: Utilizing Human Resources*, 4th ed. (Englewood Cliffs, N.J.: Prentice-Hall, 1982). This volume presents the "situational leadership" theory and applications.
5. See Don Hellriegel and John Slocum, "Organizational Design: A Contingency Approach," *Business Horizons*, Vol. 16, No. 2, 1973, 59–68.
6. Russell D. Archibald, *Managing High-Technology Projects* (New York: Wiley, 1976), 19; Jack R. Meredith and Samuel Mantel, *Project Management: A Managerial Approach* (New York: Wiley, 1985), 4–5; Daniel D. Roman, *Managing Projects: A Systems Approach* (New York: Elsevier, 1986), 2–10; John M. Stewart, "Making Project Management Work," *Business Horizons*, Vol. 8, No. 3 (Fall 1965), 54–68.
7. David Cleland and William King, *Systems Analysis and Project Management*, 3rd ed. (New York: McGraw-Hill, 1983), 191–192.
8. Keith Davis, "The Role of Project Management in Scientific Manufacturing," *IEEE Transactions of Engineering Management*, Vol. 9, No. 3, 1962, 109–113.
9. Portions of this section are adopted from Richard Johnson, Fremont Kast, and James Rosenzweig, *The Theory and Management of Systems*, 3rd ed. (New York: McGraw-Hill, 1973), 395–397.
10. Cleland and King, *Systems Analysis and Project Management*, 259.
11. Based upon W. Hofer, "Lady Liberty's Business Army," *Nation's Business* (July 1983), 18–28.
12. Archibald, *Managing High-Technology Projects*, describes general criteria for identifying major commercial, new product, R&D, capital facilities, and information systems projects. See pp. 28–31.
13. John Adams, Stephen Barndt, and Martin Martin, *Managing by Project Management* (Dayton, OH: Universal Technology, 1979), 12–13.

14. Szilagyi, *Management and Performance*, 489–490.

15. Alvin Toffler, *Future Shock* (New York: Random House, 1970).

16. This section is adapted from Daniel Roman, *Managing Projects: A Systems Approach* (New York: Elsevier, 1986), 426–429, with the permission of the publisher.

17. Based upon information compiled by Jenny Harrison from interviews with managers in Company Alpha (fictitious name).

18. Based upon information compiled by Cary Morgan from interviews with managers of the LogiCircuit Corporation (fictitious name).

19. Adapted from a case in R.L. Janson, *Production Control Desk Book* (Englewood Cliffs, N.J.: Prentice-Hall, 1978).

20. Based upon information compiled by Darlene Capodice from interviews with managers in the two accounting firms.

21. Portions of this section are adapted from Richard Chapman, *Project Management in NASA: The System and The Men* (Washington, D.C.: NASA SP–324, NTIS No. N75–15692, 1973).

22. Joseph Trento, *Prescription for Disaster* (New York: Crown, 1987).

chapter 3

Systems and Organizations

There is so much talk about the system.
And so little understanding.

Robert M. Pirsig

Zen and the Art of Motorcycle Maintenance

A project is a *system* of people, equipment, materials, and facilities organized and managed to achieve a goal. Much of the established theory and practice about what it takes to put together and coordinate project organizations comes from a perspective called "systems thinking" or the "systems approach." At the same time, work done in projects is often done for the purpose of *creating* systems. In projects, especially those in product and software development, engineering, or research in high-technology industries, methodologies such as "systems analysis," "systems engineering," and "systems management" are commonplace. This chapter and Chapter 4 introduce systems concepts that form the basis for project management, and systems methodologies used in project work.

3.1 SYSTEMS THINKING

Systems thinking is a way of viewing the world. It is the opposite of analytical thinking in which things are broken into progressively smaller parts and more highly specialized disciplines. Part of what distinguishes systems thinkers from analytical thinkers is that the former focus on "whole organisms" rather than just the parts. Even when they look at the parts, they try to keep the whole organism in mind and to understand the parts by understanding the processes taking place among them.[1]

Systems thinking means being able to perceive the "system" in a situation. It is the ability to take a confused, chaotic situation and perceive some degree of order and interrelationship. Systems thinking is a useful way of dealing with complex phenomena, especially human endeavors such as large projects. In project management theory and practice, systems thinking and analytical thinking are supplements to one another.

Although project managers have to know about the status of individual parts of the project, most of the responsibility for those parts is delegated to managers and technicians who specialize in them. Project managers are concerned with the "big picture," and as such, they must be systems thinkers. This chapter covers three fundamental topics for the project manager/systems thinker: systems concepts, general systems theory, and the systems view of organizations.

3.2 DEFINITION OF SYSTEM

The word "system" means computer to many people, yet it is so commonly used that it seems to refer to everything else, too. By definition, a system is "an organized or complex whole; an assemblage of things or parts interacting in a coordinated way." The parts could be players on a football team, keys on a typewriter, or components in a VCR. The parts need not be physical entities; they can be abstract or conceptual entities, such as words in a language or steps in a procedure. Everyday usage of the word is included with such disparate things as river systems, planetary systems, transportation and communication systems, nervous and circulatory systems, production and inventory control systems, ecosystems, urban systems, social systems, economic systems, stereo systems, philosophical systems, ad infinitum (and computer systems, too).

Thus, a system can be just about anything. So besides being an "assemblage of things," the definition of system should include three other features:

1. parts of the system are *affected* by being in the system and are changed if they leave it;
2. the assemblage of parts *does* something; and
3. the assembly is of particular interest.[2]

The first feature means that, in systems, the whole is more than the sum of the parts. The human body, for example, can be analyzed in terms of separate components—the liver, brain, heart, nerve fibers, and so on, yet if any of these are removed from the body, both they and the body will change. Parts of the body cannot live outside the body, and without the parts the body cannot exist either. The name given to a way of viewing things in terms of their "wholeness," or the whole being more than the sum of the parts, is *holism*. Holism is the opposite of "reductionism," which says that things can be understood by simply breaking them down and understanding the pieces. Certainly many things cannot be understood by simply looking at the pieces. Water, for example, is more than just the characteristics of hydrogen and oxygen combined. The idea of the parts affecting the whole and vice versa is central to systems thinking. (Related ideas appear elsewhere. Psychologists use the term *Gestalt* to describe theories and practices that emphasize the whole person and the surrounding situation. Another term, *synergy*, describes situations where several components work together to produce a combined effect.)

The second feature of systems is that they are dynamic and exhibit some kind of *behavior*; they *do* something. The kind of behavior they exhibit depends upon the particular kind of system at hand. System behavior can usually be observed in the outputs of the system or the way the system converts inputs to outputs, though the conversion process and the outputs may be quite obscure.

Third, systems are conceived by the people looking at them, which means they exist in the eye (or mind) of the beholder.[3] This is not to say that they fail to exist unless someone is there to see them, but rather that the conception of a system can be altered to suit one's purpose. For example, in diagnosing a patient, a doctor may see the whole body as "the system." The doctor may send the patient to a specialist, who sees only the digestive tract as "the system." If the problem is food poisoning and the patient files suit, her attorney may include the restaurant and food manufacturer in "the system."

Scientists and researchers who study and work with systems have tried to identify, organize, and classify facts, ideas, and even laws that apply across the board to all systems, no matter how different they seem. The body of knowledge describing system structure and behavior is called General Systems Theory.

3.3 GENERAL SYSTEMS THEORY[4]

According to Buckley, "A whole which functions as a whole by virtue of the interdependence of its parts is called a *system*, and the method which aims at discovering how this is brought about in the widest variety of systems has been called general system theory."[5] General system(s) theory classifies systems by the way their components are interrelated in order to define typical behavioral patterns for different classes of systems.

Classification Taxonomy

Kenneth Boulding devised a taxonomy for classifying various systems into a hierarchy of levels. In this hierarchy, system complexity increases from each level to the next higher one. The hierarchy, shown in Figure 3–1, is described as follows:

Level	Type of System[6]
1	Static structures, called frameworks, describe the function, position, or relationships among elements of the system: anatomy charts, maps, floor plans, and models are examples.
2	Simple dynamic systems, called clockworks, have predetermined motions: for example, machines and the solar system. Most of the theories of physics, chemistry, and economics are at this level.
3	Control mechanisms, or cybernetic systems, are self-regulating and maintain equilibrium: examples include the heating thermostat, self-guided missiles, and servomechanisms. Behavior is goal seeking, but there is no self-changing of goals.
4	Open systems, or self-maintaining, self-reproductive systems. Life begins to be differentiated from non-life at this level: for example, a cellular system.

(Continued on next page)

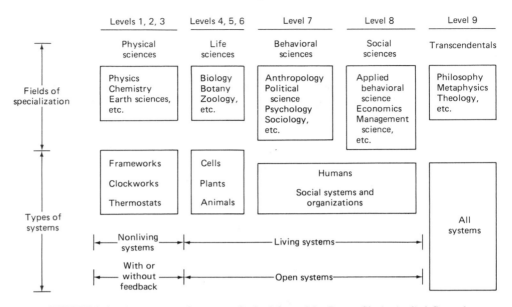

FIGURE 3–1. A taxonomy of systems. (Derived from: John P. van Gigch, *Applied General Systems Theory*, 2nd ed. (New York: Harper and Row, 1978), 39.)

Level	Type of System[6]
5	Genetic-societal systems, typified by plants and characterized by a division of labor. Distinctive stages of the life cycle are genetically programmed.
6	Animal systems, which have increased mobility, self-awareness, exogenetic information storage, and instinctive goal-seeking behavior.
7	Human systems, which have self-consciousness (awareness of being aware), goal formulation, reflection and planning, speech and symbolism.
8	Social systems, systems of human organization, and their characteristics: values, roles, history, culture, and art forms.
9	Transcendental systems, those "unknowables" which escape us and for which we have no answers.

Each level has the characteristics of all lower levels. The first three levels consist of physical and mechanical systems; they provide the basis for the physical sciences and engineering. The next three levels deal with biological systems; they are the realm of biology, botany, zoology, and medicine. The final three levels deal with the behavioral and social sciences, the arts, religions, and humanities. Empirical evidence and theoretical advances in systems theory indicate that all systems in the natural world—physical, biological, and socio-cultural—are interrelated and have evolved in sequence.[7] The practice of project management exists at level 8, but its goals, outcomes, and processes make use of or relate to systems at all levels.

3.4 SYSTEMS CONCEPTS AND PRINCIPLES

In the above discussion, some systems terms were used without being defined (in the hope that their meanings could be discerned by the context of their usage). The most common system terms will now be defined in detail.

Elements and Subsystems

Systems can be broken down into smaller and smaller parts. The smallest part of a system is an *element*. Systems can also be broken down into parts which are themselves systems, called *subsystems*. A subsystem is a system which is part of a larger system. When it is unnecessary to understand or reveal its inner workings, a subsystem can simply be thought of as an element. In Figure 3–2, a common organization chart illustrates that the Production Department may be viewed as an element in the company; if we delve into

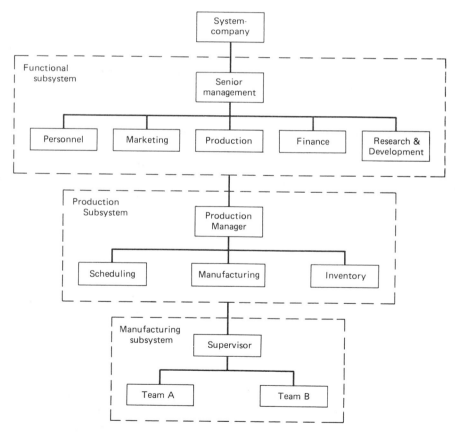

FIGURE 3–2. A company portrayed in terms of elements and subsystems.

it, however, it becomes a subsystem with elements of Scheduling, Manufacturing, and Inventory. Each element, such as Manufacturing, could in turn be viewed as a sub-subsystem containing elements. In a project, an element could be a unit of work, a person or group doing the work, or a component of the item being produced by the project.

Attributes

Systems, subsystems, and elements all have characteristics and properties that distinguish them. These *attributes* are used to describe or express the condition of systems, subsystems, and elements in qualitative or quantitative terms. The attributes of a system may be used to monitor and measure system behavior and performance. Among attributes used to describe a project, the most common are its cost and its progress at a particular point in time.

Environment and Boundary

When a system is conceptualized by someone, called the "decision maker," the system's *environment* is taken to be whatever lies outside of the decision maker's control but can affect how the system operates. The environment can include the community we live in, the air we breathe, or the people we associate with, though it is not necessarily any of these. A system is separated from its environment by a *boundary*. In many systems the boundary is somewhat obscure and it is difficult to separate the system from the environment. To determine what is the environment, the decision maker asks the questions "Can I do anything about it?" and "Is it relative to my situation or objective?" If the answer is "No" to the first question but "Yes" to the second, then "it" is part of the environment. The following table shows how to distinguish a system from its environment:

<table>
<tr><td></td><td></td><td colspan="2" align="center">Is it relevant to the system?</td></tr>
<tr><td></td><td></td><td align="center">Yes</td><td align="center">No</td></tr>
<tr><td rowspan="2" align="right">Can the
decision maker
control it?</td><td align="center">Yes</td><td align="center">System</td><td rowspan="2" align="center">The Irrelevant
Environment</td></tr>
<tr><td align="center">No</td><td align="center">Environment</td></tr>
</table>

The "irrelevant environment" includes all things outside the system which have no influence on it and do not matter. It is the background to the system. To a project manager, the planet Jupiter is part of the irrelevant environment—unless the system being produced is an interplanetary space probe, in which case it becomes part of the relevant environment and must be considered in the design of the system. From here on, mention of the environment will always refer to the *relevant* environment—factors that matter to and influence the system in some way.

Objectives

Man-made systems are designed to *do* something. They have objectives which are conceived by people. One of the greatest aids to help conceptualize, create, or investigate a system is to have a clear, concise statement of the *objectives* of the system. Frequently objectives are broken down into a hierarchy of objectives, each relating to a subsystem. For instance, the top objective of the project may be defined as "build a space station." Moving down the hierarchy are various activities and subsystems such as "select vehicle configuration," "select prime contractor," "train crew," "launch materials into orbit," "assemble components," and so on. Each activity has objectives which are *subobjectives* for the overall system.

System Structure

Elements and subsystems are linked together by relationships. The form taken by the relationships is referred to as the *structure* of the system. The functioning and effectiveness of a system is largely determined by the "appropriateness" of the structure to the objective or purpose of the system. Most complex systems have hierarchical structures consisting of organized levels of subelements within elements, elements within subsystems, and so on. The formal organization structure shown in Figure 3–2 is an example of a hierarchical structure.

Constraints and Conflicts

Systems have *constraints* or limitations imposed both from within and by the environment. These inhibit their ability to reach objectives. Time and money are two universal constraints in projects: without limitations on one or the other, almost any objective conceivable would be attainable. The trouble is that most project objectives are deemed desirable only within a limited time period and budget.

In human organizations, and especially in projects, the objectives of subsystems are frequently in *conflict*. This reduces the chances that any of them or the overall system objective will ever be achieved. Conflict in objectives is especially prevalent between different levels and functions in project systems.

Open and Closed Systems

Probably the major contribution of general systems theory is the distinction between *open* systems (levels 4 and higher) and *closed* systems (levels 3 and lower). Closed systems are *viewed* as self-contained. Take, for example, a machine: to know its workings, you need only study the machine; it is not necessary to look at anything else. Closed system *thinking* focuses on the internal operation, structure, and processes of a system without regard to the external environment. This does not mean that the environment does not affect it; it means that the person looking at the system has chosen to ignore the environment. In fact, for *many* machines, closed system thinking works fairly well.

In contrast to machines, biological and social systems are not closed. They are open systems, which means they interact with the environment and have the capability to adapt to changes in the environment. To know about them you need to know something about their environment as well.

The concept of open systems has been particularly useful in social and organization theory. It has led to the development of a way of viewing organizations in terms of structures, processes, functions, and relationships *between* components. Such a view is a key part of project management.

Natural versus Man-Made Systems

Another way of classifying systems is to contrast *natural systems* (e.g., animal organisms and planetary systems) to *man-made systems* (e.g., communication systems and human organizations). Natural systems came into being by natural processes. Man-made systems are designed and operated by man. Many projects exist for the purpose of creating man-made systems.

Among natural systems there is natural harmony, and processes tend to fall toward equilibrium. In contrast, no such harmony exists between man-made systems. They tend to be scientifically unpredictable, disruptive, and destabilizing. Natural systems can be altered by or become a part of man-made systems. An example is the alteration of a river system and formation of a lake by a dam; another is the alteration of the atmosphere and ecosystems through introduction of man-made pollutants.

Man-made systems are embedded in and utilize inputs from natural systems, and both systems interact in important and significant ways. In recent years the appearance of large-scale man-made systems has had significant, mostly undesirable, impact on the natural world. Examples abound, such as acid rain, toxic contamination of water systems, and air pollution. Such consequences are referred to as "side effects." They arise largely because planners failed to consider or ignored the possibility of their occurrence. It is becoming more and more necessary for designers of systems to adopt a wider systems view which encompasses the elements and interfaces of man-made systems with natural systems.

3.5 HUMAN ORGANIZATIONS[8]

Organization is a familiar concept. Most people belong to numerous organizations—employers, clubs, congregations, sports teams, and so on. Organizations can be looked at as goal-oriented *systems*—interacting parts, human and nonhuman, generally working toward common (though sometimes vague or uncertain) goals. All organizations have a goal or mission, stated or otherwise; it is the reason they exist.

Organizations as Open Systems

Organizations are *open* systems: they interact with the environment, receive as inputs people, materials, information, and capital, and export as outputs goods, services, information, or waste byproducts. Certain features characterize organizational systems; we will consider those relevant to project organizations:

1. Organizations are contrived by mankind, so they can have *large numbers* of objectives. For just about any "realistic"[9] goal man can conceive, a project organization can be developed to work toward it. Unlike biological systems, organizations do not necessarily die; they can be altered and reformed to sustain life and pursue different objectives. This is certainly true for many project organizations because once an objective has been achieved, an organization (its elements, technology, and structure) can be changed to pursue another one.

2. Given that organizations are open systems, the *boundaries* of organizations are permeable and tend to fluctuate with different objectives and types of activities. The boundary of large project organizations are sometimes difficult to define, especially when one considers all of the contractors, subcontractors, suppliers, customer representatives, and local and government regulatory groups that might be involved. Some of these elements are more involved, others less involved, but all are a part of the project system.

The role of management is to ensure integration and cooperation among the subsystems within the boundary, and between these and others outside the boundary in the larger environment. Project managers are "boundary agents": they work at the point of contact between subsystems where there is transfer of energy, people, materials, money, and information.

3. All complex systems are *hierarchical*—they are composed of lower-order subsystems and are part of a higher-order suprasystem. Within an organization, people combine to form organized groups, and groups combine to form departments or project teams. These make up a company, which is part of an industry, which is in an economy, and so on. Hierarchy exists for both structure—units and relationships—and processes—lower level tasks and activities combine to make up higher level tasks and activities. Much of the planning and scheduling of project work utilizes this concept of hierarchy.

4. To maintain stability in changing environments, organizations depend upon *feedback* of information from their internal elements and the environment. Negative feedback is information telling a system that it is deviating from its objectives and should adjust its course of action. In project organizations, managers must continuously gather and interpret feedback information and take action to keep the project on course; this is the vital role of project review and control. Shifts in the environment can make a project obsolete or inappropriate and require new objectives to be set or new courses of action to be charted.

The view of organizations as open systems was heralded in the 1960s and 70s as the major new paradigm in management theory and practice. Although many managers and researchers have adopted terminology from open systems theory, it appears, unfortunately, that most still practice a more closed system approach in their actual behavior.[10] One promising trend however, is the increasing number of popular books on management and organization that broadly adhere to systems principles; examples include *Beyond the Quick Fix*, *Thriving on Chaos*, and *Change Agent Skills A: Assessing and Designing Excellence*.[11] These speak of the importance of the environment, goals, subsystems, and relationships in the creation and management of effective human organizations.

Environmental Subsystems

Organizations interact with other, external, people and organizations such as customers, suppliers, unions, stockholders, and governments, to mention a few. They rely upon the environment for inputs of energy, information, and material, and they export their outputs of goods, services, and wastes to the environment (represented in Figure 3–3).

Elements of the environment can be thought of as interacting subsystems, each having goals and responsibilities related to one another. Some of the more predominant subsystems of the project management environment include:

Competitive	Legal
Cultural	Political
Economic	Psychological
Technological	Educational
Sociological	

In establishing goals and methods of operation, organizations are influenced by and must deal with these subsystems. Take, for instance, elements of the "competitive subsystem." Any organization which challenges others for the same *scarce resources*—customers, raw materials, budget allocations, etc.—is part of a competitive subsystem. All organizations compete. Projects organizations rely on technology—equipment, tools, facilities, techniques, and knowledge—that is given or loaned to them by other organizations such as suppliers, consultants, and functional departments. They must compete economically and politically to

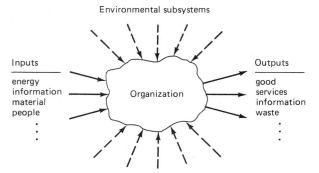

FIGURE 3–3. Organization as input-output system.

acquire the technology they need to obtain contracts and accomplish goals, indeed, to survive.

Effective project managers are familiar with the key subsystems in their environment. Many organizations try to operate as if they were isolated; they collect little information about their environment and fail to utilize the information they have. As open systems, organizations must choose goals and conduct their operations in ways that respect the opportunities and limitations afforded by the environment. Cleland and King call this the manager's "environmental problem." It requires that managers:[12]

1. appreciate the need to assess the forces in the environment;
2. understand the forces which significantly effect their organization; and
3. integrate these forces into the organization's goals, objectives, and operations.

Properties of Organizations

Organizations have been called *socio-technical systems* which means they consist of a social subsystem of individuals with a culture and a mission, as well as a technology subsystem of equipment, facilities, tools, and techniques. An organization cannot be just one or the other since both subsystems are interdependent. Human and social activities must be structured and integrated around the technology since the technology influences the types of inputs and outputs of the organization. Yet it is the social subsystem that determines the effectiveness of the utilization of technology. This is one reason why in project management, it is just as important to be aware of and *manage* the behavioral and social aspects of projects as it is to manage their technology. To the detriment of project goals, some managers behave as if the social subsystem did not exist.

Each organization has a *structural* subsystem which comprises the units of the organization and the relationships between them. The structural subsystem includes both the formal structure—described by organization charts, job descriptions, procedures, and patterns of authority and communication, as well as the informal structure—procedures and patterns of work and communication that bypass the formal structure.

A common model for the structural subsystem is the organization chart shown in Figure 3–2. It reveals formal elements of the subsystem—people, groups, departments—and formal authority and responsibility relationships that connect them. It shows who reports to whom and how groups are formally associated. Its disadvantage is that it mistakenly equates formal hierarchy with authority and control, and ignores the effects of personalities and informal interaction between peers and associates.

Organization charts look at organizations as Level 1, or static systems—a holdover from the early "classical" and bureaucratic view of organizations mentioned in Chapter 2. They are still useful, however, as long as this limitation is recognized.

"Systems models" of organization, in contrast, emphasize not only the structure but the *processes* within organizations that contribute to or detract from objectives. Systems models consider how components relate to each other and the environment.

Internal, Functional Subsystems[13]

Besides social, technology, and structural subsystems, organizations can be broken down into subsystems according to function or purpose. For example, one form of breakdown is in terms of functional specializations:

The marketing subsystem

The production subsystem

The personnel subsystem

The financial subsystem

The research and development subsystem

Project subsystems

In much the same way as the circulatory, respiratory, digestive, and other subsystems contribute to the behavior and well-being of an animal, *functional subsystems* of organizations have purposes which contribute to the well-being and goals of an organization. Projects are subsystems that, to large extent, have features similar to, yet beyond, those of all the other subsystems. This is because to accomplish their ends projects take *elements* from other functional subsystems—personnel, technology, and so on—and use them to do things which none of the functional subsystems can do alone.

Project Management Systems

Of special relevance are the *management subsystems* which internally organize the organization and are responsible for its effective performance. All management subsystems are integrated into a subsystem that manages the overall organization. Each project has its own management subsystem, hereafter called a *project management system.*

Embedded in the project management system are other subsystems for project management *control* and project management *information. Project management control* subsystems (described in Chapter 15) include the standards, policies, procedures, decision rules, and reporting requirements to monitor and control a project. Every project has its own control subsystem to monitor activities, compare them to goals and standards, and suggest corrective actions. *Project management information* subsystems (described in Chapter 16) include data requirements, collection procedures, data storage and processing, and information reporting. They collect and summarize data from internal and environmental subsystems to provide managers with information for making decisions. Each project and functional subsystem may have its own information subsystem, and all are combined into an organization-wide management information system.

To be effective, project management must have both information and control subsystems. Timely and pertinent information is necessary to exercise control, and a framework must exist to utilize that information for decision making. In subsequent chapters the concepts of management, control, and information subsystems will be related to project management.

One way to better explain the position and purpose of project management subsystems in organizations is to consider their relationship to other kinds of management subsystems.

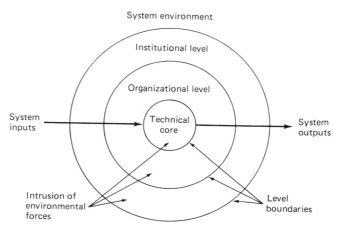

FIGURE 3–4. Management systems hierarchy. (From Thomas Petit, "A Behavioral Theory of Management," *Academy of Management Journal*, December 1967, 346.)

In general, management subsystems can be divided according to the three-level hierarchy shown in Figure 3–4:[14]

1. The underlying technical level produces and distributes goods and services. Here, work tends to be standardized and repetitive; decisions are largely programmed according to standards, policies, and procedures.

2. The organizational level organizes and integrates the work of the technical level. It coordinates inputs and outputs between functional subsystems, disseminates information to and exercises control over activities and outputs at the technical level. Some decisions at this level are programmed, but most are nonprogrammed.

3. The institutional, or highest level, is where organizational activities are related to the environment. This is the realm of the chief executive and board of directors where goals and adaptive, innovative strategies are laid out. Structures and processes are conceived to meet demands of internal and environmental subsystems. Decisions at this level are strictly nonprogrammed.

There is considerable difference in the orientation and tasks of managers at the three levels. At the bottom, technical level, managers are more task-oriented and have a relatively short time perspective. A closed system perspective is often seen here because the organization is able to close off the technical "core" from the environment. Much of the work at this level tends to be repetitive and routine, so management's role is largely to provide guidance and control.

Managers at the top, institutional level, tend to be more conceptual in orientation and have a long-range time perspective. Their principal occupation is planning. They face considerable uncertainty in dealing with inputs from the environment over which they may have little control.

Managers at the middle, organizational level, integrate the levels above and below them. They are boundary agents, working at the interfaces between the three levels. They must translate the strategies of the institutional level into procedures and practices for the technical level. Similarly, they must translate decisions by managers at the technical level for interpretation by managers at the institutional level. They take on responsibilities for translating, planning, and control.

Project managers, and the project management system, usually exist at the organizational level. A primary function of the project management system is to mediate between the institutional and technical levels, and to coordinate tasks and functions at the technical level. In carrying out the project goals of top management and integrating the project work (usually done by various functional areas), project managers do both planning and controlling. They often have limited knowledge of the functional areas, so they must rely on the expertise of managers at the technical level to get work done. In later chapters, our discussions about project managers will utilize both functional subsystem and hierarchical concepts of organizations.

3.6 SUMMARY

Systems thinking is a useful way for dealing with complex phenomena. It implies the ability to perceive the system in a situation, to take something confused or chaotic and perceive a degree of order and interrelationship in it. A system is defined as an assemblage of parts where (1) the parts are affected by being in the system, (2) the assembly does something, and (3) the assembly is of particular interest. What is called the system depends upon one's point of view and purpose. Projects are systems, and they are created for the purpose of making systems.

Human organizations are man-made, open systems. They are sociotechnical systems, meaning they are social systems organized around a technology. Organizations interact with the environment and rely upon it for input. In establishing goals and methods of operation, managers must deal with subsystems in the environment and account for how these subsystems influence the organization.

Functional subsystems in organizations provide the specializations necessary to carry out technology. Management subsystems organize other subsystems and are responsible for organization performance. Control and information subsystems monitor activities, provide information for decision making, and suggest corrective action.

Management systems are hierarchical: managers at the technical level deal directly with the tasks and technology of the organization; managers at the organization level are responsible for coordinating activities at the technical level and integrating activities across functional areas; managers at the institutional level interface with the environment and develop goals and strategies of the overall organization. Project managers typically are at the organization level.

This chapter focused on systems thinking as a way of conceptualizing and analyzing physical entities. Systems thinking also leads to a perspective for approaching problems. The next chapter describes these "systems approaches" and some well-known methodologies for analyzing, designing, and managing complex systems.

CHAPTER REVIEW QUESTIONS

1. What distinguishes "systems thinking" from "analytical thinking?" Is systems thinking something new or is it just another perspective? Explain.

2. Define "system." What notable features enable you to "see" something as a system? Describe briefly the American legal or education system in terms of these features.

3. How can several people looking at the same thing see the "system" in it differently?

4. What are Boulding's nine levels in the systems hierarchy? Which of these might be considered "living" systems?

5. Describe the following concepts and explain how they fit into systems thinking: elements, subsystems, environment, boundary, open systems, objectives, structure, and constraints.

6. Describe the difference between open and closed systems, and between man-made and natural systems. Are all natural systems open systems?

7. Is a space vehicle an open system? Is an organization an open system? Explain.

8. Why are organizations called "socio-technical" systems? Are they ever just social systems?

9. What are the limitations of traditional organizational charts? How do "systems models" of organizations differ from these charts?

10. Describe the features and properties that distinguish human organizations from other systems.

11. Name some predominant environmental subsystems. What is their place in the systems view of organizations?

12. What is the manager's "environmental problem?"

13. What are some internal subsystems of organizations? Distinguish between functional subsystems and managerial subsystems.

14. What are the three levels of the management systems hierarchy? How do the roles, perspectives, and time orientation differ between levels? Describe the three levels for a school system; for a religious organization; for a hospital; for the military; for General Motors.

15. What is the relevance of systems thinking to project management?

QUESTIONS ABOUT THE STUDY PROJECT

1. Conceptualize the project organization (the project team and the parent organization of the team) you are studying as a system. What are the elements, attributes, environment, and so on? What are its internal subsystems—functional breakdown and management-hierarchy subsystems? What are the relevant subsystems in the environment?

2. Describe the role of the project manager with respect to these subsystems, both internal and external. What is the nature of his or her responsibilities in these subsystems? How aware is the project manager of the project "environment" and what does he or she do that reflects this awareness?

3. Now, conceptualize the output or end-item of the project as a system. Again, focus on the elements, relationships, attributes, subsystems, environment, and so on. All projects, whether directed at making a physical product (e.g., computer, space station, skyscraper, research report) or a conceptual product (e.g., providing a service or giving consultation and advice), are devoted to producing

systems. This exercise will help the reader better understand what the project is doing. It is also good preparation for the topics of the next chapter.

ENDNOTES

1. Peter Schoderbek, Asterios Kefalas, and Charles Schoderbek, *Management Systems: Conceptual Considerations* (Dallas: Business Publications, 1975), 7–8.

2. John Naughton and Geoff Peters, *Systems Performance: Human Factors and Systems Failures* (Milton Keynes, Great Britain: The Open University, 1976), 8–12.

3. Ibid., 11. Innumerable systems can be perceived from any one entity. In Kenneth Boulding, *The World as a Total System* (Beverly Hills: Sage, 1985), the world is described as physical, biological, social, economic, political, communication, and evaluative systems.

4. See David Cleland and William King, *Management: A Systems Approach* (New York: McGraw-Hill, 1972), 61–70; Richard Johnson, Fremont Kast, and James Rosenzweig, *The Theory and Management of Systems*, 3rd ed. (New York: McGraw- Hill, 1973), 41–48.

5. Walter Buckley, *Modern Systems Research for the Behavioral Scientist* (Chicago: Aldine, 1968), xvii.

6. Kenneth Boulding, "General Systems Theory: The Skeleton of Science," *Management Science* (April 1956), 197–208.

7. Ervin Laslo, *Evolution: The Grand Synthesis* (Boston: Shambhala, 1987).

8. See Fremont Kast and James Rosenzweig, "The Modern View: A Systems Approach." In *Systems Behavior*, 2nd ed., ed. John Beishon and Geoff Peters (London: Harper & Row, 1976), 19–25.

9. "Realistic" is relative, and given greater time and resources, formally unrealistic objectives may become more feasible and realistic. It is possible to uniquely structure an organization that is "best suited" for working toward a particular goal, whether or not that goal is ever achieved.

10. Donde Ashmos and George Huber, "The Systems Paradigm in Organization Theory: Correcting the Record and Suggesting the Future." *Academy of Management Review*, Vol. 12, No. 4 (October 1987), 607–621.

11. See Ralph Kilmann, *Beyond the Quick Fix* (San Francisco: Jossey-Bass, 1986); Tom Peters, *Thriving on Chaos* (New York: Alfred A. Knoff, 1988); and Gerard Egan, *Change Agent Skills A: Assessing and Designing Excellence* (San Diego: University Associates, 1988).

12. Cleland and King, *Management: A Systems Approach*, 89.

13. See J. Miller, *Living Systems* (New York: McGraw-Hill, 1978) for a discussion of functional subsystems; also see Ibid., 162–164.

14. See Talcott Parsons, *Structure and Process in Modern Societies* (New York: Free Press, 1960), 60–96; and Herbert A. Simon, *The New Science of Management Decision* (New York: Harper and Row, 1960), 49–50; and Thomas Petit, "A Behavioral Theory of Management," *Academy of Management Journal* (December 1967), 346.

chapter 4

System Methodologies

The uncreative mind can spot wrong answers, but it takes a creative mind to spot wrong questions.

Anthony Jay

Management and Machiavelli

The previous chapter dealt with the basic concepts of systems and organizations. This chapter now turns to the "systems approach," which is more of a way of *doing* things than it is of *looking* at them. Three common ways of applying the systems approach, called "system methodologies," are also described; these are systems analysis, systems engineering, and systems management. Each has a different purpose and scope, but all share a similar, systems view of the world.

An appreciation of the systems approach is important for project managers because it is the approach that underlies the *process* of project management. Especially in technical projects, many of the steps and procedures are prescribed according to the methodologies of this approach. As will be shown, throughout projects there is often need to apply a problem solving approach called "systems analysis"; in large-scale engineering and developmental projects, the life cycle follows a sequence of stages using an approach called "systems engineering"; and most large projects are managed as systems, a process called "systems management." Although methodologies such as these are typically found in technical projects, they are useful for all kinds of problem solving, organizing, and integrating of work tasks, regardless of the type of project. For this reason it is good to know about them even if you do not manage technical projects.

4.1 SYSTEMS APPROACH

The *systems approach* is a strategy for problem solving, planning, and managing human affairs. It provides a framework, a way of thinking, and methodologies for implementation.

Systems Approach Framework

The systems approach is a framework for *looking* at problems as systems and for *doing* things—like solving problems and designing systems. In the framework, systems concepts such as elements, subsystems, relationships, and environment are defined. The systems approach formally acknowledges that the behavior of any one system element may affect other elements, and no single element can perform effectively without help from the others. This recognition of *interdependency* and *cause-effect* among elements is what most distinguishes the systems approach.

For example, as an element of the "world system," the internal combustion engine can be viewed in terms of the multiple chain of effects it has triggered in other world elements and subsystems. They, include, for example:

- development of rich economies based entirely on the production and distribution of petroleum,

- industrialization of previously nomadic societies and redistribution in the concentration of political power among world nations,

- development of new, improved modes of transportation which have altered patterns of world travel, commerce, markets, and population distribution, and

- alteration of the chemical composition of the atmosphere, causing ecological consequences such as air pollution, altered weather patterns, and the "greenhouse effect."

Managers who use the systems approach recognize the complexity in problems—the elements in a situation, inputs and outputs among them, and the influence of the environment—and are better able to grasp the magnitude of a problem and anticipate consequences of their actions. This leads to better decisions and better management because it reduces the chances that important elements in a situation or consequences of actions will be overlooked.

The systems approach keeps attention on the big picture and the ultimate objective, something that tends to get lost when the focus shifts away from the whole and toward parts of the system. For instance, it is possible to view a university system as separate entities of students, faculty, administrators, and alumni, and to take action on each one by ignoring their interactions with each other and the environment. But actions that focus exclusively on just parts of the system are likely to be suboptimal because they disregard the negative repercussions on other parts. For example, curtailing hiring in the faculty subsystem reduces costs in that subsystem, but it can also result in classroom overcrowding, less time for faculty to do research, fewer research grants, lower prestige to the university, and, ultimately, lower enrollments and less income. Similarly, air pollution can be reduced by enacting laws, but such laws might restrict or prohibit industry and severely damage the regional economy.

No problem can be solved simply on its own basis. Every problem is inextricably united to the environment, and attempts to solve it may cause other, more intractable problems. Churchman calls this the "environmental fallacy."[1]

Examples abound of situations where solutions for the parts have led to worse problems for the whole, examples such as trying to improve housing by replacing ghettos with public projects, trying to reduce traffic congestion by adding more roads, trying to eliminate alcohol and drug abuse by outlawing consumption, or trying to increase the "appeal" of wilderness areas by building resorts in national parks. The negative consequences of these problem solving attempts are well known. The systems approach tries to avoid the environmental fallacy.

Orderly Way of Appraisal[2]

Besides being a way of looking at problems, the systems approach is a logical *methodology* for solving problems and managing systems. By its holistic nature, it avoids tackling problems narrowly, head-on. It says "Let's stand back and look at this situation from all angles." The problem solver does this by thinking about the overall system, keeping in mind:

1. the *objectives* and the performance measures of the whole system
2. the *environment* and *constraints* of the system
3. the *resources* of the system
4. the *elements* to the system, their functions, goals, attributes, and performance measures, and
5. the *management* of the system.

First, the place to start planning for a system is with the overall *objective* of the system. Costly mistakes can be made if the true objective of the system is vague or misconstrued. The systems approach mandates hardheaded *thinking* about the *real* objective of the system and *real* ways to measure it. Project management uses this kind of thinking: it begins with the mission or objective of the system and, thereafter, all subsequent work is organized and directed to achieve that objective. The stated objective must be precise and measurable in terms of specific performance criteria. Regardless of how intangible the objective—goodwill, quality of life, happiness, or even beauty, performance measures must be established. So that system performance can be realistically assessed, performance measures should reflect the many relevant consequences of the system.

The *environment* of the system (relevant subsystems, groups, and persons who affect or are affected by the system) must also be identified—no easy matter since many external forces are hidden or work in insidious ways. The way in which the system interacts with the environment must be determined, highlighting inputs, outputs, and *constraints* imposed. Looking to the future, questions must be raised about likely changes or innovations in the environment and how they will affect the system.

System *resources*, which are internal to the system and the means by which it accomplishes its goals, must also be identified. These are assets or means the system utilizes and influences to its own advantage; they include capital, labor, materials, facilities, and equipment. Most system resources are exhaustible. The system is free to utilize them, but at the point where they are depleted they become constraints on the system. The systems approach considers availability of resources and what happens after resources are depleted.

The fourth concept is *elements* of the system. The systems approach disregards traditional boundaries and definitions for elements. The systems approach to a project, for example, views it in terms of many elements, each having performance measures directly related to performance measures of the overall project. Traditional categories such as functional departments are ignored in favor of basic "work packages" or jobs. By dividing the project into small elements or tasks, the manager can tell if the project is going smoothly and what actions need to be taken.

Finally, the systems approach pays explicit attention to the *management* of the system, that function which takes into consideration all of the other aspects of the system—objectives, environment, constraints, resources, and elements—in the planning and control of the system. This is precisely the role of project management.

The ordering of the above concepts does not mean that they are addressed in sequence. In actuality each concept might have to be dealt with several times before it is completely described and clearly defined. More importantly, each concept serves to suggest numerous open-ended questions which aid in investigating the system. In defining the system, its elements, and environment, the decision maker asks: What cause-and-effect relationships exist among them? What functions need to be performed by each? What tradeoffs may be required among resources once they are defined?[3]

Figure 4–1 illustrates how plans are developed in cyclical fashion, utilizing loops and feedback. General objectives are used to define plans, then objectives are refined, plans detailed, and so on. Objectives are used to develop requirements, but as additional data is collected, the requirements (and even the objectives) are refined.

The planning cycle in Figure 4–1 has a *systems analysis* phase and a systems *synthesis* phase. In systems analysis, each objective is clarified in terms of requirements or criteria, and alternative approaches for attainment are specified. These approaches are weighed and the best ones selected in a tradeoff study. The selected approaches are then synthesized, or integrated together into a system model or plan. The final solution and overall plans are selected and developed based upon criteria compatible with the objectives.[4]

As plans are implemented, *systems management* monitors them to insure the parts are suitably integrated and carried out. Both the plans themselves and the way they are implemented are evaluated. Management monitors the system and is prepared to modify plans in response to changes in the environment, objectives, resources, or system elements. Since none of these can be known with complete certainty, the best plans incorporate mechanisms for self-evaluation and self-change.

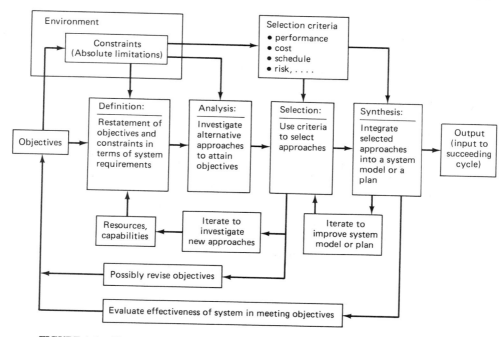

FIGURE 4–1. The systems approach. (Adapted and revised from P. Thome and R. Willard, in S.L. Optner, ed., *Systems Analysis* (Middlesex, England: Penguin, 1973), 216.)

The systems approach applies to a wide range of complex, real world problems. It is concerned with the total problem solving cycle, not just parts of it, which is one reason why it is so important to project management.

Systems Life Cycle

Complex systems change over time. Changes in systems tend to be systematic and evolutionary, with similar kinds of systems following similar cycles of evolution. One basic cycle, that of living organisms, is the pattern of birth, growth, maturity, decline, and death. Another, that of all nonliving, electro-mechanical systems, is the cycle of burn-in, normal operation, then deterioration or obsolescence. Similarly, all products follow a parallel cycle: they are conceived and introduced, capture market share, then decline and are ultimately discontinued. Some products, like the 1950s Ford Edsel, have a life cycle of only a few years. Others last for decades; Kool-Aid ® and Levi's ® jeans are examples. Organizations and projects follow life cycles too, with stages characterized by the types of problems they face, the resources they utilize, the formal structures they take on, and the expertise they employ.[5]

The *development* of a system also follows a series of phases, starting with initial conception and ending with final installation and termination. A key feature of the systems approach is recognition of the logical order of thought and action that go into developing systems, whether commercial home products, public works, or military weapons systems.

Large-scale design and development projects follow a prescribed process called *systems engineering*. The more general development of a system according to a prescribed series of logical, structured steps is called the *systems development cycle*. These topics will be discussed later in this and the next two chapters.

4.2 SYSTEMS ANALYSIS

Systems analysis is a problem solving framework to help decision makers select the best alternatives. By one definition, "systems analysis is a systematic examination of a problem in which each step of the analysis is made *explicit*. Consequently, it is the *opposite* of a manner of reaching decisions which is largely intuitive, unsystematic, and where much of the argument remains hidden in the mind of the decision maker or his advisor."[6] Thus, what distinguishes systems analysis from other forms of analysis is its *precision* in defining the elements of the analysis.

As shown in Figure 4–1, systems analysis focuses on only a part of the total systems approach (analysis), so is more narrow in scope than the systems approach. However, it is more general than disciplines like operations research since it covers problem and objective formulation,[7] or economics since it covers all kinds of problems, not just scarce resources. Systems analysis should not be confused with *computer systems analysis*, which is the narrow application of systems analysis to computers and computerized systems.

Elements of Systems Analysis

Four kinds of inquiry are required in systems analysis:[8]

1. First, the objectives of the decision maker are determined; criteria are established for deciding between alternatives to achieve these objectives.
2. Next, the alternatives are identified and their feasibility examined.
3. The alternatives which are found to be feasible are then compared in terms of cost, effectiveness, time, and risk.
4. Finally, the best alternative according to the criteria is chosen; if all are deemed lacking, better alternatives are designed or other objectives identified.

Systems analysis uses "modeling" to help decision makers understand the system and to measure alternatives against objectives. A model is a simplified representation of the world; it abstracts the essential features of the system under study. It may be a physical model, mathematical formulation, computer simulation, or simple checklist. One example of a *physical model* is a model airplane. It is simply a scaled down abstraction of the real system. It includes some aspects of the system (configuration and shape of exterior components) and excludes others (interior components and crew). Another kind of model is a *conceptual model*; it depicts the elements, structure, and flows in a system. The conceptual model in Figure 4–2, for example, helps analysts to understand relationships among the elements contributing to population size and to make limited predictions.[9] Most

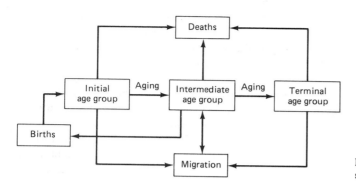

FIGURE 4–2. A generalized population sector model.

models for decision making are conceptual and are formulated in terms of mathematical equations. The models used by operations researchers involving linear programming, queuing analysis, Monte Carlo simulation, and statistical analysis are examples.

Models are used to conduct experimentation. Many systems are too expensive or risky to do "real life" experiments with. The model permits assessment of various alternatives and their consequences before a decision is made. Engineers use model airplanes in wind tunnel tests, for instance, to try out design alternatives and to measure the effect of different design parameters on performance. A good model allows the analyst to ask "what if" questions and to explore the effects of changing various inputs. This exploration is called sensitivity analysis.

Anyone doing systems analysis must be careful not to catch "modelism"—i.e., not become more interested in the model than in the real world. This tends to happen when questions result in "mathematically untidy" situations. Modelism leads to the study of irrelevant or over-idealized questions rather than answers to important questions.[10]

Most models and analytical procedures in systems analysis are quantitative, but this by no means should imply that they are intended to replace qualitative analysis. Indeed, good systems analysis employs both qualitative and quantitative methods. The value of systems analysis is that it explicitly takes into consideration all things which can be quantified, thus permitting decision makers to use judgment on those factors which can only be addressed qualitatively.

The central role of the model is seen in its relation to the other elements of systems analysis in the following list. These elements are present in every systems analysis, though not always explicitly:

1. Objective(s).   The first task in systems analysis is to discover what the decision maker *expects after the problem has been solved*. This is the objective. Objectives must be clear, concise, and—ideally—measurable. To eliminate confusion and misunderstanding about the problem or system, both the decision maker and the analyst must agree to the objectives.

2. Criteria.   Criteria are performance measures that will enable the analyst to determine how well objectives are being achieved. They are the basis for ranking the performance of alternative solutions to the problem.

3. Alternatives.   Alternatives are the solutions to problems and the means for attaining objectives. The common error in many analyses is to focus on the same alternatives and ignore new, different, or innovative solutions. One rule of the systems approach is "Don't prejudge solutions!" Early solutions should serve as guides rather than stopping points. Ideally, a wide range of alternative solutions are considered.

4. Resources and Constraints.   Resources are elements of the system—labor, time, capital, materials—available to solve the problem. They are part of the system, are controllable, and can be utilized as deemed appropriate. Constraints are elements of the environment which restrict the applicability or usefulness of alternatives. Resources and constraints determine what is feasible and reduce the number of potential solutions to a problem. All resources are limited, so they too become constraints when in short supply or exhausted.

5. Model.   The model incorporates *all* of the above elements such that consequences of alternatives can be compared in terms of attainment of objectives. As mentioned, models widely vary, ranging from a set of mathematical equations and computer programs for quantitative analysis, to a verbal description that permits consequences to be assessed using judgment alone.

The model must compare alternatives in terms of both costs and benefits. Costs are resources which when allotted to alternatives cannot be used elsewhere; benefits are the worthwhile outcomes of alternatives. It may seem obvious that both aspects must be considered to establish the overall worth of an alternative, but history is replete with cases where benefits and costs were not treated together. For example, there are instances where sophisticated weapons systems have been acquired without adequate funding for maintenance and spare parts (resulting in their being permanently "nonoperational" because of repair backlogs). When decisions are made solely in terms of anticipated system benefits (e.g., a certain type of fighter plane will fulfill a certain mission) without regard to system costs (e.g., "chopping off" maintenance capability to satisfy cost requirements) the outcome is to cancel out or greatly diminish the anticipated benefits. In systems analysis, the alternatives yielding the greatest effectiveness (benefits) are examined with respect to current and anticipated resource limitations (costs).

Process of Conducting a Systems Analysis

Systems analysis involves four overlapping phases, shown in Figure 4–3.[11]

In the first phase, *formulation,* fuzzy ideas are translated into clear definitions of the problem, objectives, and criteria measures. Sometimes the decision maker provides a clear problem formulation, though often she does not know what the problem is and the systems analyst must start from scratch.

Notice in Figure 4–3 that, *prior* to formulation, the systems analyst must establish who the *decision maker* is. The decision maker is that party (person or group) which is dissatisfied with the present or prospects for the future, and has the *desire* and *authority* to do something about it. Systems analysis is a precursor to action, but unless the true decision maker is

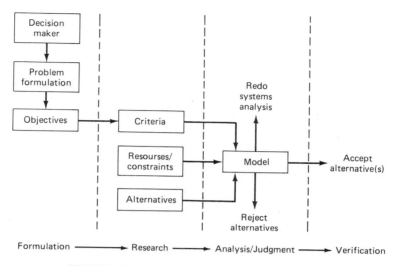

FIGURE 4–3. Elements and process of systems analysis.

involved, it will be of little avail. Many systems analyses have been shelved because they were done for parties *posing* as decision makers instead of the "real" decision makers.

During the second, *research* phase, data about the problem is collected. System components and relationships are identified, resources and constraints are defined, and potential alternative courses of action are identified.

Identifying alternatives is not always straightforward, especially when the obvious ones are inadequate and new ones must be developed. This is where *interdisciplinary teams* are beneficial. The use of interdisciplinary teams to search for broad alternatives is an outgrowth of the early application of systems analysis during World War II. Interdisciplinary teams were found to provide an effective means for combining the knowledge from experts of many fields—physics, mathematics, psychology—and for generating alternatives and solutions that transcended any one person's or one field's area of expertise.

In the third, *analysis/judgment* phase, models are developed for comparing alternatives and consequences in terms of criteria measures. Conclusions are made and a course of action is selected. The analysis is performed by the systems analyst, but the final judgment is made by the decision maker.

In the final, *verification* phase, conclusions are experimentally tested in the real world. Empirical evidence is collected to ensure that the alternative selected is the appropriate solution. Any discrepancies between actual performance and system objectives indicate the need for further analysis, revised alternatives, or different objectives.

Systems analysis seldom proceeds smoothly: objectives may be obscure, in conflict, or difficult to clarify and quantify; none of the alternatives may be adequate to reach the objective; a suitable model may be unattainable; or the decision maker may have changed his mind. One pass through the process is usually not enough and it is necessary to recycle, i.e., reformulate the problem, select new objectives and criteria, collect additional data, design new alternatives, build new models, reweigh costs and benefits, and so on until an alternative is chosen.

The Role of Systems Analysis[12]

Is systems analysis applicable to all problem situations? The answer lies in the consequences of performing systems analysis. In situations where a rapid decision must be made, systems analysis might be so time consuming that the opportunity would be lost. When speed is the decisive factor, a quick, intuitive judgment might be better than systems analysis. But in most situations where the outcome depends more on the choice of alternatives than on the speed of the decision, systems analysis is clearly more appropriate. The elements and phases of systems analysis guarantee logic and consistency, whereas purely subjective approaches do not. Since the assumptions, steps, and conclusions are spelled out, any systems analysis is reproducible. It can be resurrected and repeated if need be, and the analytical procedure itself can be scrutinized.

As an applied activity, the motivation of systems analysis is in having its results used. For results to be useful, the analysis must realistically reflect the technical aspects of the system and effectively relate findings in terms of the real world. To provide the bridge between planning and implementation, alternatives should be analyzed and evaluated in terms of the impacts they will have when actually implemented.

Systems analysis produces solutions within relatively clearly defined situations. Another methodology, *systems engineering*, produces solutions to problems which are much more complex and much less clearly defined. Unlike systems analysis, it also considers how the elements and subsystems to a solution will be integrated together. Also, it devotes much effort to conceptualizing and understanding the overall situation in which a particular solution or system must fit. Within the systems engineering process are smaller, more tidy problems, and for these systems analysis is employed repeatedly as a decision making framework.

4.3 SYSTEMS ENGINEERING[13]

Jenkins defines systems engineering as "the science of designing complex systems in their totality to insure that the component subsystems making up the system are designed, fitted together, checked and operated in the most efficient way."[14] Systems engineering emphasizes overall performance of the system, not just performance of its individual parts. Up through World War II, the term systems engineering referred to integrating existing components into a final product. Today it refers more to the conception, design, and development of complex systems where the *components themselves* must be designed and developed from scratch and integrated together to fulfill mission objectives. In contrast to systems analysis which focuses on *decisions about systems*, systems engineering is a way to actually *bring a system into being*.

All Systems Go

A good example of systems engineering is in the design and operation of a space vehicle. The expression "all systems go," popularized during the early U.S. space flights of the 1950s and 60s, means that the overall system of millions of components that make up the vehicle and its support systems, and the thousands of people in its technical and management teams, is ready to "go" to achieve the objectives of the vehicle. Every component and person is in place, working as prescribed, and ready to contribute to the overall mission.

To get to the point of "all systems go" planners must have first defined the overall system and its *objectives*. Designers must then have analyzed the requirements of the system and *broken them down* (analysis) into smaller subsystems so each component could be clearly defined, designed, and put into place. They must then *put together* (synthesis) a total system of rocket boosters, space vehicle, launch facilities, ground support, crew selection and training, and technical and management capability. In the end, every component and person must have a planned role and be *integrated* into a subsystem which is integrated into the overall system.

Systems engineering includes a much wider role than ordinary "engineering." In fact, systems engineering is not even engineering in the same context as other engineering disciplines. Rather, it is a logical *process* employed in the orderly evolution of a system from the point when a need is first identified, through planning, design, construction, and ultimate deployment and operation by a user. The process has two parts, one associated with the *development and production* of the system, the other with the way the system will *work or operate* in its environment. The process is outlined in Figure 4–4.

Stages of Systems Engineering

The stages of the systems engineering process in Figure 4–4 are discussed in detail in Appendix A. Briefly, they include the following:

1. System Concept: Clarify the problem, establish the need and value for the system; set overall mission, objectives, and operational and maintenance requirements for the system.

2. System Definition and Preliminary Design: Determine major functions of the system; cluster functions to form subsystems; perform systems analysis to evaluate design alternatives; prepare design specifications.

3. Detailed Design and Development: Describe in detail subsystems, units, assemblies; develop models to test performance and integration of designs; prepare for production of system.

4. System Production or Fabrication: Maintain construction/production operations and produce the system; prepare for installation of system.

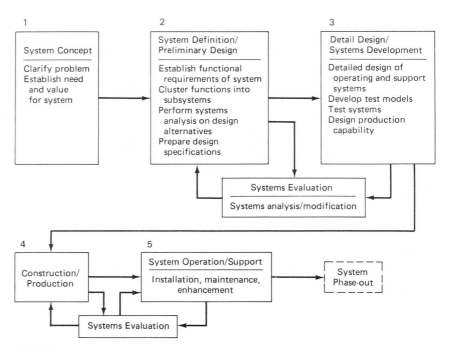

FIGURE 4–4. Systems engineering process. (Adapted with permission from B. Blanchard and W. Fabrycky, *Systems Engineering and Analysis,* (Englewood Cliffs, N.J.: Prentice-Hall, 1981), 238.

5. System Operation and Support: Check-out and install system with the user; provide maintenance, field support, and system enhancement as necessary to ensure continued compliance with objectives; phase-out system at the end of its useful life.

Throughout the systems engineering process, *systems evaluation* procedures are repeated to insure that system requirements satisfy objectives, that design criteria satisfy requirements, that fabricated units meet design criteria, and that the overall system performs within its environment to the satisfaction of users.

Because of its breadth of scope, systems engineering calls for a depth of experience which no single specialist (e.g., manager, physicist, astronomer, computer scientist, aerospace engineer, cost accountant, psychologist) can provide. It requires a team effort of specialists from many separate and divergent disciplines. Diverse people from different companies and organizations, spread over a wide geographic area, and with no common background may be involved. The difficult task, largely that of the project manager, is to get them all to work together toward a common purpose. Systems engineering provides the framework without which it would be impossible for teams to effectively communicate and coordinate their efforts.

In summary, systems engineering is a logical sequence of steps for identifying and coordinating the multitude of considerations and tasks in systems development. It provides for identification of overall system requirements and the means for developing and integrating hardware, software, personnel, facilities, and procedures. It provides for checking, cross-checking, and quality controlling, and thus helps avoid waste, oversights, and redundant effort.

4.4 SYSTEMS MANAGEMENT[15]

Characteristics

A third general application of the systems approach is *systems management*, the management and operation of organizations as if they were systems. Three major characteristics distinguish systems management. First, it is total system oriented and emphasizes achievement of the *overall system* mission and system objectives. Second, it emphasizes decisions that optimize the *overall system* rather than just subsystems. Third, it is responsibility oriented. The manager of each subsystem is given specific assignments so that inputs, outputs, and contribution to *total system* effectiveness can be measured.

Emphasis on total systems is pervasive wherever the systems approach is applied. Systems management sustains the integration, coordination, and control of subunits in the organization to achieve total system objectives. Since many large-scale systems efforts involve contributions from multiple contractors and suppliers, it is systems management which is responsible for planning, organizing, coordinating, and controlling their combined efforts.

System management works to insure that organizations, responsibilities, knowledge, and data are integrated toward achieving overall objectives. Thus, the orientation of the systems manager is to consider the interactions and interdependencies between various subsystems and with the environment. Interdependencies are recognized and plans and actions are made to take advantage of them. This contrasts with the more typical management view which is to focus on individual functions and tasks, and to enhance the performance of a unit or department, even at the expense of others or the total organization.

Systems Management, Systems Analysis, and Systems Engineering

The relationship between systems management, systems analysis, and systems engineering can partly be explained in terms of *when* they are applied during the life cycle of a system. Systems management performs the basic managerial functions of planning, organization, and control throughout the life of the system, but the focus remains on coordinating and integrating work rather than actually performing it.

As Figure 4–5 shows, systems management often works in parallel with systems engineering and utilizes the tools of systems analysis. The purpose of systems analysis is to ask questions about the goal or mission of the system, the kind and nature of resources to use, and the organization of people and facilities. In systems management, systems analysis is used for planning and controlling activities and materials (scheduling and inventory control), and for evaluating system operation to determine when and why the system is not functioning properly. During every phase of a system's life cycle, study is made of the nature and kind of information needed to carry out the kind of analysis required.

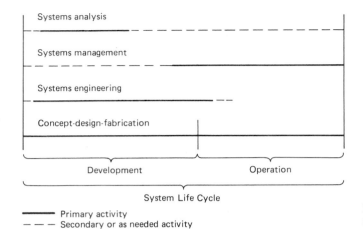

Systems analysis

Systems management

Systems engineering

Concept-design-fabrication

Development   Operation

System Life Cycle

———— Primary activity
— — — Secondary or as needed activity

FIGURE 4–5. Application of systems
methodologies during the system life cycle.

Systems management entails identification of total system requirements, control over the evolution of requirements and design, integration of technical efforts, and development of data and documentation. It is applied over the full life cycle of the system. As DeGreene notes, system management serves two broad purposes—*systems development management* and *systems operations management*—the first applies to the development and growth of a system (the management of the *development* process), the second to the actual *operation* or use of a system.[16]

Both systems analysis and systems management can be placed in the context of systems engineering. According to Cleland and King (refer to Figure 4–5):[17]

> The principle activity during [Development] is the performance of studies leading to the collection and evaluation of sufficient data on which to base a decision. In a similar fashion, the manager who is mainly concerned with managing an ongoing system will find ample opportunity to do [systems analysis]; yet his main focus will be directed toward the execution function of management, i.e., the management of an existing system [Operations]. As the system proceeds through its life cycle and grows in maturity, the manager will become more knowledgeable with respect to its capabilities and limitations. The need for redesign of the original system may be realized and…both elements of systems analysis and systems management will be involved.

4.5 SUMMARY

The primary feature of all methodologies in the systems approach is to focus on the wholeness of the situation, problem, or organization. The systems approach is action oriented; it provides a conceptual framework, a process, and a management system to guide the planning, implementing, and managing of solutions and organizations. Systems analysis, systems engineering, and systems management are ways of applying the systems approach to problem solving, developing, and operating systems.

Systems analysis is the class of approaches concerned with determining whether alternative solutions or elements of a system can sufficiently contribute to its desired objective. An essential feature of systems analysis is the use of modeling to perform tradeoff studies in selecting among alternatives. The model permits analysis of the sensitivity of system parameters in terms of interplay of systems elements and their relation to the larger environment. Although systems analysis provides a rigorous, logical, and scientific basis for analysis, judgment and intuition nonetheless play important roles in formulating objectives, generating and comparing alternatives, and making the final decision.

System engineering is an approach to designing large-scale systems to satisfy operational requirements. It refers to the process of translating operational requirements into functional requirements, then expanding these into detailed end-item equipment and support requirements. Requirements refer to the proper mix of mission hardware, software, personnel, training, procedures, and logistics support to achieve integrated, cost-effective system design. The process relates system design and development efforts with other system life cycle requirements for fabrication, installation, test, evaluation, production, maintenance, support, modification, and eventual phase-out of the system.[18]

Systems management is the process of monitoring and controlling a system to ensure fulfillment of overall system objectives. The systems view of the manager's job considers the interactions and interdependencies between various subsystems and with the environment. Systems management oversees the system life cycle process to ensure that all necessary disciplines and functional areas are integrated to satisfy system requirements.

The tools of systems analysis, the process of systems engineering, and the concepts of systems management are frequently utilized in the planning, organizing, and execution of projects, especially large-scale and technological projects. In the development of technical systems, management of the systems engineering process is synonymous with project management. Within project management, the systems analysis framework is employed for problem solving. Although project and systems management both emphasize integration of activities to achieve overall goals, a distinction between them is that the former ceases after a project is terminated, whereas the latter continues for the life of the system.[19]

This section of the book has given you an overview of project management, its origins, applications, and underlying systems philosophy. Projects are of finite (relatively limited) duration, so of course they always have a beginning and an ending. What goes on at the start, the finish, and in between comprise the life of the project. In all projects, what "goes on"—the kinds of tasks and activities—tends to follow a sequence of stages, regardless of the kind of project. Some of these activities were alluded to in the examples in Chapter 2, such as doing a feasibility study, preparing a proposal, forming a team, preparing a schedule and budget, and so on. The sequence of activities in the life of a project is called the project life cycle. The next section of the book discusses project life cycles and describes a normative approach for conducting projects called the systems development cycle.

Case Study: Glades County Sanitary District

Glades County is a region on the Gulf Coast with a population of 600,000. About 90 percent of the population is located in and near the city of Sitkus. The main attractions of the area are its clean, sandy beaches and nearby fishing. Resorts, restaurants, hotels, retailers, and the Sitkus/Glades County economy in general rely on these attractions for tourist dollars.

In the last decade, Glades County has experienced a near doubling of population and industry. One result has been the noticeable increase in the level of water pollution along the coast due primarily to the increased raw sewage dumped by Glades County into the Gulf. Ordinarily, the Glades County sewer system directs effluent waste through filtration plants before pumping it into the Gulf. Although the Glades County Sanitary District (GCSD) is usually able to handle the County's sewage, during heavy rains the runoff from paved surfaces exceeds sewer capacity and must be diverted past filtration plants, directly into the Gulf. Following heavy rains, the beaches are cluttered with dead fish and debris. The Gulf fishing trade is also temporarily affected; pollution drives away desirable fish. Recently, the water pollution level has become high enough to begin to damage both the tourist and fishing trade. Besides coastal pollution, there is also concern that as the population continues to increase, the County's primary fresh water source, Glades River, will also be polluted.

The GCSD has been mandated to prepare a comprehensive water waste management program that will reverse the trend in pollution along the Gulf Coast as well as handle the expected increase in effluent wastes over the next twenty years. Although not yet specified, it is known that the program will include new sewers, filtration plants, and stricter laws. As a first step, GCSD must establish the overall direction and mission of the program.

Wherever possible, answer the following questions (given the limited information, it is okay to advance some logical guesses; if you are not able to answer a question for lack of information, indicate how and where, as a systems analyst, you would get it):

1. What is the system? What are its key elements and subsystems? What are the boundaries and how are they determined? What is the environment?

2. Who are the decision makers?

3. What is the problem? Carefully formulate it.

4. Define the overall objective of the water waste management program. Since the program is wide ranging in scope, you should break this down into several subobjectives.

5. Define the criteria or measures of performance to be used to determine whether the objectives of the program are being met. Specify several criteria for each subobjective. As much as possible, the criteria should be quantitative, although some qualitative measures should also be included. How will you know if the criteria that you define are the appropriate ones to use?

6. What are the resources and constraints?

7. Elaborate on the kinds of alternatives and range of solutions to solving the problem.

8. Discuss some techniques that could be used to help evaluate which alternatives are best.

CHAPTER REVIEW QUESTIONS

1. Briefly, what is the "systems approach?" Where does the systems approach apply? In a sentence, what does a manager do in the systems approach that she might not do otherwise?

2. What things does the problem solver keep in mind when applying the systems approach?

3. Describe how the following elements of the systems approach apply to projects and project management: objectives, environment, resources, subsystems, and management.

4. Describe the systems approach in Figure 4–1. How does this process vary from situation to situation?

5. What is the systems life cycle? How do life cycles differ among the systems in Boulding's hierarchy? What is the importance of recognizing life cycles in systems design and management?

6. How does systems analysis compare to other types of analysis. If "analytical thinking" is different from systems thinking, then how is systems analysis a form of systems thinking?

7. Describe the elements and stages of systems analysis shown in Figure 4–3. What is the role of the "model" in systems analysis?

8. Describe some examples of physical models; of graphical models; of mathematical models.

9. Why is systems engineering a systems approach? How does it differ and how is it the same as systems analysis?

10. Describe the stages of systems engineering in Figure 4–4. Think of some projects and describe the stages of systems engineering in these projects.

11. What is the emphasis in systems management? How does it differ from just "management?" How do systems analysis, systems engineering, and life cycles fit into systems management?

QUESTIONS ABOUT THE STUDY PROJECT

1. At the end of Chapter 3 you were asked about the main *end-item* or *operating system* (i.e., the output objective) of the project you are studying. If you skipped that question before, do it now: describe the main system, subsystems, components, and the relevant environment of the output of the project. Who are the decision makers?

2. In the project you are studying, has systems analysis been used anywhere? If so, describe where it has been used, the nature of the systems analysis (the problem, objectives, criteria, and so on), the types of models used, how alternatives are evaluated and selected, and who does the analysis. If not, comment about the reasons. What kinds of decision making and problem solving approaches are used instead? How are alternatives evaluated?

3. If the study project involves engineering or integration of many components, is the systems engineering process used? Is there a section. department, or task in the project called systems engineering? If so, elaborate. Are there functions or phases of the project which seem to resemble the systems engineering process?

   As described in this chapter, besides the main *end-item* or *operating system* (i.e., the output objective of the project) systems engineering also addresses the *support system*—that system which supports installation, operation, maintenance, evaluation, and enhancement of the operating system. Describe the support system in the study project and its development.

4. What aspects of the project or parent organization appear to use systems management? What aspects do not use systems management? Describe the appropriateness or inappropriateness of systems management in the project you are studying.

ENDNOTES

1. C. West Churchman, *The Systems Approach and Its Enemies* (New York: Basic Books, 1979), 4–5.

2. Much of the discussion in this section is based upon C. West Churchman, *The Systems Approach* (New York: Dell, 1968), 30–39.

3. P.G. Thome and R.G. Willard, "The Systems Approach: A Unified Concept of Planning," in *Systems Analysis*, ed. S.L. Optner (Middlesex, England: Penguin Books, 1973), 212.

4. Ibid., 212–215.

5. The stages of technological products and their impact on competitive markets is eloquently described by Richard Foster in *Innovation: The Attacher's Advantage* (New York: Summit Books, 1986).

6. Malcolm W. Hoag, "An Introduction to Systems Analysis," in *Systems Analysis*, ed. S.L. Optner (Middlesex, England: Penguin, 1973), 37.

7. Operations research (OR) is problem-solving pertaining to the operations of an organization. OR employs mathematical methods to find the best solution to satisfy a stated objective under restriction of constrained resources. OR typically is *not* concerned with defining objectives or determining what are the resources and constraints. These, and often the alternatives themselves, must be well-defined before the techniques of OR can be applied to find a solution. See, for example, H.A. Taha, *Operations Research: An Introduction*, 3rd ed. (New York: MacMillan, 1982); and W.P. Cooke, *Quantitative Methods for Management Decisions* (New York: McGraw-Hill, 1985).

8. E.S. Quade and W.I. Boucher, eds., *Systems Analysis and Policy Planning: Applications in Defense* (New York: Elsevier Publishing, 1968), 11–14.

9. H.R. Hamilton, et al., *Systems Simulation for Regional Analysis* (Cambridge: The M.I.T. Press, 1972).

10. See Herman Kahn and Irwin Mann, *Ten Common Pitfalls*. (Santa Monica, CA.: The RAND Corporation, RM 1937, 1957).

11. Adapted from C.W.N. Thompson and G.J. Rath, "Making Your Health Systems Work: A Systems Analysis Approach" (Chicago: Annual Meeting of the American Academy of Pediatrics, October 20– 24, 1973).

12. Portions of this section are adopted from D. Cleland and W. King, *Systems Analysis and Project Management*, 3rd ed. (New York: McGraw-Hill, 1983), 96–102.

13. Portions of this section are derived from four sources: Benjamin S. Blanchard and Walter J. Fabrycky, *Systems Engineering and Analysis* (Englewood Cliffs, N.J.: Prentice-Hall, 1981), 18–52; Robert Boguslaw, *The New Utopians: A Study of System Design and Social Change* (Englewood Cliffs, N.J.: Prentice-Hall, 1965), 99–112; Harold Chestnut, *Systems Engineering Methods* (New York: John Wiley, 1967), 1–41; G.W. Jenkins, "The Systems Approach," in *Systems Behavior*, 2nd ed., ed. John Beishan and Geoff Peters (London: Harper & Row for the Open University Press, 1976), 78–101.

14. Jenkins, ibid., 82.

15. Portions of the discussion on systems management are adopted from D. Cleland and W. King, *Management: A Systems Approach* (New York: McGraw-Hill, 1972), 171–173; and R. Johnson, F. Kast, and J. Rosenzweig, *The Theory and Management of Systems*, 3rd ed. (New York: McGraw-Hill, 1973), 122–130.

16. Kenyon B. DeGreene, "Systems and Psychology," in *Systems Behavior*, 2nd ed., eds. John Beishon and Geoff Peters (London: Harper & Row for the Open University Press, 1976), 141–43.

17. Cleland and King, *Management: A Systems Approach*, 172.

18. Wilton P. Chase, *Management of Systems Engineering* (New York: John Wiley, 1974), 125.

19. The term systems management is sometimes used to pertain to systems that are designed to operate within defined organization boundaries, whereas project management often extends beyond the boundary of the organization responsible for mission accomplishment. Project management thus relies more upon persuasion than formal authority to coordinate and organize activities (this is discussed in Chapter 8). See Johnson, Kast, and Rosenzweig, *The Theory and Management of Systems*, 395.

II

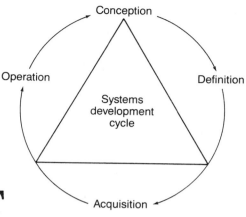

SYSTEMS DEVELOPMENT CYCLE

Most systems move inexorably through a process or series of developmental stages. In planned human systems, development occurs through an intentional, logical sequence of prescribed activities called the Systems Development Cycle. Project management takes place within the broader context of systems development and is the function responsible for planning activities and for organizing and guiding their execution. The two chapters in this section outline the process of systems development and describe the role of project management within its stages.

Chapters in this section:

chapter 5

Systems Development Cycle: Early Stages

There is...a time to be born, and a time to die; a time to plant, and a time to reap; a time to kill, and a time to heal; a time to break down, and a time to build up...

Ecclesiastes, iii, 1

An important aspect of the systems approach to management is the concept of "life cycle"—the basic pattern of change that occurs throughout the life of a system. There are two ways of considering life cycles in the systems approach: one is to recognize the *natural* process that occurs in all dynamic systems—that of birth, life, and death; the other is to incorporate this recognition into the planning and management of systems.

The practice of project management occurs within the context of such a natural process. The sequence of stages a project follows from beginning to end, which is similar for all projects, is called the *project life cycle*. There is within the project life cycle a way of logically ordering affairs in order to optimize the outcome. This ordering of activities is referred to as the *systems development cycle*. This chapter and the next will describe features of the project life cycle and show how systems development is implemented within it. This chapter discusses systems and project life-cycles in general, then focuses on the early stages of the systems development cycle. Chapter 6 will discuss the middle and later stages.

5.1 SYSTEMS LIFE CYCLES

Most systems change over time—they are dynamic. Using systems terminology, we say that the state of the system is in flux. This fluctuation in system properties is definitely not random; it tends to follow a distinct pattern that is repeated again and again. Mentioned earlier was the obvious life cycle of living organisms—birth, growth, maturity, decline, and death, and the similarity in cycles among virtually all man-made products and human organizations. Recognizing this is important because it enables us to create systems, anticipate and guide their actions, and plan appropriately for them.

Project Life Cycle

Projects are undertaken for the purpose of developing systems—either to create new ones or improve existing ones. The natural life cycle of systems gives rise to a similar life cycle in project organizations. Each project has a starting point and progresses toward a predetermined conclusion during which the state of the project organization changes. Starting with project conceptualization, projects are characterized by a buildup in "activity" which eventually peaks and then declines until project termination—the typical pattern shown in Figure 5–1. This activity in a project can be measured in various ways, such as the amount of money spent on the project, the number of people working on it, the amount of materials required, the percentage of total organizational effort devoted to it, or the amount of conflict generated between project and functional units.

Besides changes in the level of activity, the nature and emphasis of the activity also vary. For example, consider the mix of project personnel: during early stages of the project, users and planners dominate; during middle stages, designers, builders, and implementors are in charge; in later stages, users and operators take over.

Despite changes in level and mix of activity, there are *three measures* of activity that are applied over the full span of a project; these are *time*, *cost*, and *performance*. Time refers to the progress of activities and the extent to which schedules and deadlines are being met. Cost refers to the rate of resource expenditure and how it compares to constraints imposed on the project. Performance refers to specifications and requirements established for outputs of the project (for example, the speed and range of an aircraft, the consumer appeal of a new product, the results of polls for a candidate running for office) and how they compare to objectives. Project organizations attempt to achieve time, cost, and performance requirements during successive advances throughout the life of the project.

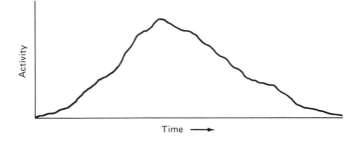

FIGURE 5–1. Level of activity during the project life cycle.

Managing the Project Life Cycle

The management of project life cycles requires special treatment. In general, management must be *adaptable*, both to changes induced by the life cycle of each individual project as well as to combined changes induced by the life cycles of multiple, concurrent projects. Unlike nonproject repetitive operations where activities tend to be stable, the project life cycle puts resources, costs, and schedules in a constant state of change. To respond, management must be flexible and changeable. Little that is done in a project can be considered repetitive or even routine. Work schedules, budgets, and tasks must be tailored to fit the stages of the project life cycle.

All life cycles contain an element of uncertainty. Unforeseen obstacles, which are virtually inevitable, can cause missed deadlines, cost overruns, and poor system performance. Management must anticipate problems and uncertainties and be able to replan activities and shift resources.

Many organizations undertake several projects at once so that at any given time each is at a different stage of the life cycle. While some projects are just being started, others have reached maturity or are being phased out. Management must be able to continuously balance resources among these projects so the individual requirements of each are fulfilled and their sum does not exceed the capacity of the parent organization.

5.2 SYSTEMS DEVELOPMENT CYCLE

A project can be thought of as *an organization which exists to develop a system to respond to a problem.* Accordingly, all projects can be divided into logical phases or stages to indicate the types of tasks or activities conducted within a period of time. Figure 5–2 shows one model for dividing a project into four phases:

1. Conception phase (Phase A)
2. Definition phase (B)
3. Acquisition phase (C)
4. Operation phase (D)

Each phase has specific content and management approaches. Between phases are points at which decisions are made concerning the preceding phase and whether the next phase should be undertaken or the project abandoned. Though the number of phases and details for each are a matter of judgment and differ for every project, the sequence is similar for virtually all projects.

This normative four-phase sequence, called the *systems development cycle,* encompasses the total developmental life cycle of systems. The phases overlap and interact, yet are clearly differentiable. They reflect the natural order of thought and action in the development of man-made systems, whether consumer products, space vehicles, computer information systems, company relocations, movie productions, or even political cam-

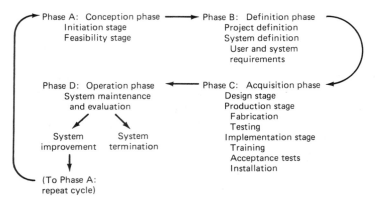

FIGURE 5–2. Four-phase model of the systems development cycle.

paigns. For some systems the development cycle overlaps identically with the project life cycle. In others, only portions of systems development are covered in the project life cycle, such as beginning with the Definition phase or terminating with the Acquisition phase.

A project can be terminated at the juncture between phases either by contractual arrangement or because management decides the project is not worth continuing. In large-scale programs such as space and weapons systems development, the span of the entire systems development cycle is considered a *program*, while each phase of the cycle is covered by a separate *project* (sometimes conducted by different contracting organizations).

The following brief description of the phases of the systems development cycle serves as an introduction to the main actors (interested parties) in the cycle. They are:

1. System *users*, also called customers or clients. These include:
   a. user top management and
   b. user operators.

2. The System Development Organization (SDO), called the *contractor*, developer, or consultant, which includes:
   a. contractor top management (corporate and functional managers),
   b. project management (project manager and staff), and
   c. the doers—professional, trade, assembly and other workers.

Users are the persons or groups for whom the project is being undertaken and who will acquire and/or operate the system when it is completed. The Systems Development Organization or contractor is the group doing the project, i.e., studying, designing, and developing the system. The project manager usually works for the contractor, though users may also have project managers to represent their interests.

Phase A. Conception

Every man-made system is an attempt to solve a problem. The first step in solving a problem is recognition or acceptance that the problem exists. The person or group facing the problem—the users, so-called because they become the ones to "use" any proffered solution—seek out someone who can help. Responding to the call is the contractor, the consultant, or SDO who believes it can develop the system to solve the problem. (The SDO comprises everyone who will work on the project—top management, project leaders, and others. In big projects it also includes both prime and associate contractors and subcontractors.) Contractor top management determines which potential users (clients or customers) they want to respond to or approach for business. Top management makes the preliminary contact with the user and selects the project management, who in turn selects and organizes the team of workers who will perform the project.

Before the project is undertaken, a sizing up takes place. The contractor (1) examines the user's environment and objectives; (2) identifies alternative solutions, requisite resources, organization, and strategies; and (3) determines the technical, economic, and environmental feasibility and practicality of undertaking the project. Given that, the contractor presents to the user a *letter of interest* or a *formal proposal* that describes the *system concept*—a suggested solution—and the contractor's capability of doing it. The user examines the solution for its appropriateness and for (his perception of) the contractor's ability to carry it off. Finally, the user makes a choice among the competing system concepts and competing contractors. All potential systems go through this rite of initiation, but only a relative few are judged to be practical, feasible, or sound enough to progress to Phase B. Most systems die in Phase A.

Phase B. Definition

The systems concept advanced in Phase A is now investigated in greater detail. All elements and subsystems of the proposed system are scrutinized and defined. The project team is expanded to enable it to identify resource requirements, system performance requirements, major subsystems, components, support systems and system interfaces, and project cost and schedule requirements. Project management assembles a comprehensive plan of activities, schedules, costs, and resources necessary to design, build, and implement the system. After contractor top management has evaluated the plan for acceptability, it is passed on to the user who similarly evaluates it to decide whether to continue or cancel the project.

Phase C. Acquisition

The Acquisition phase is so-called because at its end the user acquires the system. This phase is variously referred to as "design," "production," or "execution"— progressing from an idea to a finished end-item. All systems have a pattern or structure, and it is the design that portrays the pattern necessary for the system to fulfill requirements. To ensure requirements are satisfied, various design alternatives are evaluated through the use of models or mock-ups. Once an acceptable detailed design is chosen, the system goes into production. Production involves either fabrication of a single item or mass production. The bulk of the activity is now handled by personnel in design, development, production, and manufacturing. Project management oversees and controls resources, motivates the workers, and reports progress to the user. Top management is kept apprised of project performance and progress.

Near the end of this phase the system is moved from the realm of the contractor to that of the user. It is installed and becomes a part of the user's environment. The user is prepared to operate the system through training and technical support.

Phase D. Operation

During the final Operation phase the system is deployed. The user takes over, operates the system, and evaluates its performance according to its ability to resolve the problem for which it was designed. The contractor may remain involved by providing maintenance support and evaluation services. Some systems are "one-shot" and either succeed or fail. There is no maintenance in these systems, per se, but evaluation of their outcomes is useful for the *next* similar system to be developed. A rock concert, political campaign, or lunar landing are examples.

Phase D also includes system divestment and system improvement. All systems eventually outlive their purpose or simply wear out. System evaluation identifies when this occurs and suggests a course of action. One course is to phase out or scrap the system. The other is to retain the system but reconfigure or improve it so that it remains useful. In the latter case, system improvement becomes a new "concept" and the beginning of a new systems development cycle.

One advantage of the systems development cycle is that it enables projects to be taken in steps (called the *phased project planning* approach). Decisions are made stage by stage, and objectives and outcomes are re-evaluated between stages at increasing levels of detail. Major resource commitments are never made without thorough management review, and there is no need to commit "all or nothing" in the early stages of the project.

5.3 SYSTEM DEVELOPMENT CYCLE, SYSTEMS ENGINEERING, AND PROJECT MANAGEMENT

Perhaps you have noticed a similarity between the systems development cycle and the systems engineering process (Chapter 4 and Appendix A). The difference between them is mainly one of scope. Systems engineering focuses on the scientific and technical aspects of systems to assure that subsystems, components, support subsystems, and environmental subsystems interrelate and interface to satisfy functional requirements.[1] Although it covers the entire systems development cycle, systems engineering is mainly concerned with the Conceptual and Definition phases—formulating functional requirements, performing system tradeoff studies, and designing systems.

In contrast, the systems development cycle is much broader in scope, encompassing virtually *all* considerations in systems development, not just configuration and integration. The systems development cycle includes elements of planning, scheduling, budgeting, control, organization, communication, negotiation, documentation, and resource acquisition and allocation. In short, it includes the elements of project management.

5.4 CONSTRAINTS IN SYSTEMS DEVELOPMENT

Organizational constraints greatly influence the course of the systems development cycle. The project manager is most aware of these constraints since it is he who, regardless of constraints, must guide the project and see that the system development is a success. The major constraints in projects are labor, facilities, capital, schedules, knowledge, and technology. They affect the cycle in the following ways:[2]

Sufficient labor (analysts, designers, managers, assembly, or other workers) must be available at the right time, otherwise the work simply cannot be done. Inappropriate or insufficient labor capacity slows the development process, prevents achievement of system objectives, or forces the project to be cancelled.

Even with sufficient labor, there must be facilities for them to the conduct the work of analysis, design, development, testing, and fabrication. Labor must have the equipment, tools, and a place to work. When new facilities must be built, construction must begin in the systems development cycle long before they are needed.

Similarly, sufficient capital must be available to procure facilities, material and equipment, and support the labor force. Clearly, insufficient capital has the same impact on system development as insufficient labor or facilities: the cycle is slowed down, system performance is degraded, or the project is cancelled.

Time is always a constraint. The user or the management may impose a tight schedule in hopes of speeding up the development cycle, but unless sufficient labor, facilities, and capital are provided the effect will only be to compromise project objectives and degrade system performance.

As the systems development cycle pushes the state of knowledge, more uncertainty enters the picture and the above constraints become more imposing. Requirements of advanced or "leading-edge" systems involve experimentation that tends to slow the development process and protract the project schedule. Developmental problems may become so difficult that system requirements have to be compromised or the project abandoned.

Even with sufficient knowledge, the contractor must have the technology to utilize that knowledge. Archaic or inappropriate technology has the same impact on the systems development cycle as inadequate labor, facilities, capital, or knowledge.

It is obvious that all of these constraints relate to the three dimensions of time, cost, and system performance—these three are not only goals but also constraints which influence the course of the systems development cycle. Throughout the cycle, the project manager must balance the effect of these constraints and negotiate with management to acquire the labor, facilities, capital, and time to achieve system goals. Sometimes the project manager must negotiate with the user to adjust time, cost, and performance goals to lessen the impact of resource constraints.

Starting in the next section, the phases of the systems development cycle will be examined more closely, emphasizing the activities and outcomes that relate to the role of the project manager. The first phase, Conception, is examined in this chapter; the remaining phases, Definition, Acquisition, and Operation are covered in Chapter 6.

5.5 PHASE A: CONCEPTION[3]

The Conception phase is comprised of two separate stages. The first stage, Project Initiation, establishes that a "need" exists and that the need is worthy of investigation. The second stage, Feasibility, involves a detailed investigation and choosing a solution.

Project Initiation

The systems development process begins when the user perceives a problem, need, or opportunity. Let us just say that the user has an "idea." Ideas can originate virtually anywhere—in corporate planning, marketing, engineering, manufacturing, or research and development. The user may be in a different organization or in the same organization as the systems development group or contractor. Sometimes the user is obvious, sometimes not. The systems development group may be its own user.

Initiation is the point where the idea for a system is born. Most problems are already being addressed in some way, though the way might be outmoded, inefficient, or otherwise unsatisfactory. At initiation the user has the idea that there might be a better way for coping with the problem. The user also sees *needs* or benefits which would accrue should a better way be found. When the need grows out of competitive environmental factors, a decision about the idea must be made quickly.

Beyond perceiving the need, Project Initiation requires proving that the idea has merit and can be achieved at practical cost. It is easy to identify problems and muse about solutions, but the vast majority of ideas are ephemeral or of small worth. If the users decide to take an idea beyond speculation, they may implement the idea using a "quick and dirty" approach or, alternatively, they may undertake a more protracted, albeit systematic and thorough approach. The latter is the systems development approach. In systems development, only ideas with a reasonably high degree of success or certainty about return on investment are permitted to develop. To cull the few good ideas, the user organization undertakes a brief, initial investigation.

Many users know a problem exists but do not know what it is or how to explain it. During initial investigation, the user tries to clarify the problem and evaluate the merit of solutions. The investigation starts with fact-finding—interviews with upper level and functional managers, background research, and review of existing documentation. A clearer statement of the problem is formulated, project objectives are defined, and a list of alternative, potential solutions is compiled. In considering potential alternatives, emphasis is put on developing a *range* of solutions. No attempt is made yet to work on details of individual solutions. The emphasis is on breadth, not depth. The investigation focuses on the elements of the problem, including:

- The environment
- The symptoms, problem definition, objectives and needs
- Preliminary alternatives and the estimated costs and benefits, strengths, and weaknesses of each.
- Estimated budgets, wherever possible
- Affected individuals and organizations

The user must decide whether or not to proceed. Most systems never get farther than this; just "seeds" of ideas, they are killed before they can germinate. It is obvious why this should be: while there are endless ideas about needs and potential system solutions, organizations can commit scarce resources only to those comparative few that provide the most return and seem to have the best chances of prospering. Only well-founded ideas receive commitment.

To commit to further study, the user must be convinced that:

- Potential solutions are consistent with the goals and resources of the organization.
- A real need exists and funding is available to support it.
- The project has sufficient priority in relation to the opportunity presented by other projects, present or future.
- The project has particular value in terms of, for example, applying new technology, enhancing reputation, increasing market share, or raising profits.

The initial investigation is usually conducted by the user and is brief, a few days or a few weeks at most. If, based upon the above criteria, the idea is found to warrant a full-scale, detailed investigation of the alternative solutions, approval is given for the next stage, Feasibility.

Project Feasibility

Feasibility is the process of investigating a problem and developing a solution in sufficient detail to determine if it is economically viable and worthy of development.

There are several possible perspectives about the Feasibility stage—what it entails, when it takes place, and which parties are involved. The initial investigation by users is really a "preliminary feasibility" study. If the users decide to further pursue the idea, they will solicit alternatives for solutions from one or more contractors. Each competing contractor performs its own internal feasibility study to assess the merit of the solicitation and evaluate its capability for submitting a winning proposal and obtaining a profitable contract with the user.

The purpose of the user's solicitation (called a *request for proposal*) might be to find a contractor to perform the feasibility study, in which case the Feasibility stage begins after a contractor is selected; alternatively, the *process* that a contractor follows in responding to the request for proposal may itself be considered a feasibility study. In this case, when the user has evaluated competing responses and decided which, if any, contractor to select, the Feasibility stage is completed. In the second case, selection of the winning contractor marks the decision to advance to Phase B, Definition.

These different interpretations of the Feasibility stage are illustrated in Figure 5–3. The discussion below will focus only on Theme A where the feasibility study is undertaken during the process of responding to a user's request. This is called the "proposal preparation process." In general, a similar process is followed under Theme B as well.

Since each project requires allocation of resources and must be coordinated with other, ongoing projects in both user and contracting organizations, it must first be authorized by top management in both the user and contractor organizations. This is the purpose of the Feasibility stage—to establish which system solution and which contractor, if any, is best. Feasibility study results become the basis for determining whether or not the system should be advanced to Phase B.

The specifics of the Feasibility stage include the user requesting proposals for solutions, contractors doing feasibility studies and preparing proposals, the user evaluating

Phase A: Conceptual

Stage 1: User initiation

"Preliminary feasibility" to investigate merit
of pursuing idea in more detail

↓

Stage 2: Feasibility

User Request for Proposal (RFP) sent to SDO's

Theme A: When purpose of RFP is
to determine if idea is feasible
and to select group to do Phase B

Theme B: When purpose of RFP
is to select group to do
feasibility study

↓   ↓

SDO investigates feasibility of preparing winning proposal
and performing profitable project.

↓   ↓

SDO undertakes feasibility
study as part of the proposal
process to do Phase B.
If wins: SDO begins
Phase B.

SDO prepares proposal
to perform
feasibility study.
If wins: SDO performs
feasibility study

If user determines
concept is feasible:
Repeat RFP, proposal
process to select an
SDO to begin Phase B
(Theme A).

FIGURE 5–3. Different paths in the Feasibility stage.

the proposals, and joint user-contractor negotiations for a project contract. Each of these will be considered in the following sections.

Request for Proposal

Since a feasibility study is usually a time consuming effort that requires particular expertise, the user typically chooses to bring in a contractor. (Sometimes the contractor is brought in as early as the initial investigation.) The user notifies one or several contractors, internal or external, by sending them a document called an *RFP*—a Request for Proposal. The most common purpose of the RFP is to outline the user's idea (problem, need, etc.) and solicit suggestions for solutions. RFP's are sent to companies on the user's *bidders list* or to anyone else who wants one. Contractors not on the bidders list can learn about upcoming jobs in newsletters and bulletins. For example, the *Commerce Business Daily* is a daily publication that gives a synopsis of all federal jobs over $10,000. Many smaller contractors scan these and ask for RFP's about jobs they might be interested in bidding on.

The RFP states the user's requirements—system objectives, project scope, performance specifications, cost and schedule constraints, data requirements, and type of preferred contracting arrangement. Contractors send in proposals that comply with the RFP, then the user selects one to become the prime or associate contractor in the systems development process.

Each competing contractor must determine if it is capable of preparing a winning proposal and then, should it win, performing the proposed work. The feasibility of winning and conducting a project depend upon numerous factors, including

- whether competitors have gotten a head start
- whether the contractor has sufficient money, facilities, and resources to invest in the project
- whether performance on the project is likely to be good for (or damaging to) the contractor's reputation
- other criteria, similar to those which the user employed in the Initiation stage.

The amount a contractor spends on preparing proposals and the proportion of contracts it wins significantly effect its company overhead since expenses for lost proposals must be charged to overhead. It is only in rare cases, such as major defense contracts, that winning contractors are reimbursed for their proposal expense.

Sometimes contractors will respond to an RFP knowing that they cannot possibly win the project, doing so just to maintain a relationship with the solicitor, remain on the user's bidders list, or keep the field competitive. Sometimes *users* send out an RFP with no intent of ever signing with a contractor; they do it simply to gather ideas. Obviously this is a situation of which respondent contractors must be wary.

Sometimes proposals are submitted to potential users without an RFP. When a project group believes it has a system or solution to satisfy a need or solve a problem, the project manager works with his marketing department to identify prospective customers and then notifies them with an *unsolicited proposal*. Other times the project manager identifies follow-up work related to a current project and submits an unsolicited proposal to the current customer.

The Feasibility Study[4]

The statement of the problem as defined in the Initiation stage is frequently incomplete, vague, or even incorrect. If an RFP has been sent out it will contain such a statement. Thus one of the first steps of the contractor in responding to an RFP is to develop a more concise, accurate statement of the problem. This is the way to gaining a full and complete understanding of the user's problem situation.

The prime source of information about the problem is interviews with the user, so it is important that the contractor make sure who the *user* really is. Surprisingly, this is not always obvious. The "real" user of the system is often confused with persons of rank and position who only represent the user. If the user is an organization, the contractor must determine the individual parties whose needs are to be met. The contractor will be working closely with the user throughout the feasibility study, so it is important that "users" be found who are both familiar with the problem and the workings of the organization.

Based upon information gathered from interviews, reports, organizational records and memos, the contractor prepares a formal, documented description of the problem situation. This is the *present system*. Documenting the present system is an important step since the appropriateness of a proposed system solution depends on how well the proposer understands the present (problem) system. Documentation should identify key system elements (inputs, outputs, functions, flows, volumes, subsystems, components, relationships, and attributes) using schematics and charts. The schematic in Figure 5–4, for example, was developed by a consultant in a hospital study to find ways of improving efficiency and reducing costs in the procurement and utilization of surgical facilities and supplies. It shows components and flows in the present (problem) system and was useful for identifying areas of cost and procedural inefficiency.

Investigation of the present system also helps the contractor and user determine what the system objectives and user requirements should be. Systems objectives and user requirements delimit the scope of the work to only those areas essential to solving the problem.

Each contractor develops alternative system approaches to meeting the objectives, taking into account what the system must do (operating requirements to satisfy user needs), how it can be done (technical considerations), and the value of it (economic considerations). Alternative solutions may include new systems developed from scratch or modifications of off-the-shelf systems and existing technology. As in the Initiation stage, emphasis is on a *range* of solutions, not depth, so project leaders must engender an atmosphere that encourages creativity and stimulates free flow of ideas.

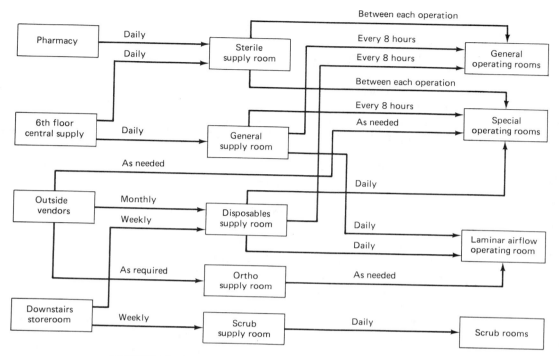

FIGURE 5–4. System schematic: Flow of supplies to the operating room.

The contractor conducts a systems analysis to evaluate solutions. Evaluative criteria are based upon system objectives and preliminary user requirements, resources of the contractor (facilities, capital, expertise), and constraints imposed by the user.

The final feasibility study document includes a summary of the data collected, a description of the existing system, the statement of the problem, the criteria and methods used to evaluate alternatives, the preferred alternative(s), and reasons for its selection. The feasibility study is combined with the project plan, bid price, and contractor qualifications to make up the project proposal.

5.6 THE PROJECT PROPOSAL

Proposal Preparation[5]

Since the contractor must commit an (often large) amount of time and money to preparing a proposal, the proposal preparation process must be authorized by top management. The proposal effort is itself a project—with cost constraints, a deadline for submittal, and performance requirements—and it should be managed like one. Upon authorization of the proposal process, a technically competent person is identified to be the project manager.

He or she may become sole manager of the proposal effort or, alternatively, may work with a proposal manager who has experience in conducting proposal-related activities. The project team, or part of it, is selected by the project manager to help prepare the proposal. Usually the rest of the project team cannot be specified until the proposal effort has been completed.

The project manager reviews the requirements of the RFP and then prepares a detailed summary for the project. This summary guides the effort and keeps the focus from shifting to irrelevant technical or managerial considerations.

In preparing the proposal the project team outlines the work to be done for the solution chosen in the feasibility study. This is referred to in the proposal as the *statement of work* (SOW). (A similar statement may exist in the RFP that identifies the user's requirements for the technical content of the proposal.) In addition to the SOW, the team provides specifications (measurable, verifiable criteria) for the work. Sometimes approximate specifications are given, to be worked out more carefully and precisely later. The SOW is reviewed with the user for clarity and correctness.

The proposal includes both the feasibility study and a plan for conducting the systems development project. The project team performs an economic evaluation to compare development and operating costs with anticipated benefits. This evaluation will become a major criterion for user management in determining the project's feasibility and priority level among other projects.

During proposal preparation the project team must think through the entire project and prepare a project plan. The project plan addresses the dimensions of time, cost, and performance. A *work breakdown structure* (WBS) is used to determine the work necessary to achieve performance specifications and subsequent work schedules and cost estimates. WBS, schedules, and cost breakdowns showing how the price was derived are included in the proposal. (These techniques are fully described in Section IV of this book.) When more than one system solution is proposed, a plan is worked out for every one.

The proposal is both a sales device and a form of contract: the more detailed it is, the easier it is to work out price, schedules, and other details, and to convince the user that the contractor knows the job; this is a big help should the contract have to be negotiated.

In complex technical projects, the WBS is a systems engineering effort; it converts system requirements into functional block diagrams and schematic diagrams which show components, interfaces, and quantitative design specifications for inputs, outputs, and processes. The effort is carried just to the level of detail needed to satisfy proposal requirements; if the contract is won, the effort is resumed to the level of detail necessary to do the work.

Those contractor functional departments which would be involved in the project, if it is won, should be called upon to provide information for the proposal. This not only increases the accuracy of proposal estimates, it helps build commitment from those who will be doing the work.

During proposal preparation, the contractor should establish a dialogue with the user to determine which requirements are dominant among time, cost, and performance, and which solutions the user prefers. Even when the RFP is clear, there is need to confer with the user about details of scheduling, costing, specifications, reporting, and so on. Dialogue is the best way to insure that terms in the proposal are clear and satisfy the user's requirements.

The feasibility study and proposal preparation may take many weeks or months to complete. While enough time must be spent to produce an acceptable proposal, not so much time should be spent that it becomes overly time-consuming and expensive. Do not do the entire project while preparing the proposal!

Throughout the proposal preparation, the project manager makes sure that all parts fit together and there is no duplication of effort. To assure nothing is overlooked, project managers typically employ checklists which, over the years, grow to accumulate the most important items on a proposal; they include, for example, key considerations for design, assembly, test, shipment, documentation, facilities, subcontractors, supplies, travel, labor rates, training, and payment.

Contractor top management is briefed frequently about the scope of the proposal and the resources being committed to the project. Prior to submission to the user, the completed proposal is sent to contractor top management for approval.

Proposals range in length from a few statements to volumes. The content varies depending on purpose, format favored by user, requirements in the RFP, relationship between user and contractor, technical complexity of the work, solicited versus unsolicited proposal, and so on. Figure 5–5 shows the main ingredients of a typical proposal.[6]

Example: Writing Proposals for Real Estate Projects at the Bigate Company

Customers come to the real estate department at Bigate Company, a "Big 8" accounting firm, for help in investigating and choosing real estate investment alternatives. A meeting is set up with the client to establish a clear definition of the investment "problem" and the client's goals. The client and several Bigate employees brainstorm about the problem to achieve the clearest, most accurate problem definition. A project "resource director" prepares a proposal that includes the problem definition, the pricing structure, and the steps to be taken in achieving a solution. In proposals that require developing a site or designing and constructing a building, a feasibility study is included in the proposal. For projects that involve simply evaluating, improving, or determining the value of a site, no feasibility study is needed. If the client likes the proposal, the resource director prepares a second proposal specifying the steps of analysis in greater detail. The second proposal includes a work breakdown structure and a modified CPM network (see Chapters 11, 12 and 13). If approved by the client, the second proposal becomes the project plan. It specifies tasks to be done, dates to be completed, and is the basis for assigning personnel to the project. Usually the second proposal calls for a feasibility study, demographic study, or analysis of financing, tax, accounting, or other ramifications of the alternatives.

The information generated by the study or analysis is then submitted to the client in a third proposal that recommends what action the client should take regarding the alternatives investigated. Although Bigate Company does not perform contracting or construction work, if the study favors site development or construction, the real estate

Cover Letter
This is perhaps the most important part of the proposal since it must convince the user that the proposal is worth considering. It should be more personal than the proposal and briefly state the qualifications, experience, and interests of the contractor, especially drawing attention to any unique or outstanding features of the proposal or the contractor's ability to do the project. The "contact" person with the contractor is identified here.

Executive Summary
A succinct summary of the project emphasizing its significant aspects to enable the reader to determine its relevance to user needs and its contribution to solving the problem. This is an important section because it is here that user management decides whether or not to have the rest of the proposal examined.

Technical Section
Indicates the scope of the work—the planned approach and the statement of work. It must be specific enough to avoid misunderstandings and demonstrate the method and appropriateness of the approach, yet not so specific as to "give away" the solution.

Anticipated Benefits
Describes realistic benefits in sufficient detail to demonstrate that user needs will be fullfilled, but not so specific or enthusiastic as to promise benefits that the contractor may have difficulty in delivering.

Schedule
A schedule of when end-items will be delivered. It should be based upon the work breakdown structure and include the major project phases and key tasks, milestones, and reviews. In developmental projects, portions of this section may have to be negotiated.

Financial Section
A breakdown of projected hours for direct, indirect, and special activities, associated labor charges and materials expenses. Preferred or required contractual arrangement (see Appendix B on contracts) and method of payment may also be included.

Legal Section
Anticipated, possible, or likely problems and provisions for contingencies; for example, appropriate procedures for handling changes to the scope of the project and for terminating the project.

Management/Qualifications
Background of the contractor organization, related experience and achievements, and financial responsibility. Organization of management, and resumes of project manager and key project personnel.

FIGURE 5–5. Contents of a proposal.

department will make recommendations about consultants, contractors, or construction firms.

As the example shows, proposal preparation is sometimes an iterative process where acceptance of one leads to the preparation of other, more detailed proposals.

Selection of Proposal[7]

The user evaluates proposals in a fashion similar to one used by the contractor in deciding which RFP's to respond to. Each proposal is evaluated according to criteria related to system performance, price, and schedule. Generally, approval and priority of projects is based upon considerations of

- Return on investment
- Relation to organizational goals
- Value of intangible benefits
- Likelihood of success
- Fit to organizational resources and technological capability

Proposal finalists are notified when the user has determined that at least one of the proposals is acceptable. Competing contractors may then be requested to provide more data or to make presentations. When a contractor has been selected, the recommendation is submitted to user top management for approval. If management accepts the recommendation, then a contract is awarded to the winner. If several contractors receive equal weight or if some terms in the proposal are unspecified or questionable then negotiation is required to settle upon final terms and a contractor. If none of the proposals are acceptable or the feasibility studies reveal that the systems development process would be too costly, too risky, too time-consuming, or have insufficient return, then the project is terminated.

Negotiating the Contract[8]

The purpose of negotiation is to clarify technical or other terms in the contract and to reach agreement on time, schedule, and performance obligations. Negotiation is not necessary on standardized items for which terms are simple and costs are fairly well known, but it is commonplace on complex systems that require much development work and involve considerable uncertainty and risk. Different contractual arrangements offer advantages to the user and contractor, depending on the nature of the project. These are discussed in Appendix B.

Although final negotiation is the last activity before a contractual agreement is reached, the negotiation process actually begins much earlier—during preparation of the proposal—since the proposal must be consistent with the kind of contract acceptable to both user and contractor. During negotiation, terms related to specifications, schedules, and price are converted into legal, contractual agreements. Ongoing negotiation improves communication and helps the user and contractor reach mutual understanding and expectations about the job. Final negotiation is the last opportunity to correct misperceptions which might have slipped through the RFP and proposal process.

Performance, schedule, and cost are interrelated, and a "package" agreement must be reached wherein all three parameters are acceptable to both parties. In highly competitive situations the user will try to play one contractor against the other. The user will try to raise performance specifications while decreasing time and cost. While raising performance requirements, corresponding costs may increase to a level unacceptable to the contractor. In that case, project managers take on the role of salespeople by pushing the merits of their proposals. Throughout negotiation, their goal is to obtain an agreement to the best advantage of their company. In countering objections to the proposal, the project manager's best defense is a well-thought-out project plan that clearly explains what can or must be done to achieve certain desired parameters. A detailed project plan is often used to define the relatively "fixed" part of the plan—the work and the schedule, leaving only the details and final price to be negotiated.

To be in the most knowledgeable and competitive position, the project manager must learn as much as possible about the user and the competition. The project manager should determine, for example, if the user is under pressure to make a particular decision, or if the user needs the system as soon as possible or faces an impending fiscal deadline. The project manager should determine if the user has historically shown a preference for one particular approach or contractor over others. The project manager must know the competition—their likely approach to the problem, their costs, competitive advantages and disadvantages. Information may be derived from historical information about past projects, published material, or even employees who once worked for competitors. (Relying on the last source is ethically questionable, and, of course, works against the contractor whenever his employees are hired by a competitor.)

To be able to negotiate tradeoffs, the project manager must be intimately familiar with the technical details of system design, fabrication, and related costs. Sometimes the contract will include incentive or penalty clauses as inducements to complete the project before a certain date or below a certain cost. To competently negotiate such clauses, the project manager must be familiar with the project schedule and time-cost tradeoffs.

The signed contract becomes the binding agreement for the project. Any changes thereafter should follow formal change mechanisms, including change notices, reviews, customer approvals, and sometimes contract renegotiation—topics discussed later in Chapter 15. Changes with legal implications should be anticipated and procedures for making changes outlined in the legal section of the proposal.

Signing the contract marks the completion of Phase A and approval to proceed to Phase B. The project is then prioritized with other previously approved projects according to availability of capital funds and resources needed to begin the project. The steps in Phase A are summarized in Figure 5–6.

5.7 SUMMARY

The systems approach to management recognizes the life cycle nature of systems. Projects, too, have life cycles which are broken into stages describing their technical and managerial activities. A common theme among project life cycles is the systems development process that divides a project into four phases of Conception, Definition, Acquisition, and Operation.

This chapter focused on the first phase and described the stages of initiating a project and evaluating the feasibility of undertaking it. This phase includes the activities of formulating the problem, defining needs and requirements, defining systems solutions, evaluating alternatives, and developing an organization and a plan to conduct the project. At the start of this phase most activities are in the hands of the user. By the end, they have been taken over by the contractor and systems specialists. The relationship between the

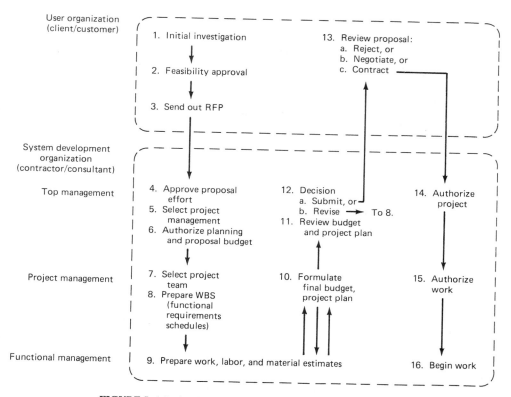

FIGURE 5–6. Project initiation, planning, and authorization process.

user and the contractor was cemented through the process of solicitation (RFP's), proposal preparation and evaluation, and contract negotiation.

Phase A is the "foundation" part of the systems development cycle; it establishes the objectives, requirements, constraints, agreements, and patterns of communication upon which the remaining phases must build. It is a crucial phase, and it is not surprising that most system ideas never get past this phase. Among those that do, the failures often have their roots planted here.

CHAPTER REVIEW QUESTIONS

1. How are projects initiated? Describe the process.
2. How is it determined if the feasibility of an idea should be investigated?
3. Who is the "user" in the systems development process?
4. How does the contractor (systems development organization) become involved in the project? Describe the ways.

5. What is the role of an RFP? Describe the contents of an RFP.
6. What is a feasibility study? Describe its contents and purpose.
7. Who is involved in preparing the proposal? Describe the proposal preparation process.
8. Describe the contents of the proposal.
9. How is the best proposal selected? Describe the process and the criteria used.
10. Describe the different kinds of contracts (refer to Appendix B). What are the relative advantages and disadvantages of each to the user and the contractor?

QUESTIONS ABOUT THE STUDY PROJECT

As appropriate, answer the above questions 1–9 regarding your project. Also answer the following question: How are contracts negotiated and who is involved in the negotiation?

ENDNOTES

1. Traditionally, the practice of Systems Engineering has been applied to large-scale, hardware development systems. In concept however, Systems Engineering is just as applicable for developing complex software systems or solving difficult problems in social systems.

2. D. Meister and G.F. Rabideay, *Human Factors Evaluation in System Development* (New York: John Wiley, 1965), 37–39.

3. The initiation stage is covered in greater detail in C.L. Biggs, E.G. Birks, and W. Atkins, *Managing the Systems Development Process* (Englewood Cliffs, N.J.: Prentice-Hall, 1980), 51–59; and J. Allen and B.P. Lientz, *Systems in Action* (Santa Monica: Goodyear, 1978), 41–63.

4. Other aspects of the feasibility study are discussed in Biggs, Birks, and Atkins, 59–80; and Allen and Lientz, 65–89.

5. A thorough description of proposal preparation is provided by V.G. Hajek, *Management of Engineering Projects,* 3rd ed. (New York: McGraw-Hill, 1984), 39–57; a good, succinct overview is given by M.D. Rosenau, *Successful Project Management* (Belmont, CA:, Lifetime Learning, 1981), 21–32.

6. See D.D. Roman, *Managing Projects: A Systems Approach* (New York: Elsevier, 1986), 67–72, and Rodney Stewart and Ann Stewart, *Proposal Preparation* (New York: Wiley, 1984) for comprehensive coverage of proposal contents and the proposal preparation process.

7. Analysis and selection of projects is a broad subject. Models for analysis and selection are discussed in L. Bussey, *The Economic Analysis of Industrial Projects* (Englewood Cliffs, N.J.: Prentice-Hall, 1978); also see issues of *IEEE Transactions on Engineering Management, Management Science,* and *Research Management* for titles regarding project evaluation and selection.

8. See Hajek, *Management of Engineering Projects.*, Chaps. 8 and 9; and Rosenau, *Successful Project Management,* 34–41.

chapter 6

Systems Development Cycle: Middle And Later Stage

When one door is shut, another opens.

Cervantes, Don Quixote

The result of Phase A is a formalized "systems concept." It includes (1) a clear problem formulation, (2) a rudimentary but well-conceptualized systems solution, (3) an elemental plan for the project, and (4) an agreement between the user and the contractor about all of these. The project is now ready to move on to the "middle" and "later" phases of systems development and to bring the systems concept to fruition.

6.1 PHASE B: DEFINITION

The Definition phase can also be called the "analysis of the solution" phase because it is here that the *solution* is first scrutinized in great detail. Most of the effort in Phase A was devoted to investigating the problem—what is it, if it is significant, if it should be resolved, and can it be resolved in an acceptable fashion. Despite the effort and expense devoted to initial investigation and feasibility studies, most of the work remained focused on the problem. Any work on the solution was preliminary and rudimentary.

As Figure 6–1 shows, with approval of the project in Phase A the thrust of the effort is now turned toward definition, design, production, and implementation of the

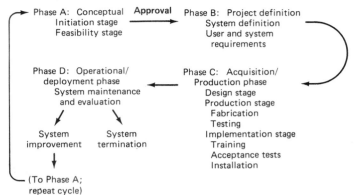

FIGURE 6–1. Four-phase model of the Systems Development Cycle.

solution. In Phase B the system solution is analyzed and defined in sufficient detail so that designers and builders can produce a system with the greatest likelihood of solving the user's problem. The Definition phase has two thrusts: first, preparation of a detailed project plan; second, determination of final, detailed systems specifications.

Detailed Project Planning

Going into Phase B, a portion of the project definition work has already been performed. At minimum, some definition work was necessary in Phase A to prepare project plans and system specifications for inclusion in the proposal. Although the proposal may contain considerable detail, it is still the result of a proposal-sized effort and usually contains only a detailed *outline* of what is to come. During the Definition phase the contractor must fill in the outline and expand and elaborate on details of the project plan. This includes attention to details such as: lower-level schedules and networks; cost accounts, budgets, and cost control systems; support documentation about policies, procedures, and job descriptions; the project team, including leaders, supervisors, and workers from functional areas, subcontractors, and project support staff.

A full-sized project team begins to evolve out of the skeletal group which worked on the proposal. Selection of team members generally follows a cascade pattern. First the project manager selects project team leaders who, in turn, select team members to fill positions under them. The project manager negotiates with functional managers to get specific individuals and the requisite expertise assigned to the project. Sometimes user approval is sought for key members of the project team. This practice is advisable in cases where users and team members must work closely and where it is possible that the user *might* have an objection. Good user-project team rapport is crucial to maintaining a healthy user-contractor relationship.

Once key members of the project team have been assembled, they begin preparation of the detailed project plan. The plan includes:

1. Work schedules and deadlines
2. Budgets, cost accounts, and a cost control system
3. Detailed WBS and work packages
4. Areas of high risk and uncertainty and contingency plans
5. Personnel plan and resource utilization plans
6. Plans for testing the system
7. Documentation plan
8. Change control and work review plan
9. Initial plans for implementing the system

(Details of the plan and the planning process are discussed in Section IV; a sample project plan is given in Appendix C.) Most of the planning on large projects is delegated to subordinate members of the project team. The project manager coordinates and oversees subplanning efforts and checks that everything is covered and that all subplans tie together. The final plan is reviewed for approval by top management and by the user. Contractor management makes sure that the plan fits into existing and upcoming organizational projects and capabilities. User management checks that the plan conforms with specifications in the contract agreement.

Anxious to get the project underway, many contractors avoid reviewing the project plan with the user. This is shortsighted since the plan may contain elements to which the user may object. A project is not conducted and implemented in isolation but in the user's ongoing system. Everything on the plan must fit: the project schedule must fit the user's schedule; project cash flow requirements must meet the user's payment schedule; personnel and procedures of the contractor must complement those of the user; and materials and work methods must be acceptable to the user. To avoid problems later, it is best to check the plan with the user before starting work.

Planning is a process that continues throughout the project. Although a summary plan must be developed to cover the project from start to finish, details are often not available until later. As the project moves from stage to stage and new information becomes available, plans are detailed and revised in a rolling wave fashion. The overall summary plan is adhered to, but the gaps are filled in. The summary plan enables planners to integrate and coordinate the stages of the project and tells them about what other information is needed to develop more detailed plans.

Besides a detailed project plan, the Definition phase also involves preparing a well-defined technical solution called the *system specifications*. The work of defining system specifications parallels that of project planning because the specifications affect elements of the project plan. Two categories of systems specifications will be considered: user requirements and systems requirements.

User Requirements

The first step in defining a system is to get *user requirements*. These describe what the user wants the finished system to be and do. User requirements are the measures the user will employ to determine whether or not the final system is acceptable. The project manager has responsibility for making sure that the user is well-informed and that final user requirements are adequate, clear, and accurate. When the project is completed and the contractor says "Here's the system you ordered," the user should be able to say "Yes, it certainly is," meaning "Yes, it satisfies my requirements." User requirements are formally documented and become the ultimate reference for the system solution. They are, in a word, the "quality" measures of the project.

Detailed user requirements come from one source: the user. When an architect-contractor discusses with a client what is wanted in a new home, she is gathering user requirements. The contractor and client work together to formulate requirements. Just as users sometimes need help in determining what the problem is, so they sometimes need help in determining what their requirements for the solution should be. They may be not be aware of the cost, schedule, or other ramifications of requirements, nor understand what is needed in a system to fulfill them. The project team should not accept just any requirements from the user, but should help the user to define them. Once the user and contractor agree upon the requirements, the requirements should be documented using the user's own terminology and language.

Preliminary definition of user requirements happens during proposal preparation, and summary user requirements are always included in the final contract. In simple systems, user requirements rarely exceed a few sentences. In big systems, however, they might have to be expanded and detailed, and eventually fill volumes. An example of the former is user requirements for a contract to perform a one day management seminar; an example of the latter is user requirements for (what became) the nine year, multibillion dollar Delta Project to prevent the North Sea from flooding the Netherlands.

System Requirements

User requirements are employed to derive another set of requirements called *system requirements*. Whereas user requirements are stated in the language of the user, system requirements are stated in the technical jargon of the specialists. System requirements are a *translation* of user requirements; they tell system designers what the system must be and do, and what they must put into it. To develop system requirements, the architect, engineer, systems analyst, or consultant thinks about the user's requirements, then translates them into the dimensions, arrangements, quantity, capacity, etc. of the components and materials necessary to achieve the user's requirements. System requirements identify all of the significant functions to be performed by the system. They identify functions and related components and indicate how functions interface with the rest of the system. They are the *functional requirements* of systems engineering. System requirements are often stated in terms of required resources (e.g., type, quality, or capacity of engines, materials, systems, personnel, hardware). Following are some examples of system requirements and the user requirements they are derived from:

User Requirements	*System Requirements*
1. Vehicle must accelerate from 0 to 60 mph in 10 seconds, and accommodate six people.	Vehicle size and weight, engine horsepower, kind of transmission.
2. House must be spacious for a family of four.	Number and size of rooms.
3. House must be luxurious.	Quality of materials; number, quality, and expense of decorative features.
4. Space station must operate life support, manufacturing, and experimental equipment.	Type and kilowatt capacity of power generating equipment.
5. Computer system must provide summary reports on a daily basis.	Type of manual and electronic systems, hardware and software; collection, entry, storage, and processing procedures.

Another kind of system requirement, called a performance requirement, specifies the output of the system in technical terms—miles per hour, miles per gallon, turning radius, decibels of sound, acceleration, percent efficiency, bauds per second, labor turnover rate, operating temperature, BTU's, operating cost, and so on. These are specifications that systems specialists will use to measure performance of the system against the user's requirements. Users may provide a set of system performance specifications as part of the user requirements.

Following are types of specifications placed on the system, its subsystems, and its components:[1]

1. *Compatibility.* The ability of subsystems to be integrated into the whole system and to contribute to objectives of the whole system.
2. *Commonality.* The ability of a component to be used interchangeably with an existing component of a different type. A "high commonality" system is composed of many available (off-the-shelf) components; a "low commonality" system contains many components unique to the system which must be developed (from "scratch").
3. *Cost Effectiveness.* The total cost to which the user *may be subjected* if a particular design is adopted. Cost effectiveness requires analysis of cost of the design, as well as the cost to the user to implement and operate the design to achieve a given level of benefit.
4. *Reliability.* The ability of a system or component to function at a given level without failing, or to function for a given period of time before failing.
5. *Maintainability.* The ability of a subsystem to be repaired within a certain period of time (i.e., the *ease* with which it can be repaired).
6. *Testability.* The degree to which a subsystem enables systematic testing and measuring of its performance capabilities.

By the end of the Definition phase, a detailed list of user requirements and system requirements has been compiled. In combination they comprise the *system specifications*.

Both will be used in Phase C to design, build, and test the system, and in Phase D to implement and evaluate the performance of the system in real-life operation.

System specifications should be reviewed with the user. During review the user and contractor should check for the accuracy and completeness of user requirements, the fit of system requirements to user requirements, the fit of system requirements to time and cost constraints in the project plan, as well as the need to modify, add, or delete specifications. As soon as the project plan and systems specifications have been approved the project can proceed to Phase C.

6.2 PHASE C: ACQUISITION

The Acquisition phase variously includes stages of *design*, *development*, *procurement*, *construction/production*, and *implementation*; depending on the project, it involves some or all of these activities in sequence. For example, in hardware development projects Acquisition includes stages of design, development, and production; in construction projects it includes stages of design and construction; in consulting projects it includes stages of report outline and compilation. Virtually all projects that have a physical end-item—a product, building, system, or report—also have an implementation stage where the end-item is given to the user. Our discussion will divide the Acquisition phase into three nominal stages: Design, Production, and Implementation.

Design Stage

During the design stage specifications are converted into plans, sketches, or drawings. The output of design varies depending on the industry and the type of system, but usually it is some form of pictorial representation of the system—blueprints, flow charts, or schematic diagrams showing relationships, arrangements, and dimensions of components.

In the design process the system is broken into subsystems, then subsystems are divided into tiers of components and parts. Various design possibilities are reviewed for compatibility with each other and with higher level systems, and for their ability to satisfy system specifications and system cost, schedule, and performance requirements. The breakdown of system design into tiers and components uses the block diagramming approach described in Appendix A and the WBS approach described in Chapter 11.

The design process involves two interrelated design activities. The first is preparation of a design that shows the system components and relationships necessary to achieve system objectives. This is essentially the thrust of the systems engineering process described in Chapter 4. The second is preparation of a design that shows what the system will physically look like. This is the "drafting" process or the making of working drawings and schematics.

The purpose of the first design activity is to determine *logically* what functional elements are necessary and how they should be interconnected to achieve the purpose of the system. This design is based upon functional analysis of the system and results in block diagrams. Two examples from Schmenner are shown. Figure 6–2 shows the functional design for an automobile assembly line and Figure 6–3 shows the functional design for a paper processing plant.

The second kind of design shows what the actual system will look like, its component parts, their sizes, shapes and relative location—that is, the *physical* appearance of a system which satisfies the requirements of the functional design. This design activity involves producing engineering, manufacturing, architectural, or other types of drawings. These drawings show details necessary for system fabrication, assembly, and maintenance. Sometimes they reveal places where the functional design is impractical or infeasible because of assembly, maintenance, or appearance considerations. In such cases it is necessary to return to the functional design, revise it, then go back and redo the drawings.

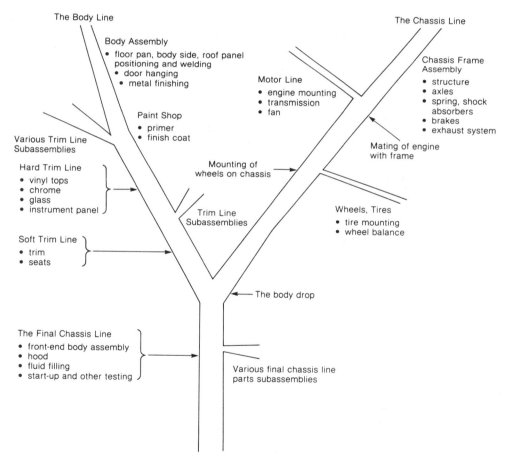

FIGURE 6–2. Functional design plan for automobile assembly. (Reprinted with permission of MacMillan Publishing Co. from *Production/Operations Management: Concepts and Situations:* 3rd ed., by Roger W. Schmenner. Copyright © 1987. Science Research Associates, Inc.)

Design often follows an evolutionary, trial and error process. A trial design is prepared, modeled, then tested against system performance specifications. If it fails, the design is modified and retested. This process is followed to varying degrees in virtually all development projects for new or innovative high-technology systems. When a system has been designed which finally satisfies system specifications, the result is a physical description, picture, or model. Figure 6–4 shows such a "picture," the blueprint design for the paper processing plant derived from the functional design in Figure 6–3.

The Project Manager in the Design Stage

The size of the project team and the level of project activity continually grow as the project moves through Phase C. As the system is defined in greater detail and more activities are identified, the project manager assigns project tasks to group leaders in the systems development organization. Project tasks are broken down into small, clearly identifiable segments called *work packages*, each of which becomes the basis for project scheduling, budgeting, and control for the duration of the project. Work package breakdown, planning, and control are described later in Section IV.

As the size of the project organization increases, so does the amount of work required of the project manager. Design activities require participation from groups throughout the contractor organization and its subcontractors. The project manager coordinates their efforts to ensure accurate information exchange, effective interfacing, and work that is on schedule and according to budget. Throughout, the project manager keeps the effort directed toward system requirements to prevent irrelevant or impractical things from sidetracking the project or degrading project performance.

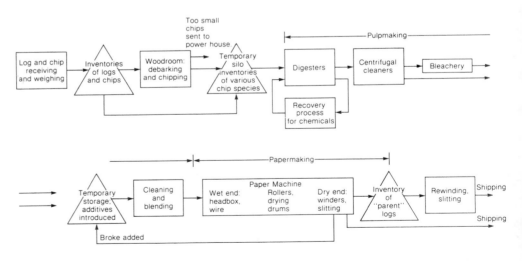

FIGURE 6–3. Functional design for paper-manufacturing process. (Reprinted with permission of MacMillan Publishing Co. from *Production/Operations Management: Concepts and Situations:* 3rd ed., by Roger W. Schmenner. Copyright © 1987. Science Research Associates, Inc.)

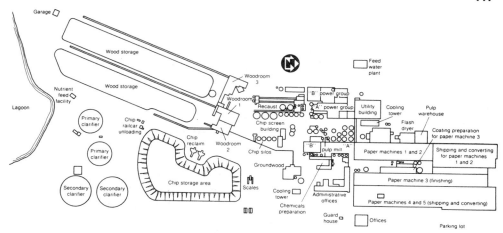

FIGURE 6–4. Blueprint design for paper manufacturing plant. (Reprinted with permission of MacMillan Publishing Co. from *Production/Operations Management: Concepts and Situations:* 3rd ed., by Roger W. Schmenner. Copyright © 1987. Science Research Associates, Inc.)

During the design stage, reviews are conducted at key milestones to insure that objectives, requirements, and specifications are being met. Although reviews are planned and scheduled by the project manager, they are, ideally, conducted and chaired by objective "outsiders." Functional and final designs are approved by the user to ensure that functions, interfaces, and flows satisfy user requirements, and that the final design suits the user's personal tastes, needs, and budget.

During design, development, and review, changes to initial designs may be necessary because of new technology, intractable technical problems, or new requirements by the user. These inevitably necessitate changes in work activities and significantly affect the project plan, its schedules, costs, and so on. Such changes must be approved by the user. Those changes which drastically alter the project plan may require amendments to or renegotiation of the contract.

Project management is responsible for monitoring design changes, determining their impact on the project, communicating the impact to all affected parties, obtaining approvals, and updating schedules, budgets, and plans. Although design changes add to project costs, as shown in Figure 6–5, typical design costs are a small fraction of production costs. Prolonging the design stage to get it right is usually less financially risky than extending the production stage to incorporate omissions or eliminate errors. Still, at some point all designs must be *frozen* so that the project can progress fully to the next stage.

Planning for Production

During the design phase, the project manager or production coordinator begins to plan the production stage by dividing it into individual tasks such as tool and machine design, equipment and materials purchasing, metal work, subsystem and final assembly, compo-

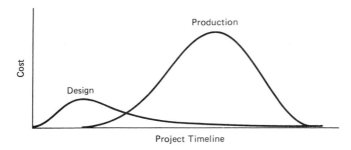

FIGURE 6–5. Relative costs for design and production.

nent testing, integration testing, packaging, and so on. A schedule is then prepared for these tasks based upon dates when design inputs are expected. Since the design work might not be completed all at once, production tasks may have to be scheduled in phases. Planning and scheduling of phased production involves considerable coordination of personnel, materials, and facilities. Project leaders and supervisors prepare detailed schedules which are combined and integrated into the master schedule by the project manager and key functional managers.

6.3 PRODUCTION STAGE

With detailed designs in hand, the contractor is now ready to begin production of the system. For one-of-a-kind items this means that the system is ready to be constructed. For mass-produced items, this means the system is ready for manufacture. In either case, the system is ready to be fabricated.

System Fabrication

Fabrication of the system begins when design work is completed and the project manager authorizes fabrication work areas to begin. The project manager monitors the work, coordinates production efforts among departments, and makes sure that expenditures and schedules conform to the project budget and master schedule.[2] The project manager, in conjunction with manufacturing or construction managers, is responsible for production planning and control. The control process involves releasing orders, monitoring, inspecting, and documenting progress, and comparing planned versus actual results (the process is described in Chapter 15). Project control and summary reports are released showing budgeted and scheduled work versus actual costs and work completed. These enable managers to make cost and work predictions and take corrective action when they spot deviant trends.

   One measure of project performance is the extent to which the system achieves quality specifications. As with most tasks in production, quality control of components and system assembly is not, per se, the responsibility of the project manager. However, since the quality of the final system is the responsibility of the project manager, she must make sure that the construction or manufacturing manager has implemented a quality control program that will achieve the quality objectives of the project.

Concurrent with system assembly are three other major activities that the project manager oversees and coordinates: system testing, preparation of training materials, and implementation planning.

System Testing

Throughout Phase C, a variety of tests are performed to insure that the system meets requirements. In new product development, testing occurs continuously throughout the project. Testing falls into three categories: tests by the contractor to make sure that (1) the system design is adequate, and (2) that the design is being followed by the producers or builders, and (3) tests by the user to make sure the system meets user requirements and other contractual agreements.

If the system is inadequate because of faulty or poor design, then the design stage must be repeated. If the design problem lies in the specifications, then the Definition phase must also be repeated. The most costly situation is where errors or omissions are not found until final integration tests or user acceptance tests—near the end of Phase C. The process of repeating stages is costly and time-consuming, so tests should be devised to catch problems as early as possible.

Tests are also needed to insure that the design is being correctly implemented by the producers. Even when design is adequate, the system as produced will be inadequate if the builders fail to follow the design or cut corners on materials and procedures. Quality control tests will help determine the acceptability of system components and workmanship.

Additionally, verification tests, reviews, and audits should be conducted throughout the project by the user to insure that system requirements are being met and that test documentation is complete and accurate.

To minimize the chances of having to redesign whole systems because of faulty components, testing should follow the sequence of measuring components first, subsystems next, then the whole system last. Individual parts are tested first to ensure they function individually; parts integrated into components are then tested to ensure they work together; next, components integrated into subsystems are tested to insure that subsystems perform; and finally subsystems integrated into the entire system are tested to guarantee total system performance.

Tests are performed against the earlier developed system objectives and systems specifications. In addition, the system might be tested in excess of specifications to determine where its actual capacity or point of failure lie. In *stress tests* an increasingly severe test load is applied to the system to determine its ability to handle heavier than probable conditions. In *failure tests* the system is loaded until it fails so that its ultimate capacity can be measured.

Test criteria are sometimes defined in the contract. In development projects, the contractor establishes design requirements and performance criteria, then specifies during the design stage the types of tests needed to verify the system.

The project manager is responsible for overseeing test plan preparation and coordinating the testing effort. A detailed test schedule should be prepared to ensure that tests occur at the right places and to catch problems at the earliest stage possible. The project manager must ensure that the tests are adequate to verify the system and components, that human and facility resources are available to perform tests, and that test results are well documented and filed for later reference.

Planning for Implementation

Implementation is the process of turning the system over to the user. The two prime activities in implementation are installing the system in the user's environment and training the user to operate the system. Plans and resources for the implementation stage must be developed in advance so that implementation can begin as soon as system fabrication is complete (if not sooner). Although implementation planning should be started earlier, it must happen no later than during the production stage.

While the implementation plan is being prepared, the contractor accumulates materials to enable the user to learn about the system and how to operate and maintain it. Simple systems require only a brief instruction pamphlet and a warranty. Complex systems require much more, such as lengthy manuals for procedures, system operation, repair, and service, testing manuals, manuals for training the trainers, and schematics, drawings, special tools, servicing, and support equipment. Much of the information for these manuals is derived from documentation accumulated during the design stage. The difference is that information for user-oriented manuals must be translated into user terms so it is clear, understandable, and *usable* by the user.

The plans to install the system must also be finalized.[3] The project team must develop an implementation strategy which addresses:

1. activities for converting from the old system to the new system.
2. sequencing and scheduling of implementation activities.
3. acceptance criteria for the new system.
4. the approach to phasing out the old system and reassigning personnel.

During Phase B an initial implementation plan might have been included as part of the master project plan. Now, in Phase C a more detailed plan is prepared with the participation of people who will be affected in both the contractor and user organizations. The final implementation plan should contain a user training plan and training schedule, system installation plans (for installation, check out, and acceptance of all central and remote systems), site preparation requirements and schedules (addressing security, access, power, space, equipment, etc.), a conversion plan for phasing the old system out and the new system in, and a systems test plan adequate enough to enable sign off on the system.

Agreement must be reached about when the project will be "completed," that is, when the system will be considered accepted and the project terminated. Misunderstandings about termination, such as "acceptance only after modification" arrangements, can make a project drag on indefinitely.

The project manager coordinates preparation of the implementation plan, making sure that all key user and contractor participants are involved or kept informed, that activities are scheduled, budgeted, and adhere to the project plan, that approvals are obtained, and that clear agreement is reached on conditions governing project termination.

6.4 IMPLEMENTATION STAGE

At implementation the system is turned over to the user. In some systems this happens in an instant, like when you purchase a clock. If the clock is simple, you just plug it in. If it is a digital alarm clock with a radio, you may need to read the instruction booklet to see how to set it. If the clock is a nuclear clock like the one used by the Bureau of Standards, you may need several manuals and a training program to learn how to use it. If the clock is a replacement for an existing clock connected to a timing device that controls lighting and heating in a large skyscraper, you will have to develop a strategy for substituting one clock with the other in order to minimize the disruption and inconvenience to people in the building. These are some of the issues considered in implementation.

User Training

The purpose of user training is to teach the user how to operate, maintain, and service the system. At one extreme, training is a simple instruction booklet; at the other, it is an extensive, ongoing program with an annual budget of tens of thousands of dollars. The first step is to determine the training requirements—the type and extent of training required. This will dictate the kind of materials needed (manuals, video tapes, simulators), the personnel to be trained (existing or newly hired personnel), the techniques to be used (classroom, independent study, role plays), the training schedule (everyone at once, in phases, or ongoing), and the staffing (contractor, user, or subcontracted training personnel). Users must be heavily involved in training. They should review and approve all training procedures and documents before training begins and have input afterwards to modify and improve the training.

Frequently the user will take over training after the contractor's trainers have trained user-trainers. In new systems where users may be unfamiliar with training requirements, the contractor should review the user's training program to make sure it is complete.

Good user training addresses the issue of how the system fits into the whole system. Training should provide an overview of system objectives, scope, operation, and its interface with other elements of the user organization and environment. This will enable the user to better understand the system as part of the total user environment and to integrate the new system into existing systems.

Training should be aimed at relieving user anxiety. All new systems create fear, stress, and frustration; training should include all people who are affected by the system and address their points of concern.

User Acceptance Testing

The final system test before installation is the user acceptance test. The user relies on the results of this test to determine if the system satisfies requirements sufficiently to warrant (1) adoption or installation as is, (2) installation pending modifications or adjustments, or (3) complete rejection.

User training must be adequate enough so that the user is able to competently try out the system to determine if it is acceptable. These tests differ from those in the production stage since users will have their own kinds of tests. Previous tests conducted by the contractor should anticipate and exceed the test requirements of users. Nonetheless, the contractor should prepare for the possibility that the system will fail portions of user tests.

Ideally tests of acceptance will be performed by users with minimal assistance from the project team. When the user is unable to perform the tests, the project team must act as surrogate user and make every effort to view the system *as the user would*. This means putting aside biases or vested interests and assuming a role largely devoid of system related technical expertise. Lack of user participation in acceptance testing is likely to lead to long-term implementation problems, so even in the role of surrogate the contractor must make sure that the user is on hand to witness tests.

The user is likely to discover things about the system that will require modifications or alterations. This is to be expected and, despite the added cost, is still preferable and less costly then discovering the need for changes after implementation is finished. Following modifications, acceptance tests and tentative user approval, the system is ready to install.

System Installation and Conversion Stage

System installation and conversion is conducted according to the implementation plan. Virtually all systems are, in a sense, designed to substitute other, existing systems, so a major issue is the strategy to be used for replacing the old system with the new one; this is called *conversion*. Possible strategies include:

1. *Parallel installation*: both new and old systems are operated until the new system is sufficiently proven.
2. *Pilot operation*: the new system is operated in a limited capacity until it is proven, then the old system is phased out as the new one is phased in.
3. *Cold turkey* (The Big Bang): in one fell swoop, the new system is moved in and the old one is moved out.

During conversion, equipment must be installed, tested, fine-tuned, and deemed operable to the fulfillment of requirements. Selecting the best conversion strategy is no simple matter; it involves complicated considerations of costs, risks, and logistics. For example, the first strategy seems the safest: if the new system fails there is still the old one.

But it is also the most expensive since two complete systems must be operated simultaneously. There is also the problem of finding the staff to operate both systems at once. With the second strategy, costs and risks are low, and staff can be trained in stages. But being a pilot operation, however, it may not be representative of the full system operation. Often, only after the full system has been phased in (and the old one phased out) will certain critical problems become apparent. The last strategy is the fastest and potentially least costly, but it is also the most risky. The question is, when will there be time to train the staff (they must operate the old system until they switch over to the new system) and what happens if the new system fails?

Prior to actual installation, implementation plans should be reviewed and updated to reflect the most current conditions. Schedules and procedure for training and conversion should also be reviewed and revised as needed. The project manager must update all plans and schedules, gain approval for revisions, and renew the commitment from involved groups in the contractor and user organizations. Plans must account for the significant increase in user organizational resources that any conversion requires. Interpersonal and organizational adjustments are necessary, and enough time must be scheduled to enable careful, thorough, and systematic installation. Implementation is a high stress stage, particularly for the user, and the project manager must make certain his team is patient and sensitive to the questions, concerns, and fears of the user.

Once the system has been installed, it remains to be proven that it performs successfully in the user's environment. The contractor will continue to monitor the new system and perform tests to ensure that system design is adequate, that the system has been installed properly, and that it interfaces with other systems in the user environment. After a breaking in period and resolution of discrepancies, the new system is turned over to the user, and the remains of the old system are phased out. User management and project management work together in the process.

One of the final tasks of the contractor before termination is to prepare a *postcompletion project summary* document. This document is largely for the benefit of the contractor. The summary should use the project plan as a framework and enumerate everything that happened in the project—bad as well as good. The summary serves two purposes: (1) a learning document to help the contractor know what was right, what was wrong, and how to avoid making the same mistakes twice; and (2) a reference document about details of the system for possible future use. The postcompletion project summary is described further in Chapter 17.

6.5 PHASE D: OPERATION

The conclusion of Phase C marks either (1) the formal termination of the project and the final involvement of the contractor, or (2) the beginning of still another phase: operation. This depends on whether or not the project end-item is a physical system or procedure which the user must operate or adhere to. Some projects, the *one shot* ones such as rock concerts, company moves, or audits, produce no physical system which must be maintained afterward. In such cases, the contractor's last project-related effort is installation. Just as often, however, the project output is a physical system or product which becomes operational, that is, the user must operate it. The contractor sometimes remains involved during this phase, either on a continual basis through contractual arrangement or through a new project with the same system. We will discuss these latter cases.

System Evaluation and Maintenance

The contractor may perform the system evaluation either as part of the original contract agreement or by additional agreement. The evaluation may occur as the last scheduled activity of the contractor in the form of a *postinstallation review*, the purpose of which is to evaluate system performance and to discover any maintenance or design-related problems that arise after the system has become fully operational. The subject of postinstallation review is discussed in Chapter 17.

The involvement of the contractor in system evaluation and maintenance may *extend* thereafter, usually through a contractual agreement to provide periodic review and/or service on a continuing basis. Sometimes the agreement is a warranty type of arrangement where the contractor provides review and maintenance during a pre-specified period as part of the original contract. Other times, it is an "extended" warranty type of arrangement which continues the contractor's involvement for a longer specified time period. The contractor may assign *system representatives* and technicians to the user site to perform periodic, preventive maintenance (parts replacement/system update at regular intervals) as specified by the agreement. Alternatively, the contractor may make system repairs or updates, but only at times as requested by the user and for an additional fee.

Improving the System

System requirements change—either because the user's tastes, needs, or budget change, or because the user's environment changes. In the first case, the user changes his objectives even though the environment is largely the same. In the second case, the user's environment (consumer wants, competition, government regulation, resource availability) changes—whether the user likes it or not. Either way, the system becomes inadequate and must be replaced. Replacement occurs by scrapping the existing system and getting a new one, or by modifying or enhancing the existing system so it satisfies new requirements.

The urgency of deciding what to do depends on the reason for the change. A homeowner-user may decide to add a den simply to acquire more space for leisure and recreation. This is a different case from the manager-user who is forced to expand production facilities because of rising competition or an increase in product sales. Changes in user tastes and wants are discretionary and, although the existing system may not live up to the new requirements, it will continue to function adequately as originally designed, *without changes*. When the user's environment changes the situation is potentially more critical since these changes can render the system infeasible, inoperable, obsolete, inefficient, or in other ways delimit or incapacitate it. In short, the system *must* be replaced or modified.

For whichever reason, the decision to expand, enhance, or otherwise modify the system from its original requirements marks the beginning of a new system development cycle. The contractor that originally developed the system may be called back to do the work, or a new contractor may be selected in a competitive bidding process. Mankind engages in few dead-end projects; each one spurs others, and the systems development cycle keeps rolling along.

Most projects follow a pattern somewhat similar to the four-phase cycle described in this and the previous chapters. Following are examples taken from a variety of settings showing how the cycle is included in projects of widely differing size and purpose.

6.6 SYSTEMS DEVELOPMENT IN INDUSTRIAL AND SERVICE ORGANIZATIONS

The following four cases illustrate the systems development cycle in projects in industrial R&D, real estate operations, a company relocation, and reorganization of a public agency.

New Product Development[4]

Jamal Industries is a medium-sized, diversified manufacturing firm which produces various products for major retailers under the retailer's own label; e.g., Sears, True Value, etc. All of Jamal's development and production work is done in phases similar to the systems development cycle, i.e., *initiation*, *feasibility*, *analysis*, *design*, and *manufacturing*. The R&D director is the project manager for Jamal's development projects. Most projects are initiated and implemented internally, though sometimes development and manufacturing work is contracted out. In such cases, Jamal assumes the role of a user. The following example of the development and production of a computerized lighting timer is just such a case.

In this project there was little formal emphasis on the initiation stage. A competitor had just introduced a computerized timer that would likely have a major impact on Jamal's market share. In essence, this project was initiated by Jamal's competition. To examine project feasibility, Jamal engineers investigated samples of the competitor's device to see if they could come up with their own version quickly enough to maintain market share. The purpose of their analysis was to see if a device as good or better could be made and sold with the retailers' private labels for 20 percent under the competitor's price. As an alternative, Jamal could seek other distribution channels and try to sell the product efficiently with its own label. The feasibility study indicated that Jamal could not design and produce the product in-house and remain 20 percent below the competitor's price, though sufficient channels were available to sell the product with the Jamal label.

An in-depth analysis was made to determine how Jamal could contract out for design and production, alleviating the capital investment which the feasibility study showed Jamal could not afford. For four months, the R&D director and his engineering staff analyzed alternatives for contracting out the work. They developed a complete MRP system to help investigate alternatives. The final decision was to use a general contractor who would be responsible for all tasks of product design, manufacture, and packaging. A foreign contractor was found that could make a competitively superior timer that Jamal could market at a price that was 12 dollars under the competition. Much of the planning, scheduling, and budgeting associated with the project was delegated to this contractor.

A goal was set for design, manufacture, and distribution of the product so that it could be on store shelves within one year. At present, production of the device has just begun. Having oversight of the product design, Jamal is now involved in monitoring the production progress. As manufacturing progresses, Jamal will devote more of its resources to marketing.

As long as Jamal markets the timing device, the foreign contractor will remain the vendor. The R&D director will continue to monitor the contractor and insure that quality control standards are being maintained. The rest of the Jamal project team will be transferred to other projects.

Computerization of Bank Real-Estate Operations

Another example of the cycle, described by Linn Struckenbruch, is in a large California bank which decided to implement project management into operations that involved multiple functional areas.[5] To implement project management, the bank hired a consultant. He suggested that the bank execute projects in four phases:

1. *Concept*: recognize problem or need
2. *Preliminary Study*: feasibility study
3. *In-depth Study*: define project characteristics
4. *Product Development and Implementation*: develop and deliver the system or solution.

Struckenbruch describes how these phases were conducted in the "Real Estate Loan and Escrow Operations Project." The goals of this project included reducing the operating costs of the real estate department, standardizing compliance with government agencies, increasing control over credit procedures, shifting more control to management, and ridding the bank of problems related to the centralization of its real estate activities. The Senior V.P. of Corporate Banking was appointed project manager; the consultant reported to him as project director.

During the concept phase the need for the project was established and the above goals were defined in detail. The preliminary study phase was granted a budget of $15,000 and a scheduled completion date of thirty days. This phase generated a report that suggested an in-depth study to assess three possible operational alternatives. These recommendations were brought before the Administrative Planning Committee, which approved the project for the in-depth phase.

The in-depth phase lasted nine months during which a study was conducted, resulting in a recommendation to purchase two computer systems and relocate the entire real estate department to Santa Ana, California. It was estimated that this move could save the bank $5 million annually. With approval of the recommendations the project proceeded into the final, development and implementation phase. The project was completed on time and within budget, 21 months later.

Relocation of a Company Division[6]

The relocation of any large facility should be considered a project since it is a unique, complex undertaking which must be completed within a limited budget and time period. Usually a "relocation director" is assigned responsibility for overseeing and coordinating elements, maintaining a schedule of events, and tracking costs. The activities involved in a typical relocation parallel the phases of systems development in many ways, as illustrated in the following case of one division of a major data-processing organization.

Over recent years, the Information Systems division had grown at such an unanticipated rate that it became obvious it would soon have to relocate to obtain greater work area and more equipment. Phase I, project *concept*, occurred by mandate: either the division relocate or it would "suffocate" itself out of business. Three other phases comprised the project: Phase II, *definition* (finding a location to move to, defining facilities and equipment needs, and obtaining designs and construction drawings); Phase III, *acquisition* (new facilities construction and equipment purchasing); and Phase IV, *implementation* (relocating the division and monitoring it during a settling-in period). Many of these phases overlapped. Phase II started with a needs analysis to determine the requirements of the new site. It was determined that the division needed space for the current 80 employees, expandable to include 25 more, and additional space for a computer room. Major considerations in finding a suitable location were the company's client base and the distance to the company's other offices.

Preliminary budget figures were prepared taking into account how many square feet would be needed and whether the site should be bought or leased. Based upon the needs analysis, it was decided that 30,000 square feet were required and that the site should be leased. Three suitable sites were considered. The company hired a real estate broker and legal consultant to help select the site and conduct contract negotiations. For the site evaluation, preliminary space designs were prepared for each site showing location of work stations and work flow. A detailed budget was prepared with leasing arrangements, improvement and construction expenses, furniture, fixture, and telecommunication costs, moving expenses, and plant and office costs. Based upon budget and design considerations, a site was selected.

During the latter half of Phase II, detailed design and construction drawings were obtained for company offices and the computer room. A detailed needs analysis was performed and the space design was analyzed in greater detail. For the computer room it was necessary to consider requirements for power, air conditioning, and both corporate and local data inputs to the system. Bids were secured from local distributors and installation groups, and a furniture manufacturer was selected. After the final interior design was selected, bids were taken on general construction drawings for space design, HVAC engineering, electricity, architecture, lighting, telephone, and computer equipment.

When the preliminary work was completed and contracts signed, Phase III began. A team of corporate and general contractor personnel was given responsibility to oversee and supervise construction. Numerous vendors—electrical, sheet metal, dry wall, painters, HVAC, plumbers, plasterers, and carpenters—performed the work. Phase III also involved equipment needs analysis and equipment purchase, such as data circuitry, cabling requirements, choice of vendors, purchasing or leasing arrangements, maintenance agreements, and employee training.

Bids from several moving companies were reviewed, one was selected, and a moving schedule was prepared. At the same time, bids were received for procurement and installation of plant and office equipment such as word processors, photocopy machines, vending machines, and security systems. Bids and maintenance agreements were negotiated and contracted.

Under the supervision of the project management team, Phases III and IV (facility construction, move to the new site, and equipment installation) were performed according to schedule. Before, during, and after the move an orientation program was conducted for division employees. Following the move, a final check-out was conducted to insure that all steps had been carried out and that all equipment was working properly. During the last phase, management established amicable working relationships with the local municipality and services environment—city hall, the community college, the fire department, and utilities companies.

Reorganization of Human Services Administration

Even though many projects, especially those that are small or in the service sector, tend not to follow the exact stages described in this chapter, they do follow a series of phases that is roughly *analogous* to the systems development process. These phases nominally include *initiation*, *problem definition*, *analysis of solutions*, *implementation*, and *operation*. The following example is an illustration.[7]

Human Services Administration (HSA) is a city welfare agency that provides limited financial assistance in the form of money, medical care, and drug rehabilitation treatment to eligible recipients. In administering these services HSA became plagued by a number of bureaucratic problems, the worst being:

- Inefficient control measures that allowed for mismanagement and errors in the payment system.
- High increases in the annual cost of the system.
- Inadequate control in applicant approvals leading to fraudulent client abuse.
- Employee productivity below 40 percent.

- Excessive tardiness and absenteeism among employees.

The city's mayor allotted 10 million dollars annually for the implementation and maintenance of a new administrative system to resolve these problems. A group of outside professionals would be hired to comprise a project team whose purpose was to overhaul the system. After the team had resolved the problems it would become a permanent part of HSA.

The project was to be conducted in four phases. During the first phase, *initiation*, HSA would define overhaul objectives and hire the professionals who would form the project team. In the second phase, *analysis*, the project team would identify problems and related objectives, and recommend solutions. In the third phase, *implementation*, the solutions would be executed, giving priority to the most severe problems. In the fourth phase, *operation*, the project team would be interweaved into the existing organization and become an ongoing staff function.

During the initiation phase, the following project objectives were stated:

1. Create a project management organization that depicts clear-cut responsibilities and authority for the newly hired project team.
2. Eliminate opposition by some members of the existing organization to the planned overhaul.
3. Work on and produce solutions to smaller problems so confidence can be gained and talent identified for working on larger problems.
4. Gain taxpayer confidence through media attention to the overhaul project.

Conforming to the first objective, outside professionals were hired and a project management team was created.

In the second phase the project management team identified specific problems areas. The team then divided the problems into five categories: new applications, photo identification, addicts, eligibility, and fraud. They then reorganized HSA to create a task force for each category. Each task force was to define problems, document the system, and suggest long range recommendations and alternatives to the current system.

Problems needing immediate attention were singled out and worked on first. Parts of the second and third phases overlapped as solutions to some problems were implemented while other, longer-range problems were still being analyzed. Among the changes introduced by the overhaul were: a new photo identification system for clients, a more efficient system for processing clients, tighter controls on client eligibility, a computer system for processing procedures and validating payments, tighter auditing controls, greater accountability of personnel, and tighter management controls.

In the final phase, HSA was reorganized again, this time on a more functional basis but keeping roughly the same structure as the original project task forces. Most of the project management team stayed with HSA to assume management and staff positions.

6.7 SYSTEMS DEVELOPMENT IN LARGE GOVERNMENT PROGRAMS

Following are two illustrations of the systems development cycle in large-scale government programs: a NASA planetary exploration program and Air Force weapons procurement.

Planetary Exploration Program

A good example of the concepts in the last two chapters is NASA's "Phased Program Planning" approach. This comprehensive planning and review process is designed to keep projects aligned to NASA goals and within available resources, without premature commitment to a particular course of action.

The NASA system for organizing and managing projects varies from project to project, but common to all are the stages of (A) *conceptualization*, (B) *study*, (C) *design and development*, and (D) *operations*. Throughout a typical spacecraft program, the project manager has responsibility for all phases, from initial study and project planning, to fabrication and integration of spacecraft and experiments, to launch and subsequent acquisition and use of experimental data. An example of a typical large scientific space flight project is the hypothetical project "Cosmic," a series of spacecraft for the collection and analysis of geophysical measurements of the planet Mercury.[8]

Phase A, concept, is initiated when, at the urging of scientists, the director for Lunar and Planetary Programs (LPP) at NASA headquarters asks the director of Goddard Space Flight Center to begin preliminary analysis of how NASA might send either a probe or a satellite to Mercury to conduct geophysical experiments. The purpose of Phase A is to determine if the mission is feasible and should be pursued. This involves looking at alternative project approaches, identifying ones for further refinement, defining project elements such as facilities, operational and logistics support, and identifying necessary research or technology development. Phase A is conducted at NASA installations by a study team of NASA scientists and engineers appointed by the director of Goddard. The person chosen as study team leader is someone capable of becoming *project manager* should the analysis prove favorable. The person selected is currently spacecraft manager of a satellite project that is being completed.

At the same time, the director of LPP in Washington assigns a liaison with the Goddard study team. The liaison officer is chosen with the approval of the director of Goddard to assure a smooth working relationship. If the project is approved the liaison officer will become the *program manager*. The distinction between project and program managers was discussed in Chapter 2.

The preliminary analysis is favorable and the study team recommendation to prepare a proposal and proceed to Phase B is approved by Goddard management. Phase B, definition, involves detailed study, comparative analysis, and preliminary systems design. The study team leader and the liaison officer draft the project proposal and a project approval document. The approval document outlines resources and the field installation to oversee work (Goddard), specifies project constraints, and defines the number of spacecraft, type of launch vehicle, and allocation of funds and manpower. It is for approval of Phase B only.

The liaison officer coordinates and receives all necessary approvals from other involved program divisions and operating offices at NASA headquarters. The approval document is then sent to the top NASA administrator for a decision. With this approval, project Cosmic is authorized to begin.

Management formally names the Cosmic program manager (the liaison officer) and the Cosmic project manager (the study team leader). The project manager assembles a skeleton team to develop specifications for study contracts which will provide data to determine whether or not to proceed further. Estimated schedules and resource requirements for the total project are developed. The project team works with major project functional groups such as launch vehicle, reliability, data acquisition, and launch operations. Relationships are established to provide the necessary lead time for equipment manufacture, testing, and operations. A detailed project plan is prepared outlining technical specifications, manpower, funds, management plans, schedules, milestones, and launch and tracking requirements to meet project objectives.

The project plan is approved by management at Goddard and NASA headquarters and becomes a contract between them. Headquarters sets up a formal information and control system and formally makes available necessary financial resources. The project manager sends monthly (later weekly) reports to the program manager. This is important since, should the project run into difficulties, the program manager can work quickly to obtain or reallocate funds to support it.

The original approval document is updated throughout Phase B and becomes the authorization document for Phase C (design) or for both Phase C and Phase D (development and operations). During Phase B, appropriate experiments are selected and the number of flights of Cosmic is put at three. At the completion of Phase B, project Cosmic appears on NASA information and control systems that review financial, schedule, and technical progress. As of this point, less than ten percent of total project costs have been incurred.

During Phase C contractors become involved in detailed engineering design, development of mock-ups, and completion of detailed specifications on all major subsystems of the Cosmic spacecraft. The project team completes design and supporting studies and develops RFP's for design, development, fabrication, and test of final hardware, and project operations.

The project manager has two associates, one who facilitates coordination between the project and the experimenters, another who coordinates activities for modification of the launch vehicle to meet requirements for the three flights. Members of the project team are also working at Cape Kennedy in preparation of launch, and at Jet Propulsion Laboratory in California which handles data acquisition from deep space probes.

When spacecraft fabrication begins, the project manager travels to the contractor plants where he spends considerable time in design and test reviews and in conferences for quality assurance, components testing, and system integration. Meanwhile the program manager keeps tabs on the project and keeps it "sold" at NASA. Both managers participate in formal reviews to catch errors at critical points in the project. Usual reviews include:

1. *Conceptual design reviews* (at end of Phase B) to evaluate preliminary designs and the design approach.
2. *Detailed design reviews* after design is frozen and before assembly begins to review design approach testing.
3. *Flight qualification reviews* to determine hardware status and evaluate tests.
4. *Flight readiness reviews* before the spacecraft is shipped to Cape Kennedy.
5. *Flight operations review* to evaluate orbital operations and spacecraft-ground support interface.
6. Other reviews to determine the state of readiness of communication networks, ground stations, and support facilities and personnel.

Phase D nominally begins with final preparation and launch of the first Cosmic spacecraft. The project manager oversees efforts of the multiple key teams working in this phase, including the (1) NASA launch team, (2) NASA project management team, (3) NASA program management, (4) scientists whose experiments are on the spacecraft, (5) prime contractors and subcontractors who built the spacecraft and launch vehicle, and (6) the Air Force team which controls the missile range. The spacecraft is "mated" with the launch vehicle and tested. During the last few moments of countdown, only the project manager has authority to make the final irrevocable decision to "go."

Launch data are recorded during the time between rocket lift-off and when the spacecraft is successfully placed in orbit to Mercury. Problems are analyzed so that they will not be repeated with the next spacecraft. Once the spacecraft is on its way and communication and instrumentation are verified as working and returning usable data, the project manager turns attention to Cosmic II—now in the early fabrication stage (Phase C). He continues to monitor Cosmic I operation since lessons from it will be applied to improve the design of Cosmic III, which is now in Phase B.

Air Force Weapons Systems Programs

NASA's four-phase process is an outgrowth of the weapons systems procurement process used by the military. For many years the Department of Defense (DOD) pressed companies in the aerospace industry to develop standardized management, planning, and control tools. When standardization did not occur, the Air Force in 1964 introduced a series of manuals designed to administer consistent management control to all of its future systems. A program package concept was designed to relate planning and budgeting to defense requirements.

The program package outlines four phases that a defense system must go through. The phases, as well as the series of manuals, are still in use today. During Phase I, *concept formulation*, experimental and test studies are performed to develop the system concept and establish its feasibility in terms of technical, economic, and military criteria. Each contractor must perform certain steps for the Air Force, which, in turn, must do the same for the DOD. When the best technical approach has been selected, the DOD makes sure that the cost effectiveness of the approach weighs favorably in relation to the cost effectiveness of competing systems on a DOD-wide basis.

Phase II, *contract definition*, has three stages. Stage A involves screening contractors and negotiating requirements on proposals. The DOD finances contract definitions for, usually, two contractors. In Phase B competing contract definitions are submitted by the contractors; these include complete technical, managerial, and cost proposals for the proposed system development. In Phase C an advisory committee reviews the competing proposals and selects a contractor.

Phase III and Phase IV overlap toward the end of the project. Phase III, *acquisition*, is the detailed design, development, procurement, and testing of the system. In Phase IV, *operation*, the system is delivered, placed in service, and follow-up evaluated to make sure it is effective. After systems have been tested and accepted by the Air Force, they are transferred to a "user command" and made operational with active logistic support.

6.8 SUMMARY

There are good reasons why the Systems Development Cycle appears in so many kinds of projects. First, it emphasizes continuous planning, review, and authorization. At each stage results are examined and used as the basis for decisions and planning for the next stage. Second, the process is goal oriented—it strives to maintain focus on system objectives. Review and evaluation help ensure that mistakes and problems are caught early and corrected before they get out of control. If the environment changes, timely action can be taken to modify the system or terminate the project. And third, with the system objective always in sight, activities are undertaken so that they are coordinated and occur at the right time, in the right sequence.

The four-phase Systems Development Cycle of the last two chapters outlines the nominal phases, stages, and activities for projects. It is just an outline, however, and should not be taken as a description of what does or should happen in all projects. As the examples show, it can be altered or simplified so that some stages receive more emphasis, some less, some are deleted, and some even appear in different sequence—depending on the project. Nonetheless, in preparing for any project it is a good idea to mentally review all of the stages described to make certain that nothing will be missed.

In the last two chapters the work of project organizations (the contractor or SDO) was described, but little was said about the organizations themselves or the teams and people that comprise them. The next section shifts focus away from what project organizations do to the organizations themselves. It is concerned with the subjects of behavior—organizational, leadership, group, and individual—and managing behavior. It is an important area, not only in terms of project performance, but also for the well-being of the groups and individuals who work in projects.

CHAPTER REVIEW QUESTIONS

1. When does the project manager become involved in the project?
2. How is the project team created?
3. How are the various functional areas and subcontractors involved in the planning process?
4. Describe briefly the contents of a project summary (master) plan.
5. What are user requirements and system requirements? Give examples. How are they related?
6. Describe the process of developing user requirements and system requirements.
7. What happens during the design stage? Who is involved? What do they do? What is the role of the project manager? How are design changes monitored and controlled?
8. What happens during the production or building stage? How is work planned and coordinated? Who oversees the work?
9. How is the project end-item tested and checked out for approval?
10. How is the system implemented? Describe the important considerations for turning the system over to the user.
11. Describe ways of converting to the new system.
12. How are projects "closed out" or terminated?
13. Describe the post-completion project summary. What is its purpose?
14. Describe the post-installation review. What is its purpose?
15. Describe what happens during the operation stage. What is the role of the systems development organization?

QUESTIONS ABOUT THE STUDY PROJECT

As appropriate, answer the above questions 1–10, 12–15 with regard to your project. Also, answer the following questions:

1. When the end-item is a product, system implementation includes marketing, promotion and distribution of the product. If the end-item in your project is a product, when does the planning begin for marketing, promotion, and distribution, and who is responsible? Where does the plan fit into the project master plan?
2. If the end-item is a building or other "constructed" item, how is it turned over to the user? Describe the testing, acceptance, training, and authorization process.
3. What happens to the project team when the project is completed?
4. How does the organization get reinvolved in the next project?

ENDNOTES

1. V. Hajek, *Management of Engineering Projects*, 3rd ed. (New York: McGraw-Hill, 1984), 35–37.
2. The production authorization process is described by Hajek, ibid. 195–197.

3. Portions of this section are derived from C.L. Biggs, E.G. Birks, and W. Atkins, *Managing the Systems Development Process* (Englewood Cliffs, N.J.: Prentice-Hall, 1980), 187–193. This reference focuses on implementation planning for computerized systems but the topics are generalizable to other types of systems.

4. Based upon information collected and documented by Cary Morgen from interviews with managers of Jamal Industries (fictitious name).

5. Based upon Linn C. Struckenbruch, *The Implementation of Project Management* (Los Angeles: Project Management Institute, 1981), 189–199.

6. Based upon an actual company relocation and data collected from interviews with company managers by Pam Paroubek. The title of the division is fictitious.

7. This example is adapted from K.L. Harris, "Organizing to Overhaul a Mess," *California Management Review,* Vol. 17, No. 3, 1975, 40–49.

8. Based upon R.L. Chapman, *Project Management in NASA: The System and the Men* (Washington, D.C.: NASA, SP–324, 1973), 13–19.

III

Leadership Structure

Project
organization

Teamwork

ORGANIZATION BEHAVIOR

Project outcomes depend on the way individuals and groups are organized and how they interact. As human endeavors, projects are both influenced by and have influence on the behavior and well-being of the groups and individuals that belong to them. The four chapters in this section focus on the major behavioral issues surrounding the management of projects and the teams and individuals that comprise them. They describe ways that groups are organized into projects, styles of leadership used by project managers, roles and responsibilities of project team members, and ways groups and individuals are managed to increase effectiveness and reduce the negative consequences of working in projects.

Chapters in this section:

Chapter Seven. Project Organization Structure

Chapter Eight. Project Roles, Responsibility, and Authority

Chapter Nine. Managing Projects through Participation and Teamwork

Chapter Ten. Managing Conflict and Stress in Projects

chapter 7

Project Organization Structure

How can you expect to govern a country that has 246 kinds of cheese?

Charles de Gaulle

The systems approach views organizations as human and physical elements interacting to achieve goals of the overall organization. As with all types of systems, organizations are partly described by their *structure*—the form of relationships that bond their elements.

In organizations two kinds of structures coexist. One is the *formal organization* structure, the *published* one, that describes normative superior-subordinate relationships, chains of command, and subdivisions and groupings of elements. The other is the *informal structure*, comprised of relationships that are *evolved* through the interactions of people. Whereas the formal organization prescribes how people are supposed to relate, the informal organization is how they want to relate. It is the groupings, authority figures, and communication lines that exist in the organization, but nowhere do they appear on the organization chart.

This chapter deals primarily with formal organization structure, particularly the kinds of structures applicable to projects. There is no one best way to structure project organizations, but there are structural patterns and specific roles that enhance project performance. Though project managers are seldom involved in organization design decisions, they should understand the kinds of organizational designs used in project management and their relative advantages and disadvantages. Sometimes project managers can affect the project structure, even if only through suggestions to top management. The chapter will conclude with a brief discussion about features of the informal structure and those which project managers may be able to influence.

7.1 FORMAL ORGANIZATION STRUCTURE

Concepts of organizational structure apply to all kinds of organizations—companies, institutions, agencies—as well as to their subunits—divisions, departments, projects, teams, and so on. Formal organization structure is publicized in a chart like the one for NASA in Figure 7–1; a quick glance reveals both the organizational hierarchy and groupings for specialized tasks. By looking at the chart in Figure 7–1, for example, one can see:

1. The range of activities in which the organization is involved (space flight, space sciences, aeronautics and space technology....).
2. The management hierarchy and reporting relationships (e.g., the directors at Ames, Lewis, and Langley all report to the associate administrator for aeronautics and space technology).
3. The major subdivisions of the organization (e.g., communications, commercial programs, exploration....).
4. The type of work and responsibility of each subdivision (e.g., each associate administrator is responsible for an "office," each of which addresses a separate activity—space sciences, technology, exploration, and so on.)
5. The official lines of authority and communication (the administrator is the highest authority, the deputy administrator is the next highest, and so on; communication moves formally along the lines from one box to the next, up or down).

There are many things the chart does not show. For example, it does not show informal lines of communication and personal contacts whereby, say, workers at Lewis talk directly to workers at Goddard on the telephone, not (as the chart implies) via the directors of these centers, nor does it indicate areas of status and power that develop at lower levels. Nonetheless, the chart does give a fundamental overview of elements and relationships of the formal organization, and in this way it is useful.

7.2 ORGANIZATION DESIGN BY DIFFERENTIATION AND INTEGRATION

There is no "best" kind of organization structure. The most appropriate structure depends on the organization's goals, type of work, and environment. Organization structures typically develop through a combination of planned and evolutionary responses to ongoing problems. Organizations create specialized roles and units, each with suitable expertise and resources needed to resolve certain classes of problems efficiently. As organizations grow or the environment changes, additional subdivisions and new groupings are imple-

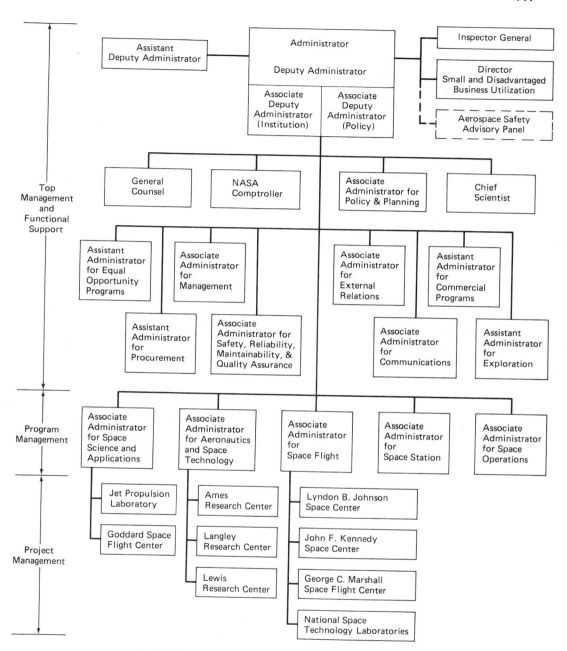

FIGURE 7–1.   NASA organization chart. 1987.

mented to better handle emerging problems. For example, as a company increases its product line, it may subdivide its manufacturing area into product-oriented divisions so each can better address problems specific to just one product. As a company expands its sales territory, it may subdivide its marketing force geographically to better handle problems of regional origin. This subdivision into specialized areas is called *differentiation.*

Obviously, subunits of an organization do not act as independent entities but must interact and support each other. The degree to which they interact, coordinate, and mutually adjust their actions to fulfill organizational goals is called *integration.*

Traditional Forms of Organization

How an organization chooses to classify and address its problems is referred to as the *basis* for differentiation. The six bases are functional, product, process, geographic, customer, and project. The project form will be discussed in detail. First we will look briefly at the other five "traditional" forms of organization.

Functional Differentiation.
The functional form of organization is so called because it is divided into functional subunits such as marketing, finance, production, personnel, and research and development; the structure of the Standard Industrial Gadgets (STING) Company in Figure 7–2 is an example. Most of the integration between subunits, is handled by rules, procedures, coordinated plans, and budgets. When discrepancies occur that cannot be resolved by these, the managerial chain of command takes over. When a problem involves several subunits, it is collectively resolved by managers over all subunits affected.

This form of organization works well in repetitive, stable environments because there is little change, and the rather low level of integration afforded by rules, procedures, and chain-of-command gets the job done. The functional form has a long history. The Roman Army was an early organization that used functional differentiation, rules and procedures, and chain-of-command. The functional form remains today as the most prevalent basis for organization structure.

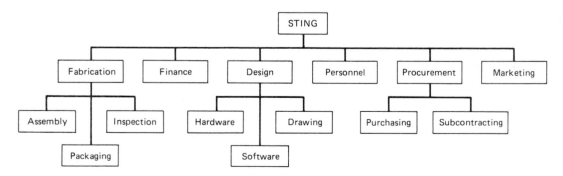

FIGURE 7–2. Formal organization structure for STING company showing functional breakdown.

Geographic Differentiation.   Most organizations have more than one basis for differentiation. The Roman Army was also geographically differentiated, that is, structured according to region or location. Organizations subdivide according to region (e.g., Atlantic, Mid-Western, and Pacific states, European branch, Far East command, etc.) to tailor themselves to the unique requirements of local customers, markets, enemies, and so on. Within each geographic subunit, functional differentiation is often retained. Regional subunits may operate relatively autonomously with little integration between them. Integration, usually achieved through standardized accounting and reporting procedures, simplifies upper management's monitoring of subunits.

Product Differentiation.   Firms that produce a variety of products use product-based differentiation. Corporations such as General Motors, General Foods, and General Electric are split into major subdivisions wherein each designs, manufactures, and markets its own product line. Within each subdivision is a functional, geographic, or other form of breakdown. As with geographically differentiated organizations, integration between product subdivisions tends to be low and is achieved by standardized financial and reporting rules and procedures.

Customer Differentiation.   Organizations also differentiate by customer. For example, companies with large military sales often establish a separate division since federal requirements for proposals, contracting, and product specifications differ substantially from those for commercial customers. The level of integration between customer divisions depends on the degree of interdependence between their product lines; typically though integration is low.

Process Differentiation.   In the process differentiated form, some logical process or sequence of steps (e.g., design, then development, then assembly, then inspection...) is the basis for differentiation. Such a basis is used for the subunits in the Fabrication Department of STING, shown in Figure 7–2. A higher level of integration is required among process differentiated subunits since they are sequentially related and problems in one area directly impact the other areas. These subunits tend to rely on coordinated plans and schedules as the primary means of integration. Other means, such as task forces and teams, are necessary when unanticipated problems arise or as task uncertainty increases. These will be discussed later.

Drawbacks of Traditional Forms of Organizations

By their very design, traditional forms of organization can only address certain anticipated, classifiable kinds of problems. As the environment changes and new kinds of problems arise, they react by further differentiating subunits and adding more rules, procedures, and levels of management. The price paid for adding layers of management, rules, procedures, and subunits is less flexibility and greater difficulty in integrating subunits.

Most traditional organization forms work on the assumption that problems can be neatly classified and resolved within specialized areas. Thus, subunits in traditional forms tend to work independently and toward their own goals. When a problem arises that requires participation from multiple subdivisions, there may no person or group to see that it gets resolved. Such problems fall through the cracks.

One way to handle unanticipated, unclassifiable problems is to adapt (redesign) the organization whenever they arise. But the process of adapting organization structure to suit unique problems is slow and expensive, reflecting both the inertia of systems as well as resistance to change by people in systems. The alternative to redesign is to bump problems up the chain-of-command. This works as long as it is not done too often; but when the number of unanticipated problems becomes large, the chain of command gets quickly overloaded. Management's response to overload is to add more managers and more staff groups, which further stifles the process and makes the organization even less flexible. In short, traditional organizations are not well-suited for environments where there is high uncertainty and frequent change.

7.3 REQUIREMENTS OF PROJECT ORGANIZATIONS

Projects environments are characterized by complexity, change, uncertainty, and unpredictability. Projects typically require the resources and coordinated work effort of multiple subunits and organizations. Each project is a new undertaking to satisfy a new goal. Subunits must work together to estimate their resource requirements, combine the requirements into a coordinated plan, and conduct work according to that plan. Changes or mistakes in one area have consequences on all others. Uncertainty is inherent in projects since each project is unique and may have no precedent. As the size of the project increases so do the number of subunits involved and the potential number of small errors or problems in each.

Projects in advanced technologies such as software development, pharmaceuticals, biomedicine, space exploration, and product and weapon systems development can routinely expect the unpredictable. As a result, they need to be able to adjust to changing goals and environmental forces, and to deal with the uncertainty that accompanies these changes. They must, in a word, be *organic*, which means be highly differentiated to accommodate a large variety of potential problems, highly integrated to respond rapidly to problems involving multiple subunits, and highly flexible and able to alter structure as goals change.

To achieve this, all project organizations have two properties:

- they integrate subunits using horizontal relations, and
- they have organization structures suited to the unique requirements of the project and the environment.

These properties are discussed next.

7.4 INTEGRATION OF SUBUNITS IN PROJECTS[1]

Traditional organizations are characterized by their verticalness, or reliance upon up-and-down patterns of authority and communication. As mentioned, this makes them clumsy and ineffective in the face of rapid change and high uncertainty. In contrast, project organizations are characterized by their *horizontalness* or use of direct communication between the parties involved in a problem. Horizontal relations cut across lines of authority and move decisions down to the level of the parties affected.

All organizations have horizontal relations, mostly in the form of personal contacts and friendships. These contacts are particularly helpful for expediting communication and getting problems resolved between subunits. For example, whenever the Assembly Department in Figure 7–2 experiences a minor parts shortage, George, the assembly foreman, phones Helen in Purchasing for a "rush order" favor. The call bypasses the formal structure (via each of George's and Helen's managers) and speeds up the ordering procedure.

The drawback with personal contacts like this is that they do not insure that everyone is involved who should be, or that everyone gets the necessary information. For example, Helen must charge all purchases to an account, but if George is not privy to the dollar amount in the account it is possible that his informal requests will deplete the account before additional funds can be credited (which involves a third party). Also, if George does not tell anyone else about the parts shortages, the reason for the problem—pilferage, defective parts, or under- ordering—never gets resolved. Finally, George's requests might be too late; i.e., informal processes do not always occur when needed.

Project organizations improve upon informal, personal contacts by incorporating horizontal relations into the formal structure. They do this through the use of functions referred to as *integrators*—which reduce the number of decisions referred upward and facilitate communication between units working on a common task. Like informal processes, integrators bypass traditional lines of authority and speed up communication. They are better, however, because they ensure that everyone affected by a problem gets involved and has the necessary information.

Several kinds of integrators are used in projects. They are listed below in order of increasing authority, need, and cost. In this list, the latter kinds take on all the authority and responsibility of the former kinds.[2]

> Liaison role
> Task forces and teams
> Project expeditors and coordinators
> Project managers
> Matrix managers
> Integrating contractors

7.5 LIAISON ROLES, TASK FORCES, AND TEAMS

The *liaison role* is a specialized person or group that links two departments at lower levels. Figure 7–3, for example, shows the liaison role of "inventory controller." Besides other duties in the Assembly Department, this person links the Assembly and Purchasing departments by notifying Purchasing of impending shortages and keeping track of orders placed. The role relieves the foreman of this responsibility and, by legitimizing the process, ensures that orders get placed and are documented.

But the liaison role is not always effective. Though the inventory controller in the example expedites parts ordering, the reason for part shortages goes unresolved. To unravel the problem it is necessary to involve people from other areas of the company. This is where the next kind of integrative function, interdisciplinary *task forces* and *teams*, comes into play.

A *task force* is a temporary group of representatives from several areas that meet to solve a problem. For example, when a shortage problem occurs, the Assembly foreman might call together liaison people from Inspection, Accounting, Purchasing, Marketing, or any other area that should be involved. The task force meets once, several times, or as needed, and when the problem is worked out it is dissolved. The most effective task forces are short-lived and typically have ten members or less.[3]

To be effective, members of the task force must have information relevant to the group task and authority to make commitments for their functional areas. If they lack knowledge, the group's decisions will be faulty; if they lack authority, they will be unable to take action on decisions. Functional departments which do not have people with the knowledge and authority to serve on task forces may have to restructure themselves to develop such positions.

Problems which are novel but call for continuous coordinated interaction of subunits require the attention of *permanent teams*. Teams have the same characteristics as task forces except they convene on a regular basis and for longer periods of time. For example, if the STING company produces several products and each requires repeated design changes throughout the year then representatives from Design, Fabrication, Procurement, and other areas would have to meet as a team on a frequent basis. Only through repeated face to face association would the team be able to coordinate decisions about changes in market conditions and product design. Members may be assigned to teams part-time or full-time.

In most projects there are many teams; some convene during just one stage of the project life cycle, others for the full duration of the project. One kind of permanent team in development projects is called a *change board*, a multifunctional team that meets every week to discuss and approve changes in design. Change boards are discussed in Chapter 15.

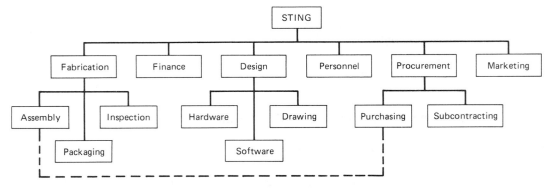

FIGURE 7-3. Liaison role linking Assembly and Purchasing Departments

Organizations are created around people, not the reverse, and it is sometimes difficult to find people with the knowledge, authority and inclination to serve on multifunctional teams. People develop attitudes and goals oriented toward their specialization, and though this helps them be effective in their own functional area, it restricts their ability to interact with people from other areas. For interdisciplinary teams to be effective, it is essential to have members who are aware of other peoples' functional orientations and receptive to their opinions and attitudes.

7.6 PROJECT EXPEDITORS AND COORDINATORS

Teams form the core of project organizations. The simplest projects consist of one team within a single functional area. A task force created to solve a special problem or answer a particular question is one type of project organization. The most complex projects are performed by a consortia of multifunctional teams from numerous contractors, subcontractors, and users. Tens or hundreds of teams are created and dissolved throughout the systems development cycle. Despite the many ways to structure project teams and multiteam project organizations, the one feature common to all of them is emphasis on integration. In project management, *the leader's primary role is integration.*

The simplest kind of project organization is a single, small group of people, a task force or team formed on a full-or part-time basis to perform an assignment. This kind of organization is used in projects that are not large or important enough to warrant "disrupting" the existing organization. Project groups like this can exist inside one functional area or span over several functional areas.

Projects within One Functional Area

It makes sense that a project that affects only one functional area or is the responsibility of one area should be located in that area. For example, a project to survey customer attitudes about a new product would ordinarily be placed within the Marketing Department because all the necessary resources and expertise are located there. The team does all the tasks itself—it prepares the survey questionnaire, obtains mailing lists, distributes the survey, and processes the results. With few exceptions, all of these can be done by members inside the Marketing Department. Project teams like this are managed by a *project expeditor,*[4] a staff assistant selected by the manager of the area where the project lies. The expeditor coordinates decision making, monitors schedules, makes suggestions, and keeps the executive apprised. The expeditor typically has no formal authority over team members and must rely on persuasion, personal knowledge, and information about the project to influence team members. A single team, project expeditor organization is shown in Figure 7–4.

Multifunctional Project Teams

An example of a project that might use a *multifunctional team* is the development of a Materials Requirements Planning (MRP) system. This team includes representatives from

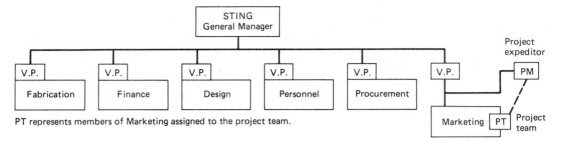

FIGURE 7–4. Project within a single functional subunit.

all the departments that will provide inputs to the system or will utilize its outputs, such as inventory control, purchasing, manufacturing, engineering, and data processing. The team is responsible for establishing the system requirements and overseeing development and installation of the system. Multifunctional teams like this are typically used on projects that are large but that do not require the resources to merit a complete reorganization.

One of the best places to use multifunctional teams is in product development. By using closely knit teams of engineers, designers, manufacturers, assemblers, marketers, lawyers, suppliers, dealers, and customers, phases of the systems development cycle usually done sequentially can be done simultaneously. The team approach eliminates cross-functional barriers and can result in higher quality and lower cost. A good example is the Ford team that created Sable and Taurus. The team not only came up with car models that won quality and design-excellence awards, but they did it for half a *billion* dollars under the proposed development budget.[5]

The multifunctional project team is located either in the functional area most responsible for the project or at a higher level position, such as reporting to the general manager as shown in Figure 7–5. The latter arrangement imputes greater importance to the project and improves coordination between the areas involved. The person managing the project is designated the project *coordinator*. Though this person has no line authority over

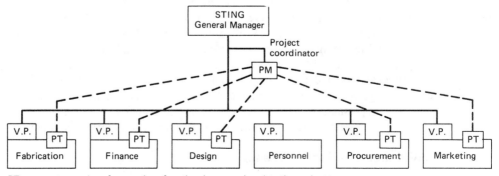

FIGURE 7–5. Multifunctional project team.

team members, he does have authority to make decisions about project budgets, schedules, and work performance, and to command action based upon these decisions. Besides the high level position of reporting to the general manager, the coordinator's influence, like the expeditor, originates in his knowledge about the project and by being at the center of everyone involved.

7.7 PURE PROJECT ORGANIZATIONS

Projects that entail high level complexity, major resource commitments, and heavy stake in the outcome require a *pure project* form of organization. A pure project is a separate organization, almost like another company, especially created for and singularly devoted to achievement of the project goal. Whatever the project needs to afford it the highest priority—all necessary human and physical resources—is incorporated into the pure project organization. These organizations are able to react quickly to changing demands of the environment, the user, and the parent organization. They rely heavily on the use of liaisons, task forces, and teams.

Heading the pure project organization is the *project manager*. Unlike the coordinator, the project manager has full authority over all people and physical resources assigned to the project and, thus, maximum control. For those areas which cannot be placed under her control, the project manager has authority to contract out for resources, both from internal functional areas as well as from external subcontractors and suppliers. The pure project manager is involved in the project from start to finish: during proposal preparation, she prepares forecasts, requests plans from functional areas, and reconciles discrepancies among plans; after acceptance, she allocates budgeted money to buy resources and hire personnel; during the project, she reallocates resources and approves all changes to requirements and the project plan. When personnel must be "borrowed" from functional areas, she is the one who negotiates to get the best people.

When resources are not internally available, the project manager heads selection of and negotiations with subcontractors. She oversees their work and coordinates it with other work being done. The project managers in Jamal Industries, the company relocation, and NASA in Chapter 2 are examples of pure project managers.

Pure Project Variations

Three common variations of the pure project structure are the *project center*, the *stand-alone project*, and the *partial project*.

In the *project center* the structure of the parent organization remains the same except for the addition of a separate "project arm" and project manager. This form is shown in Figure 7–6 for the Logistical Online (LOGON) project. Resources and personnel are borrowed from functional and staff areas for as long as needed. General Motors used a project center when it chose 1,200 key people from various divisions for the task of determining how to downsize all of the corporation's automotive lines. The project center developed suggestions, turned them over to the automotive divisions for implementation,

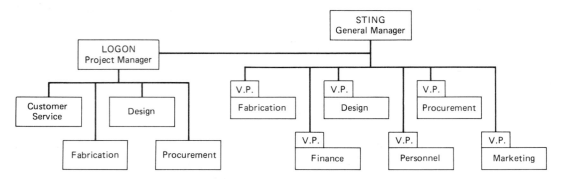

FIGURE 7–6. Pure project as "arm" to functional organization.

and then was disbanded. In another corporation, a project center was used to oversee the relocation of its offices. By creating a relocation-project center to work full time on the tricky problems of relocation, the rest of the organization was able to continue its work as usual.

The *stand-alone project* is an organization newly created especially for the purpose of accomplishing the project. It is not part of any one existing organization but is made up of areas from several participating organizations. It is typically used for large-scale government or public works projects that involve one or more prime contractors, dozens of subcontractors, and hundreds of smaller supporting organizations, suppliers and consultants. The NASA space station development program and Quebec's LaGrande Complex (Hydro) project are examples. When these projects are completed, only an operating function remains and the rest of the organization is dissolved. Stand alone projects are discussed later in this chapter in the section on integration of large-scale projects.

In a *partial project*, the functions critical to the project (such as construction or engineering) are assigned to the project manager while other, support-oriented functions (such as procurement and accounting) remain with the functional areas. In Figure 7–6, for example, the project manager might only control design and fabrication, while the areas of Finance, Marketing, and Personnel give functional support. The manager of a partial project has direct control over all major project tasks, but he also receives assistance from support areas in the parent company over which he does not have control.

Disadvantages

The chief disadvantage of the pure project organization is its *cost* to the parent organization and project personnel. Since each pure project is a completely or partially independent organization it must be fully or substantially staffed. Each project becomes a self-centered empire; between projects there is often little sharing or cross-utilization of resources. Companies with multiple pure projects incur considerable duplication of effort and facilities.

Since resources are not always available at the time they are needed, project organizations must begin acquiring them in advance. The author was one of dozens of engineers hired in advance of obtaining a large government contract, a necessary move so that the project could begin as soon as the contract was signed. But the contract was never awarded so eventually everyone assigned to the project had to be transferred or laid off. The payroll loss alone amounted to hundreds of man-months.

This suggests still another expense: outplacement of personnel. Whenever there is no follow-up work to a project the organization faces the problem of what to do with its work force. Personnel on long-term projects become so highly specialized that it is difficult to put them in other projects requiring more generalized or up-to-date skills. Companies add to this cost when they delay breaking up a project organization in hopes of acquiring new work. When there is no follow-up work the only option is to release workers and sell facilities. This was the experience of the aerospace industry in the early 1970s when, after completion of the Apollo Lunar Program, facilities were closed and thousands of scientists and engineers had to be let go.

Pure project organizations are strictly temporary, and as the work draws to a close the uncertainty about the fate of the team leads, understandably, to a decline in morale and enthusiasm. Project managers may become so preoccupied with generating new contracts, extending old contracts, or finding jobs for themselves and the team that they neglect the project they are currently working on.

7.8 MATRIX ORGANIZATION

Although the pure project form often provides the only way to do a large-scale, one time project, its disadvantages make it impractical for businesses that *continually* operate on a project basis. Examples of such businesses include: architecture and construction, where every building, bridge, dam, or highway is a new project; product development, where every product concept, design, manufacture, and promotion is a new project; computer systems, where every hardware and software installation is a new project; law and accounting, where every case and audit is a new project; and aerospace, where every transport, weapons, and space system is a new project. Though some of these projects are small enough to be handled by task forces or teams, most are not because they are too large, too complex, and have too much at stake. In addition, most of these businesses are *multiproject* organizations, meaning they are involved in more than one project at a time. They need the capability to quickly create large project groups without the personnel and cost disadvantages associated with pure project organizations.

To achieve this capability a new form of organization was evolved. First adopted in the aerospace industry by such firms as Boeing and Lockheed, it is called the *matrix*. The matrix, shown in Figure 7–7, is a grid-like structure of authority and reporting relationships created by the overlay of a project organization on a traditional, functional organization.[6] This overlay gives the matrix three unique capabilities.

First, the functional part provides the repository for the technical expertise and physical resources needed by the project. The project manager creates a project group by

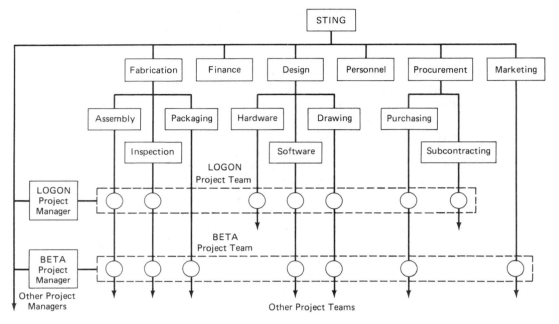

FIGURE 7–7.   Matrix form of project organization.

negotiating with functional managers and then "borrowing" the expertise and physical resources needed for the project. Each project is composed of workers who are on loan but who work together as a project team during the course of the project. Since the same work force is time shared among several projects, duplication of effort is reduced.

Second, while in their "functional homes" workers associate with colleagues in their fields of specialization; this not only keeps them current in their profession or trade, but makes them more assignable to new projects. Each functional area has, at a given time, many individuals who are working on different projects. Sharing ideas and exchanging points of view makes them more effective in their respective projects.

Third, when individual assignments are fulfilled or a project completed, workers go back to their functional homes for a new assignment. Large fluctuations in the work force and in worker morale and anxiety are thus reduced.

The primary effort of the project manager in the matrix (sometimes called the *matrix manager*) is integration. The authority granted the matrix manager varies from having judicious control over functional managers to being under their control. Typically, the project manager is considered on the same hierarchical level as functional managers. Functional managers provide the necessary technical counsel, advice, and support, while the project manager integrates and unifies their efforts to meet project goals. The project manager works *with* functional managers to accomplish the project.

The matrix makes it easy to create unique organizations to accomplish particular goals. It shares the virtue with the pure project organization of having dedicated resources and a project manager to give the project priority.

In multiproject organizations the matrix makes it easier to balance schedule and resource requirements among several projects at once. The prioritizing and balancing of resources between projects is the responsibility of the *manager of projects*, shown as the "vice-president of projects" in Figure 7–8. The manager of projects attends to the short- and medium-term requirements of current and upcoming projects and relieves top management of most project operations responsibility.

Problems with Matrix Organizations

The strong point of the matrix organization—its combination vertical-horizontal structure—is at the same time the root cause of its problems.[7] The matrix is not just a structure but a whole different way of doing things. To be successful it must be reinforced by information systems and human behavior that support two-dimensional information flow and dual reporting relationships.

Many organizations have tried and found the matrix impossible to implement. Most organizations are accustomed to hierarchical decision making and vertical information processing. With its emphasis on horizontal relations, lateral information flow, and

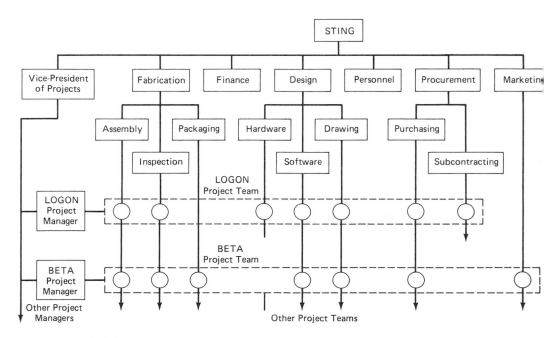

FIGURE 7–8. Location of the vice-president of projects in a matrix organization.

decentralized decision making, the matrix is clearly contrary. It superimposes a lateral system on a functional system, so companies adopting the matrix must add horizontal information processing systems to existing vertical accounting and command systems. It can be done, but tends to be somewhat complicated and expensive. Dual processing schemes for project planning, monitoring, and control are described later in Section IV.

In human terms, the major drawback of the matrix is that it is conflict inducing. Theoretically, the two-dimensional structure promotes coordinated decision making among functional areas and enables tradeoff decisions to be made for the benefit of the project. It assumes that both functional-technical and project related issues have equal priority and that a balance of power exists between functional and project managers. Often, however, authority in the matrix is unclear and functional and project managers jockey to control one another. Functional managers control project resources, but project managers seldom control functional managers. In multiproject organizations additional conflict is generated over which project gets priority and which project manager gets the best resources.

Since each worker in the matrix has two bosses, one functional manager and one project-matrix, the matrix violates a major principle of management: single, scalar chain-of-command. The project manager directs the worker on the project, but it is the functional manager who evaluates the worker's performance. The inevitable result is role conflict or confusion over allegiance.

The matrix strives to give equal priority to functions and projects, but sometimes neither gets priority. For workers to avoid the chaos and confusion in the matrix, everyone must have a common reference. For this to happen, organizations must establish clear, stable values and priorities. At Boeing, for example, which has used the matrix successfully for many years, priorities are established day to day: people operate *either* in a project team *or* in a functional area. Whichever they are in, that is the one on which they put priority.[8]

Any attempt to adopt the matrix must be accompanied by both attitudinal and cultural change. Some group and interpersonal skills to help facilitate these changes are discussed in the next two chapters.

7.9 SELECTING A PROJECT FORM

Although project managers seldom have the responsibility for designing the organizations they lead, they can offer suggestions to the managers who do. It is impossible to state which form is always best, but general criteria can be listed to help decide the most appropriate form for a given project. Figure 7–9 shows the approximate applicability of different project organization forms depending upon four criteria:

- Frequency of new projects (how often, or to what degree the parent company is involved in project-related activity).

- Duration of projects (how long a typical project lasts).

- Size of projects (level of human, capital, or other resources in relation to other activities of the company).

- Complexity of relationships (number of functional areas involved in the project and degree of interdependency).

    Matrix and pure project forms are more applicable to projects of medium and higher complexity and of medium or larger size. These kinds of projects have greater resource and information requirements and need project managers and integrators with strong central authority. In particular, the matrix works best where there are a variety of different projects going on at once and where all can share functional resources on a part-time basis. In contrast, when there is less variety among projects, when specialists must be devoted full-time, and when complete project authority is desired, then the pure project form is better. Both forms are applicable when projects are an organization "way of life," although they can also be applied temporarily to one shot, infrequent projects when the stakes are high. As mentioned, the complexity of the matrix and the enormous human and facility requirements of the pure project can present major problems to the parent company, so both should be avoided when simpler forms would work as well.

    For smaller projects involving several functional areas, task forces and teams which link functional areas are more appropriate. Short-term projects in one or a few functional areas can be effectively handled by part-time task forces managed by expeditors in one functional area. When several areas are involved, a multifunctional task force with a

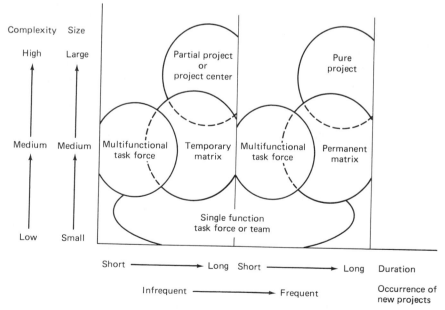

FIGURE 7–9. Some criteria for selecting project organizational form.

coordinator who reports to the general manager is more suitable. Projects of longer duration, but small in scope and low in complexity are best handled by full-time project teams with coordinators. When the team size needed to accomplish the task becomes large and interrelationships become too complex, then a temporary matrix or partial project should be set up. Teams, task forces, and project centers are appropriate when the normal structure and work flow of the organization cannot be disrupted.

Other criteria important to selecting a project form are the stake of the project, the degree of technological uncertainty, the criticalness of time and cost goals, the uniqueness of the project, and the relative importance of the criteria.[9] For example, task forces and teams are generally appropriate when the project task involves high certainty and little risk, and when time and cost are not major factors. When the risk and uncertainty is great, when time and cost goals are critical, or when there is much at stake, matrix and pure project forms better afford the obligatory high level of integration and control. When a project differs greatly from the normal business of the firm, it should be made a partial or full pure project.

These considerations all relate to the project, which, in fact, sometimes is less important than attributes and experiences of the parent company. For example, matrix and pure project forms are seldom used in small organizations simply because they have insufficient resources and managers to commit. Top management's attitudes about how much responsibility and authority is appropriate for the project manager also specify the acceptable form of organization by dictating the allowable degree of centralized project control. The most important factor is the company's experience with projects and management's perception of which project forms work best. Firms with little project experience should avoid the matrix because it is difficult to adjust to. Faced with a complex project, they might do better by adopting a partial or project center approach.

Often, project organization structure *evolves* to suit the preferences of management, which is to say that it develops through a trial-and-error process. An example follows.

Changing Organization Structure Midstream: The Case of MARTA

The Metropolitan Atlanta Rapid Transit Authority (MARTA) system is a rapid transit, rail system built during the 1970s at a cost of 3.5 billion dollars. The study by Lammie and Shah of the MARTA project management process illustrates the kinds of structural changes that take place *during* a project.[10]

Early in the MARTA project, a typical general engineering consultant (GEC) construction organization was established. This consisted of a group of field resident engineers reporting to field area managers who, in turn, reported to the construction manager and project director (Figure 7–10a).

Given that nearly everyone in the field organization represented the GEC, MARTA disliked this structure because it gave them little ability to supervise the work. The structure was modified to (1) include a joint management team of MARTA area supervisors and GEC field managers at the field level, and (2) eliminate all delegated approval authority from resident engineers. The GEC project director was removed from the line of contractual

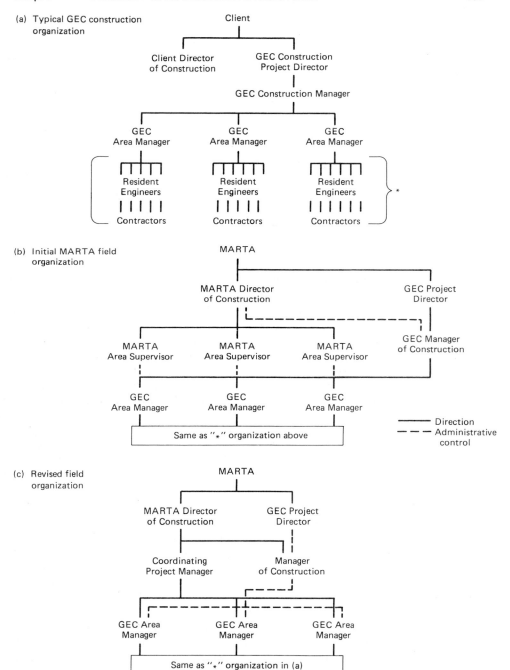

FIGURE 7–10. Evolution of MARTA project organization.

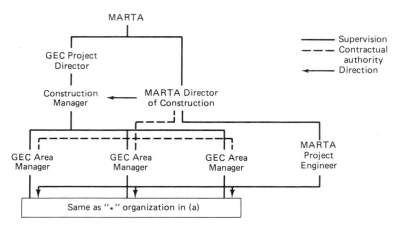

FIGURE 7–10.   (Continued).

authority to allow the MARTA director of construction to communicate directly with the GEC construction manager (Figure 7–10b).

Within a year it was determined that this structure was also problematic because it had too many layers. Since engineers and managers in the field had so little authority, contractors had to deal directly with the MARTA director of construction. In revising the structure, a position of project engineer was established to monitor field work, and the MARTA field supervisor positions were eliminated (Figure 7–10c). This structure was later altered, moving authority from the MARTA director of construction to the GEC area managers, then finally back to the resident engineers. Both the GEC construction manager and project director became so involved in contractual matters, that the MARTA director of construction started to lose ability to supervise details. A new organization structure was finally agreed to which allowed MARTA and the GEC to work more as an integrated team (Figure 7–10d). This organization, according to Lammie and Shah, reflected a "mutual respect with a defacto delegation of authority on many items beyond that specified in approved procedures."[11]

Project organization structures are not cast in stone, though sometimes they are treated as if they are. When an organization is ineffectual it should be changed. Although restructuring causes consternation and confusion in the short run, an organization should make whatever changes are necessary to get the structure best suited for its requirements.

7.10 PROJECT OFFICE

The term *project office* has dual meaning: it refers first to a support staff group which reports to the project manager, and second to a physical place where the project team meets. Our discussion will focus on the *project staff*, although it is stressed that all projects, even the smallest ones, should have a physical project office to serve as an information center and place where the team can meet and keep reports.

The major purpose of a project office staff is to coordinate the project efforts of functional areas and subcontractors. The staff is responsible for planning, directing, and controlling all project activities and for linking project teams, users, and top management. When projects are small and coordinating procedures are well-established, the responsibility of the project staff is handled by one person, the project manager.

Composition of the Project Office

The function and composition of the project office depend upon the authority of the project manager, and the size, importance, and goal of the project. The project office shown in Figure 7–11 is for a large-scale engineering development effort. Of the functions shown, one of the most important is planning and control. During project concept and definition this function prepares and implements work breakdown structures (WBS), project schedules, budgets, and PERT/CPM networks (topics covered in Section IV). In later phases, it monitors work, forecasts trends, updates schedules and budgets, and distributes reports to functional, upper-level, and user management.

Also shown are functions for systems engineering and configuration management, both headed by the project engineer. These activities are closely tied together and to the tasks of planning and control. The systems engineering function oversees systems analysis, requirements definition, and end-item specifications (discussed in Appendix A), and furnishes inputs to both planning and

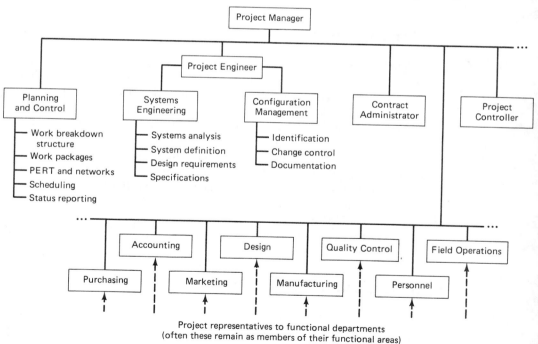

FIGURE 7-11   Project office for a large development project.

control and configuration management. Configuration management (discussed in Chapter 15) defines the initial product configuration and controls changes in product requirements resulting in (or from changes to) project plans and systems engineering requirements.

As shown in Figure 7–11, the project office also has functions for contracting, financial control, and for representing every functional area.

In staffing the project office, the project manager must avoid duplicating the effort of the functional areas. The purpose of the project office is to *coordinate* work and advise the functional areas on *what* they should do, not *how* to do it. To keep the full-time size of the project office to a minimum, on small projects all functional representatives and most specialists remain physically within their functional areas.

The project integration effort is best served when the project office is structured to mirror the functional areas it integrates.[12] This is achieved (see Figure 7–11) by having a representative from each functional area who will coordinate activities in that area with the overall project. Each representative is a specialist in a functional discipline, but while in the project office his prime charge is integrating his discipline with others in the project.

Thus, the way the project manager integrates the functional areas is by *coordinating the representatives* in the project office. She facilitates integration by, for example, having the project staff work in the same physical office, making the office open and accessible to all functional areas, and encouraging frequent meetings and using consensual decision making among representatives. Techniques for facilitating interaction are further discussed in chapters 9 and 10.

Office of Projects and the Program Office

Multiproject organizations also have an *office of projects* (not to be confused with the project office). This was shown in Figure 7–8 as the office of the vice-president of projects. When projects are small the office of projects substitutes for individual project offices and handles proposals, contracting, scheduling, cost control, and report preparation for every project. When projects are large or overlap, the office of projects is used *in addition* to project offices and serves the purpose of coordinating the combined requirements of all the projects.[13]

When projects are part of a program there is also a *program office* to ensure that the projects supplement one another and "add up" to overall program goals. The program office handles external to project interfaces, maintains user enthusiasm and support, keeps project managers informed of problem buildups, and handles interfaces and integration between projects. The NASA program office described in Chapter 2 is an example. When programs are very large, the integration work of the program office is supplemented by outside "integration contractors."

7.11 THE INFORMAL ORGANIZATION

Despite the importance of the formal project organization, its usefulness depends on the strength and support of the emergent *informal organization*. We will consider just one facet of the informal organization, informal communication.

Informal communication—the most familiar vehicle of it is the *grapevine*—certainly has its drawbacks. It is neither thorough nor dependable, it tends to garble messages from one person to the next (even jokes loose their punch after going through just a few people), and it never guarantees that people who need information will ever get it. Nonetheless, informal communication is largely beneficial and essential. It fulfills social and work needs and it conveys information more quickly and directly than most formal systems. Some management theorists posit that vast networks of informal communication are essential for organizations to perform well.

Managers cannot control informal communication, but they can influence it. Peters and Waterman described several means of doing this.[14] One way is to remove status barriers and inspire casual conversation, particularly between managers and workers, by *insisting* on informality. For example, at Walt Disney, everyone—from the president on down—wears a name tag; at Hewlett Packard, people are urged to use first names; and at Delta Airline and Levi Strauss, the management philosophy is "open door." MBWA (management by walking around) or getting managers out of the office and talking to people (instead of relying solely on reports) is another way to stimulate informal information exchange. The physical layout of the office is also instrumental. Intermingling the desks of workers from interrelated functional areas, removing walls and partitions, "family groupings" of chairs and desks, and spot placement of lounges are ways of increasing face to face contact.

Project management attempts to do what the informal organization sometimes does: to allow the people involved in a problem or decision to directly communicate and make decisions. One way or another, people affected by a decision or problem talk about it, form ideas and make decisions, though often the formal organization overlooks or stifles these ideas. After management has adopted the appropriate formal structure it should then encourage the right informal processes to support it.

7.12 ADVANCED TOPIC: INTEGRATION IN LARGE-SCALE PROJECTS

Any party which works toward the project goal is part of the project organization. In large-scale projects (LSP), numerous parties—sponsors, prime contractors, subcontractors, consultants, and suppliers—are all part of one effort. Figure 7–12 shows the principal contributors and relationships in a LSP. Relationships are complex and lines of authority connecting the parties are often weak (sometimes based only on contracts and purchase orders). If Figure 7–12 appears somewhat confusing it simply reflects the fact that relationships in LSP's are, well, sometimes confusing.

To increase the level of integration, roles likes project managers, coordinators, liaisons, and task forces are used. Notice in Figure 7–12 the relationships, both horizontal and hierarchical, among contributors' management as well as between functional areas in different organizations. Direct lines of communication between, for instance, the sponsor's design group and the contractors' and subcontractors' design groups accelerate decision making and improve integration.

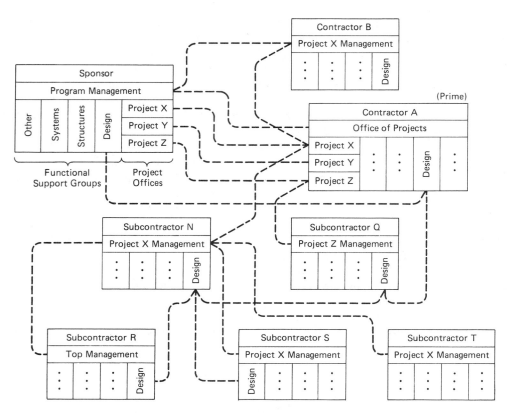

FIGURE 7–12.   Integration relationships in a large-scale project.

Examples of LSP's include space systems (e.g. the NASA space station), construction projects (Canada's LaGrande hydroelectric venture, Holland's Delta flood control project, the trans-English Channel Tunnel), as well as company relocations (involving the client, movers, construction companies, recruiters, consultants, suppliers) and corporate mergers (dual clients, consultants, and attorneys).

Most technological LSP's are devoted to development and production of complex systems. The total effort is subdivided among a number of contributors, each responsible for a specific subsystem or component to be integrated with the others to form the overall system. Figure 7–13, for example, shows the major subsystems in Skylab and the major organizations involved.[15] The figure is simplified and excludes the launch rocket, crew descent vehicle, and ground support systems, each involving many more organizations.

In public works and government projects, integration is usually the responsibility of the sponsoring agency, but sometimes the engineering and management problems are too difficult and outside help is required.

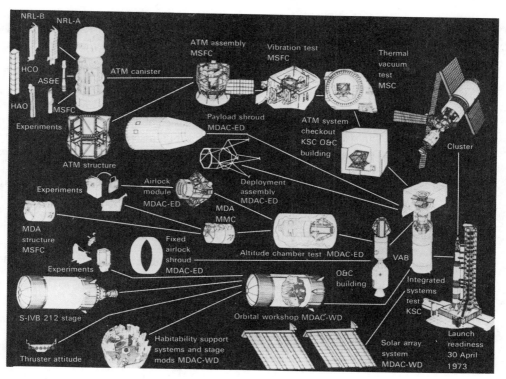

FIGURE 7–13.   Major subsystems and organizations in the hardware and assembly of Skylab.
(Adopted from W.D. Compton and C.D. Benson, *Living and Working in Space: A History of Skylab*
(Washington, D.C.: NASA, 1983), 198.)

Among the first LSP's to experience the problems inherent to integrating subsystems
were weapons system development projects during World War II.[16] The components
which made up a system such as a bomber were purchased by separate offices within, say,
the Air Force. These components—airframe, engines, and electronics were then furnished
to the airframe manufacturer to assemble. As systems grew more complex, procurement
by several separate organizations no longer worked. Sometimes the subsystem interfaces were different so plugs and fasteners would not fit, or the size of components
was greater than planned and the entire system had to be redesigned. To overcome
these difficulties, the military established detailed specifications and committees to
coordinate subsystem interfaces. The result was massive red tape and long delays, as
exemplified by Livingston:

A contractor wished to change the clock in an airplane cockpit from a one-day to an eight-day
mechanism. A justification was written and given to the military representative, who for-
warded it to the military technical group. The group requested from the contractor more

detailed reasoning for the change. The contractor acknowledged and sent it to the group. The group approved the request and sent it to the change committee. The committee reviewed it, accepted the change, then sent an authorization back to the contractor to replace the clock. This simple request took *three months* to process.[17]

Today, the integration process is expedited by giving responsibility to a single "oversight" body, similar to the role of a wedding consultant or general contractor, but on a larger scale. The job of integrating a LSP requires considerable manpower and a wide range of technical skills. Usually, the *lead* or *prime* contractor is assigned the responsibility for systems integration, though the sponsor retains other responsibilities such as contracting with *associate* contractors (subsystem manufacturers), making major decisions, as well as resolving conflicts between the prime and associates. The associates become subcontractors to the prime contractor, take their orders from the prime, and are subject to its surveillance and approval. Figure 7–14 shows the relationships among the sponsor, prime, and associate contractors for a large urban transit project. Notice the different types of relationships.[18]

Sometimes the prime contractor is given greater responsibility, like assisting the sponsor in selecting associates, pricing subsystems, and allocating project funds. This

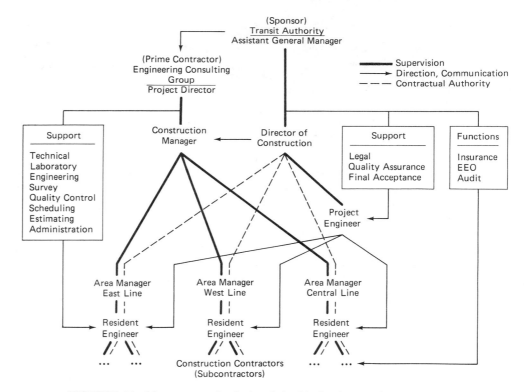

FIGURE 7–14. Management and authority relationships in a large public construction project.

presents a problem when the prime contractor and the subcontractors are competitors, since subcontractors are hesitant to divulge concepts that the prime might need to integrate the system.

Sometimes even the largest prime contractors need assistance and it is necessary for them to submit a joint proposal as a *team* where one company serves as leader and is responsible for systems engineering and management of the others. This appeals to small and medium-sized firms which ordinarily would not have the resources to contract independently. The problem with this approach is that unless the lead company is strong there can be serious interface problems. It also reduces competition, and since no team is likely to have all the best subsystems, the sponsor may require the team leader to open up subsystems to competition and, if necessary, change the members of the team.

When the prime contractor lacks the capability to perform the integrating work, a separate consulting firm, or *integration contractor* is engaged entirely for the purpose of integration and engineering advice.[19] These contractors, which sometimes employ thousands of workers, are better able to quickly pull together all the necessary resources. The problem is that they are often in the same business as the contractors they integrate, which puts them in the awkward position of managing their competitors and being able to learn their secrets.

7.13 SUMMARY

Organization structure is the way organizations attempt to achieve goals and respond to problems in the environment. Two key features of structure are differentiation and integration; the former is the subdivision of organizations into specialized subunits, the latter is the linking of subunits to coordinate actions. Organizations traditionally differentiate along functional, geographic, customer, and process lines. They integrate subunits with rules and procedures, coordinated plans, and the chain-of-command. These kinds of differentiation and integration are effective when there is stability in the environment and certainty in the task, but they are ineffective when there is frequent change, high complexity, and high uncertainty in the task.

Project organizations are characterized by being able to adopt structures suited to changing goals. They achieve high integration through formal integration functions that emphasize horizontal relations. The simplest project organization is a task force or team with a project expeditor or coordinator to oversee and coordinate work efforts. Project expeditors and coordinators lack formal authority and must rely upon technical skills, information, and diplomacy to influence project members.

When a project task involves just one specialty, the project team is put in one functional area. When it is multifunctional, members are drawn from several functional subunits and the group is positioned physically outside the bounds of any functional area. The team leader reports to the chief executive overseeing the multiple areas.

When projects are large and involve substantial resource commitment and stake in the outcome, pure project organizations are used. This form commits major functional areas directly to the project and gives the project manager direct authority and control. The advantage is that it gives highest priority to the project. The disadvantage is that it is costly and results in large fluctuations in resource requirements. The matrix organization was developed to mitigate these problems.

The matrix superimposes project teams on the functional organization and permits sharing of resources across projects. But it requires two-dimensional information systems that are difficult to implement, and non-traditional dual reporting relationships that cause conflict. It also requires much commitment and project experience to succeed.

Thoroughbred organizations such as those just described are seldom found. Most projects are hybrids and a pure project may be subdivided into portions which are matrixes, and vice versa. Projects rarely stand alone as the only basis for organization. Matrix forms and project centers coexist in companies that have functional, product, geographic, or customer bases, and where there are smaller project teams and task forces.

The appropriate project organization structure depends upon characteristics of the project and the preference of the parent organization. Among the criteria for project organization selection are project frequency, duration, size, complexity, stake, uncertainty, uniqueness, and importance of cost and schedule. The size of the company, its experience in projects, and the desired degree of project authority are also important.

In large projects the project manager has the assistance of a staff of specialists and representatives called the project office. This office handles all project-specific tasks such as contracting, planning, scheduling, and controlling, but its major role is integrating functional areas. Two other staff groups, the office of projects and the program office, oversee and coordinate activities in multiproject situations. When projects and programs involving multiple contributing organizations cannot be fully integrated or technically managed by the sponsor, the lead contractor or a special, integration contractor may be assigned to integrate work efforts.

All human organizations also have an informal structure that influences organizational performance. Informal communication is an important aspect of informal structure that project managers can influence to enhance integration and problem solving.

Project organizations overcome many shortcomings of functional organizations, but they are not perfect. Like other kinds of organizations, project organizations become self serving, compete with each other, and attempt to acquire ever greater resources and more influence. They are well-suited to achieve their goals, but like functional organizations, they become corrupted and their processes and goals are not always in the best interest of the larger organization. This is a problem with all organizations, and projects are no exception.

Exercise: The LOGON Project

The Standard Industrial Gadgets Company (STING) is a medium-sized engineering and manufacturing firm specializing in warehousing and materials handling systems. STING purchases most of the subsystems and components for its product systems, then modifies and assembles them to satisfy customer requirements. Most of STING's customers are in manufacturing or distribution.

Every STING system is made to customer specification and most of the firm's work is in system design, assembly, installation, and checkout. The firm's 250 employees are roughly divided equally among five divisions: engineering, design, fabrication, customer service, and marketing. Recently, competition has forced the firm to expand into computerized warehousing systems despite the fact that its experience and computer expertise is currently rather limited.

The company has been awarded a large contract for a robotic system for placement, storage, retrieval, and routing of shipping containers for truck and rail by the Midwest Parcel Distribution Company. This system, called the Logistical Online System, or LOGON, is to be developed and installed at the company's main distribution center in Chicago. The contract is for a fixed price of 1.462 million dollars which includes design, fabrication, and installation at the center. The contract was awarded because it was the lowest bid and because of STING's outstanding record for quality and customer service. A clause in the contract imposes a penalty of 1000 dollars daily for failure to meet the contract delivery date.

At various times throughout the estimated 47-week project, personnel will be involved from the functional divisions of design, fabrication, procurement, and customer service. Most personnel will be involved on a full-time basis for at least four or as many as 18 weeks. In the past, the company has set up ad hoc project management teams comprised of a project coordinator and members selected from functional areas. These teams are then responsible for planning, scheduling, and budgeting, but the actual work is done by the functional departments. Members of the teams serve primarily as liaisons to the functional areas and work part-time on the teams for the duration of the project.

The LOGON contract differs from other STING systems, both in its heavy usage of computer, real-time operation via remote terminals, and in its size. The company has no experience with real-time warehousing systems and has only recently hired people with the background needed for the project. (However, a contract has been signed with CRC, a major computer manufacturer, to provide hardware, programming support, and to assist with system installation and checkout.)

The LOGON contract is roughly 40 percent greater than anything STING has done before. At present, STING is in the middle of two other projects that absorb roughly three-fourths of its labor capacity, is winding down on a third that involves only the customer service division, and has two outstanding proposals for small projects under review.

Discuss how would you organize the LOGON project if you were the president of STING. Discuss the alternatives available for the STING project and the relative advantages and disadvantages of each. What assumptions must be made?

CHAPTER REVIEW QUESTIONS

1. What do the terms differentiation and integration mean?
2. What are the five traditional forms of differentiation? List some companies that presently use each.
3. List the various forms of integration. Gives examples of each. Which of these are "lateral" forms of integration?

4. What are the advantages of functional organizations? What are the disadvantages?

5. What distinguishes "project forms" from other forms of organization?

6. Describe the responsibility and authority for each of the following:

 Project expeditor

 Project coordinator

 Project leader in a pure project

 Project leader in a matrix

7. Describe the applications, advantages, and disadvantages for each of the following:

 Project task force

 Project team

 Pure project and project center

 Matrix

8. Give some examples of organizations where each of these project forms has been used.

9. What is the project office? Describe its purpose? Who is in the project office? How should members be selected for the project office?

10. What is meant by the informal organization? Give some examples. How does it help or hinder the formal organization? How can its beneficial aspects be influenced by the project manager?

11. Describe the role of the prime contractor and integration contractor in large projects.

12. One form of an integration contractor is the wedding consultant, another is the consultant who organizes high school reunions. For each of these:

 • List the various groups, organizations, and individual parties that are involved and must be integrated;

 • Describe the relationship among these parties and how the consultant coordinates their efforts, both prior to and during the wedding or reunion.

13. An important element of informal organization not covered here is groups. Discuss informal groups—how they arise and why. Give some examples. How can informal groups be an asset to the project? How can they be a problem? In what ways can project managers encourage "beneficial" informal groups; how can they discourage "problematic" groups?

QUESTIONS ABOUT THE STUDY PROJECT

1. In your project, how is the parent organization organized—functionally, geographically, etc.? Show the organization chart, its overall breakdown, and relationships.

2. How does your project fit into the overall organization chart of the parent organization?

3. What kind of form is used in your project? Show the chart of the project organization; indicate the key roles and the authority and communication links between them.

4. How was the project structure developed? Has it "evolved" during the project? Who designs or has influence on the project structure? What role did the project manager have in its design? Is the design similar to those used in other, similar projects in the organization?

5. Critique the project design. Is it appropriate for the project goal, the parent organization, and the environment?

6. Is there a project office? Is there an office of projects or a program office? In each case: (a) describe the physical office and how it is used; (b) describe the members of the project or program office staff—representatives, specialists, etc. What is the purpose of the staff of the project office? Describe the various tasks and functions in the project office. What are the members' participation in the project office—full-time, as needed, etc? What is the reporting relationship between the project manager and members of the project office?

7. How does the project manager integrate functional areas?

8. Are there prime and associate contractors involved? If so, what is the function of the company you are studying (prime contractor, subcontractor, supplier?) and how does it fit into the structure of all the organizations contributing to the project? If applicable, discuss the involvement of integration contractors or team leader contractors.

9. Does the project manager encourage open, informal communication? If so, in what way? If not, why not?

ENDNOTES

1. Detailed discussion of the organization structure, coordination, and integrating mechanisms in high technology environments is given by Jay Galbraith, "Environmental and Technological Determinants of Organizational Design," in *Studies in Organization Design*, eds. J.W. Lorsch and P.R. Lawrence (Homewood, Ill.: Irwin-Dorsey, 1970), 113–139.

2. See Jay Galbraith, *Designing Complex Organizations* (Reading, Mass.: Addison-Wesley, 1973).

3. Thomas Peters and Robert Waterman, *In Search of Excellence* (New York: Warner Communications, 1984), 127–130.

4. See Keith Davis, "The Role of Project Management in Scientific Manufacturing," *IEEE Transactions of Engineering Management*, Vol. 9, No. 3 (1962), 109–113.

5. Tom Peters, *Thriving on Chaos* (New York: Alfred A. Knopf, 1988), 212–13.

6. A discussion of the matrix organization, its applications and implementation is given by S.M. Davis and P.R. Lawrence, *Matrix* (Reading, Mass.: Addison-Wesley, 1977).

7. J. McCann and J.R. Galbraith, "Interdepartmental Relations," in *Handbook of Organizational Design*, eds. P.C. Nystrom and W.H. Starbuck (New York: Oxford University Press, 1981), Vol. II, No. 61; J.R. Meredith and S.J. Mantel, *Project Management: A Managerial Approach* (New York: John Wiley & Sons, 1985), 104.

8. Peters and Waterman, *In Search of Excellence*, 307–308.

9. See R. Thomas, J. Keating, and A. Bluedorn, "Authority Structures for Project Management," *Journal of Construction Engineering and Management*, Vol. 109, No. 4 (Dec 1983), 406–422. This provides an overview of how to create a project organization.

10. Based on J.L. Lammie and D.P. Shah, "Construction Management: MARTA in Retrospect," *Journal of Construction Engineering and Management*, Vol. 110, No. 4 (Dec 1984), 459–462.

11. Ibid., 462.

12. James Burns, "Effective Management of Programs," in *Studies in Organizational Design*, eds. J.W. Lorsch and P.R. Lawrence (Homewood, Ill.: Irwin-Dorsey, 1970), 140–152.

13. See Chapter 4, "Multiproject Management," in Russell Archibald, *Managing High-Technology Programs and Projects* (New York: John Wiley & Sons, 1976).

14. Peters and Waterman, *In Search of Excellence*, 121–125.

15. Adopted from W.D. Compton and C.D. Benson, *Living and Working in Space: A History of Skylab* (Washington, D.C.: NASA SP–4208, 1983). This work describes the managerial and technical integration problems encountered in the development of one large-scale project.

16. This discussion is based on J.S. Livingston, "Weapons System Contracting," *Harvard Business Review* (July–August, 1959), 83–92.

17. Ibid., 85.

18. Adopted from J.L. Lammie and D.P. Shah, "Construction Management: MARTA in Retrospect," 459–475.

19. A more complete discussion of integration contractors is given in L.R. Sayles and M.K. Chandler, *Managing Large Systems: Organizations for the Future* (New York: Harper & Row, 1971), 253–271.

chapter 8

Project Roles, Responsibility, and Authority

All the world's a stage,
And all the men and women merely players.

William Shakespeare, As You Like It

When an organization wants to accomplish a new goal without completely restructuring itself, it uses a project team, matrix team, or task force. Responsibilities are assigned within the project, but unless it is a pure project most people are "borrowed" from other departments. Project management "gets work done through outsiders"—people from various technical, functional, and professional groups scattered throughout the parent company and outside subcontractors.[1] As Sayles and Chandler describe, project management

> calls for a new set of skills and procedures. It is dealing laterally, but not in the informal-group, informal-organization sense. It requires a capacity on the part of the manager to put together an organizational mechanism within which timely and relevant decisions are likely to be reached [as well as] a conceptual scheme for "working" interfaces...[It is a] dynamic, interactive, iterative, and intellectually challenging concept of the managerial role.[2]

Being a project manager means monitoring and influencing decisions without giving orders or making decisions in the same way as other managers. Most project managers have considerably more responsibility than authority, so they need different skills and approaches than traditional managers.

8.1 THE PROJECT MANAGER

Project Manager's Role

The project manager's role is so central that without it there would not even be project management. The project manager is the glue holding the project together and the mover and shaker spurring it on. To be a project manager, a person has to wear a lot of different hats, many at the same time; they include the hats of an integrator, communicator, decision maker, motivator, evangelist, entrepreneur, and change agent.

The importance of integration in project work was emphasized earlier. Project management integrates diverse activities and scattered elements to achieve time, cost, and performance goals. As the central figure in project management, the project manager's prime role is to *integrate everything and everybody* to accomplish these goals. The project manager has been called the organizational "metronome," the person who keeps the project's diverse elements responsive to a single, central beat.[3]

The project manager is the *hub for project communication*, the end of the funnel for all reports, requests, memoranda, and complaints. The project manager takes inputs from more sources and directs information to more receivers than anyone else. In between the sources and receivers, she refines, summarizes, and translates information to make sure that project contributors are well-informed about policies, objectives, budgets, schedules, requirements, and changes.

Being the center of communication puts the project manager in the central position of making difficult *decisions*, such as reallocating resources, changing project scope and direction, and balancing schedule, cost, and performance criteria. Even when she lacks the authority to make high-level decisions, the project manager is still best situated to influence the decisions and actions of those who do.

The prime motivation in any diverse group is strong commitment to a central goal. In a project organization, it is the project manager who instills *sense of direction* and commitment to action. There are many motivating aspects associated with project work such as spontaneity, achievement, and excitement, but these are sometimes difficult to uphold, especially when the project is long and stressful. Lack of precedent, part-time personnel, diverse specialties, infrequent contact, and spatial distance between workers are among the factors reducing motivation in projects. The successful project manager is able to foster enthusiasm, team spirit, confidence, and a reputation for excellence.

The project manager is an *evangelist* who conveys faith in the project, its value, and workability. During the conceptual phase, the would-be project manager is often the only person who sees the big picture. Whether or not it gets funded depends on her ability to gain the endorsement of top management.

The project manager is an *entrepreneur*, driven to procure funds, facilities, and people to get the project off the ground and keep it flying. She must win over reluctant functional managers who will question assigning their better people to the project. Even after work is underway, the project manager must continue to champion the cause. At any stage she might find herself fighting for the project's very existence. In the end, success or failure, the project manager is the person ultimately held accountable.

The project manager is also the *change agent* who initiates passage into new and promising areas. She is always alert to developments which could impinge on the project, ready to adopt new and innovative ideas, and striving to overcome resistance to change. As the composition and size of the project (and so the communication and reporting channels) change, the project manager is the person who orchestrates and facilitates the change. At the same time, while facilitating big changes, she resists those little ones which unnecessarily increase the scope, cost, or duration of the project.

Job Responsibilities

The project manager's principal responsibility is to deliver the project end-item within budget and time limitations, in accordance with technical specifications, and, when specified, in fulfillment of profit objectives. Other, specific responsibilities vary depending on the project manager's capabilities, the current stage of the project, the size and nature of the project, and the duties delegated by upper management. Delegated responsibility ranges at the low end from the rather limited influence of a project expeditor (where, in essence, the real project manager is the manager to whom the expeditor reports) up to the highly centralized, almost autocratic control of a pure project manager.

Though responsibilities vary, usually they include:[4]

- Planning project activities, tasks, and end results, including work breakdown, scheduling, and budgeting.
- Organizing, selecting, and placing the project team. Coordinating tasks and allocating resources.
- Interfacing with constituencies:
    Negotiating with and integrating functional managers, contractors, consultants, users, and top management.
    Serving as contact with the user.
- Effectively using project team and user personnel.
- Monitoring project status.
- Identifying technical and functional problems.
- Solving problems directly or knowing where to find help.
- Dealing with crises and resolving conflicts
- Recommending termination or redirecting efforts when objectives cannot be achieved.

Spanning all of these is the umbrella responsibility for integration, coordination, and direction of all project elements and life-cycle stages. This responsibility involves (1) identifying interfaces between the activities of functional departments, subcontractors, and other project contributors, (2) planning and scheduling so the efforts are integrated, and (3) monitoring progress, identifying problems, communicating the status of interfaces to contributors, and initiating and coordinating corrective action.

Risks and uncertainty are unavoidable in project environments, and the likelihood of managerial crisis, if not a certitude, is at least substantially higher than in non-project situations. The project manager takes overall responsibility for the advance planning necessary to anticipate and avoid crises.

Most project managers report in a line capacity to a senior-level executive. Their responsibility is to monitor and narrate the technical and financial status of the project and to promptly report current and anticipated errors, problems, or overruns.

Competency and Orientation

Because project managers work at the *interface* between top management and technologists they must generally have managerial ability, technical competence, and other broad qualifications. They must feel as much at home in the office talking with administrators about policies, schedules, and budgets as in the plant or on site talking to specialists and supervisors about technical issues.

The relative importance of technical awareness versus managerial competence depends on the project. In R&D projects, project management requires greater emphasis on the former because of the greater complexity of technical problems and technical orientation of members of the project team. In product development and non-technical projects, project management requires more emphasis on managerial ability because of the greater involvement of multiple, diverse functional areas. Regardless of the project, project managers must have sufficient technical awareness to understand the problems; it is stressed, however, that too much technical emphasis can lead project managers to neglect their role as manager. There is no substitute for a strong managerial orientation in the role of the project manager.

Broad background is also essential. The more highly differentiated the functional areas, the more prone they are to conflict and the harder it is to integrate them. To effectively integrate multiple, diverse functional areas, the project manager needs to know something about all of them, their techniques, procedures, and contribution to the project.

Studies indicate that the most effective project managers have goals, time, and interpersonal orientations intermediate to the functional units they integrate. In other words, they take a balanced outlook.[5] For instance, to integrate the efforts of a production department and a research department, the project manager's time perspective should be intermediate between production's short-term, weekly outlook and research's long-term, futuristic outlook.

Though most project managers cannot be expert in all functional areas of the project, they must be familiar enough with the basics to intelligently ponder ideas offered by specialists and to evaluate and make appropriate decisions. Along the same lines, to deal effectively with top management and the user, they must know about the workings and business of both parent and user organizations.

The project manager's broad background includes knowledge and proficiency in using management tools. Project managers have cost responsibility for the project, so they must understand concepts like cost estimating, budgeting, cash flow, overheads, incentives, penalties, and cost-sharing ratios. They are involved in contract agreements, so they must be informed about contract terms and implications. They are responsible for the phasing and scheduling of work to meet delivery dates, so they must be familiar with the tasks, processes, and resources necessary to execute the contract. They are responsible for enforcing schedules, so they must be knowledgeable about tools and techniques for monitoring and controlling project schedules. Many of these tools are covered in other parts of this book.

Project managers must also be effective communicators and listeners. They must be sensitive to the attitudes of project contributors regarding policies, time limits, and costs. Many members of the project team, especially non-managers, have disdain for anything nontechnical and resent the constraints imposed by schedules and budgets. Project managers must be able to communicate with and convince others about the importance of policies, budgets, schedules, and other support functions.

Project managers must be able to work *with* people and to delegate responsibility. They should be willing to prepare budgets and schedules with the cognizance and assistance of those who will have to live by them. Project managers must understand personalities, attitudes, and characteristics of people as team members and as individuals, and know how to best utilize talent even when it does not measure up to project requirements. They must be sensitive to human frailties, needs and greed, and be interventionists skilled at resolving conflict, managing stress, and coaching and counseling.

8.2 PROJECT MANAGEMENT AUTHORITY

Traditional Authority

Authority is an important subject in project management. In general, *authority* refers to a manager's power to command others to act or not to act. There are different dimensions to authority, the most familiar is that conferred by the organization, called *legal authority*. Legal authority is written in the manager's job description. It refers to delegated power, hierarchical reporting, and the control of resources. Given legal authority, people in higher offices are viewed as having the "right" to control the actions of subordinates. Often associated with legal authority is *reward power*, the power to evaluate and reward subordinates.

Another kind of authority, *charismatic authority*, stems from the power one gains by personal characteristics such as charm, personality, and appearance. People both in and outside the formal authority system can increase their ability to control others by using charisma.

Traditional management theory says that authority is always greater at higher levels in the organization and is delegated downward from one level to the next. This is presumed to be right because managers at higher levels are assumed to know more and be in the best position to make decisions, delegate responsibility, and give "command." This point has been challenged on the grounds that modern managers, particularly in technology-based organizations, cannot possibly know everything needed to make complex decisions. They often lack the necessary technical expertise and so, increasingly, rely upon subordinate specialists for advice. Even managers who are technically skilled cannot always perform their management tasks alone; they rely upon staff groups for personnel and budgetary assistance.

Influence

It is important for project managers to distinguish between legal authority and the *ability* to influence others. Managers with legal authority have the power to influence subordinates by giving orders and controlling salaries and promotions. Generally however, the most effective managers are able to influence others *without* "commanding" them or making issue of their superior- subordinate relationship (this is especially true when subordinates are well-educated or highly experienced). In fact, managers who rely solely on their legal authority are often relatively ineffective at influencing people.

In other words, even without legal authority and reward power, it is possible to influence people by using other sources of influence such as (1) *knowledge* and (2) *personality*.[6] The first source of influence, called *expert power*, refers to a special level of knowledge or competence attributed to the holder of the power. The recipient of the power believes that the information possessed by the holder is relevant and that he himself does not have that information. Simply, the power holder is seen as being right because of his knowledge, and others readily defer to his opinions or directives.

The other source of influence, called *referent power*, is power derived from rapport, personal attraction, friendship, alliances, and reciprocal favors. The recipient identifies with the power holder and conveys certain rights or additional weight to him.

Given expert power and referent power, the issue of influence in organizations can be approached irrespective of the formal hierarchy and legal authority. Clearly these two kinds of power provide ample means for people to gain influence over others *despite* the formal authority system. In the informal organization, for example, they allow one member in a work group to influence all the rest (sometimes more than the group's supervisor). Even within the formal hierarchy, referent and expert power can subtly reverse the authority relationship. A subordinate may exert considerable influence over her superior if the superior comes to rely upon the subordinate for information or advice, or if a bond of trust, respect, or affection develops between them. Everyone has seen this happen, and history is replete with examples: Alexandria was Queen of Russia; Rasputin was a lowly priest.

Authority in Projects

Most kinds of managers rely upon multiple forms of influence—knowledge, expertise, persuasion, and personal relationships; when these fail, however, they still have their legal power to fall back on. But in project management this is seldom the case. Except in the extreme case of the manager of a pure project, most often the typical project manager *lacks any form of traditional legal authority.*

Unlike traditional organizations where influence and authority flow vertically, in project management influence and authority flow horizontally and diagonally. The project manager exists *outside* the traditional hierarchy. The role is only temporary, superimposed on the existing structure, and so is not privy to the leverage afforded by hierarchical position. Project managers work across functional and organization lines and (except for members of the project office) have no subordinates reporting to them in a direct line capacity. The issue is further complicated in matrix organizations because, although project managers have a permanent role, they must share formal authority with functional managers.

Thus, despite the considerable degree of responsibility they carry, most project managers do not have the formal authority to carry it out. They have instead what is called *project authority*, meaning they can make decisions about project objectives, policies, schedules and budgets, but cannot give orders backing up those decisions.

This disparity between much formal responsibility and little formal authority has been referred to as the *authority gap*.[7] What it means is that project managers must rely upon other forms of influence. "How to make friends and influence people" is not an academic issue for project managers.

Project Manager's Authority

Regardless of the size of the authority gap, most project managers handle it in much the same way. In cases where project managers are given no legal authority they have no choice but to rely entirely upon influence derived from expert power and referent power. Yet even in larger projects where they do have legal authority, their strongest source of influence tends to be in their professional reputations. This is because in virtually all projects—task force, matrix, or pure project, project managers *depend* on others to get the job done. They have few resources of their own and must rely upon functional managers and support units for personnel and facilities. Numerous decisions must be made for which project managers lack time or expertise, so they depend upon others to investigate and suggest courses of action. To successfully implement decisions, people must be committed to supporting them. Project commitment cannot be achieved through force but must be made at the personal level and come from mutual understanding and agreement with functional managers and supervisors.

The project manager's real source of influence tends to reside in a network of alliances, the quality of which depend heavily upon her reputation and personal achievements. Such reputations are gained through recognition of accomplishment, not by organization charter. Even when project managers have legal authority, they seldom resort to it since unilateral decisions and commands are inconsistent with the need for reciprocity and tradeoffs in projects. Recognizing that not all information and decisions need to be channeled through them, effective project managers encourage direct contact between individuals involved, regardless of level.

In summary, successful project managers, no matter how much formal authority they possess, tend to rely upon knowledge, experience, and personal relationships for influence (Figure 8–1). To build expert-based power, effective project managers must be perceived as technically and administratively competent (initially through their experience and reputation, later through the correctness of their decisions). To build referent-based power, they must develop effective interpersonal, persuasion, and negotiation skills.

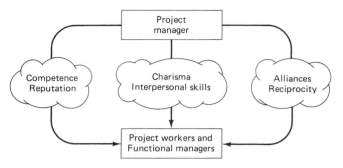

FIGURE 8–1. Project manager's sources of influence.

This does not mean that the project manager never uses legal authority or the power of command. *If* the project manager has such authority, there are doubtless many cases where she needs to use it. These are situational, depending on the task at hand and the willingness of subordinates to take responsibility. This subject is discussed more in the next chapter.

The Balance of Power

Since project managers (with the sometime exception of the pure project managers) share authority with functional managers, what relative balance of power between them is optimal? Some theorists say that project and functional managers should share power equally. But the concept of power has several dimensions, and according to some research not all of these dimensions should be balanced equally.[8] In the best performing projects, authority is clearly differentiated: project managers are given the power to obtain the backing of top management, to procure critical resources and coordinate work efforts, and to mediate conflicts; in contrast, functional managers are given greater power to make decisions over technical problems and the technology used.

Even in the usual circumstance where project managers do not have reward power, it is beneficial for them to be *perceived* by workers as having the same or greater reward power as functional managers. This is important because (whether or not true) unless project personnel see *both* managers influencing their salaries and promotions, they will tend to follow only the one with the most influence.

8.3 SELECTING THE PROJECT MANAGER

Four categories of qualifications can be listed for the successful project manager: personal characteristics, behavioral skills, general business skills, and technical skills.

Personal Characteristics

Archibald lists the following as essential personal characteristics:[9]

- flexible and adaptable
- preference for initiative and leadership

- confidence, persuasiveness, verbal fluency
- effective communicator and integrator
- able to balance technical solutions with time, cost, and human factors
- well-organized and disciplined
- a generalist rather than a specialist
- able to devote most of his time to planning and controlling
- able to identify problems and to make decisions
- able to devote the time and effort and to maintain a proper balance in use of time

These characteristics are important because of both the environment where the project manager works and the responsibilities and restrictions placed on the role. Obviously, project managers must be able to work in situations where there are constant deadlines, great uncertainty, starts ups and close outs, and constant change in goals, tasks, people, and relationships. At the same time, they must be able to gain the respect, trust, and confidence of others.

Behavioral Skills

A project manager needs strong behavioral and interpersonal skills.[10] In particular, she must be an active listener, active communicator, and able to capitalize on informal communication channels. To be an active listener, a project manager must master the art of questioning for clarification and paraphrasing to insure she understands verbal messages. She must know how to build trust, promote team esprit, and reward cooperation through praise and credit (often the only forms of reward she has). To be able to facilitate communication and integrate technical work she has to know the jargon used by specialists.

General Business Skills

The project manager is, after all, a *manager* and so should have general business skills too. These should include:

- An understanding of the organization and the business.
- An understanding of general management—marketing, control, contract work, purchasing, law, personal administration, and (in profit environments) the general concept of profitability.
- An ability to translate business requirements into project and system requirements.
- A strong, active, continuous interest in teaching, training, and developing subordinates.

Technical Skills

To make informed decisions, project managers must be able to grasp the technical aspects of the project. In non- or low-technology environments, understanding can be developed through experience and informal training. In high-technology projects, qualifications are more rigorous, usually including a career molded in the technology environment and a knowledge of many fields of science or engineering.[11]

Although project managers seldom do technical analysis, they must be technically qualified and have the intuition to formulate and make technical judgments. In a technical project, the project manager:

> must be capable of both integration and analysis, and must understand that the rigorous training of professional technologists with its emphasis on analysis sometimes impairs their integrative ability.[12]

To fulfill management requirements for both technical and general business competence, projects sometimes have two managers—one technical and one administrative. This often happens in construction projects where the architect is responsible for technical matters while the so-called project manager handles administrative "paperwork." The arrangement tends to complicate problems of coordination, communication, and authority because the two of them must share responsibility. Further, when the project manager becomes subservient to the architect, his ability to perform the role is compromised. Another example is the motion picture industry. The movie *producer* is the person who manages the resources, schedules, and budgets (in essence, the project manager), while the *director* is the person who oversees technical-artistic matters. Sometimes they are the same person, though often not. Because the shooting of a motion picture is an artistic pursuit, directors need flexibility in budgets and shooting schedules that allow them to create, but since costs matter too, the producer is always faced with the question "what price creativity?" It is no surprise that they do not always have an amicable relationship.[13] Still, in the eyes of the movie industry the role of the project manager is highly regarded. When the Academy Award is given for "Best Picture," it is always awarded to the picture's producer.

Selection and Recruiting

Project managers are selected from among the ranks of product and functional managers, functional specialists, and experienced project managers. Though the last source is preferred (provided the chosen manager has a successful project record) it is often the least feasible. It is difficult to find an experienced project manager who has the right mix of qualifications and whose current project ends just when the new one is to begin. As a result when experienced project managers are needed they often must be recruited from the outside. This is readily observable in the Sunday job listings of most major metropolitan newspapers (Figure 8–2 shows a sampling). The problem with recruiting outsiders is the time it takes for them to make friends, build alliances, and learn organizational procedures and policies. These problems are offset by benefits, however, such as when the project needs an objective outsider to overhaul procedures, or when all of the insider candidates are seen as enemies by their colleagues.

The role of project manager is also filled by transferring or promoting functional managers. The problem with this is the difficulty they sometimes experience in shifting from a functional to a project perspective. A functional manager must make the adjustment from working in just one area to overseeing and integrating the work of all areas, an adjustment that requires considerable effort and inclination. Also, unless he has abundant well-rounded experience he will be perceived by other managers as just another functional manager.

Senior Project Manager

We need aggressive, innovative, top-flight professionals to manage large-scale, complex building design projects. Degree and registration, plus a minimum of 10 years solid U.S. experience in putting buildings together.

Complete management responsibilities for scheduling, resource planning, feasibility studies, design and design/build for multi-million dollar projects.

PROJECT ENGINEERS

5-6 years of project management experience in the design of electro-mechanical products. Your track record of managing projects from inception thru completion should include: project and material planning, costing and product testing. A BSME is required with exposure to electrical engineering preferred. Supervisory and decision making skills.

PROJECT COORDINATOR

Move into this key position with the company that moves America...

Here you will assist/support a project team which analyzes the work flow/efficiency of several departments. Position involves: Heavy utilization of a PC; analyzing and assembling reports; independent research; identifying information pertinent to various projects; maintenance and control of all files; designing and developing PC forms and reports. Candidate will also perform various other duties as needed.

Requirements include 3-5 years of equivalent project coordination experience, preferably within a corporate environment, highly developed PC, communication and organization skills

PROJECT MANAGER

We are a rapidly growing ENR 400 firm with an outstanding opportunity for a Project Manager. Responsibilities relate to activities for environmental audits and site assessments.

The successful candidate should have project management capabilities and hazardous waste background. Business development experience is also desirable.

SYSTEMS PROJECT ANALYSTS/LEADERS

Federal Savings and Loan Association has excellent professional opportunities for experienced Systems Project Analysts/Leaders. Immediate opportunities are available in the areas of telecommunications, McCormack and Dodge financial systems, and savings and loan financial systems, including installment lending and mortgage banking applications.

Ideal candidates must possess a college degree in business administration, or computer science with a business administration background, and have at least 5 years of experience in systems project implementation, operations analysis, and finance/accounting. Direct exposure and/or experience in savings and loans, other financial institutions, or mortgage banks is desirable.

Specific systems experience should include structured project management experience, through implementation. Candidates must also possess project supervisory and excellent communication skills.

CORPORATE PROJECT MANAGER

National manufacturer of transportation equipment is seeking an experienced individual to assume responsibilities as their Corporate Project Manager.

Candidates must possess a Bachelor of Science degree including some programming training. Three to five years experience within Production or Engineering Management within the primary metal fabrication industry is desired with experience working with mini and micro computers. Additionally, the preferred candidate will be experienced in modern inventory control techniques within a heavy manufacturing environment. Initial responsibilities of this function will be the analysis and installation of systems within a manufacturing environment with the successful incumbent becoming a candidate for executive management responsibility.

PROJECT ENGINEER

Design Company, the nation's leading manufacturer of private label vitamins, over-the-counter drugs and beauty products has an immediate need for a Project Engineer.

RESPONSIBILITIES. This position will be responsible for managing a variety of specification, design, and implementation projects in our manufacturing process area, and will also include providing assistance to the maintenance group and other engineering departments as needed.

QUALIFICATIONS. A BS in Mechanical Engineering, Chemical Engineering or related degree will be required, as well as 5 years project experience, preferable in a processing manufacturing environment.

PROJECT MANAGER TECHNICAL SERVICES

Our client, a leading organization located in Texas, has retained us to assist them in recruiting a top level ELECTRICAL ENGINEER to manage hardware and software projects which support the services provided by the company's operating units.

The successful candidate will report to corporate manager of Technical Services and must possess a BS degree in Electrical Engineering and a minimum of 5 years experience. Experience should include: electronic hardware design, assembly language programming.

Project Supervisor

Looking for a challenging career with the leader in the communications industry? An opportunity is currently available for the qualified professional with knowledge and skill in communications.

As a member of the Advanced Service Organization, the successful candidate will be involved in coordinating the installation of communications technology.

Strong interpersonal skills are essential as is the ability to work productively in a fast-paced, unstructured environment. This position requires a background in coordinating project installations and/or the communications industry.

PROGRAM DIRECTOR

A major social service agency in Chicago is seeking a Program Director for an adult day training program for persons who are blind & developmentally delayed. Responsibilities include planning, organizing and supervising the activities

PROGRAM DIRECTOR

is seeking a Program Director for an 85 bed inpatient chemical dependency treatment center. Doctoral level psychologist or MSW with extensive management experience in large inpatient facility required.

FIGURE 8–2.   Advertisements for project management positions.

Project management assignments are also filled by promoting non-managerial specialists (engineers, scientists, system analysts, product specialists, etc.). The problem with this is the same as with putting any non-manager into a management role: he must first learn how to manage. Administrative and technical abilities differ sharply, and just because a person is a good engineer or auditor does not mean he will be a good project manager. Besides learning how to manage, specialists must learn how to separate themselves from their area of specialty and become generalists.

Ideally, the person selected as project manager is someone who can stay with the project for its duration and whose assignment will not conflict with existing lines of authority or reporting relationships. It is a bad idea, for example, to put a functional specialist in a project management position having authority over her former manager.

Training

Since project management skills cannot be learned quickly, organizations devote substantial time and expense in preparing individuals for careers in project management. Some sponsor internal training programs that focus on the special requirements of their organizations; others use external seminars and university programs. Recent years have seen a rapid proliferation in both kinds of training programs.

There is no substitute for real experience. Many organizations allow people of promise who aspire to become project managers to benefit from on-the-job training.[14] As part of their career paths, technical specialists work full or part-time as administrative assistants to experienced project managers—like serving an apprenticeship. Not only does this give them management exposure, but it tests their aptitude and talent for being a manager. Valued specialists with little managerial aptitude or ability are given other career opportunities commensurate with their skills and interests.

Moving into the Role

Project management responsibilities range from few and mundane on simple projects to extensive and challenging on complex projects. Presumably, the person in the role of project manager is qualified and wants the responsibility; still, his burden can be eased if, upon moving into the role, he has the following:[15]

- an understanding of what has to be done
- an understanding of his authority and its limits
- an understanding of his relationship with others in the project
- knowledge of what specific results constitute a job well done
- knowledge of when and what he is doing exceptionally well, and when and where he is falling short
- an awareness of what can and should be done to correct unsatisfactory results

- the belief that his superiors have an interest and believe in him
- the belief that his superiors are eager for him to succeed

The effect of not having these is to diminish the project manager's effectiveness. Senior management must give the project manager the necessary assurances and information; ultimately, however, it rests with the project manager to obtain these and ensure that they will continue throughout the project.

8.4 WAYS OF FILLING THE PROJECT MANAGEMENT ROLE

Organizations use various titles for the role of project manager including "program manager," "project director," "task force chairman," or others. The titles "task force coordinator" and "project engineer" are also used, though these usually imply more focused roles with less responsibility than other forms. The most effective project manager role is when one person becomes involved during proposal preparation and stays on until the project is completed. Since it is often difficult to find someone early in the project who is competent enough to see the project through (or have someone who will not be transferred before the project is completed), the role is filled in other ways. For example, the role can be assumed by the general manager or plant manager, though most top managers have neither the time to devote to a project nor the flexibility to shift roles. Alternatively, the role can be assigned temporarily to a functional manager. The consequence is that she must divide her time between the project and her department, and both may suffer. Also, these combination functional-project managers may have trouble gaining cooperation from other functional managers because they are seen as competitors for status and resources. In long-term projects, responsibility is sometimes passed from one functional manager to the next as the project progresses. The problem here is that the process lacks an oversight person who can insure continuity from one phase to the next. Managers at later stages inherit problems developed earlier for which they are not responsible and may not be aware.

Sometimes project responsibility is divided among several people, one each for scheduling, budgeting, marketing, technical performance, and so on. This is common practice in technological projects where, as mentioned earlier, responsibility is split between a technical project manager and an administrative project manager. The problem with this arrangement is in having two or more project management roles with no one to integrate them.

The project management role is optimally filled by one person. Normally the position is a full-time project manager, though it can be part-time or time shared among multiple projects as long as project management responsibilities are adequately fulfilled. The practice of one person managing multiple small projects can be an advantage because it puts the project manager in a good position to resolve resource and priority conflicts between projects and to negotiate resources for several projects at once with functional managers.

8.5 ROLES IN THE PROJECT TEAM

In the early stages of a project, the project manager and functional managers divide the overall objective into work tasks. This division is used to determine skill requirements and is the basis for personnel selection and subcontracting. Anybody who contributes to the project at any time, such as people from functional support areas, contractors, and the project office, is considered part of the *project team*. This section describes roles and responsibilities of members of the project team.

Members Serving the Project Office

Chapter 7 described the purpose of the project office and its place in the organization. This section focuses on specific roles of members of the project office. The example shown in Figure 8–3 is for an engineering-development project like the one discussed in Chapter 7. Besides the project manager and representatives to functional departments, the following roles typically serve in the project office:

The *project engineer* shoulders responsibility for coordinating technological areas and assuring integrated design of the project end-item. The responsibility encompasses system analysis and engineering, design, interface control, system integration and test, and configuration management.[16] When several functional areas are involved, the project engineer

1. oversees product or system design and development;
2. translates performance requirements into design requirements;
3. oversees communication, coordination, and direction of functional areas and sub-contractors;
4. plans, monitors, evaluates, and documents progress in design and test of subsystems; and
5. plans, monitors, and evaluates system integration tests.

The project engineer also oversees configuration management—the purpose is to have uniform communication media for all areas and activities for identifying, document-ing, and controlling information. Configuration management is used in projects where it is necessary to review frequent changes during system design and development, and to control and document these changes in ways that account for their impacts on related components and the overall system.

The title project engineer sometimes denotes a person having full project manager responsibilities; more typically it refers to the more limited role described here.

The *contract administrator*[17] is responsible for project legal aspects such as autho-rizations to begin work and subcontracting with outside firms. Contract administrators are involved in preparing the proposal, defining and negotiating the contract, integrating contract requirements into project plans, assuring the project fulfills contractual obliga-tions, identifying and defining changes to project scope, and communicating the comple-

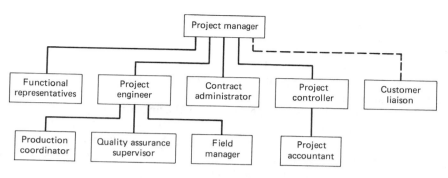

FIGURE 8–3.   Members in a project office

tion of milestones to the customer. During closeout, they notify customers of fulfilled obligations, document customer acceptance of the end-item, and initiate formal requests for payment. They are also responsible for collecting and storing RFP's, project correspondence, legal documents, contract modifications, bills, payment vouchers, and other records and documents.

The *project controller*[18] assists the project manager in planning, controlling, reporting, and evaluation. She works with functional managers to define tasks and interrelationships on the work breakdown structure, and to identify individuals responsible for controlling tasks. She also maintains work package files and cost summaries, releases approved work authorization documents, monitors work progress, evaluates schedule and cost progress, and revises estimates of time and cost to complete the project. The project controller prepares and negotiates revisions to budgets, schedules, and work authorizations, drafts progress reports to users and upper management, and closes cost accounts upon completion.

The *project accountant* provides financial and accounting assistance to the project manager. He establishes procedures for utilizing the PMIS (see Chapter 16), assists in identifying tasks to be controlled, establishes cost account numbers, prepares cost estimates for tasks, validates reported information, and investigates financial problems.

The *customer liaison* is the customer's or user's technical representative. She participates in technical discussions and ongoing reviews (within the bounds of the contract) and helps expedite contract changes. She is responsible for maintaining amicable contractor-customer relations.

The *production coordinator* plans, monitors, and coordinates production aspects of the project. His responsibility includes reviewing all engineering documents released to manufacturing; developing requirements for releases, equipment, and parts; monitoring procurement and assembly of parts, materials, and processes for the end-item; monitoring manufacturing costs; developing schedules for production related activities; and serving as liaison between project management and the production department.

The *field manager* oversees installation, testing, maintenance, and handing over to the customer of the project end-item. Her responsibilities include scheduling field operations, monitoring field operations costs, supervision of field personnel, and liaison with the project manager.

The *quality assurance supervisor* establishes and administers inspection procedures to assure fulfillment of all quality related requirements. Overall, his responsibility is to raise awareness of quality and to institute means for improving work methods and producing zero defects.

Members of the office charge their work time to the project or to an overhead account. They are assigned to the office only as necessary—when they must be in frequent contact with the project manager or other project office personnel, or when their services are required continuously and for an extended period. When their tasks are completed they return to their functional departments.

The project manager should try to keep the office staff small. This increases the flexibility of functional staffing to the project, minimizes duplication of personnel costs and reassignment problems, and requires less effort from the project manager.

Functional Managers

Often the glamour of the work sits on the project side and functional managers see their roles diminished. Nonetheless, if earlier discussions led to the impression that functional managers are somehow subservient to the project manager, that was not the intention. Both functional and project organizations depend on each other to achieve project goals. Functional managers are responsible for maintaining the technical competence of their disciplines and for staffing, organizing, and executing project tasks *within their functional areas*. They and the project manager work together to define tasks and develop plans, schedules, and budgets for each work package.

Since personnel in project organizations are shifted from one project to another, their only permanence is in a functional "home." Unlike the project manager who tends to solicit "human resources" solely in terms of what is best for her project, a functional manager is more likely to look out for the interest of the people being solicited. The functional manager is responsible for the hiring, performance review, compensation, professional development, and career paths of the people in his area.

In most project organizations, functional managers retain much the same authority and responsibility as in nonproject environments. Nevertheless, some functional managers believe that the project manager undercuts their authority and that they could handle the project better if it were exclusively in their domain. Project managers who try to establish empires, undermine the authority, or otherwise confirm the suspicions of captious functional managers will have difficulty in obtaining the functional support they need.

It is important that the technical role of the functional manager not be allowed to diminish. Before a project begins, technical responsibilities and contributions to technical content should be clearly delineated and defined for each functional manager.[19] This insures maintenance of a continued strong technical base for all projects and alleviates much of the animosity between functional and project managers.

Project Functional Leaders and Work Package Supervisors

In large projects each functional manager (sometimes with the help of the project manager) selects someone as *project functional leader*. This person serves as project-functional liaison between the project manager and the functional manager. Through the project manager, this person plans his department's portion of the total project plan, makes sure it is consistent with total project objectives, and supervises all project work performed by the department.

In still larger projects, the work for a project in a given department is divided into multiple, clearly defined tasks called work packages. Responsibility for each work package is delegated to a *work package supervisor* who reports to the functional leader. The work package supervisor prepares the plan, schedule, and budget for the work package, supervises the technical effort, and reports progress.

8.6 ROLES OUTSIDE THE PROJECT TEAM

The Manager of Projects

The *manager of projects* (called the vice-president of projects, director of projects, or other title) is positioned in the hierarchy at the same level as functional executives. The manager of projects oversees multiple projects and relieves top level managers of most project related responsibilities. The manager of projects:[20]

- Directs and evaluates the activities of all project managers.
- Ensures that the stream of projects is consistent with the strategic objectives of the organization.
- Works with functional heads to allocate resources and resolve priority conflicts between projects.
- Assists in development of project management policies, planning and control techniques and systems.
- Ensures consistency among projects and that changes in any one are integrated with the cost, schedule, and performance objectives of the others.

In matrix organizations, the manager of projects also serves as liaison between the Office of Projects and top management.

Top Management

Top management is usually restricted to establishing organizational missions and goals and developing policies and strategies to accomplish them. Depending on the size of the organization and the nature of the project, its involvement with project management varies. In smaller organizations top management takes on the responsibilities of the manager of projects. To ensure that projects are consistent with organizational goals, top management usually makes all final evaluations and approvals. In addition, top management approves the project feasibility study, selects the project manager, and authorizes the project to begin. In very small organizations, the company manager or general manager is the project manager.

Top management is ultimately responsible for successful implementation of project *management*. For project management to be effective, top management must first:[21]

- Clearly define the project manager's responsibility and authority relative to other managers.
- Define the scope and limitations on the project manager's decision making responsibilities.
- Establish policies for resolving conflicts and setting priorities.
- Prescribe the objectives against which the project manager's performance will be evaluated.
- Plan and give support to a project management system that provides information necessary for planning, control, review, and evaluation of projects.

Project managers exercise the authority granted by, and on behalf of, the senior executive or manager of projects, as stated in the organization charter. In complex situations, critical negotiations, or unresolvable conflict, top management may pre-empt the authority of the project manager.

8.7 INTERFACES AMONG PROJECT AND FUNCTIONAL ROLES

Clearly no project manager works in a vacuum. Perhaps in more than any other managerial position, the project managers' authority and responsibilities are defined by their relationships with other roles. Because of the multiple interfaces in the role, and the disparity between responsibility and authority, relationships in project management are neither simple nor self-explanatory.

For example, if misunderstood or neglected, the project-functional interface can easily result in competition for resources and conflict in reporting relationships. All involved functional and project managers should jointly participate in preparing and documenting policies that define their authority/responsibility relationships. The roles, responsibilities and relationships in the project can then be summarized as in Figure 8–4.[22] The numerous subdivision of roles and responsibilities shown in the example are for a large project; in smaller projects the relationships would be similar, but with less delegation and fewer roles. In small projects, functional managers are the project-functional interface and take on the responsibilities of project-functional leaders and work package supervisors.

8.8 SUMMARY

Central to project management is the role of project manager. Project managers work at the project-functional-user interface to integrate project elements to achieve time, cost, and performance objectives. They have ultimate responsibility for the success of projects.

Despite their pivotal role most project managers are outside the traditional hierarchy and have little formal authority. To achieve their ends, they tend to rely heavily upon negotiations, alliances, favors, and reciprocal agreements. Their strongest source of influence is in the respect they gain through skillful and competent administration.

In high performing projects, project managers have influence over matters concerning critical resources and organizational support, while functional managers have authority over technical matters. Successful project managers are perceived as both technically and administratively competent. They have a strong business orientation as well as an understanding of the technology of the project. They also have strong behavioral skills and the ability to function effectively in risky, changing environments.

The role of project manager is best filled by one person who becomes involved at proposal preparation and stays on until the project is completed. Sharing or rotating the role among several people is usually less effective.

Project managers get work done through a team composed of people from various functional and support groups scattered throughout the parent company and outside subcontractors. Part of the team, the project office, provides administrative assistance and services. Others, the functional managers, contribute primarily to the technical content of the project, though they also share responsibility for developing tasks, plans, schedules and budgets for work in their areas. They maintain the technical base upon which projects draw. The project team may also include project-functional leaders and work package supervisors who are responsible for the tasks and work packages performed in individual functional departments.

Top management and the manager of projects also play key roles in project management. Top management establishes the policies, responsibilities, and authority relationships through which project management is conducted. The manager of projects insures that projects are consistent with organization goals and resolves priority and resource conflicts between multiple projects.

In project work there is always some risk and uncertainty, and in project organizations there is always some confusion and conflict. Many people find project work challenging, rewarding, and exhilarating; but without question, many also find it taxing, distressful, even destructive. It is when the distressful aspects of projects overcome the motivating ones that projects fail. One qualification of a good project manager is the ability to see projects in human terms—as systems of individuals and groups of people. To increase the chances of project success—and to minimize human casualties along the way—a project manager must have behavioral skills for dealing with groups and individuals. These skills include being able to take disparate individuals and groups and mold them into a single, cohesive team, and to recognize and deal effectively with personal and work conflicts and emotional stress. These are the subjects of the next two chapters.

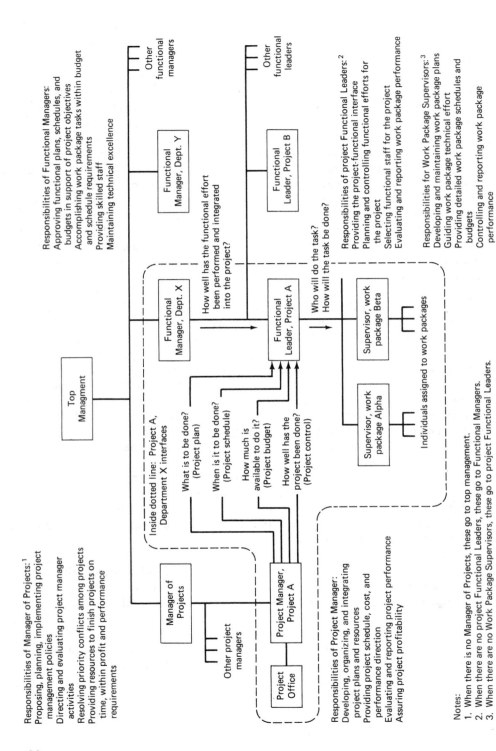

FIGURE 8–4. Summary of managerial roles, responsibilities, and interrelationships. (Adopted with permission from David Cleland and William King, *Systems Analysis and Project Management*, 3rd ed. (New York: McGraw-Hill, 1983) 332, 353.)

Exercise: The LOGON project

Top management of the STING Company has decided to adopt a project-management form of organization for the LOGON project. As a consultant to top management you have been given two tasks to help implement this. First, you must develop a project management policy statement and a project manager job description. Your policy statement should define the project manager's role with respect to other functional managers, as well as clarify the role of functional managers in the project. Your job description must define the specific responsibilities and legal authority of the project manager. You should consider the reactions of functional managers to the policy statement and job description and how best to get them to "buy into" them. How can you give the project manager sufficient authority to manage the LOGON project without usurping the authority of other managers who must give their support (many of whom have been with the STING company for over twenty years)? You should also suggest to top management what forms of evaluation can be used on project team members as an incentive to work together toward project goals. Remember, the functional departments are also currently involved in other repetitive and project activities.

Your second task is to specify and document the qualifications for the position of LOGON project manager. After considering the nature of the project (technical scope, risks, complexity, etc.) as described in the previous chapter, prepare a list of specific qualifications—general background and experience, personality characteristics, managerial, technical, and interpersonal skills—to be used to screen candidates and make the final selection. STING has some employees who have worked as project coordinators and expediters, but no one with experience as a pure project or matrix manager. Consider the assumptions and pros and cons of selecting a functional manager or technical specialist from inside STING or an experienced project manager from outside the company. A contract has been signed and LOGON is to begin in four months.

CHAPTER REVIEW QUESTIONS

1. What is the project manager's primary role?
2. What is meant by "the project manager is an evangelist, entrepreneur, and change agent?"
3. Does the fact that the project manager must be resistant to change contradict being a change agent?
4. Describe the typical responsibilities of a project manager. In what ways are responsibilities such as budgeting, scheduling, and controlling considered to be integration and coordination responsibilities?
5. Discuss the relative need for both technical and managerial competence in project management.
6. Why is a "broad background" essential for the project manager? What *is* a broad background?
7. Describe what is meant by legal authority. How does it differ from charismatic authority?
8. Describe how and in what ways people in organizations, regardless of hierarchical position, influence others.
9. How does the authority of the typical project manager differ from authority of other managers?
10. What is meant by the "authority gap?"

11. What is the most frequently used source of influence among project managers? How does the project manager use this and other sources of influence to induce functional managers to release their personnel to the project?

12. List the ideal qualifications—personal, behavioral, technical—for project managers. How do they differ from the qualifications for functional managers? How do these vary depending on the project?

13. Discuss the considerations in selecting a project manager from among each of the following groups: experienced project managers, functional managers, functional specialists.

14. Discuss the pros and cons in the various ways of filling the role of project manager (e.g., part-time, multiple project managers for one project, one manager for multiple projects, etc.).

15. How are project managers trained on the job? What are the advantages and drawbacks of relying upon on-the-job training as a source for project managers?

16. Describe the responsibilities of key members of the project office for a large-scale project.

17. Describe the responsibilities of the manager of projects.

18. Describe the project related responsibilities of top management.

19. Describe the responsibilities of the functional manager, the project *leader*, and the work-package supervisor in project management, and their interfaces with one another and with the project manager.

QUESTIONS ABOUT THE STUDY PROJECT

1. In your project, what is the formal title given to the role of project manager?

2. Where in the organization structure is the project manager? Show this on an organization chart.

3. Describe in one sentence the overall role for the project manager of your project. Now, list his or her *specific* responsibilities.

4. In your opinion, is the so-called project manager the REAL project manager or is someone else controlling the project? If the latter, what effect does this have on the project manager's ability to influence the project?

5. Would you describe the project manager's orientation as being more technical or more managerial? Explain.

6. Describe the project manager's professional background. Has it helped or hindered his or her ability to be a project manager? (You might pose this question to the project manager.)

7. Describe the kind of authority given to the project manager. (How much legal authority and reward power does the project manager have?) How does he or she *know* this; is his or her authority specified in the organization charter, the job description, or elsewhere?

8. How big would you say is the project manager's authority gap? Explain. Does the project manager have any complaints about it?

9. From where does this organization get its project managers? Does it have a procedure or seminars for training and selecting project managers? Where did the manager of your project come from?

10. How does this project manager fill the role: part- or full-time, shared or rotated with other managers, manager of several projects at once? Explain. Does the project manager have enough time to do an effective job? Would another way of filling the position be more effective?

11. Is there a project office? If not, how are the responsibilities (e.g., for contract administration) handled? If so, who is in the project office (a project engineer, contract administrator, field representative, etc.)? Are they on loan, full-time, or part-time? Describe their responsibilities.

12. What functional managers are involved in this project? Describe their responsibilities in the project, decisions they make unilaterally, and decisions they share with the project manager.

13. Is there a manager of projects? If so, describe his or her responsibilities and influence on this particular project.

14. What has been the role of top management in your project? What, in general, is the involvement of top management in projects in this organization?

ENDNOTES

1. L.R. Sayles and M.K. Chandler, *Managing Large Systems: Organizations for the Future* (New York: Harper and Row, 1971), 204.

2. Ibid., 212.

3. Ibid., 204.

4. Russell Archibald, *Managing High-Technology Programs and Projects* (New York: Wiley-Interscience, 1976), 35; William Atkins, "Selecting a Project Manager," *Journal of Systems Management* (October 1980), 34; and Daniel Roman, *Managing Projects: A Systems Approach* (New York: Elsevier, 1986), 419.

5. Paul Lawrence and Jay Lorsch, *Organization and Environment: Managing Differentiation and Integration* (Boston: Graduate School of Business, Harvard University, 1967), Chap. III.

6. These bases of interpersonal power were first described by J.P.R. French and B. Raven, "The Bases of Social Power," reprinted in *Group Dynamics*, 3rd ed., D. Cartwright and A. Zander, eds. (New York: Harper and Row, 1968), 259–269.

7. Richard Hodgetts, "Leadership Techniques in the Project Organization," *Academy of Management Journal*, Vol. 11 (June 1968), 211–219.

8. R. Katz and T.J. Allen, "Project Performance and the Locus of Influence in the R&D Matrix," *Academy of Management Journal*, Vol. 28, No. 1 (March 1985), 67–87.

9. Archibald, *Managing High-Technology Programs*, 55.

10. J.R. Adams, S.E. Barndt, and M.D. Martin, *Managing by Project Management* (Dayton: Universal Technology, 1979), 137.

11. P.O. Gaddis, "The Project Manager," *Harvard Business Review* (May–June 1959), 89–97.

12. Ibid., 95.

13. An example is the 1984 movie *Heaven's Gate* where the director was allowed to virtually dominate the movie's producers. Originally scheduled for completion in six months at a cost of $7.5 million, the production ended up being released a year late and $28 million *over* budget. The movie was a box office flop and helped clinch the demise of United Artists Corp. which had to underwrite the expense. From: Steven Bach, *Final Cut* (New York: William Morrow, 1985).

14. Roman, *Managing Projects*, 439–440.

15. Harold Kerzner, *Project Management: A Systems Approach to Planning, Scheduling, and Controlling* (New York: Van Nostrand Reinhold, 1979), 99.

16. These responsibilities are for project engineers in engineering-development projects, as described in W.P. Chase, *Management of Systems Engineering* (New York: Wiley- Interscience, 1974), 25–29.

17. According to Archibald, *Managing High-Technology Programs*, 124–128, 199.

18. Ibid., 128–131.

19. Katz and Allen, "Project Performance and the Locus of Influence," 83–84.

20. David Cleland and William King, *Systems Analysis and Project Management*, 3rd ed. (New York: McGraw-Hill, 1983), 358.

21. Ibid., 362–363.

22. Ibid., 332 and 353.

chapter 9

Managing Projects Through Participation and Teamwork

Eh! je suis leur chef, il fallait bien les suivre.
Ah well! I am their leader, I really ought to follow them!

Alexandre Auguste Ledru-Rollin, 1857

A leader is best when people barely know that he exists.
Of a good leader, who talks little, when his work is done, his aims fulfilled, they will say, "We did this ourselves."

Lao-tzu, The Way of Life

During the manned landings on the moon in the early 1970s, a study was conducted of NASA project management by researcher Richard Chapman.[1] This was during NASA's heyday—a period marked by extraordinary achievements and a time when NASA was upheld as exemplary of a large agency that worked, and worked well. It is interesting and instructive to begin this chapter with a few of Chapman's comments about the project managers of that era:

> [In addition to technical competence and management capacity] all agree that the project manager must have the ability...to build a cohesive project team. (p.93)
>
> Those project managers who [developed the most closely- knit project teams emphasized] decentralized decision making [and] technical problem-solving at the level where both the problem and most experience reside. [They encouraged project members] to feel a sense of responsibility for problem-solving at their respective levels, within the assigned guidelines... (p.83)
>
> Most project staffs believe that they receive generous support and attention from the project manager. Most also acknowledge that the project manager is vigorous and fair in bestowing recognition on team members and in rewarding them to the best of his capability. (p.82)

In another NASA study, E. H. Kloman compared the performance of two large projects, Lunar Orbiter and Surveyor. Lunar Orbiter was a success and fulfilled objectives within time and resource limits, Surveyor was less so and met cost escalation and schedule delays. The study characterized Lunar Orbiter's customer/contractor organizations as being tightly knit *cohesive* units, with good *teamwork* and mutual *respect* and *trust* for their project counterparts. In contrast, teamwork in Surveyor was characterized as "slow and fitful" to grow and "spurred by a sense of anxiety and concern."[2] Kloman concluded:

> What emerges perhaps most forcefully from a broad retrospective view is the importance of the human aspects of organization and management. Both projects demonstrated the critical nature of human skills, interpersonal relations, compatibility between individual managers, and teamwork. (p.39)

These remarks are the crux of this chapter: that behavioral issues like decentralized decision making, interpersonal skills, supervisory support, and teamwork are chief factors in effective project management. It is unfortunate that, like other important behavioral issues, they are often overlooked in project practice or given short shrift in project management education, largely because inexperienced managers and specialists in the "hard" disciplines (scientists, engineers, businesspeople) see them as "soft" issues of little consequence and with no precise answers. But in reality these issues are not soft. They are as hard as nails. The fact is, as experienced managers know, they often have more effect on project performance than do other technical matters.

This chapter and the next discuss issues broached by the two studies cited above: participative decision making, high-level teamwork, conflict resolution, and the related matter of emotional stress in work. For years behavioral scientists have been investigating practical methods for building cohesive teams, resolving interpersonal and intergroup conflict, and managing stress. We will review the methods most relevant to project environments.

9.1 LEADERSHIP IN PROJECT MANAGEMENT

Leadership Style

Chapter 7 described a variety of organizational forms apropos for different purposes and types of work. Likewise there are a variety of suitable leadership styles depending on the situation. Leadership is the ability to influence the behavior of others to accomplish something; *leadership style* is the way a leader achieves that influence.

Leadership style can generally be divided between the two extremes of *task-oriented* and *relations-oriented*. Task-oriented leaders show high concern for the goal and the work and tend to behave in a more autocratic fashion. Relations- oriented managers show greater concern for people and tend to exercise a more democratic kind of leadership.

Numerous studies have been directed at finding the most appropriate or effective leadership style. Most management theorists agree that no one leadership style is best for all situations. Effective style depends upon characteristics of the leader, the follower, the leader's interpersonal relationship with followers, and the nature and environment of the task. This perspective is called the *contingency approach* to leadership. There are many different contingency theories; all suggest that the leader should use the style that best fits the work situation and should not try to apply the same style to all employees and situations. Brief mention will be made of two of these theories—those of Fred Fiedler and Hersey and Blanchard.

Contingency Model

According to Fiedler[3] the three variables that most affect a leader's influence are whether (1) the work group accepts or rejects the leader, (2) the task is relatively routine or complex, and (3) the leader has high or low formal authority. Fiedler contends that the most effective leadership style depends upon the *combination* of these variables. The eight possible combinations of the three variables are shown in Figure 9–1.[4]

Although he might encounter any of these situations, the most common one for a project manager (as described in the previous chapters) is likely to be:

- he has relatively low formal authority,
- he gets along with team members and is respected for his ability and expertise,
- the task is relatively complex and requires a good deal of judgment or creativity.

Fiedler's research indicates that under these three conditions a *relations-oriented* style is the most effective. In this style the most prominent behavior is the leader's positive emotional ties with and concern for subordinates.[5]

Situational Leadership

Though Fiedler's model suggests that leader behavior is either task-oriented or relations-oriented, evidence indicates that the two styles are independent. Both Blake and Mouton[6]

Variables	1	2	3	4	5	6	7	8
Leader-member relations	Good	Good	Good	Good	Poor	Poor	Poor	Poor
+								
Task structure	High	High	Low	Low	High	High	Low	Low
+								
Position power	Strong	Weak	Strong	Weak	Strong	Weak	Strong	Weak
lead to	↓	↓	↓	↓	↓	↓	↓	↓
Effective leadership styles	T	T	T	R	R	R	R	T

T = Task-oriented style   R = Relationship-oriented style

FIGURE 9–1. Fiedler's contingency model. (Adopted with permission from Fred Fiedler, *A Theory of Leadership Effectiveness* (New York: McGraw-Hill, 1967), 37.)

and Hersey and Blanchard[7] have developed "two-dimensional" leadership models where it is possible to be high or low in *both* task and relations behavior. The framework of Hersey and Blanchard, called *situational leadership*, weighs the interplay of three variables: (1) the amount of direction and guidance a leader gives (task behavior), (2) the amount of socio-emotional support he gives (relations behavior), and (3) the readiness of followers to perform the task (maturity). The last variable, "maturity," has two aspects: a person's *skill or ability* to do something and a person's *motivation or willingness* to do something. According to the framework the most effective leader behavior depends upon the maturity level of the followers. The curve in Figure 9–2 shows the appropriate leadership style in terms of task and relations behavior depending on the follower's maturity.

Project managers seldom manage shop-floor people. They deal with technical specialists, staff personnel, managers, and other highly trained people. Thus, they tend to work with people in the M3 and M4 maturity categories in Figure 9–2. These people are either able but perhaps unwilling to do what the manager wants (M3), or both able and willing to do what he wants (M4). For the M3 group the model suggests a *participating* style as most effective. The thrust of a participating leadership style is on facilitating, supporting, and communicating with followers. Both managers and followers share the decision making.

For the M4 group, the model suggests a delegating style as most effective. The manager identifies the problem or goal and gives the followers responsibility for carrying out the task. Followers are permitted to solve the problem and determine how, where, and when to do the task.

In research on managing scientific and technical personnel, Hersey and Blanchard found that people with higher levels of education and experience respond better to participating and delegating management. They also found that the same people do not respond well to high levels of task behavior and supervision, though sometimes they do need socio-emotional support.[8]

Of course, this is not to say that project managers never face workers who are unwilling to follow instructions or will not take initiative. In cases where delegation or diplomacy fail, a project manager with legal authority may need to use it. Like other managers, he sometimes has to cajole, give orders, and fire people to get the job done.

Project Circumstances

The most effective style of leadership also depends on project circumstances, especially project length and intensity. For example, a less participating, more directive style might be more appropriate when there is less time and high pressure to complete the work. The *pace* of the work sometimes constrains the available leadership options, and in situations where there is high intensity and involvement, these may act as a "substitute for leadership." It is difficult for people to build trust and confidence when the job has to be completed in only a few days. Especially with subcontractors, where there might be no more than an arms-length association, and when the work force is transient and unfamiliar, the project manager might have to be more directive and assertive.[9] As with other aspects of the project manager's role, he has to be able to wear many leadership-style hats and be able to change them quickly.

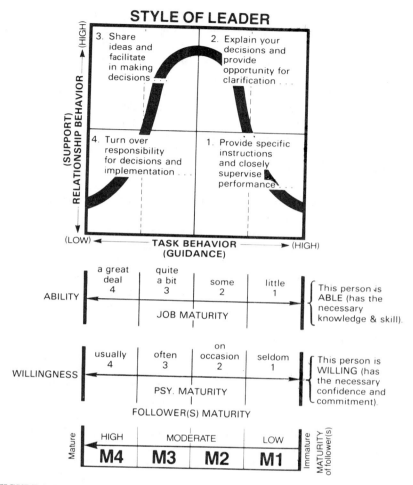

FIGURE 9–2. Hersey and Blanchard's situational leadership mode. (Adopted with permission from Paul Hersey and Kenneth Blanchard, *Management of Organization Behavior: Utilizing Human Resources,* 4th ed. (Englewood Cliffs, N.J.: Prentice-Hall, 1982), 161 and 205.)

9.2 PARTICIPATING MANAGEMENT

The models of both Fiedler and Hersey and Blanchard offer similar conclusions about project management situations—that the most effective leadership style for project managers is a high relations style, i.e., supportive, facilitative, and encouraging. As mentioned, this is not to say that they must never use high task behavior or tell people what to do; rather it says that in *most* project management situations high relations behavior works best, even when in combination with high task behavior.

This conclusion is further supported by Sayles and Chandler who report that the preferred style of leadership in large aerospace projects is *participating management*. They observe that project managers seldom give orders to the individuals they influence. They say that this is partly because most of these individuals are not the project manager's subordinates, and also because order giving induces a "no, we can't do it" reaction. Project managers use participating management because they have to deal with specialists and other managers who *must* share in the decision making. Although project managers have a purview of the total system, they are farther removed from problems than the specialists and do not know the answers to technical questions.[10]

Motivation

Project work can be stimulating, satisfying, and provide a great sense of achievement. The constant pressure to meet project goals is highly motivating to many people. Elements inherent to project management systems—contractual agreements, work breakdown structures, responsibility matrixes, and work package orders—can also be motivators. They provide clear goals which, when combined with financial and career rewards, motivate people in the same way as the management-by- objective approach.

But there are many de-motivators, too, in project work. Too much pressure leads to stress, tension, and conflict. On large jobs individuals lose sight of the end-item and feel alienated. The formal mechanisms of control can also be threatening and, by themselves, a turnoff. One advantage of participating decision making is that it helps overcome many potential de-motivators in projects by stimulating workers' commitment to project decisions.

Participating project managers do not relinquish responsibility, they delegate it. Even when they have legal authority, effective project managers involve others by, for example, acquainting them with problems, consulting their opinions, and giving frequent feedback. Workers knowledgeable enough are allowed to help prepare project plans and budgets. The process enables them to see how and where their work fits in; this encourages them to associate themselves with the project and to care about its success. As suggested before, people and situations vary, so the project manager must determine how much responsibility individual workers can be given and how much they have to be monitored and directed.

Management Development

Most project managers use a great deal of human- relations skills to influence action. They work hard at being supportive, involving others in decision making, and not being dogmatic or impatient with the participating process. In those projects where there is great potential for conflict, project managers need to develop good personal relationships, especially during the early phases of the project when patterns are set. To do this they have to invest considerable emotional energy in their work, be open with people, take risks, and work hard at trusting and gaining the trust of others.

Simply telling people to shift from traditional management style (high task-oriented) to project management style (high-relations *and* task-oriented) is not enough. Especially in matrix organizations, unless project managers and workers receive support in adjusting to relations-oriented leadership, there is a great likelihood of failure; left alone, patterns of behavior develop naturally to destroy participation, trust, and cooperation.[11] A planned process of individual and group development—team building and training in interpersonal skills—is often necessary to help managers and subordinates make the transition. Unfortunately, one consequence of becoming a relations-oriented project manager is that it is difficult to move—after the project is finished—back into traditional management roles that might require more authoritarian, autocratic leadership styles.

In the words of Bennis and Nanus, the most effective leaders are able to "align" the energies of people and groups behind the goal. They lead by "pulling rather than by pushing; by inspiring rather than by ordering"; and by creating achievable, challenging expectations and rewarding progress toward them rather than by manipulating.[12] And the ample evidence, both anecdotal and empirical, is that the most effective project managers are strong leaders who, through participating management, are able to do just this.

9.3 TEAMS IN PROJECT MANAGEMENT

All project organizations, whether task forces, pure projects, or a matrix, are comprised of groups. As Figure 9–3 illustrates, in a large project some groups are comprised of people from within one organization (the project office, middle level management, and functional

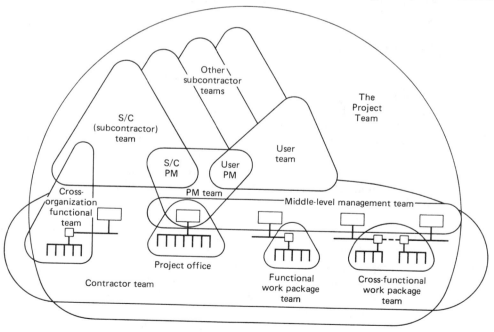

FIGURE 9–3. Groups comprising the project team.

and multifunctional work package teams) and some of people from multiple organizations (cross-organizational project management and functional groups, and so on). In many of these groups the membership overlaps and people serve dual roles that link the groups together.

The term *project team* is used to refer to any group in the project or to all of them in combination. Thus it can be said that virtually all work accomplished in a project, whether decisions or goods, is the product of teams. To be successful, however, a project needs more than just teams. It needs *teamwork*.

The Trouble with Teams

Failures in projects can often be traced to the failure of a team to make the right decisions or perform the right tasks. The major reason for these team failures stems from the maladies that teams suffer: internal conflict, member anxiety and frustration; time wasted on irrelevant issues; and haphazard decisions made by the dictate of senior people, by coalitions, or by default. Team members are often more concerned with getting the task done than with doing a *good* job. Many teams never even know what the *purpose* of the team is, so they never know when, or if, they achieved it.

In projects with multiple teams, each one has different attitudes, orientation, and goals. Some teams may be physically isolated and maintain separate offices that create and reinforce boundaries separating them. Each may develop an "us versus them" attitude that leads to intergroup competition, resentment, and conflict. This makes for a portentous project environment and bodes ill for the success of the project.

High Performing Systems

In contrast, successful projects are the result of the efforts of *effective* teams, teams which succeed in achieving what they set out to do regardless of purpose. Effective teams in projects means that individuals and groups work together as a single cohesive unit.

What makes a team effective? Peter Vaill has studied a large number of effective teams, teams which "perform at levels of excellence far beyond those of comparable systems."[13] The prominent feature he found in all of them is that the team knows what it must do and commits to doing it. Members are never confused about why the team exists or what their role is. Leaders inculcate belief in the purpose of the team, transform doubts about it, and embody it. He also found that:

- Commitment to the purpose of the system is never perfunctory and motivation is always high.
- Teamwork is focused on the task. Distinctions between task and process functions dissolve. Members develop behaviors that enable them to do what they must.
- Leadership is strong, clear, and never ambivalent. Leaders are reliable and predictable, regardless of style.
- The system is clearly bounded from other systems; members have a consciousness that "we are different."

Vaill found three characteristics *always* present in the behavior and attitudes of leaders and members of high performing systems. He calls them *time, feeling, and focus*:

First, leaders and members devote extraordinary amounts of time to the task. They work at home, in the office, in taxicabs, anywhere. They fully commit themselves for the duration of the project. Second, they have very strong feelings about the attainment of the goal. They care deeply about the team's purpose, structure, history, future, and the people in it. And third, they focus on key issues; they have a clear list of priorities in mind. In high performing teams, time, feeling, and focus are always found together.

Vaill encourages would be leaders to "Seek constantly to do what is right and what is needed in the system (focus). Do it in terms of your energy (time). Put your whole psyche into it (feeling)."[14]

High performing systems function as a whole. Everyone devotes lots of time, intensely values the system and its purpose, and is clear about priorities. Successful project organizations are high performing systems. For project managers, Vaill's findings underscore the importance of clear definition of project objectives, clarification of the roles and tasks of everyone, strong commitment to achieving objectives, strong project leadership, and a "project spirit" that bonds everyone together.

Time, Feeling, and Focus in Project Management: Renovating the Statue of Liberty

The renovation of the Statue of Liberty is a good example of the kind of commitment and effort that go into managing a successful large-scale project.[15] Over 25 firms submitted proposals for the task of leading the some 500 engineers, architects, artisans, and craftsmen who would do the renovation. Selected for the job was the small construction management firm of Lehrer/McGovern, Inc.

As Hofer describes the firm's partners: Lehrer is soft spoken and generally conservative in appearance; McGovern clean- shaves his head, has a handlebar mustache, and wears cowboy boots. Despite differences in appearance, the two share similar goals and broad experience as civil engineers and construction managers.[16]

Did they devote a lot of time to the project? To coordinate the more than 50 businesses doing the job, Lehrer and McGovern worked as many as 16 hours a day. As managers they handled everything from helping architects and craftsmen to implement plans, to making arrangements with subcontractors and insuring materials were ordered and delivered on time.

Did they instill feeling for the project? Said Lehrer, "this project is a labor of love. The spirit and pride of hundreds of men and women involved bring out the best of us as Americans."[17] They expected and they inspired feelings like that from everyone else, too. They only hired people who had "the same commitment and dedication as we do, who are aggressive and ambitious and understand that virtually nothing is impossible."[18] Before beginning they gave each subcontractor a lecture about the importance of the job and that nothing be allowed to damage the "crown jewel of the United States."

Did they maintain focus? Their major emphasis was on top quality work. The two partners believe that management's staying closely and personally involved is crucial to quality, so they made frequent visits to the site and personally supervised or handled thousands of details.

Obviously this was an exceptional project; it was highly publicized, it faced a lot of political pressure to succeed, and it had to be completed in time to celebrate the Statue's centennial anniversary. But many prominent, highly charged projects in the past have bombed. In this case, prominence did not diminish the significant role that time, feeling, and focus had in bringing about success.

Effective Project Teams

Because people in project teams have to rely on and accept one anothers' judgments, project work is high collaboration work: managers must share information and consult with each other to make decisions, and groups must support each other and accept others' viewpoints. Individual persons, departments, or organizations must be committed to *project* objectives rather than their own. Tightly knit, highly committed project teams are essential for project success.

One way to increase collaboration in a project team is to stimulate interaction between its members. In some cases this can be achieved by having members share the same office quarters. Presumably, individuals with frequent daily contact are more likely to feel like one group.

But although close physical proximity *can* increase members' feeling of affiliation with a group, it is not enough to make them an effective, *cohesive* team. Vaill's findings indicate that effective teams are clear about their purpose, are committed to it, know their role, and know how to function as a team. But in most projects people have never worked together before and do not have enough time to become friends, develop group work habits, or build team spirit. In fact, it is common in many projects that patterns of effective group work never develop. This is why team building is essential in project management.

9.4 THE TEAM BUILDING APPROACH[19]

The importance of teamwork to project success is well known. In a study of two NASA research centers, 36 experienced project managers were asked to rank the most important principal functions of their job. The function of collecting, organizing, directing, and motivating the *project team* and supporting groups was ranked as first by 20 managers from one center and as second by 16 managers from the other center.[20] In another study involving 32 project groups in research and product development, the *single most* important factor to achieving budget, schedule, and quality goals was found to be *group cohesiveness.*[21]

Effective groups do not just happen. Like any other purposeful system, every team and organization is a system which must be developed. This is the purpose of *team building*. It is a procedure whereby a team formally looks at how it works with the purpose of improving its functioning and output. Team building considers such issues as decision making, problem solving, team objectives, internal conflict, and communication. These are called *group process issues*, referring to the process or means by which a team gets things done. Ordinarily these are considered responsibilities of the team leader, though in fact many leaders ignore them. In effective groups, members openly monitor these issues whether or not the leader is present.

The idea of formally looking at group process is new for most people because it is something groups usually do not do. In team building a group looks at whatever process issues its members consider important, and then it *plans* for how it will handle these issues and perform its work.

When It Is Needed

The need for team building depends on the people in the team and what the task is. Generally, the more varied the backgrounds and responsibilities of team members, the greater the need for team building. For example, members of multidisciplinary or multiorganizational teams have different work backgrounds and goals with different outlooks on planning and doing work. Some members take the wider perspective, others are detail people. Team building helps them accept their differences and define a common goal.

Projects involving innovation, new technology, high risks, changes in policies and procedures, tight schedules, or large investments typically place teams under heavy stress. Stress may actually improve the output of a group, but after a point it is detrimental. Team building helps the group to avoid or to deal with problems that arise from stress. Stressful problems are brought into the open and resolved as they occur, before they escalate and interfere with team performance.

Team building efforts can be applied to experienced teams, new teams of strangers, or several teams which must work together as if they were one.

Aspects of Team Building Efforts

The purpose of team building is to improve group problem solving and group work efforts. To this end, it strives to achieve norms such as the following:

1. Effective communication among members.
2. Effective ways of resolving group process problems.
3. Techniques for using conflict in a constructive way.
4. Greater collaboration and creativity among team members.
5. A more trusting, supportive atmosphere within the group.
6. Clarification of the team's purpose and the role of each team member.

Three features common to all team building efforts are (1) it is carefully planned and "facilitated," usually by a human relations consultant or a professional staff person; (2) data on the functioning of the group is collected and "worked through" by the group during a diagnostic/problem solving workshop; and (3) provisions are made for later self-evaluation and follow-up. Following are some examples.

9.5 IMPROVING ONGOING WORK GROUPS

First consider how team building is applied to an experienced team such as a functional or project office group which is having problems that reduce its effectiveness. These problems might include inability to reach agreement, lack of innovation, too much agreement, too much conflict, or complacency of the members.

Initially a human relations consultant or someone else with group process skills is employed to facilitate the effort. Her function is to help the group *solve its own* problems by drawing attention to the *way* the group's behavior is affecting its decision quality and work performance.

Prior to the team building workshop, the consultant collects data from members using personal interviews or questionnaires. The consultant then summarizes the data, keeping individual sources anonymous. This summary will later be presented so the team can see its problems and analyze its behavior.

The consultant shares the results with the group leader (project manager, functional leader, or work package supervisor) and coaches him on how to prepare for the upcoming team building workshop. The consultant remains impartial to the team leader and team members; the *entire team* is her client.

A workshop is convened so members can review and analyze the group's problems. The workshop differs from ordinary staff meetings in many ways. It is convened at an off-site location away from interruptions, it may last for several days, and all team members are present. The atmosphere is open and candid, without the usual superior-subordinate restrictions. Usually the workshop is facilitated by the consultant who may alternate with the group leader depending on the agenda.

The workshop specifics vary.[22] One common format is this:[23]

1. The workshop begins with an open discussion of what is going to take place. Team members describe what they would like to have happen and what they do not want to happen.

2. The consultant presents the summary results from the interviews or questionnaires. These are posted on the wall for easy reference. Discussion may be necessary to make sure everyone understands the issues. The consultant may post (anonymous) quotes from interviews. A variety of problems can be expected, for example:

> "Our meetings are always dominated by the same two or three people."
> "Our way of getting things done is slow and unorganized."
> "I have no voice in decisions that affect my functional group."
> "Even though the team leader asks for our opinions, I know she ignores them."
> "This group works a lot of overtime because there is no scheme for how we should fit new projects into our existing workload."
> "There is no clear cut definition distinguishing between the roles of engineers and researchers in this project."

3. Given the summary results and the time constraint of the workshop, the team sets priorities about which problems it wants to resolve.

4. The group works to resolve the priority issues plus any additional ones generated during the workshop. In the meantime:

a. The consultant monitors the session and reports her observations, pointing out dysfunctional group behavior, encouraging members to express their feelings, confronting behaviors of individuals that lead to defensiveness or distrust, and reinforcing effective behavior.

b.   The group periodically critiques itself. After working through a problem the group pauses to discuss things it did which helped or hindered it.

c.   The group prepares a formal action plan that indicates solutions, target dates, and persons responsible. The plan may include "operating guidelines" for *how* the group will function. (Typical guideline topics are described in section 9.6, step 4.)

The author has worked with project groups where problems ranging from technical issues to interpersonal conflict were resolved with this process.[24]

The purpose of the workshop is twofold: it provides a structured way for the team to resolve interpersonal or group process issues as well as a forum where the group examines itself as a team. Participants often find these sessions a refreshing change. They gain stimulating insight into the dynamics of groups and develop a model of behavior to follow in the future.

To ensure that action steps are implemented and process issues continue to be addressed, team building always includes follow-up sessions. These take place formally at two or three month intervals or, less formally, during regular meetings. The team takes stock of its functioning, what improvements it has made, and what is still needed. As the group becomes more effective, the consultant is no longer needed and the group itself takes on the role. Whenever follow-up sessions reveal new problems on the rise, the process is repeated. The full cycle is summarized in Figure 9–4.

Two conditions are necessary for team building to succeed. First, it must have management's *support*. The team leader and upper managers must be willing to face the issues uncovered and to assist in (or provide resources for) working toward solutions. Second, team members must *want* to resolve the group's problems. They must be open and honest in providing data and be willing to share in the responsibility for having caused problems and for working toward solutions.

9.6 BUILDING NEW TEAMS

With small variation, team building can be applied to *new* project teams. The major tasks of a new team are similar to those of an experienced group—to develop a plan for working together and to build good working relationships and a good working environment. New teams have the advantage of not having established bad habits or poor working relationships.

The first task of a newly formed team is to reach agreement on its purpose, how it will achieve its purpose, and the roles of its members. It then asks itself: How can we effectively work together in a manner that will allow us to accomplish our purpose and leave us feeling good about one another?

A team building workshop facilitated by a consultant is convened to help members become acquainted and to reach agreement on objectives and how they will function as a team. In *Team Building: Issues and Alternatives*, William Dyer describes several workshop agendas. The following is one possible application to new project teams:[25]

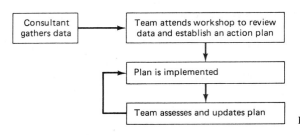

FIGURE 9–4. The team building cycle.

Step 1: Develop a priority level.   Members of the team may differ widely in the priority they place on the team task. Especially in ad hoc teams or task forces with part-time members, some members give the project high priority while others give it low priority. One way of communicating this is to have each member indicate on a scale of 1 to 10 the priority of the project compared to other work. They can also indicate the amount of daily or weekly time they will devote to the project. The information is tallied and posted on a chart similar to Figure 9–5. A group discussion follows about commitments to the task and about which people are willing to accept heavier duties than others. People who desire can explain their position on the chart. This discussion helps reduce the resentment of some members carrying more work than others.

Step 2: Share expectations.   Each person is asked to think about the following questions: (1) What would this team be like if everything worked ideally? (2) What would it be like if everything went wrong? (3) In general, what kinds of problems occur in work groups? and (4) What actions do you think need to be taken to insure an effective team? Each person's responses are shared verbally and then posted. Concerns and answers are discussed. Differences that surface will be worked through later in Step 4.

Step 3: Clarify purpose and objectives.   The team discusses and writes down its central goal. Sometimes this is straightforward, as for a work package team where the goal has already been set; other times the group will have to define the goal on its own. Either way, goals and objectives should be clearly defined and accepted by all members. The group goal is the standard against which all plans and actions will be measured. The group then develops subgoals and specific objectives so members can be given specific assignments.

Step 4: Formulating operating guidelines.   Much conflict in groups arises over different expectations about work roles, job assignments, and how the group ought to work. Problems can be reduced by establishing guidelines for the group to follow. Areas where guidelines can be formulated include:

1. How will the team make decisions—by dictate of the leader, by vote, by consensus, or by other means? Who should be involved in decisions? Not everyone should be

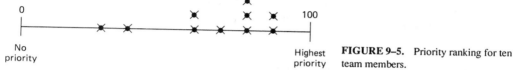

FIGURE 9–5.   Priority ranking for ten team members.

required to work on all problems since some will involve only two or three members. In most cases, only the best informed people should make decisions. Total group decision making should be done as often as necessary, but as little as possible.[26]

2.   How will the team resolve differences among members and subgroups? Disagreements waste a lot of time, so guidelines should address the kinds of conflicts likely to arise and options for resolving them—consensus, vote, or calling in a mediator.

3.   How will the work be assigned? The team should specify which activities the whole group will handle and which are subgroup activities. Tasks may be divided according to expertise, position of authority, or personal preference. If several people can handle a task, who will be chosen?

4.   How will the team ensure that work is completed? One person falling behind can delay the work of others. The team must ensure that assignments and completion dates are clear and that corrective action is taken when efforts lag or are out of control.

5.   How will the team ensure open discussion? The team must ensure that members are able to openly discuss issues so that ideas are not ignored or suppressed and that personal problems do not block team effectiveness.

6.   How frequently and where will the team meet? What do members expect about attendance?

7.   How will the team evaluate its performance and make changes? There should be procedures for periodic review and evaluation of the team and to allow the team to change its mode of operation and guidelines.

Teams can also discuss roles and responsibilities of group members and points of ambiguity, overlap, and conflict. This option is discussed in Chapter 10.

New teams do not have to wait for problems to arise before they take action; they can stop potential problems before they begin. Team building helps members to develop the common expectations necessary to build trust and mutual commitment.

Disbanding Teams

Successful teams generate close ties and strong relationships, but when projects end, so do their teams. People are usually reluctant to give up relationships, and the breakup of a cohesive team produces feelings of loss. These feelings need to be acknowledged, shared, and accepted. The disbanding of a project team should be preceded by a ceremony—a banquet, party, informal workshop or get-together—both to give the team recognition for its accomplishments and to help individuals make the transition out of the team.

9.7 INTERGROUP PROBLEM SOLVING

Intergroup problem solving (IGPS) is a technique for improving working relationships *between* several teams in a project. Its purpose is to permit confrontation of issues such as communicating or withholding information, competition or collaboration, or coordination of joint efforts. Following is a general design for an IGPS intervention:[27]

The two (or more) groups are brought together for a day long session. First, each group meets separately to compile four lists: (1) what they believe are the responsibilities of the *other* group, (2) how they feel about the *other* group, including its strengths and weakness, (3) what they think are their own responsibilities, and (4) what they anticipate the other group feels about them (strengths, weaknesses, etc.).

The groups then meet to share their lists. The only discussion allowed is to clarify points on the lists so that both groups can get information about each other's expectations, perceptions, and feelings.

The groups again separate, this time to discuss what they learned from the other's lists, to review points of disagreement, and to prioritize items to be resolved. The groups then meet together to discuss their differences and to develop an action plan for resolving them. A few weeks later at a follow-up session they meet to determine how well their plan is working. The result of the procedure is usually a much improved understanding of what each group expects from the other and a more effective working relationship.

IGPS can be applied whenever groups interface or must work together. Examples are project and user teams, or project teams from different organizations and functional areas. Without IGPS, groups often try to optimize their *own goals*, and overall project goals suffer. Problems arise because members of one group do not understand the requirements of another group or do not share expectations about what they should do. IGPS is useful whenever there are interdependencies, deadlines, or situations that induce intergroup conflict and stress.

Participants in an intergroup session are likely to have a "gee whiz" experience. Through IGPS each group may find that what it expects of itself and what the other group expects of it are very different (and often conflicting). This realization is a first and necessary step to bringing expectations into line and for planning ways to resolve differences.

One caveat is that groups should *not* be brought together for IGPS whenever they are experiencing severe *internal* problems. A group must have its own internal affairs in order before it can handle relationships with other groups.

Example: Team building and IGPS at Ruxten Software Corporation

Ron Granger is the manager of a two-year software development project involving six programming teams at three Ruxten sites in California. Each team is headed by a team leader who reports directly to Ron on project matters. Ron also has a support staff of eight systems analysts in the project office whose function is to monitor and integrate the work of the teams. Ron and his support staff spend most of their time traveling between teams and checking their work.

After eight months, the project was already running two months behind schedule. As Ron struggled, unsuccessfully, to get it back on track, he started to feel that a major obstacle was the conduct of his own staff. Whereas Ron felt it might be better to give the team leaders more autonomy, his staff wanted more control over them.

Ron had attended a team building session at corporate headquarters and decided one was needed for his staff. He called in a consultant and they discussed with the staff the possibility of doing a team building program. The staff agreed, and the first step of the consultant was to interview each analyst about changes they wanted and how they felt about the project manager.

The first team building session lasted two days. It began with the project manager asking the staff to air their complaints. The main ones were that (1) he did not back their orders to team leaders, and (2) he did not replace team leaders who they felt were "incompetent." In their view, he was a weak and indecisive project manager. Afterwards, Ron described *his* dissatisfaction with their way of working, including their attempts to dominate the team leaders. He reasserted that their purpose was to coordinate work, not to direct it.

Ron then announced his goal for team building: to get the project back on schedule. The staff agreed that this goal made obvious sense and discussed some ways to reach it. They felt that, given the importance of the team leaders' commitment to that goal, Ron should have a similar meeting with the team leaders, then a joint meeting with both team leaders and staff.

The next team building meeting involved Ron, the project staff, two team leaders, and the consultant. The two team leaders agreed about the importance of putting the project back on target, but they felt it would be impossible given all of the specifications they had to meet. They also felt that their relationship to the eight staff members had deteriorated and would have to change first. The meeting lasted one and a half days.

The third meeting included Ron, all six team leaders, and the consultant; it lasted two days. Ron stated that the purpose of the meeting was to break down their working relationship and put it together in a better way. He asked the team leaders to bring up any issues that bothered them, including *him*. In venting their feelings, the team leaders revealed that they felt harassed by the people who were supposed to be helping them (the staff), but still they were highly motivated by the project. They discussed ways in which both the staff and members of their own teams could be more helpful. Their solution was that the staff should be made *jointly* responsible with them for the performance of their teams, and that only Ron should monitor them through monthly performance reviews. Ron was not yet ready to commit to these suggestions, but after the meeting he met with every team leader to discuss performance goals.

The final meeting was an intergroup problem solving session. The eight members of the staff, the six team leaders, Ron, and the consultant met together for two days. Working in small groups, the team leaders and staff disclosed what they liked and did not like about their relationship and what they wanted to change. Each group presented the other with its complaints and suggestions for solutions. After much discussion and argument, they reached agreement on the following solutions:

1. The staff would have fewer meetings with Ron and instead associate more with the team leaders, working participatively and taking equal responsibilities.

2. The team leaders would involve their own programmers more in decision making.

3. There would be no more on-site checking by the staff. Performance would be monitored by weekly written reports from the team leaders to Ron. When necessary, Ron would make inspections and include other team leaders, but not the staff. The purpose of inspections would be to spot and solve problems, not to trap anyone or "point the finger."

4. Whenever a team leader needed help he could request the project manager to form a task force including other team leaders and members of other teams.

5. Monthly team reviews with the project manager would be conducted *with the total project group* so people could learn from each other, help one another, and maintain project team esprit de corps. The reviews would also be used to critique the progress of each team.

The changes were implemented within two months. This made it possible for project members to shift their energy and talent away from policing and self-defense toward mutual assistance and problem solving. Within the year the project was back on schedule.

9.8 SUMMARY

According to contingency theories of leadership the most effective style of leadership in project management is relations-oriented. Effective project managers often use participating decision making because they must rely upon the decisions and opinions of specialists and other managers to gain commitment to action. Research suggests that participation is the preferred and most common style among project managers.

Project organizations are comprised of teams. A significant factor in superior project performance is cohesive project teams and close teamwork. Teamwork does not just happen; it must be developed and nurtured. Especially when a project is comprised of team members from divergent backgrounds or exposes members to high stress, groups need help in developing effective teamwork. Two team development techniques are particularly relevant. One, team building, is useful for resolving problems in experienced teams and for building teamwork in new groups. The other, intergroup problem solving, is useful for building teamwork between two or more groups.

Team development methods are applicable throughout all phases of the systems development process. With slight variation they can be adapted to bring users, subcontractors, and suppliers together at the start of a project. They can also be used to unify work groups following changes in project organization or plans, and to prepare team members for new job assignments just before a project is completed.

The next chapter focuses on two common negative forces which, uncontrolled, can splinter the project organization and damage the health and vitality of team members and work groups. They are the forces of destructive conflict and emotional distress.

CHAPTER REVIEW QUESTIONS

1. Explain the difference between task-oriented and relations-oriented leadership styles.
2. Describe the contingency approach to leadership. According to this approach, what is the best way to lead?
3. What are the differences between the leadership models of Fiedler and Hersey-Blanchard? What do they say about leading in the situations faced by project managers?

4. In what ways is participative management useful for motivating and gaining commitment?

5. Why is teamwork important in projects? Isn't it enough to have individual workers who are highly skilled and motivated?

6. What characteristics are common to Vaill's "high performing systems?"

7. What is meant by group "process" issues? What kinds of issues do they include?

8. What is the purpose of team building? Where is team building needed?

9. Outline the steps in a team building session for a group that has been working together. Outline the steps for building a new project team.

10. Outline the steps in the IGPS process.

11. What conditions of management and the participating members are necessary for team building interventions to succeed?

12. Describe some situations that you know of where team building could be used.

13. What do you think are the reasons why team building is not used more often? What barriers are there to applying team building?

QUESTIONS ABOUT THE STUDY PROJECT

1. How would you characterize the leadership style of the project manager in your project? Is it authoritarian, laissez faire (do-nothing), or participative? Is the project manager more task- or more relations-oriented, or both?

2. What kind of people must the project manager influence? Given the theories of this chapter, is the style of leadership used appropriate? Despite the theories, does the style used by the project manager seem to be effective?

3. What do you think are the primary work motivators for people in this project? Discuss the relative importance of salary, career potential, formal controls, and participation in decision making.

4. Describe the different groups (management teams, project office, functional groups) that comprise the "project team" in this project.

5. What mechanisms are used to link these teams—coordinators, frequent meetings, close proximity, etc.?

6. What kinds of formal and informal activities are used to increase the cohesiveness of the project team? Can any of these be termed as team building?

7. What kinds of activities are used or steps taken to resolve problems involving multiple groups?

8. How would you characterize the level of teamwork in this project?

9. Ask the project manager if he or she knows about formal team building and intergroup problem solving procedures like those described in this book.

10. At the end of this (or other projects), what does the organization do to disband a team? Are there any procedures for giving recognition or dealing with members' feelings about disbanding?

ENDNOTES

1. Richard L. Chapman, *Project Management in NASA: the System and the Men* (Washington, D.C.: NASA SP–324, NTIS No. N75–15692, 1973). The project team Chapman refers to is the project

office staff which numbered from one or two members on small matrix projects to as many as 70 in large pure project organizations.

2. E.H. Kloman, *Unmanned Space Project Management* (Washington, D.C.: NASA SP–4102, 1972), 23.

3. Fred Fiedler, *A Theory of Leadership Effectiveness* (New York: McGraw-Hill, 1967).

4. Ibid., 37.

5. To conserve space the other seven combinations are not discussed here. The reader is encouraged to read Fiedler, ibid., about these since, although less likely, project managers might encounter any of them.

6. Robert R. Blake and Jane S. Mouton, *The Managerial Grid* (Houston: Gulf Publishing, 1964).

7. P. Hersey and K. Blanchard, *Management of Organization Behavior: Utilizing Human Resources*, 4th ed. (Englewood Cliffs, N.J.: Prentice-Hall, 1982), 150–173.

8. Paul Hersey and Kenneth Blanchard, "Managing Research and Development Personnel: An Application of Leadership Theory," *Research Management* (September 1969).

9. A. Bryman, M. Bresnan, A. Beardsworth, J. Ford, and E. Keil "The Concept of the Temporary System: The Case of the Construction Project," *Research in the Sociology and Psychology of Organizations*, Vol. 5, 1987, 253–83.

10. L.R. Sayles and M.K. Chandler, *Managing Large Systems: Organizations for the Future* (New York: Harper & Row, 1971), 219.

11. S.M. Davis and P.R. Lawrence, *Matrix* (Reading, Mass.: Addison-Wesley, 1977). See 108–109 for a discussion of the interpersonal and leadership requirements for the matrix.

12. Warren Bennis and Burt Nanus, *Leadership: Strategies for Taking Charge* (New York: Harper & Row, 1985), 224–5.

13. Peter Vaill, "The Purposing of High-Performing Systems," *Organizational Dynamics* (Autumn 1982), 23–39.

14. Ibid., 38.

15. This discussion is largely based on W. Hofer, "Lady Liberty's Business Army," *Nation's Business* (July 1983), 18–28; see also Alice Hall, "Liberty Lifts Her Lamp Once More," *National Geographic* (July 1986), 2–19.

16. Hofer, ibid.

17. Ibid., 28.

18. Ibid., 21.

19. John Nicholas, "Developing Effective Teams for System Design and Implementation," *Production and Inventory Management* (Third Quarter 1980), 37–47; and John Nicholas, "Organization Development in Systems Management," *Journal of Systems Management*, Vol. 30, No. 11 (November 1979), 24–30. Much of the following discussion is derived from these sources.

20. The other functions of project management were defined to be project planning, information and control, and consultation. See Chapman, *Project Management in NASA*, 59–62.

21. R.T. Keller, "Predictors of the Performance of Project Groups in R&D Organizations," *Academy of Management Journal*, Vol. 29, No. 4 (December 1986), 715–726.

22. See for example William Dyer, *Team Building: Issues and Alternatives*, 2nd ed. (Reading, Mass.: Addison-Wesley, 1987) and John Nicholas, "Organization Development in Systems Management," 24–30.

23. A.J. Reilly and J.E. Jones, "Team Building," in *Annual Handbook of Group Facilitators*, eds. J.W. Pfeiffer and J.E. Jones (LaJolla, Calif.: University Associates, 1974).

24. Nicholas, "Organization Development in Systems Management."

25. This discussion is largely based on Dyer, *Team Building*, 100–6.

26. Davis and Lawrence, *Matrix*, 134.

27. R.R. Blake, H.A. Shepard, and J.S. Mouton, *Managing Intergroup Conflict in Industry* (Houston: Gulf Publishing, 1965).

chapter 10

Managing Conflict
and Stress
in Projects

Kenka ryosei bai.
In a quarrel, both sides are at fault.

Japanese proverb

Illness is the doctor to whom we pay most heed:
to Kindness, to Knowledge we make promises only;
Pain we obey.

Marcel Proust, Cities of the Plain

This chapter deals with human conflict and emotional stress, two subjects which, perhaps, seem out of place in a textbook on project management. But they are included here for a good reason—because of the paramount influence they have on the performance of project organizations and team members. Ask any project manager and you will hear about the problems of interpersonal conflict and emotional stress that surround projects. The consequences of ignoring or mismanaging these problems can be as severe as faulty planning or bad management control. The purpose of this chapter is make new project managers aware of what to expect, and to offer all project managers tools for managing and reducing the damaging effects of conflict and emotional stress.

10.1 ORIGINS OF CONFLICT

In all organizations, differences in objectives, opinions, and values lead to arguments and friction. Project organizations are far from the exception; if anything, they are predisposed to friction and conflict. Conflict arises between users and contractors, between project staff and functional groups, and between functional departments. It occurs between people on the same team, people in different groups, and groups in different organizations. Some conflict is natural; too much is destructive.

Between User and Contractor

Seeds of conflict between the user and the contractor are sown during early contract negotiations. People representing the two parties are usually less concerned with developing trust and teamwork than with driving a hard bargain for their own best interests. The user wants to minimize cost, the contractor wants to maximize profit. One's gain is the other's loss. In the extreme, each strives for an agreement which provides an "out" in case one side cannot keep its part of the bargain; each makes the other side responsible in case of failure, and each gives oneself final rights to all benefits of the project. In technology based firms where scientists and engineers rule, the nontechnical, legal "types" who negotiate contracts may try to enlarge their function by using highly legalistic frameworks which try to cover all eventualities.[1] Says one manager,

> "You start with science and engineering, but a project, once it's decided on, has to be costed. You have to select contractors and get budgets approved. Then you turn to the contractors working with you and write contracts that say you don't trust one another. What starts as a fine scientific dream ends up being a mass of slippery eels."[2]

After negotiations the contract itself becomes a source of conflict. In cost-plus agreements (see Appendix B) where profit is a percentage of costs and there is little incentive for the contractor to control expenses, the user must closely supervise and question everything. Such scrutiny is a constant irritant to the contractor. In fixed price contracts, costs may have to be periodically renegotiated and revised upward. This is also a source of friction. Any contract that is vaguely worded or poorly specified in terms of cost, schedule, or performance is likely to have multiple interpretations and lead to conflict.

Within the Project Organization

Functionalism is based upon and promotes differences in ideas and objectives. This is good for functional departments because it makes them better at what they do, but it is bad for projects because the functional areas have to work together. High-level interdependency between functional areas in projects increases the level of contact between them and, at the same time, the chances of conflict. Each functional area has different ideas and goals and comes up with different solutions for similar problems—differences that must frequently be resolved without the benefit of a common superior.

In addition, the wants of functional areas are often incompatible with the needs of the project. Functional areas often request changes to the project plan that the project manager has to evaluate and sometimes refuse. The project manager often must compromise the high scientific and technical standards of research and engineering areas with time and cost considerations of the project. Even when project managers defer to the technical judgment of specialists, they often disagree over the means of implementation.

Work priorities, schedules, and resource allocations are further sources of conflict. Functional areas working in multiple projects must set priorities which sometimes conflict with priorities of project managers. Although cost estimates and schedules are originally set by functional areas, they are revised by project managers; often the final schedules conflict with other jobs and the allocation of funds is perceived as insufficient.

In matrix organizations there is potential for conflict at every interface. Functional managers see project managers as impinging on their territory and resent having to share planning and control with them. They sometimes refuse to release certain personnel to projects or try to retain authority over the personnel they do release. Workers who have dual reporting relationships are often confused about priorities and loyalties.

Moreover, given that projects are temporary, goal driven systems, workers are under constant pressure to meet time and cost objectives. People are ordinarily reluctant to accept change, yet in projects change is the norm. Expansions and contractions in the labor force make it difficult to establish obligations and reporting relationships once and for all. Administrative procedures, group interfaces, project scope, and resource allocations are always subject to change.

Finally, projects inherit feuds that have nothing to do with them. Regardless of the setting, clashes arise from differences in attitudes, personal goals, and individual traits, and from people trying to advance their careers. These create a history of antagonisms which set the stage for conflict even before a project begins.

10.2 CONSEQUENCES OF CONFLICT

Conflict is inevitable in human systems and is not always detrimental. Properly managed, a certain amount of conflict is necessary and beneficial. On the positive side conflict helps:[3]

1. produce better ideas
2. force people to search for new approaches
3. cause persistent problems to surface and be dealt with
4. force people to clarify their views
5. cause tension which stimulates interest and creativity
6. give people the opportunity to test their capacities.

In fact, it is an unhealthy sign when there is no conflict. Called *groupthink*, lack of conflict is a sign of overconformity. It causes dullness and sameness and results in poor or mediocre judgment. In contrast, conflict over differences in opinion or perspective stimulates discussion and can enhance problem solving and innovation. In project groups charged with exploring new ideas or solving complex problems, conflict is essential.

Conflict between groups in competition is beneficial because it increases group cohesion, spirit, loyalty, and the intensity of competition. But, of course, groups in competition do not need to *cooperate*.

Conflict between cooperating teams in a project can be devastating. Groups in conflict develop an "us versus them" attitude; they selfishly strive to achieve their own objectives and block the objectives of other teams. Left uncontrolled and unresolved, destructive conflict spirals upward and creates more hostility and conflict. Conflict fosters lack of respect, lack of trust, and destroys communication between groups and individuals. Ideas, opinions, or suggestions of others are rejected or discredited. Project spirit breaks down and the organization splinters apart.

10.3 CONFLICT IN THE PROJECT LIFE CYCLE

In a well-known study of 100 project managers, Thamhain and Wilemon[4] investigated seven potential causes of conflict. They determined that, on the average, the three greatest sources of conflict are project schedules, project priorities, and the work force—all of those areas over which project managers generally have limited control and must negotiate with functional managers. In decreasing order of importance, other sources of conflict are technical opinions and performance tradeoffs, administrative and organizational issues, interpersonal differences, and costs. Costs are a relatively minor cause of conflict, the authors surmise, not because costs are unimportant but because they are difficult to control and usually dealt with incrementally over a project's life.

The study also revealed that the sources of conflict change as projects move from one phase to the next. Figure 10–1 summarizes the four major sources of conflict in each phase.

During project formation (conception phase), the most significant sources of conflict are priorities, administrative procedures, schedules, and labor. Disputes between project and functional areas arise over the relative importance of the project compared to other activities, the design of the project organization, the amount of control the project manager should have, the personnel to be assigned, and scheduling the project into existing workloads.

During project buildup (definition phase), the chief source of conflict remains priorities, followed by schedules, procedures, and technical issues. Priority conflicts extend from the previous phase, but new disputes arise over the enforcement of schedules and functional departments' efforts to meet technical requirements.

During the main (acquisition) phase, friction arises over schedule slippages, technical problems, and labor issues. Deadlines become more difficult to meet because of accumulating schedule slippages. Efforts aimed at system integration, technical performance of subsystems, quality control, and reliability also encounter problems. Labor requirements grow to a maximum and strain the available pool of workers.

Start ——————— Project Life Cycle ————→ Finish			
Project Formation	Project Buildup	Main Project Effort	Project Phase-out
Priorities	Priorities	Schedules	Schedules
Procedures	Schedules	Technical	Personality
Schedules	Procedures	Manpower	Manpower
Manpower	Technical	Priorities	Priorities

FIGURE 10–1. Major sources of conflict during the project life cycle. (Adopted with permission from H.J. Thamhain and D.L. Wilemon, "Conflict Management in Project Life Cycles," *Sloan Management Review* (Spring 1975), 31–50.)

During the final (phase-out) effort, schedules continue as the biggest source of conflict as accumulated slippages make it more difficult to meet target completion dates. Pressures to meet objectives and growing anxiety over future projects increase tensions and personality related conflicts. The phasing in of new projects and the absorption of personnel back into functional areas create major conflicts in the work force.

Conflict Resolution

How do project managers deal with these conflicts? In general there are five ways to handle conflict; they are to:

1. Withdraw or retreat from the disagreement.
2. Smooth over or de-emphasize the importance of the disagreement (pretend it does not exist).
3. Force the issue by exerting power.
4. Compromise or bargain to bring at least some degree of satisfaction to all parties.
5. Confront the conflict directly; work through the disagreement with problem solving.

All of these are at times appropriate. In a heated argument it may be best to withdraw until emotions have calmed down or to de-emphasize the disagreement before it gets distorted out of proportion. Neither of these solves the problem and it is likely to arise again. The project manager might force the issue by using authority; this gets the action done but it risks creating hostility. As discussed earlier, if authority must be used, it is better if it is based upon knowledge or expertise. To use bargaining or compromising both sides must be willing to give up something to get something. Ultimately, both sides may feel they lost more than they gained, and the result is not necessarily optimal for the project. Of the five approaches the only one which works at resolving underlying issues is *confrontation*.[5]

Confrontation involves, first, recognizing potential or existing problems, then facing up to them. At the organization level this starts by having all areas involved in the project reach consensus on project objectives, administrative plans, labor requirements, and priorities. Careful monitoring of schedules, quick reallocation of resources to problem areas, close contact between project groups, and prompt resolution of technical problems are all important steps in reducing conflict.[6]

At the individual level, project managers resolve conflicts by raising confrontational questions and challenges such as:[7]

How do you know that this redesign is likely to solve the problem? Prove it to me.

What have you done to correct the malfunctions that showed up on the test we agreed to?

How do you expect to catch up on lost time when you haven't scheduled overtime and there is no additional staffing?

Questions like this demonstrate that the project manager is vitally interested, alert, and that everything is subject to question. It is a crucial part of effective project management.

But there is a catch to confrontation: the very *process* of setting plans, schedules, and priorities, and enforcing them with confronting questions is, itself, a source of conflict. Attempts to prevent or resolve conflict through planning and control become a source of conflict at the *interpersonal* level. Frequently, what begins as a conflict of schedules, priorities, or technical matters degenerates into a struggle for power and a conflict of "personalities" between parties.

For confrontation to work, conditions must be right. This is where team building and related approaches play a key role.

10.4 MANAGING CONFLICT[8]

A presumption in project management is that conflict is inevitable, healthy, and best resolved by confrontation. But successful confrontation assumes a lot about the individuals and groups involved. It assumes that they are willing to reveal why they favor a given course of action. It assumes that they are open to and not hostile toward differing opinions. It assumes that they are all working toward a common goal. And it assumes that they are willing to abandon one position in favor of another.

The simple fact is, many groups and managers are highly critical of differences in others. Faced with differences, they tend to operate emotionally, not analytically. For individuals to use confrontation as a way to resolve conflict, they must first be able to manage their emotions. This implies fundamental changes to the interpersonal styles and processes normally used by many groups and individuals. In some cases it requires nothing short of radical change in the way people behave and in the culture of the organization.

Expectation Theory of Conflict[9]

When two people do not get along it is common to say they have a "personality conflict." The presumption is that features of their personalities—attitudes, values, experiences—are so different that they cannot possibly get along. Groups also develop personality conflicts when their values, tasks, or objectives differ.

Dyer suggests a more constructive way of looking at conflict, that it is a *violation of expectations*. Whenever a person or group violates the expectations of another, there is a negative reaction. Between groups and managers working on a project, some may feel that others are favored, have better facilities, or get more credit. When they expect more equitable treatment and do not get it they react using verbal attacks, placing blame, or severing relations. Negative responses violate the expectations of others who reciprocate further with more negative reactions.

10.5 TEAM METHODS FOR RESOLVING CONFLICT

Conflict confrontation assumes that parties can discuss issues frankly and level with one another. One way the project manager can make confrontation work is with team building. As discussed in Chapter 9, team building helps members develop attitudes more accepting of differences and leads to greater openness and trust. It attacks conflict directly by getting to the source and engaging members in problem solving. Following are team building methods that focus on conflict stemming from work roles and group interaction.

Role Clarification Technique[10]

Much conflict in projects arises because people have mixed expectations about work plans, roles, and responsibilities. In particular, disagreements arise because:

- The project is new and people are not clear about what to do and what others expect of them.
- Changes in projects and work reassignments have made it unclear how functions and positions should interact.
- People get requests they do not understand or hear about things in the grapevine that they think they should already know.
- Everyone thinks someone else is handling a situation when no one is.
- People do not understand what their group or other groups are doing.

The *role clarification technique (RAT)* is a systematic procedure to help resolve these sources of conflict. The title "role clarification" suggests its goals: that everyone understand the major requirements of their own positions and duties, that others also understand everyone else's positions and duties, and that everyone knows what others expect of them.[11]

RAT has many similarities with team building. It includes data collection, a meeting which lasts for one or two days, and a consultant who serves as facilitator. When incorporated as part of team building for a new team, it allows the project manager and team to negotiate team member roles. It is especially useful in participative management where responsibilities are somewhat ambiguous.

Clarifying Roles for a Team.   Role clarification for an existing team begins with each person answering a questionnaire prior to a meeting. Questions might include:[12]

1. What does the organization expect of you in your job?
2. What do you actually do in your job?
3. What should others know about your job that would help them?
4. What do you need to know about others' jobs that would help you?
5. What difficulties do you experience with others?
6. What changes in the organization, assignments, or activities would improve the work of the group?

For a new team the questions would be modified to reveal job expectations and anticipated problems.

At the start of the group meeting, the announced ground rules are that people be candid, give honest responses, express their concerns, and that everyone agrees to decisions.

The meeting begins with each person reading the answers to the first three questions. As each person reads, others have a chance to respond. It is important that each person hears how others see their job and what they expect of them.

Each person then reads the answer to question 4 and gets responses from the people identified. Issues in question 5 that have not already been resolved are addressed next. Throughout the process, emphasis is placed on solving problems and not placing blame. The group then discusses question 6 and tries to reach consensus about needed changes.[13]

Clarifying the Role of One Person.   A similar process is followed for clarifying the role of just one person. It begins with the "focal person" identifying people relevant to her role—anyone who interacts with her and expects certain behavior from her to meet work obligations (boss, subordinates, members of other departments relating to the focal person). The purpose is to have these people meet together so they can clarify their expectations to the focal person.

At the meeting the focal person discusses her job responsibilities and covers topics such as those in the first five questions above. The other people in the meeting then state their expectations of the focal person. Special attention is given to ambiguities, inconsistencies, or incompatibilities between their expectations. When consensus is reached, the focal person writes a description of her role and gives a copy to everyone. The description is reviewed to ensure that it is clear, specific, and as internally consistent as possible.

RAT is especially useful in matrix situations where role ambiguity can lead to power struggles between the managers and to role conflict in the workers that report to them. In projects where relationships and job descriptions are in perpetual change, a less formal procedure can be used to help redefine and reclarify roles on a frequent basis.

Intergroup Conflict Resolution[14]

When several groups are in conflict because of mixed expectations, a procedure similar to intergroup problem solving can be used. The procedure begins by each group preparing a list of what they would like the other groups to start doing, stop doing, and continue if their relations are to improve. As a variation, the groups also predict what the others think about them and want from them. Guesses are often accurate and facilitate reaching an agreement.

The groups share their lists and negotiate an agreement stating what each will do in return for equitable changes on the part of the other. The focus is on finding solutions, not fault. A consultant may facilitate the negotiation. To increase the groups' commitment the agreements are written.

Another approach is to have Team A select a subgroup of members to represent it. Names in the subgroup are given to Team B, which selects three or four members from the Team A list. Team B also prepares a list of names and gives it to A. This creates a mixed team of representatives that both sides agree to. The mixed team tries to resolve problems between the teams. It can interview people in other teams, invite a facilitator, and so on. The mixed team then prepares a list of actions, people to be responsible, a time frame, and ways to prevent problems from reoccurring. This is a common approach because it is easy to implement without a consultant. It requires less involvement from members than the first method, but it also tends to have less impact.

There are several preconditions for team building to be useful in resolving conflict. The conflicting parties must agree that they have problems, that the problems should be solved, that they both have a responsibility to work on them, and that they need to come together to solve them. Often it is easier to get people to deal with conflict if they realize that the goal of team building and confrontation is not to get them to like each other but to understand and to work with each other.

10.6 EMOTIONAL STRESS

There are numerous "down" sides to working in projects. Long hours, tight schedules, high risks, and high stakes take a severe toll in terms of the organizational well- being, social and family relationships, and individual mental and physical health. Projects achieve great things, but they also instigate bankruptcy, divorce, mental breakdown, and heart attacks. One of the major problems associated with working in projects—and which is both a contributor to and the result of individual, family, and organizational difficulties—is emotional stress. It is a problem which affects the achievement and health of project organizations and their workers, and which all project managers have to grapple with. This section is a brief introduction to the topic of emotional stress, its symptoms, causes, and ways for project managers to deal with it. Readers are encouraged to see the accompanying references to understand it more.[15]

Definition of Stress

Stress is an unconscious psychological and physical reaction of people to their environment. The potential for stress exists whenever a situation is perceived to present demands which threaten to exceed a person's capability and resources to meet it. Some stress is necessary for life; our concern is with negative stress or "distress."

How much stress a person experiences and whether that experience is positive or negative depends upon the fit between two factors: the demands or threats of the environment and the adaptive capabilities of the person. Work-related stress depends upon a person's perception of the demands or opportunities of the job and his self-perceived abilities, self-confidence, and motivation to perform. A manager faced with impending failure to meet a deadline might experience stress if the schedule is supposed to be met, but no stress if it is assumed the deadline will be missed. Stress is a reaction to prolonged internal and environmental conditions which overtax a person's adaptive capabilities. To cause distress, an individual's capabilities must be overtaxed for a prolonged period.

Any discussion about stress or stressful situations can only be in regard to individuals since stress is only experienced by individuals. Everyone responds differently to stressful situations, and what is distressful to one person may be stimulating and challenging to another. The cause of stress can be psychological or environmental. Even when a person has the ability to handle a situation, he will still feel distress if he lacks self-confidence or cannot make a decision.

Consequences and Symptoms

Stress occurs naturally and has beneficial as well as destructive consequences. On the positive side, stress stimulates energy and contributes to innovation and learning. Under stress, the body responds with greater speed, strength, endurance, concentration, and sharper intellect.

However, at excessively high or low levels and for prolonged periods the effects of stress are mentally and physically destructive. The relationship is shown in Figure 10–2. Long projects with high stakes and project managers who are chronically demanding and unsupportive provoke tension, anxiety, and frustration among project workers. Symptoms include ailments like mental illness, high blood pressure, ulcers, backaches, and heart disease; they result in high absenteeism, turnover, low commitment, low performance, and accidents. They disrupt social and family ties which further add to stress on the job.

The signs of distress may increase so slowly over time that people are unaware of them. When people work under perpetual stress they forget how it felt to be free of tension. Some people, called "Type A's," constantly elevate their energies as if they were responding to stressful situations even when they are not. They show the same symptoms as if they were actually subjected to prolonged environmental stress.

Sources of Stress

The stress a person feels is related to features of the individual, the environment, and their interaction. Seldom is there a single cause.

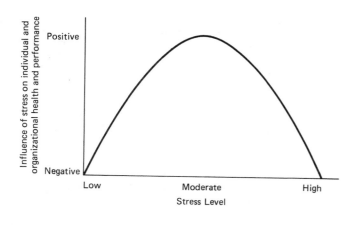

FIGURE 10–2. Stress level and influence on health and performance.

Features internal to the individual both cause stress and influence the way a person copes with stressful events in the environment. When a person is by nature fearful, nervous and anxious she experiences degrees of stress in all situations. She creates her own stress. When a person has low self-esteem, she feels more stress because she more often perceives situations as threatening or overwhelming. She distorts situations and makes them stressful. A person with high achievement needs also experiences more stress, especially when her ambitions exceed her ability or opportunities. Many people have a high resistance to stress. Depending on their self-confidence, flexibility, and ability to blow off steam, they are able to withstand more anxiety and pressure than others.

Internal stressors predominate in Type A people—people who are aggressive, work-aholic, and competitive. Most managers are Type A, either fully or borderline. They have low tolerance for uncertainty, are hard-driving and impatient. Despite the grave conse-quences to emotional and physiological health, organizations reward this kind of self-in-duced stressful behavior.

The second source of stress, the environment, includes aspects of the job (tasks, schedules, work climate, roles, relationships, and career progress) and of the family and life events (marriage, children, health, loved ones, finances, and so on). Problems or conflicts in any of these induce stress. Although we are focusing on the work environment, it should be noted that stressful nonwork events and personal problems aggravate a person's stress on the job and influence her ability to cope. The sources and consequences of stress are reviewed in Figure 10–3.

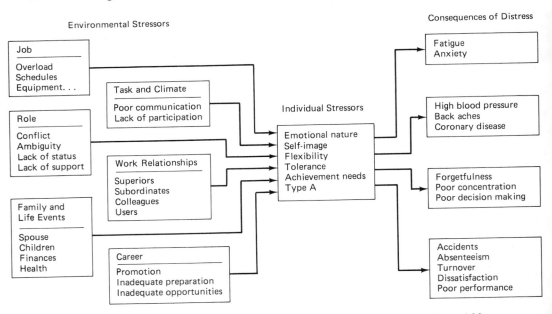

FIGURE 10–3. Model of job distress. (Adopted with permission from J. Ivancevich and M. Matteson, "Optimizing Human Resources: A Case for Preventive Health and Stress Management," *Organizational Dynamics,* Vol. 9 (Autumn 1980), 17.)

10.7 STRESS IN PROJECTS

These are numerous causes of stress in projects, including the rapid pace, transient work force, anxiety over discrepancies between project performance and goals, cost overruns, and impending failure to meet schedules or contract requirements. The project manager herself is exposed to considerable stress; for example in construction, in the words of Bryman, et al.:

> "The fact that the [project manager] is in the front line controlling the labor force; he's answerable to the client, to his organization at a high level; he's responsible for million of pounds [or $] worth of work. . . In a very fragile environment he is at the mercy of the weather, material deliveries, problems with labor, and problems with getting information."[16]

The ability to cope with this stress is an important aspect of project management. We will restrict discussion to three general causes of stress in projects: work overload, role conflict, and interpersonal relations.

Work overload in projects is experienced in two ways. One is simply by having too much work or doing too many things at once, with time pressures, long hours, and no letup. The other is having work that exceeds one's ability and knowledge. Overload can be self-induced by an individual's need to achieve (being Type A) or it can be imposed by managers and the responsibilities of the job. Job induced work overload is prevalent during crash efforts to recover lost ground and when projects are rushed toward completion. When work overload is in balance with abilities, it is positive and motivating. When it exceeds ability, it is distressful. A related problem, *work underload*, occurs when there is too little work or work that is beneath a person's ability. Project workers suffer from underload whenever there is a long hiatus between projects.

Another cause of stress in projects is called *role conflict*. As described earlier, work roles are the expectations of a person and others about how he should do a job. Two or more people, for instance a functional manager and a project manager, which send contradictory or incompatible expectations cause the worker in the middle to experience stress. Role conflict and stress are also felt when a person has two roles with incompatible requirements. A project manager, for instance, may find that he has to do things to be a good administrator that conflict with his values as a professional engineer.

A related source of stress is *role ambiguity*. This results from inadequate or confusing information about what a person needs to do to fulfill his job, or about the consequences of meeting or failing to meet requirements of the job. Role ambiguity is stressful because the person knows neither where he stands nor what to do next.

Role conflict and role ambiguity are common in projects because people have to interact with and satisfy the expectations of many others. Role ambiguity causes greater stress among managers because typically they have lower tolerance for uncertainty. Project managers in particular might find their work frustrating and stressful because the authority they need to carry out project responsibilities is often unclear or inadequate.

Stress also develops from the demands and pressures of *social relations*. Having a boss or partner who is self-centered and authoritarian causes stress. Irritable, abrasive, or condescending personalities are hard to work with; they make others feel unimportant and provoke anxiety (which people try to suppress and it builds up internally) or anger and outbursts (which generate still more tensions).

In summary, the typical project has many environmental stressors and emotional stress is inevitable. Like conflict, however, there are ways to manage stress to reduce its negative consequences.

Stress Management

Most people accept distress as the price of success. Although stress is inevitable, distress is not. Project managers must be able to anticipate which work demands are most stressful and know how to ameliorate the negative effects.

In general, means for reducing negative stress at work are aimed either at changing the organizational conditions that cause stress or at helping people to better cope with stress. Since stress results from the interaction of people with their environment, both are necessary. Organizational level means are aimed at task, role, physical, and interpersonal stressors; individual level means are aimed at peoples' ability to manage and respond to stressful demands. Following are some methods which can readily be applied by project managers.

10.8 ORGANIZATIONAL LEVEL MEANS FOR MANAGING STRESS[17]

One general way to reduce the distress of people in projects is to create a less distressful project environment. Various avenues include:

1. Setting reasonable work plans and schedules.
2. Delegating responsibility and increasing individual autonomy.
3. Clarifying responsibilities, authority, and performance criteria.
4. Clarifying goals, procedures, and decision criteria.
5. Giving consideration and support in leadership.

The first way calls for pre-planning and scheduling to allow for reasonable work hours and time off. Good planning and scheduling helps balance work loads and familiarizes workers with what is expected. It helps avoids ambiguity in expectations, work overload, and the "crunch" that precedes milestones and project close out.

Good planning and scheduling are "technical" means for reducing stress; these methods and procedures are well described in the next section of this book. The other four items on the list are "behavioral" means for managing stress. They consist of ways for altering work demands, relationships, and individual behavior, and center around participating management, team building, and conflict resolution.

Modifying Work Demands Through Participation

The distressful influence of some kinds of leadership styles is well-known. Dictatorial, self-centered leaders (the too bossy boss) cause frustration, annoyance, and stress; the opposite kind, the do-nothing, understimulating boss is just as bad. In contrast, it makes sense (and there is supporting research) that the participating style of leadership is the least stressful.[18] Most projects are demanding; one way to reduce distress is to give project workers decision latitude and autonomy commensurate with work demands and their ability. Participating leaders set goals and define task limits, but allow greater freedom about how goals will be achieved. This latitude gives workers greater flexibility and results in less anxiety and tension. Participating decision making takes longer, but it is a fair trade-off if the result is less tension and greater commitment to the decision.

Modifying Work Relationships

Work roles and relationships are important to mental well-being. In project environments where there is considerable change and complexity, distress is caused by confusion, ambiguity, and conflict about work roles. One useful means for reducing role-related work stress is the role analysis technique described previously. By clarifying role demands and minimizing contradictions in role expectations, stress originating from role conflict and role ambiguity is reduced. Like good project planning, this should be done early so that work roles and expectations are clear from the beginning.

Social Support

Another way to reduce stress arising from work roles and relationships is to increase the *social support* within project teams. Social support is the assistance one gets through interpersonal relationships. Generally, people are better able to cope with stressful situations when they feel that others care about and are willing to help them.[19] Social support at work comes in the form of giving emotional support (listening and caring), appraising performance and behavior, and giving advice, information, and direct assistance in a task.[20]

Vital sources of social support are family, close friends, a supportive boss, and good relations with coworkers and subordinates. Social support from managers and coworkers does not necessarily alter the stressor but it does help people to better cope. Supportive managers act as a barrier against destructive stress, and their subordinates are less likely to suffer harmful consequences than those with unsupportive managers.[21] Coworker social support in groups is equally important, though often their supportiveness correlates with the amount of support modeled by the leader.[22] Caught between the conflicting expectations of a functional manager and project manager, a person who has the support of coworkers will be better able to deal with the conflict and feel less troubled by her inability to meet both expectations.

Training for Social Support

How do people become supportive? Simply telling someone to be supportive does not work. Even when managers try to be supportive by giving advice they often leave the distressed worker worse off. Giving someone physical assistance is easy, but true emotional support is difficult and more subtle. Empathic listening, understanding, and real concern are essential parts of support often missing in naive efforts to help. Usually it is necessary to provide training in social support skills, then reinforce and reward the usage of these skills. Unfortunately, as with many other behavioral aspects of management, empathy and sensitivity are considered "soft" issues and are often devalued as "nonproductive."

Team Building for Social Support

Cohesive teams are not only more productive, they help reduce distress through the support members give and receive. As part of a team building program procedures can be included to help groups confront and resolve stressful issues. For example, during the data collection phase of team building members can be asked to describe features of their task or the group which cause stress. Once uncovered, the group can work to resolve stressful issues by devoting some time at each meeting to handle one or two issues. Alternatively, the group can meet at a workshop to prepare a strategy for minimizing distress. The assistance of a third party may be needed. Although there may be little time in projects to follow the formal steps of stress diagnosis, resolution, and follow-up, many causes of stress can be reduced or eliminated through early team building and pre-planning.

10.9 INDIVIDUAL LEVEL MEANS FOR MANAGING STRESS

Even with preventive activities such as participating management and team building, project workers will still face stressful work demands. In high stress project environments, project managers are advised to implement a *stress management program*. Such programs vary widely in focus; some are aimed at altering the perception of potential stressors, others at treating stress-induced problems. They range from training in relaxation and personal coping to lifestyle management and physical exercise.

Comprehensive stress management programs are directed at three levels: perceived stressors in the environment, people's responses to stress, and clinical treatment. Techniques at the first level aim to reduce stressors in the environment. Since something must first be perceived as stressful to actually become stressful, one way to reduce stress is to alter perceptions. By developing creative perceptual frames of reference people can learn to face problems in ways that are not psychologically destructive. For example, people in stressful decision making positions are encouraged to think "I will give this project all I have to offer, but if I make a mistake it will not be the end. I don't have to be liked by everyone to be effective. It is enough to do my job well and be respected."[23] Individuals learn to interpret situations in ways that increase their resistance to stress. Other approaches focus on how to effectively manage time, obligate and de-obligate responsibilities, and effectively plan activities.

Techniques at the second level are directed at improving the way people respond to stressful situations. They include, for example, relaxation training (meditation, Zen, biofeedback, relaxation response, and other techniques), and physical and emotional outlets such as sports, relaxing with friends and family, and diversions from work-related problems.

Third level methods are directed at reducing the physical effects of distress. They include counseling, psychotherapy and medical care. Most stress management programs emphasize the first two levels to try to minimize the need for third-level steps.

Stress management programs should involve everyone in the project team who needs help from distress. Project managers are among the most stressed individuals because they are caught in the middle and are under pressure by everyone else. They usually need a stress management program as much or more than anyone.

10.10 SUMMARY

Some conflict is inevitable in organizations. Properly managed, it is even beneficial. In projects, the primary sources of conflict are schedules, priorities, manpower levels, technical opinions, administrative issues, interpersonal conflicts, and costs. The relative importance of these varies with the stage of the project life cycle.

In project management the assumption is that, generally, conflict is best dealt with through confrontation. Confrontation examines the underlying issues and attempts to resolve the conflict at its source. It presumes, however, that people will be open, honest, and willing to work together to resolve the conflict. Lacking these conditions or poorly handled, confrontation can lead to hostility and personality conflicts.

Conflict often occurs because of a violation of expectations between parties. Sharing, clarifying, and mutual agreement of expectations is one way to eliminate such conflict. This is the basis for conflict resolution using the role analysis (RAT) and intergroup problem solving (IGPS) techniques.

Stress in projects is inevitable, though distress is not. Stress induces energy, increases vitality, and helps people deal with the demands of work. But stress from too few or too many work demands can be debilitating. In projects, the main sources of stress are demanding goals and schedules, work tasks, roles, and social relations. Good project planning helps reduce many technical sources of stress. Participating management, role analysis, and social support help reduce destructive stress from work tasks, roles, and social relations. Participating managers lessen tensions by providing greater decision latitude and flexibility. Stressors from work roles are inevitable, but role analysis helps reduce ambiguity and conflict. Social support assists individuals in their capacity to deal with stressful work demands which cannot be altered. Most individuals need training in social support skills; team building can be used to help foster more supportive team behavior.

As leaders, project managers share responsibility with each individual for the health of project team members. In high stress projects, managers can sponsor stress management programs and set an example by taking advantage of these programs. Project managers may be in the best position to diagnose the stress of the organization by using their own stress level as a barometer.

CHAPTER REVIEW QUESTIONS

1. What are the sources of conflict between the user and the contractor? How do contracts lead to conflict?
2. What are the sources of conflict between parties in the project organization?
3. Describe how the sources of conflict vary with the phases of the project life cycle.
4. What are the negative consequences of conflict in projects?
5. Some conflict is natural and beneficial. Explain why.
6. Describe five ways of dealing with conflict.
7. Explain how the project manager uses confrontation to resolve conflict.
8. What are the assumptions in using confrontation (i.e., what conditions must exist for it to be successful)?
9. Describe the "expectation theory" of conflict. How does the expectation theory compare with your experiences of conflict in work situations?
10. Describe the role analysis technique. What sources of conflict does it resolve?
11. Describe what happens in intergroup problem solving. What sources of conflict does it resolve?
12. List and compare environmental and individual stressors.
13. Describe each of these major sources of stress in the project environment: project goals and schedules, work overload, role conflict and ambiguity, and social/interpersonal relations. Describe your work experiences with these sources of stress.
14. What are the benefits of stress? What are the negative consequences of too much or too little stress (distress) on individuals and organizations?
15. Describe the means by which (a) participating management and (b) role analysis help to reduce work stress.
16. What is "social support?" What are the sources of social support? How does social support reduce job stress?
17. What are some ways of improving social support among project team members?
18. Name some techniques that individuals can use to manage or reduce their stress levels.
19. Investigate further, through outside reading or discussion, the techniques listed in question 18.

QUESTIONS ABOUT THE STUDY PROJECT

Ask the manager or others involved in the project that you are studying about the major sources of conflict.

1. How prevalent is conflict and what effect does conflict have on individual and project performance?
2. What responsibility does the project manager take in resolving these conflicts?
3. How does the project manager resolve conflict? Is confrontation used?
4. Are any formal procedures used, such as RAT or IGPS, to resolve conflicts?

Emotional stress is a personal issue and most people are hesitant to speak about it other than on a general level. Still, you might ask the project manager or other team members about stresses they personally feel or perceive in the project:

5. Is this a high stress or low stress project? Explain. If it is a high stress environment, is it taken for granted that that is the way it must be or do people feel that steps could be taken to reduce the stress?

6. Are there any noticeable consequences of distress on individuals or project performance? Explain.

7. Does the project manager try to help team members deal with job stress? Explain.

8. Does the organization make available to its employees programs on stress management? Have any of the people on the project team had experience or formal training in stress management techniques?

ENDNOTES

1. L.R. Sayles and M.K. Chandler, *Managing Large Systems* (New York: Harper & Row, 1971), 277–8.

2. Ibid., 278.

3. W.H. Schmidt, "Conflict: A Powerful Process for (Good or Bad) Change," *Management Review*, Vol. 63, (Dec. 1974), 5.

4. H.J. Thamhain and D.L. Wilemon, "Conflict Management in Project Life Cycles," *Sloan Management Review* (Spring 1975), 31–50; and H.J. Thamhain and D.L. Wilemon, "Diagnosing Conflict Determinants in Project Management," *IEEE Transactions of Engineering Management*, Vol. 22 (February 1975).

5. It is not only the best approach, it is also the one most favored by project managers (followed by compromise, then smoothing, then forcing and withdrawal). See Thamhain and Wilemon, "Conflict Management in Project Life Cycles," 42–44.

6. Ibid., 46–47.

7. Sayles and Chandler, *Managing Large Systems*, 216.

8. This section focuses on managing conflict from a group level perspective. For an individual level perspective, see Marc Robert, *Managing Conflict from the Inside Out* (Austin: Learning Concepts, 1982).

9. This discussion is based upon W.G. Dyer, *Team Building: Issues and Alternatives*, 2nd ed. (Reading, Mass.: Addison- Wesley, 1987), 116–18. See Herb Bisno, *Managing Conflict* (Newbury Park, CA: Sage, 1988) for another perspective.

10. This discussion is based upon Dyer, *Team Building*, 109– 16.

11. Ibid., 111.

12. Ibid., 112.

13. Ibid., 113–14.

14. This section based upon Dyer, ibid., 116–17, 135.

15. Portions of this section are adapted from E.F. Huse and T.G. Cummings, *Organization Development and Change*, 3rd ed. (St. Paul: West, 1985), Chap. 12; J.C. Quick and J.D. Quick, *Organizational Stress and Preventive Management* (New York: McGraw Hill, 1984); and J.C. Williams, *Human Behavior in Organizations*, 2nd ed. (Cincinnati: South-Western, 1982), Chap. 9.

16. A. Bryman, et al., "The Concept of the Temporary System: The Case of the Construction Project," *Research in the Sociology and Psychology of Organizations*, Vol. 5, 1987, 253–83.

17. Portions of this section are adapted from Huse and Cummings, *Organization Development and Change* ; Quick and Quick, *Organizational Stress and Preventive Management* ; Williams, *Human Behavior in Organizations* ; J.S. House, *Work Stress and Social Support* (Reading, Mass.: Addison-Wesley, 1981); and L.J. Warshaw, *Managing Stress* (Reading, Mass.: Addison-Wesley, 1982).

18. See research cited in Quick and Quick, *Organizational Stress and Preventive Management*, 170.

19. House, *Work Stress and Social Support*, 30–38.

20. Ibid., 22–26.

21. Ibid., 98.

22. Ibid., 99.

23. Williams, *Human Behavior in Organizations*, 221.

IV

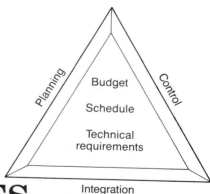

Planning

Control

Budget

Schedule

Technical
requirements

Integration

SYSTEMS
AND PROCEDURES

It is possible for a project manager to use participating management, foster high level esprit de corps, skillfully manage conflict, and yet—after all that—still have virtually nothing to show for it. Successful project management is more than just managing people and groups, it is defining the work they must do, then providing leadership and direction to ensure it gets done. Overall project goals need to be articulated into shorter term objectives with carefully plotted plans, schedules, and budgets to accomplish them. Controls are then needed to make sure plans and schedules are carried out as intended.

Over the years an impressive collection of methods has been developed to help project managers collect and use information for defining and directing work. The next seven chapters describe these, including techniques and procedures for specifying, scheduling, and budgeting project activities, organizing and keeping track of them, and monitoring and controlling work to achieve project goals.

Procedures are best conducted within the framework of a system to ensure that all elements are accounted for, properly organized, and executed. The so-called Project Management System and the various structures, activities, and frameworks that comprise it—work breakdown structures, cost accounting systems, management information systems, and many others—are also described in this section.

The concluding chapter discusses failure and success in the practice of project management. It summarizes lessons learned and ties together the major topics and tenets of the book.

chapter 11

Work Definition and Scheduling

Big fleas have little fleas
Upon their backs to bite 'em
Little fleas have lesser fleas
And so ad infinitum.

Old rhyme[1]

As we have seen, successful project management calls for selecting the appropriate organization form, choosing skilled and influential project leadership, and building an integrated, coordinated project team. Yet all of this is not enough: the project manager and project team need to know *what to do*. Deciding what to do is the function of project planning. Making sure it is done right is the function of project control.

During the planning and control process three things happen: (1) before the project begins (and during the conception and definition phases) a *plan is prepared* specifying project goals, work tasks, schedules and budgets; during the project (in the acquisition phase) (2) the *plan is compared to actual* time, cost, and performance figures so that, if there are discrepancies from the plan, (3) *corrective action can be taken* and time and cost estimates for the project can be updated. Planning and control are essential parts of project management; they enable people to understand what is needed to meet project goals, and reduce the uncertainty of outcomes. Planning is the subject of the next four chapters.

11.1 PLANNING STEPS

Top management gives the authorization to begin planning shortly after a contract request or RFP is received. This authorization releases funds so that plans, schedules, and budgets can be prepared. These plans are then used to justify additional funds and authorize work for the remainder of the project.

Since every project is different there is never an apriori, established way specifying how it should be done. New projects pose new questions. For starters, the project team has to answer questions about *what* has to be done, *how* it has to be done, by *whom*, in *what order*, *for how much*, and by *when*. The formalized way to answer these questions is through the planning process. The process addresses the questions in roughly the following steps:

1. Project *objectives* and *requirements* are set. These specify project end-items, desired results, and time, cost, and performance targets. (What, for how much, and by when?)

2. The specific *work activities*, tasks, or jobs to achieve objectives are broken out, defined, and listed. (What?)

3. A *project organization* is created specifying the departments, subcontractors, and managers responsible for work activities. (Who?)

4. A *schedule* is prepared showing the timing of work activities, deadlines, and milestones. (When, in what order?)

5. A *budget* and *resource plan* is prepared showing the amount and timing of resources and expenditures for work activities and related items. (How much and when?)

6. A *forecast* is prepared of time, cost, and performance projections for the completion of the project. (How much is needed, what will it cost, and when will the project be finished?)

These steps need to be followed every time because every project is somewhat unique, requires different resources, and must be completed to specific time, cost, and performance standards to satisfy users' requirements. Whenever projects are similar, much of the planning relies on past experience and historical records for assistance; when they are first-of-a-kind, much of the planning proceeds from scratch.

Functional areas of the organization assigned to the project should be involved in the planning process. Although each area develops its own plan, all plans are derived from and become a part of a single, overall project plan. This overall plan is referred to as the *project summary plan* or project master plan.

11.2 THE PROJECT SUMMARY PLAN

The project is initiated with the preparation of a formal, written summary plan. The purpose of this plan is to guide the project manager and team throughout the project life cycle; to tell them what resources are needed, when, and how much they will cost; and, later, to enable them to measure progress, determine when they are falling behind, and know what to do to catch up.

Common sources of project failure such as scheduling and cost overruns could often be avoided if more thought were given to planning. The process of preparing a summary plan should be thorough and begun early, even before the project is authorized. In most cases, this means that project planning begins during formulation of the project proposal. During proposal preparation, a rudimentary project team is organized and major decisions for resource acquisition are made. The team prepares a summary project plan for inclusion in the proposal using the same (albeit more abbreviated) procedures as they will use later to develop more elaborate and detailed plans. When management approves the plan it gives the project manager tacit authority to conduct the project in accordance with the plan.

Contents of Summary Plans

The contents of summary plans vary depending on the size, complexity, and nature of the project. Typically, the plan has four major sections:[2]

I.   Introduction. Definition of the project and summary of its background and history. This may be combined with the management summary.

II.   Management Summary. An overview description of the project oriented toward top level management. It includes a brief description of the project, objectives, overall requirements, constraints, problem areas (and how they will be overcome), and the master schedule showing major events and milestones.

III.   Management and Organization Section. Overview of organization and personnel requirements for the project. It includes:

   1.   Project management and organization. Details how the project will be managed and identifies key personnel and authority relationships.
   2.   Manpower. Estimates of work force requirements in terms of skills, expertise, and strategies for locating and recruiting qualified people.
   3.   Training and development. Summary of the executive development and personnel training necessary to support the project.

IV.   Technical Section. Overview of major project activities, timing, and cost. It includes:

   1.   Statement of work. Generalized breakdown of project showing major activities and tasks.
   2.   Project schedules. Generalized project and task schedules showing major events, milestones, and points of critical action or decision. May include Gantt charts, project networks, and PERT/CPM diagrams.
   3.   Budget and financial support. Estimates and timing of capital and development expenses for labor, materials, and facilities.
   4.   Testing. Listing of things to be tested, including procedures, timing, and persons responsible.

5. Documentation. List of documents to be produced and how they will be organized and maintained.

6. Implementation. Discussion and guidelines showing how the customer will convert to, or adopt, the results of the project.

7. Work review plan. Procedures for periodic review of work, noting what is to be reviewed, when, by whom, and according to what standards.

8. Economic justification. Summary of alternatives in meeting project objectives showing tradeoffs between costs and schedules.

9. Areas of uncertainty and risk. Contingency plans for areas of greatest uncertainty in terms of potential work failure or missed milestones. (This section is often excluded because it scares users and management.)

Depending on the client or type of project contract, some plans require additional, special items not outlined here.[3] In small or low cost projects, it is possible to delete certain sections, taking care not to overlook the crucial ones. It is usually good practice to systematically cover every item in the four sections even if only to verify that some of them are "N/A" (not applicable). An example of a project summary plan is given for the LOGON Project in Appendix C.

You might notice a similarity between the sections of the summary plan and the contents of the proposal described in section 5.6. Though the format is slightly different, there is indeed a similarity. In many cases the proposal, revised and updated to reflect current agreements and contract specifications, becomes the project summary plan. At other times, when the project summary needs to be expanded and defined in greater detail, the proposal serves as an outline. Since the primary audience of the final summary plan is the project team and not the user, the technical section is usually larger and in greater detail than what appears in the project proposal.

As the following example shows, the development of a project plan is an evolutionary process.

Developing a Project Plan at Master Control Company

The Master Control Company (MCC), a medium-sized engineering firm, was approached by Bier Publishing Company to develop a control unit for tracking the production process of two multistage, high efficiency printing presses. The Bier engineering department initiated the project by sending MCC a list of requirements for power, wiring, performance, and possible future enhancements for the unit. MCC appointed a project manager to oversee design and development and to prepare a proposal.

MCC's engineering group conceived an initial, theoretical design to cover all specifications and circumvent any design flaws. Throughout the process they consulted with engineers from Bier, and the design was altered and redone several times. The final design consisted of blueprints, a manual of operational specifications, and a bill of materials and parts.

With this design the MCC marketing department performed a detailed analysis of the price of parts and cost of labor. The manager of the production department also examined the design and, together with the project manager, prepared a work breakdown structure and tentative project plan outlining major work tasks.

A meeting was held with representatives from project management, engineering, marketing, and production, to review the project plan, costs, and feasibility. The production department supplied information about the kind of labor expertise needed, the availability of parts, and a forecast of the time required to produce the unit. Marketing provided information about the costs of labor, parts and supplies, and the overall project. Having this information, the project manager was able to expand the project plan, develop a bid price, and combine the two into a proposal. Notice that, in terms of the systems-development process, the stages of initiation, feasibility, definition, and most of the design were completed before the proposal was even sent to Bier.

Following contract negotiation and signing, the project manager and production manager developed a final, detailed master plan. This plan contained the same information as the proposal but was updated and expanded to include a schedule for materials and parts purchases, a schedule of labor distribution for work tasks, a management and task responsibility matrix, and a detailed master schedule.

Seldom does project planning occur all at once or at a particular point in time. As this example shows, the plan is developed gradually, expanded and modified as information is accumulated and after it has been reviewed, refined, and finally accepted by project participants.

Learning from Past Projects

During development of the project plan, reference should be made to earlier, similar projects (including plans, procedures, successes, and failures) for whatever applications seem relevant. Indeed, when they exist, this is one purpose of the *postcompletion project summary* (described in Chapter 17), that is, to enable planners to avoid reinventing the wheel and repeating past failures. Often projects are approached as *too* unique, and the lessons of history—dilemmas, mistakes, and solutions—are ignored. Simply, this means that in preparing for any project it is important to scrutinize what others have done before. Although this approach is somewhat common among researchers and scholars, it is less so among persons who consider themselves more "action-oriented."[4]

Tools of Project Planning

Much of the technical content of project plans is derived from the basic tools described in this chapter; these are:

1. *Work breakdown structure* and *work packages*—used to define the project work and break it down into specific tasks.
2. *Responsibility matrix*—used to define project organization, key individuals, and their responsibilities.
3. *Events* and *milestones*—used to identify critical points and major occurrences on the project schedule.
4. *Gantt Charts*—used to display the project master schedule and detailed task schedules.

Additional planning tools such as networks, critical path analysis, PERT/CPM, cost estimating, budgeting, and forecasting are covered in subsequent chapters.

11.3 WORK DEFINITION

Once project objectives have been set they must be translated into specific, well-defined elements of work. A big list is needed telling the team what tasks, jobs, or activities need to be done to accomplish the project. On large, new projects it is easy to overlook or duplicate activities. So that no activities are missed and the relationships between them are clearly understood, a systematic, formal approach is used to define the work elements. This is called the work breakdown structure.

Work Breakdown Structure

Complex projects consist of numerous smaller, interrelated tasks and work elements. As the rhyme at the beginning of the chapter alludes, the goal or end-item of a project is a system which can be broken down into subsystems, which themselves can be broken down, and so on. The procedure for dividing the overall project into sub-elements is called the *work breakdown structure* or *WBS*. The purpose of a WBS is to divide the total project into small pieces, sometimes called *work packages*. Dividing the project into work packages makes it possible to prepare project schedules and cost estimates and to assign management and task responsibility.

The first step in creating a WBS is to divide the total project into major work categories. These major categories are then divided into subcategories which, in turn, are subdivided, and so on. This level-by-level breakdown continues so that the scope and complexity of work elements is reduced with each level of breakdown. The resulting WBS is analogous to a product structure diagram.

The objective of the analysis is to reduce the project into work elements that are so clearly defined that they, individually, can be thoroughly and accurately defined, budgeted, scheduled, and controlled. The WBS approach helps insure that all elements, even minor ones, are accounted for.

A typical WBS might consist of the following five levels (in actuality the number of levels varies; the name of the element description at each level is arbitrary):

Level	Element Description
1	Project
2	Category
3	Subcategory
4	Sub-subcategory
5	Work package

Level 1 represents the total project. At Level 2 the project is broken down into several (usually 4 to 10) major categories of work. All of the categories' efforts, when taken together, must make up the *total project effort*. Each category, in turn, is broken down into subcategories, the sum of which must comprise the effort of the category. At the lowest level, whatever level that might be, is a work package. Figure 11–1 shows the typical hierarchical structure of a WBS.

Figure 11–2 illustrates the WBS for building a house. The top part of Figure 11–2 shows the project objective (Level 1) and the major categories of items (Level 2) necessary to accomplish it. Notice that, for the most part, the items in the breakdown are *hardware-* or *product-oriented*. This makes it easier to assign specific responsibilities and to hold people accountable for specific *units of work* with expected performance, cost, and schedule requirements. As will be demonstrated later, using a thorough, product-oriented WBS facilitates in the scheduling and budgeting of projects.

In contrast to the top WBS in Figure 11–2, the WBS in the middle is *less desirable*. This is because it is *functionally-oriented*, and associated with each function (e.g., carpentry) are numerous products (such as cabinets, walls, floors, trim, doors, stairs, and windows), all of which require work that must eventually be scheduled at various times in the project. The point is, to plan for the project it would be necessary to eventually break each of these functions down into *products* anyway.

There are, however, a few places in the WBS where a *task oriented* breakdown might be necessary or desirable. This is the case for tasks such as "design," "engineering," or "management," which are *common* to more than one element in the WBS or involve *integrating* elements in the WBS into the total system.

Continuing with the example in Figure 11–2, Level 2 items would be further elaborated into a work breakdown at Level 3 (shown at the bottom of Figure 11–2), and

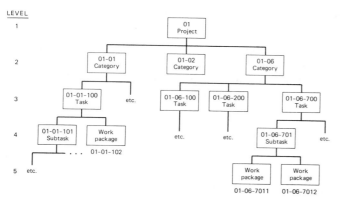

FIGURE 11–1. Elements of a work breakdown structure.

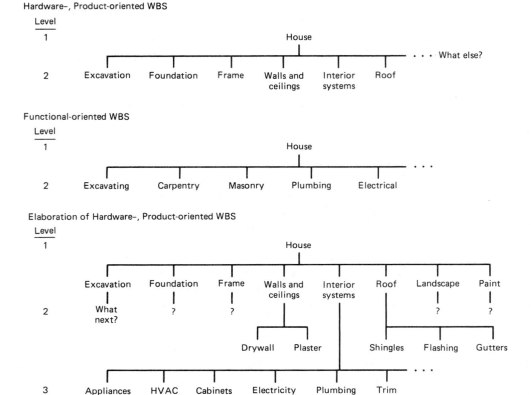

FIGURE 11–2.   Example of WBS for building a house.

each of these items would be further broken down as necessary at Level 4, and so on. Concurrent with the development of the WBS is the process of *work definition*. As each element of the WBS is identified and broken down, project work is further elaborated and more clearly specified. By the time the WBS is completed, all work on the project has been completely defined.

During the WBS process, the questions "What else is needed?" and "What's next?" are constantly being asked. The WBS is reviewed again and again to make sure everything is there. Supplementary or missed items are identified and added to the structure at appropriate levels. For example, nowhere in the WBS in Figure 11–2 are blueprints, budgets, and work schedules indicated, even though construction cannot begin without them. These are items associated with the planning phase of the project, things that must be completed prior to construction. They could be included in the WBS by expanding Level 2 and inserting categories for "design" and "administration and management," then by putting "architectural and engineering blueprints" at Level 3 under "design" and "budget and work schedules" at Level 3 under "administration and management." It might also be necessary to expand Level 2 so that other considerations like site location and building maintainability could be included.

The WBS should be checked by the various project participants to insure that nothing is missed. In cases like building a house where the work is pretty standardized, the likelihood of overlooking something is remote. However, the larger and less standardized the project, the easier it is to miss something and the more valuable the WBS becomes. Nothing must be overlooked. Training, documentation, and project management activities should all be included.

As another example of the process of developing a WBS, consider the Logistical Online Network (LOGON) illustration project. Initially, the project manager and project office staff "rough out" the major categories of work and the functional areas responsible. This is the Level 2 breakdown. The project manager then meets with managers from the functional areas identified for approval of the Level 2 breakdown. The functional managers then work with planners and supervisors in their areas to prepare a Level 3 breakdown. Supervisors then prepare a Level 4 breakdown.

The result is shown in Figure 11–3. Level 2 divides the project into the major work elements of basic design, hardware part A, fabrication, and so on. At Level 3, hardware part A is subdivided into design and drawings. These become the work packages for hardware part A since they are the lowest elements in that part of the structure. The resulting WBS is reviewed for final approval by the project manager, functional managers, and supervisors.

Another example is shown in Figure 11–4. This breakdown subdivides the project according to categories of major system assemblies, then divides the assemblies into subassemblies. Each subassembly would be assigned to a functional work group which would then do a work breakdown to elaborate the items and tasks to produce that subassembly.

To help keep track of project activities, each category, task, etc. should be coded by a unique number. Usually the number at each level is based on the next higher level. For example in Figure 11–1, the six categories in Project "01" were numbered 01–01 through 01–06. Then, for example, in the last category, 01–06, the seven tasks were numbered 01–06–100 through 01–06–700, and so on. The coding scheme is established by managers during development of the WBS. The scheme must be accepted by everyone as being neither "too broad" nor "too detailed." The kind of numbering system varies depending on the control scheme used. It should be emphasized, however, that of paramount importance is the correct partitioning of WBS elements, not the numbering scheme. The numbering scheme shown in Figure 11–4 is another example.

As mentioned, the WBS should be product-, hardware-, or task-, but *not* functionally-oriented. This means that elements on the WBS should correspond to subsystems or

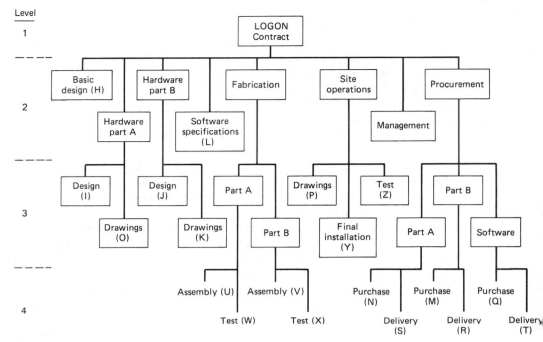

FIGURE 11–3. Work breakdown structure for the LOGON Project. Work packages are lettered H through Z.

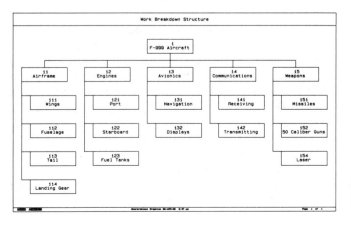

FIGURE 11–4. Typical WBS based upon primary hardware. (Courtesy, Metier Management Systems.)

components (hardware or software) of the end-item system, or to work tasks (assembly, test, delivery, etc.), but *not* to functional departments like Personnel, Finance, Engineering, etc. Generally there is little or no correspondence between divisions and levels in the WBS and the functional hierarchy of organizations.

How far down does the breakdown structure go? Simply, as far as is needed to deduce the following: a good definition of the work, how long it will take, what resources it will require, and what it will cost. Sometimes these will be known at level 2, though usually a level 3 or higher breakdown will be necessary.

On the other hand, the breakdown must not continue *so* far that it unnecessarily encumbers the system. Too much breakdown will actually increase the amount of time needed to do the project. A large number of individual tasks require greater time and cost than fewer tasks. Each work package is the focal point of management planning and control and, as such, requires paperwork, time, and cost to monitor. Notice that different "branches" on the WBS do not necessarily have the same number of levels; this is because each branch is developed separately.

WBS in the Planning and Control Process

The WBS becomes the central feature of the project planning and control process. It is used in three ways:

1. During the WBS analysis, functional managers and others who will be doing the work are identified and become involved. Their approval of the WBS helps insure accuracy and completeness of work definition, and gains their commitment to the project.

2. The WBS and work packages become the basis for budgeting and scheduling. The cost and time estimates for each work package show what is expected to complete that work package. The sum of work package budgets plus overhead and indirect expenses becomes the target cost of the entire project. These budgets and schedules are the baselines against which actual figures will later be compared to measure project performance.

3. The WBS and work packages become the basis for project control. When the project is underway, actual work completed for each work package is compared to work that was scheduled to have been completed. This gives an estimate of time and schedule variance. Similarly, a comparison of actual expenditures to date with the value of the work accomplished gives an estimate of cost variance. Schedule and cost variances for the project as a whole are determined by summarizing all schedule and cost data throughout the WBS. These procedures are described in later chapters.

The WBS should never be a mere copy of the WBS for a previous project. No matter how similar projects might seem, scrutiny and care should go into preparing every WBS. To reduce oversights, it is a good idea to have two or more WBS's prepared independently.

Also, the WBS should be as flexible as possible to permit revisions in case there are changes in project objectives or scope. Since it is the basis for project schedules, budgets, and control mechanisms, even small changes to the WBS can be difficult and costly to make and cause problems in procurement, staffing, and cash flow. Whenever changes are needed, a systematic "change control" procedure for revision and communication is necessary so that all changes are authorized and communicated to affected parties. This is discussed in Chapter 15.

Work Packages

Within the WBS, work packages should represent jobs of about equal magnitude of effort and be of relatively small cost and short duration compared to the total project. Sometimes, to reduce the proliferation of work packages in large projects, several related activities or small work packages are aggregated to form work packages on the basis of cost and time. For example, DOD/NASA guidelines specify that work packages should be of three months' duration and not exceed $100,000 in cost. These are guidelines however, not strict limits. The dollar size and duration of work packages depend on many factors, including the control practices of the industry, stage of the project (usually design work packages have a longer duration, and fabrication work packages have a larger cost), size of the project (smaller projects have smaller work packages), and the detail and shape of the WBS.

Each work package represents either a subcontract of work to be performed by outsiders or, more likely, an "internal contract" of work to be performed by an inside functional unit. A typical work package description includes:[5]

- A summary of the work to be accomplished.
- Inputs required from other project tasks (predecessors).
- The manager and organizational unit responsible.
- Product specifications.
- Subcontracts and purchase orders.
- Resource estimates for labor, material, equipment, and facilities.
- Total cost and budget.
- Work orders.
- Scheduled dates and milestone events.
- Specific results: hardware, software, tests, documents, drawings, deliveries, etc.

Table 11–1 gives a partial description—the time, cost, and labor estimates—for work packages in the LOGON project.

Specific start and finish events should be identified for work packages where the output is a tangible result or physical product. For tasks directly related to the project but that have no definable end result—overhead and management are examples—there should be a separate part of the WBS. Other tasks that also have no end product, such as inspection and maintenance, must also be identified as work packages. Cost and time figures for these activities are determined as a percentage of other work elements. More will be said about this in Chapter 14.

TABLE 11–1. Activities, Time, Cost, and Labor Requirements (Result of Work Breakdown Analysis)

Activity	Time (weeks)	Weekly Direct Cost ($K)	Total Cost ($K)	Weekly Labor Requirement (workers)
H	10	10	100	5
I	8	8	64	4
J	6	16	96	8
K	4	4	16	2
L	2	18	36	6
M	4	21	84	3
N	4	20	80	2
O	5	10	50	5
P	5	12	60	6
Q	5	16	80	2
R	5	0	0	0
S	3	0	0	0
T	3	0	0	0
U	1	14	14	9
V	5	16	80	14
W	2	12	24	6
X	3	12	36	6
Y	8	13	104	14
Z	6	11	66	5

Total Direct Cost—$990K

As can be seen, the concept of the work package is central to project management. All of the major functions of management—planning, organizing, motivating, directing, and control—are carried out with reference to individual work packages:[6]

- Projects are planned by subdividing them into work packages and then aggregating the plans of work packages.
- Projects are organized by organizing work packages. This involves assembling resources and delegating responsibility to persons who will manage work packages.
- The project effort is motivated by motivating people who are doing individual work packages.
- Projects are directed by directing how activities within work packages should be done.
- Projects are controlled by controlling work packages. This involves monitoring each work package with respect to target costs, performance requirements, and completion dates.

11.4 PROJECT ORGANIZATION STRUCTURE AND RESPONSIBILITIES

Integrating WBS and Project Organization

As the WBS is being developed, it is related to the project organization by identifying the areas of the organization that will have functional and budgetary responsibility for each work package. As an illustration, the LOGON project is being conducted by the Standard Industrial Gadgets (STING) Company. Figure 11–5 represents the integration of the WBS for LOGON with the organizational structure for STING. On the left are company departments and on the top are LOGON work packages. The box at the intersection of a department with a work package, called a *cost account*, represents assignment of responsibility for that work package to that department. It means that the department is "accountable" for that work package. Like the work package itself, each account has prespecified start and finish dates, a budget, resource requirements, and a manager or supervisor responsible for overseeing the work. In general, each box represents a "contract" with a department, subcontractor, or supplier to complete a task within work package requirements. Cost accounts are described more in Chapter 14.

While relationships exist between all levels of the WBS and the project organization, for effective planning and control accounts should be established at the lowest levels of the WBS—at the work package level and possibly lower. Once work package responsibility has been assigned to a department, more detailed subdivisions can be made within the work package by assigning responsibility down to still lower management and technical levels.

Responsibility Matrix

The intersection of the WBS and the organizational structure can be represented by a chart called a *responsibility matrix* or "responsibility chart." In Figure 11–6, the responsibility matrix format is shown for one functional position and one work package. The position of project engineer has the responsibility of "approval" for the work package of "basic design."

The responsibility matrix in Figure 11–7 shows the organizational relationships among all work packages and key personnel for the LOGON project. Each row on the responsibility matrix shows all of the persons or functional positions involved in one work package and the type of involvement. Each column shows all the work tasks or work packages for which a single person or functional position is responsible.

An advantage of the matrix is that project personnel can easily see what their responsibility is to work packages and to other individuals in the project. When further breakdown of assignments is necessary, those listed in the matrix can subdivide their respective tasks and make assignments to additional individuals.

The kind of responsibility defined for each organizational position/work package intersection should be determined by mutual agreement of the workers listed and their managers and other affected parties. This insures consensus about the nature of responsibilities and enables everyone to share what they think is expected of them and what they

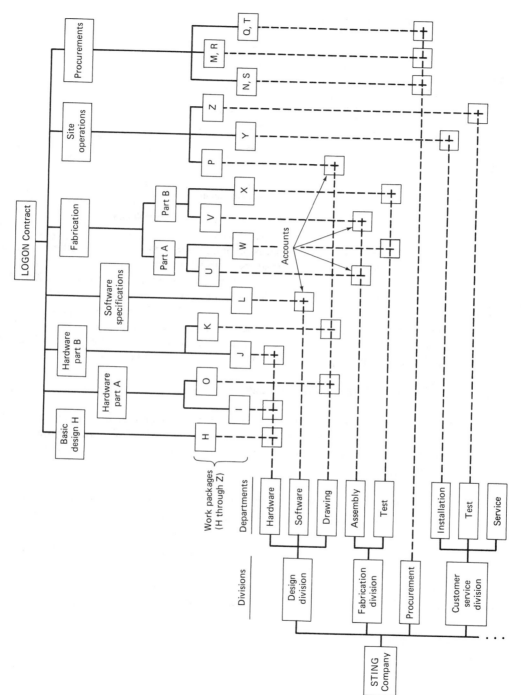

FIGURE 11–5. Integration of WBS and project organization.

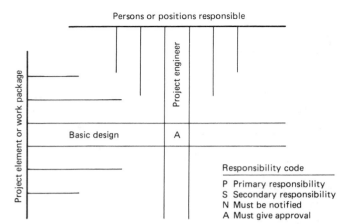

FIGURE 11–6. Structure of a responsibility matrix.

expect from others. To prevent confusion or conflict, the matrix can be filled in during a team building session using role analysis or similar techniques described earlier.

Since the responsibility matrix prescribes how units in the organization *should* perform, it is useful for monitoring and assessing how well responsibilities are being carried out. It permits managers and others to know where responsibilities lie and helps avoid "passing the buck." However, it obviously expresses only formal relationships and not necessarily *how* people really interact or other aspects of informal organization. Nonetheless, it is a useful planning device and helps reduce misunderstandings and conflict later on.

11.5 PROJECT MANAGEMENT SYSTEM

The system around which the managerial functions of planning, organizing, communicating, and control are structured and consolidated is called the Project Management System (PMS). Briefly, the structural elements and activities that jointly comprise the PMS for each project follow:[7] PMS structures include:

1. A *work breakdown structure and work packages* to define all work to be done.
2. An *organization structure* to integrate people and functional areas with the WBS and assign responsibilities.
3. *Project schedules* to provide a basis for work package resource allocation and work timing.
4. *Cost accounts* to provide a basis for project cost and performance control.
5. *Budgets* to define expected costs for each cost account and work package.

PMS activities which utilize the above structures include:

6. Means for collecting and storing *project management information* and performing *evaluation*.

Persons Responsible

Responsibility Code

P Primary responsibility
S Secondary responsibility
N Must be notified
A Must give approval

Project Task or Activity	Project Manager	Project Engineer — Design						Drawing				Software				Site Operations					Assembly A					Assembly B		Fabrication Manager
	F.W.	J.M.	S.E.H.	R.L.Q.	P.J.	D.V.R.	R.L.P.	O.E.M.	P.V.R.	D.M.N.	R.L.	L.S.F.	J.R.S.	D.V.Q.	F.W.N.	J.M.M.N.	L.O.T.	A.U.A.	D.A.R.	S.O.B.	E.N.	G.G.F.	R.T.T.	B.V.L.	B.J.	T.T.Y.	H.R.D.	B.V.–Purchasing
Project coordination	P	S																	S									
Project development	A	P	A	P	S	S																					N	
Project design	A		A	P	S																							
H Basic design	N					A					N	N			A				N								N	
I Hardware design A		A	A	P		N					N																	
J Hardware design B		A	A	P		N					N																	
K Drawings B		A	A					A	S	P																		
L Software specs	N	N			A							A	P	S	S													
M Parts purchase B	N	N																									P	
N Parts purchase A	N	N																	N	A							P	
O Drawings A					A	A		A	S	P									A	A								
P Installation drawings						A		A		P					N				N	A							P	
Q Software purchase	N													N					A	A	A	P	S	A				
U Assembly A	N													N	N				N	N	A	A	P	S				
V Assembly B	N													A	A				A	N				A	P	S		
W Test A	N													N	N	A	P	S	A	A								
X Test B	N													N	P	P	S		A	P							P	
Y Final installation	N													A	A	P	S											
Z Final test	N																											

FIGURE 11–7. Sample responsibility matrix for LOGON Project (with initials of persons responsible).

7. Means for *reporting information*.

8. Means for *management direction*, decisions and corrective action.

These PMS structures and activities will be discussed in later chapters; they are mentioned in this chapter to emphasize the importance of having a thorough, accurate WBS with work packages or other work elements related to the project organization. The WBS, work packages, and project organization become the bases for establishing other structures in the PMS and the focal points around which PMS activities revolve. Later, in Chapter 16, we will look at the Project Management Information System (PMIS); this is the primary means for consolidating all PMS structures (points 1–5) and accomplishing PMS activities (points 6–8).

11.6 SCHEDULING

Next to the WBS analysis, the *scheduling* of work elements is the most important step in planning since it is the basis for allocating resources, estimating costs, and tracking project performance. Schedules show the timing over which work elements occur and denote when specific events and milestones take place.

Events and Milestones

Project plans are like road maps: they show not only how to get to where you want to go, but how much progress you have made along the way. Work packages are what you must do; taken together, they are the road to project goals. Along the way are signposts called *events* and *milestones* that show how far you have progressed. When the last event is passed, the project is completed.

Events and milestones should not be confused with work packages, activities, or other kinds of tasks. A *task* is the actual work planned (or being done) and represents the *process* of doing something (like *driving* a car to get somewhere); it consumes resources and time. In contrast, an *event* signifies only a *moment in time*, usually the instant when something is *started* or *finished* (like beginning a trip, or arriving at the destination). On some project schedules, tasks are depicted as line segments (the road) which connect two nodes representing the events of starting and completing that task. For example, in Figure 11–8, the line labeled "Task A" represents the duration or time to do the job (the actual doing of the job), while events 1 and 2 represent moments when the job is started and finished, respectively. Schedules reflect the specific calendar dates (day, month, and year) when events are planned to occur.

There are two kinds of events in project plans: interface and milestone events.[8] An *interface event* denotes changes in responsibility or the completion of one task and simultaneous start of one or more subsequent tasks. With interface events, tasks are completed and the results, management responsibility, or both are transferred so that subsequent tasks can begin. Important management decisions and approvals, and avail-

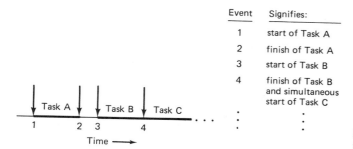

Event	Signifies:
1	start of Task A
2	finish of Task A
3	start of Task B
4	finish of Task B and simultaneous start of Task C

FIGURE 11–8. Relationship between tasks and events.

ability of facilities and equipment necessary for a task to begin are also interface events. Event 4 in Figure 11–8 is an interface event.

A *milestone event* signifies a major occurrence such as completion of several critical or difficult tasks, a major approval, or the availability of crucial resources. Milestone events signify progress and are important measures of project performance. Final approval of a design or successful completion of tests are often designated as milestones because they signify that the project is ready to proceed to another stage of the systems development cycle. Missing a milestone usually signifies that budgets and schedules will have to be revised.

Kinds of Schedules

At least two kinds of planning schedules are commonly used: project schedules and task schedules. Others may be used in larger projects, but these are usually more detailed versions of project schedules.

One kind of project schedule is the *project master schedule*. It is used by project managers and upper management for planning and reviewing the entire project. It shows the major project activities without too much detail. The project master schedule is developed during project initiation and is continually refined thereafter. Project managers develop the project master schedule in a top-down fashion, making bottom-up refinements as the more detailed task schedules are developed by functional managers.

Task schedules show the specific activities necessary to complete a task. They permit lower level managers and supervisors to focus on tasks without being distracted by other areas that they have no interaction with. Task schedules are prepared by functional managers and incorporate interface and milestone events as shown on the master schedule.

Schedules take many forms including Gantt charts, milestone charts, networks, and time-based networks. All of these should be related to the WBS and account for interrelationships between individual work elements.

11.7 PLANNING AND SCHEDULING CHARTS

Gantt Charts

The simplest and most commonly used scheduling technique is the *Gantt chart* (or bar chart) named after the famous management consultant Henry L. Gantt (1861–1919).

During World War I, Gantt worked with the U.S. Army on a method for visually portraying the status of the munitions program. He realized that time was a common denominator to most elements of a program plan and that progress could easily be assessed by viewing each element's status with respect to time. His approach used standardized setup and processing times and depicted the relationship between production jobs planned and completed. The Gantt chart became widely adopted in industry. Today it has many versions and is used in a variety of ways.[9]

The chart consists of a horizontal scale divided into time units—days, weeks, or months—and a vertical scale showing project work elements—tasks, activities, work packages, etc. Figure 11–9 is an example of a Gantt chart for the LOGON project using the work times given in Table 11–1. Work packages are listed on the left-hand side and work weeks are listed along the bottom. The starting and completion times of jobs are indicated by the beginning and ending of each bar.

Preparation of the Gantt chart comes after a WBS analysis; the work packages or other tasks are the work elements to be scheduled. During WBS analysis, time estimates are prepared for each work element by functional managers, others responsible for the work (as shown in the responsibility matrix), or project planners who confer with them. Work elements are then listed in sequence of time, taking into account which elements must be completed before others can be started.

As an example, consider how the first nine work elements in Figure 11–9 (elements H through P) were scheduled. In any project there is a precedence relationship between the jobs (some jobs must be completed before others can begin) and this relationship must

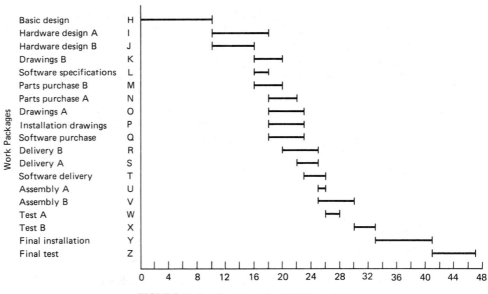

FIGURE 11–9.   Gantt chart for LOGON project.

be determined before jobs can be scheduled. Suppose that during the WBS analysis for LOGON it was determined that before elements I and J could be started, element H had to be completed first; that before elements K, L, and M could be started, element J had to be completed; and that before elements N, O, and P could begin, that I had to be finished. That is,

this must be completed...	before these can be started
H	I,J
J	K,L,M
I	N,O,P

On the Gantt chart this sequencing logic must be maintained. Thus, as shown in Figure 11–10 (using times from Table 11–1), only after week 10—after element H has been completed—can elements I and J be scheduled. After J has been completed in week 16, elements K, L, and M can be scheduled next; finally, after I has been completed in week 18, elements N, O, and P can be scheduled. As each work element is added to the chart, care is taken that it is scheduled only after all work elements which must precede it have been completed.

This example uses work packages as the elements being scheduled, but in fact any level of work can be scheduled depending on the level of detail desired.

The big advantage of the Gantt chart is that it gives a clear pictorial model of the project. One reason it is so widely used is because it is simple to construct and easy for everyone in the project to understand.

After the project is underway the Gantt chart becomes a means for assessing the status of individual work elements and the project as a whole. Figure 11–11 shows progress

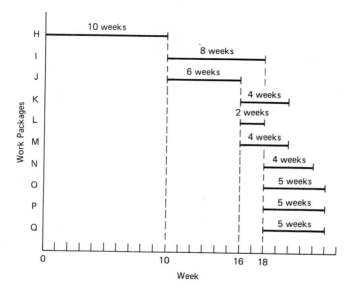

FIGURE 11–10.   Setting up a Gantt chart.

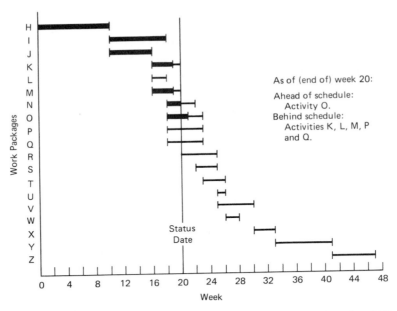

As of (end of) week 20:

Ahead of schedule:
    Activity O.
Behind schedule:
    Activities K, L, M, P
    and Q.

FIGURE 11–11.   Gantt chart for LOGON project showing work progress as of week 20.

as of week 20, the posted "status date." Work that has been completed is indicated by the heavy portion of the bar. The part of the bar not covered by a heavy line represents the amount of work unfinished, or the time still needed to complete the task.

This method is particularly effective for showing which elements are ahead of or behind schedule. For example, as of week 20, work package N is on schedule and work package O is ahead of schedule. Work packages K,L,M,P, and Q are all behind schedule, with L the furthest behind. This might suggest to the project manager that she should shift resources temporarily from O to L.

The amount of time the project is behind schedule is sometimes assumed to roughly correspond with the element on the schedule that is the furthest behind. Corresponding to the delay in work package L, the project in Figure 11-11 is about four weeks behind schedule. As the next chapter will show, however, the project is not *necessarily* four weeks behind schedule. More information is needed to say this for certain, information not available on a simple Gantt chart.

When the Gantt chart is used like this to monitor work progress, it is only as good as the most current information. Thus it must be updated on a daily or weekly basis. Posting the chart to show progress is one way to help keep the team motivated and the project on schedule.

Expense Charts

Gantt charts can be used for manpower planning, resource allocation, and budgeting. Graphs can be constructed based upon information from the Gantt chart to show period by period and cumulative figures such as expenditures, labor, and resource requirements. As an example, in

Table 11–2 the "activities during the week" column (column 2) was derived from the Gantt chart in Figure 11–9. Summing across activities in a given week gives the weekly labor requirements (column 3), weekly direct expense (column 4) and cumulative expense (5).

The information in the last two columns is shown graphically in Figure 11–12. Graphs like this clearly reveal capital funds, labor, and other requirements and are useful for planning the allocation of resources and for monitoring work progress. For small projects like the example they can be used to reschedule activities so resource requirements are compatible with resource availability. This will be discussed in Chapter 13.

Hierarchy of Charts

As the size of the project increases it becomes difficult to present on one chart sufficient information about all of its work elements. The problem is resolved by using a *hierarchy* of charts, as shown by the three levels in Figure 11–13. The top level plan, usually the project master schedule, outlines the principle work packages or aggregates of work packages and provides estimates of major milestones and target dates. The computer generated master schedule in Figure 11–14 is another example.

At the intermediate level, charts expand on the detail of the top level. The activities represented are usually of the cost-account, work package, or subwork package size. The chart in Figure 11–9 is an example. This level schedule is of sufficient detail to permit labor and resource planning by project and functional managers. In a small project the top-level and intermediate-level schedule is one and the same.

A more detailed, bottom-level schedule is necessary on most projects. These are derived from intermediate-level schedules and are the task schedules mentioned before. They are used by work package supervisors and technical specialists to plan and control activities on a daily or weekly basis.

Figure 11–15 is a multilevel schedule. It shows in the upper portion the master schedule from Figure 11–14 and in the lower portion the detailed tasks for one work package, "preliminary design."

Disadvantages of Gantt Charts

There are disadvantages to the Gantt chart. For one, it does not explicitly show interrelationships among work elements so there is no way of knowing from it what the effect is of one work element falling behind schedule on other elements. In most projects, certain work elements must be completed by a specific date to insure that the project is completed on target, while others can be delayed without delaying the project. Gantt charts alone provide no way of distinguishing elements which can be delayed from those which cannot. Neither does a hierarchy of Gantt charts necessarily permit timely assessment of the impact of schedule slippages. Computerized project systems ease the problem, but making changes or updates to hierarchical schedules still can be difficult, especially as the number of activities and planning levels increase.

Gantt charts are often manually maintained. This is an easy task and an advantage in small projects, but it is burdensome in large projects, causes apathy, and results in

TABLE 11–2. LOGON project Weekly Labor Requirements and Expense

Week	Activities During Week	Weekly Labor Requirements	Weekly Expense ($K)	Cumulative Expense ($K)
1	H	5	10	10
2	H	5	10	20
3	H	5	10	30
4	H	5	10	40
5	H	5	10	50
6	H	5	10	60
7	H	5	10	70
8	H	5	10	80
9	H	5	10	90
10	H	5	10	100
11	I,J	12	24	124
12	I,J	12	24	148
13	I,J	12	24	172
14	I,J	12	24	196
15	I,J	12	24	220
16	I,J	12	24	244
17	I,K,L,M	15	51	295
18	I,K,L,M	15	51	346
19	K,M,N,O,P,Q	20	83	429
20	K,M,N,O,P,Q	20	83	512
21	N,O,P,Q	15	58	570
22	N,O,P,Q	15	58	628
23	O,P,Q	13	38	666
24	---	0	0	666
25	---	0	0	666
26	U,V	23	30	696
27	V,W	20	28	724
28	V,W	20	28	752
29	V	14	16	768
30	V	14	16	784
31	X	6	12	796
32	X	6	12	808
33	X	6	12	820
34	Y	14	13	833
35	Y	14	13	846
36	Y	14	13	859
37	Y	14	13	872
38	Y	14	13	885
39	Y	14	13	898
40	Y	14	13	911
41	Y	14	13	924
42	Z	5	11	935
43	Z	5	11	946
44	Z	5	11	957
45	Z	5	11	968
46	Z	5	11	979
47	Z	5	11	990

charts becoming outdated. Computerized project graphics systems eliminate this problem as long as the input data is frequently and periodically revised. The computer generated Gantt chart in Figure 11–16 is an example; notice the comparison of actual versus scheduled task times.

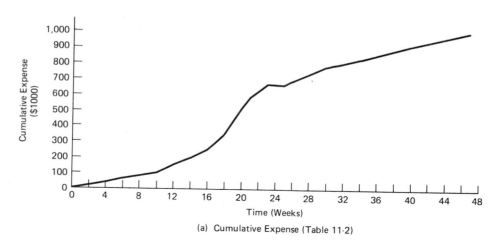

(a) Cumulative Expense (Table 11-2)

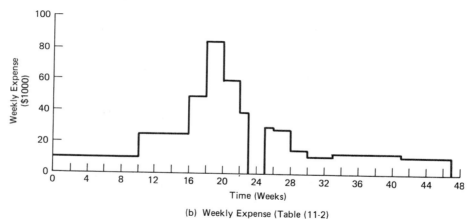

(b) Weekly Expense (Table (11-2)

FIGURE 11–12. Planned weekly and cumulative expenses for the LOGON project.

11.8 SUMMARY

The purpose of project planning is to determine the way in which project goals will be achieved—what must be done, by whom, when, and for how much. Project planning strives to minimize uncertainty, avoid cost and scheduling overruns, and uphold project performance requirements.

This chapter addresses methods for determining the what-who-when issues of projects. The Work Breakdown Structure (WBS) is a formal process that involves managers and specialists in answering the question "what must be done?" The result of the WBS process are work packages or other work elements each small enough to be understood, planned, and controlled. Virtually all functions of management and the Project Manage-

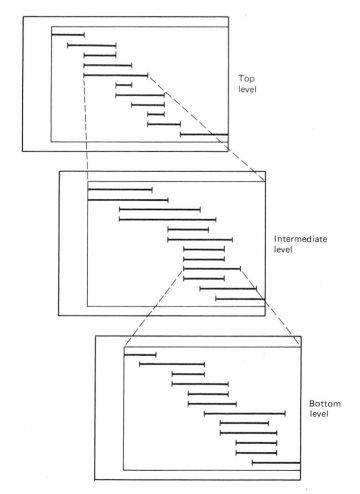

Top level

Intermediate level

Bottom level

FIGURE 11–13. A hierarchy of bar charts.

ment System—scheduling, budgeting, resource allocation, tracking, and evaluation—are subsequently carried out with reference to the WBS and work packages.

The responsibility matrix integrates the project organization with the WBS. It prescribes which units and individuals, both internal and among subcontractors, have project responsibility and the kind of responsibility. It is valuable for achieving consensus, insuring accountability, and reducing conflict among project participants.

Project schedules show the timing of work and are the basis for resource allocation, cost estimation, and performance tracking. Depending on the amount of detail required, different types of schedules are used. Project-level schedules show clusters of tasks and work packages which comprise the project. Task-level schedules show the jobs needed to complete individual work packages or smaller work elements.

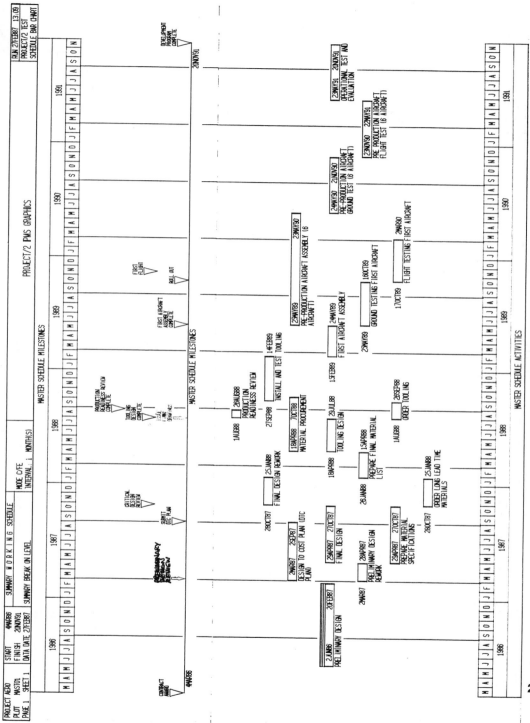

FIGURE 11–14. Master schedule with milestones. (Courtesy, Project Software & Development, Inc.)

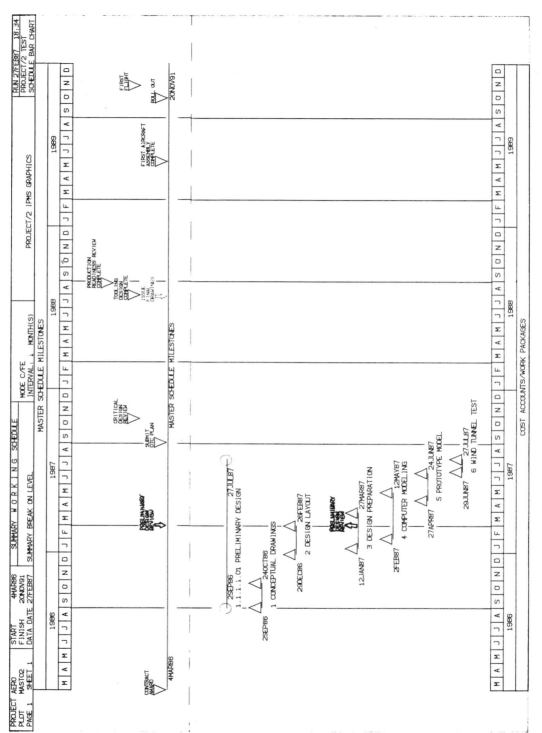

FIGURE 11-15. Multi-level schedule. (Courtesy, Project Software & Development, Inc.)

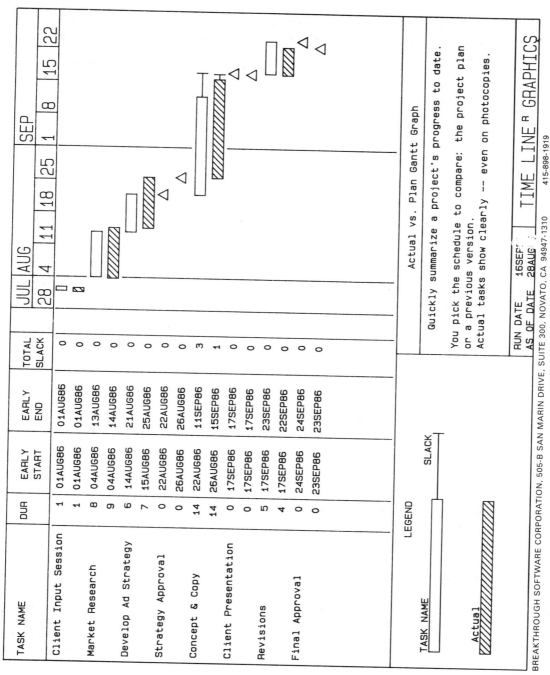

TASK NAME	DUR	EARLY START	EARLY END	TOTAL SLACK	JUL AUG SEP
Client Input Session	1	01AUG86	01AUG86	0	
Market Research	8	04AUG86	13AUG86	0	
Develop Ad Strategy	9	04AUG86	14AUG86	0	
	6	14AUG86	21AUG86	0	
Strategy Approval	7	15AUG86	25AUG86	0	
	0	22AUG86	22AUG86	0	
Concept & Copy	0	26AUG86	26AUG86	3	
	14	22AUG86	11SEP86	1	
Client Presentation	14	26AUG86	15SEP86	0	
	0	17SEP86	17SEP86	0	
Revisions	0	17SEP86	17SEP86	0	
	5	17SEP86	23SEP86	0	
Final Approval	4	17SEP86	22SEP86	0	
	0	24SEP86	24SEP86	0	
	0	23SEP86	23SEP86	0	

Actual vs. Plan Gantt Graph

Quickly summarize a project's progress to date.

You pick the schedule to compare: the project plan
or a previous version.
Actual tasks show clearly -- even on photocopies.

RUN DATE   16SEP
AS OF DATE 28AUG

TIME LINE ® GRAPHICS

415-898-1919

BREAKTHROUGH SOFTWARE CORPORATION, 505-B SAN MARIN DRIVE, SUITE 300, NOVATO, CA 94947-1310

FIGURE 11–16.   Actual versus planned Gantt chart. (Courtesy, Symantec Corp.)

The most commonly used device for portraying schedules is the Gantt chart. As a visual planning device it is effective for showing when work is supposed to be done and which work elements are behind or ahead of schedule.

The concepts and techniques in this chapter are foundation tools for planning and scheduling. The next few chapters look at techniques that augment these ideas and compensate for their limitations. Later we will consider the role of WBS, work packages, and project schedules in cost estimating, budgeting, and project control.

CHAPTER REVIEW QUESTIONS

1. What questions must be answered every time a new project is planned? What are the steps in the planning process which answer these questions?

2. What is the purpose of a project summary plan? At what stage of the project should this plan be prepared?

3. Can a project be undertaken without a summary plan? What are the possible consequences?

4. Which items, if any, could be eliminated from the summary plan for projects with small budgets? Which could be eliminated for projects of short duration (say,a few weeks or months) that have relatively few tasks?

5. The subsection on "Areas of risk and uncertainty" is frequently left out of the project summary plan. What are the potential pitfalls of doing this?

6. Think of a somewhat complicated task that you are familiar with and develop a work breakdown structure for it. (Examples: a wedding, a high school reunion, a questionnaire survey, a motion picture or stage play, etc.). Now do the same for a complicated job that you are not very familiar with. At what point would you need the assistance of "functional managers" or specialists to help you break down subtasks?

7. In a WBS, how do you know when you have reached the level where no further breakdown is necessary?

8. Could the WBS in Figure 11–3 have started with different elements at level 2 and still ended up with the same work packages? In general, can different approaches to a WBS end with about the same results?

9. In what ways is the WBS important to project managers?

10. What is the role of functional managers in developing a WBS?

11. What is the impact of altering the WBS after the project has started?

12. What should a "well-defined" work package include?

13. What is the relationship between the WBS and organization structure? In this relationship, what is the meaning of an "account?"

14. Figure 11–6 shows some possible types of responsibilities that could be indicated on a responsibility matrix. What other kinds of responsibilities or duties could be indicated?

15. Using a WBS which you developed in problem 6, construct a responsibility matrix. In doing this, you must consider the project organization structure, the managerial/technical positions to be assigned, and their duties.

16. What function does the responsibility matrix have in project control?

17. Do you think a responsibility matrix can be threatening to managers and professionals? Why?

18. Distinguish between an event and an activity. What problems can arise if these terms are confused by people on a project?

19. Distinguish between an interface event and a milestone event. What are some examples of each? When is an interface event also a milestone event?

20. How are project level and task level schedules prepared? What is the relationship between them? Who prepares them?

21. Construct a Gantt chart similar to the LOGON project in Figure 11–9 using the following data:

Task	Start time (wks.)	Duration (wks.)
A	0	5
B	6	3
C	7	4
D	7	9
E	8	2
F	9	8
G	12	7

When will the last task be completed?

22. How must the Gantt chart you drew in problem 21 be changed if you were told the C and D could not begin until B was completed, and that G could not begin until C was completed? What happens to the project completion time?

23. Is the Gantt chart an adequate tool for planning and controlling small projects?

24. For problem 21, suppose the weekly direct expenses are as follows:

Task	Direct expense ($1,000/wk)
A	10
B	15
C	25
D	35
E	10
F	20
G	10

Construct charts, as in Figure 11–12, showing weekly and cumulative direct expenses. Use the start dates given in problem 21.

25. Repeat problem 24 using the assumptions given in problem 22. What is the effect on weekly and cumulative expenses?

26. In a hierarchy of charts, how does changing a chart at one level effect charts at other levels?

27. How would you decide when more than one level of charts is necessary for planning?

28. If a hierarchy of charts is used in project planning, explain if there should be a corresponding hierarchy of plans as well.

QUESTIONS ABOUT THE STUDY PROJECT

1. Describe the Project Summary Plan for your project (the plan developed at the *start* of the project). What is in the contents? Show a typical summary plan.

2. Who prepared the plan?

3. At what point in the project was the plan prepared?

4. What is the relationship between the summary plan and the project proposal? Was the plan derived from the proposal?

5. How, when, and by whom was the Work Breakdown Structure (WBS) prepared? Describe the process used in preparing the WBS.

6. How is "project management" included in the WBS?

7. Was the concept of "work package" used? If so, describe what is included in a work package. How is the work package defined?

8. How were ongoing activities like management, supervision, inspection, and maintenance handled? Was there a work package for each?

9. How were responsibilities in the WBS assigned to the project organization (i.e., how was it determined which functional areas would be involved in the project and which tasks they would have)?

10. How were individual people assigned to the project? Describe the process.

11. Was a responsibility matrix used? Show an example.

12. How were activities in the WBS transferred to a schedule? How were times estimated? Who prepared the schedules?

13. Show examples of project-level and task-level schedules. Who prepared each one? How were they checked and integrated?

ENDNOTES

1. Cited in Robert Boguslaw, *The New Utopians* (Englewood Cliffs, N.J.: Prentice-Hall), 38.

2. Contents of summary plans are listed in D.I. Cleland and W.R. King, *Systems Analysis and Project Management*, 3rd ed. (New York: McGraw-Hill, 1983), 461–469; J. Allen and B.P. Lientz, *Systems in Action* (Santa Monica: Goodyear, 1978), 95.

3. See, for example, Cleland and King, ibid., 461–469.

4. Seymour Sarason in *The Creation of Settings and The Future Societies* (San Francisco: Jossey-Bass, 1972) argues the importance of knowing the beginnings, origins, and history of any new "setting" before initiating it, especially to learn about and prepare for the struggles, obstacles, and conflicts which will later be encountered.

5. R.D. Archibald, *Managing High-Technology Programs and Projects* (New York: John Wiley & Sons, 1976), 147.

6. Cleland and King, *Systems Analysis and Project Management*, 258.

7. F.L. Harrison, *Advanced Project Management* (Hants, England: Gower, 1981), 30–31.

8. Archibald, *Managing High-Technology Programs and Projects*, 65 and 156.

9. James L. Riggs, *Production Systems: Planning, Analysis, and Control*, 4th ed. (New York: John Wiley & Sons, 1987), 549–552.

chapter 12

Network Scheduling and PERT

I know why there are so many people who love chopping wood.
In this activity one immediately sees the results.

Albert Einstein

Gantt charts require that the sequence of work tasks be considered as the tasks are being listed, but they do not explicitly show the relationships among tasks nor the impact of delaying activities or shifting resources. Planning and scheduling methods using networks do not have this inadequacy. They clearly show interdependencies among activities and enable planning and scheduling functions to be performed separately. Alternative plans can be analyzed and, afterwards, they can be scheduled according to the availability of resources.

This chapter and the next treat the topic of project network development and describe the two most widely used network based approaches to project planning—the Program Evaluation and Review Technique (PERT) and the Critical Path Method (CPM).

12.1 LOGIC DIAGRAMS AND NETWORKS

The simplest kind of network, called a logic diagram, shows the major elements of a group of tasks and their logical relationship. It clearly exposes those tasks that must be completed before others can be started; this is called the "precedence." Figure 12–1 is a logic diagram for "getting up in the morning and getting dressed" (for a male). The boxes represent tasks (or activities) and the arrows connecting them show the order in which they should occur (e.g., put on shirt *before* tie, put on pants *and* socks *before* shoes, etc.).

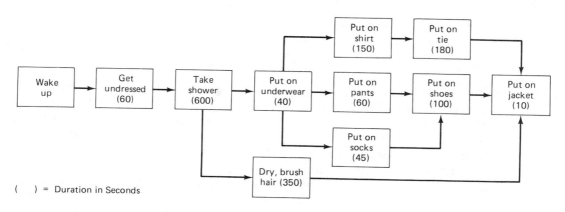

FIGURE 12–1.   Logic diagram for getting up in the morning and getting dressed.

The two common methods for constructing network diagrams are called *Activity-on-Node (AON)* and *Activity-on- Arc (AOA)*. Both were developed independently during the late 1950s—AON as part of the CPM planning method, and AOA in the PERT method. Most of our discussion will center on the AOA method, but we will start with the AON method since it is slightly easier to learn.

Activity-on-Node Diagrams

Network diagrams describe a project in terms of sequences of activities and events. An *activity* is a work task; it is something to be done. It can be a unit of work at any level of the WBS—a work package, a cluster of work packages, or an individual job smaller than a work package, depending on the desired detail. An activity is something that requires time and utilizes resources. In contrast, as mentioned in section 11.6, an *event* represents an instant in time. It is an "announcement" that something has or will happen. Typically it signifies the start or finish of an activity. A significant event is a *milestone.*

Figure 12–2 shows how an activity is represented using the AON method. The *node* (the circle) represents an activity with its associated events; in this case the activity is "take shower" and the events are the times when the shower is started and finished.

Referring back to Figure 12–1, we see that this is an AON type diagram for a group of activities. To construct an AON project network like this start by drawing the first activity in the project (e.g. "wake up") as the beginning node. From this node draw lines to the activities that happen next. As shown in Figure 12–1, activities are added one after another, in sequence or parallel, until the last activity is included.

Of course, before activities can be included in a network their relationships to each other must be known first; in general, this involves knowing for each activity:

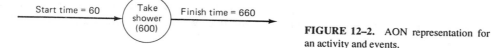

FIGURE 12–2.   AON representation for an activity and events.

- What activities are its predecessors?
- What activities are its successors?
- What activities can be done at the same time as it?

Every activity except the first one has *predecessors*, or activities which must be completed ahead of it. In Figure 12–1 for example, "put on shirt" is a predecessor for "put on tie." Similarly, every activity except the last has *successors*, activities which cannot begin until the current activity is completed. "Put on tie" is a successor of "put on shirt," which is a successor of "put on underwear," and so on.

However, to construct a network it is really only necessary to identify each activity's *immediate predecessors*—those activities that immediately precede it. For example, although "wake up" and "get undressed" are both predecessors for "take shower," only "get undressed" is the immediate predecessor and needs to be identified. Given the information in, for example, Table 12–1 (and Table 12–1 alone) it is easy to construct the network in Figure 12–1 by starting with the first activity (the one with no immediate predecessors) and then linking activities one by one to their respective immediate predecessors.

TABLE 12–1

Activity	Immediate Predecessors	Duration (Seconds)
Get undressed	—	60
Take shower	Get undressed	600
Put on underwear	Take shower	40
Dry, brush hair	Take shower	350
Put on shirt	Put on underwear	150
Put on pants	Put on underwear	60
Put on socks	Put on underwear	45
Put on tie	Put on shirt	180
Put on shoes	{ Put on pants Put on socks	100

Put on jacket	{ Put on tie
	  Put on shoes
	  Dry, brush, hair
		15

Once you have constructed the network you can easily see which activities are sequential and which are parallel. Two activities which have a predecessor/successor relationship are *sequential* activities. One follows the other. For example, "take shower," "put on underwear," and "put on shirt" are sequential activities because they occur in that order, one after another. Two or more independent activities which can be performed at the same time are *parallel* activities. For instance, "put on shirt," "put on pants," "dry, brush hair" and "put on socks" are parallel because they can be done in *any* order or (though difficult in this case) *all at the same time.*

Immediate predecessors should be determined during the WBS analysis. Relationships are then checked for completeness and logical consistency when the project network is constructed.

A second example is given in Table 12–2. The network diagram for this project begins at Activity A. Since activities B and C both have A as their common immediate predecessor, both are connected directly to A. Then, since D has two immediate predecessors, B and C, it is connected to both of them; similarly, so is activity E. The result is shown in Figure 12–3. Each node is labelled to identify the activity and its duration time. Nodes labeled "start" and "finish" are included so there is always a single place for the beginning and ending of the project. In Figure 12–3, for example, it would otherwise be difficult to determine if the project was completed with activity D or activity E. The "finish" node indicates that *both* D and E must be completed to finish the project.

TABLE 12–2

Activity	Immediate Predecessor
A	—
B	A
C	A
D	B,C
E	B,C

As another example, Table 12–3 shows the predecessor relationships for the LOGON project using work packages from the WBS in Chapter 11 as activities. Figure 12–4 is the corresponding network.

Activity-on-Arc Diagrams

The other common method for diagramming networks is the *Activity-on-Arc*, or *AOA* technique. The major feature that distinguishes it from AON is the way activities and events are denoted. Figure 12–5 shows the AOA representation for one activity and its events.

Notice that in the AOA method the activity is represented as a directed line segment (called an *arc* or *arrow*) *between* two nodes. The number over the line is the activity duration. The direction of the arrow indicates the flow of time in performing the activity. The *length* of the line has *no* significance (unlike in Gantt charts where it is proportional to the time required).

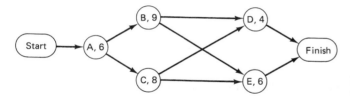

FIGURE 12–3. AON diagram corresponding to Table 12–2.

TABLE 12–3 LOGON Project

Activity[*]	Description	Immediate Predecessors	Duration (Weeks)
H	Basic design	—	10
I	Hardware design for "A"	H	8
J	Hardware design for "B"	H	6
K	Drawings for B	J	4
L	Software specifications	J	2
M	Parts purchase for B	J	4
N	Parts purchase for A	I	4
O	Drawings for A	I	5
P	Installation drawings	I,J	5
Q	Software purchases	L	5
R	Delivery of parts for A	M	5
S	Delivery of parts for B	N	3
T	Software delivery	Q	3
U	Assembly of A	O,S	1
V	Assembly of B	K,R	5
W	Test A	U	2
X	Test B	V	3
Y	Final installation	P,W,X	8
Z	Final system test	Y	6

[*]Work packages from WBS, Figure 11–3.

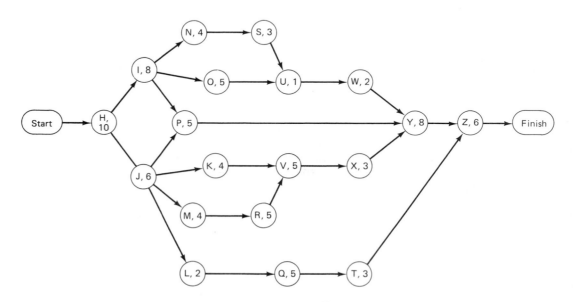

FIGURE 12–4. Network diagram for LOGON project.

"Start"
event

"Finish"
event

8 weeks

14 ⟶ 15

Activity Y:
Final installation

FIGURE 12–5. Arrow representation for an activity and its events.

Also notice that in the AOA method events are *explicitly* denoted by circles or nodes at each end, as shown in Figure 12–5. (The numbers inside the nodes have no significance here. In general, however, they are used to identify each event. The numbers do not need to be in any specific sequence, but every event must have a unique number.)

An activity can be defined in two ways, either directly or by the nodes at the ends. For example, the activity in Figure 12–5 can be referred to as either "Activity Y: final installation" or as "Activity 14–15."

As in the AON method, a network for a project is developed by drawing directed lines and circles in the sequence that activities must occur. An AOA network diagram is constructed by first drawing a node to represent the *origin* event; this represents the *start* of the first activity in the project. A directed line is drawn from this event to another node to represent the finish of the first activity. Activities to be performed next are then added in sequence or in parallel from the last node. The final or *terminal* node in the network represents the project completion. Every network has only *one origin* and *one terminal* event. All arcs must progress toward the end of the project, and there can be no doubling back or loops.[1]

As with the AON method, the activities must follow the order of precedence as defined by their immediate predecessors. As an example, consider the project in Table 12–4.

TABLE 12–4

Activity	Immediate Predecessors	Duration (Days)
A	—	6
B	A	9
C	A	8
D	B,C	4
E	B	6
F	D,E	6

The diagram for this project begins with activity A. Since activities B and C both have activity A as their common immediate predecessor, they are both connected to the terminal event of A, as shown in Figure 12–6. Event 2 represents the completion of A and, concurrently, the start of B and C.

When an activity has more than one immediate predecessor the network must show that it cannot be started until *all* of its immediate predecessors have been completed. This is the purpose of a special kind of activity called a dummy.

Dummy Activities

A *dummy activity* is used to illustrate precedence relationships in AOA networks. It serves only as a "connector" and represents neither work nor time. Figure 12–7 indicates a way

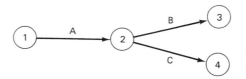

FIGURE 12–6. Two activities with a common immediate predecessor.

of diagramming the project in Table 12–4 using dummy activities as represented by the dotted arcs. It shows that both B and C must precede D, and that both D and E must precede F. Notice that the purpose of the dummy activities is to "connect" activities D and F to their respective immediate predecessors.

To help understand why dummies are necessary, look at just activities B and C: why couldn't they both be connected directly to D without dummies? The answer is because of the rule followed by the AOA method that says an arc connecting any two events can represent at most *one* activity—which means that if two or more activities are performed in parallel they must be represented by separate arcs. Thus, activities B and C must each be represented by an individual arc in Figure 12–7 (as must activities D and E). Given that any two parallel activities must be represented by two separate arcs, it follows that the only way a *common* successor can be connected to both of them is to use something like a dummy activity.

Another question, then, is why can't we represent two parallel activities as two arcs between two nodes, creating something such as Figure 12–8? The answer is because the use of several arcs between the same two nodes is confusing and leads to possibly incorrect answers. For example, the network in Figure 12–8 is confusing because it leaves out information. It shows event 3 as representing two things—the ending of activities B and C, as well as the start of D and E. Unless B and C had exactly the same duration they would be completed at two different times; since node 3 represents one event which—by definition—is *one instant in time*, the implication is that B and C are finished at the same time, which is not true.

The network in Figure 12–8 is also misleading. It implies that both B and C are immediate predecessors for *both* D and E, which according to Table 12–4 is not true. It also implies that D and E are started and completed at the same time, which is again not true.

In practice, dummy activities should be used sparingly to keep the network as simple as possible. The appropriate way to diagram the project in Table 12–4 using the minimum

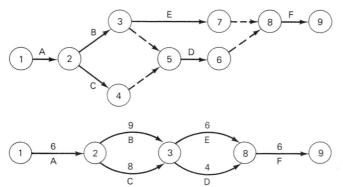

FIGURE 12–7. Network with dummy activities.

FIGURE 12–8. Network using no dummy activities (incorrect).

necessary dummy activities is shown in Figure 12–9. Notice that no information is lost even though there is only one dummy activity. The network still clearly shows that D must be preceded by B and C, and F must be preceded by E and D.

As a second example, consider the project described earlier in Table 12–2. Several possible arrow diagrams for this project are shown in Figure 12–10. Notice in (a) that D is connected to immediate predecessors B and C with two dummies, and E is connected directly to C and indirectly, with a dummy, to B. In contrast, the four diagrams in (b) all convey the same information, but with one less dummy. In large projects especially, economizing of dummy activities is important because it reduces network "clutter" and helps to improve interpretation of the network.

In constructing networks by hand, as a rule it is easiest to start by putting in dummy activities wherever they seem necessary, then removing them from places where they are not essential. The "*overriding rule*" is that *dummies cannot be removed* **whenever it results in** *two or more activities that run between the same two start and finish nodes.* (An example is Figure 12–8 where activities B and C have the same start and finish nodes, as do activities D and E. This violates the rule.) *As long as they do not result in that rule being violated*, the following rules suggest where to eliminate dummies:[2]

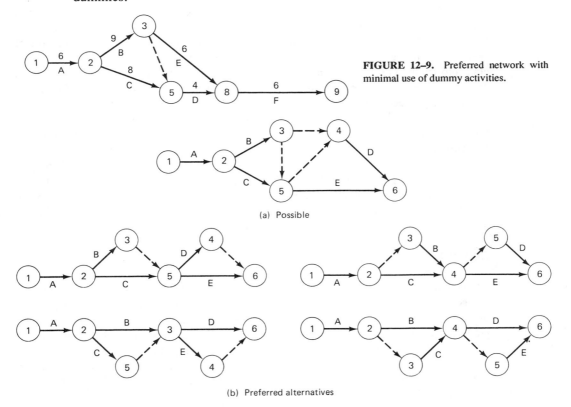

FIGURE 12–9. Preferred network with minimal use of dummy activities.

(a) Possible

(b) Preferred alternatives

FIGURE 12–10. Possible and preferred network diagrams for project in Table 12–2.

1. If a dummy is the *only* activity emanating from its initial node, it can be eliminated (e.g., dummies 4-5, 7-8, and 6-8 in Figure 12–7).

2. If a dummy is the *only* activity going to its final node, it can be eliminated.

3. If two or more activities have the same identical predecessors, then they both can emanate from a single node connected to their predecessors. (E.g., in Figure 12–10a, dummies 3-4 and 5-4 can be eliminated, resulting in something similar to the alternatives on the left in Figure 12–10b. Dummy 4-6 was added in Figure 12–10b in order not to violate the above "overriding rule.")

4. If two or more jobs have identical successors, they can be joined at their final node and connected with a dummy to their successors. (E.g. in Figure 12–10a, [as an *alternative* to rule 3 above] dummies 3-4 and 3-5 can be eliminated, resulting in something similar to the alternatives on the right in Figure 12–10b. Dummy 2-3 was added in 12–10b in order not to violate the "overriding rule.")

5. Dummy jobs which show relationship already implied by other activities are redundant and can be removed.

Using these rules it is possible to create networks with relatively few dummies. Figure 12–11 shows the network plan for an exaggerated version of changing a flat tire. It indicates, for example, that "jack up car" (activity 5-8) has immediate predecessors of "set parking brake" (2-5) and "remove tools, tire, and jack" (4-5), while "put jack, tools, etc., into trunk" (13-14) has immediate predecessors of "tighten lug nuts" (11-12) and "jack down car" (11-13). The last activity "turn on ignition, drive away" (15-17), has immediate predecessors of "close trunk" (14-15), "release parking brake" (13-15), and "replace hub cap" (12-15). The dummy activity 16-17 indicates that when "turn off flashers" and "turn on ignition, drive away" are both completed, then the changing flat tire project is completed too.

As a final example, Figure 12–12 shows the AOA network for the LOGON project based on information from Table 12–3 (and corresponding to the AON network in Figure 12–4). Notice the use of dummy activities 3-4 and 5-4. Event 4 could have been connected directly to Event 3 or Event 5, thus eliminating one dummy activity, but the rule of minimal use of activities was relaxed here to clarify the presentation.

Redundant Activities

All activities in a project except the first have predecessors. Although only the immediate predecessors need be known to construct a network, it is easy to accidentally specify *more* predecessors than are necessary. Table 12–5 shows a list of project activities and their predecessors. It shows activity D as having A, B, and C as predecessors, although listing A is *redundant* since A is the predecessor of B and C. Similarly, listing A, B, and C as predecessors for activity E is redundant since all of them are predecessors for D. As shown in the last column, only the immediate predecessors need be listed and redundancies should be eliminated; this has no effect on the logic of the network.

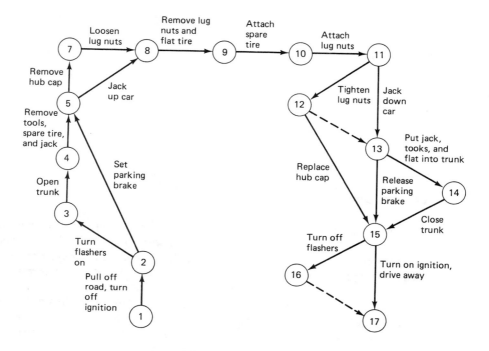

FIGURE 12–11. Network plan for changing a flat tire.

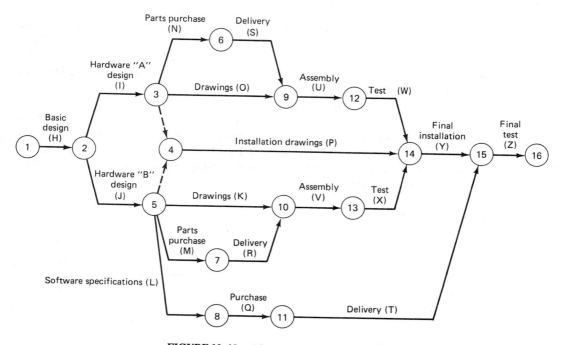

FIGURE 12–12. AOA Network diagram for LOGON project.

TABLE 12–5

Activity	Predecessors	Redundant Predecessors	Immediate Predecessors
A	—		
B	A		A
C	A		A
D	A,B,C	A	B,C
E	A,B,C,D	A,B,C	D
F	A,B,C	A	B,C

Level of Detail

The level of detail in a network must be sufficient to reveal any scheduling restraints and important predecessor relationships. This is illustrated in Figure 12–13. The upper diagram is a portion of the network in Figure 12–12. In the middle diagram, Hardware B Test (activity X) has been divided into two sequential activities, "main bus test"[3] (X1) and "remaining tests" (X2). The shaded node denotes the event "complete main bus test." Should activity X have been subdivided like this? That depends. If the situation were such that *all* subtasks in Hardware B Test must be completed before "final installation" (activity Y) is started, then there would be no need to subdivide activity X in two. The event "complete main bus test" would not even be shown.

But suppose we wanted to advance the start of "final installation," and suppose to do so we need *only* to complete the main bus part of the test. In this case, "complete main bus test" should be identified as an event since "main bus test" is the immediate predecessor of "final installation." The lower diagram in Figure 12–13 should be used since it shows "final installation" beginning *as soon as main bus test is completed*. It also shows that although the "remaining tests" (X2) are not needed to begin "final installation," they are needed to begin "final test" (Z).

Although whole work packages are often of sufficient detail to be used as activities in a network, sometimes they must be subdivided to reveal precedence relationships among tasks within them. In the above example, it was necessary to subdivide the work package Hardware B Test because the work package (X) did not have insufficient detail nor show a precedence relationship permitting "final installation" to be started earlier.

AON versus AOA

The different ways that work activities are represented in AOA and AON results in two kinds of networks. Because AON networks are constructed without use of dummies they are simpler in form and easier to construct (compare Figure 12–3 with Figure 12–10). Nonetheless the AOA method is used just as often, probably because it was developed first and is better suited for PERT procedures. The PERT model, described later, places emphasis on project *events*, and in the AOA method events are specifically designated by nodes. Also, since AOA diagrams use line segments (the arcs) to represent the flow of

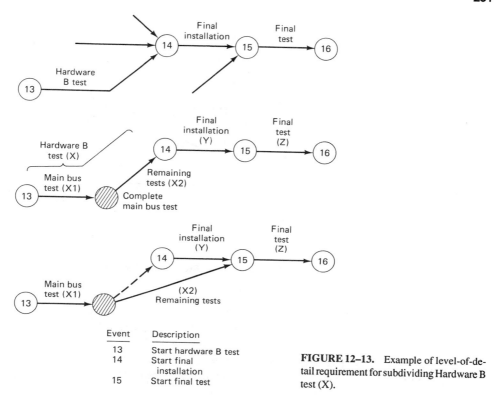

Event	Description
13	Start hardware B test
14	Start final installation
15	Start final test

FIGURE 12–13.   Example of level-of-detail requirement for subdividing Hardware B test (X).

work and time, it is easy to construct schedules similar in appearance to Gantt charts but incorporating the advantages of networks. Most project software packages create AOA networks that look like Gantt charts. Still, the AON technique is very popular among certain industries, particularly construction, and its use is on the rise both in North America and Europe. Many project planning computer packages create both AOA or AON networks.

In a particular project, it is best to select one form of technique, AOA or AON, and stick with it. Most examples in this book are in the AOA format.

Event Oriented Networks

Both AON and AOA formats produce "activity-oriented" networks; i.e., they describe projects in terms of tasks or jobs, which makes them especially useful in planning activities in projects. But for managers who are more concerned with getting activities *completed*, "event-oriented" networks are more useful. Figure 12–14 shows part of an event-oriented network. It is similar to an AOA network except the activity names are deleted, and the nodes are drawn large enough to contain event descriptions (in past tense). This kind of network is useful for reviewing *completion* of jobs.

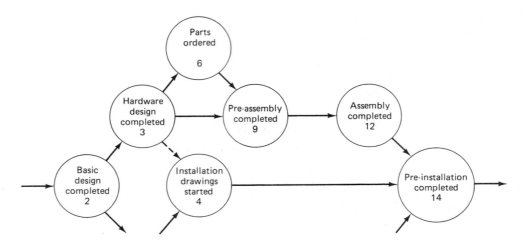

FIGURE 12–14. Event-oriented network.

Creating a Network

A network is developed by starting with a list of activities (for example, work packages from the WBS) and their immediate predecessors. If done by hand the process is trial and error, and the network might have to be redrawn several times before it is complete and correct. Networks of 50 to 100 activities can be constructed easily by drawing the obvious sub-networks first and then connecting them.

For small projects, computer software packages greatly ease the task; for large projects, they are a must. Even in large projects, however, before entering the data into a computer it is a good idea for the project manager to first sketch out the network by hand showing major clusters of activities. This affords the project manager a better intuitive "feel" for the project. Whenever a computer is used, the resulting network should be reviewed for accuracy, omissions, or mistakes in data entry. Examples of computer generated networks are shown near the end of this chapter and in Chapter 16.

12.2 THE CRITICAL PATH

How are networks used in project planning? The major use of project networks is scheduling—determining *how long* the project will take (the *expected project duration*) and *when* each activity should be scheduled.

The expected project duration, T_e, is determined by finding the *longest path* through the network. A "path" is any route comprised of one or more arcs (activities) connected in sequence. The longest path from the origin node to the terminal node is called the *critical path*; this gives the expected project duration.

These concepts are illustrated in the following example. The firm of Kelly, Applebaum, Nuzzo, and Earl, Assoc. (KANE) is working on the Robotics Self-Budgeting (ROSEBUD) project. Table 12–6 lists the project activities and Figure 12–15 shows the network. The first phase in the project is systems design (activity J). After that, simultaneously (a) the robotics hardware is procured, assembled, and installed (M-V-Y), and (b) the computer software is specified and procured (L-Q). The last phase of the project is system and user testing of the combined hardware and software (W-X).

The first activity J (system design) takes six weeks. Notice in Figure 12–15 that after J has been completed, both the "hardware activities" and "software activities" can begin. It will take $4 + 6 + 8 = 18$ weeks to do the hardware activities (path M-V-Y), and $2 + 8 = 10$ weeks to do the software activities (path L-Q). Since activity J takes six weeks, the *hardware* will be ready for activity W (system test) in $6 + 18 = 24$ weeks, and the *software* will be ready in $6 + 10 = 16$ weeks. But since *both* the hardware and the software activities must be finished before activity W (system test) can begin, the earliest activity W can begin is in week 24. Two weeks later, after activity W and activity X (user test) are completed,

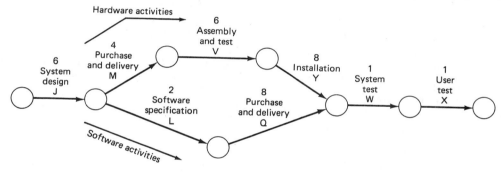

FIGURE 12–15.   Network diagram for ROSEBUD project.

TABLE 12–6   ROSEBUD Project

Activity	Description	Immediate Predecessors	Duration (weeks)
J	Systems design	—	6
M	Hardware purchase and delivery	J	4
V	Hardware assembly and test	M	6
Y	Hardware installation	V	8
L	Software specification	J	2
Q	Software purchase and delivery	L	8
W	System test	Y,Q	1
X	User test	W	1

the ROSEBUD project will be completed. Thus, the project duration is $T_e = 24 + 1 + 1 = 26$ weeks.

Notice that there are two paths from the origin node to the terminal node. The shorter path J-L-Q-W-X is 21 weeks long; the longer path J-M-V-Y-W-X is 26 weeks long. In general, *the longest path gives the duration of the project*. This is called the *critical path*, and the activities that comprise it are called *critical activities*. The path is "critical" in the sense that, should it be necessary to reduce the project completion time, the reduction would have to be made by shortening activities on the critical path. Shortening any activity on the critical path by, say, one week, would have the effect of reducing the project duration by one week.

In contrast, shortening activities not on the critical path, L or Q, has no effect on project duration. If either activity is reduced by one week, then the software activities will be completed in week 15 instead of week 16. However, this would not change the project duration since activity W still has to wait for completion of hardware activities, which is not until after week 24.

The critical path is important for another reason: a delay in any activities along the critical path will result in a delay in the completion of the project. Should any critical activities be delayed by, say, one week, the project completion will be delayed by one week.

Notice, however, that noncritical activities L and Q *can* be delayed somewhat without delaying the project. In fact, together they can be delayed up to eight weeks. This is because they will be completed in week 16, which is eight weeks earlier than the hardware. Thus, although the software can be ready at the end of week 16, it is okay if it is not ready until the end of week 24.

As a further example, look at the network in Figure 12–16. This network has four paths leading from origin to termination:

a.   H-J-P-Y-Z
b.   H-J-K-V-X-Y-Z
c.   H-J-M-R-V-X-Y-Z
d.   H-J-L-Q-T-Z

The lengths of the four paths are, respectively, 35, 42, 47, and 32; the critical path is c, the longest, and T_e is 47.

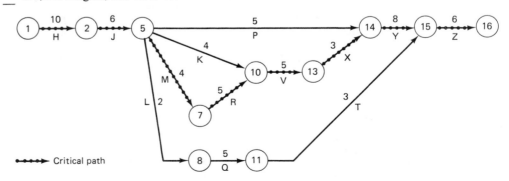

FIGURE 12–16. Example network showing the critical path.

Multiple Critical Paths

Can a project have more than one critical path? Why not? Suppose activity L in Figure 12–15 had a duration of length ten weeks instead of two; then the project would have *two* critical paths, J-M-V-Y-W-X and J-L-Q-W-X, both 26 weeks. In that case, a delay along *either* path would *extend* the project beyond 26 weeks. Suppose, however, you wanted to *reduce* the project duration to less than 26 weeks; you would then have to shorten *both* paths. This means you could reduce the time on activities J, W, or X, or, if you reduce either M, V, or Y by a certain amount, then you must *also* reduce either L or Q by the same amount.

Early Expected Time—T_E

Every event in the network has an "earliest expected time," called the *early time* T_E. This is the earliest possible time that the event can occur. (Be careful not to confuse T_E with T_e, the expected duration of the project.) Usually the early time represents the earliest an activity can be started, though it can also mean the earliest time an activity can be finished.

Determining T_E 's for the start of an activity is what is termed *lead time analysis*. Virtually everything—design, development, fabrication, procurement—has a lead time. To know when you can schedule an activity to begin, you have to first know the lead time—which is how long it will take to complete all of its predecessors.

In general, the T_E for any event is found by taking the sum of all activity durations along the path that lead to that event. When more than one path leads to an event, T_E is the time of the *longest path*. The longest path represents the time when the latest immediate predecessor will be completed and, hence, the earliest that the next activity can be started. For example, in Figure 12–15, if the project is started at time zero, the T_E for the start of activity W is 24 weeks because that is the longest path of its predecessors.

A larger example is illustrated in Figure 12–17. If the project is started at time zero, the T_E for Event 2 is 10 weeks, meaning the earliest time that activity H can be completed and activity J can be started is in 10 weeks. Similarly, T_E for Event 5 is 16 weeks, the earliest time when J can be completed and the earliest time when activities P, K, M, and L can be started. Now look at activity V. Before it can begin, *both* of its immediate predecessors—K and R—must be completed. Coming through activity K, the length of the path up to event 10 (the start of V) is $16 + 4 = 20$. Coming through activities M and R, the length of the path is $16 + 4 + 5 = 25$. Thus, T_E at event 10 is 25 since this is the longer of the two paths that lead to it. Thus, the earliest that activity V can be started is in 25 weeks.

The same happens at Event 14. The immediate predecessors for activity Y are P and X. P will be completed in $16 + 5 = 21$ weeks, X will be completed in $25 + 5$(for V) + 3 (for X) = 33 weeks. Thus $T_E = 33$ weeks, which represents the earliest time that *all* of activity Y's immediate predecessors will be completed and, hence, the earliest that Y can be started. Finally, as you should verify, T_E for Event 15 is 41 weeks and T_E for Event 16

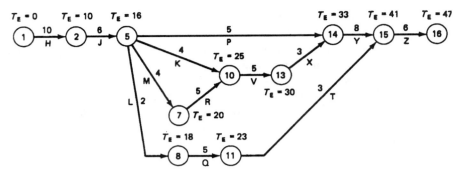

T_E = The earliest time (date) on which an event (start or finish) can be expected to take place.

FIGURE 12-17. Example network showing T_E's.

is 47 weeks. Notice that the T_E for the terminal event is the same as the expected duration of the project, T_e.

In summary, T_E's are computed by taking a "forward pass" through the network. When an activity has only one immediate predecessor, the T_E for its start event is simply whenever the predecessor is completed. When an activity has several immediate predecessors, the T_E for its start event is the *latest* (longest path) among *all* of its immediate predecessors; this represents the time when the latest immediate predecessor will be completed and, hence, the earliest possible time that the activity can begin.

Latest Allowable Time—T_L

It was mentioned earlier that activities not on the critical path can be delayed without delaying the project. We will now determine by how much they can be delayed.

Like T_E, every event in the project has a *late time*, T_L, which is the "latest allowable time" the event can occur in order not to delay the completion of the project. The late time can represent the latest time an activity must be completed or the latest time another can be started.

The T_L for any event is computed by starting at the *terminal* node of the project. Begin by assigning a *target completion date* T_s to that node. Often T_s is selected to be the same as the expected project duration T_e ; however, a larger value can be used when the project does not have to be completed by the earliest time. Now, referring to Figure 12–18, we will show that the method of calculating T_L is largely just the reverse of calculating T_E.

Starting at Event 16, we make a "backward pass" through the network. If T_s is 47, then the latest that activity Z must begin is $47-6=41$. Thus at event 15, $T_L=41$. Likewise at event 14, $T_L=41-8=33$. Now, whenever an event is encountered which has *multiple* paths leading back to it, it is the *longest backward path* which becomes the basis for T_L. For example, there are four paths leading back from Event 15 to Event 5. Coming via activity P, the T_L would be $41-8-5=28$; coming via activity K, the T_L would be

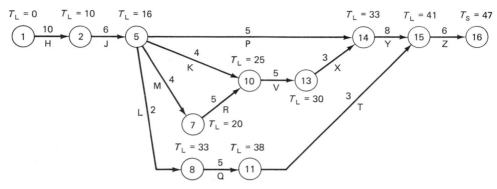

T_L = the latest time (date) an event can take place without extending the project completion date beyond T_S.

FIGURE 12–18. Example network showing T_L's.

41–8–3–5–4 = 21; coming via activity M, the T_L would be 47–8–3– 5–5–4 = 16; coming via activity L, T_L would be 41–3– 5–2 = 31. Notice that the longest path back gives the smallest time, or the *earliest* T_L, which is 16 weeks. This means that the latest J can be completed is in 16 weeks. This is because enough time has to be allowed so that the longest sequence of remaining activities, M-R-V-X-Y-Z, can be completed in 47 weeks.

In summary, calculations for T_L's start at the terminal node and work backwards. When there is more than one path leading back to an event, use the longest path back. This gives the smallest, or earliest T_L value, the one which allows the longest sequence of successors to be finished on time. Having completed forward and backward passes, we now have both the earliest possible times and the latest allowable times for every event in the network.

The examples in Figures 12–17 and 12–18 are portions of the LOGON network. You should verify the T_E and T_L values for the entire LOGON project as shown in Figure 12–19.

Total Slack

Referring to Figure 12–19, notice that T_E and T_L are not always the same at each event. The difference between T_E and T_L is referred to as the *slack* (or the "float") of an event. Slack is the range of allowable variation between when an activity *can* be scheduled and when it *must* be scheduled for the project to be completed on target. The *total slack* of a given activity is computed by subtracting both the T_E of its "start node" and the activity duration time (*t*) from the T_L of its "finish node":

$$\text{Total Slack} = T_L \text{ (finish)} - T_E \text{ (start)} - t$$

On Figure 12–19, the total slack for activity H is 10 – 0 – 10 = 0 weeks; for activity I it is 23 – 10 – 8 = 5 weeks; for activity J it is 16 – 10 – 6 = 0, and so on.

The total slack for activities on the critical path in Figure 12–19 is zero, meaning that a delay in any of the critical activities would delay the project. One reason why the longest path is called the "critical" path is because, besides being the longest path, slack

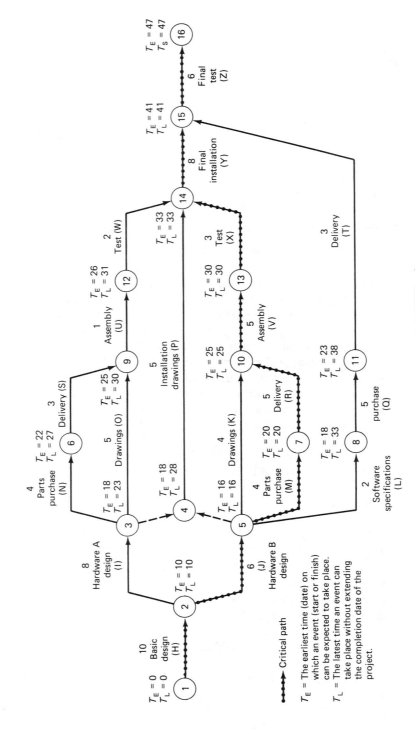

FIGURE 12-19. PERT network diagram for LOGON project.

along the critical path is always the *smallest slack* of anywhere in the project; activities on the critical path are thus more "critical" to completing the project by its target date. Activities not on the critical path (noncritical activities) can be delayed by their amount of total slack without affecting the completion date.

Notice that the total slack time for any one activity on a subpath refers to the amount of slack for *all* activities on that subpath. This is because when activities are in sequence, delaying earlier activities automatically delays later ones and reduces the remaining slack times. In Figure 12–19 for example, on the bottom subpath, activities L, Q, and T all have the same total slack of 15 weeks. This is the amount of slack available for *all* of them. If the first one in the sequence, L, is delayed by five weeks, then Q and T will have only 10 weeks total slack remaining. If, in addition, Q is delayed by 10 weeks, then activity T will have no remaining slack and must be started as soon as Q is completed. Thus, the total slack for any activity always assumes that it will be started at the earliest possible time (T_E).

For noncritical activities, the total slack is the maximum time they can be delayed. Once their total slack time is used up, noncritical activities become critical and further delays will delay the project completion date.

Free Slack

Some noncritical activities can be delayed without affecting the slack of successor activities. The term *free slack* is used to refer to the amount of time an activity can be delayed without affecting the start time of any successor activities. The free slack of an activity is computed by subtracting both the T_E of its "start node" and the activity duration (t) from the T_E of the start node of its earliest successor:

$$\text{Free Slack } = T_E \text{ (start of earliest successor) } -T_E \text{ (start) } - t$$

For example, in Table 12–7, activity I has a total slack time of 5 weeks but a free slack is $18 - 10 - 8 = 0$ weeks (18 is the T_E of its successors, N, O, and P). It has no free slack since *any* delay in it will delay the start of activities N and O (and if N, then S also). Activity O, on the other hand, has a free slack of $25 - 18 - 5 = 2$ weeks (25 is the T_E of its successor, U). It can be delayed 2 weeks without affecting the early start of any successors.

As with total slack, computation of free slack assumes the activity will begin at its earliest start time. Thus, the free slack for activity O is 2 weeks only as long as activity I is started at its earliest possible date. If any slack is used up on activity I, then the free slack on activity O will be reduced by that amount.

Table 12–7 summarizes these concepts, showing T_E and T_L for start and finish nodes, and total and free slack times for the LOGON project in Figure 12–19. Notice that on the critical path both free and total slack are zero.

One apparent inconsistency in Table 12–7 needs explanation: the T_E's shown in the "finish node" column for activities K, O, P, T, and W are not the same as shown in Figure 12–19. The reason is because the T_E's in this column represent the earliest an activity can be *completed*, whereas the T_E's in Figure 12–19 always represent the earliest an activity can be *started*.

Table 12-7 LOGON Project Time Analysis (From Figure 12–19)

Activity (1)	Duration (Weeks) (2)	Start node T_E (3)	Start node T_L (4)	Finish node T_E (5)	Finish node T_L (6)	Total* slack = (6)− (3)−(2)	Free** slack = [(3) of earliest successor] − (3)−(2)	Note
H	10	0	0	10	10	0	0	CP
I	8	10	10	18	23	5	0	
J	6	10	10	16	16	0	0	CP
K	4	16	16	20	25	5	5	
L	2	16	16	18	33	15	0	
M	4	16	16	20	20	0	0	CP
N	4	18	23	22	27	5	0	
O	5	18	23	23	30	7	2	
P	5	18	28	23	33	10	10	
Q	5	18	33	23	38	15	0	
R	5	20	20	25	25	0	0	CP
S	3	22	27	25	30	5	0	
T	3	23	38	26	41	15	15	
U	1	25	30	26	31	5	0	
V	5	25	25	30	30	0	0	CP
W	2	26	31	28	33	5	5	
X	3	30	30	33	33	0	0	CP
Y	8	33	33	41	41	0	0	CP
Z	6	41	41	47	47	0	0	CP

*Total slack is the spare time on an activity which, if used, will affect the slack on succeeding jobs (i.e., will delay the jobs and reduce their slack).

**Free slack is the spare time on an activity which, given that previous jobs have been carried out on time, if used up will not affect the early start time of any succeeding activities (i.e., will not affect the total slack nor delay those activities).

For example, the T_E (finish) for activity K is shown in Table 12–7 to be 20, which is the earliest it can be finished since the earliest it can be started is in week 16, and its duration is four weeks; but in Figure 12–19 the T_E at the "end" of K (event 10) is shown to be 25. The difference is because in Figure 12–19 event 10 is intended to signify the *start* of the next activity, V, rather than the completion of activity K. With the exception of terminal event 16, all of the T_E's and T_L's in Figure 12–19 refer to the *start* of an activity. Since the start time of one activity does not necessarily coincide with the completion time of all of its immediate predecessors—just the latest one—the T_E figures for some activities in Figure 12–19 had to be adjusted in Table 12–7 to reflect early finish times.

Changes in Project Target Completion Date

We assumed in discussing total slack time that the target completion date, T_s, was the same as the earliest expected completion date, T_e. In actuality the target completion date can be varied, making it either later to provide for more total slack or earlier to reflect wishes of the client.

Setting the target date *later* than the earliest completion date has the effect of *increasing* total slack for every activity by the amount $T_s - T_e$. All activities will have this amount of slack in addition to what they had when T_s and T_e were the same. Activities on the critical path will now have this additional slack instead of zero slack. Although slack on the critical path is no longer zero, it is still the smallest slack anywhere in the network. For example, if the target completion date T_s for the project in Figure 12–19 were increased to 50 weeks, then the total slack in Table 12–7 would be three weeks for all critical activities, and three weeks more for all noncritical activities.

If the T_s is set *earlier* than T_e, then total slack times throughout the network will be reduced by the amount $T_s - T_e$, and activities along the critical path will have negative slack times. Negative slack is an indication that time must be cut from a path to meet the desired target date.

All of this has no influence on free slack times since they depend on early start and finish times, both of which are affected by the same amount when changing T_s.

Using AON Diagrams

Until now all the examples for determining early, late, and slack times have used AOA diagrams. How do these concepts work on AON diagrams? Since on AON diagrams the node represents an activity and there is no specific feature to demarcate events, all four possible events for an activity—early start (ES), early finish (EF), late start (LS), and late finish (LF)—must be indicated at each node. Figure 12–20 is the AON network for the LOGON project corresponding to the AOA diagram in Figure 12–19. The calculations of the ES, EF, LS, and LF times follow a procedure similar to finding T_E and T_L on AOA diagrams: ES and EF are computed with a forward pass through the network, then LF and LS are computed with a backward pass.

The AON diagram requires more numbers and is more time-consuming to prepare (a non-consideration if software is used). For the LOGON project in Figure 12–20, 76 numbers show the early and late times for the project's 19 activities (excluding start and finish). The AOA diagram in Figure 12–19 gives the similar information with only 32 numbers. However, there is a difference in the information. The AON diagram gives the exact early finish time for every activity, whereas the AOA does not. Comparing Figure 12–20 to Table 12–7, notice that ES and LS correspond exactly to T_E (start) and T_L(start), and that EF and LF correspond exactly to T_E (finish) and T_L(finish). Thus the AON diagram gives *all* of the necessary scheduling information for every activity, including exact early finish times, whereas in the AOA diagram some of it must be inferred.

12.3 PROGRAM EVALUATION AND REVIEW TECHNIQUE (PERT)

The two most commonly used network methods for project planning, scheduling, and control are the *Program Evaluation and Review Technique (PERT)* and the *Critical Path Method (CPM)*. Other network techniques such as PERT/Cost, PDM, GERT, and Decision

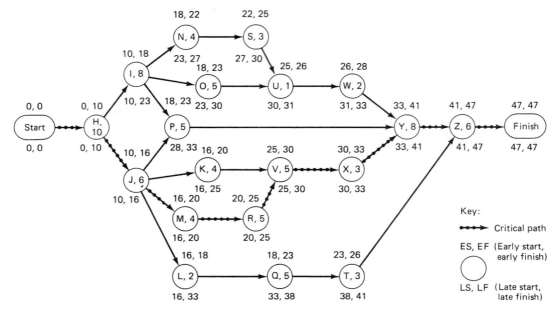

FIGURE 12–20. AON diagram for LOGON project showing earliest and latest times.

CPM are largely extensions and modifications of these original two. Both PERT and CPM are termed *critical path methods* since both use the critical path to compute expected project duration, early and late times, and slack. The two are frequently described under one term, *PERT/CPM*. Despite their similarity, PERT and CPM were developed independently in different problem environments and industries. The subject of PERT will be introduced here. CPM will be discussed in the next chapter.

PERT was developed for application in projects where there is much uncertainty about the nature and duration of activities. It was originated in the late 1950s during the U.S. Navy's Polaris Missile System program. In complex research and development programs such as this there are questions about the kind of research to be done, how long it will take, what stages of development are necessary, and how fast they can be completed—largely because of the uncertainty about what the final outcome of the project will be like. Such projects are contracted while new developments are still occurring and before problems in technology, materials, and processes can be resolved.

To accelerate the Polaris program a special operations research team was formed in 1958 with representatives from the Navy's Special Projects Office, the consulting firm of Booz, Allen, and Hamilton, and the prime contractor Lockheed Missile Systems. As a way of handling uncertainties in the estimating activity times, the team developed PERT.[4]

Three Time Estimates

Earlier we computed the critical path and slack times using *best* estimates for activity duration times. Instead of using one estimate for activity duration, PERT addresses uncertainty in the duration by using three time estimates—*optimistic, most likely,* and *pessimistic.* These estimates are then used to calculate the "expected time" for an activity. The range between the estimates provides a measure of variability which permits statistical inferences to be made about project events at particular times.

The *optimistic time, a,* is the minimum time an activity could take—the situation where everything goes well. There should be little hope of finishing before this time. A normal level of effort is assumed with no extra shifts or personnel. The *most likely* time, *m,* is the normal time to complete the job. It is the time that would occur most frequently if the activity could be repeated. Finally, the *pessimistic* time, *b,* is the maximum time an activity could take; it is the situation where bad luck is encountered at every step. It includes likely problems in development or fabrication, but not environmental snags such as strikes, power shortages, bankruptcy, fire, or natural disasters. The estimates are obtained from the most qualified people—expert estimators or those who will actually perform or manage the activity. They should be the people most knowledgeable about difficulties likely to be encountered and about the potential variability in time.

The three estimates are related in the form of a *Beta* probability distribution with parameters *a* and *b* as the end points, and *m* the modal, or most frequent, value (Figure 12–21). The PERT originators chose the Beta distribution since it is unimodal, has finite end points, and is not necessarily symmetrical—properties which seem desirable for a distribution of activity times.

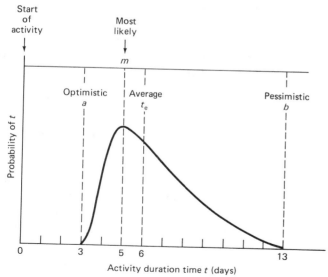

FIGURE 12–21. Estimating activity duration time.

Based on this distribution, the *mean* or *expected* time, t_e, and the *variance*, V, of each activity are computed with the three time estimates using the following formulas:

$$t_e = \frac{a + 4\,m + b}{6}$$

$$V = \left(\frac{b-a}{6}\right)^2$$

The expected time, t_e, represents the point on the distribution in Figure 12–21 where there is a 50-50 chance that the activity will be completed earlier or later than it. In Figure 12–21

$$t_e = \frac{3 + 4\,(5) + 13}{6} = 6 \text{ days}$$

The variance, V, is a measure of variability in the activity completion time:

$$V = \left(\frac{13 - 3}{6}\right)^2 = (1.67 \text{ days})^2 = 2.78$$

The larger V, the less reliable t_e, and the higher the likelihood that the activity will be completed much earlier or much later than t_e. This simply reflects that the farther apart a and b, the more dispersed the distribution and the greater the chance that the actual time will be significantly different from the expected time t_e. In a "standard job" estimates of a and b would be close to each other, V would be small, and thus t_e more reliable.

Probability of Finishing by a Target Completion Date

The expected time t_e is used in the same way as the estimated activity time t was used before. Since statistically the expected time of a sequence of independent activities is the sum of their individual expected times, the expected duration of the *project*, T_e, is the sum of the expected activity times along the critical path:

$$T_e = \sum_{CP} t_e \qquad \text{where } t_e \text{ are expected times of the activities on the critical path}$$

In other words, the project duration in PERT is not a single estimate but an estimate subject to uncertainty owing to the uncertainties of the activity times along the critical path. Since the project duration T_e is computed as the sum of average activity times along the critical path, it also follows that T_e is an average time. Thus, the project duration can be thought of as a probability distribution with an average of T_e. So the probability of completing the project prior to T_e is less than 50 percent, and the probability of completing it later than T_e is greater than 50 percent.

The variation of the distribution of T_e is computed as the sum of the variances of the activity durations along the critical path:

$$V_P = \sum_{CP} V$$

where V are variances of the activities on the critical path.

These concepts are illustrated in the network in Figure 12–22.

The distribution of project durations, T_e's, is approximated using the familiar bell-shaped, normal distribution.[5] Given this assumption, the probability of meeting any target project completion date T_s which does not coincide with the expected date T_e can be determined.

As examples, consider two questions about the project shown in Figure 12–22: (1) what is the probability of completing the project in 27 days?; (2) what is the *latest* likely date by which the project will be completed? Both questions can be answered by determining the number of standard deviations which separate T_s from T_e. The formula for the calculation is:

$$z = \frac{T_s - T_e}{\sqrt{V_P}}$$

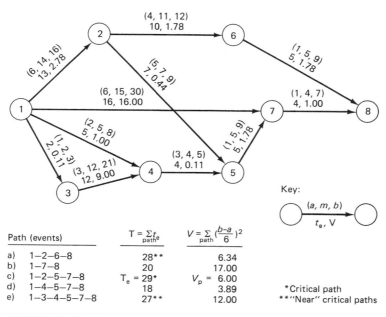

Path (events)		$T = \sum\limits_{path} t_e$	$V = \sum\limits_{path} (\frac{b-a}{6})^2$
a)	1–2–6–8	28**	6.34
b)	1–7–8	20	17.00
c)	1–2–5–7–8	$T_e = 29*$	$V_p = 6.00$
d)	1–4–5–7–8	18	3.89
e)	1–3–4–5–7–8	27**	12.00

*Critical path
**"Near" critical paths

FIGURE 12–22. PERT network with expected activity times and activity variances.

To answer the first question, use $T_s = 27$ since the question asks the probability of finishing within a target completion date of 27 days. From the network, the expected project duration, T_e, is computed as 29 days. Therefore

$$z = \frac{27 - 29}{\sqrt{6}} = -0.82$$

The probability of completing the project within 27 days is equal to the area under the normal curve to the left of $z = -0.82$. Referring to Table 12–8 and interpolating, the probability is 0.207, or about 21 percent.

To answer the second question, suppose we rephrase it to ask: at what date is there a 95 percent probability that the project will have been completed? Again, using the table

TABLE 12–8

Z	Probability of Completing Project by T_S *
3.0	.999
2.8	.997
2.6	.995
2.4	.992
2.2	.986
2.0	.977
1.8	.964
1.6	.945
1.4	.919
1.2	.885
1.0	.841
.8	.788
.6	.726
.4	.655
.2	.579
0.0	.500
-.2	.421
-.4	.345
-.6	.274
-.8	.212
-1.0	.159
-1.2	.115
-1.4	.081
-1.6	.055
-1.8	.036
-2.0	.023
-2.2	.014
-2.4	.008
-2.6	.005
-2.8	.003
-3.0	.001

*Based on the area under a standard normal curve.

and interpolating, a probability of 0.95 is seen to have a z value of approximately 1.645. As before, we calculate

$$1.645 = \frac{T_s - 29}{\sqrt{6}}, \text{ so } T_s = 33.03 \text{ days}$$

In other words, it is "highly likely" (95 percent probable) that the project will be completed within 33 days.

Near-critical Paths

PERT statistical procedures have been criticized for providing overly optimistic results.[6] The criticism is well justified. First, notice in the example in Figure 12–22 that there are two paths which are "near" the critical path in length. The variance of these paths is large enough that if things went wrong, either one could easily end up becoming critical by exceeding the 29 days on the original critical path. In fact, as you may wish to verify using the statistical procedure described above, the probability of not completing path a and path e within 29 days is 33 percent and 28 percent, respectively. So there is more than a slight chance that these paths will become critical. One problem with putting too much emphasis on the critical path is that it leads managers to ignore other paths that are near-critical or have large variances, and which themselves could easily become critical and jeopardize the project.

Furthermore, the 50 percent probability of completing the project in 29 days presumed with the normal distribution is overly optimistic. Since all activities in the network must be completed before the project is finished, the probability of completing the project within 29 days is really the same as the probability of completing *all* five paths within 29 days. While the probability of completing paths b and d within 29 days is close to 1.00, the probabilities of completing paths a and e by then is 67 percent and 72 percent, respectively, and the probability of completing c, the critical path, is only 50 percent. So the chance of completing all paths by 29 days is the product of the probabilities (1.0 x 1.0 x 0.67 x 0.72 x 0.5), which is less than 25 percent.[7]

Meeting the Target Date

When there is negative slack or when the probability is low of completing the project by a certain target date, planners must consider moving the target date back and/or revising the project network to shorten critical and near-critical paths. When the original activity time estimates are good, they should not be adjusted merely to meet the target date. Some possible actions that could shorten the project include:[8]

1. Look for activities on the critical path which could be removed from the path and put in parallel with it.
2. Add more resources or transfer resources from activities having large slack times to critical and near-critical activities.

3. When time is of the utmost importance, substitute activities which are less time consuming or delete activities which are not absolutely necessary.

There are no general guidelines and individual activities must be scrutinized to determine if any of these are feasible.

Putting activities in parallel that normally lie in sequence can be risky, especially when failure of one would negate the effort of the other. For example, promoting a new product at the same time it is under development risks building customer expectations despite the possibility that the development effort might fail.

Adding more resources to speed up activities or transferring resources from one activity to another usually increases the cost. Besides the added expense of overtime wages and additional shifts, there is the cost of making changes to plans and schedules. Also, managers tend to resist temporary buildups of resources because, besides the direct cost, it poses the problem of what to do with the resources—labor and facilities—after work is completed. Ideally, managers desire work schedules that maintain uniform utilization of resources, and they resist changes that result in over- or under-utilization. (This is the "resource leveling" problem described in the next chapter.)

The final alternative, substitution or elimination of activities, is sometimes risky because it jeopardizes project performance. Elimination or substitution means making "cuts" with the potential consequence of degraded end-item performance or quality of work.

Simulating a PERT Network

Monte Carlo computer simulation is a procedure that takes into account the effects of near-critical paths that might become critical. Times for project activities are randomly selected from probability distributions and the critical path is computed using these times. The procedure is repeated thousands of times so that a distribution of project durations can be generated. The resulting average project duration and standard deviation is more realistic than simple PERT probabilistic analysis.[9] The procedure also gives the probabilities that other paths might become critical.

Simulation allows the use of a variety of probability distributions besides Beta, including distributions based upon historical data. The result is that the generated project durations are more likely to represent the range of time that could be expected. The method also avoids some limitations of PERT assumptions, such as independence of activities and normality of the project duration distribution. A simulation procedure called GERT is described in the next chapter.

12.4 DISADVANTAGES AND CRITICISMS OF NETWORK METHODS AND PERT

PERT and other network methods have been criticized since their inception, partly because they are based upon assumptions and yield results which sometimes pose problems to their users.[10]

PERT assumes that a project can be completely defined as a sequence of identifiable, independent activities with known precedence relationships. In many projects however, problems cannot always be anticipated, and not all activities can be clearly defined. Rather, projects "evolve" as they progress.

Also, it is often difficult to demarcate one activity from the next, and the point of separation is more or less arbitrary. Sometimes successors can be started before predecessors are finished, so the two "overlap" in the sequence. While overlap of activities shortens the estimated project duration, the arbitrariness of demarcating the activities increases its variation. One method described in the next chapter called PDM helps overcome this problem.

Still, precedence relationships are not always fixed, and the start of one activity may be contingent upon the outcome of an earlier one which may have to be repeated. The results of a test activity, for example, may necessitate redoing analysis and design, which in a network is a "loop back" to activities that preceded the test. The GERT method discussed in the next chapter deals somewhat with these inadequacies.

Many of these criticisms are problems with *any* planning scheme, not just PERT. It can be argued that PERT, even if not perfect, is still helpful for getting the best schedule estimates possible. To allow for contingencies of outcomes, the PERT method can be applied to several alternative networks to reflect various possible project outcomes.

PERT assumes that activity times are independent and can be accurately estimated. But time estimates are usually subjective and reflect the estimators' personal biases. This problem is compounded when the people planning the project and making the estimates are not the same as those who implement the plans—problems that are not unique to PERT. Ideally, estimates are made by persons knowledgeable about the tasks and best qualified to make estimates—usually seasoned experts or the workers themselves. With PERT, the pessimistic estimate removes the burden of having to make a single estimate which cannot account for possible setbacks. If a "history" can be developed of similar activities from previous projects, activity time estimates can be improved.

Contractual arrangements also influence time estimates. Incentive type contracts can lead to overestimating of times, while cost-plus contracts can lead to underestimating of times. But, of course, these problems are not the fault of PERT.

The assumption of independence of activity times has also been criticized. The duration of an activity is influenced whenever resources originally planned for it are transferred to other activities that need expediting. In other words, activities are not independent because one's gain is the other's loss. This problem, a conflict of necessary resources, can be minimized if it is dealt with early enough in the planning and scheduling phases of the project.

The three time estimates used in PERT also pose problems. Getting three estimates instead of one adds to the work involved, and unless there is good historical data all three are *guesses*; there is not much improvement over a single "best" guess. In fact, the requirement for good historical data upon which to base estimates makes PERT more appropriate for projects that are somewhat "repeatable," not for the research and first time kinds of projects for which it was originated. For this reason the three time estimate is used primarily in construction and standardized engineering projects, but seldom elsewhere.

Two other criticisms of PERT are that it leads to overly optimistic results and that the Beta distribution gives large errors in estimating T_e. As mentioned, looking only at the critical path to determine expected project duration can be misleading, and the influence of near-critical paths must also be considered. About the Beta distribution: other formulas have been suggested to reduce statistical error but with relatively little consequence. The reason is because in practice most of the errors in T_e come from faulty time estimates, not the Beta distribution.

12.5 CALENDAR SCHEDULING AND TIME-BASED NETWORKS

After a project network has been created and finalized the resulting schedule times should be converted into a *calendar schedule* plan—a plan that expresses the schedule in terms of actual calendar dates (day, month, year). Resource constraints such as availability of funds and personnel, and calendar restrictions such as weekends, holidays, and vacations must be taken into account. Some resources may have to be shifted because they are limited or work loads need to be leveled out; this requires shifting and rescheduling of jobs—topics that are discussed in the next chapter.

To complete the calendar schedule, the network is converted into a *time-based network*, such as shown in Figure 12–23. Another example, Figure 12–24, shows the LOGON project time-based network derived from the network in Figure 12–19. On top is a simple Gantt chart altered to show the critical path. The middle figure is the time-based version of the network in Figure 12–19 using the calendar format of the Gantt chart and early times. The bottom figure is the same time-based network using late times.

The schedule in Figure 12–24 uses weeks and assumes no work on weekends. However, it does not indicate holidays and vacations, which would extend T_e beyond 47 weeks. Figure 12–25 shows the LOGON schedule produced by Microsoft Project® software and incorporating weekend and holiday time off. Notice the schedule has increased from 47 weeks to approximately 52 weeks. Most computerized project scheduling packages use calendar scheduling and generate time-based networks.

Time-based networks have the advantages of both Gantt charts and networks since they show the calendar schedule as well as relationships among activities. As with Gantt charts, once the project is underway the network must be monitored and kept "current."

12.6 MANAGEMENT SCHEDULE RESERVE

The T_e first computed from the network is usually not the duration specified as the contractual completion time. A *management schedule reserve* is established by setting the required target time T_s at some amount *greater than* the time of the final scheduled event T_e. Generally, the greater the uncertainty of the project, the larger the schedule reserve. The schedule reserve and a management budget reserve, described later, comprise a "safety

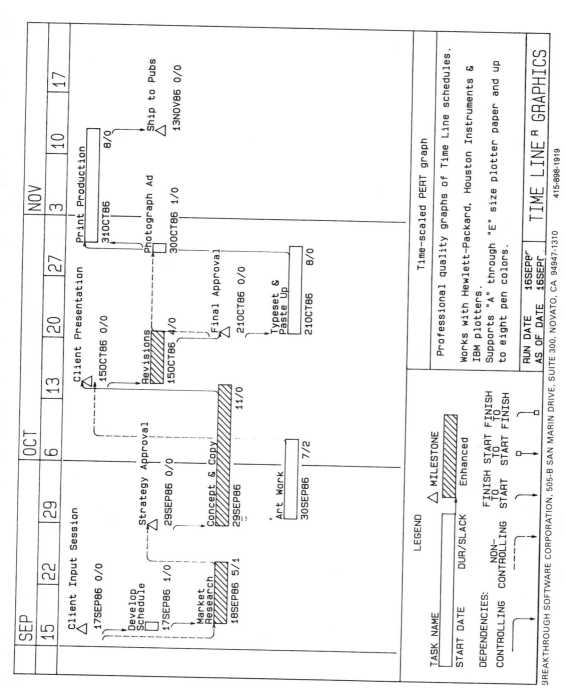

FIGURE 12-23. Time-based PERT network. (Courtesy, Symantec Corp.)

301

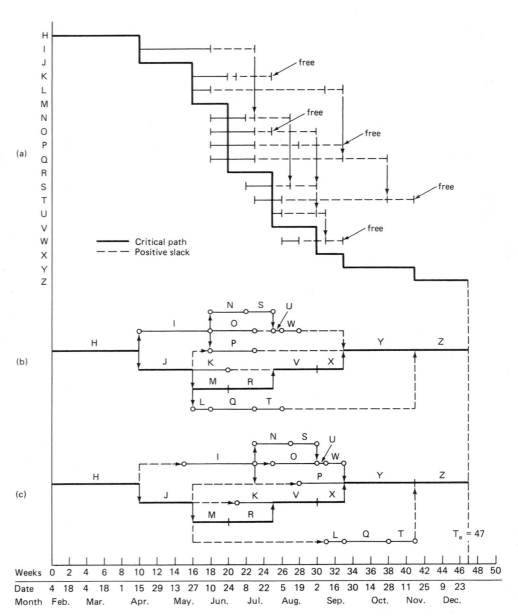

FIGURE 12–24. LOGON project: (a) Gantt chart, and corresponding time-based networks using (b) early start times, and (c) late start times.

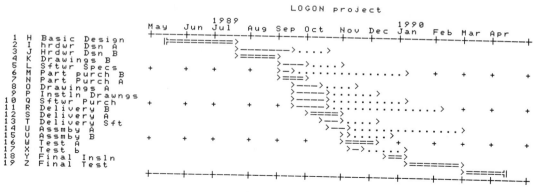

FIGURE 12–25. Time-based schedule for LOGON adjusted for weekend and holiday time off.

buffer" that the project manager can utilize to overcome problems or delays that threaten project performance.

12.7 SUMMARY

This chapter introduced network methods and PERT for scheduling project activities. The advantage of networks is that they clearly display the interconnectedness of project activities and show the scheduling impact that activities have on each other. This feature enables planners to determine critical activities and slack times, both essential variables in project planning. The PERT method includes statistical procedures to help planners better account for uncertainties in scheduling project activities. PERT is one of two well-known network scheduling methods, the other is CPM.

The next chapter describes CPM and network methods useful for scheduling activities when project resources are limited. It also briefly introduces two other, more advanced methods, PDM and GERT, which overcome many of the shortcomings of PERT/CPM. Below is a summary list of the symbols introduced in this chapter and a summary illustration problem.

Summary List of Symbols

T_e **Expected Project Duration:** the expected length of the project.

T_s **Target Project Completion Date:** the contracted or committed date for project completion.

T_E **Earliest Expected Time for an Event:** the earliest possible time an event can be reached.

T_L **Latest Allowable Time:** the latest allowable time an event can be reached and still complete the project by the target completion date, T_s.

ES **Early Start for an Activity:** the earliest feasible time an activity can be started.

EF **Early Finish for an Activity:** the earliest feasible time an activity can be completed.

LS **Late Start:** the latest allowable time an activity can be started to complete the project on target.

LF **Late Finish:** the latest allowable time an activity can be completed to complete the project on target.

t **Activity Time:** the most likely, or best guess of the time to complete an activity.

t_e **Expected Activity Time:** in PERT, the mean time to complete an activity, based on optimistic (a), most likely (m), and pessimistic (b) estimates of the activity duration.

V	**Variance of an Activity:** the variability in activity completion time.
V_p	**Variance of the Project Duration:** the variability in the expected project completion time.

Summary Illustration Problem

I. AON representation:

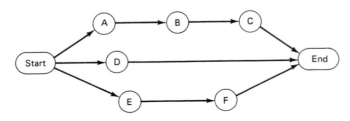

II. AOA representation, same example:

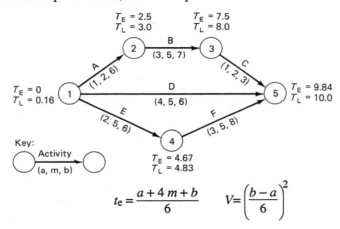

$$t_e = \frac{a + 4m + b}{6} \qquad V = \left(\frac{b - a}{6}\right)^2$$

Activity	t_e	V	ES	EF	LS	LF	Slack Total	Slack Free
A	2.5	0.694	0	2.5	0.5	3.0	0.5	0
B	5.0	0.444	2.5	7.5	3.0	8.0	0.5	0
C	2.0	0.111	7.5	9.5	8.0	10.0	0.5	0.5
D	5.0	0.111	0	5.0	5.0	10.0	5.0	5.0
E*	4.67	0.444	0	4.67	0.16	4.83	0.16	0
F*	5.17	0.694	4.67	9.84	4.83	10.0	0.16	0.16

*activities on Critical Path

$$T_e = \sum_{CP} t_e = 9.84 \qquad V_P = \sum_{CP} V = 1.138$$

CHAPTER QUESTIONS AND PROBLEMS

1. What are the advantages of networks over Gantt charts?
2. How is a WBS used to create a network?
3. Can a Gantt chart be created from a network? Can a network be created from a Gantt chart? Explain.
4. Why is it vital to know the critical path? Explain the different ways the critical path is used in network analysis and project planning.
5. Explain the difference between "total" and "free" slack.
6. Explain the difference between AOA and AON diagrams.
7. Explain the difference between "event oriented" and "activity oriented" diagrams.
8. Explain the difference between T_E, T_L, and ES, EF, LS, and LF.
9. When does the EF for an activity not correspond to its "end node" T_E on the AOA diagram?
10. Consider each of the following "projects":
    a. Composing and mailing a letter to an old friend
    b. Preparing a five course meal (you specify the courses and dishes served)
    c. Planning a wedding for 500 people
    d. Building a sundeck for your home
    e. Planning, promoting, and conducting a rock concert
    f. Moving to another house or apartment
    g. Developing, promoting, manufacturing, and distributing a new packaged food item.
    h. Developing and installing a computerized information system, both hardware and software.

    Now, answer the following questions for each project:
    1. Using your experience or imagination, create a WBS.
    2. List the activities or work packages.
    3. Show the immediate predecessors for each activity.
    4. Draw the network diagram using the AOA scheme.
    5. Draw the network diagram using the AON scheme.
11. Draw the AON network diagrams for the following projects:

a.

Activity	Immediate Predecessor
A	–
B	A
C	A
D	B
E	D
F	D
G	D
H	E,F,G

b.

Activity	Immediate Predecessor
A	–
B	A
C	A
D	B
E	B
F	C
G	D
H	D
I	G
J	E,F,H,I

c.

Activity	Immediate Predecessor
A	–
B	A
C	–
D	–
E	D
F	B,C,E

d.

Activity	Immediate Predecessor
A	–
B	–
C	–
D	C
E	A
F	B
G	E
H	F,G,J
I	A
J	D,I

12. Redraw the networks in Problem 11 using the AOA method.
13. Redraw Figure 12–11 using the AON method.
14. Redraw the following networks, eliminating unnecessary dummy activities.

a.

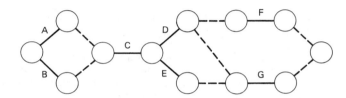

b.

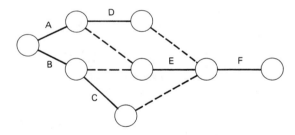

c.

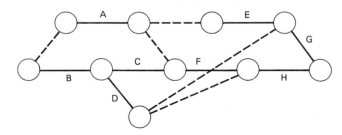

15. Eliminate redundant immediate predecessors from the following lists.

a.

Activity	Immediate Predecessor
A	–
B	–
C	–
D	B
E	C
F	A
G	B,D,C,E
H	A,B,C,D,E,F,G

b.

Activity	Immediate Predecessor
A	–
B	A
C	A
D	A,B
E	A,B
F	A,C
G	A,B,C,D,E,F
H	A,B,C,D,E,G

c.

Activity	Immediate Predecessor
A	–
B	–
C	A
D	A
E	B
F	B
G	A,C
H	A,B,D,E
I	B,F
J	C,D,E,F,G,H,I

16. For each of the following AOA networks:
compute T_E for each event
compute T_L for each event
find the critical path
determine the total slack and free slack

a.

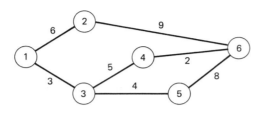

b.

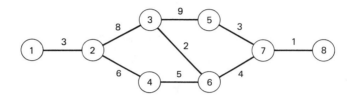

c

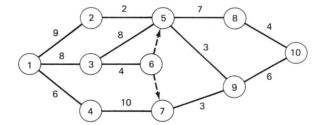

d.

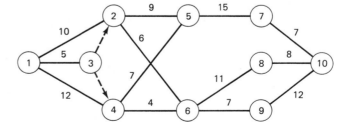

17. For each of the following AOA networks:

compute ES and EF for each activity

compute LS and LF for each activity

find the critical path

determine the total slack and free slack

    a.

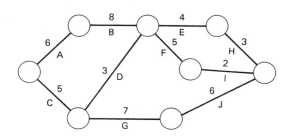

    b.

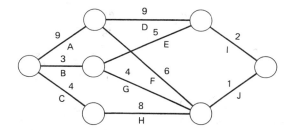

    c.

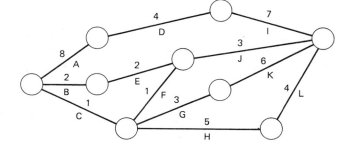

.8. For the following networks, given a, m, b for each activity, compute:

t_e and V for each activity

T_E and T_L for each event

T_e and V_p for the project.

a.

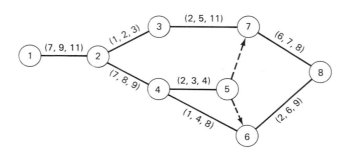

b.

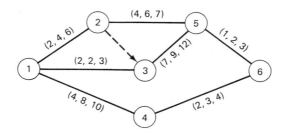

19. Referring to problem 18a above:

    a. what is $P(T_e < 23)$?

    b. what is $P(T_e < 32)$?

    c. for what value of T_s is the probability 95 percent that the project will be completed?

20. Referring to the network shown in Figure 12–22 of this chapter, what is the probability of completing each of the five paths within 30 days? What is the probability of completing *all* five paths within 30 days?

QUESTIONS ABOUT THE STUDY PROJECT

1. Were PERT-type networks used for scheduling? If so, describe the networks. Show examples. What kind of computer software system was used to create and maintain them? Who was responsible for system inputs and system operation? Describe the capabilities of the software system.

2. At what point in the project were networks created? When were they updated?

3. How was the "schedule reserve" determined and included into the schedule?

4. Were the networks used for probabilistic analysis of project completion times? Describe the applications and show examples.

ENDNOTES

1. Loops are permitted in a special form of network analysis called GERT. This is discussed in the next chapter.

2. See J. D. Weist and F. K. Levy, *A Management Guide to PERT/CPM*, 2nd ed. (Englewood Cliffs, N.J.: Prentice-Hall, 1977), 20–22.

3. A "bus" is a connector that runs through lots of devices, each one taking something from the bus or putting something into it. An electrical circuit is a form of bus.

4. The method first appeared in the article by the originators of PERT: D.G. Malcolm, J.H. Roseboom, C.E. Clark, and W. Fazar, "Application of a Technique for Research and Development Program Evaluation," *Operations Research*, Vol. 7, No. 5 (1959), 646–670.

5. This approximation is inferred from the Central Limit Theorem which specifies that the sum of a large number of independent random variables will be normally distributed no matter what the distribution of the individual random variables. Strictly speaking, this implies the requirement for a "large number" of activities on the critical path—but the approximation is always used, regardless of the number of activities.

6. See A.R. Klingel, "Bias in PERT Project Completion Time Calculations for Real Networks," *Management Science*, Vol. 13 (1966), 194–201.

7. This computation assumes that paths are independent, which, in fact, they are not since portions of paths overlap (e.g., paths a and c both contain activity 1–2; c and d both contain 5–7–8; and so on). This fact makes the computation of the probability of finishing within a given time period very difficult, so difficult that it is never done. Nonetheless, the criticism that PERT gives overly optimistic results still holds.

8. See R.W. Miller, *Schedule, Cost, and Profit Control with PERT* (New York: McGraw-Hill, 1963), 58; and Harold Kerzner, *Project Management: A Systems Approach to Planning, Scheduling, and Controlling* (New York: Van Nostrand Reinhold, 1979) 346–348.

9. See R.M. Van Slyke, "Monte Carlo Methods and the PERT Problem," *Operations Research*, Vol. 11, No. 5 (1963), 839–860.

10. See M. Krakowski, "PERT and Parkinson's Law," *Interfaces*, Vol. 5, No. 1 (November 1974); and A. Vazsonyi, "L'Historie de la grandeur et de la decadence de la methode PERT," *Management Science*, Vol. 16, No. 8 (April 1970) (written in English). Other problems of PERT/CPM are described by Kerzner, *Project Management*, 356–358; Miller, *Schedule, Cost, and Profit Control with PERT*, 39–45; and J. D. Weist and F. K. Levy, *A Management Guide to PERT/CPM*, 2nd ed. (Englewood Cliffs, N.J.: Prentice-Hall, 1977), 57–58, 73, 166–173.

chapter 13

CPM, Network Resource Allocation, and Extensions

> Look beneath the surface: never let a thing's
> intrinsic qualities or worth escape you.
>
> *Marcus Aurelius, Meditations*

The planning methods described so far ignore the influence that limited resources like capital, labor, and equipment have on project scheduling. They disregard the availability of resources and assume that whenever an activity is scheduled the requisite resources will be on hand. The fact is, necessary resources are not always available, so activities must be scheduled around when they can be obtained. Also, project cost and project duration are interdependent variables. Altering project schedules influences costs, and it is possible to alter schedules to achieve the optimum project-cost, completion date tradeoff.

This chapter covers the topics of Critical Path Method (CPM) and constrained resource planning—methods which enable project managers to see the exchange between project schedules, costs, and resource utilization. First we look at CPM—a method similar to PERT except that it explicitly includes cost as a scheduling consideration; we then consider the topic of activity scheduling, taking into account the utilization and allocation of limited resources. The chapter ends with a brief discussion of PDM and GERT, two advanced methods that surmount some of the problems and limitations of PERT/CPM.

13.1 CRITICAL PATH METHOD (CPM)

The *Critical Path Method* or *CPM* originated in 1957 through an effort initiated at the DuPont Company and expanded to include Remington Rand and Mauchy Associates.[1] CPM was developed in an industrial setting (a plant construction project for DuPont) and gives relatively more emphasis to project costs. It contrasts to PERT which, developed in a research and development setting, gives greater emphasis to uncertainty but none to cost.

At first glance both CPM and PERT appear the same: both employ networks and use the concept of critical path. Underlying, however, are two points of divergence. First, CPM is a "deterministic" approach: only one time estimate is used for each activity, and there is no statistical treatment of uncertainty. Variations in activity times can be included, but as planned variations instead of random variations as presumed in PERT. The other difference is that CPM includes a mathematical procedure for estimating the tradeoff between project duration and project cost. CPM features analysis of reallocation of resources from one job to another to achieve the greatest quickening of project time for the least cost.

Time-cost Relationship

The Critical Path Method assumes that the estimated completion time for a project can be shortened by applying additional resources—labor, equipment, capital—to particular key activities. It assumes that the time to perform any activity in the project is variable, depending on the amount of effort or resources applied to it.

Unless stated otherwise, any given activity is assumed to be performed at a *normal* (usual and customary) work pace. This is the "normal" point shown in Figure 13–1. Associated with this pace is the *normal time*, T_n—how long the activity will take under normal work conditions. (Usually the normal time is assumed to represent the *longest estimated duration* for an activity.) Also associated with the normal pace is the *normal cost*, C_n, the price of doing the activity in the normal time. (Usually the normal pace is assumed to be the most efficient and thus *least costly* pace. Extending the activity beyond the normal pace will not cause any additional savings and might well increase the cost.)

To reduce the time to complete the activity, more resources are applied in the form of added personnel and overtime. As more resources are applied the duration gets shorter, but the cost rises. When the maximum effort is applied so that the activity can be completed

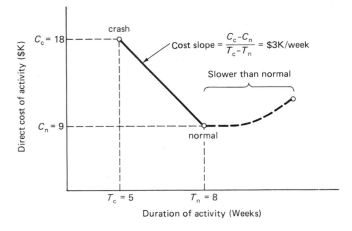

FIGURE 13–1. Time-cost relationship for an activity.

in the shortest possible time, the activity is said to be *crashed*. The crash condition represents not only the shortest activity duration, but the *greatest* cost as well. This is the "crash" point shown in Figure 13–1.

As illustrated in Figure 13–1, the time/cost of completing an activity under normal conditions and crash conditions theoretically define two extreme points. The line connecting these points, called the *cost slope*, represents the time-cost relationship, or marginal trade off of cost-to-time for the activity. Every activity has its own unique cost slope. Since the shape of the actual time-cost relationship is often not known, a simple linear relationship is assumed.[2] Given this assumption, the formula for the cost slope is

$$\text{cost slope} = \frac{C_c - C_n}{T_c - T_n}$$

where C_c and C_n are the crash and normal costs, respectively, and T_c and T_n are the crash and normal times for the same activity. The cost slope is how much the cost of the job would change if it were sped up or slowed down. In general, the steepness of the cost slope increases with the cost of accelerating an activity.

Using the above formula, the cost slope for the activity in Figure 13–1 is $3K per week. Thus, for each week the activity duration is reduced (sped up) from the normal time of eight weeks, the additional cost will be $3K. To complete the activity one week earlier (i.e., in seven weeks) would increase the cost of the activity from the normal cost of $9K to the "sped up" cost of $9K + $3K = $12K; to complete it still another week earlier (in six weeks) would increase the cost to $12K + $3K = $15K; completing it yet another week earlier (in five weeks) would increase the cost to $18K. According to Figure 13–1, this last step puts the activity at the crash point, the shortest possible completion time for the activity.

Reducing Project Completion Time

The cost-slope concept can be used to determine the most efficient way of shortening a project. Figure 13–2 illustrates this with a simple example. We start with the preliminary project schedule by assuming a normal pace for all activities: the project in the figure can be completed in 22 weeks at an expense of $55K. Suppose that we want to shorten the project duration. Recall from Chapter 12 that the project duration is the length of the critical path. Since the critical path A-D-G is the longest path (22 weeks) the way to shorten the project is to simply shorten any critical activities—A, D, or G. Reducing an activity increases its cost, but since the reduction can be made *anywhere* on the critical path, the cost increase can be kept to a minimum by selecting the activity with the smallest cost slope. Thus, activity A would be selected since it has the smallest cost slope. Reducing A by one week shortens the project duration to 21 weeks and adds $2K (the cost slope of A) to the project cost, bringing the project cost up to $55K + $2K = $57K. This step does not change the critical path so, if need be, an additional week can be cut from A to give a project duration of 20 weeks for a cost of $57K + $2K = $59K.

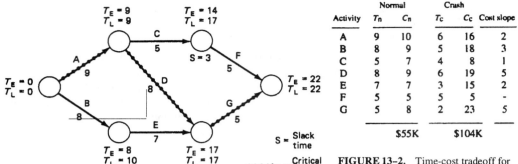

Activity	Normal		Crush		
	T_n	C_n	T_c	C_c	Cost slope
A	9	10	6	16	2
B	8	9	5	18	3
C	5	7	4	8	1
D	8	9	6	19	5
E	7	7	3	15	2
F	5	5	5	5	-
G	5	8	2	23	5
		$55K		$104K	

FIGURE 13–2. Time-cost tradeoff for example network.

With this second step the nature of the problem changes. As the top network in Figure 13–3 shows, all of the slack on path B-E has been used up, so the network now has two critical paths: A-D-G and B-E-G. Any further reduction in project duration must be made by shortening both paths since shortening just one would leave the other at 20 weeks. The least costly way to reduce the project to 19 weeks is to reduce A and E each by one week, as shown in the bottom network in Figure 13–3. The additional cost is $2K for A and $2K for E, so the resulting project cost would increase to $59K + $2K + $2K = $63K. This last step reduces A to 6 weeks, its crash time, so no further reductions can be made to A.

If a further reduction in project time is desired, the least costly way to shorten both paths is to reduce G. In fact, since the slack time on the noncritical path C-F is three weeks, and since the crash time for G is two weeks (which means, if desired, three weeks *can* be taken out of G), the project can be reduced down to 16 weeks by reducing G by three weeks. This adds $5K per week, or 3($5K) = $15K to the project cost. With this last step, all slack is used up on path C-F, and all paths through the network (A-C-F, A-D-G, and B-E-G) become critical.

Any further reductions in the project must reduce *all three critical paths*. As you may wish to verify, the most economical way to reduce the project to 15 weeks is to cut one week each from E, D, and C, bringing the project cost up to $86K. This step reduces the time of C down to its crash time, which precludes shortening the project completion time any further. The sequence of steps is summarized in Table 13–1.

TABLE 13–1

Step	Duration (T_e, wks.)	Activities on CP With Least Cost Slope	Cost of Project ($)
1*	22		$55
2	21	A ($2)	$55 + $2 = $57
3	20	A ($2)	$57 + $2 = $59
4	19	A ($2),E ($2)	$59 + $2 + $2 = $63
5,6,7	18,17,16	G ($5)	$63 + $5 + $5 + $5 = $78
8	15	E ($2),D ($5),C ($1)	$78 + $2 + $5 + $1 = $86

*Time/cost using normal conditions

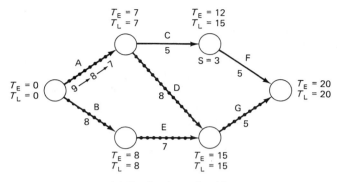

(a) Results of steps 2 and 3.

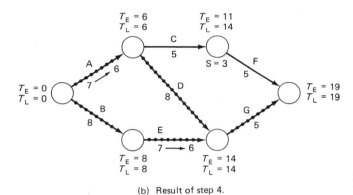

(b) Result of step 4.

FIGURE 13-3. Reducing project completion time.

Thus far we have been looking at how to decide which activities to speed up to make a project progressively shorter and shorter. This stepwise reduction of the project duration eventually leads to the shortest possible project duration and its associated cost. However, if we want to directly find the *shortest possible project duration* and avoid the intermediate steps, a somewhat simpler procedure is to immediately crash all activities at once. This, as Figure 13–4 shows, also yields the project duration of 15 weeks.

The expense of crashing all activities is $104K (table in Figure 13–2). However, this expense is artificially high since, as will be shown, it is not necessary to *crash* every activity to finish the project in the shortest time.

The project completion time of 15 weeks is the time along the critical path. Since the critical path is the longest path, other (noncritical) paths are of shorter duration and, consequently, have no influence on project duration. So it is possible to "stretch" or increase any noncritical activity by a certain amount without extending the project. In fact, the non-critical activities can be stretched until all the slack in the network is used up.

Just as reducing an activity's time from the normal time increases its cost, so stretching its time from the crash time *reduces* its cost. As a result, the project crash cost of $104K can be reduced by stretching noncritical jobs. To do so, start with those non-critical activities which will yield the greatest savings—those with the greatest cost slope. Notice in Figure 13–4 that since path B-E-G has a slack time of five weeks, activities along this path can be stretched by up to five weeks without extending the project. Three weeks can be added to activity B (bringing it up to the normal time of eight weeks) without lengthening the project. Also, two weeks can be added to E and one week to D, both without changing the project completion date. The final project cost is computed by subtracting the savings made by stretching B, E, and D from the initial crash cost:

$$\$104K - 3(\$3K) - 2(\$2K) - 1(\$5K) = \$86K.$$

In general, noncritical activities with the greatest cost slope are stretched in order to use up available slack and provide the greatest cost savings. An activity can be stretched up to its normal time; beyond that, given the usual assumption that the normal time is the least costly time (Figure 13–1), there is no additional cost advantage.

Total Project Cost

The above analysis dealt only with direct costs—costs immediately associated with individual activities and which increase directly as the activities are expedited. But the cost of conducting a project includes more than just direct activity costs, it also includes *indirect* costs such as administrative and overhead charges. (The distinction between direct and indirect cost is elaborated upon in the next chapter.) Usually indirect costs are a function of, and increase proportionately to, the duration of the project. In other words, indirect costs, in contrast to direct costs, *decrease as the project duration decreases.*

The mathematical function for indirect cost can be derived by estimation or by a formula as established in an incentive type contract. As an illustration, suppose indirect costs in the previous example are approximated by the formula

$$C = \$10K + \$3K(T_e)$$

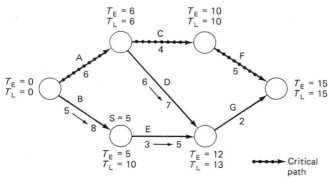

FIGURE 13–4. Example network using crash times.

where T_e is the expected project duration in weeks. As shown in Figure 13–5, the total project cost is computed by summing indirect and direct costs. Notice from the figure that by combining indirect costs and direct costs it is possible to determine at what point to stop shortening the project. This is the point where further shortening results in an increase in total project cost. Figure 13–5 shows that the point to stop shortening is at 20 weeks since, from a cost standpoint it is the "optimum" project duration.

Besides direct and indirect costs, other cost elements that influence total project cost and, hence, the optimum T_e are *contractual incentives* such as *penalty* charges and *bonus* payments.[3] Penalty charges are late fees imposed on the contractor to account for failing to complete a facility or product on time. Bonus payments are negative penalties—cash inducements—for completing a project early. The specific terms of penalties and bonuses are specified in incentive type contracts such as described in Appendix B.

Suppose, in the previous example, the contract agreement is to complete the project by week 18. The contract provides for a bonus of $2K per week for finishing before 18 weeks, and a $1K per week penalty for finishing after 18 weeks. Figure 13–6 shows these incentives and their influence on total project cost. Notice that the optimum completion time (for the contractor) is at 19 or 20 weeks, not the contractual 18 weeks. (This example reveals that a formal incentive agreement alone is not necessarily enough to influence performance. For the incentive to motivate the contractor it must have "teeth," i.e., have sufficient magnitude with respect to other project costs to affect performance. Had the penalty been raised to an amount over $2K (instead of $1K) per week for finishing after 18 weeks, the optimum completion time would have shifted to 18 weeks.

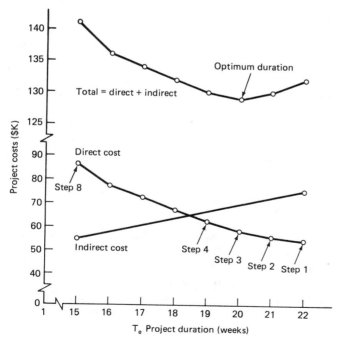

FIGURE 13–5. Total time-cost tradeoff for the project.

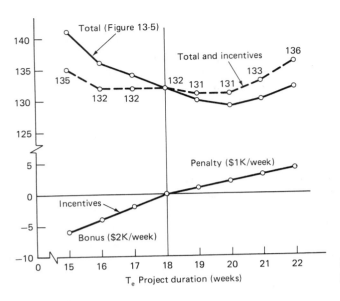

FIGURE 13.6 Time-cost tradeoff for the project with incentives.

Criticisms of CPM

Like PERT, CPM has its critics. First, CPM assumes that time and cost are linearly related. While this seems plausible, it is often difficult to prove. For many activities, actual data may not be available and educated guesses must be used. It can be argued, however, that educated guesses are still useful because they enable the project manager to perform time-cost tradeoff analysis, even if imprecisely. Otherwise there is no way to know where the "normal" schedule lies in relation to possible lower cost schedules.

Another criticism of CPM is that many alternatives must be enumerated to determine which activities should be shortened and the resulting effect on the critical path. Time-cost tradeoff analysis is time consuming, and repetitive computation precludes tradeoff analysis for large scale projects. This criticism is somewhat impertinent since advanced mathematical approaches and computers now make possible trade off analysis for most smaller projects and for portions of large projects.

13.2 SCHEDULING WITH RESOURCE CONSTRAINTS

Until now the discussion of work scheduling has assumed implicitly that any resources needed to do the work would always be available. The only scheduling restriction was that predecessor activities must be completed first. A different, additional restriction will now be considered: constrained resources. While many resources are available in sufficient quantity so as not to pose scheduling problems (such as air, unless the project is being conducted under water or in outer space where air is limited), all resources are finite and many are scarce. In many cases, limited availability of skilled workers, machinery, equipment, and working capital dictate that activities must be scheduled at times other than the early, or even late start date. This is especially true when multiple activities requiring the same resources are scheduled for the same time. When resources are not adequate to satisfy the requirements of all of them, some will have to be rescheduled.

The same problem occurs in multiproject organizations such as the matrix which depends upon resources from a common pool. To schedule activities for any one project, managers must take into account resource requirements of other concurrent projects. The result is that project schedules are largely determined by when resources will be freed from other higher priority projects.

In the following sections, two resource related problems will be considered. The first concerns scheduling of activities so that utilization of a given resource is somewhat balanced throughout the project. The objective is to reduce the extreme highs and lows of resource requirements typical in project life cycles. The second concerns the scheduling of activities so that strict constraints placed on the availability of a resource are not violated.

Resource Leveling

The process of scheduling activities so that the utilization of a certain resource is balanced throughout the project (or "smoothed" so the resource utilization is somewhat uniform) is called *resource leveling*. The concept can be applied to all kinds of resources including capital, equipment, facilities, or labor. Without resource leveling, resource requirements tend to fluctuate dramatically. The usual pattern of work effort and associated resource utilization in projects is a steady buildup of effort, a peak, then a steady decline. As a result, most projects have small demand for resources in their early and late stages, and large demand in the middle (the resource "crunch"). This is problematical for functional managers who have to support a stable pool of workers and equipment, regardless of project requirements.

Consider, for example, the important resource of labor. Figure 13–7 shows the labor utilization, or *worker loading*, for the LOGON project. This diagram was created with the project schedule and the weekly labor requirements shown in Table 13–2, using a procedure similar to that for creating the cost schedules in Chapter 11. For example, activity H is the only activity scheduled for the first ten weeks, so the loading stays at 5 workers. Over the next six weeks, activities I and J are scheduled so the loading is $4 + 8 = 12$, and so on.

TABLE 13–2   LOGON Project Weekly Labor Requirements

Activity	H	I	J	K	L	M	N	O	P	Q	R	S	T	U	V	W	X	Y	Z
Duration (weeks)	10	8	6	4	2	4	4	5	5	5	5	3	3	1	5	2	3	8	6
Weekly Labor Requirements (workers)	5	4	8	2	6	3	2	5	6	2	0	0	0	9	14	6	6	14	5
Weekly Equipment Requirements (hours)	8	2	6	1	2	2	0	0	6	0	4	4	0	8	8	8	8	8	8

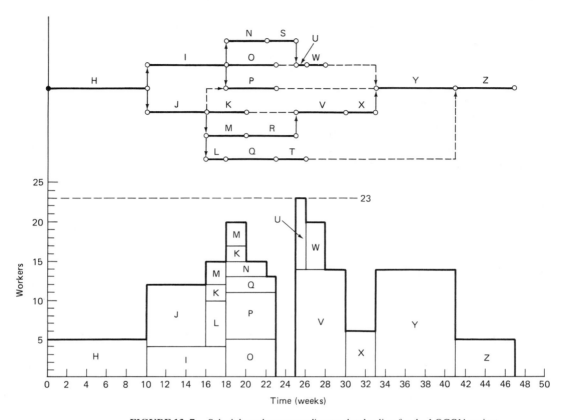

FIGURE 13–7. Schedule and corresponding worker loading for the LOGON project.

The loading for the LOGON project is potentially a problem since it varies from a maximum of 23 workers in week 26 to a minimum of zero workers in weeks 24 and 25. The question facing the manager of LOGON is what to do with excess workers during slow periods and where to get additional workers during busy periods. To reduce the problems of hiring and layoffs it is desirable to try to attain a balanced work effort so that the worker loading is somewhat uniform over the duration of the project.

The problem can be reduced by "juggling" activities around. This is done by taking advantage of the slack time and delaying noncritical activities so that the resulting shifting of resources will cause loading peaks to be leveled and valleys to be filled. A smoothed worker loading, achieved by delaying activities P and Q each two weeks and U and W each five weeks, is shown in Figure 13–8. Of course, it should be recognized that in reality, rarely can projects attain the ideal leveling.

In the example, an even more uniform loading could be achieved if each activity could be split up and pieces scheduled at different times. Whether this is feasible depends on whether the work, once started, can be interrupted and then restarted later. As we have seen, the designation of work packages takes place during the process of creating the WBS, and the final

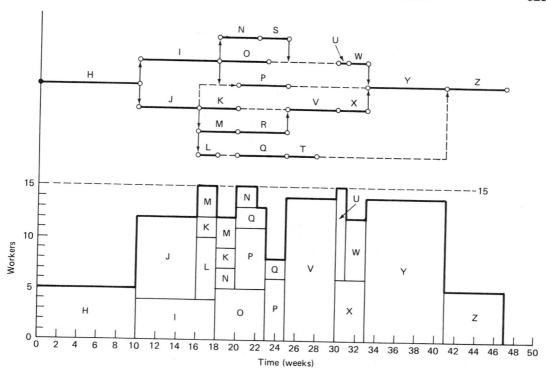

FIGURE 13–8.   Smoothed worker loading for the LOGON project.

breakdown is used to establish schedules, cost accounts, and so on. Once an activity is defined as an "activity" in the WBS, it is difficult later to divide it since this might also require changing the cost account structure, budgets, schedules, and other control mechanisms. Consequently, the usual assumption in PERT/CPM is that once started, an activity must be carried out uninterrupted. However, some project software packages, and some PERT/CPM "extensions" such as PDM (discussed later) do permit splitting activities.

Leveling can easily be applied to any single resource, but it is difficult when several resources must be balanced simultaneously. Since work packages often require resources from more than one functional unit or subcontractor, a schedule that provides a smooth loading for one organizational unit may cause problems or hardships for others. Also, projects require numerous resources, and a schedule that levels one resource inevitably produces irregular loadings for others. For example, based on the weekly equipment requirements for LOGON shown in Table 13–2, the schedule in Figure 13–8 (which provides for a level worker loading) yields the erratic equipment loading shown in Figure 13–9. Any attempt to smooth this equipment loading by adjusting or delaying the schedule will result in disrupting the loading of workers and other resources (as you can verify—the schedule in Figure 13–7 that produced the erratic worker loading yields a relatively balanced equipment loading).

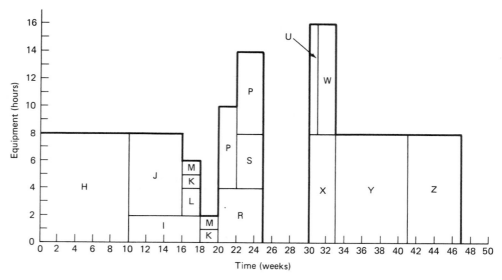

FIGURE 13–9.   Equipment loading for LOGON project.

It is impossible to level requirements for all resources. The best that can be done is to apply the scheduling equivalent of the "Parieto optimum", i.e., schedule the activities in the best interests of the project, but among organizational units try to minimize the number of conflicts and problems caused by the schedule. When considering multiple resources simultaneously, schedules are adjusted to provide a level, smooth loading for those "priority" resources where irregular loadings would be the most costly to the project or demoralizing to workers. The high financial and social costs associated with hiring, overtime, and layoffs often dictate that "human resources"—the workers—be given the highest priority. Some project software packages perform scheduling analysis with simultaneous leveling of multiple resources.

Delaying activities is one method of leveling resource utilization. Three other alternatives are to:

- Eliminate some work segments or activities
- Substitute less resource consuming activities
- Substitute resources.

These alternatives eliminate or alter work segments or tasks to consume fewer or different resources. For example, when the most qualified workers are not available, work requiring their expertise can be eliminated from the plan, or less qualified workers can be called in. These options are compromises which reduce the scope or quality of the work. When employing any of these alternatives there is always the attendant risk of not meeting project performance requirements.

Resource Loading

What happens when the number of personnel, pieces of equipment, or working capital available restricts what can be scheduled? This is called the *resource loading* problem: activities must be scheduled so that the utilization of a particular resource does not exceed a specified maximum. It is different from resource leveling in that less attention is given to the variability in resource utilization than to the *maximum availability*. As each activity is to be scheduled, the sum of the amount of resources it requires plus the resource requirements for activities already scheduled must be checked against the available amount. This problem is more than just leveling resources; it calls for rescheduling jobs and often delaying them until such time when resources become available.

In the LOGON project, for example, suppose only 14 workers are available in any given week. The "leveled" schedule in Figure 13–8 results in a maximum loading of 15 workers. It is not possible to reduce the maximum loading to any number less than this and still complete the project in 47 weeks. To reduce the loading to the 14 worker maximum, some activities will have to be delayed beyond their late start dates. This will delay the project. In problems like this something has to give: it is infeasible to both satisfy the resource restriction and to complete the project by the earliest completion time.

Figure 13–10 shows a schedule which satisfies the 14 worker constraint. This schedule was determined by trial and error, making certain to violate neither the precedence requirements nor the loading constraint of 14 workers. Notice that the project now requires 50 weeks to complete since activity X had to be delayed three weeks beyond its late start date.

While solutions can be determined manually for small projects, resource loading becomes difficult for large ones. Unless several alternative solutions are tried, there is no way of knowing what better solutions might exist. Some manual heuristic procedures for allocating resources in project scheduling are discussed by Weist and Levy[4]; however, as in resource leveling, virtually all but the smallest problems call for computerized analysis.[5]

The following section introduces two extensions of PERT/CPM called PDM and GERT. These are relatively more advanced techniques developed to handle limitations and shortcomings of PERT/CPM. The purpose of this section is make you aware of these methods; more thorough coverage, necessary to apply these techniques, is beyond the scope of this book. Interested readers should refer to the references in the endnotes.

13.3   ADVANCED TOPIC: PERT/CPM EXTENSIONS

PDM Networks[6]

Critical path methods using PERT/CPM assume a strict sequence of activities where the start of a job is predicated upon the completion of its predecessors. This precludes any representation of those types of jobs which can be started when their predecessors are only *partially* (but not fully) completed. For example, when a company is being relocated, the "employee move-in" can start as soon as *some* of the office furniture has been moved in.

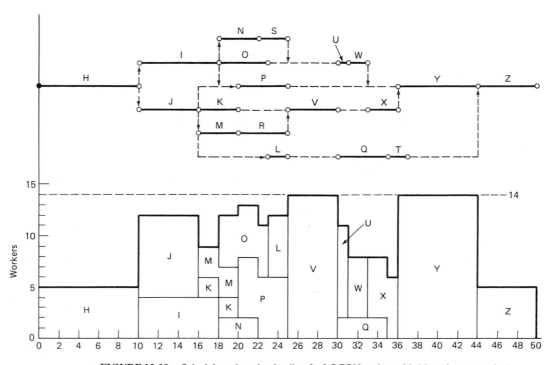

FIGURE 13-10. Schedule and worker loading for LOGON project with 14 worker constraint.)

Although it might be necessary to have completed "furniture move in" before completing "employee move in," the point is that the activity "employee move in" can begin *before* all of its immediate predecessor "furniture move in" has been completed. The *Precedence Diagramming Method* (*PDM*) allows for this and other situations in a project.

Using a network similar to the AON method, the following special cases are allowed:

1. The start of B can occur n days at the earliest after the start of A, its predecessor. (B starts no sooner than n days after A starts.) For example, "employees move in" (B) can start n days after "move furniture in" (A) starts.

This is diagrammed in Figure 13–11.

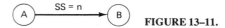

FIGURE 13–11.

2. The finish of B can occur n days at the earliest after the finish of A. (B finishes no sooner than n days after A finishes.) For example, "paint dividing lines" (B) cannot finish until n days after "lay asphalt" (A) has been finished. See Figure 13–12.

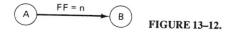

FIGURE 13–12.

3. The finish of B can occur n days at the earliest after the start of A. (B finishes no sooner than n days after A starts.) For example, "phase-out old system" (B) cannot be finished until n days after "test new system operation" (A) begins. See Figure 13–13.

FIGURE 13–13.

4.   The start of B can occur n days at the earliest after the finish of A. (B starts no sooner than n days after A finishes.) For example, "tear down scaffolding" (B) can start no sooner than n hours after "plaster walls" (A) to allow time for drying and inspection. (Note: This is the one and *only* kind of relationship permitted in PERT/CPM, i.e., where FS=0.) See Figure 13–14.

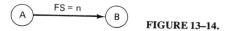

FIGURE 13–14.

The ROSEBUD Project will be used as an example. Figure 13– 15 shows the AON diagram for ROSEBUD and Figure 13–16 shows the corresponding time-phased network. The network will now be altered to permit the following special relationships:

1. Activity L can begin three days after activity G begins, but it cannot be finished until G is finished too.
2. Activity Y can begin two days after activity V begins, but it cannot be completed until at least five days after V is completed.
3. Activity W can begin five days after activity Y begins, but it cannot be completed until Y is completed too.

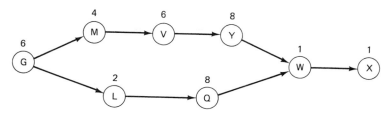

FIGURE 13–15.   AON diagram for Rosebud project.

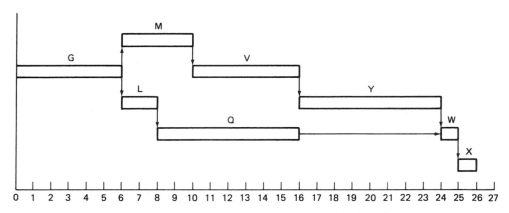

FIGURE 13–16. Time–phased network for ROSEBUD project.

4. Activity X cannot be started until at least one day after activity W is completed.

The PDM network in Figure 13–17 shows these relationships. Figure 13–18 shows the time-phased network assuming earliest start dates and allowing for interruptions in activities.

Although PERT/CPM can handle relationships where FS>0 by creating artificial activities, it has no way of incorporating SS, FF, or SF. The obvious advantage of PDM is that it permits a greater degree of flexibility. The tradeoff is that PDM networks are more complex and require greater care both in their creation and interpretation. Since activities do not follow a neat start-to-finish sequence, finding the critical path and slack times is not so simple. The complex precedence relationships also cause counter intuitive results. For example, in a simple CPM network, the way to reduce the project completion time is to reduce the time of activities along the critical path; but doing the same thing in a PDM network does not necessarily produce the same results. In the above example, the critical path is path G-M-V-Y-W-X. Suppose we decide to reduce the time on activity Y. Since the precedence requirement is that Y cannot be finished sooner than six days before V is finished, the completion date

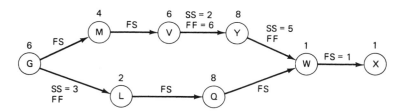

FIGURE 13–17. PDM network for ROSEBUD project.

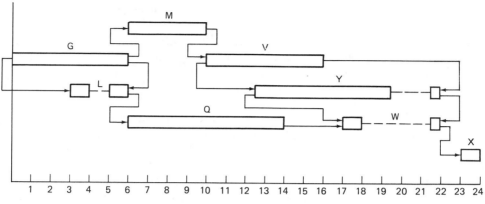

FIGURE 13-18. Revised time-phased network.

of Y cannot be changed. Thus, any shortening of the duration of Y serves to *move back* the start date of Y. Because of the precedence requirement, moving back the start date of Y results in moving back the start date of W and, as a result, the start date of X. In other words, shortening critical activity Y actually causes an *increase in the project duration*.

In general, interpreting PDM networks requires more care than ordinary PERT/CPM networks. However, these and other difficulties are relatively less of a burden now that PDM is included in a number of computerized project management software routines.

GERT[7]

In addition to the limitations of PERT/CPM cited above, others include:

1   All immediate predecessor activities must be completed before a given activity can be started.

2. No event can be repeated and no "looping back" to predecessors is permitted.

3. The duration time for an activity is restricted to the Beta distribution for PERT and a single estimate (deterministic) for CPM.

4. The critical path is always considered the longest path even though variances include the likelihood of other paths being longer.

5. There is only one terminal event and the only way to reach it is by completing all activities in the project.

Although these are only minor limitations for some projects, for others they are major drawbacks. Take the situation, for example, of a product development project which involves the stages of research, design, assembly, and test. At a given time, multiple research groups might be in pursuit of a product "breakthrough," and success of any one of them would lead to a go-ahead for the rest of the project. Although there are several research activities taking place at once, not all of them need to be completed to begin successor activities (limitation # 1).

In some situations it is necessary to repeat activities. Product tests can reveal inadequacies in performance and dictate changes to design or fabrication. Especially in development-oriented projects, it is likely that tests will reveal places where improvements or adjustments are necessary and the project must "loop back" to repeat the stages of design or assembly (limitation # 2).

Depending on the nature of the activity, its duration might follow any of a variety of distributions other than the Beta (limitation # 3).

The last chapter discussed "near critical" activities and it was shown that, because of the variance in path durations, there is a high likelihood that other paths will become critical and extend the project duration. Even in relatively less complex projects, it is difficult to accurately statistically assess the impact of path variability on project completion times (limitation # 4).

Just as individual activities like tests can have multiple outcomes, so can projects. In a research and development project, the result can be failure, partial success leading to further product development, or complete success leading to manufacture and distribution of any one of numerous different products. Different outcomes of activities lead to different paths of successors and, ultimately, to different outcomes for the project (limitation # 5).

The GERT technique (Graphical Evaluation and Review Technique) overcomes these limitations. It is similar in many ways to PERT except that it permits alternative time distributions (in addition to Beta) and allows looping back so previous activities can be repeated. The major distinction of GERT, however, is that it utilizes complex "nodes." In PERT, a node is an event that represents the start or finish of an activity. A node cannot be realized until all of its immediate predecessors have been realized (e.g., a "start event" cannot occur until the "finish event" has been reached for *all* of its immediate predecessors). Also in PERT, once a node is reached *all* of its successor nodes must then be realized (e.g., reaching the "finish event" for an activity signals the "start event" for successor activities).

GERT utilizes *probabilistic* and *branching* nodes that specify both the number of activities leading to them which must be realized, as well as the potential multiple branching paths which can emanate from them. For example, the node in the following figure represents that that node will be reached if *any* m of its p immediate predecessors are completed. The node can be reached more than one time (through looping), but in subsequent times it will need *any* n of its immediate predecessors to be completed. When an "A" is inserted in the node, it means that all predecessors (m or n) must be completed to reach it (as in conventional PERT).

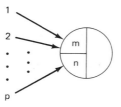

The node in the next figure represents a probabilistic output where any of q outputs or branches are possible. Each possible branch has an assigned probability; the sum of the probabilities over all the branches is 1.0. When no probabilities are given for the branches, it is assumed that the probability is 1.0 for *each one* (as in PERT, where every branch must be taken).

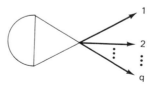

The symbols may be combined to represent a large variety of situations, like the two shown in the next figure. The first represents a node which can be reached the first time by completing any two of the input activities a, b, or c; subsequently, only one of the possible inputs need be completed. This node also represents that upon reaching it, both d and e can be started. The second node represents that both a and b must be completed before the node can be reached. The infinity means that it cannot be reached subsequently, i.e., no loops are permitted back to it. It also shows that upon being reached, activities c, d, or e will start with probabilities of 0.3, 0.4, and 0.3, respectively. This discussion covers only a few of the available nodal representations. Several other options are available in GERT; these are discussed in the references.[8]

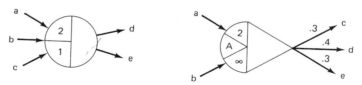

A simple example follows to illustrate the application of GERT. A basic network diagram for the ROSEBUD Project is shown in Figure 13–19. It is similar to the diagram for ROSEBUD in Chapter 12 except it has been expanded to include the possibility of failure following each of three tests for hardware, system, and the user. Specifically:

1. a failure in the hardware test would require adjustments to the equipment;
2. a failure in the system test would require either adjustments to the installation, minor redesign of the hardware, or minor respecification of the software, depending on the nature of the failure;
3. a failure in the user test would require either minor system adjustments or major system adjustments followed and a new system test.

The example is greatly simplified, and you can probably see numerous other places where loops and branches would likely occur in a project like this. For example, there could be multiple branches at each of the activities for design, delivery, and adjustments.

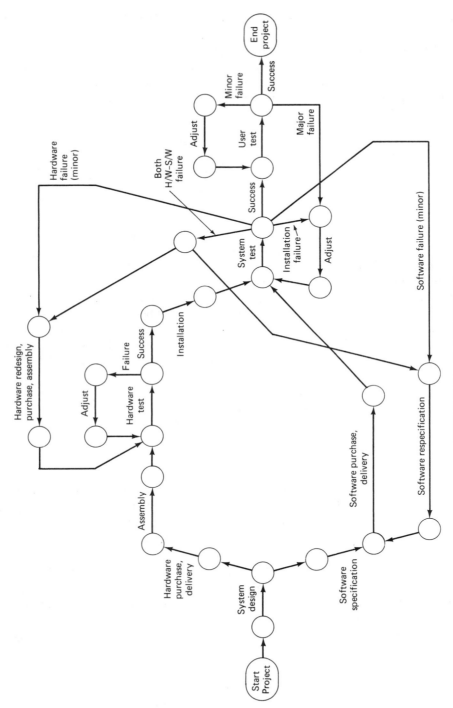

FIGURE 13-19. The ROSEBUD project.

Figure 13–20 illustrates the corresponding GERT network for the project. Notice that for probabilistic nodes the probabilities are given for the output branches. For example, the node for complete user test (the node following node 14) ends with success, 0.7; minor adjustments, 0.2; and major adjustments, 0.1. Also notice node 12 represents failure in both hardware and software and the need to redesign both. Although not indicated on the figure, each activity would also have an assigned probability distribution type (e.g., normal, Beta, Erlang, uniform, constant, and so on) as well as distribution parameters (mean, variance, maximum, and minimum).

Given the network and distributions, a Monte Carlo computer simulation model can be prepared to derive statistics about the project. For example, the project could be simulated 1000 times to gather statistics on the mean, variance, and distribution of times to successfully assemble the hardware, complete the system test, and complete the project. Similar information can also be gathered and tallied for other nodes in the network. It is also possible to collect information about the distribution of failure times (the time when failures are most likely to occur)—an important item of information for estimating the ultimate cost of the project. As the network stands, there is the possibility, though small, that it could loop back infinitely without ever reaching an end.

13.4   PERT/CPM: DISCUSSION AND SUMMARY

CPM is a network-based method developed to help project managers analyze the effect of project duration on cost. Project cost is just one constraint that prescribes project schedules. Scarce resource such as the labor, equipment, materials, and capital required over the duration of the project also delimit the scheduling of activities. The resource loading and leveling techniques in this chapter are helpful for reconciling conflicts between project time schedules and scarce resources and for balancing resources to reduce fluctuations. When activities require more resources than are available, some activities must be delayed until those resources can be made available.

Despite the advantages of CPM, PERT, and related applications described in the last two chapters, such methods have gained only marginal acceptance outside the construction and aerospace industries. In contrast, simpler techniques such as Gantt charting have remained in widespread usage. Probably the reason for this lies in the fact that network methods require considerably more data and computation than Gantt charts. On large projects the amount of time spent planning and managing the *network itself* can be large. When PERT/CPM was first developed it received much fanfare and acquired numerous advocates. Many organizations eagerly attempted to utilize the techniques, often without considering the appropriateness of the application or the best way to go about it. For a while, PERT was *required* of all contractors of the U.S. government. In either case, the techniques were frequently poorly understood, misapplied, and fell into disfavor with managers. Except in a few key industries such as construction and defense, critical path methods have since remained widely ignored by managers.

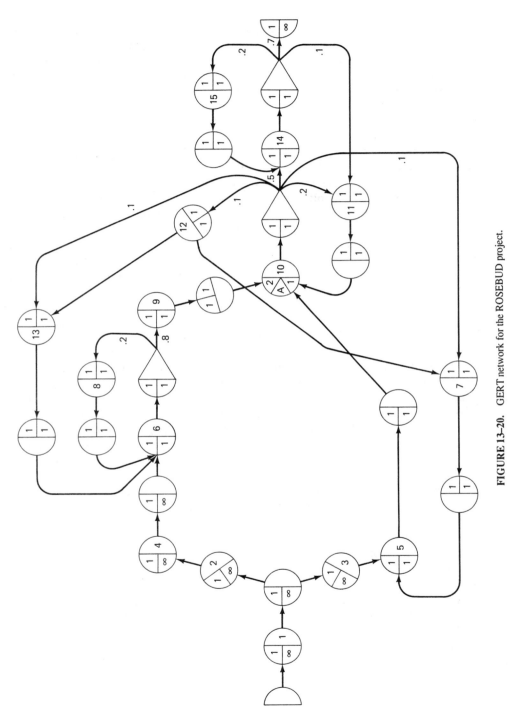

FIGURE 13–20. GERT network for the ROSEBUD project.

Nonetheless, the merits of PERT/CPM stand. Most of the computational difficulties are no longer a problem with the widespread availability of user-friendly project management computer systems. Dozens of software packages are available suitable for projects ranging in size from hundreds to tens of thousands of activities.[9]

PERT/CPM must be understood for what it is: a planning tool for grappling with the problems of arranging and scheduling work. It is not a substitute for other planning and control techniques; Gantt charts, WBS's, responsibility matrices, and additional planning and scheduling tools are still necessary.

Like other management methods such as management by objectives or quality circles, managers should first understand the logic behind the method and its costs and limitations before they decide when and where to apply PERT/CPM and related methods. PERT/CPM methods should be adopted when the potential benefit of their application is estimated to be greater than the time and cost of using them. It is likely that the widespread availability of easy to use, inexpensive, quality software will increasingly put these methods back in favor.

The next chapter rounds out our coverage of planning techniques. It focuses on the "accountant's" perspective of project planning, namely, the subjects of cost estimating and budgeting.

Summary List of Symbols

C_n **Normal Activity Cost:** the direct cost of completing an activity under normal work effort; usually, the lowest cost for completing an activity.

C_c **Crash Activity Cost:** the direct cost of completing an activity under a crash work effort; usually, the highest cost for completing an activity.

T_n **Normal Activity Duration:** the expected time to complete an activity under normal work effort; usually, assumed to be the longest time the work will take.

T_c **Crash Activity Duration:** the expected time to complete an activity under a crash work effort; the shortest possible time in which an activity can be completed.

CHAPTER QUESTIONS AND PROBLEMS

1. How do CPM and PERT differ? How are they the same?

2. Define "crash" effort and "normal" effort in terms of the cost and time they represent. When would a *project* be crashed?

3. What does the cost slope represent?

4. The cost slope always has a negative (-) value. What does this indicate?

5. Time-cost tradeoff analysis deals only with direct costs. What distinguishes these costs from indirect costs? Give examples of both direct and indirect costs. (The answer to this question is covered in detail in the next chapter, but take a guess now.)

6. What are the criticisms of CPM? How and where is CPM limited in its application?

7. Distinguish resource loading from resource leveling.
8. Why is leveling of resources preferred to large fluctuations?
9. Discuss the implications of resource allocation for organizations involved in multiple projects.
10. The following project network and associated costs are given:

(T in days, C in $1000's)

Activity	Normal		Crash		Cost slope
	T_n	C_n	T_c	C_c	
A	4	210	3	280	70
B	9	400	6	640	80
C	6	500	4	600	50
D	9	540	7	600	30
E	4	500	1	1100	200
F	5	150	4	240	90
G	3	150	3	150	—
H	7	600	6	750	150

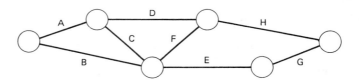

a. Verify that the normal completion time is 22 days and that the direct cost is $3050.
b. What is the least costly way to reduce the project completion time to 21 days? What is the project cost?
c. What is the least costly way to reduce the completion time to 20 days? What is the project cost?
d. Now, what is the *earliest* the project can be completed and what is the least costly way of doing this? What is the project cost?

11. The following project network and associated costs are given:

(T in days, C in $1000's)

Activity	Normal		Crash		Cost slope
	T_n	C_n	T_c	C_c	
A	6	6	3	9	
B	9	9	5	12	
C	3	4.5	2	7	
D	5	10	2	16	
E	2	2	2	2	
F	4	6	1	10	
G	8	8	5	10	

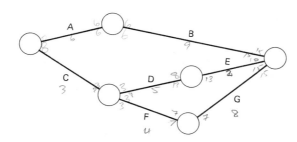

a. What is the earliest the project can be completed under normal conditions? What is the direct cost?

b. What is the least costly way to reduce the project completion time by *two* days? What is the project cost?

c. What is the *earliest* the project can be completed and what is the least costly way of doing this? What is the project cost?

12. The following table gives information on a project:

(*T* in days, *C* in $100's)

Activity	Immediate predecessors	Normal T_n	C_n	Crash T_c	C_c
A	--	6	10	2	38
B	--	4	12	4	12
C	--	4	18	2	36
D	A	6	20	2	40
E	B,D	3	30	2	33
F	C	10	10	6	50
G	F,E	6	20	2	100

a. Draw the project graph. Under normal conditions, what is the earliest the project can be completed? What is the direct cost? What is the critical path?

b. What is the cost of the project if it is completed one day earlier? Two days earlier?

c. What is the earliest the project can be completed? What is the lowest cost for completing it in this time?

d. If overhead (indirect) costs are $2000 per day, for what project duration are total project costs (direct + indirect) lowest?

13. The network and associated requirements for systems analysts and programmers for the GUMBY Project are as follows:

Activity	J	M	V	Y	L	Q	Z
Duration (weeks)	6	4	6	8	2	8	2
Systems Analysts (weekly)	8	5	3	2	5	3	5
Programmers (weekly)	3	4	2	3	3	2	3

GUMBY Project

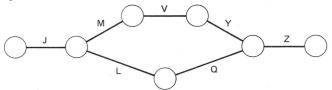

a. Compute T_E's, T_L's, and total slack times.
b. Then show the separate resource loadings for systems analysts and programmers, assuming T_E start times.
c. Suppose the maximum weekly availability is eight systems analysts and five programmers. Can activities be scheduled to satisfy these constraints without delaying the project?

PDM QUESTIONS AND PROBLEMS

1. What limitation of PERT/CPM does PDM overcome? What limitations does it not overcome?
2. Give examples of applications of PDM. Take a project you are familiar with (or invent one) and create a PDM network.
3. For the PDM network in Figure 13–17, calculate ES, EF, LS, and LF for all activities.
4. Suppose in Figure 13–17 everything is the same except: Activity Y can start 4 days after Activity V starts, but cannot be finished until 6 days after Activity V is finished. Show how this changes the values for ES, EF, LS, and LF.

GERT QUESTIONS

1. Describe how GERT overcomes the limitations of PERT/CPM.
2. Give some examples of projects where GERT could be used.
3. Take an existing PERT network (such as for LOGON); using your imagination (and the rules of GERT), redraw it as a GERT network.

QUESTIONS ABOUT THE STUDY PROJECT

1. In the project you are studying, discuss which of the following kinds of analysis were performed:
   a. time-cost tradeoff analysis
   b. scheduling with resource constraints
   c. PDM
   d. GERT

2. Discuss how they were applied and show examples. Discuss those applications which were not applied but which seem especially applicable to the project

ENDNOTES

1. CPM first appeared in the article by its originators: J.E. Kelley and M.R. Walker, "Critical Path Planning and Scheduling," *Eastern Joint Computer Conference* (Boston, Mass., 1959), 160-173.

2. A piece-wise approximation can be used for nonlinear relationships. See J.D. Wiest and F. K. Levy, *A Management Guide to PERT/CPM*, 2nd ed. (Englewood Cliffs, N.J.: Prentice-Hall, 1977), 81-85.

3. See R.W Miller, *Schedule, Cost, and Profit Control with PERT* (New York: McGraw-Hill, 1963), 123-124.

4. Resource allocation techniques, both manual for small projects and computer programs for large projects, are described by Wiest and Levy, 103-132.

5. For an evaluation of four widely used mainframe computer resource allocation packages, see Luis Suarez, "Resource Allocation: A Comparative Study," *Project Management Journal* Vol. XVIII, No. 1 (March 1987), 68-71.

6. Weist and Levy, *A Management Guide to PERT/CPM*, 134-146.

7. E.R. Clayton and L.J. Moore "PERT Versus GERT," *Journal of Systems Management*, Vol. 23, No. 2 (February 1972), 11-19; L.J. Moore and E.R. Clayton, *GERT Modeling and Simulation: Fundamentals and Application* (New York: Petrocelli/Charter, 1976); and Wiest and Levy, *A Management Guide to PERT/CPM, 150-158*.

8. Ibid.

9. Over 120 project planning software packages are described in Jack Guido, *Project Management Software Directory* (New York: Industrial Press, 1985).

chapter 14

Cost Estimating and Budgeting

A billion here and a billion there. Pretty soon it starts to add up to real money.

Senator Everett Dirkson

Besides work definition and work scheduling, the two other major focal points of project planning are cost estimating and budgeting. The concepts described in Chapters 11, 12, and 13 are used in this chapter to show how estimates and budgets are combined with WBS's and schedules into a single, integrated plan.

Cost estimates, budgets, WBS, and schedules are interrelated concepts. Estimates for project costs are based upon elements of the WBS and are made at the work package level; when the cost of a work package cannot be estimated because it is too complex, the work package is broken down further until it can be. Project schedules dictate rates of expenditures and cash flows, but, as described in the last chapter, the converse is also true; when working capital and other resources are limited, schedules must be adjusted to accommodate them.

It is necessary in projects to put practical constraints on costs so that realistic budgets can be established. Failing to do so results in projects being prematurely terminated for lack of funds, or being completed but at exorbitant expense. Both occurrences are relatively commonplace.

Cost estimating, budgeting, and cost control are thought to be the exclusive concerns of accountants, but in projects they should be the concern of everyone. Project participants who have the best understanding of the work—the engineers, scientists, systems specialists, architects, or others who are the closest to cost sources—should be involved in the estimating and budgeting process (though it is common for these same people to be disdainful of budgets or ignorant of why they are necessary and how they work). Project managers too must be involved. They do not have to be financial wizards, but they should have an accountant's skill for organizing and using cost figures.

This chapter describes cost aspects that project managers should be familiar with and the cost estimating and budgeting process. Even with this knowledge, it is a good idea for the project manager to have a cost accountant on the project staff.

14.1 COST ESTIMATING

The initial cost estimate can seal a project's financial fate. When project costs are overestimated (unrealistically high), chances are high that the contract will be lost to a lower bidding competitor. Just as harmful is when the cost is underestimated. A $50,000 bid might win the contract, but it is too bad if the project ends up costing $80,000. Underestimates are often accidental, the result of being overly optimistic; but they are sometimes intentional and result from trying too hard to beat the competition. In a practice called *buy in*, the contractor takes an initially realistic estimate and reduces it just enough to win the contract, hoping somehow to cut costs or renegotiate higher fees after the work is underway. The practice is risky, unethical, and, sadly, relatively commonplace.

A very low bid signifies more than the desire to get a contract. It may imply that the contractor has cut corners, left things out, or is just sloppy. The consequences for both client and contractor can be catastrophic, from operating at a loss to going bankrupt.

Cost estimates are used to develop budgets and become the baseline against which project performance is evaluated. The rate of actual cost expenditure compared to the estimated rate of expenditure (as indicated on the budget) is an important measure of project work performance, and throughout the project actual costs are continuously compared with estimated, budgeted costs. Without good estimates it is impossible to evaluate work efficiency or to determine how much the finished project will cost.

14.2 COST ESCALATION

Accurate cost estimating is sometimes a difficult task, largely because it has to be done in the feasibility stage, well before all necessary, final information about the project is available. The less well-defined the project, the less information there is, and the greater the chances that the estimated costs will substantially differ from final, actual figures. As a rule, the difference will be on the side of a cost overrun. The amount by which actual costs increase to overrun estimated costs is referred to as *cost escalation.*[1]

Some escalation can be expected; up to 20 percent is relatively common. Usually the larger and more complex the project the greater the *potential* for escalation. Cutting edge, high-technology and R&D projects frequently show cost escalations upwards of several hundred percent. The Concorde supersonic airliner cost more than five times its original estimate, nuclear power plants frequently cost two to three times their estimates, and NASA spacecraft often exceed estimates by a factor of four to five. How does this happen? Following are the reasons—many are avoidable, some are not:

- Uncertainty and lack of accurate information
- Changes in design or requirements
- Economic and social variables in the environment
- Work inefficiency, poor communication, and lack of control
- Ego involvement of the estimator
- Kind of project contract

Uncertainty and Lack of Accurate Information

Much of the information needed to make accurate estimates is simply not available in the early planning stages when cost figures are first developed. In NASA, for example, lack of well-defined spacecraft design and unclear definition of experiments is the principal reason for cost overruns. Not until later, when the design is finalized and work activities are well-defined (usually after the Definition phase or later) can material and labor costs be accurately determined. In most research and development projects the activities are unpredictable, of doubtful duration, or have to be repeated.

To minimize escalation from uncertainty, management must strive for the most definitive scope of work and the *clearest, most specific project objectives*. The clearer the objectives, scope, and work definition, the better the requirements definition, and the easier it is to make accurate cost estimates.

Whenever major changes in product design or project schedule are needed—because of, for example, changes in state of the art or product concept, developmental barriers, strikes, legal entanglements, or skyrocketing wage and material costs—then the original cost estimate should be updated. This new estimate then becomes the new baseline for controlling project costs.

In large projects which involve substantial technical uncertainties, work can be divided into successive phases where each one is estimated, budgeted, and evaluated for performance; as each phase is completed, the decision is made to proceed or terminate the project. This process is referred to as *phased project planning*. Sometimes competitive bids are received and new contracts negotiated for each phase.

To make allowances for uncertainty, a small sum, called a *contingency fund* or management *budget reserve*, is added to the original estimate.[2] This is the budget equivalent to the management *schedule reserve* mentioned earlier. The fund is set up as a central account for the entire project, overseen by the project manager, with strict rules for its allocation. The amount of the fund is proportionate to the uncertainty of the work, so phases of the project with greater uncertainty are allotted a higher contingency amount. When possible, the percentage contingency is derived from records of similar tasks and projects. A common project contingency amount is 10 percent.

Contingency funds are intended to offset small variations arising from estimating errors, small omissions, minor design changes, small schedule slippages, and so on. Each time the cost estimate is updated, so is the contingency fund. The contingency fund is not a "slush" fund. When no longer needed as intended, it should be cut from the project cost in order not to be used elsewhere; otherwise, there is a tendency for costs to rise to expend whatever remains in the fund.

Changes in Requirements or Design

Another major source of cost escalation comes from discretionary, nonessential changes to system requirements and plans. These are changes that come from a change in mind, not from oversights, mistakes, or changes in the environment which would make them imperative. The routine tendency is for users and contractors alike to want to continually modify systems and procedures—to make "improvements" to original plans throughout the project life cycle. These kinds of changes are especially common in the absence of exhaustive planning or strict control procedures.

Many contracts include a *change clause* which allows the customer to make certain changes to contract requirements, sometimes for additional payment, sometimes not. The clause gives the customer flexibility to incorporate requirements not envisioned at the time of the original contract agreement. The clause can be exercised at anytime and the contractor is obligated to comply. Any change, no matter how small, causes escalation. To implement a change requires some combination of redesigning or reorganizing work, acquiring new or different resources, altering previous plans, and undoing or scrapping earlier work. The further along the project, the more difficult and costly it is to make changes.

When accumulated, even small changes have substantial effect on schedules, costs, and performance. In many projects, formal mechanisms such as a *change control system* or *configuration management* procedure are used to reduce the number of discretionary or imperative changes, and to contain their influence on escalation. These topics are discussed in the next chapter.

Economic and Social Factors

Even with good initial estimates and few changes, cost escalation occurs because of social and economic forces beyond the contractor's or user's influence. Variables such as labor strikes, legal action by consumer and public interest groups, trade embargoes, and materials shortages can neither be precisely anticipated nor factored into plans and budgets, but they all serve to stifle progress and increase costs. Whenever work on a project is suspended or interrupted, administrative and overhead costs continue to mount, interest and leasing expenses continue to accrue on borrowed capital and equipment, and the date when payback begins and profit is earned is set back. Rarely can such problems be anticipated and their impacts incorporated into the contingency fund.

One economic factor that has major influence on cost escalation and project profitability is *inflation*.[3] The contractor can try to offset increases from inflation by inflating the price of the project, but often he is confined by the actions of competitors or federal restrictions on price increases. Some protection from inflation may be gained by including clauses in the contract that allow increases in wages or material costs to be appended to the contract price,[4] but the protection may be limited. Inflation is not one dimensional; it varies depending on the labor, materials, and equipment employed, the geographical region, and the country. Subcontractors, suppliers, and clients use different kinds of contracts which have different inflation protection clauses and which may be to the advantage or disadvantage of other parties in the project.

Inflation causes cash flow difficulties, too. Even when a contract includes an inflation clause, payment for inflation related costs is tied to the publication of inflation indices which always lags behind the inflation. While contractors pay immediately for the effects of inflation, it is not until later that they are reimbursed for these effects.

Trend analysis of inflation in the industry and the economy can improve the accuracy of cost estimates. In long-term projects especially, wage rates should be projected to indicate what they will be at the time they must be paid. This is done by starting with best estimates of labor hours and wage costs in current dollars, then applying inflation rates over the project's length.

Initial cost estimates are based upon prices at the time of estimating. After that, whenever actual costs are compared with initial estimates, adjustments for inflation must be made so there remains a common basis upon which to identify variances and take corrective action. Either the estimates must be adjusted upward or actual expenses adjusted downward.

Inefficiency, Poor Communication, Lack of Control

Another source of cost escalation is work inefficiency. Primarily this is the result of poor management, lack of supervision, and weak planning and control; in large projects especially, poor coordination, miscommunication, and sloppy control lead to conflicts, misunderstandings, duplication of effort, and mistakes. But this is *one* source of cost escalation where management can have a substantial influence. Meticulous work planning, tracking and monitoring of activities, team building, and good control all help improve efficiency and keep (at least this source of) cost escalation to a minimum.

Ego Involvement of The Estimator

Cost escalation also comes from the *way* people estimate. Most people are overly optimistic and habitually underestimate the amount of time and cost it will take to do a job, especially in areas where they have little experience. Have you ever estimated how long it would take for you to paint a room, tile a floor, or replace a muffler? How long did it *really* take? Most people think of an estimate as an "optimistic prediction." They confuse estimates with incentives or goals, and see the estimate as a reflection on themselves, not an honest prediction of what it will take. The more "ego involvement" of the estimator in the job, the more unreliable the estimate.

The problem can be lessened by having professional estimators, people different than those who will actually do the work. Remember the earlier contention about the necessity of involving project participants in planning the project? Most experienced workers are much better at estimating tasks, materials, and schedules than they are costs. While the doers (those who do the work) should *define* the work—the WBS, work packages, tasks and schedules—and provide *initial* estimates of time and costs, professional estimators should review the estimates for accuracy, check with the doers, and then prepare *final* cost estimates.[5]

A cost estimate should not be something to strive for; it should be a reasonable prediction of what will happen. Estimators must be, organizationally, in a position where they will not be coerced to provide estimates that conform to anyone's desires.

Project Contract

Appendix B describes the relative merits of different forms of contracts. Some of the merits are related to the contract's influence on cost escalation.[6]

Consider, for example, differences between the two basic kinds of contract: fixed-price and cost-plus. A fixed-price agreement gives the contractor incentive to control costs because, no matter what happens, the amount paid for the project remains the same. In contrast, in a strictly cost-plus contract there is only slight incentive to control costs. In fact, in cases where profit is computed as a percentage of costs, cost-plus agreements tend to motivate contractors to "allow" controllable costs to escalate. Other forms of legal agreements, such as the incentive contracts described in Appendix B, permit cost increases but at the same time encourage cost control and provide some motivation to try to reduce escalation.

14.3 COST ESTIMATING AND THE SYSTEMS DEVELOPMENT CYCLE[7]

Development of the cost estimate is closely tied to the first three phases of the Systems Development Cycle:

A. Conception: initiation/feasibility
B. Definition: detailed planning/analysis
C. Acquisition: design/fabrication/implementation

The first cost estimate is made during project conception. At this time very little hard cost information is available so the estimate is the least reliable that it will ever be. This is illustrated in Figure 14–1 by the largest "region of time-cost uncertainty" shown at project initiation. How much the project will *really* cost and how long it will *really* take are very much open to question. Typically the estimate is based upon standards of what it should take—labor time, materials, and equipment—to do a certain job. The project is compared to other, similar projects, and adjustments made for differences. This approach is less useful

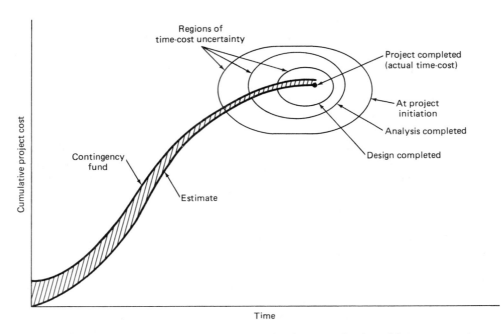

FIGURE 14–1.   Time-cost graph showing cumulative project cost and regions of time-cost uncertainty.

when there is much development work involved because fewer of the tasks can be classified as "standard" and no other projects are similar. On large development projects the initial estimates are largely "guesstimates" and might end up being nowhere close to actual costs.

Unless the project is strictly routine, uncertainty in estimates dictates that contracts awarded during the conception phase be of the cost-plus form. Only after most of the definition phase and some design work are completed can the uncertainty be reduced. As more of the design is finalized, material costs become known and reliable estimates of labor requirements and rates can be made. It is then possible to obtain solid cost estimates for fabrication and installation. This is illustrated by the shrinking time-cost uncertainty regions in Figure 14–1.

By the time design work is half completed, cost estimates may be reliable enough to award incentive-type or (in well-defined situations) fixed-price contracts. In fact, the awarding of contracts is often put off for as long as possible, well into the design stage, just so that the cost estimate can be more certain. This requires contractors to do a lot of front end work without assurances that they will be awarded the job. When contractors are required to bid before the design phase is reached, they usually include substantial contingencies to cover the uncertainty of their estimates.

As the project moves into the middle and later phases, with work actually being completed and funds expended, cost estimates become more certain. The contingency fund can be decreased, starting from 10 to 20 percent in the conception phase, down to only a few percent to cover small corrections after the work is finished.

Once the cost estimate has been developed and approved it is used to establish the budget and becomes the baseline against which progress and performance will be evaluated. Thus, it is bad practice to change the estimate frequently during the project life cycle because it destroys the purpose of having a baseline. However, sometimes escalation factors render the initial estimate obsolete and require it to be revised periodically.

14.4 INITIATION, PLANNING, AND AUTHORIZATION PROCESS

Using the WBS

The WBS process breaks the project down into work packages each roughly small enough to permit accurate estimation of labor, materials, and costs. A meeting is held with representatives from functional and subcontracting units to discuss the WBS, work requirements, and work packages, and to assign work packages to the units that will be responsible for them.

To prevent duplication of effort the project team tries to identify tasks in the WBS which are similar to existing designs and could readily be adopted. Work is classified either as *developmental* or as an adaptation of existing or *off-the-shelf* designs, techniques, or procedures. Developmental work requires considerable effort in design, testing, and fabrication setup, and cost estimating is more difficult because of the greater uncertainty about what needs to be done. Overruns for developmental work are common, especially because of the difficulty in estimating labor hours. Estimation of standard, off-the-shelf items is more straightforward because it is based upon records of material and labor costs for similar systems or tasks. It is thus beneficial to try to make use of existing design and technology in as many work packages as possible; this helps reduce estimating errors and may afford cost savings.

Estimated costs are also classified as *recurring* and *nonrecurring*.[8] Recurring costs happen more than once; they are associated with tasks periodically repeated and include costs for labor, materials, tooling, quality assurance, and testing. Nonrecurring costs happen only once and are associated with unique tasks or procurement of special items; they include development, fabrication, and testing of one-of-a- kind items.

In the pure project form of organization the project manager assigns responsibility for estimating, directs the estimating effort, and combines the estimate results for presentation to management. In a matrix organization, estimating is the joint responsibility of the project and functional managers, though the project manager coordinates the effort and accumulates the results. Close coordination and communication during the estimating effort is crucial for reducing redundancies and omissions—especially for estimates from groups working jointly on interfacing work packages.

Estimating Procedure

After the work packages have been assigned to and accepted by particular functional and subcontracting units, they are broken into more fundamental, or "basic areas" of work. For example, a work package assigned to a functional unit might be divided into two basic areas, "engineering" work and "fabrication" work. The manager of the unit then asks his supervisors to estimate the hours and materials needed to do the work in each basic area. The supervisor overseeing engineering work might further divide it into the tasks of structural analysis, computer analysis, layout drawings, installation drawings, manuals, and reproduction, then develop an estimate for each task of how long it will take and the labor grade or skill level required. In similar fashion, the fabrication supervisor might break the work down into—for example, fabricated materials (steel, piping, wiring), hardware, machinery, equipment, insurance, and so on—then estimates how much (quantity, size, length, weight, etc.) of each will be needed. The supervisors' estimates of time and materials are determined by reference to previous, similar work, standards manuals, reference documents, rules of thumb ("one hour for each line of code"), and rough estimates. The more developmental and the less standardized the task, the more guesswork involved; even with routine, off-the-shelf items, good estimating is an art. The supervisors submit their estimates to the unit manager who checks, revises, and then passes them on to the project manager.

The project manager and independent estimators or pricing experts in the project office review the time and material estimates to be sure that: no costs were overlooked or duplicated, estimators understood what they were estimating, correct estimating procedures were used, and allowances were made for risk and uncertainty.[9] The estimates are then aggregated, as shown in Figure 14–2, and converted into dollars by multiplying by standard wage rates and material costs (current or projected). Finally, the project manager tallies in any project-wide overhead rates (to cover project management and administrative costs) and company-wide overhead rates (to cover the burden of general company expenses) to come up with a cost estimate for the total project. (The topic of overhead rates will be discussed later.)

The final cost estimate and project schedule is reported to company management. The project manager may also include forecasts showing time and cost effects of likely, potential escalation factors such as inflation, project risks, and so on. Management then decides to accept the estimate or have it revised.

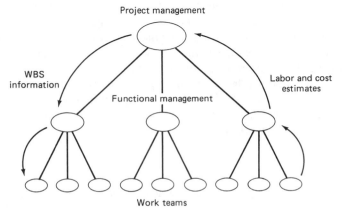

FIGURE 14–2.   The estimating process.

This upward accumulation of work package estimates to derive the project estimate is called the "bottom-up" approach. The resulting total estimate is compared against the "top- down" or gross estimate from top management. If the gross estimate is substantially larger, the project manager reviews each work package estimate for oversights or over-optimism (the ego involvement of estimators). If the gross estimate is much smaller, the work package estimates are examined for incorrect assumptions or padding.

To reconcile differences between estimates, top management sometimes exercises an across-the-board cut on all estimates. This is poor practice since it fails to account for judgmental errors or excessive requests on the part of just a few units. It also unfairly penalizes unit managers who tried to produce fair estimates and were honest enough not to pad them. Such indiscriminate, across-the board cuts induce everyone to pad estimates for their own protection.

Mistakes in estimation run in both directions. The project manager should approve bottom-up estimates for work packages, but functional units should approve top-down estimates for the work expected of them. Final estimates should be mutually agreed upon by both project and functional managers.

Project estimating procedures using computerized management systems are mentioned in section 14.6 and Chapter 16.

Reducing Costs

What happens if competition or insufficient funding force upper management to reduce costs? Managers and workers will want to retain a share of the project and none will want to see their budget or staff reduced. Nonmanagement professionals such as engineers, scientists, or systems analysts, unless actively involved in the budgeting process, are often unaware of budget constraints and resist cuts. Here is where effective communication, negotiation, and diplomacy between project management, functional management, and staff is necessary to get project team members to accept a share of budget reductions. When this fails, the project manager must try to alter the work plan to reduce labor requirements. The final resort is to appeal to top management.[10]

The extent to which a contractor is willing to cut costs depends partly on the existing and projected work load. A company with current or expected excess capacity is usually much more willing to take on projects with little or no profit just to absorb its fixed overhead costs.

Suppose you are the project manager and it is clear that management wants to buy in with a budget too low to perform the work. There are only two courses of action: either undertake the project and attempt wholeheartedly to meet the budget, or hand it over to another manager.[11] If you decide on the former, you should document your disagreement with the estimate and report it to top management; later, the client might agree to changes in the project which would enable it to be completed within budget. If the contract is cost-plus, then the risk is low because additional costs will be reimbursed. If, on the other hand, the contract is fixed-price, and the budget is so grossly underfunded as to result in shoddy workmanship or an uncompletable project, then you should try to get the project cancelled or step down as project manager. Not only is this good business practice, it is the only ethical alternative.

14.5 ELEMENTS OF BUDGETS AND ESTIMATES

The similarity between budgets and estimates is that both state what it will cost to do something. The difference is that the estimate comes first and is the basis for the budget. An estimate may have to be refined many times, but once it is approved it becomes the budget. Organizations and work units are then committed to performing work according to the budget: it is the agreed to contracted amount of what the work should cost and the baseline against which expenditures will be compared for tracking and control purposes. Project budgets are similar to fiscal operating budgets with the difference that the former covers the life of the project, while the latter only covers a year at a time.

Estimates and budgets share most or all of the following elements:

direct labor expense
direct nonlabor expense
overhead expense
general and administrative expense
profit
total billing

Direct Labor Expense[12]

Direct labor expense is the charge of labor for the project. From the total number of hours or days of work for each task indicated on the project schedule, an estimate is made of how many people will be needed in each labor grade and for how long. This gives the distribution of labor hours or man-days required for each labor grade. The labor hours for the various grades are then multiplied by their respective wage rates. The work package in Figure 14–3 is an example, showing the wage rates for three labor grades and the associated labor hours time-phased over a six-month period.

When the wage rate is expected to change over the course of the work, a weighted average wage rate is used. In Figure 14–3, suppose the initial rate for assistant is expected to increase from $20 to $25 in months 3, 4, and 5. The labor cost for assistant in months 2, 3, 4, and 5 would then increase from $8000 to $100(\$20) + 100(\$25) + 100(\$25) + 100(\$25) = \$9500$. (The average wage rate would thus be $9500/400$ hours $= \$23.75$/hour.) Notice that the average wage rate changes whenever the distribution of hours changes. In the example had the work been evenly distributed 100 hours/month over months 1 through 4 (instead of over months 2 through 5) the average wage for assistant would have been $9000/400$ hours $= \$22.50$/hour.

Project __CASTLE__		Date __April 1, 1592__							
Department __Excavating__		Work Package __Moat__							

Charge	Rate	Months[+]						Totals	
		1	2	3	4	5	6	Hours	Cost
Direct labor Professional Associate Assistant	$35/hr $30/hr $20/hr	50	 100	 100	 100	50 100		100 400	3,500 8,000
Direct labor cost Labor overhead Other direct cost*	 75%	1,750 1,312	2,000 1,500 100	2,000 1,500	2,000 1,500	3,750 2,813			11,500 8,625 100
Total direct cost General/adminstration	 10%	3,062 306	3,600 360	3,500 350	3,500 350	6,563 657			20,225 2,023
Total costs Profit	 15%	3,368	3,960	3,850	3,850	7,220			22,248
Billing total									

[+]Should extend for as many months as required by the project.
*Should be itemized to include costs for materials, freight, subcontracts, travel, and all other nonlabor direct costs.

FIGURE 14-3.   Typical six-month cost report for a work package.

Direct Nonlabor Expense

Direct nonlabor expense is the total expense of nonlabor charges applied directly to the task. It includes subcontractors, consultants, travel, telephone, computer time, material costs, purchased parts, and freight. Material costs include allotments for waste and spoilage and should reflect anticipated price increases. Material costs and freight charges sometimes appear as separate line items called *direct materials* and *overhead on materials*, respectively; computer time and consultants may appear as *support*.

Direct nonlabor expenses also include items necessary for installation and operation such as maintenance manuals, engineering and programming documentation, instruction manuals, drawings, and spare parts. Note that these are costs incurred only for a specific project or work package. Not included are the general or overhead costs of doing business, unless the costs are tied to the specific project.

On smaller projects all direct nonlabor expenses are individually estimated for each work package. In larger projects, a simple percentage rate is applied to cover travel and freight costs. For example, 5 percent of direct labor cost might be included as travel expense and 5 percent of material costs as freight. These percentages are estimated in the same fashion as the overhead rates discussed next.

Overhead and General and Administrative Expenses

Direct expenses for labor and materials are easily charged to a specific work package. Many other expenses cannot be easily allocated to specific work packages, nor even to a specific project. These expenses, termed *overhead* or *nondirect expenses* are the cost of doing business. They include whatever is necessary to house and support the labor, including building rents, utilities, clerical assistance, insurance, and equipment. Usually overhead is computed as a percentage of the direct labor cost. Frequently the rate is around 100 percent but it ranges from as low as 25 percent for companies that do most of their work in the field to over 250 percent for firms with laboratories and expensive equipment.

The actual overhead rate is computed by estimating the annual business overhead expense, then dividing by the projected total direct labor cost for the year.[13] Suppose projections show that total overhead for next year will be $180,000. If total anticipated direct labor charges will total $150,000, then the overhead rate to apply is 180,000/150,000 = 1.20. Thus, for every $1.00 charged to direct labor, $1.20 is charged to overhead.

While this is the traditional accounting method for deriving the overhead rate, for project management it results in a somewhat arbitrary allocation of costs. This is counterproductive for project control since the sources of many overhead costs are independent of project performance. Overhead costs in projects should thus be treated differently. They should be divided into two categories: *direct overhead*, which can be allocated in a logical manner; and *indirect overhead*, which cannot. Direct overhead costs can be traced to the support of a particular project or work package, so these costs are allocated only among the specific activities for which they apply. If a department is working on four projects then its overhead is apportioned among the four projects based on the percentage of labor time it devotes to each. Department overhead should not be allocated to projects that it is not involved in.

Indirect overhead includes general expenses for the corporation. Usually referred to as *general and administrative* expenses, or *G&A*, it includes taxes, financing, penalty and warranty costs, accounting and legal support, proposal expenses on lost contracts, marketing and promotion, upper management, and employee benefits packages. These costs are not tied to any specific project or work package, and are allocated across all projects, to certain projects, or parts of projects.

Corporate or company level expenses are allocated across all projects, project management costs are allocated on a per project basis, and departmental overhead is allocated to specific project segments in which the department did work. Overhead expenditures are allocated on a time basis so that as the duration of a given project is extended, so is the period over which G&A is charged.

The actual manner in which indirect costs are apportioned varies in practice. The example for the SETI Company in Table 14–1 shows three methods for distributing indirect costs between two projects, MARS and PLUTO.[14] Notice that although company wide expenses remain the same, the cost of each project differs depending on the method of allocating indirect costs.

Clients want to know the allocation method used by the contractor, and the contractor should know the allocation method used by subcontractors. For example, method I is good for the client when the project is labor (DL) intensive, but bad when it is direct nonlabor (DNL) intensive. Method III is the opposite and gives a lower cost when the project is relatively nonlabor intensive (i.e., when labor costs are low but material and parts

TABLE 14–1 Examples of Indirect Cost Apportionment

SETI Company
Company wide (indirect costs)
Overhead (rent, utilities, clerical, machinery)   OH   120
General (upper management, staff, benefits, etc.)   G&A   40
                                                                                     Indirect Total 160

Project Costs	MARS Project	PLUTO Project	Total
Direct Labor (DL)	50	100	150
Direct Nonlabor (DNL)	40	10	50
	90	110 Direct	
		Total	200
		Direct and Indirect Total	360

Some methods for apportioning indirect costs:

I. Total indirect proportionate to total direct costs

	MARS	PLUTO	Total
DL and DNL	90	110	200
OH and G&A	72	88	160
	162	198	360

II. OH proportionate to direct labor only; G&A proportionate to all direct costs

	MARS	PLUTO	Total
DL	50	100	150
OH on DL	40	80	120
DNL	40	10	50
G&A on (DL and DNL)	18	22	40
	148	212	360

III. OH proportionate to direct labor only; G&A proportionate to DL and OH and DNL

	MARS	PLUTO	Total
DL and OH and DNL	130	190	320
G&A	16.25	23.75	40
	146.25	213.75	360

expenditures are high). This can be seen in Table 14–1 by comparing MARS (somewhat nonlabor intensive) to PLUTO (somewhat labor intensive).

Profit and Total Billing

Profit is the amount left over for the contractor after expenses have been paid. It is an agreed to fixed fee or a percentage of total expenses. (Different ways of determining profit are discussed in Appendix B.) Total billing is the sum of total expenses and profit. Profit and total billing are included for estimates of the project as whole, for large groups of work packages, and for subcontracted work. Usually they do not appear on budgets for lower level work elements.

14.6 PROJECT COST ACCOUNTING AND MANAGEMENT INFORMATION SYSTEMS

Projects are complex systems of workers, materials, and facilities, all of which the cost must be estimated, budgeted, and controlled. Hundreds or thousands of items may be involved. To reduce confusion, maintain accuracy, and expedite operations, a system is needed to compute estimates, combine budgets, and track costs. The term *Project Cost Accounting System (PCAS)* refers to a structure and methodology, manual or computerized, which allows systematic planning, tracking, and control of project costs. The PCAS is set up by the project manager, project accountant, and involved functional managers. Although the PCAS emphasizes project costs, by relating project costs to schedules and work performance it also permits tracking and control of schedules and work progress. When combined with other project planning, control, and reporting functions, it is more generally referred to as a *Project Management Information System (PMIS)*.

During project planning, cost estimates of work packages are accumulated through the PCAS to produce a total project estimate. These estimates later become the basis upon which total project and work package budgets are created.

After work on the project begins, the PCAS enables total project and subactivity costs to be accumulated, credited, and reported. Time-phased budgets are created to help managers monitor costs to insure they are allocated against appropriate work, and to verify that work has been completed and charged. The system also provides for revision of budgets.

The functions of the PCAS are reviewed in Figure 14–4.

Example: Using a PMIS for Estimating Labor Requirements and Costs[15]

Sigma Associates is a moderately large architectural/engineering firm with a staff of over 100 architects, engineers, and draftsmen supported by 40 data processing and office personnel. The firm has developed its own PMIS which, in addition to planning and scheduling functions, stores information about all Sigma projects since 1978.

The project manager begins planning a project by creating a WBS to identify the major work activities (e.g., architectural schematics, design administration, construction cost estimating). Using a menu in the PMIS, she then reviews the history of similar work activities in previous projects and the kind and amount of labor required to do them. By entering factors related to relative project size, relative construction costs, and type of clients, the project manager can forecast the labor requirements for every activity in the project.

The PMIS combines these labor requirements with requirements for existing projects to make a one year, manpower loading forecast. The forecast enables the project manager to determine whether or not sufficient labor is available. If it is not, the system aids the project manager in

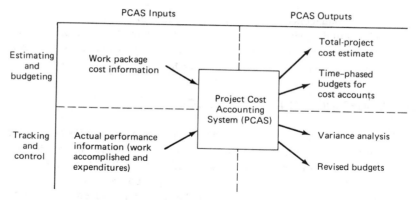

FIGURE 14–4.   Elements of project cost accounting system.

reviewing options, including modifying her original schedule, scheduling overtime, and so on (using resource loading procedures as discussed in Chapter 13).

The labor requirements plan is then given to the comptroller to establish a budget. The comptroller uses the PMIS to apply one of two hourly rates to each activity in the plan. The first is the average hourly rate of all employees who might work on the activity, the second is the average rate associated with all hours charged to that kind of activity in the last 90 days. The second rate is used more often because it reflects the actual mix of personnel currently employed in similar work. The comptroller then applies factors to account for employee benefits and labor overhead. The result is a budget for direct labor cost.

With information from the company general ledger, the comptroller computes the indirect overhead rate in terms of overhead amount per labor dollar. The project is then charged with this rate for its share of company-wide expenses. Project related, nonlabor expenses that will not be reimbursed by the client (e.g., travel, reproduction, communications) are forecast and through the PMIS rolled up into the total budget.

With the forecasted total budget completed the comptroller analyzes the project plan for profitability. If the plan shows a reasonable profit, the project is accepted. If not, a more profitable plan which maintains the same high quality standards is tried out. When both the controller and project manager agree to a plan, the project is accepted.

Time-phased Budgets

In most projects it is difficult to control work schedules and cost expenditures simultaneously. The project manager needs some way of knowing how the project is progressing, what changes are happening, and where problems are developing.

The two primary tools for controlling projects, the project schedule and the project budget, can be consolidated using a cost equivalent to the project schedule called the *time-phased budget*. This is roughly a scheme showing how budgeted costs are distributed over time according to project schedules. Figure 14–3 is an example showing the distribution of costs over one six month period. Throughout the duration of the project the PCAS would generate time-phased reports similar to Figure 14–3 for every work package. This allows managers to review planned expenditures on a monthly basis and to compare them with actual expenditures. The reports are also used to perform variance analysis of costs (discussed in Chapter 15) to insure that work is completed and accurately charged, and to revise estimates and budgets as needed.

14.7 BUDGETING USING COST ACCOUNTS[16]

On small projects, planning and performance monitoring is done using one simple budget for the project as a whole. This budget, perhaps similar to the one in Figure 14–3, is used as the basis for comparison to actual costs throughout the project.

On larger projects, however, a single, project-wide budget is too insensitive; once the project is underway and actual costs begin to exceed budgeted costs, it is difficult to quickly locate the source of the overrun. To overcome this problem the project-wide budget is broken down into smaller segments called *cost accounts* where each segment is monitored individually. On very small projects there is only one cost account—the budget for the project as a whole. Larger projects have tens of cost accounts; very large projects have many hundreds.

The cost account is the basic project tracking and control unit of the PCAS. A system of cost accounts is set up in a hierarchy, similar or identical to the WBS. Although the lowest level cost account usually corresponds to a work package, cost accounts may also be formed on the basis of several work packages, especially when the number of work packages in a project is very large. A numerical coding scheme is used to organize, communicate, and control the accounts. For example,

Level	Numerical Assignment (Cost Account Number)
1	01-00-0000....
2	01-01-0000....
3	01-01-1000....
3	01-01-2000....
2	01-02-0000....
3	01-02-1000....
4	01-02-1010....

Cost accounts and work packages are analogous. Each cost account includes:

- A description of the work
- A time schedule
- Who is responsible
- A time-phased budget
- Material, labor, and equipment required

Notice that, with the exception of the time-phased budget, this information is determined from the WBS analysis. The time-phased budget is derived from the work schedule and shows the distribution of costs over the period of the work. In practice, both the schedule and time-phased budget are developed simultaneously to account for resource and cash flow limitations.

Cost accounts are also established for *nondirect* project costs—costs not readily attributable to any work packages or specific tasks. For example, monies allocated to a project for general purpose items, materials or equipment that can be used by anyone on any task, or for jobs nonspecific to activities, such as administration, supervision, or inspection jobs which apply across the project, are budgeted to separate cost accounts, or, where appropriate, to special work packages for general project items. These accounts are usually set up for the duration of the project and extended, period by period, as needed or as funds are appropriated.

With the PCAS and the cost-account structure, performance can be monitored for a work package, groups of work packages, and the project as a whole. As an example consider again the Robotics Self-Budgeting (ROSEBUD) project. Figure 12–15 in Chapter 12 is the project network; in Figure 14–5 is the WBS and organization chart for the ROSEBUD contractor, KANE & Associates. The shaded boxes represent locations of cost accounts. Notice each represents all or part of a work package for which a single functional area is responsible.

The WBS for ROSEBUD results in nine work packages performed by four functional departments plus an additional work package for project management. During the estimating phase each department submits a cost estimate for its part of the project. Through the PCAS these estimates are accumulated upward to derive the total project estimate. Upon approval, with additions for overhead and G&A, each departmental estimate becomes a budget.

In Figure 14–5 the shaded boxes represent where initial estimates are made and where budgets will be set up. In this example, they also represent cost accounts. The total project budget is the sum of the ten budgets. In particular, Figures 14–6 and 14–7 show, respectively, the time-phased budget portions of the cost accounts for the Programming Department and for work packages L and W.

14.8 COST SUMMARIES[17]

The cost account structure can be a matrix. If desired, higher level accounts can be developed by consolidating cost accounts through the WBS and organizational hierarchies. With a computerized PCAS, cost-summary information is easily obtained, though for small projects it can also be developed manually.

Consolidating basic cost-account information is useful for monitoring the performance of individual departments and segments of the project. For example, consolidating accounts horizontally results in a cost account for each functional department or subcontractor. Figure 14–8 shows this in the time-phased budget summary for the Programming Department, which is the sum of the programming costs for work packages L and W. This is the budget for the ROSEBUD cost account for the Programming Department.

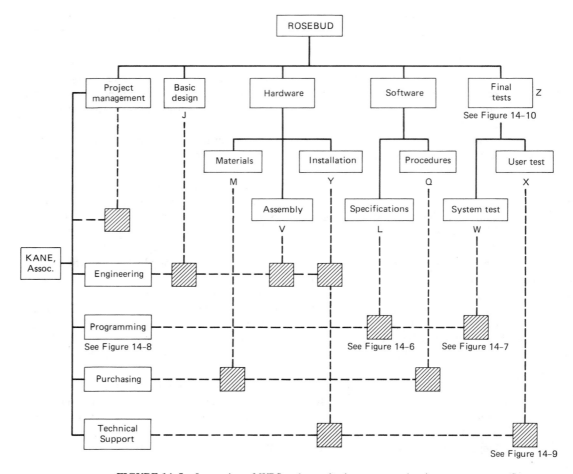

FIGURE 14–5. Integration of WBS and organization structure showing cost accounts. (See Figures 14–6 through 14–10 for details.)

Cost accounts can also be consolidated vertically through the WBS. This information is useful for tracking and controlling individual work packages, clusters of work packages, or the project as a whole. Figure 14–10 shows this in the budget summary for final tests, which represents costs from work packages W (Figure 14–7) and X (Figure 14–9).

The highest level cost accounts are for the project and the company. Figure 14–11 shows how costs are aggregated vertically and horizontally to derive these costs. Through the PCAS and cost-account structure, any deviation from budget at the project level can readily be traced to the work packages and departments responsible. Chapter 15 describes specifically how this is done.

Most PCAS's can be used to create a variety of cost summaries, depending on purpose. Table 14–2 is an example, showing the allocation of certain budget elements—

Project __ROSEBUD__								Date _____	
Department __Programming__						Work Package __L- S/W Specifications__			

Charge	Rate	Months+						Totals	
		1	2	3	4	5	6	Hours	Cost

Direct labor
  Professional
  Associate
  Assistant
	$35/hr.
	$30/hr
	$20/hr
			130
			50
				100
				100
								130
								150
								100
									4,550
									4,500
									2,000

Direct labor cost Labor overhead Other direct cost*	75%		6,050 4,538	5,000 3,750				11,050 8,288 	0
Total direct cost General/administrative	10%		10,588 1,059	8,750 875				19,338 1,934	
Total costs Profit	15%		11,647 1,747	9,625 1,444				21,272 3,191	
Billing total			13,394	11,069				24,463	

+ Should extend for as many months as required by the project.
* Should be itemized to include costs for materials, freight, subcontracts, travel, and all other nonlabor direct costs.

FIGURE 14-6. Budget for Programming Department for work package L.

Project __ROSEBUD__								Date _____	
Department __Programming__						Work Package __W- System Test__			

Charge	Rate	Months+						Totals	
		1	2	3	4	5	6	Hours	Cost

Direct labor
  Professional
  Associate
  Assistant
	$35/hr
	$30/hr
	$20/hr
							20
							50
								20
								50
									700
									1,500
									0

Direct labor cost Labor overhead Other direct cost*	75%						2,200 1,650 0	2,200 1,650 0	
Total direct cost General/administrative	10%						3,850 385	3,850 385	
Total costs Profit	15%						4,235 635	4,235 635	
Billing total							4,870	4,870	

+ Should extend for as many months as required by the project.
* Should be itemized to include costs for materials, freight, subcontracts, travel, and all other nonlabor direct costs.

FIGURE 14-7. Budget for Programming Department for work package W.

Project __ROSEBUD__   Date _____

Department __Programming__   Work Package __All__

Charge	Rate	1	2	3	4	5	6	Hours	Cost
Direct labor									
Professional	$35/hr		130				20	150	5,250
Associate	$30/hr		50	100			50	200	6,000
Assistant	$20/hr			100				100	2,000
Direct labor cost			6,050	5,000			2,200		13,250
Labor overhead	75%		4,538	3,750			1,650		9,938
Other direct cost*									0
Total direct cost			10,588	8,750			3,850		23,188
General/administrative	10%		1,059	875			385		2,319
Total costs			11,647	9,625			4,235		25,507
Profit	15%		1,747	1,444			635		3,826
Billing total			13,384	11,069			4,870		29,333

+ Should extend for as many months as required by the project.
* Should be itemized to include costs for materials, freight, subcontracts, travel, and all other nonlabor direct costs.

FIGURE 14–8. Budget summary for Programming Department.

Project __ROSEBUD__   Date _____

Department __Technical Service__   Work Package __X– User Test__

Charge	Rate	1	2	3	4	5	6	Hours	Cost
Direct labor									
Professional	$35/hr						10	10	350
Associate	$30/hr						40	40	1,200
Assistant	$20/hr								
Direct labor cost							1,550		1,550
Labor overhead	75%						1,163		1,163
Other direct cost*						1,200	2,107		3,307
Total direct cost						1,200	4,820		6,020
General/administrative	10%					120	482		602
Total costs						1,320	5,302		6,622
Profit	15%					198	795		993
Billing total						1,518	6,097		7,615

+ Should extend for as many months as required by the project.
* Should be itemized to include costs for materials, freight, subcontracts, travel, and all other nonlabor direct costs.

FIGURE 14–9. Budget summary for user test work package.

Project __ROSEBUD__		Date _____							

| Department __A11__ | | Work Package __(W + X) Final Tests__ | | | | | | | |

Charge	Rate	Months[+]						Totals	
		1	2	3	4	5	6	Hours	Cost
Direct labor									
Professional	$35/hr						30	30	1,050
Associate	$30/hr						90	90	2,700
Assistant	$20/hr								0
Direct labor cost							3,750		3,750
Labor overhead	75%						2,813		2,813
Other direct cost*						1,200	2,107		3,307
Total direct cost						1,200	8,670		9,870
General/Administrative	10%						120	867		987
Total costs						1,320	9,537		10,857
Profit	15%						198	143		1,628
Billing total						1,518	10,967		12,485

[+] Should extend for as many months as required by the project.
* Should be itemized to include costs for materials, freight, subcontracts, travel, and all othe nonlabor direct costs.

FIGURE 14–10.   Budget summary for final tests.

direct labor, overhead, materials, and G&A—among the four departments and seven work packages that comprise the ROSEBUD project.

14.9 COST SCHEDULES AND FORECASTS[18]

Questions arise during planning and budgeting about what the rate of project expenditures will be, which periods will have the heaviest cash requirements, and how expenditures will compare to income. To help answer these questions and others the project manager analyzes the "pattern of expenditures" using work package estimates of costs and forecasts of costs derived from the project schedule. Following are some examples.

Cost Analysis with Early and Late Start Times

One simplifying assumption used in cost forecasts is that costs in each work package are incurred uniformly over its duration. For example, a two-week, $22,000 work package is assumed to have a weekly cost of $11,000 per week. With this assumption a *cost schedule* for the project can be easily created by adding costs, period by period, for the work packages scheduled in each time period. As an example look again at the LOGON project and Figure 14–12 which shows the time-based network using early start times. Table 14–3 shows LOGON work packages and corresponding time, total cost, and resulting average weekly

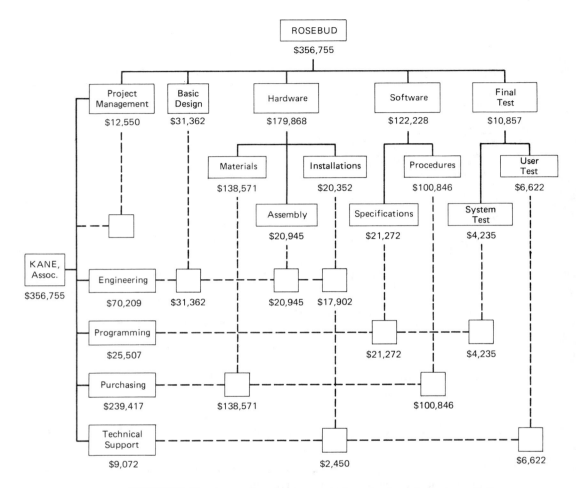

FIGURE 14–11. Aggregation of cost account information by project and organization.

direct cost (derived using the simplifying assumption). For example, the average weekly direct cost for activity H is computed as $100K/10 weeks = $10K/week.

Using the early start schedule in Figure 14–12, the total weekly project cost can be computed by summing the weekly cost for all activities on a week-by-week basis. In the first ten weeks only activity H is scheduled, so the weekly cost stays at $10K. Over the next six weeks only activities I and J are scheduled, so the weekly cost is their total, $16K + $8K = $24K. Further along, in weeks 17 and 18, four work packages—I, K, L, and J—are scheduled, so the weekly expense is their total, $8K + $4K + $18K + $21K = $51K. These weekly expenses, summarized in Table 14–4, represent the cost schedule for the project. Table 14–4 also shows the cumulative project expense, which also can be interpreted as the forecasted project cost as of a given week. These costs are shown graphically in Figure 14–13.

TABLE 14-2 Cost Summary ROSEBUD Project

	Labor ($)				Overhead ($)						Total Cost
	Engineering	Programming	Purchasing	Technical Support	Engineering	Programming	Purchasing	Technical Support	Materials	General and Administrative	
Total Project	22800	13250	2230	2850	22800	9938	1673	2138	235236	31290	356755
Project Management											12550
Activity J	7200				7200				14111	2851	31362
Activity L*		11050				8288				1934	21272
Activity M			1100				825		124050	12596	138571
Activity Q			1300				818		89700	9168	100846
Activity V	8200				8200				2641	1904	20945
Activity Y	7400			1300	7400			975	1427	1850	20352
Activity W	2200					1650				385	4235
Activity X				1550				1163		602	6622

*Refer to Figure 14–6 to see, for example, how costs in this row were developed.

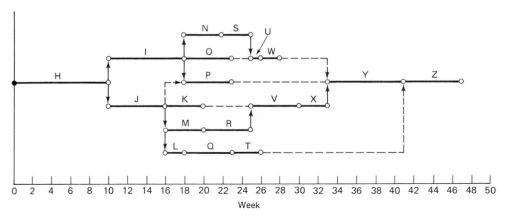

FIGURE 14–12. Time-based network for the LOGON project using early start times.

TABLE 14–3   Activities, Time, Cost, and Labor Requirements (Result of Work Breakdown Analysis)

Activity	Time (weeks)	Total Cost ($K)	Weekly Direct Cost ($K)	Weekly Labor Requirements (workers)
H	10	100	10	5
I	8	64	8	4
J	6	96	16	8
K	4	16	4	2
L	2	36	18	6
M	4	84	21	3
N	4	80	20	2
O	5	50	10	5
P	5	60	12	6
Q	5	80	16	2
R	5	0	0	0
S	3	0	0	0
T	3	0	0	0
U	1	14	14	9
V	5	80	16	14
W	2	24	12	6
X	3	36	12	6
Y	8	104	13	14
Z	6	66	11	5

Total Direct Cost—$990K

Project cost schedules and cost forecasts can be prepared in the same fashion using late start times. Figure 14–14 is the time-based network for LOGON using late start times, and Table 14–5 is the associated weekly and cumulative costs.

Given the two cost profiles in Table 14–4 and 14–5 it is possible to analyze the effect of delaying activities on project costs and budgets. The cost and budget implications of

TABLE 14–4   LOGON Project Weekly Expense Using Early Start Times ($1000)

Week	Activities During Week	Weekly Expense	Cumulative Expense
1	H	10	10
2	H	10	20
3	H	10	30
4	H	10	40
5	H	10	50
6	H	10	60
7	H	10	70
8	H	10	80
9	H	10	90
10	H	10	100
11	I,J	24	124
12	I,J	24	148
13	I,J	24	172
14	I,J	24	196
15	I,J	24	220
16	I,J	24	244
17	I,K,L,M	51	295
18	I,K,L,M	51	346
19	K,M,N,O,P,Q	83	429
20	K,M,N,O,P,Q	83	512
21	N,O,P,Q	58	570
22	N,O,P,Q	58	628
23	O,P,Q	38	666
24	—	0	666
25	—	0	666
26	U,V	30	696
27	V,W	28	724
28	V,W	28	752
29	V	16	768
30	V	16	784
31	X	12	796
32	X	12	808
33	X	12	820
34	Y	13	833
35	Y	13	846
36	Y	13	859
37	Y	13	872
38	Y	13	885
39	Y	13	898
40	Y	13	911
41	Y	13	924
42	Z	11	935
43	Z	11	946
44	Z	11	957
45	Z	11	968
46	Z	11	979
47	Z	11	990

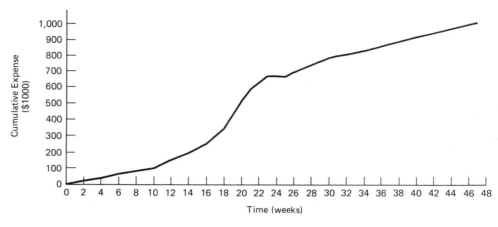

(a) Cumulative expense forecast (Table 14-4)

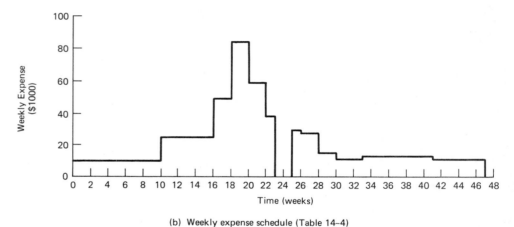

(b) Weekly expense schedule (Table 14-4)

FIGURE 14–13. Planned weekly and cumulative expenses for the LOGON project.

using early start times versus late start times is shown in Figure 14–15. Even if escalation factors are disregarded, it is apparent that changes in the project schedule significantly influence project cost. The shaded area in the top figure represents the *feasible budget region*, the range of budgets permitted by changes in the project schedule. The lower part of the figure shows the weekly impact on the cost schedule of delaying activities.

When budgetary restrictions put constraints on project expenditures, cost schedules reveal places of conflict. For example, Figure 14–15 shows a peak weekly expense of $82,000 in weeks 18 and 19. What if the budget ceiling is only $60,000? In that case the

TABLE 14–5   LOGON Project Weekly Expense Using Late Start Times ($1000)

Week	Activities During Week	Weekly Expense	Cumulative Expense
1	H	10	10
2	H	10	20
3	H	10	30
4	H	10	40
5	H	10	50
6	H	10	60
7	H	10	70
8	H	10	80
9	H	10	90
10	H	10	100
11	J	16	116
12	J	16	132
13	J	16	148
14	J	16	164
15	I,J	24	188
16	I,J	24	212
17	I,M	29	241
18	I,M	29	270
19	I,M	29	299
20	I,M	29	328
21	I,R	8	336
22	K,I,R	12	348
23	K,R	4	352
24	K,R,N	24	376
25	K,R,N	24	400
26	N,O,V	46	446
27	N,O,V	46	492
28	S,O,V	26	518
29	S,O,P,V	38	556
30	S,O,P,V	38	594
31	U,P,X	38	632
32	W,P,X,L	54	686
33	W,P,X,L	54	740
34	Y,Q	29	769
35	Y,Q	29	798
36	Y,Q	29	827
37	Y,Q	29	856
38	Y,Q	29	885
39	Y,T	13	898
40	Y,T	13	911
41	Y,T	13	924
42	Z	11	935
43	Z	11	946
44	Z	11	957
45	Z	11	968
46	Z	11	979
47	Z	11	990

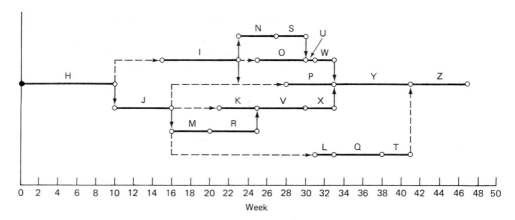

FIGURE 14–14. Time-based network for the LOGON project using late start times.

late start times would be preferred because they provide a more "leveled" cost profile and a peak expense of only $54,000. (The general method for leveling resources discussed in Chapter 13 is also applicable to minimizing variation in costs. Costs are treated as just another resource.)

The forecasts in the above example were based upon the total budgeted costs for each work package. Similarly, cost schedules and forecasts can be prepared for other specific kinds of costs or portions budgets—such as direct labor or materials. Table 14–6 shows the labor cost schedule for the ROSEBUD project using early start times. This kind of cost schedule is useful for spotting periods where scheduling changes may be necessary to meet payroll ceilings (i.e., when the monthly total direct labor cost cannot exceed a payroll ceiling).

Effect of Late Start Time on Project Net Worth

The time value of money results in work farther in the future having a lower net present value than the same work done earlier. Delaying all activities in a lengthy project can thus provide substantial savings because of differences in the present worth of the project. For example, suppose the LOGON project had a long duration, say 47 *months* instead of the 47 weeks used so far. If an annual interest rate of 24 percent were used, compounded monthly at 2 percent per month, the present worth for the project would be $649,276. This is computed by using the monthly expenses in Table 14–4 (again, assuming the weeks shown to be months instead) and discounting the amounts back to time zero. Now, when the late start times are used instead, the present worth is only $605,915—a savings of $43,361.

Does this mean that activities should always be delayed until their late start date? Not necessarily. Remember, delaying activities uses up slack time and leaves nothing for unexpected problems. If a problem arises, slack is needed to absorb the delay and keep the project on schedule. Thus, whether or not an activity should be delayed depends on the *certainty of the work*. Activities that are familiar and unlikely to encounter problems can

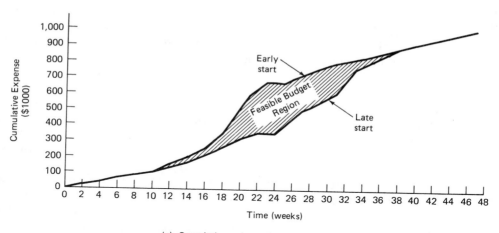

(a) Cumulative cash requirements profile

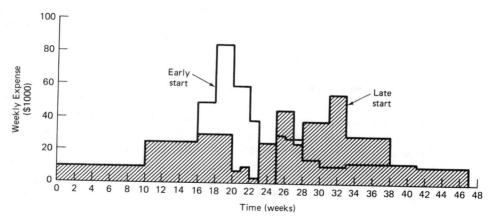

(b) Total cash requirements profile

FIGURE 14–15.   Comparison of cash requirements, early versus late start times.

TABLE 14–6   Labor Cost Schedule, ROSEBUD Project

Department	Monthly Cost ($)						Total Cost
	1	2	3	4	5	6	
Engineering (Project)	7200	4800	3300	5100	2100	300	22800
Programming*		6050	5000			2200	13250
Purchasing		1100	580	550			2230
Technical Service				800	500	1550	2850
Total direct labor cost	7200	11950	8880	6450	2600	4050	41130

*Refer to Figure 14–8, for example, to see how costs in this row were obtained.

be started later to take advantage of the time value of money. But it is risky to intentionally eliminate slack in schedules of uncertain activities. Activities that are less familiar, such as research and development work, should be started earlier to retain valuable slack that might be needed to absorb unanticipated delays.

Material Expenditures and Cash Flow

Cost schedules and forecasts are also used for estimating cash requirements to meet payments for materials, parts, and equipment.[19] There are several ways, depending on purpose, to prepare such a forecast. The forecast, for example, might represent the cost of materials "when needed," that is, the cost of materials corresponding to the date when the materials must actually be on hand for use. Alternatively, the forecast might represent the date when actual payments for materials must be made. This forecast will be different from the "when needed" forecast since often a portion of the payment must accompany the order—i.e., the expense *precedes* when the item is needed. Other times payment can be delayed until after the order is received—i.e., the expense *follows* when the item is needed. The costs shown in the time-phased budget usually reflect costs of materials when needed and not when actual payments are due. Since the times when actual expenditures must be made seldom correspond to the times when these amounts are shown on time-phased budgets, forecasts should be made to reveal major discrepancies. Figure 14–16 illustrates this point.

A problem often facing the project manager is maintaining a positive cash flow. Throughout the project, the difference between cash in and cash out ideally will be kept small.[20] The project manager must do a juggling act to hold income from the client in balance with expenditures for labor, subcontractors, materials, and equipment. To help keep the cash flow in balance management can, for example, use the time lag between when materials are needed and when payment for them is required.

Figure 14–17 shows an example of forecasted cash flow. All sources of income over the life of the project based on contractual agreements are compared to all foreseeable

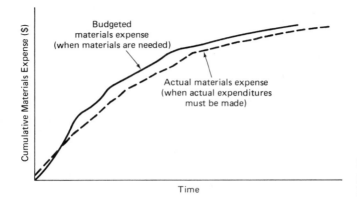

FIGURE 14–16. Forecasted materials expense showing budgeted versus actual expenditures.

expenditures—direct and indirect, as well as any penalty costs (should the project have to be terminated early). The deficit between forecasted income and estimated expenditures represents the amount of invested or working capital needed to meet payment commitments. Once such a cash flow forecast is completed, a *funding plan* must be created to assure that sufficient working capital will be available.[21]

14.10 SUMMARY

Cost estimation and budgeting are major parts of the project planning process. Cost estimation logically follows work breakdown and precedes project budgeting. Accurate cost estimates are necessary to establish realistic budgets and to provide standards against which performance will be measured; they are thus crucial to the financial success of the project.

Costs in projects have a tendency to escalate beyond original estimates. The accuracy of estimates can be improved and cost escalation minimized by using good management, employing skilled estimators, and anticipating the effects of escalation factors such as inflation.

Accuracy in estimates is a function of the time during the systems development cycle when the estimate is prepared; the further along in the cycle, the easier it is to produce accurate estimates. The problem is that good estimates are often needed early in the project. Clearly defining objectives and project scope at the earliest possible point and employing standardized technology and procedures helps improve the accuracy of estimates. The more standardized the work of the project, the greater the certainty and precision of estimates.

The aggregate of cost estimates for all subelements of the project plus overhead costs becomes the cost estimate for the overall project. In larger projects a systematic methodology, or Project Cost Accounting System (PCAS), is useful for aggregating estimates and for maintaining a system of cost accounts for budgeting and control. Cost accounts are derived from the WBS and project organization hierarchies and are the financial equivalent to work packages.

Cost schedules reveal patterns of costs and expenditures over time. They are used to identify cash and working capital requirements for labor, materials, and equipment.

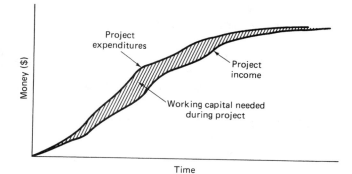

FIGURE 14–17. Balancing project income and expenditures.

The last four chapters described steps in the project planning process—things that should be done *before* the project can begin. Planning precedes action, but only in the simplest sense. The greater the uncertainty in the project, the more that actions dictate that changes be made to the plan. This is to be expected since planners do not have perfect information. Still, under the circumstances, planners work with the intent of creating the best possible plan. The better the plan, the easier it is for participants to communicate intentions, the more prepared they are for contingencies, and the easier it is for them to successfully complete the project.

The last four chapters described elements of project plans—work packages, schedules, and budgets, as well as the structures and systems that tie them together—WBS, cost-account structure, responsibility matrix, and PCAS. The next few chapters discuss what to do with them after the project begins.

CHAPTER REVIEW QUESTIONS

1. Why are accurate cost estimates so important, yet so difficult, in project planning? What are the implications and possible consequences of overestimating costs? Of underestimating costs?
2. Define "cost escalation." What are major sources of cost escalation?
3. What is the purpose of a contingency fund (management reserve)? How is the contingency fund used and controlled?
4. Describe what the term "phased project planning" means.
5. How do "changes" in requirements cause cost escalation?
6. How does the type of contractual agreement influence the potential for cost escalation?
7. What is the relationship between phases of the project life cycle and cost escalation?
8. Describe the process of using the WBS to develop cost estimates. How are these estimates aggregated into total project cost estimates?
9. What is the role of individual functional and subcontracting units in cost estimating?
10. Describe the Project Cost Accounting System (PCAS). What is its purpose and how is it used in project planning?
11. What is a time-phased budget? What is the difference between a budget and a cost estimate?
12. Distinguish recurring costs from nonrecurring costs.
13. What are six cost elements shared by most estimates and budgets?
14. How are direct labor expenses determined?
15. What expenses are included under direct nonlabor?
16. How is the overhead rate determined?
17. What is a cost account and what kinds of information does it contain? How does a cost account fit into the structure of the PCAS?
18. How are cost accounts aggregated "horizontally" and "vertically?" Why are they aggregated like this?
19. How are time-based forecasts prepared and how are they used?
20. What are the reasons for investigating the influence of schedules on project costs? What is the "feasible budget region?"

21. What might happen if top management submitted a bid for a project without consulting the management of the areas to be involved in the project?

22. The example in Table 14–1 shows three possible ways of apportioning total direct costs. Suppose, using the same example, the Direct Nonlabor (DNL) cost and G&A are broken down as follows:

Direct Nonlabor

	MARS	PLUTO		G&A
Materials	30	5	Freight	8
Other	10	5	Other	32
	40	10		40

Assuming all remaining costs shown on Table 14–1 are unchanged, compute the project costs for MARS and PLUTO using the following apportioning rules:

a. Overhead (OH) is proportionate to direct labor (DL).
b. Freight G&A is proportionate to materials.
c. Other G&A is proportionate to DL, OH, DNL, and freight.

23. Chapter 13 discussed the impact of "crashing" activities and the relationship of schedules to cost. The assumption was that as activity duration was decreased, the direct cost increased owing to the increase in direct labor rates from overtime. Overhead rates may also vary, although the overhead rate is often *lower* for overtime work. For example, the overhead rate may be 100 percent for regular time but only 20 percent for overtime. In both cases, the overhead rate is associated with the wage rate being used.

Suppose in the MARS project in Table 14–1, 1000 direct hours of labor are required at $50 per hour, and the associated overhead rate is 100 percent for regular time. Now suppose for overtime, the wage rate is time-and-a-half and the overhead rate is 10 percent.

Compare the project cost if it were done entirely on regular time with the cost if it were done entirely on overtime. Which is less expensive?

24. Use the following network and table to answer questions about the ARGOT project:

Activity	Time (Wks)	Weekly Cost ($K)	Total ($K)
A	4	3	12
B	6	4	24
C	3	5	15
D	4	5	20
E	8	3	24
F	3	4	12
G	2	2	4
			111

ARGOT project

a. Compute the T_E's and T_L's for the project. Assume T_s is the same as the earliest project completion date.
b. Construct a time-phased network for the project like Figure 14–12 (use early start times).

    c. Construct two diagrams like those in Figure 14–13 showing the weekly and cumulative project expenses.

25. Using the data in problem 24, repeat steps b and c using late start times. Then identify the feasible budget region using the cumulative curves.

QUESTIONS ABOUT THE STUDY PROJECT

1. How were project costs estimated? Who was involved? Describe the process.
2. When did estimating take place? How were estimates checked and accumulated? How were they related to the WBS?
3. What, if any, were the principle causes of cost escalation in the project?
4. How often and under what circumstances were cost estimates revised during the project?
5. How were overhead costs determined? What basis was used for establishing overhead cost rates?
6. How were cost estimates tallied to arrive at a total project cost estimate? Who did this?
7. What kind of "project cost accounting system" (PCAS) was used? Was it manual or computerized? Describe the system and its inputs and outputs. Who maintained the system? How was it used during the project?
8. Describe the process of creating the project budget. Show a sample budget (or portion thereof).
9. How were management and supervisory costs handled in the budget?
10. Was the project budget broken down into "cost accounts?" If so:
    a. how were they related to the work packages and WBS, and
    b. how were they tied into the PCAS?
11. What kinds of costs summaries were prepared? Who were they sent to? How were they used? Show some examples.
12. Did the PCAS produce time-phased cost schedules and forecasts? Show some examples. How were they used by the project manager?

ENDNOTES

1. See F.L. Harrison, *Advanced Project Management* (Hants, England: Gower, 1981), 147–148.
2. See R.D. Archibald, *Managing High-Technology Programs and Projects* (New York: John Wiley & Sons, 1976), 167–168.
3. See Harrison, *Advanced Project Management*, 148–152.
4. Harrison, ibid., 172–173, gives an example of an escalation clause.
5. Politically, how independent should the estimators be? So independent, says DeMarco, that the project manager has "no communication with the estimator about how happy or unhappy anyone is about the estimate." See Tom DeMarco, *Controlling Software Projects* (New York: Yourdon Press, 1982), 19.
6. A more complete discussion is found in Harrison, *Advanced Project Management*, 162–171.

7. Ibid., 154–161.

8. Archibald, *Managing High-Technology Programs and Projects*, 171.

9. A complete discussion of the pricing review procedure is given by Harold Kerzner, *Project Management: A Systems Approach to Planning, Scheduling, and Controlling* (New York: Van Nostrand Reinhold, 1979), 402–404.

10. See Milton Rosenau, *Successful Project Management* (Belmont, Ca.: Lifetime Learning, 1981), 91.

11. Ibid., 91–92.

12. A thorough discussion of labor pricing is given by Kerzner, *Project Management*, 372–379. This example is derived from Kerzner.

13. See Kerzner, ibid., 379–385, for examples of overhead rate computation.

14. This example is derived from a similar one in Rosenau, *Successful Project Management*, 89–91.

15. This example is derived from Thomas Wilson and David Stone, "Project Management for an Architectural Firm," *Management Accounting* (October 1980), 25–46.

16. See Harrison, *Advanced Project Management*, 199–202 for further discussion of cost accounts.

17. The kinds of cost summaries used often depends on what is available in the software, though many software packages permit customizing of reports.

18. J.D. Wiest and F.K. Levy, *A Management Guide to PERT/CPM*, 2nd ed. (Englewood Cliffs, N.J.: Prentice-Hall, 1977), 90–94.

19. See Kerzner, *Project Management*, 396–398, for an example of a material expenditure forecast.

20. Harrison notes that keeping cash in balance in foreign contracts is especially difficult because foreign currency use must be managed: "In many cases, the profits from [currency dealings] can exceed the profits from the project; in others, if this is not managed effectively, the losses from foreign currency commitments can bring about large losses on a project and lead to bankruptcy." See Harrison, *Advanced Project Management*, 185.

21. See Archibald, *Managing High-Technology Programs and Projects*, 168.

chapter 15

Project Control

> The rider must ride the horse, not be run away with.
>
> *Donald Winnicott, Playing and Reality*

It is impossible at the onset of a new project to foresee all problems or to anticipate all changes that the project might need. Still, every effort is made throughout the project to regulate work, minimize changes to the plan, and guide the project toward pre-established performance, cost, and schedule objectives. The process of keeping the project on target and as close to plan as feasibly possible is the subject of *project control*.

To keep the project close to plan, obviously there must first be a plan. Thus the initial step in project control is project planning, though, in a sense, the two are interrelated and it is sometimes difficult to tell where planning stops and control begins. In contrasting the two, author Daniel Roman notes that planning *anticipates* action, whereas control *initiates* action.[1] Both work toward similar ends:[2]

- Planning concentrates on setting *goals* and *directions*; control *guides* the work toward those goals.
- Planning *allocates resources*; control ensures effective, ongoing *utilization* of those resources.
- Planning *anticipates* problems; control *corrects* the problems.

- Planning *motivates* participants to achieve goals; control *rewards* achievement of goals.

15.1 THE CONTROL PROCESS

As Roman states, the control process

> is concerned with assessing actual against planned technical accomplishment, reviewing and verifying the validity of technical objectives, confirming the continued need for the project, timing it to coincide with operational requirements, overseeing resource expenditures, and comparing the anticipated value with the cost incurred.[3]

In general, the process is achieved in three phases: setting performance standards, comparing these standards with actual performance, then taking necessary corrective action.

In the first phase, *performance standards* are defined and expressed in terms of technical specifications, budgeted costs, schedules, and resource requirements. Performance standards are derived from the user requirements, the project plan, and the statement of work. These standards precisely define the cost, schedule, and technical factors to be regulated and the boundaries within which they must be maintained.

In the second phase, the standards are compared with the actual project *performance to date*. Schedules, budgets, and performance specifications are compared to current expenditures and work completed. The time and cost of work still remaining are estimated and used to forecast the anticipated date and cost of the completed project.

Finally, whenever actual performance significantly deviates from standards, *corrective action* is taken. Either the work is altered or expedited, or the plans and standards revised. When work performance is deficient, resources are added, shifted, or altered. When original estimates or expectations prove unrealistic, then project goals are changed and the performance standards themselves revised. The project control system and the project organization itself might have to be restructured.

15.2 INFORMATION MONITORING

To enable timely and effective control related decision making, the project must be systematically tracked and observed. This requires setting up a project *monitoring function*. Two activities comprise project monitoring: data collection and information reporting.

It is during the first phase of the control process—while performance standards are being set—that a system of data collection and information reporting is established. Data for monitoring the project must be directly related to the project—its plans, outputs, schedules, budgets, and standards. Typical data sources include materials purchasing invoices, worker time cards, change notices, test results, and attitude surveys. A balance must be struck between gathering too much data and too little. Too much data is costly to collect and process, and will be ignored; too little does not capture the project status and allows problems to go unchecked.

The monitoring function must ensure that all levels of management receive reports in sufficient detail and frequency to enable them to identify problems and take corrective action while they are small. It must guarantee that significant deviations from the plan, called *variances*, will be flagged.[4]

The timing of measurement and reporting, daily, weekly, or monthly, is also important. Data can be collected periodically or topically, and reported periodically or by exception. The distinction is crucial to the effectiveness of the monitoring function. At minimum, reports should coincide with significant project milestones and be available in sufficient time to permit problems to be spotted while they are still small.

15.3 INTERNAL AND EXTERNAL PROJECT CONTROL

Both internal and external control systems are used to monitor and regulate project activities. *Internal control* refers to the contractor's systems and procedures for monitoring work and taking corrective action. *External control* refers to the additional procedures and standards imposed by the client, including taking over project coordination and administration functions. Military and government contracts, for example, impose external control by stipulating the following of the contractor:

- frequent reports on overall project performance
- reports on schedules, cost, and technical performance
- outside inspections by government program managers
- inspection of books and records of the contractor
- strict terms on allowable project costs, pricing policies, and so on.[5]

External controls can be a source of annoyance and aggravation to the contractor because, superimposed on internal controls, they create management turmoil and increase the cost of the project. Nonetheless, they are sometimes necessary to protect the interests of the client. To help minimize conflicts and keep costs down, contractors and clients should work together to establish agreed upon plans, compatible specifications, and joint methods for monitoring work.

15.4 TRADITIONAL COST CONTROL

In traditional cost control, the method of measuring performance is called *variance analysis*. This involves comparing actual costs with planned costs to see if the amount spent was more or less than budgeted. In project management, cost variance analysis is, by itself, inadequate because it indicates neither how much work has been completed nor what the future expenses are likely to be.

Consider the following weekly status report for a software development work package:

Budgeted cost for period = $12,000	Actual cost for period = $14,000	Period variance = $2,000
Cumulative budget to date = $25,000	Cumulative actual to date = $29,000	Cumulative variance = $4,000

The report indicates apparent overruns for both period and cumulative costs, with to date cumulative costs running $4,000 (16 percent) over budget. However, because we do not know how much work has been completed for the $29,000, it is difficult from this data to determine if the project is really over budget.

Suppose that the $25,000 indicated was the amount budgeted for, say, completing 50 percent of software development work. That is, as of the week of this report, 50 percent of the work package should have been completed. Now, as of the week of the report, if only 30 percent of the work had been completed, then the project would be over budget and behind schedule, and additional cost overruns could be expected just to get caught up; if 50 percent of the work had been completed (as intended), then the project would be on schedule but still over budget. Something would have to be done to reduce future expenditures and eliminate the $4,000 overrun. If, however, as of the week of the report, 70 percent of the work had been completed—20 percent more than was scheduled—then the project would actually be ahead of schedule; future expenditures would probably be less than budgeted, possibly reducing or eliminating the $4,000 variance by project completion. In other words, in the last case the project is probably not over budget because substantially more work has been completed than was planned for this date.

The point of this example is to show that cost variance information alone is inadequate; it is also necessary to have information about *work progress*—information such as percentage of work completed, milestones achieved, or whatever—to be able to assess the status of the project and suggest a course of action. In project management, work progress as of a given status date is expressed using the concept of *earned value*. This concept will be discussed later.

There are times when even work progress information is not enough. Whenever large developmental problems, schedule delays, or changes to the scope of work arise, then the plans, schedules, and budgets are invalidated. It is then necessary to modify the plans and update the budgets and schedules themselves. Effective project control requires comparisons not only of actual cost and work performance data to planned cost and performance, but potentially of planned cost and performance to *revised estimates* of what will be needed to complete the project.

15.5 COST ACCOUNTING SYSTEMS FOR PROJECT CONTROL

PERT/Cost Systems

The previous section showed that traditional cost variance analysis alone is insufficient and that information is also needed on work progress. Early attempts to correct for this using PERT/CPM went to the opposite extreme by ignoring costs and focusing entirely on work progress. If PERT/CPM users wanted to integrate cost control with network planning methods they had to develop their own systems.

In 1962 the U.S. government developed a PERT-based system which incorporated cost-accounting with scheduling. Called *PERT/Cost*, the system became mandatory for all military and R&D contracts with the Department of Defense and National Aeronautics and Space Administration (DOD/NASA).[6] Any contractor wanting to bid to DOD/NASA had to demonstrate the ability to use the system and to produce the necessary reports. Although this mandate increased usage of PERT/Cost it also created resentment. Many firms found the project-oriented PERT/Cost system an expensive duplication of, or incompatible with, existing functionally oriented accounting systems. Interestingly, many firms not involved in DOD/NASA bidding voluntarily adopted PERT/Cost with far fewer complaints.[7]

PERT/Cost was a major improvement over traditional cost-accounting techniques because it blended costs with work schedules. Just as important, it spurred the later development of other more sophisticated systems which track and report work progress and costs on a project rather than a fiscal/functional basis. PERT/Cost was the original network-based PCAS. Hereafter the term PCAS will be used to refer to any network-based cost-accounting system which incorporates PERT/Cost principles.

Most PCAS's integrate work packages, cost accounts, project schedules, and networks into a unified project control package. They permit cost and scheduling overruns to be identified and causes to be quickly pinpointed among numerous work packages or cost accounts. Rapid identification and correction of problems is the single greatest advantage of modern PCAS's. Two elements common to most of these systems are use of work packages and cost accounts as basic data collection units, and the concept of earned value to measure project performance.

Work Package and Cost Account Control

Earlier chapters described the importance of work packages and cost accounts as planning tools. It is no coincidence that they are also major elements of project control. Each work package is considered a contract for a specific job, with a manager or supervisor responsible for overseeing costs and work performance. Cost accounts are comprised of one or more work packages; both include similar information such as work descriptions, time-phased budgets, work plans and schedules, people responsible, resource requirements, and so on. During the project, work packages and cost accounts are the focal point for data collection, work progress evaluation, problem assessment, and corrective action.

Early PERT/Cost systems were inadequate for two reasons. First was the problem of how to handle *overhead* expenses. Typically work packages are identified in either of two ways, (1) as *end products* when they result in a physical product and have scheduled start and finish dates, or (2) as *level of effort* when they have no physical end product and are "ongoing"—such as testing or maintenance. Given that there is usually no direct connection between company overhead and either of these kinds of work packages, there is a problem with arbitrarily allocating overhead expenses to them. Any arbitrary allocation of expenses reduces expense control and distorts the apparent performance of work packages. Work package managers have little influence on overhead, yet such costs are a frequent source of overruns.

In current PCAS's the problem is resolved in two ways. First, any expenses such as supervisory and management overhead which can be traced to specific work packages are allocated directly to them. Second, any overhead which cannot be traced to specific work packages is kept separate by using either an "overhead" work package for the entire project (lasting for the duration of the project) or a series of shorter duration overhead work packages. Overhead work packages are kept "open" for the duration of the project and extended as needed if the project is delayed.

Another problem with early PERT/Cost systems was that some of them consolidated and reported information *only* at the project level, making it difficult to sort through hundreds of work packages to locate sources of cost or schedule overruns. Other systems reported information *only* at the work package level, which was fine for project control but conflicted with the functionally organized cost and budgeting systems that most organizations use. In modern project management the individual work package remains the central element for control, but PCAS's now permit consolidation and reporting of information for *any* level of the project, from the individual cost account or work package up to the project level. Additionally, most also permit consolidation and reporting of project information using a functional breakdown.

For instance, when cost accounts are established for work packages, the PCAS can aggregate them vertically through the WBS or horizontally through the project-functional organization. Figure 14–11 in Chapter 14 is an example, showing how cost-account information is aggregated for the ROSEBUD project. Since higher level accounts in the cost-account structure are built up through the WBS and organizational hierarchies, variances in costs and schedules at any project level can be tracked through the structure to identify the work packages causing the variances. Similarly, cost or schedule variances observed at the project level can be traced back through the account structure to find the functional departments responsible for the variance.

Earned Value Concept

Costs are budgeted period-by-period for each work package or cost account (time-phased budgeting); once the project begins, work progress and actual costs are tracked every period and compared to these budgeted costs. Managers measure and track work progress using the concept of *earned value*. Roughly, earned value represents an estimate of the "percentage of work completed" thus far. (The variable "BCWP," discussed later, is the identical concept.)

The earned value of work completed in a project is determined by the combined status of all work packages at a given time. It is computed by taking (1) the sum of the budgeted costs of all work packages thus far completed, plus (2) the sum of the earned value (costs or subjective estimates) of all "open" (started but not yet completed) work packages. If, for example, as of June 30 work packages A, B, and C had been completed, and if they had been budgeted to cost $20K, $10K, and $12K, respectively, and if, additionally, work package D had been budgeted to cost $20K but was only 75 percent completed, then the earned value for the project on June 30 would be

$$\$20K + \$10K + \$12K + (0.75)\,\$20K = \$57K.$$

Like expense data, the earned value for the project, individual work packages, or levels in between can be summarized and reported through the PCAS. Use of earned value to track work progress overcomes the problem of control associated with ordinary cost variance analysis. The application of earned value to project performance analysis will be discussed later.

15.6 PROJECT CONTROL PROCESS

The remainder of this chapter focuses on five nominal stages of the project control process: work authorization, data collection and tally, performance analysis, reporting, and corrective action.

Work Authorization

As shown in Figure 15–1, *work authorization* begins with upper management, moves down through middle management, and ends with the work teams. Before they accept responsi-

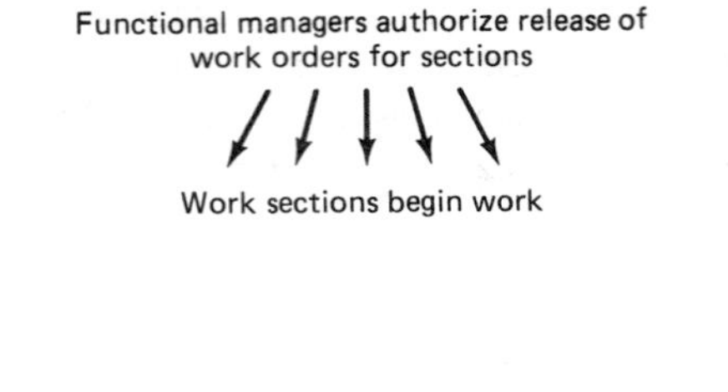

Upper management authorizes project via contract
release or project work release

Project manager authorizes departmental
work via incremental work orders

Functional managers authorize release of
work orders for sections

Work sections begin work

FIGURE 15–1. Project work authorization process.

bility, each level should review tasks they are authorized to perform according to the specified statement of work, schedule, and budget.

Authorization formally occurs upon completion and top management acceptance of the project plan. This authorizes the project manager, functional managers, and supervisors to begin expending project funds for labor and materials. Similar authorization is extended to subcontractors and suppliers.

On large projects authorization is subdivided into the stages of *contract release, project release*, and *work order release*. After a contract has been awarded the contract administrator prepares a contract release document that specifies contractual requirements and gives project management the go-ahead. The comptroller or project accountant then prepares a project release document that authorizes funding for the project.

Actual work begins when a department or work unit receives a *work order* release which might be an "engineering order," "shop order," "test order" or similar document, depending on the kind of work. Each work order is a small but crucial part of project control; it specifies how requirements are to be fulfilled, the permissible resources to be expended, and the time period over which the work should span. Work orders include:[8]

- Statement of work
- Time-phased budget of direct labor hours, materials, and other direct costs
- Schedules, milestones, and relationships to other work packages
- Position of the task in the WBS
- Specifications and requirements
- Cost account number and position in the cost-account structure
- Signatures of person authorizing and person accepting responsibility.

Before any task can begin a work order or other such order is required. As the start date for a given task draws near, the project office releases authorization to begin work using the work order document. Each work order is assigned to a cost account and is updated whenever new information is available or as new requirements arise. Other authorization documents such as purchase orders, test requests, and tool orders are released as needed.

Data Collection and Tally

Work orders and their cost accounts are the fundamental elements of project control. For each work order, data about *actual* costs and work progress is periodically collected and entered into the PCAS. The PCAS tallies and summarizes information up through the WBS and project organization structure in a process similar to creating the budget summaries described in the last chapter. Using work order information, the PCAS generates performance reports on a period-by-period basis for every work package, the entire project, every department or section, and at various levels of the WBS.

Assessing the impact of work progress on work schedules is the responsibility of the functional manager or team supervisor in charge of the work order. Each week the supervisor tallies the labor hours for each task as indicated on time cards. She notes tasks completed and tasks still "open," and estimates the time still needed to complete open tasks. Progress is recorded on a Gantt chart showing completed and open tasks. Figure 15–2 is an example showing the status of the LOGON project as of week 20. Notice that work packages K, L, M, and Q are all behind schedule.

The work order supervisor documents any changes in estimates or schedules for remaining work and submits it to the project manager for approval. Using network methods the impact of current work on remaining work is reassessed. Project plans are reviewed to determine where changes are needed and ways to minimize or eliminate anticipated delays.

Each week the work package manager or supervisor also tallies current expenses. Labor hours reported on time cards are converted into direct labor cost. The supervisor adds direct labor, material, and level-of-effort costs for completed and open tasks to the cost of work done in prior periods, then applies the overhead percentage rate to applicable direct charges. Late charges and outstanding costs (a frequent source of cost overruns) are also included.[9]

The work package supervisor validates all expenditures as actually contributing to the work order. As each task is completed its cost account is closed to prevent additional, unauthorized billing. Each week a revised report is prepared showing costs of all work completed in prior periods plus work accomplished in the current period. This is reviewed, verified, and signed by the supervisor before forwarding it to the project manager.

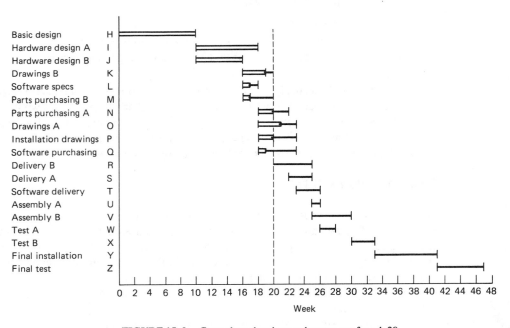

FIGURE 15–2. Gantt chart showing work status as of week 20.

Once work package information has been validated by the project manager it is entered into the PCAS so that costs to date can be accumulated across all work packages and summary reports prepared. Each month the project manager reviews the summary reports to reassess the project and prepare estimates of the work and cost still needed to complete the project. These estimates plus the record of project costs and work progress to date provide a forecast of the completion date and project cost at completion. This forecast of the cost of work and time needed to complete the project is described later.

15.7 PERFORMANCE ANALYSIS

Data collected and tallied through the PCAS is used by the project manager to assess project work progress, schedule, and cost performance. Several analytical methods for assessing performance are described next.

Cost and Schedule Analysis with Budgeted Cost of Work Performed

The status of the project or any portion of it can be assessed with three variables: BCWS, ACWP, and BCWP.

1. *BCWS* is the *Budgeted Cost of the Work Scheduled*—the sum cost of all work, plus apportioned effort, scheduled to be completed within a given time period as specified in the *original budget*. It is the same as the time-phased budget mentioned before. For example, Table 14–4 in Chapter 14 shows the cumulative and weekly BCWS for the LOGON project. In week 20, for example, to date BCWS is $512,000 and weekly BCWS is $83,000.

2. *ACWP* is the *Actual Cost of the Work Performed*—the actual expenditure incurred in a given time period. It is the sum of the costs for all completed work packages plus all "open" work packages and overhead.

As one measure of project performance, ACWP can be compared to BCWS. Suppose in the LOGON example that the ACWP as of week 20 is $530,000. This is $18,000 more than the budgeted amount of $512,000 (Chapter 14, Table 14–4). Remember, however, that whether or not this represents a cost overrun depends on how much work has been completed. The additional $18,000 might mean that some tasks were performed ahead of schedule, meaning that the project is not overbudget but rather is ahead of schedule. As mentioned before, project work progress must be known before project performance can be judged. This is where the next variable comes in.

3. *BCWP* is the *Budgeted Cost of the Work Performed*. This variable is the same as the *earned value* concept mentioned earlier. It is determined by looking at work tasks performed thus far (completed and open work packages, plus overhead) as well as their *corresponding budget* to see what they were *supposed* to cost. Then,

- The BCWP for a completed task is the same as the BCWS for that task.
- BCWP of a partially completed work package is estimated more subjectively, using formulas or an actual tally of the work completed so far. It is sometimes computed by taking 50% of BCWS when the work package is started, then the remaining 50% when it is completed at the finish. For LOGON, assume BCWP = $429,000.

Following is a simple example illustrating how to compute BCWP.[10]

BCWP versus BCWS: The Parmete Company

The Parmete Company has a $200,000 fixed-cost contract to install 1000 new parking meters. The contract calls for removing old parking meters from their stands and replacing them with new ones. The cost for doing this is $200 for each meter.

Parmete estimates that 25 meters can be installed each day. On this basis, the Budgeted Cost of the Work *Scheduled* (BCWS) as of any given day in the project is determined simply by multiplying the number of working days completed times 25 meters, times $200 for each. Thus, for example, as of the 18th working day,

$$BCWS = 18 \text{ days} \times (25 \text{ meters}) \times (\$200) = \$90,000.$$

Another way of saying this is that the $90,000 represents what the project *is budgeted, or supposed to cost as of the 18th day.* Notice that cumulative BCWS is always associated with a specific date on the schedule. At a rate of 25 meters/per day and a cost of $200/meter, the project should take 40 working days to finish and have a final BCWS of $200,000.

In contrast, the Budgeted Cost of the Work *Performed* (BCWP), or the *earned value*, shows for any day in the project how much work has *actually* been done in terms of the budgeted costs. It is, in this project, the number of meters *actually* installed to date times the $200 budgeted for each. Suppose, for example, that as of the 18th working day 400 meters had been installed; thus,

$$BCWP = (400 \text{ meters}) \times (\$200) = \$80,000$$

In other words, as of the 18th working day, $80,000 worth of work has been performed. Now, given that $90,000 was the amount of work that was *supposed* to have been performed, the project is $10,000 worth of work behind schedule. Notice that the $10,000 does not represent a cost savings, but rather that the project is *behind schedule.* $10,000 represents 50 parking meters, or two days worth of work, which means that as of day 18 the project is two days behind schedule. (The two days is referred to as the *time variance*, or *TV*.) Thus the concept of BCWP enables project cost to be translated into project work progress. As of day 18, this project has made only 16 days worth of work progress. This is represented on the graph for BCWS and BCWP in Figure 15–3.

As stated before, besides completed tasks, the BCWP must also reflect tasks started but not yet completed (open tasks). For example, suppose that before quitting at the end of the 18th

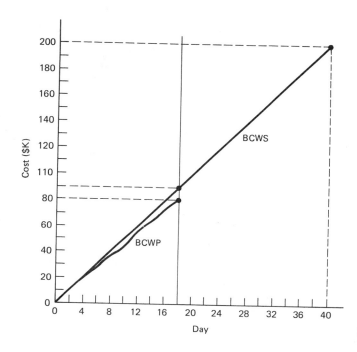

FIGURE 15-3.   BCWS and BCWP graph.

day the meter installer had just enough time to remove an old meter but not to put in a new one. The work on that task was, say, 50 percent completed. If this was the 401st meter, then BCWP would be the full cost for the first 400 meters plus 50 percent of the cost for the 401st:

$$BCWP = \$80,000 + (0.50)(\$200) = \$80,100$$

Thus, as of day 18 the BCWP would be $80,100, which is slightly more than 16 days of work completed. (Actually, it represents $80,100/(25 \times \$200) = 16.02$ days of work, which puts the project 1.98 days behind schedule, but such precision is usually unwarranted.)

When taken together, the variables BCWS, ACWP, and BCWP can be used to compute variances which reveal different aspects about the status of a project. Four kinds of variances can be determined: accounting, schedule, cost, and time. For the LOGON project shown in the graph in Figure 15-4, for example,

1. AV = BCWS − ACWP (Accounting Variance) = -$18,000
2. SV = BCWP − BCWS (Schedule Variance) = -$83,000
3. TV = SD − BCSP (Time Variance) = about 1 week (SD is the "status date" (here week 20) and BCSP is the date where BCWS = BCWP (here, about week 19))
4. CV = BCWP − ACWP (Cost Variance) = -$101,000.

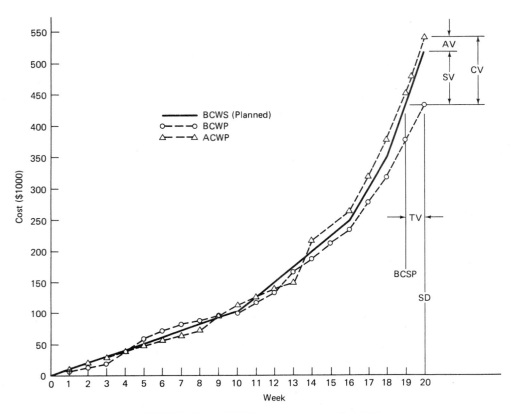

FIGURE 15–4. LOGON project status as of week 20.

The accounting variance (AV) of -$18,000 is the difference between the current budget and current actual expenditures. As Figure 15–4 reveals, as of week 20, actual expenses were $530,000 even though only $512,000 was budgeted.

The schedule variance (SV) shows that the total work completed as of week 20 is -$83,000 less than planned, suggesting that the project is behind schedule.

The time variance (TV) shows approximately how much the project is behind schedule, about one week. This is because only $429,000 worth of work has been completed (BCWP), which is roughly the amount of work scheduled (BCWS) to have been completed a week earlier.

The cost variance (CV) of -$101,000 also takes into account the status of work indicating, again, that LOGON is behind schedule. Given that it compares actual work completed with actual costs, it is a more valid measure of cost performance than SV.

Still, taken alone, even CV can be misleading. Sometimes a positive CV (overrun) arises because of factors that are outside of project control—such as overhead rates. Sometimes a negative CV (underrun) occurs because bills have not yet been paid (or are paid in periods other than when expenses are incurred). In the end, individual cost sources should be scrutinized.

Technical Analysis

Besides costs and schedules, project performance depends on how well the project is meeting technical requirements of the end-item. At certain milestones, e.g., the completion of major design, development, or production tasks, a technical review should be performed to evaluate and flag differences between achievements to date and expectations. The actual value of technical parameters as determined by estimates, analytical measurements, or empirical tests must be compared to technical parameter objectives. Since costs and schedules are related to technical performance, technical difficulties usually lead to cost and scheduling problems. Performance analysis should enable early detection of technical problems and prediction of their impact on project costs and schedules.

Work Package Analysis and Performance Indices

For the project manager to know the status of the project, she needs information on the performance for all work packages and participating functional areas. With information from the PCAS, graphs similar to Figure 15–2 and Figure 15–4 can be prepared for every work package and cost account.

   Consider the status of the LOGON project as of week 20. Referring to Figure 15–2, activities H, I, and J have been completed and are closed accounts, activities K through Q are "open" and in progress. This Gantt chart gives a general *overview* of work package and project status, but to determine the origins of project problems it is necessary to assess each work activity in more detail. For this, two kinds of *performance indices* are used to assess the schedule and cost performance of work packages and the relative size of problem areas:

1. SPI = BCWP/BCWS (Schedule Performance Index)
2. CPI = BCWP/ACWP (Cost Performance Index).

   Values of SPI and CPI greater than 1.0 indicate that work is ahead of schedule and underbudget, respectively; values less than 1.0 represent the opposite.

   Table 15–1 shows cost and variance information for all LOGON activities as of week 20. The performance indices CPI and SPI show trouble spots and their relative magnitude. Notice that L, M, and Q are the most behind schedule (they have the smallest SPI's) and that L and M have the greatest cost overruns relative to their sizes (they have the smallest CPI's). The overall project is "somewhat" behind schedule and overcost (SPI = 0.84, CPI = 0.81).

   Focusing on *only* the project level or *only* the work package level to determine project status can be misleading, and the project manager should scan both, back and forth. If the project manager looks only at the project level, good performance of some activities will overshadow and hide poor performance in others. If she focuses only on individual work

TABLE 15–1　LOGON Performance Report Week 20 Cumulative To Date.

Activity	BCWS	ACWP	BCWP	SW	CV	SPI	CPI
H*	100	100	100	0	0	1.00	1.00
I*	64	70	64	0	-6	1.00	0.91
J*	96	97	96	0	-1	1.00	0.99
K	16	12	14	-2	2	0.88	1.17
L	36	30	18	-18	-12	0.50	0.60
M	84	110	33	-51	-77	0.39	0.30
N	40	45	40	0	-5	1.00	0.89
O	20	28	24	4	-4	1.20	0.86
P	24	22	24	0	2	1.00	1.09
Q	32	16	16	-16	0	0.50	1.00
Project	512	530	429	-83	-101	0.84	0.81

*Completed

packages, the cumulative effect from slightly poor performance on many activities can easily be overlooked. Even small cost overruns on many individual work packages can add up to large overruns for the project.

The importance of examining detailed variances at both project and work package levels is further illustrated in the following two examples. The SV = $83,000 in Figure 15–4 would suggest that the LOGON project is behind schedule; this project level analysis says it is about one week behind (TV = 1). However, scrutinizing Figure 15–2 reveals that one of the work packages behind schedule, activity M, is on the critical path (see Chapter 12, Figure 12–19). Since this activity appears to be about three weeks behind schedule, the project must also be three weeks behind schedule, *not* one week as estimated by the project level analysis.

The importance of monitoring performance at the work package level is further illustrated by the following example from the ROSEBUD project. Figure 15–5 is the cost report for work package L for month 2. This report would likely be available to managers about two or three weeks into month 3. The numbers in the BCWS columns are derived from the month 2 column in the budget plan in Figure 14–6, Chapter 14. Current and cumulative numbers are the same since work package L begins in month 2.

The performance indices for (total costs) for work package L are

$$SPI = BCWP/BCWS = 0.80$$
$$CPI = BCWP/ACWP = 0.74$$

which indicate both schedule and cost overruns as of month 2. Suppose the project manager investigates the costs for work package L and finds the following:

First, although ACWP and BCWS for direct labor are equal, BCWP reflects the estimate that only 80 percent of work scheduled for the period was actually performed (BCWP = BCWS x SPI = 6050 x 0.80 = 4850). Second, although ACWP and BCWS for

Project	ROSEBUD	Date	Month 2
Department	Programming	Work Package	L Software specifications

Charge	Current Period					Cumulative To Date				
	BCWS	BCWP	ACWP	SV	CV	BCWS	BCWP	ACWP	SV	CV
Direct Labor Professional Associate Assistant										
Direct labor cost Labor overhead Other direct cost	6,050 4,538	4,840 3,630	6,050 5,445	−1,210 −908	−1,210 −1,815	6,050 4,538	4,840 6,330	6,050 5,445	−1,210 −908	−1,210 −1,815
Total direct cost General/adminstrative	10,588 1,059	8,470 847	11,495 1,150	−2,118 −212	−3,025 −303	10,588 1,059	8,470 847	11,495 1,150	−2,118 −212	−3,025 −303
Total costs	11,647	9,317	12,645	−2,330	−3,328	11,647	9,317	12,645	−12,330	−3,328

Note: BCWP is for 80 percent of work scheduled and labor overhead is increased
to 90 percent of labor cost.
SPI: BCWP/BCWS = .80   CPI: BCWP/ACWP = .74

FIGURE 15-5.   Cost chart as of month 2.

direct labor are equal, the corresponding labor overheads are different. Suppose in this example that the difference was due to a rate increase in labor overhead from 75 percent to 90 percent during month 2 because of changes in company work load. If other projects required fewer direct labor hours than planned, projects such as ROSEBUD would have to carry a larger percentage of overhead expenses. The project manager has no control over factors such as this, yet they affect his costs.

Now look at Figure 15–6, the cost report for the same work package for month 3. The performance indices for cumulative total costs are

$$SPI = BCWP/BCWS = 1.00$$
$$CPI = BCWP/ACWP = 0.92$$

Notice that, first, direct labor ACWP for the month is the same as direct labor BCWS, but more work was performed than expected for the month (BCWP>BCWS). The result is that the task was completed on schedule, as indicated by the cumulative SPI = 1.00. Also notice that there was a negative cost variance, but the project manager knows that it is not the project's fault, since the contributing factor is the increased overhead rate, which remained at 90 percent during months 2 and 3.

Of the numerous factors that affect project work progress and costs, some are simply beyond the project manager's control. Thus, to determine the sources of variance and places where action can or must be taken requires close scrutiny of costs and performance at the work package level. A project level analysis is simply inadequate.

Project	ROSEBUD					Date	Month 3				
Department	Programming					Work Package	L Software specifications				

	Current Period					Cumulative To Date				
Charge	BCWS	BCWP	ACWP	SV	CV	BCWS	BCWP	ACWP	SV	CV

Direct Labor
  Professional
  Associate
  Assistant										

Direct labor cost Labor overhead Other direct cost	5,000 3,750	6,050 4,538	5,000 4,500	1,050 788	1,050 38	11,050 8,288	11,050 8,288	11,050 9,945	0 0	0 1,657
Total direct cost General/administrative	8,750 875	10,588 1,059	9,500 950	1,838 184	1,088 108	19,338 193	19,338 193	20,995 2,100	0 0	1,657 166
Total Costs	9,625	11,647	10,450	2,022	1,196	21,272	21,272	23,095	0	1,823

Note: BCWP is for 121 percent of work scheduled, but for cumulative it is 100 percent (made up for delay in Period 2). $1,823 CV reflects increase in overhead rate.

FIGURE 15–6.   Cost chart as of month 3.

15.8 FORECASTING "TO COMPLETE" AND "AT COMPLETION"

As the project moves along, the project manager reviews not only what has been accomplished so far, but what remains to be done. Throughout the project, the expected final cost and completion date might have to be revised repeatedly, depending on its current status and direction. Significant schedule and cost overruns or underruns early in a project often indicate that the planned completion date and final cost estimate will have to be revised. In the LOGON example, large cost and schedule overruns as of the 20th week would likely lead the project manager (and others) to wonder when the project will actually be completed and at what cost.

Each month the project manager should prepare what is called a *to complete* forecast. This is a forecast of the time and cost remaining to complete the project. This forecast plus the current actual status of the project provide a revised estimate of the date and cost of the project *at completion*.

The following formulas are used to estimate the cost remaining to complete the project (to complete cost) and the approximate final project cost (at completion cost):

FCTC (Forecasted Cost To Complete Project) =
  (BCAC – BCWP)/CPI, where BCAC is the *Budgeted* Cost at Completion
    for the project. This is the same as the BCWS as of the target completion date.
FCAC (Forecasted Cost At Completion) = ACWP + FCTC.

In the LOGON project at week 20,

$$CPI = 429,000/530,000 = 0.81$$
thus, $FCTC = (990,000 - 429,000)/0.81 = \$692,593$, and
$$FCAC = 530,000 + 692,593 = \$1,222,593.$$

As shown in Figure 15–7, the revised project completion date is estimated by extending the BCWP line, keeping it parallel to the BCWS line, until it reaches the level of BCAC, \$990,000. The *horizontal* distance between the BCWS line and the BCWP line at BCAC (\$990,000) is roughly the amount the project will be delayed. On Figure 15–7 this is roughly one or two weeks, meaning the project completion date should be revised from week 47 to between week 48 and 49.

The estimated revised completion date remains to be verified since the actual delay depends on whether any of the activities behind schedule are on the critical path. (From

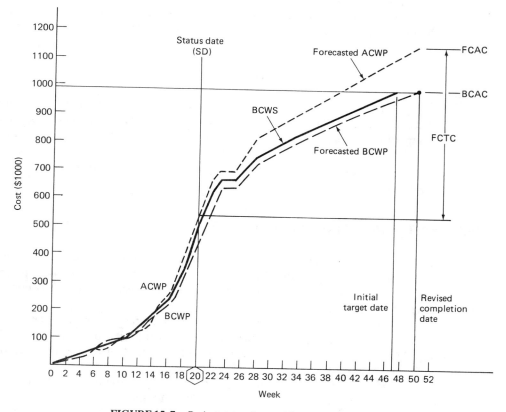

FIGURE 15–7.   Project status chart and forecasts as of week 20.

the previous discussion we know that because Activity M is on the critical path, LOGON is almost three weeks behind schedule; the revised completion date should thus be week 50.)

As shown in Figure 15–7, another line, the "Forecasted ACWP" can be drawn by extending the current ACWP line up to the level of FCAC ($1,159,630) at the revised completion date. In effect, this gives a running estimate of what the "actual" costs should be until project completion.

The forecasted completion cost and completion date assume that conditions and resources will not improve (nor, of course, will they worsen either). The project manager should question the validity of these assumptions in light of the project environment. In LOGON, for example, given the size of the current overrun ($101,000 as of week 20), he should question the reasonableness of the forecasted completion cost of $1,159,530. Given that the project is less than half finished, is it likely that all remaining work will be completed for only $629,630 more without *additional* overruns? If the answer is no, the figure should be revised further according to best guess estimates.

If the *schedule performance* does not improve, it is likely that the project will be completed somewhat later than the current revised estimate of week 48 or 49. As of week 20, the BCWP is equivalent to the BCWS at week 19. This means, in terms of budgeted cost, there are still

$$47 \text{ weeks (target date)} - 19 \text{ weeks} = 28 \text{ weeks}$$

to go. But given the current schedule performance index SPI = 0.84, it is more likely that there are 28/0.84 = 33.3 weeks to go. Since we are now in week 20, the revised completion date is 20 + 33.3 = 53.3; that is, the project will be completed sometime in week 54. This revised estimate takes into account current levels of schedule performance and is probably a more realistic estimate than the graphical estimate of week 48 or 49 in Figure 15–7.

15.9 PERFORMANCE INDEX MONITORING

Although project managers should analyze individual work packages to validate project forecasts, in large projects they frequently have to rely more on analysis at the project level. This is because, quite simply, there are so many work packages that it is impossible to investigate everyone on a frequent basis.

Project level forecasts may be somewhat inaccurate, but at least they provide the manager with a quick, periodic "ballpark" estimate of project performance. It is better to get this slightly inaccurate information in sufficient time than to receive very accurate information too late.

One way for the project manager to track project status and performance trends is to follow a plot of SPI against CPI. The plot in Figure 15–8 is an example. It shows performance for the LOGON project as starting out somewhat poor, recovering, then drifting disturbingly back to and *remaining* in the poor region. In a case like this the project manager has to rely on the appraisal and judgment of functional managers to

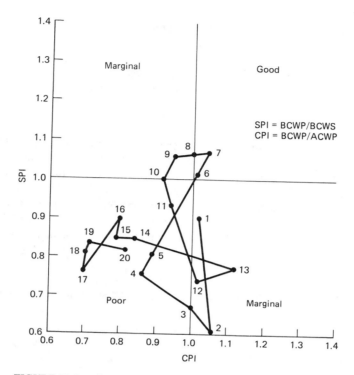

FIGURE 15–8. Cost/schedule performance index plotted for months 1-20.

help identify causes of problems at the work package level. Plots similar to Figure 15–8 for individual work packages and cost accounts can also be maintained to help the project office recognize sources of trouble.

15.10 VARIANCE LIMITS

Seldom do actual and planned performance measures coincide, and as a result, non-zero variances are more the rule rather than the exception. This leads to the question: what amount of variance is acceptable before action must be taken? Such is the purpose of *variance limits*.

At each level of the project organization—work package, departmental, and project—critical values are established as "acceptable." When a variance falls outside this acceptable range it is necessary to take measures of corrective action. Some variance limits, like those shown in Table 15–2, are set at the beginning of the project and remain constant for its duration. For jobs where there is considerable uncertainty, such as in a research project, variance limits are varied to permit a larger acceptable range during earlier, riskier phases, and a smaller acceptable range during later, less risky, phases. This is shown in Figure 15–8.

TABLE 15–2   Example of variance boundaries

Work Package A	Variances greater than $2,000
Work Package B	Variances greater than $18,000
Department C	Variances greater than $6,000
Department D	Variances greater than $38,000
Project	Variances greater than $55,000

Note that lower as well as upper variance limits can be used. This is as expected since there should be both maximum and minimum acceptable standards. Upper limits are necessary on technical parameters—not to keep performance down, but to minimize costs from excessive or unnecessary development. Upper and lower limits are important for cost and schedule control, too. A project running far ahead of schedule and under budget—an apparently desirable situation—should be scrutinized for oversights, corner cutting, and shoddy workmanship. Variance limits help point out places where cost and schedule underruns might be hurting work quality.

15.11 TAKING CORRECTIVE ACTION AND CONTROLLING CHANGES

When cost and schedule variances become too large, often the result is that the project plan and schedule must be revised or the end-item system redesigned. Changing the plan involves modifying the work, reorganizing or adding personnel, and making time, cost,

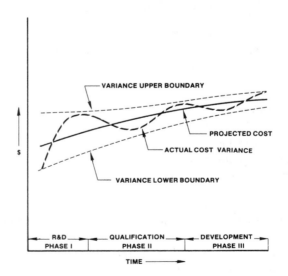

FIGURE 15–9. Variance tolerance boundaries. (Source: H. Kerzner, *Project Management: A Systems Approach to Planning, Scheduling, and Controlling* (New York: Van Nostrand Reinhold, 1979), 439, reprinted with permission.)

and performance tradeoffs. Redesigning the system often involves altering specifications and sacrificing technical performance to meet time and cost restrictions.

Whenever a project manager has to revise the project plan or reschedule work, the two most common constraints are:

- The project *must* be finished by a certain date.
- Resources are strictly *limited*.

With the first constraint it is likely that additional resources will have to be employed so deadlines can still be met. With the second constraint, however, the project usually will be delayed or the project scope altered. In either case, resources are a central issue and problems associated with rescheduling constrained resources, as described in Chapter 13, must be addressed.

The Impact of Changes

It is a fact that any project plan will have to be changed before the project is completed; generally, the larger and more complex the project, the larger the number of changes and the greater the deviation of actual costs and schedules from original objectives. But there is a reverse causality too: not only do emergent project problems require that the plan be changed, but changes to the plan *cause* problems to the project. In fact, changes to the project plan are a chief cause of cost and schedule overruns, low worker morale, and poor relationships between project and functional managers and clients.

In general, the further along the project, the more detrimental the effect of these changes. The more work that has already been done, the more that has to be undone. Since changes in the design of one system or component require redesign of other interrelated systems and components, changes in designs made after the design stage has been passed usually have the effect of significantly increasing the scope and cost of the project and delaying its completion.

Changes made still later, during construction or installation, are even more detrimental. Work is disrupted, things must be torn down and started again, materials are scrapped, and so on. Morale is affected also. People see their work being dismantled, discarded, and redone, usually on a rush basis to try to reduce overruns.

Reasons for Changes

Harrison lists the typical kinds of changes sought or required during a project. They include:[11]

1. Changes in project scope and specifications during the early stages of development. The greater the uncertainty of the work, the more likely that the scope and specifications will have to be altered during development. Such changes must be evaluated carefully since they are expensive to implement once the plan has been approved.

2. Changes in design, necessary or desirable, because of errors, omissions, afterthoughts, or revised needs. Mistakes, errors, and omissions must be corrected, but "desirable" changes requested by clients should be questioned, especially when they alter the original, contractual scope of the project. Customer representatives sometimes try to squeeze in changes (for the same price) that are beyond original specifications.

3. Changes imposed by government mandate (health, safety, labor, or environmental codes), labor contracts, suppliers, the community or other parties in the environment. There is usually no choice but to alter the plan to incorporate these.

4. Changes which are believed to improve the rate of return of the project. Such changes often cannot be justified because of the difficulty in estimating rate of return. Decisions of this nature should be referred to upper management.

5. Changes perceived as improvements upon original requirements. People have a tendency to want to improve upon their work. Apparently desirable, these changes can lead the project beyond its original intended scope and requirements. The project manager should distinguish necessary from "nice" changes and resist the latter.

Examples of the above changes include: (Type #1) After development has begun, increasing the payload requirements on a space probe to allow for necessary, additional hardware; (Type #2) after work is well along, modifying a computer software package or a building floor plan to give the user room for expansion; (Type #3) interrupting work because of labor problems or violations of municipal environmental codes; unexpected large increases in the cost of materials; (Type #4) increasing the capacity of a refinery under construction to speed up its payback; (Type #5) adding more and more refinements to an already acceptable product design.

Change Control System and Configuration Management

Because of their adverse effect on project cost and schedule objectives, project managers usually resist changes. As a result, disagreements over the necessity for changes and the impact of changes on project scope, cost, and schedule are a common source of conflict with functional managers and clients. Often these disagreements have to be resolved by upper management and require renegotiation of contracts.

One way to reduce the number of changes and their negative impact on project performance is to employ a formal system for change review and control. Since changes, like other aspects of project work, must be defined, scheduled, and budgeted, the process of drafting and implementing changes is similar to the original planning process. To quickly process and communicate the many changes a large project can generate, a formal *change control system* is used. The purpose of this system is to review and authorize design and work changes, weeding out all but the necessary ones, and to make sure that related work is also revised and authorized. According to Harrison,[12] such a system should:

1. Continually identify changes as they occur.

2. Reveal their consequences in terms of impact on project costs, project duration, and other tasks.

3. Permit managerial analysis, investigation of alternative courses of action, and acceptance or rejection.

4. Communicate changes to all parties concerned.

5. Specify a policy for minimizing conflicts and resolving disputes.

6. Insure that changes are implemented.

7. Report monthly a summary of all changes to date and their impact on the project.

Early in the project, preliminary baseline specifications are established to be used as a means for identifying changes and measuring their consequences. In projects with considerable uncertainty, initial estimates for technical specifications are based on rough approximations, to be revised and improved as more information becomes available. Throughout the project, the change control system should enable managers to trace the sources of differences between estimates to specific changes or to appraise the impact of proposed changes on current estimates and project plans. In some industries, the formal process of systematic change control and coordination, integrated into the systems development cycle, is referred to as *configuration management.*

The frequency and necessity for changes can be controlled and minimized through a configuration management approach, which emphasizes such strict procedures as:[13]

- Insuring that original work scope and work orders—with specific schedules, budgets, and statement of work—are clearly stated and *agreed to* by persons responsible.

- Close monitoring of the work to insure it is *meeting* (not exceeding) specifications.

- Careful screening of tasks for cost or schedule overruns (which may signify increase in work scope) and quick action to correct the problem.

- Requiring that all engineering and work changes are (1) *documented* as to their effect on work orders, budgets, schedules, and contractual prices, (2) formally *reviewed*, and (3) *authorized* by sign off. A typical change authorization form, similar to a task authorization form, is shown in Figure 15–10. This process is often handled by a change control committee (described below).

- Requiring similar control procedures of all subcontractors and for all purchase orders, test requests, and so on.

- At a predefined phase, freezing the project against all nonessential changes. The freeze point must be agreed to by management; the sooner the plan can be frozen, the less changes will adversely affect scheduling and cost.

In larger projects, a *change control board* consisting of the project manager and managers from engineering, manufacturing, purchasing, contract administration, and other

TASK AUTHORIZATION				.PAGE OF
TITLE				
PROJECT NO.	TASK NO.	REVISION NO.	DATE ISSUED	
STATEMENT OF WORK:				
APPLICABLE DOCUMENTS:				
SCHEDULE START DATE:		COMPLETION DATE:		
COST:				
ORIGINATED BY:	DATE:	ACCEPTED BY:		DATE:
APPROVED BY:	DATE:	APPROVED BY:		DATE:
APPROVED BY:	DATE:	APPROVED BY:		DATE:

FIGURE 15–10. Example of work authorization change request document. (Source: M.D. Rousenau, *Successful Project Management*, (Belmont, CA: Lifetime Learning, 1981), 183, reprinted with permission.)

areas should meet weekly to review change requests. Prior to the meeting, the effects of changes should be estimated so that the board can determine which to reject or to adopt.

Any proposed or enacted change that impacts the time, cost, or nature of work of a single task or other related tasks must be identified and reported. Since everyone involved in the project has the potential to recognize or originate changes, everyone must watch for changes and be held accountable for bringing them to the attention of others.

15.12 CONTROL PROBLEMS

No matter how thorough and control conscious the project manager is, and no matter how sophisticated the control systems are, control problems still occur. Roman notes the following common kinds of project control problems:[14]

1.   Only one factor such as cost is emphasized while others such as schedule and technical performance are ignored. This happens when control procedures are issued by one functional area, like accounting or finance, and other areas are left out. Forcing compliance to one factor alone, like cost, distorts the control process and usually results in excesses or slips in other areas, such as schedule delays or shoddy workmanship.

2.   Control procedures are resisted or do not receive compliance. Individuals who do not understand the benefits or necessity of using formal controls resent attempts at evaluating and controlling their work. Management encourages noncompliance with control procedures when it fails to exercise sanctions against people who defy the procedures.

3.   Information is inaccurately or partially reported. The people first aware of a problem may not understand the situation or, if they do, they may be hesitant to reveal it. The information reported may be fragmented and difficult to piece together.

4.   Self-appraisal kinds of control systems force people to act defensively and cannot provide unprejudiced information. Bias is one of the biggest obstacles to achieving accurate control.

5.   Managers are diffident on controversial issues, believing that with time problems resolve themselves. This gives some workers the impression that management doesn't care about the control process, an attitude likely to spread to others throughout the project.

6.   Managers in charge of several projects sometimes misrepresent charges so that poor performance in one is offset by good performance in others. The practice is common in organizations with multiple government contracts as a means of avoiding the bureaucracy and, overall, satisfying the requirements on all contracts. Not only does this distort the overall control process, it is unethical because clients are mischarged for the work.

7.   Information reporting and accounting mechanisms are misleading. For example, subjective measures such as the earned value of open work packages can suggest that more work was completed than actually was. Similarly, by altering accounting procedures, a bad situation can be made to look favorable.

To minimize these problems, upper management, functional managers, and project managers must actively support the control process, and all project workers must be shown the relevance of the control process and how it benefits them and the project. To be effective, control procedures must be impersonal, objective, and uniformly applied to all people, tasks, and functional areas.

15.13 SUMMARY

The purpose of project control is to guide work toward project goals, ensure effective utilization of resources, and correct problems. Project control assesses actual against planned accomplishment, confirms the continued need for the project, and updates expectations about project outcomes and requirements. It requires an effective system for collecting and disseminating information.

Project control utilizes cost, schedule, and work progress variance information. Using the concept of earned value and BCWP, project progress is assessed from the progress of all work packages at a given time.

The focal point of control is the work package and cost account. All activities—authorization, data collection, work progress evaluation, problem assessment, and corrective action—occur within the work package or cost account. Since higher level cost accounts are built up through the WBS and organizational hierarchies, project cost and schedule variances can be traced through the cost account structure to locate the sources of problems.

The control process begins with authorization, specifying time, cost, and technical specifications against which work will be evaluated. Once work begins, data is collected for each work order and corresponding cost account. Costs and schedules are tracked and correlated on a period-by-period basis. Performance to date is reviewed and figures for the cost and date of the project at completion are revised.

Cost and schedule variances are compared to pre-established limits. When variances move beyond acceptable limits, the work must be replanned or rescheduled. Changes are inevitable, but every effort is made to reduce their impact on cost and schedule overruns. A formal change control system minimizes the frequency and scope of changes, and configuration management insures that all changes are authorized, documented, and communicated.

A formal PCAS or, more generally, project management information system (PMIS) is required to accumulate, store, integrate, process, and report project information. The next chapter describes the customary requirements and features of PMIS's and reviews some software systems for computerizing the tasks of project management.

Summary of Variables

$$BCWS = \text{budgeted cost of work scheduled}$$
$$ACWP = \text{actual cost of work performed}$$
$$BCWP = \text{budgeted cost of work performed (the earned value)}$$
$$AV = \text{accounting variance} = BCWS - ACWP$$
$$SV = \text{schedule variance} = BCWP - BCWS$$
$$CV = \text{cost variance} = BCWP - ACWP$$

SPI = schedule performance index = BCWP/BCWS
CPI = cost performance index = BCWP/ACWP
FCTC = forecasted cost to complete project = (BCAC – BCWP)/CPI where BCAC is the budgeted cost at completion
FCAC = forecasted cost of project at completion = ACWP + FCTC

CHAPTER REVIEW QUESTIONS AND PROBLEMS

1. What are the three phases of the project control process?
2. Explain the differences between internal and external project controls.
3. How are overhead expenses allocated in work packages?
4. If a cost or schedule variance is noticed at the project level, how is it traced to the source of the variance?
5. What are the five steps of project control?
6. Describe the typical pattern of work authorization. What is usually included on a work order?
7. Describe the process of collecting data about the cost, schedule, and work accomplished.
8. Explain BCWS, ACWP, and BCWP, and how they are used to determine the variances AV, SV, CV, and TV. Explain the meaning of these variances.
9. What does it signify if cost or schedule index figures are less than 1.00?
10. Explain what is meant by a forecast "to complete," and how this forecast is related to the "at completion" forecast?
11. Discuss reasons why the project manager frequently resists project changes.
12. What should a change control system guarantee? Describe procedures that minimize unnecessary changes.
13. What are some difficulties encountered when attempting project control?
14. In the LOGON project suppose the status of the project as of week 22 is as follows:

$$BCWS = \$628,000$$
$$ACWP = \$640,000$$
$$BCWP = \$590,000$$

Answer the following questions:

   a. What is the earned value of the project as of week 22?
   b. Compute AV, SV, and CV.
   c. Using a graph similar to Figure 15–4, plot BCWS, ACWP, and BCWP. Show AV, SV, and CV. Determine TV from the graph.
   d. Compute SPI and CPI. Has the project performance improved or worsened since week 20?
   e. Using BCAC = \$990,000, compute FCTC and FCAC. How does FCAC compare to the week 20 estimate of \$1,222,593? Draw a status chart similar to Figure 15–7 and use it to determine the revised completion date. How does it compare to the revised date (week 48–49) as of week 20?
   f. Are the results from part (e) consistent with the results from part (d) regarding improvement or deterioration of project performance since week 20?

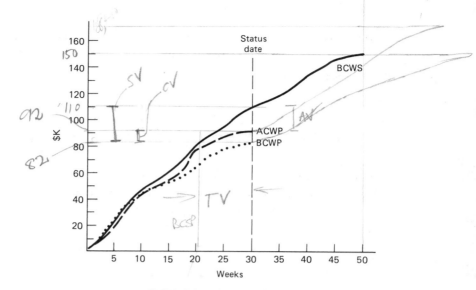

FIGURE 15–11. Status chart.

15. For a particular work package, the budgeted cost as of April 30 is $18,000. Suppose, as of April 30, the supervisor determines that only 80 percent of the scheduled work has been completed and the actual expense is $19,000. What is the BCWP? Compute AV, SV, CV, SPI, and CPI for the work package.

16. Using the status chart in Figure 15–11:

    a. Estimate AV, SV, CV, and TV, and compute SPI and CPI for week 30. Interpret the results.

    b. Compute FCTC and FCAC. Estimate the revised completion date and sketch the lines for forecasted ACWP and forecasted BCWP.

QUESTIONS ABOUT THE STUDY PROJECT

1. What kinds of *external* controls, if any, were imposed by the client on the project?

2. What kinds of internal control measures were used; e.g., work package control?; cost account control?; other? Describe.

3. Describe the project control process; e.g.:

How was work authorized to begin? Describe and show examples of work authorization orders.

How was data collected to monitor work? Explain the methods and procedures (time cards, invoices, etc.)

How was the data tallied and summarized?

How was the data validated?

4. Was the concept of earned value (budgeted cost of work performed) used?

5. How was project performance monitored? What performance and variance measures were used? Who did it? How often?

6. How were problems pinpointed and tracked?

7. Were the concepts of forecasting "to complete" and "at completion" used? If so, by whom? How often?

8. Were variance limits established for project cost and performance? What were they? How were they applied?

9. When cost, schedule, or performance problems occurred, what action did the project manager take? Give examples of problems and what the project manager did.

10. What changes to the product or project goal occurred during the project? Describe the "change control" process used in the project. How were changes to the project plan and systems specifications reviewed, authorized, and communicated? Show examples of change request and authorization documents.

ENDNOTES

1. Daniel Roman, *Science, Technology, and Innovation: A Systems Approach* (Columbus, Ohio: Grid Publishing, 1980), 369.

2. A.D. Szilagyi, *Management and Performance*, 2nd ed. (Glenview, Ill.: Scott, Foresman, 1984), 507–508.

3. Roman, *Science, Technology, and Innovation*, 382.

4. Here the terms "variance" and "deviation" are used interchangeably, although it should be noted that in some contracts, variance refers to "small" changes in the project plan for which compensation or correction is expected, whereas deviation refers to "large" changes that require a formal contractual response.

5. Ibid., 383.

6. *DOD & NASA Guide, PERT Cost Accounting System Design* (Washington, D.C.: U.S. Government Printing Office, June 1962).

7. J.D. Wiest and F.K. Levy, *A Management Guide to PERT/CPM* (Englewood Cliffs, N.J.: Prentice-Hall, 1977), 86.

8. Russell Archibald, *Managing High-Technology Programs and Projects* (New York: John Wiley & Sons, 1976), 184.

9. Ibid., 195.

10. A good explanation of ways of determining BCWP is given by T.G. Pham, "The Elusive Budgeted Cost of Work Performed for Research and Development Projects," *Project Management Quarterly* (March 1985), 76–79.

11. F.L. Harrison, *Advanced Project Management* (Hants, England: Gower, 1981), 242–244.

12. Ibid., 245–246.

13. Archibald, *Managing High-Technology Programs and Projects*, 187–190; Harrison, ibid., 244.

14. Adopted from Roman, *Science, Technology, and Innovation*, 327–328, 391–395.

chapter 16

Project Management Information Systems

An individual without information cannot take responsibility; an individual who is given information cannot help but take responsibility.

Jan Carlzon, Riv Pyramidera!

If this is the best of possible worlds, what then are the others?

Voltaire

The formal methods for planning, budgeting, and control in the last five chapters might seem too sophisticated, complicated, or time-consuming to be practical. Whether that is true or not depends upon *how* they are implemented. Those chapters illustrated the kind of information needed to manage projects, but they presume that the project manager is "organized" and has the means for collecting, storing, and processing the information. Generally, formal methods for planning and control do not require any more input data or information than is, or *should be*, available in any project. What they *do* require, however, is a framework and methodology, a *system*, for collecting, organizing, storing, processing, and disseminating that information. Such a framework and methodology is called a *Project Management Information System (PMIS)*.

The term PMIS can pertain to a manual or automated system, but commonly it refers to the latter. With the growing importance of computers in management and the proliferation of computerized PMIS's, it is important that project managers understand the uses of computers, know the kinds of computerized PMI software and hardware systems available, and appreciate the issues in selecting and implementing computer PMIS's. These are the topics of this chapter.

16.1 FUNCTIONS OF THE PMIS

It is almost impossible for any contemporary manager to do her job adequately without using some kind of manual or computerized *management information system* (MIS). Virtually all managers use information systems for functions such as payroll, billing, ordering, accounting, and inventory control. Project managers as well use these systems. The major difference between these and PMI systems is that the latter are dedicated solely to the function of project management. They are utilized primarily by project managers and staff to fulfill the unique requirements of project management.

Traditional Management Information Systems

Most traditional MIS's perform somewhat repetitive and routine functions for lower, technical core level managers (discussed in Chapter 3). Most are "data processing" systems that suit the needs of a particular functional area such as accounting, sales, personnel, or production. Typically these systems generate information on a periodic basis, usually daily or weekly. Though useful for planning and control purposes within specific functional areas, they are not very flexible or useful to managers at other levels. To assist managers at higher levels in solving complex problems, other kinds of MIS's are used; these are called *decision support systems* (DSS). DSS's assist managers in developing models for decision making and are primarily used for longer-range planning. They are helpful for solving unstructured kinds of problems, but the drawback is that they are not very useful for purposes of scheduling, budgeting, and control.

The information generated from traditional MIS's and DSS's can and is used by project managers, but it is inadequate for most project planning and control purposes. The simple reason goes back to the differences between project work and repetitive work and between project organizations and functional organizations—differences that extend to the information needed to manage projects. Projects are unique, temporary, complex activities that exist outside the traditional organizational structure. Since most traditional MIS's are designed to serve repetitive, ongoing, functional, stable information needs, they are often unsuited for project management. In addition, project managers need systems that they can use as both decision making aids and as tools for scheduling, budgeting, and control purposes.

Information Requirements of Projects

Since the information needed to manage projects tends to vary depending on the project, PMIS's must be flexible. Every project operates on a different schedule and has information requirements that change throughout stages of the project life cycle. Thus, unlike traditional information systems which routinely provide the same kind of information on a periodic basis, the outputs of PMIS's must coincide with project schedules and with the changing information needs of the project team.

PMIS's must also be able to handle the multifunctional nature of projects and support the project manager's "integrator" role. They must provide information that cuts across all levels, ties together activities in all functional areas, and integrates information on work performance, costs, and schedules.

Most PMIS's have capabilities that assist project managers in planning, budgeting, and resource allocation. Many PMIS's additionally perform assorted analyses such as variance, performance, and forecasting for any level of the WBS and project organization. A good PMIS enables facile control of changes to system configuration and project plans as well. These PMIS's allow for quick review and easy periodic updating; they filter and reduce data to provide information on summary, exception, or "what if" bases. With an effective PMIS the project manager does not have to wait for days or comb pages of data to identify problems and determine project status.

16.2 COMPUTER TOOLS

Automated PMIS's are increasingly taking over the role of managing project information. This is happening because they fulfill a need initially recognized in the 1950s when computers first came to project management. In those days the role of the computer was limited to network planning. The computer's main advantage was that it could rapidly process large amounts of information, something very important especially in large-scale construction and defense projects. But because of the great expense of computers this usage was restricted to only the very largest projects. As costs dropped during the next decade, computer network planning was more widely adopted, though still primarily within the defense and construction industries.

About the same time, many of the advanced methods of project control described in the last chapter were being developed. If you think about it, methods such as earned value analysis, forecasting, change control, and configuration management involve processing and integrating great quantities of information. These methods "roll up" work package information to the project level (or start at the project level and break down information) so problems can be traced back to their source. But they also presume the capability to process lots of information in a short time. As computers are good at doing this, they came to be seen as essential tools not just for planning but for control as well. In fact, without computers it would be difficult to do much of the analysis necessary to control large projects.

Until recently computer PM software required mini- or mainframe hardware and were predisposed to large projects. Despite proven advantages they remained cost prohibitive for small and even medium-sized projects. In the last several years all that has changed. What has made the difference is the micro or personal computer—the *PC*. Not only has the cost of hardware plummeted so that it is affordable to every manager, but the quality and capability of inexpensive project management software has greatly improved. Low cost PC's and software now make it possible for managers of small projects to plan and control activities with nearly the same sophistication as their large-scale counterparts.

Benefits of Computer PMIS's

The leading benefits of computer PMIS's over manual systems are speed, capacity, efficiency, economy, accuracy, and ability to handle complexity.

The major advantage is speed. Once data have been collected and input, practically any manipulation can be done more rapidly by computers. To create or revise printed plans, schedules, and budgets takes days or weeks with a manual system, but seconds, minutes, or hours with computers.

Computer PMIS's store large amounts of information more easily than manual systems, and they more quickly access, prioritize, and summarize that information. Manual systems for large projects are tedious to maintain, difficult to access, and provoke people to try to work around them or avoid them.

Manual systems require the efforts of numerous support personnel to maintain and use their outputs for analysis. Computer PMIS's can perform much of this analysis, reduce the requirement for clerical personnel, and relieve managers and support personnel from having to do computations. This frees them to use analysis results for making decisions.

The speed, capacity, and efficiency of computers afford still another benefit: economy. In most cases, computers offer a significant cost advantage over manual systems for storing and processing information. Assuming input data are correct, computers produce fewer computational errors and reduce the cost of correcting mistakes.

Finally, computer PMIS's are much better at handling and integrating complex data relationships. Large projects with thousands of work tasks, hundreds of organizations, and tens of thousands of workers cannot be managed efficiently without computers. In large projects, computers are regarded as virtual necessities, but even in small projects computers simply make them easier to manage.

The usage of project management software is growing so rapidly that there is no longer any doubt about their benefit and usefulness in project management. The question is no longer *will* an organization computerize its information requirements, but *when*? Although the answer for most project managers is "now," many others are holding back.

Perceived Drawbacks to Computer PMIS's

Despite the availability of PC's that rival the mainframes of a few years ago, many project managers continue to rely entirely on manual systems. Their reasons often stem from drawbacks that are more perceived than real.

PC's are still a relatively new phenomenon in business life. It is only in recent years that they have gained widespread acceptance in business, and even more recently that very good, affordable PM software has come to the market. Many managers see the computer as a dramatic change and, often, as threatening. They are wary about replacing tried and tested manual systems which seem satisfactory with a technology which they know little about. To use any new system they have to first learn it, and many are too busy or too skeptical to invest the time.

Even as general acceptance of business PC's grows, there will still be managers who resist them. This is a continuing frustration for younger project staff members who, trained in modern methods and computers, are eager to utilize their skills. Part of the resistance stems from the difficulty in choosing among the sometimes confusing plethora of hardware and software systems. As computer awareness has increased and the market has grown, so has the number of manufacturers and range of products. Project managers now have dozens of PC's and project software packages to choose from. Software packages vary greatly in capability and flexibility; generally, as the size and capability increase, so does the price. The degree of technical support accompanying software packages varies, which means sometimes it is difficult to get help or assistance from the software developer when it is needed. As if choosing the right software were not enough of a problem, the project manager must *also* determine the right combination of computer and peripheral devices—monitors, printers, plotters, modems, and add-on's. Choosing the right hardware/software combination is time-consuming, frustrating, and sometimes just too much to handle.

Generally, a computer system's outputs are only as good as its inputs. To perform well the computer system must be given adequate and accurate input data; stored data must be periodically updated; and information outputs must be distributed to the people who need them. In short, any computer system needs a good manual support system. Sometimes when human failings result in improper maintenance or utilization of the information system, it is the computer that gets blamed. One "bad experience" with a computer can leave its mark for a long time.

Many a project manager's first experience is with a low budget, limited capability system (hardware/software configuration), one that is inadequate for her management needs. Often the manager selected the system because it would be easy to learn and simple to install. When she discovers that the system does not provide all the expected benefits, she generalizes that the same must be true for *all* computer PMIS's.

Since satisfaction depends on how well system capabilities match user expectations, it is important at the start to have the "right" expectations. Simpler PMIS's have limited capability, but they are usually good at what they can do, and they *can* be of tremendous benefit. Also, once mastered, they make it is easy to upgrade to more sophisticated systems.

Computer Applications in Project Management

There are myriad hardware/software configurations with various applications in project management. Many of these are general purpose business tools which, though not

PMIS's, can be of assistance in certain limited aspects of project management. Other kinds of software (or hardware/software) systems are "dedicated" to project management, and many of these can be termed true PMIS's. For a project manager to be able to assess how satisfactory a given computer application is he must first know both the information requirements of the project and the capabilities of the computer application. Often, to satisfy all information requirements—data, text, and graphics—it is necessary to use more than one kind of software.

We will first discuss general purpose kinds of software with applications in project management, then software systems that are solely devoted to the business of project management.

16.3 GENERAL PURPOSE BUSINESS SOFTWARE

As the term implies, general purpose business software can be employed in a wide variety of business (and non-business) situations. The four categories of general purpose software most useful for project management are: spreadsheet, data base management, word processing, and mathematical/statistical modeling packages. Although each has a rather limited application, it can serve as a *partial* function of a PMIS and can be useful for decision making and project communication. Some can be utilized in combination with, or to augment, the capabilities of dedicated PMI systems.

Spreadsheet Software

Spreadsheet software are useful for project accounting, cost analysis, and financial projections. They utilize an accounting ledger format for data input and perform computations yielding column and row totals, averages, variances, and other statistics. Results can be reported in a variety of tabular and graphical formats. The construction budget in Figure 16–1 was prepared and printed with a spreadsheet software package.

Spreadsheet software are useful for project managers who want to keep close track of expenditures but also want a system that is relatively easy to master. They are valuable as planning tools and for performing "what if" kinds of analysis, for example, estimating effects of budget, funding, and cost changes on project objectives. Their biggest advantage is to relieve managers of doing tedious, repetitive computations. Many can be programmed to do rudimentary scheduling computations and to print crude Gantt charts.[1] Most spreadsheet software can store large amounts of data and have a limited data base capability (discussed next), though they cannot pool data or store information about data relationships. As discussed later, "add-in" software may be available so the spreadsheet package can also be used for scheduling. Among the best known spreadsheet packages are Lotus 1-2-3,® VisiCalc,® and SuperCalc.®

```
                                      CONSTRUCTION BUDGET

     ANALYSIS OF BUILDING COST
                                    COST      FOR 67843
     COMPONENT                      PER SF       SF
     -----                          -----      -----
  1. HVAC
       BASE BUILDING                 6.16
       TENANT IMPROVEMENTS           9.18
                                    -----
       TOTAL                        15.34

  2. TENANT FIT-UP                  10.38

  3. FOOD SERVICE                    1.51

  4. RAISED FLOOR AND CARPET         3.79
                                    -----
                    SUBTOTAL        31.02    2104489.86

  5. DATA CENTER ESTIMATE
     (17603 SF @ $100/SF)                    1760300.00
                                             -----
                    SUBTOTAL                 3864789.86

  6. PLUS CONTINGENCY @ 5%                     193239.49
                                             -----
                    SUBTOTAL                 4058029.35

  7. GENERAL CONDITIONS @ 4.5%                182611.32
                                             -----
                    SUBTOTAL                 4240640.67

  8. GENERAL CONTRACTOR'S FEE @ 4.5%          190828.83
                                             -----
                    SUBTOTAL                 4431469.50

  9. LESS: HVAC CREDIT                       -207000.00
                                             -----
                 GRAND TOTAL                 4224469.50


                                             =====
contingency usage - change order log
------------------------
opening balance                              193239.49
1 - p+w hvac redesign                         -5500.00
2 - carlson analysis of lyndhurst ups         -9500.00


                                               ---
remaining balance                            178239.49
                                               ===
```

FIGURE 16–1. Spreadsheet cost report.

Data Base Management Systems

Data base management systems (DBMS) are software which permit data to be stored using a "relational data structure"; this means that each element or unit of stored data can be related to, or cross-referenced to, every other element of data. In this way separate sets of data (about costs, schedules, resources, and so on) can be rearranged, combined, and displayed in many ways enabling the project manager to create tailor-made reports. With a DBMS, information about material availability and usage, task completion status, quality control, work changes, specifications, and labor hours can easily be stored, processed, and quickly accessed. A DBMS can be programmed to raise warnings about, for example, budget overruns, late delivery dates, or low material inventories. Among popular DBMS's are dBase III,® R:BASE 5000,® and R:BASE System V.®[2] Many of these are compatible with and can be used to enhance the capability of dedicated PMIS software. This will be discussed later.

Word Processing

Projects generate numerous miscellaneous documents such as contracts, proposals, work authorizations, directions, approvals, and other correspondence. Particularly for lengthy documents such as contracts that use standardized formats or must be periodically revised and rewritten, *word processing* software (called "word processors") are an excellent means for reducing the time to produce and modify them. Many word processors can be used in combination with computer graphics, drawing, and "desktop publishing" packages to produce high quality charts and graphs, project proposals, and newsletters. No matter what other computer applications are employed in project management, the efficiencies offered by word processing stand alone. All of the text in the LOGON project plan (Appendix C) was prepared using a word processor. Among popular word processors are WordPerfect,® Wordstar,® Microsoft Word,® and Pfs:Write.®

Integrated Systems

Spreadsheet, data base, word processing, and graphics applications are separate software tools, but some developers offer "integrated" software packages that combine features of all four into one. These systems permit, for example, data to be stored using complex relationships, then retrieved for spreadsheet computations, then results to be stored or displayed graphically with accompanying text, all in one system. A "menu" enables the user to select particular applications—spreadsheet, DBMS, word processor, and so on, and to readily move data from one to the other. Lotus Hal® and Symphony,® Microsoft Excel,® and Boreland Quatro® are examples.

Mathematical, Statistical, and Creativity Packages

There are a large number of mathematical, statistical, simulation, and related software packages which can be used for project modeling and analysis. Although these packages do not classify as PMIS's they are still of great value in project management because they help decision makers ask "what if" questions, assess alternatives, make projections, and develop scenarios. When combined with a project data base they provide a form of DSS for the project manager. Many of these packages require somewhat higher level mathematical sophistication on the part of the user.

Also useful in project management are software packages that help "thinkers" to organize thoughts. These are designed to enhance creativity and are particularly useful during the early conceptual phase of the project for laying out ideas and preparing rough plans. Most of these "creativity aids" are easy and fun to use.

Despite their usefulness, all general purpose software applications are somewhat limited in project management because they address only *portions* of the information requirements needed to manage projects. Even spreadsheet and DBMS's do not meet the requirements of a complete PMIS, largely because they were not designed with projects in mind. This contrasts to dedicated PMIS's which are software packages (or hardware/software configurations) for *exclusive* use with projects. However, as discussed next, even among dedicated PMIS's, capabilities vary considerably; there is no guarantee that using one will satisfy all the information requirements of project management.

16.4 DEDICATED COMPUTER PMI SYSTEMS

A computerized PMIS *should* be able to:

- Create and update files containing information necessary for planning, control, and summary documents.
- Enable data from other computer information systems to be transferred to the project data base.
- Integrate work, cost, labor, and schedule information to produce planning, control, and summary reports for project, functional, and upper-level managers.

Among the many available PMIS's, the fact is that few have all of these features. Many do not even perform the most essential functions of project management. The following sections discuss the kinds of features and options available in computer PMIS's and their appropriateness for planning and control functions.

Features of PMIS's

Here is a list of the kinds of analytical capabilities, outputs, and other features offered by various PMI systems.

Scheduling and Network Planning.   Virtually all project software systems do project scheduling using a network-based procedure. These systems compute early and late schedule times, slack times, and the critical path. Among the capabilities a user must assess are the type of procedure (PERT, CPM, PDM, or multiple types), event or activity oriented outputs (or multiple types), and use of probabilities. Capabilities also vary with regard to the maximum number of allowable activities, the way activities and events are coded (some use a WBS scheme), and the quality and clarity of the output format (e.g., network, Gantt chart, tabular reports, or multiple types). The kind of calendar also varies: most systems allow input of nonwork periods such as weekends, holidays, and vacations, and produce schedules accordingly, but details of input and output differ greatly.

Resource Management.
Most project systems also perform resource loading, leveling, allocation, or multiple functions, although the analytical sophistication and quality of reports vary tremendously between systems. The major considerations are: the maximum number of resources permitted per activity or project, the kind of resource loading/scheduling techniques used (resource-limited, time-limited, or both), split scheduling (stopping activities, then starting later), interchangeable usage of different resources, and using resources which are consumed.[3]

Budgeting.
In many project systems it is possible to associate cost information with each activity, usually by treating it as a resource. But software vary greatly in the way they handle fixed, variable, and overhead costs, and in their ability to generate budget and cost summary reports. In many systems cost and expense information are not treated explicitly; in others, cost accounting is a major feature. The ability of a system to handle cost information and generate budgets is a significant variable in the system's usability for both planning and control.

Cost Control and Performance Analysis.
Here is where project system capabilities differ the most. To perform the control function a system must be able to compare actual performance (actual costs and work completed) to planned and budgeted performance. Many systems cannot do this, while others can but with much variation in how well. Among the features to consider are the system's ability to compute and report cost and schedule variances, earned values (BCWP), and various performance indices, as well as to forecast by extrapolating past performance. The most sophisticated PMIS's "roll up" results and allow aggregation, analysis, and reporting at all levels of the WBS. They also permit modification and updating of existing plans through input of actual start and finish dates and costs.

The most comprehensive PMIS's *integrate* network, budget, and resource information and allow the project manager to ask "what if" questions under various scenarios while the project is underway. They allow the user to access, cross-reference, and output any information on reports or to other data bases.

Reporting and Graphics.
Project systems also vary greatly in the number, kind, and quality of reports they produce. This is an important consideration because it affects the speed with which PMIS outputs are communicated and the accuracy of their interpretation. Many systems provide only tabular reports or crude schedules; others generate networks and resource histograms; still others offer a variety of graphics

including pie charts and line graphs. The main features to consider are the number, quality, and type of available reports and graphics. Many systems generate only a few standardized types of reports, others a wide range, including custom created ones to satisfy any format or information requirement. The quality often depends on the system's ability to use different output devices. All systems produce reports on standard printers, and many show the report on the terminal screen as well; the highest quality reports and graphics are produced on plotters.

Interface, Flexibility, Ease of Use.   Some systems are compatible with and can tie into existing data bases such as payroll, purchasing, inventory, MRP, cost-accounting, or other PMIS's. Some can be used with popular DBMS and spreadsheet systems. They can also be used to provide input data for systems that do modeling and mathematical analysis. Many larger PMIS's allow data from different projects to be pooled so *multiproject* analysis can be performed.

The capability for a PMIS to interface with other software from which existing data files have been created is an important selection criterion. Many firms have had to spend considerable time and money developing interfaces so they could use a commercial PM package with their existing data and other PMI systems. Most small, inexpensive systems are stand alone and have limited interface ability.

Systems also vary widely in flexibility. Many systems are limited and perform a narrow set of functions which cannot be modified. Others allow the user to develop new applications or alter existing ones depending on needs. Among the potential additional applications and reports sometimes available are change control, configuration management, responsibility matrixes, expenditure reports, cost and technical performance reports, and technical performance summaries.

Finally, there is the consideration of user friendliness: how easy is it to learn and operate the system. Systems vary greatly in the style of system documentation, thoroughness and clarity of tutorials, ease of information input, clarity of on screen presentation and report format, helpfulness of error messages, and the training and operating support offered by the developer. Ease of use is also somewhat influenced by the sophistication and flexibility of the system. Generally, the more sophisticated the system, the more difficult it is to learn and to use.

Functions of Computer PMIS

Since the purpose of a PMIS is to support project management decisions and to provide information necessary to conduct the project, the functions of PMIS's closely parallel those of project management—in most projects, these are:

1. planning and budgeting,
2. work authorization and control,
3. control of changes, and
4. communicating all of these.

What is important to note is that currently most dedicated PMIS software systems are able to support only the first, and to a limited extent, the last functions on this list. As Levine notes, this is because for software to be able to perform the control function several features are required beyond those for planning; these include the ability to:[4]

1. save an old version of the data base as a baseline for comparison with current status and actual costs;
2. enter actual start and finish dates, and revise task durations without having them override the plan dates;
3. enter actual costs incurred, for comparison to budget; and
4. record actual resource usage.

Many popular project management packages lack these capabilities. Thus, although they can help the project manager in the early project phases of planning and definition, *once the project begins* they are of little help and cannot provide assistance in the place where, perhaps, it is needed most—project control. This is unfortunate because, as mentioned, project control is an area where computers offer a tremendous advantage over manual systems. For procedures that require the capability to integrate time, cost, and performance information, to "roll up" this information through the WBS, and to do it quickly and efficiently, computers are the only practical means.

Hence, unless it is to be used solely for that purpose, the project manager must be wary of software packages that can only do planning. Finding software that can also be used for project control is not always easy because, as Levine states, "software specifications and magazines rarely note that this capability [for control] is missing."[5]

16.5 REPRESENTATIVE COMPUTERIZED PMI SYSTEMS

Categories of PMI Systems

As discussed previously, commercially available PMIS's vary greatly in capability. They fall roughly into three categories:[6]

Category 1.   Software for developing Gantt charts or PERT/CPM analysis. Sometimes these enable inclusion of labor, costs, and resources in scheduling. They are easy to use but are severely limited and cannot be utilized for control.

Category 2.   Software for cost, labor, and resource control. These compare actual and planned labor and costs to identify period and cumulative variances. Sometimes they permit summary reporting by WBS, organizational structure, or cost-account structure.

Category 3.   Software that integrate cost, schedule, and resource information. Some permit detailed project modeling and control of changes. These software are the most comprehensive and combine features from both the above categories.

There is, of course, an association between the cost of software and its capability. While Category 1 packages cost as little as $200, Category 2 packages may cost $500 to several $1000's, and Category 3 systems still more, not including hardware costs. Cost, capabilities, required hardware and peripherals, ease of use, flexibility, format and configuration, and project environment must all be considered in selecting a PMIS. Computer journals frequently provide reviews of software, and books such as the ones by Jack Gido and Harvey Levine[7] give detailed descriptions of project management software packages.

Most PMIS software for small or medium-sized projects are designed for use on PC hardware. In recent years this software has proliferated; there are now over 100 project management packages for the PC.[8] PMIS's for larger projects usually require the storage capacity of minicomputer or mainframe hardware. The largest PMIS's use mainframe hardware/software configurations dedicated solely to project management. The following paragraphs provide a sampling of some "typical" computer PMI systems and look at five well-known systems that cover the gambit of available software. One cautionary note: these descriptions are intended just to give you a "running start." In a competitive, rapidly changing market like software it is difficult to give up-to-date assessments. During the course of writing this book some of the following software has undergone three revisions.

PMIS's for Small Projects

The following two PMIS's are for use on PC's using the MS/PC-DOS® operating system (IBM PC's® and compatibles). They are "high end" Category 1 software with some features of Category 2. Both are "user-friendly"—relatively simple to learn, and easy to use.

Time Line®[9]

Time Line® Version 3.0 by the Breakthrough Software Division, Symantec Corporation, can handle projects with up to 1600 tasks, under $100 million total cost, and 300 resources per schedule, 24 per task. The package creates Gantt and PERT charts (Figures 16–2 through 16–4) and several reports and tables including cost, resource, and detailed task reports. It also does resource leveling, displays resource histograms on the screen, and creates an earned value, cost-to-complete report (Figure 16–5). Other features enable users to prepare schedules in outline fashion and to create and store notes about project details.

Microsoft Project®[10]

Microsoft Project® Version 4.0 by Microsoft Corporation can handle projects with 255 tasks and up to $999 billion cost. It can also link files so that the number of tasks becomes virtually limitless. Up to 255 resources per file can be specified, 8 per activity. The package creates Gantt and PERT charts (e.g., Figure 16–6), resource loading charts (Figure 16–7),

```
Schedule Name:   Magazine ad schedule for new Bontano release.
Project Manager: Account Executive
As of date:        8-Jul-85 12:59am    Schedule File: B:MANAGE

Copy for November publications must be in by 9-1-85.


                                  85
                                  Jul                Aug              85
                      Who   Status 8    15   22   29  5   12   19   26  Sep
                                                                      3    9
Client Input Session  AE,Client  D =  |
Develop Schedule      AE,Art  D+      ++--       .    .    .    .    .    .    .
Market Research       AE, Crtv   C     ======    .    .    .    .    .    .    .
Develop Ad Strategy   AE, Crtv   pC    | ======  .    .    .    .    .    .    .
Strategy Approval     Client,AE  C     |    .>>M .    .    .    .    .    .    .
Concept & Copy        AE, Crtv   C     |    .  =============.   .    .    .    .
Art Work              Art Dir,+  p     |    .  =========---.    .    .    .    .
Presentation Prep     AE         C     |    .    .    ==.   .    .    .    .    .
Client Presentation   AE,Clien+  C     |    .    .  >M.  .    .    .    .    .
Copy/Layout Revisions CopyWrit+  C     |    .    .   =====  .    .    .    .    .
Copy/Layout Approval  AE,Clien+  C     |    .    .    . >M  .    .    .    .    .
Prep for Photo Shoot  Art Dir,+        |    .    .    .  ====-   .    .    .    .
Typeset Copy          AE         C     |    .    .    .  ======  .    .    .    .
Photo Sessions        Art Dir,+  C     |    .    .    .    ==   .    .    .    .
Paste Up              Art Dir,+  C     |    .    .    .    . == .    .    .    .
Final Approval        AE,Client  C     |    .    .    .    . == =   .    .    .
Print Production      Prod Mgr   C     |    .    .    .    .    ==  .    .    .
Ship to Pubs          AE         C     |    .    .    .    .    .=========.   .
                                                                     . M.   .
------------------------------------------------------------------------------
D Done              === Task          - Slack time (==---), or
C Critical          +++ Started task    Resource delay (---==)
R Resource conflict   M Milestone     > Conflict
r Rescheduled to avoid resource conflict  p Partial dependency
Scale: Each character equals 1 day
------------------------------------------------------------------------------
```

FIGURE 16–2.   Time line Gantt chart.

```
Schedule Name:   Magazine ad schedule for new Bontano release.
Project Manager: Account Executive
As of date:        8-Jul-85  1:03am    Schedule File: B:MANAGE

Copy for November publications must be in by 9-1-85.
```

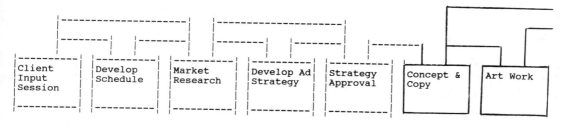

FIGURE 16–3.   Time Line PERT chart.

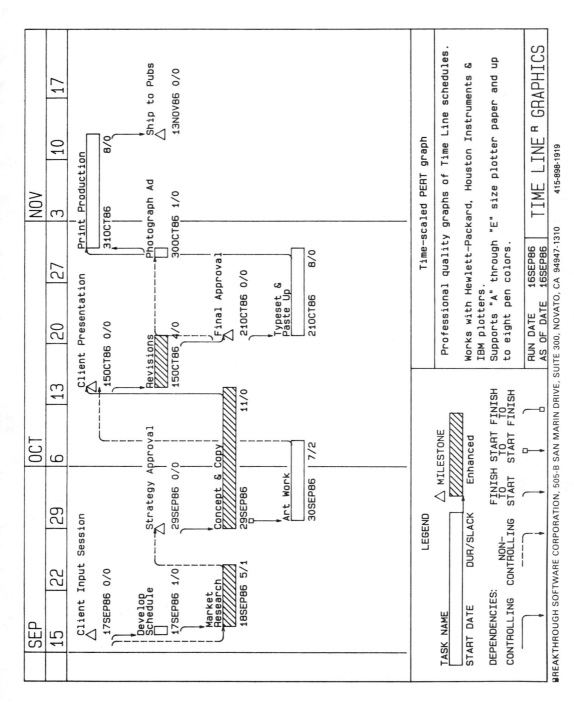

FIGURE 16—4. Time Line time-phased PERT network.

Schedule Name: Magazine ad schedule for new Bontano release.
Project Manager: Account Executive
As of date: 8-Jul-85   1:31am   Schedule File: B:MANAGE

Copy for November publications must be in by 9-1-85.

Task	Early Start	Early End	Time to Complt	% Time to Complt	% Cost to Complt	Done Cost Accrued	Startd Task Cost Accrued	Startd Task Cost to Complete	Future Cost to Complete
Client Input Session	1-Jul-85	1-Jul-85	0 hours	0		60	0	0	0
Develop Schedule	2-Jul-85	2-Jul-85	0 days	0		0	273	0	0
Market Research	8-Jul-85	12-Jul-85	1 week	100	100	1,398	0	0	0
Develop Ad Strategy	11-Jul-85	17-Jul-85	5 days	100	100	16,305	0	0	0
Strategy Approval	18-Jul-85	18-Jul-85	0 days	100	100	0	0	0	0
Concept & Copy	18-Jul-85	1-Aug-85	11 days	100	100	0	0	0	1,500
Art Work	19-Jul-85	30-Jul-85	7 days	100	100	0	0	0	3,075
Presentation Prep	1-Aug-85	1-Aug-85	1 day	100	100	0	0	0	429
Client Presentation	2-Aug-85	2-Aug-85	0 weeks	100	100	0	0	0	16
Copy/Layout Revisions	2-Aug-85	7-Aug-85	4 days	100		0	0	0	562
Copy/Layout Approval	8-Aug-85	8-Aug-85	0 days	100	100	0	0	0	0
Prep for Photo Shoot	8-Aug-85	12-Aug-85	3 days	100	100	0	0	0	919
Typeset Copy	8-Aug-85	14-Aug-85	5 days	100	100	0	0	0	1,148
Photo Sessions	14-Aug-85	14-Aug-85	1 day	100	100	0	0	0	3,227
Paste Up	15-Aug-85	16-Aug-85	2 days	100	100	0	0	0	1,172
Final Approval	19-Aug-85	19-Aug-85	1 day	100	100	0	0	0	159
Print Production	20-Aug-85	29-Aug-85	8 days	100	100	0	0	0	1,273
Ship to Pubs	30-Aug-85	30-Aug-85	0 weeks	100	100	0	0	0	1,000
			53 days			17,762	273	0	14,479
						55%	1%		45%
						18,034			14,479

FIGURE 16-5. Time Line earned value analysis report.

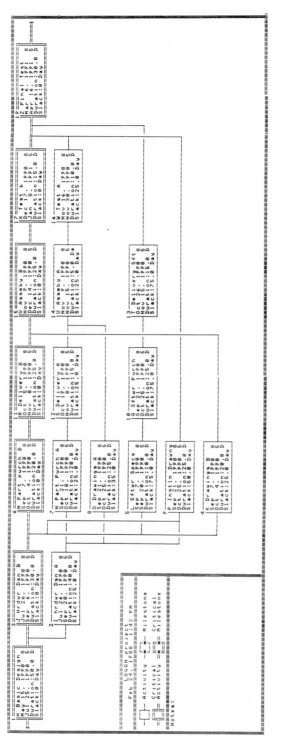

FIGURE 16–6. Microsoft PERT network.

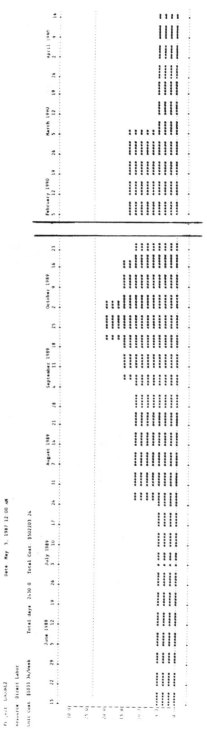

FIGURE 16–7. Microsoft resource loading chart.

and a variety of predefined task, cost, and variance tables and reports (e.g., Figures 16–8 and 16–9), as well as custom reports. Schedules can be rearranged to shorten durations, balance resources, or reduce costs.

Data on Microsoft files can be converted to files for *Primavera Project Planner®* (described next) which has the additional capacity to merge multiple projects and handle larger projects. Microsoft also has plotter capabilities to produce color graphics.

Some additional popular, well-rated software in Category 2 (a few with some Category-3 features) are *QWICKNET Professional,®* *PROMIS,*TM *Harvard Total Project Manager,*TM *Advanced Project Workbench,®* *Project Scheduler Network,*TM and *SuperProject Plus.®* There are literally dozens more with varying capabilities and quality. Additionally there are "add-in" software packages which enable spreadsheet owners to perform limited scheduling functions using PERT, CPM, or PDM. *Project Calc,*TM an add-in for *Lotus 1-2-3,®* is an example. Compared to other project management software, add-ins have relatively limited capability; their chief advantage is ease of use with spreadsheet data and low cost.

A good way to contrast the capabilities of these and other project-management software is to follow the reviews in professional and software journals. These journals frequently publish assessments of individual packages or provide comparative reviews and charts of various project software packages.[11]

```
                            Sample
                        Activity Analysis
                           Report

   Project: DEVELOP            Date:   Dec 11,1984 8:00 AM
   ---------------------------- Report Type:   DURATION
                                            -----------------
                    FORECAST        ACTUAL              VARIANCE
   Activity                                     Difference   Percent
   --------------------------------------------------------------

   1  Gen mktg plans
                    15.0 days      17.2 days     +2.2 days    +15.0

   2  Assign responsiblites
                     5.0 days       3.0 days     -2.0 days    -40.0

   3  Consolidate plans
                     5.0 days       5.0 days      0.0 days      0.0

   4  Review product lines
                    15.0 days      20.0 days     +5.0 days    +25.0

   5  Hire prototype artists
                    12.0 days      10.0 days     -2.0 days    -17.0

   6  Design prototypes
                    30.0 days      45.0 days    +15.0 days    +50.0

   7  Hire layout artist
                     5.0 days       5.0 days      0.0 days      0.0
   --------------------------------------------------------------
   Total Project Duration:
                   182.0 days     195.5 days    +13.5 days     +7.4
```

FIGURE 16–8.   Microsoft variance analysis report.

Sample
Resource Cost
Report

Project: DEVELOP   Date: Jun 3, 1985   8:00 AM

# Resource	Capacity	Unit cost	Per	Days to Complete	Cost to Complete
1 Forecaster	No limit	$1800.00	Month	35.0	$2907.90
2 Production mngr	No limit	$2550.00	Month	70.0	$8239.06
3 Recruiter	No limit	$2355.00	Month	32.0	$3478.40
4 WP operator	No limit	$55.00	Day	37.5	$2062.50
5 WP equipment	No limit	$26.00	Day	35.0	$910.00
6 Production VP	No limit	$3700.00	Month	22.0	$3757.20
7 Prototype artst	No limit	$235.00	Day	30.0	$7050.00
8 Graphic artst	No limit	$115.00	Day	65.0	$7475.00
9 Production sup	No limit	$2000.00	Month	20.0	$1846.29
10 Marketing VP	No limit	$3700.00	Month	20.0	$3415.64
11 Ad writer	No limit	$250.00	Day	40.0	$10000.00
12 Marketing mngr	No limit	$2750.00	Month	3.5	$444.26
13 Ad mngr	No limit	$2400.00	Month	2.5	$276.94
14 Paste-up artst	No limit	$75.00	Day	7.5	$562.50
15 Pr mngr	No limit	$1900.00	Month	5.0	$438.49

Cost to complete: $52864.18   Total cost of project: $52864.18

FIGURE 16–9. Microsoft resource cost report.

PMIS for Medium to Large Projects[12]

Typical among PMIS software for medium to large projects is *Project Planner (P3)*®
by Primavera Systems, Inc. *P3* is for use on IBM-PC's and compatibles. Although not
as easy to use as most Category 1 software, it is representative of Category 2 software
with many features of Category 3. It can handle projects of up to 10,000 activities and
unlimited resources per project and activity. Besides the usual critical path scheduling,
it can use the precedence diagramming (PDM) format. It integrates scheduling, resource allocation, and cost control analyses. Activities are coded according to WBS,
cost account, or user defined codes (department, manager, job, phase, etc.).

Among the types of analyses offered by *P3* are resource leveling and smoothing,
estimation of cost of completing the project, and earned value analysis. Among the
tables and reports provided are network logic diagrams, detailed task reports, cash flow
statements, Gantt charts, resource histograms, budget-to- actual control reports, cumulative cost reports, and earned value analysis reports (e.g., Figures 16–10 and 16–11).

Primavera has several add-on products that utilize *P3* files for producing enhanced, high quality graphics and reports (e.g., Figure 16–12).

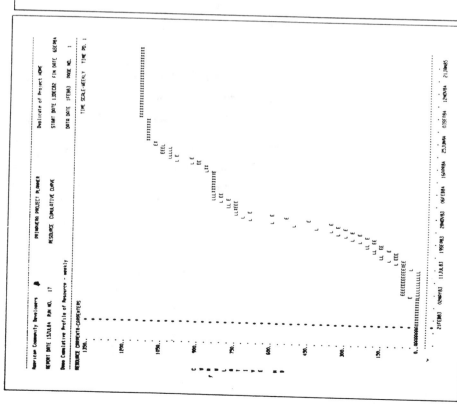

FIGURE 16-10. Primavera cost/resource reports.

Cost Control Report by Resource

Cumulative Resource Profile

Earned Value Report (Cost)

FIGURE 16–10.   (Continued.)

PMIS's for Very Large Projects

Most software for very large projects integrate schedule, cost, and resource information. These are Category 3 systems. All provide for reporting of cumulative, variance, earned value, and forecasting information. Most have enhanced graphics capabilities. Following are two examples.

Metier ARTEMIS[TM]13

ARTEMIS[TM] by Metier Management Systems is a high level application system for use on micro, mini, and mainframe computers. Planning and scheduling, cost estimating and control, and technical information are linked and integrated with a relational data base so that the impact of changes in one function on all other functions are immediately shown. Examples of integration are cost and schedule, cost and material, material and schedule, and cost, schedule, and material. *ARTEMIS* provides the ability to manage multiple projects and integrate information across projects.

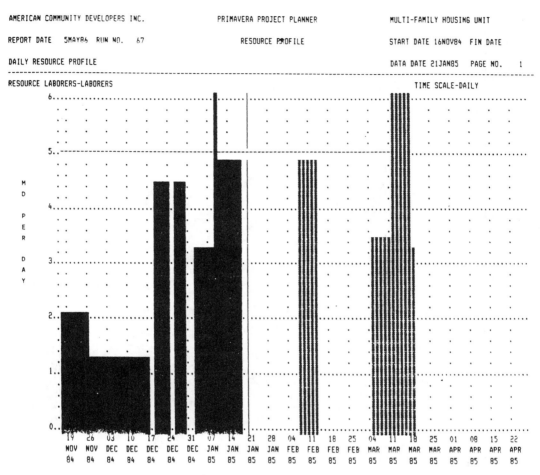

FIGURE 16–11. Primavera resource histogram.

Standard functions on *ARTEMIS* provide for checking network logic, ascertaining the critical path, performing resource analysis, leveling of resource requirements, determining project costs, and summarizing data. It can perform project scheduling under constrained resources, three-value PERT, and risk analysis using a Monte Carlo sampling technique. It can perform cost related analyses such as budget baseline, earned value, actual cost, trend analysis, and project summary (e.g., Figure 16–13). *ARTEMIS* also provides materials management analysis and reporting, vendor tracking, and packaging of work details into job cards and task lists. The *ARTEMIS* data base can also be used in records management for such applications as change control, configuration management, engineering, and drawings control (Figure 16–14).

The interactive query nature of the *ARTEMIS* language allows users to ask and get the answers to questions such as "what if material is delivered late?" or "what if laborers

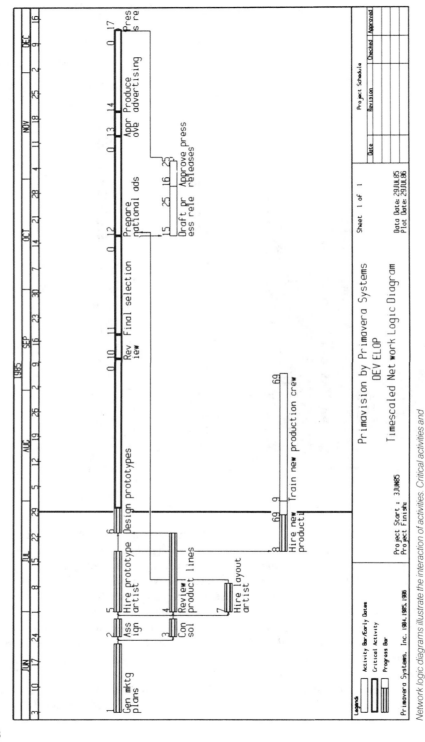

Network logic diagrams illustrate the interaction of activities. Critical activities and activity progress can be highlighted in color.

FIGURE 16–12. Primavera time-phased PERT network.

REPORT : SMM1S
COMPANY : ANY COMPANY - USA
PROJECT : DEMONSTRATION PROJECT

ACCOUNTING PERIOD: 8501

PAGE : 2
AS OF DATE : 31-JAN-85
REPORT DATE : 31-JAN-85

WPKG / Row	PREV %	PREV QTY	PREV COST	PREV CUM %	PREV CUM QTY	PREV CUM COST	MODE/TYPE	CUR %	CUR QTY	CUR COST	CUR CUM %	CUR CUM QTY	CUR CUM COST	AT COMPL QTY	AT COMPL COST
AC00100102 420DOCCTL LABOR — Discrete							T CP								
BCWS	6.2	327	4165	17.7	956	12155		5.4	280	3598	23.8	1236	15754	5188	68792
BCWP		324	4128		920	11695		7.0	375	4815	24.0	1294	16510		
AC00200201 310SYSSUP COMPUTER — Discrete							T C								
BCWS															6455
BCWP															
AC00200201 420DOCCTL LABOR — Discrete							T CP								
BCWS	4.1	2894	36885	25.9	17478	221496		5.1	3360	43179	31.4	20838	264675	66309	871743
BCWP		2735	34870		17197	217936		3.0	2038	26152	28.0	19235	244088		
AC00200202 310SYSSUP LABOR — Discrete							T CP								
BCWS	30.3	1832	34452	30.3	1832	34452		20.1	1020	19340	56.2	2852	53792	5076	96471
BCWP		1539	28941		1539	28941		22.0	1121	21224	52.0	2660	50165		
AC00200202 420DOCCTL LABOR — Discrete							T Q								
BCWS														14067	188408
BCWP															
AC00200202 430TCHWRT LABOR — Discrete							T CP								
BCWS	7.1	1774	24553	50.8	11280	155099		8.0	1720	24006	60.6	13000	179105	21447	299360
BCWP		1513	20955		10888	149680		6.0	1290	17962	56.0	12178	167641		
AD002001 210SCHDUL COMPUTER — Discrete							T CP								
BCWS	3.0		80000	22.0		502000		3.7		80000	26.9		582000		2166000
BCWP			64980			476520		8.0		173280	30.0		649800		
AD002001 210SCHDUL LABOR — Level of Effort							T Q								
BCWS	4.0	1774	29556	25.4	11324	187454		3.9	1730	29066	29.3	13054	216520	44532	767934
BCWP		1774	29556		11324	187454		3.9	1730	29066	29.3	13054	216520		
AD002001 230CNFMGT LABOR — Discrete							T CP								
BCWS	4.1	1774	27703	26.0	10434	162031		4.4	1710	26929	31.4	12144	188960	38647	623916
BCWP		1599	24957		10048	155979		3.0	1190	18717	28.0	11238	174696		
AD002002 220CSTMGT COMPUTER — Discrete							T CP								
BCWS	1.0		10110	36.0		206000		29.2		173000	63.9		379000		593001
BCWP			5930			213480		22.0		130460	58.0		343940		
AD002002 220CSTMGT LABOR — Level of Effort							T Q								
BCWS	6.8	992	15026	31.9	4637	69892		5.6	820	12524	37.6	5457	82416	14526	225805
BCWP		992	15026		4637	69892		5.6	820	12524	37.6	5457	82416		

FIGURE 16-13. ARTEMIS earned value report.

DRAWINGS AND CHANGES

XYZ Contractors Inc.

Singapore Office Building

REPORT: REP13

PAGE: 1   DATE: 30-APR-85

ACTIVITY		DRAWING NUMBER	DRAWING DESCRIPTION	CHG. NO.	CHANGE DESCRIPTION	CHANGE COST
4	CLEAR AND GRADE	S14320	Site Plan			-
4	CLEAR AND GRADE	S14352	Drainage Schematic			-
4	CLEAR AND GRADE	S14810	Foundation Layout			-
50	STEEL & DECK ERECTION NORTH	122001	Girder layout plan			-
50	STEEL & DECK ERECTION NORTH	122002	12" beam layout	1	Adjust beams to 16" center	67000
50	STEEL & DECK ERECTION NORTH	122003	16" beam layout			-
50	STEEL & DECK ERECTION NORTH	122004	Girder & beam detail joint	1	Delete beam reinforcing	-34000
50	STEEL & DECK ERECTION NORTH	FL3765	North Floor Plan			-
50	STEEL & DECK ERECTION NORTH	ST0342	North Girder Layout	1	Replace 6" beams with 8"	45000
52	STEEL & DECK ERECTION CENTER	FL3766	Center Floor Plan			-
52	STEEL & DECK ERECTION CENTER	ST0343	Center Girder Layout	1	Replace 6" beams with 8"	38000
54	STEEL & DECK ERECTION SOUTH	FL3767	South Floor Plan			-
54	STEEL & DECK ERECTION SOUTH	ST0344	South Girder Layout	1	Replace 6" beams with 8"	48000

FIGURE 16–14. ARTEMIS change report.

get a wage increase?" or "what if management imposes a new deadline?" In addition to standard reports, the system creates ad hoc and customized reports. *ARTEMIS* also has graphics capabilities to create histograms, piecharts, Gantt charts and network diagrams (e.g., Figure 16–15).

The range of capabilities of *ARTEMIS* vary greatly depending on the hardware. *ARTEMIS* for mainframes can handle projects with 256,000 activities; for minis it can handle 32,000; for micros, 2,000. One configuration is shown in Figure 16–16.

Project Software & Development Project/2®

Project/2® by Project Software and Development, Inc. (PSDI) is a high level language and application package which handles projects with up to 32,767 activities and unlimited resources. It operates on a range of equipment including DEC VAX or IBM 3000 and 4300 class computers. *Project/2* integrates project planning, scheduling, and cost management functions with graphics and relational data base capabilities. It is designed to cover the full range of planning and control activities over the project life cycle (Figure 16–17).

The system checks for errors in input and network logic. Over 60 standard reports, all of which can be customized, are available including tables, bar charts, curves and histograms. Plotter graphics are available for network diagrams, histograms, curves, Gantt charts, and logical bar charts.

Project/2 is comprised of several modules which can be integrated or used independently. The main modules are for schedule, cost, graphics, and relational data base. Data base information can be accessed and transferred among all modules. Standard scheduling features include calculating original and updated schedules, time progress reporting, multiple calendars, resource assignment and resource leveling, and "what if" analyses (Figure 16–18). Levels within a schedule can be defined so project, intermediate, and detail level schedules can be integrated. Both time-limited and resource-limited scheduling can be performed. Advanced scheduling features include discontinuous scheduling, resource assignment to portions of activities, advanced leveling techniques, automatic network generation, sequence scheduling, and probabilistic risk analysis.

The cost module allows for cost breakdowns according to project work (WBS) and project responsibility (organization breakdown). For each element of the breakdown, a three-dimensional spreadsheet is available to calculate and store user defined cost types and categories, such as original and revised budget, commitment, actual, forecast, and variance figures. Data entered into higher level elements can be allocated to lower-level elements. It can perform cost ratings, create distribution of project data, and calculate cumulative and grand totals for forecasting, trend analysis, and earned value analysis (e.g., Figure 16–19).

The graphics module produces Gantt charts, network and WBS diagrams, cost account bar charts, cash flow curves, histograms, and others (e.g., Figure 16–20). With the relational data base, tables of related items such as drawings, purchase orders, materials inventory, and contracts can be linked together for easier tracking and control.

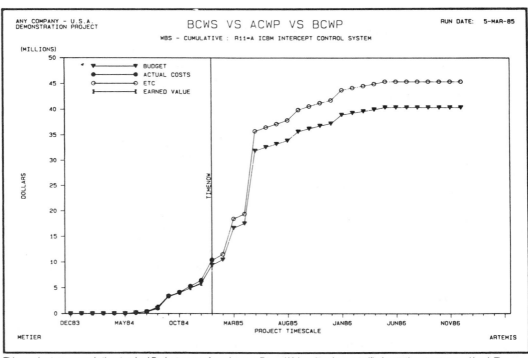

This x,y chart or s-curve is the standard Budget versus Actual versus Earned Value chart by a specified reporting structure and level. The values in this chart are cumulative.

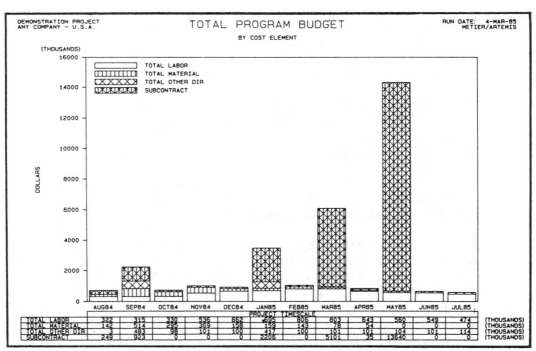

Histogram of cost elements with table values. This is a stacked histogram as defined by Reporting Structure Three (Cost Elements) over time. Cost Element Quantities are included in the table below the histogram.

FIGURE 16–15. ARTEMIS graphics.

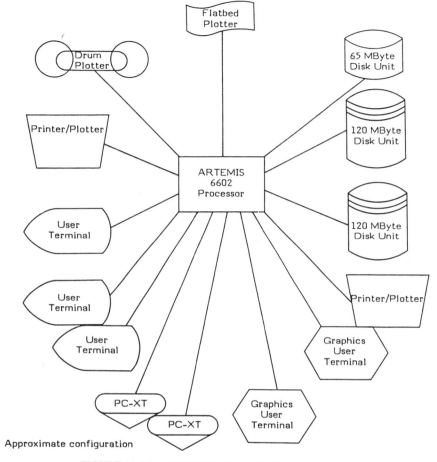

FIGURE 16–16.   ARTEMIS configuration for very large projects.

16.6 APPLYING COMPUTER PMI SYSTEMS

PMIS in the Project Life Cycle

A good computer PMIS can assist the project manager throughout all phases of the project life cycle. Referring to Figure 16–17, you can see the range of managerial tasks and functions where a PMIS can help. Following are ways a sophisticated PMIS with both dedicated project management and general purpose software are applied in project management.

Conceptual.   During the conceptual phase, mathematical/statistical and "thought organizer" software are employed for feasibility analysis, cost-benefit studies,

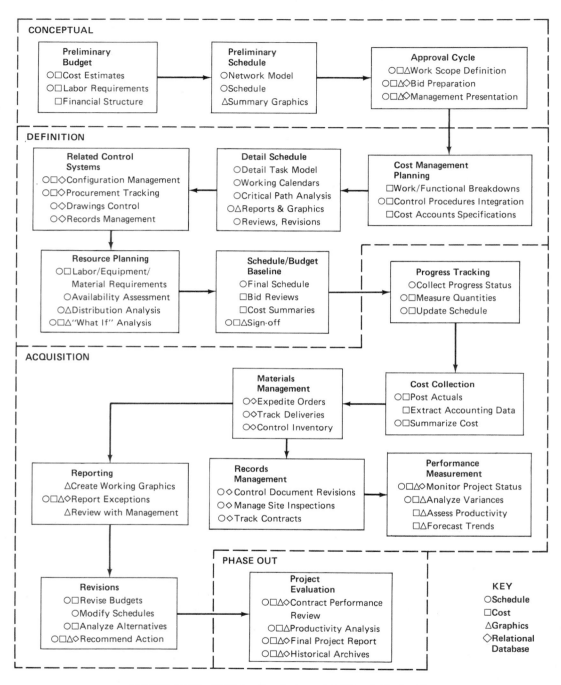

FIGURE 16–17. PMIS functions in the project life cycle (Project/2).

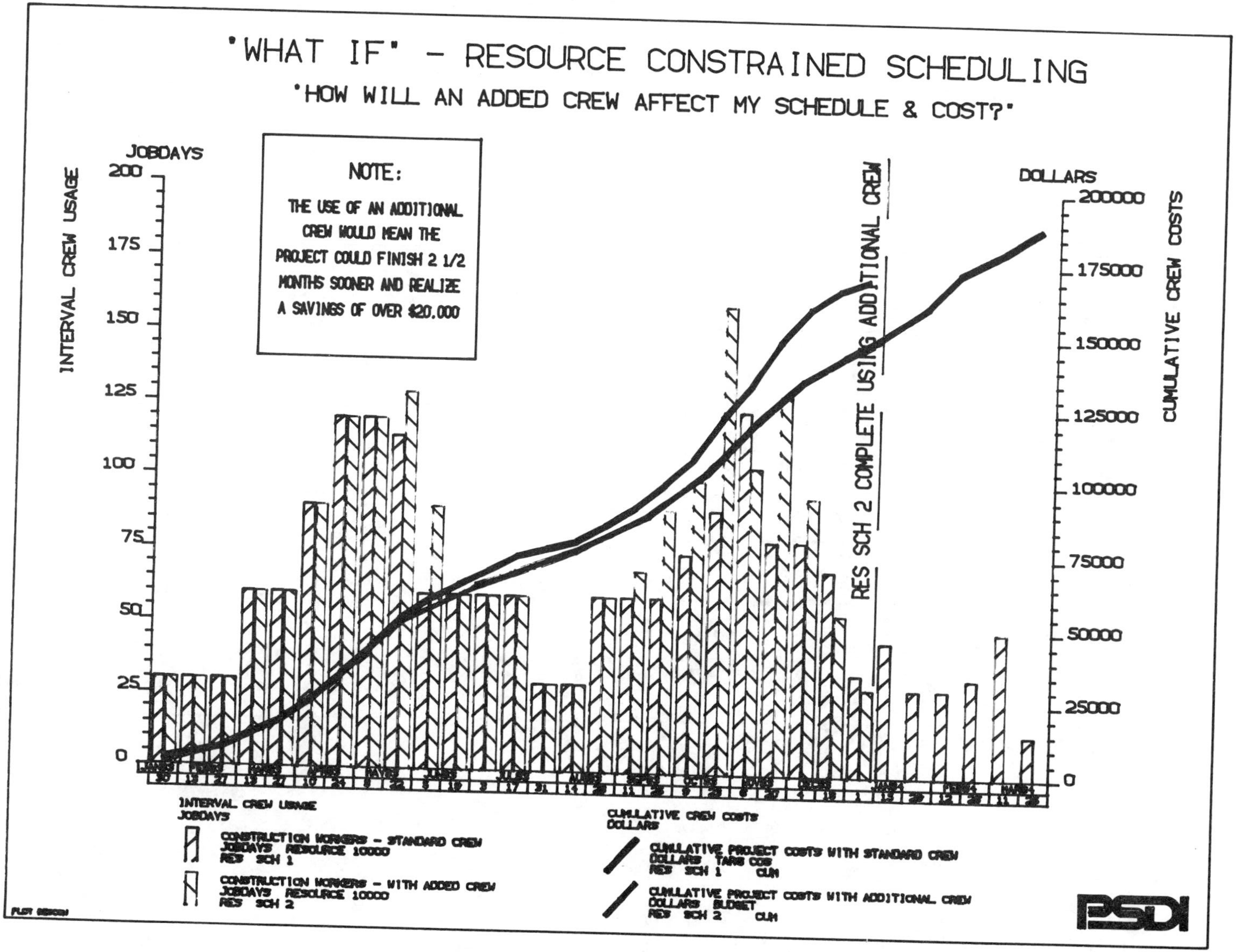

FIGURE 16-18. Project/2 what if analysis.

435

```
PROJECT/2 INTEGRATED PROGRAM MANAGEMENT SYSTEM                                                              PAGE    1

                              C O S T   A C C O U N T   E X C E P T I O N   R E P O R T

CONTRACT NAME:  AERO                      CURRENT PERIOD:   31JAN87  TO 27FEB87                 DATE:  27FEB87 2041
TO:                                                   CC:
------------------------------------------------------------------------------------------------------------------
Cost Account: 1.1.1.1.01        Description: PRELIMINARY DESIGN
                                                          |         Per Period Variance & Tolerance
                                           Variance       |      Schedule Variance      |       Cost Variance
                                    ----------------------|-----------------------------------------------------
     Type of Problem                |     $      |   %    |  Period    |     $       |   %   |     $      |   %   |
                                    |---------------------|-----------------------------------------------------|
[ ]  Cum. To Date Schedule (BCWP-BCWS) | -31599.00 | -25.5 | Current Mon |  -10222.20  | -27.9 |  -100.91  |  -0.4 |
                                    |            |        |            |             |       |            |       |
                                    |            |        | tolr range | 5000  -5000 | 25 -25 | 5000  -5000 | 10 -10 |
[ ]  Cum. To Date Cost (BCWP-ACWP)  |  -3190.84  |  -3.5  |-----------------------------------------------------|
                                    |            |        | Last Mon   |   18943.20  | -56.0 |  -3013.99  | -10.7 |
                                    |            |        |            |             |       |            |       |
[ ]  Cost at Compl. (BAC-EAC)       |  -3190.84  |   0.0  | tolr range | 5000  -5000 | 30 -30 | 5000  -5000 | 10 -10 |
                                    |            |        |-----------------------------------------------------|
                                    |            |        | Mon Bfr Last|  -28080.00 | -100.0 |     0.00   |   0.0 |
[ ]  Technical Performance          ----------------------|            |             |       |            |       |
                                                          | tolr range | 5000  -5000 | 10 -10 | 5000  -5000 | 30 -30 |
                                                          |-----------------------------------------------------|
                                                          |  NSS = Not Scheduled to Start     NWP = No Work yet Performed

------------------------------------------------------------------------------------------------------------------
```

FIGURE 16–19. Project/2 cost analysis reports.

PROJECT/2 INTEGRATED PROGRAM MANAGEMENT SYSTEM

CONTRACT NAME: AERO

S T A T I S T I C A L   A N A L Y S I S   R E P O R T

CURRENT PERIOD: 31JAN87 TO 27FEB87   DATE: 27FEB87 1816

| COST ACCOUNT / WORK PACKAGE | BCWS | BCWP | ACWP | THIS PERIOD | | | | | | | TO DATE | | |
				COST VAR $	%	SCHED VAR $	%	PERF INDICES CPI	SPI	S/C	PERF INDICES CPI	SPI	S/C
CA 1.1.1.01 PRELIMINARY DESIGN													
WP 01 CONCEPTUAL DRAWING											1.00	1.00	1.00
WP 02 DESIGN LAYOUT		12240	11812	428	3	12240		1.04			1.03	1.00	1.03
WP 03 DESIGN PREPARATION	31104	9137	8905	232	3	-21967	-71	1.03	0.29	0.30	0.89	0.45	0.40
WP 04 COMPUTER MODELING	5500	5005	5766	-761	-15	-495	-9	0.87	0.91	0.79	0.87	0.91	0.79
1.1.1.01 TOTAL	36604	26382	26483	-101	0	-10222	-28	1.00	0.72	0.72	0.97	0.74	0.72
CA 1.1.1.03 STRUCTURES DESIGN DEVELOPMENT													
WP 01 PRELIMINARY STRUCTURAL DESI	42358	26428	23501	2927	11	-15930	-38	1.12	0.62	0.70	0.91	0.73	0.66
WP 02 PROTOTYPE MODEL - GRAPHICS	11000	11000	10899	101	1			1.01	1.00	1.01	1.01	1.00	1.01
WP 03 PROTOTYPE MODEL	28771	28771	28615	156	1			1.01	1.00	1.01	1.02	2.00	2.04
WP 04 PROTOTYPE MODEL - MATERIAL	57500	57500	60291	-2791	-5			0.95	1.00	0.95	0.95	1.00	0.95
WP 05 MATERIAL EVALUATION - STUDY	9331	9331	10157	-826	-9			0.92	1.00	0.92	1.04	1.00	1.04
WP 06 STRUCTURAL DESIGN ANALYSIS	4274	4274	4589	-315	-7			0.93	1.00	0.93	0.93	1.00	0.93
1.1.1.03 TOTAL	153234	137304	138052	-748	-1	-15930	-10	0.99	0.90	0.89	0.96	0.95	0.91

FIGURE 16-19. (Continued).

COST PERFORMANCE REPORT - WORK BREAKDOWN STRUCTURE

CONTRACTOR: PROJECT SOFTWARE	CONTRACT TYPE/NO.:	PROGRAM NAME/NUMBER:	REPORT PERIOD:	SIGNATURE, TITLE & DATE:	FORM APPROVED
LOCATION: CAMBRIDGE, MA	CPIF/XX-1003	AERO KZ-1027	ENDING 27FEB87		OMB NUMBER 22R0280
RDT&E [X] PRODUCTION [ ]					

QUANTITY	NEGOTIATED COST	EST COST AUTH, UNPRICED WORK	TGT PROFIT/FEE %	TGT PRICE	EST PRICE	SHARE RATIO	CONTRACT CEILING	EST CONTRACT CEILING
1	650175	0	32509/5%	682684	720530	80/20	N/A	N/A

ITEM	CURRENT PERIOD BUDGET COST WORK SCHE	BUDGET COST WORK PERF	ACTL COST WORK PERF	VARIANCE SCHE	VARIANCE COST	CUMULATIVE TO DATE BUDGET COST WORK SCHE	BUDGET COST WORK PERF	ACTL COST WORK PERF	VARIANCE SCHE	VARIANCE COST	REPROGRAMMING ADJUSTMENTS COST VARIANCE	BUDGET	AT COMPLETION BUDGET	LATEST REVIS ESTIMT	VARIANCE
(1)	(2)	(3)	(4)	(5)	(6)	(7)	(8)	(9)	(10)	(11)	(12)	(13)	(14)	(15)	(16)
WORK BREAKDOWN STRUCTURE															
PHOENIX AIRCRAFT															
1.0 AIR VEHICLE	19341	18030	20106	-1312	-2076	117105	134746	151221	17640	-16475	0	0	244510	271326	-26815
2.0 DATA	9464	7994	8032	-1470	-38	39875	33297	34445	-6578	-1148	0	0	98723	96555	2167
3.0 COMMON SUPPORT EQUI	7618	8631	8497	1013	134	47457	52688	54286	5231	-1598	0	0	117441	126280	-8839
4.0 SYSTEM ENGINEERING	4491	4510	4528	19	-18	22431	21870	22056	-561	-186	0	0	46384	45370	1014
TOTAL PHOENIX AIRCRAFT	40915	39165	41163	-1750	-1998	226868	242601	262009	15733	-19408	0	0	507058	539531	-32472
COST OF MONEY	818	783	823	-35	-40	4537	4852	5240	315	-388	-	-	10141	10791	-649
GEN AND ADMIN	3682	3525	3705	-158	-180	20418	21834	23581	1416	-1747	-	-	45635	48558	-2923
UNDISTRIBUTED BUDGET	/////	/////	/////	/////	/////	/////	/////	/////	/////	/////	/////	/////	57340	/////	/////
SUBTOTAL	45416	43473	45691	-1943	-2218	251824	269287	290830	17464	-21543	-	-	620175	656219	-36044
MANAGEMENT RESERVE	/////	/////	/////	/////	/////	/////	/////	/////	/////	/////	/////	/////	30000	30000	0
TOTAL	45416	43473	45691	-1943	-2218	251824	269287	290830	17464	-21543	-	-	650175	686219	-36044
RECONCILIATION TO CONTRACT BUDGET BASE															
VARIANCE ADJUSTMENT	/////	/////	/////	/////	/////	/////	/////	/////	/////	/////	-	-	/////	/////	/////
TOT CONTRACT VARIANCE	/////	/////	/////	/////	/////	/////	/////	/////	/////	/////	-	-	-	-	-

(DOLLARS IN 1000'S)

FORMAT 1

FIGURE 16–19. (Continued).

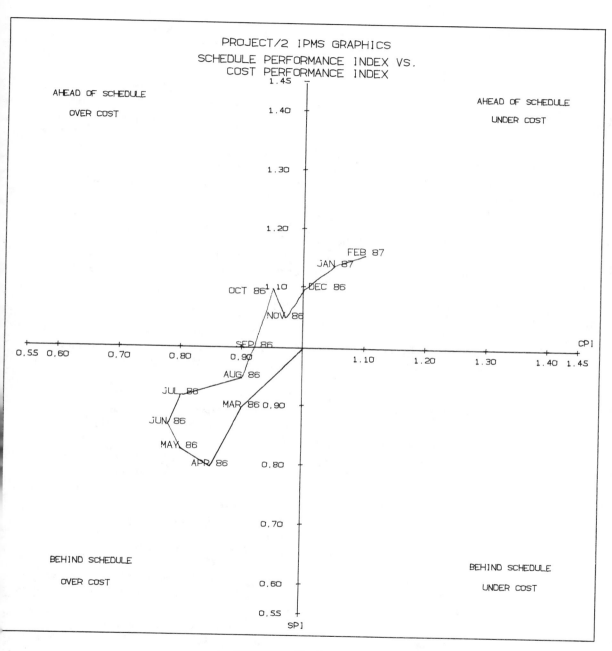

FIGURE 16–20. Project/2 CPI vs. SPI.

and assistance in project development. Dedicated PMI software is used to model variations of the work breakdown structure, to create preliminary budgets and schedules, and to prepare documents and presentations to management. Integrated software combining data base, spreadsheet, word processing, and graphics are used for performing tradeoff and feasibility studies and preparing proposal and contract documents.

Definition.   Once objectives and work tasks have been defined, they are input to dedicated PMI software to check precedence relationships and to produce networks and Gantt charts with schedule dates, slack times, and critical path. These outputs are used for detailed analysis to determine necessary resources and to prepare more detailed schedules and budgets. A dedicated PMIS performs "what if" analyses to evaluate the interactive effects of altering project scope, resources, and schedules, and to prepare a final baseline plan specifying the cost-account structure, detailed work tasks, labor/equipment/material requirements, and final schedules down to the work task level.

Acquisition.   Once the project is underway, current information is input to the project data base of a dedicated PMIS so it can be compared to the baseline plan and project progress tracked. Computer generated reports and graphics help facilitate comprehension and communication of progress information. Key parameters held in the system monitor performance and give warnings whenever variances move outside tolerable limits. The PMIS provides cost and schedule forecasts based on current project performance, and helps the project manager develop scenarios about alternative, corrective strategies. It also helps her identify and investigate opportunities to reduce costs or finish early by altering resources or schedules. A PMIS linked to purchasing and inventory files assists in expediting orders, tracking deliveries, and controlling inventories.

The PMIS enables the manager to take corrective action by providing timely, accurate reports of deviations from cost, schedule, or technical performance objectives. Information is rapidly reported to upper management and the user when critical decisions affecting project objectives, scope, and resources must be made. The computer is especially useful when decisions must be evaluated about resource transfers which affect multiple projects. Mathematical and statistical packages are used to model problems and assess alternatives.

When changes must be made, dedicated PMI systems that integrate time, cost, and resources help managers make revisions to schedules, budgets, and plans, and report them to project participants. Design changes and their effects on project plans are swiftly communicated using computer generated change documents.

Phase-Out, Termination.   During phase-out, the PMIS is used for reviewing requirements to insure contract commitments have been fulfilled. The PMIS is used with the word processor to create the final project report document. Throughout the project, all information—from original studies and the baseline plan, to the most recent plan for completion—has been stored in the project data base. This information, properly organized, provides a complete set of project archives. Maintaining such archives is an important, though often neglected, function of project management. If the data base is indexed by date, critical information about any stage or element of the project can be retrieved and sequenced into a series of "snapshots" to outline the project's history. This information can be assembled to provide a portion of the postcompletion project summary (described in the next chapter).

Example: Sigma Associates' PMIS for Project Planning and Control

Sigma Associates, the architectural/engineering firm mentioned in Chapter 14, relies on a computerized PMIS for most of its planning and control functions. So ubiquitous is Sigma's PMIS that employees think of it as a member of the team; they call it "Sally." Recall from Chapter 14 that each project manager uses Sally, the PMIS, to help estimate project labor requirements, to create original project schedules, and to adjust schedules to make allowances for labor availability. The comptroller uses Sally to forecast labor expenses, overhead costs, and to prepare project budgets. Information combined from the two constitutes the project plan.

Once a project is approved Sally's function changes from planning assistance to monitoring and control. Sally's major purpose is to routinely compare the project plan with actual performance, to raise warnings about discrepancies, and to forecast project outcomes (schedule and cost at completion). Sally "knows" the original project plan because labor hours, labor cost budgets, schedules, and activity completion dates are input at the beginning of the project.

Each week, information about current costs is input to Sally. Labor expense information taken directly from time cards is used to estimate the weekly time spent on each activity. Nonlabor expenses and client reimbursements are input through the company's general ledger system.

Project managers make biweekly estimates of hours anticipated to complete each activity. Sally converts the anticipated hours to-complete into a percentage completed for each activity. The system multiplies budgeted labor hours by the percentage completed to determine the estimated labor hours intended to bring the activity to its current level of completion (a form of BCWP). By comparing this estimate with actual labor expenditures from time cards, the project manager can determine whether the activity is moving at its budgeted pace.

Sally makes these comparisons and reports discrepancies. Project managers employ these reports to spot problems and locate causes. Sally also revises and reports the cost and date of the project at completion.

When project managers fail to make the biweekly estimates of anticipated hours, Sally makes its own estimates based upon the amount of labor hours that were charged since the last time anticipated hours were input.

Sally uses the anticipated hours to-complete to prepare estimates of labor requirement loads for the remainder of the project. These estimates are used to adjust the remaining labor loadings and to make necessary revisions to schedules.

The comptroller also uses Sally to forecast the timing and amounts of client billing, and even the timing of expected payments according to each client's payment history. Based on the percentage of work completed, the system computes an estimate of earned client fees. These fees are compared to actual labor costs, overhead costs, and nonlabor expenses in a monthly profit/loss analysis. Sally does the computation and generates monthly reports of net profit for project-to-date and year-to-date, summarized by office, department, and project manager. It also combines net profit for all projects to give a picture of the company's financial health.

Sally is also able to satisfy one time needs. If a project manager sees costs running higher than expected because of an improper personnel mix, he can request a report showing the personnel assigned to the project and the extent of their involvement. The comptroller can delve deep into cost details by requesting reports, such as one showing the printing expenses for a building design. Though not a part of Sally's standard output, these reports are easy to produce because of the system's versatile data retrieval capabilities.

Sally also checks much of its input, for example, that the number of hours charged on time cards is correct. Hours charged are compared with dates on the schedule. A card with discrepancies is withheld and a memo describing the error is sent to the employee. A summary report of rejected or uncorrected cards is sent each week to the comptroller.

Sally is an example of a sophisticated, comprehensive PMIS: it serves all the functions (and more) that might be expected of a dedicated PMIS. As pointed out before, not all dedicated PMIS's are so comprehensive.

Fitting the PMIS to the Project

Though most PMI packages (especially for PC's) are no match for the capabilities of Sally, that is not a problem if these capabilities are not required. Just as the project team should carefully plan and define the project before it begins, so it should plan and define the information requirements of the PMIS; the PMIS it then chooses should be the one that satisfies these requirements most economically and effectively.

The idea of having a computer PMIS, in the words of Palla, is to "get the right information to the right person at the right time so the right decision can be made for the project."[15] Whatever kind of PMIS is able to do this is the right one. But, as alluded earlier, making this decision is not easy. When a computer PMIS is being chosen and implemented for the first time it is a good idea to start out with a small-scale project and a limited PMIS application—a "prototype" system that can be developed quickly and at low cost to test its feasibility. The project staff should carefully evaluate the productivity of the system to determine how well it fulfills the information requirements of the test project. The evaluation should indicate what features need to be added or enhanced, or if the system should be discontinued and a new system tried instead.

Choosing, developing, and implementing a PMIS is a *project* and so it is very appropriate to apply the project management principles espoused in this book to insure that it fulfills its goals and satisfies its users. Once the system is installed, someone who is knowledgeable should be held accountable for its operation—if not the project manager, then the project controller, or a special project information systems coordinator.

Many firms use more than one kind of PMI package—for example, a Category 2 package for smaller projects and a Category 3 package for large ones. Some firms rely on a highly user-friendly package to help clients feel comfortable with the output data, then transfer the data to a more powerful package for planning and control.[16]

16.7 SUMMARY

Modern methods of project planning and control require a system, manual or computerized, to handle information efficiently. Some kind of system is necessary for integrating multifunctional tasks and for tieing schedules, costs, and work performance together. Such a system is the Project Management Information System or PMIS.

For most projects, major project management functions of scheduling, budgeting, and control are greatly facilitated by using computer PMI systems. For managing medium- and large-scale projects, computers have become essential. In recent years, PC's and low cost, high quality software have made computer PMIS's commonplace. A myriad of computer tools are available for application in project management, including general purpose tools like spreadsheets, data base managers, and word processing. While these are useful for handling portions of information management in projects, the best computer project management tools are dedicated PMIS's developed exclusively to fit the unique information requirements of projects.

Most dedicated PMIS's offer such features as network scheduling, resource management, budgeting, and to a lesser extent, cost control and performance analysis. The capabilities of available PMIS software vary greatly, and while all can be used for project planning, many cannot be used for project control. A sophisticated PMIS should be able to assist in numerous planning and control tasks throughout the entire project life cycle, from conception to close out. Among commercially available PMIS's, there is considerable variation in technical capabilities, flexibility, ease of use, and interface and integration capability. As a result, their usefulness varies greatly.

Most smaller computer PMIS's, like the ones described in this chapter, assist in scheduling, budgeting, resource allocation, and, to a lesser extent, project control. Most larger computer PMIS's provide integrated planning, scheduling, costing, control, and reporting functions. These systems utilize practically all of the planning and control techniques described in this book.

This chapter concludes the discussion of project planning and control. The next chapter discusses the topics of project evaluation and reporting, and the last stage of the project life cycle, project termination.

CHAPTER REVIEW QUESTIONS

1. What is the role of the PMIS in project management? Describe the differences between a PMIS and an ordinary MIS.

2. What are some of the information requirements of projects?

3. Why has the computer become an almost essential tool in project planning and control? What kinds of managerial functions are better performed using a computer PMIS?

4. What are the major advantages of computer PMIS's over manual PMIS's?

5. Discuss why many project managers still do not use computer PMI systems.

6. Discuss kinds of general purpose software which can be used in project management. What are their limitations as PMI systems?

7. List the major features available on commercial dedicated PMIS software.

8. What capabilities must a PMIS have so that it can be used for the function of project control?

9. Discuss the uses of the PMIS throughout the phases of the project life cycle.

10. Discuss the considerations in selecting and implementing a computer PMIS.

QUESTIONS ABOUT THE STUDY PROJECT

1. Describe the PMIS used in the project you are studying. Was it the same one used for cost-accounting (PCAS) and project scheduling? Does it combine scheduling, budgeting, authorization, and control, or were several different systems used? If several systems were used, how were they integrated?

2. What are the strong and weak points of the system? Does the system adequately satisfy the information requirements needed to plan and control the project? Are inadequacies in the system the fault of the computer PMIS, or of the manual support system which provides inputs and utilizes the outputs? What improvements would you suggest to the system?

3. If a computer PMIS is not being used, why? How effective is the current manual system and what parts of it could be supplemented or replaced by a computer system? Given the information requirements of the project, what kinds of available PMIS software might be appropriate? How would you suggest going about implementing a computer PMIS for this organization?

ENDNOTES

1. For example, see E.S. Gardner, "Project Manager, Part 1" and "Project Manager, Part 2" in the January and February 1988 issues of *Lotus*.

2. See J.L. Harrington, *Relational Database Management for Microcomputers: Design and Implementation* (New York: Holt, Rinehart, Winston), 1987; R.W. Palla, "Introduction to Micro-computer Software Tools for Project Management," *Project Management Journal* (August 1987), 61–68.

3. D. Roman, *Managing Project: A Systems Approach* (New York: Elsevier), 1986, 181, 184; L.F. Suarez, "Resource Allocation: A Comparative Study," *Project Management Journal*, Vol. 18, No. 1, (March 1987), 68–71.

4. H.A. Levine, *Project Management Using Microcomputers* (Berkeley, Ca.: Osborne McGraw-Hill, 1986), 7.

5. Ibid.

6. H. Kerzner and H.J. Thamhain, "Commercially Available Project Tracking Systems," *Project Management Journal* (September 1986), 89–97; H.A. Levine, *Project Management Using Microcomputers*, 67–88.

7. J. Gido, *Project Management Software Directory* (New York: Industrial Press, 1985); H.A. Levine, *Project Management Using Microcomputers*.

8. Edward Wasil and Arjang Assad, "Project Management on the PC: Software, Applications, and Trends," *Interfaces*, Vol. 18, No.2 (March–April, 1988), 75–84.

9. Materials in this section are used with the permission of Symantec Corporation, Breakthrough Software Division, Novato, CA.

10. Materials in this section are used with the permission of Microsoft Corp., Redmond, WA.

11. See, for example, A. Assad and E. Wasil, "Project Management Using a Microcomputer," *Computers and Operations Research*, Vol. 13, No. 2/3 (1986), 231–260; M. Faust, "Firms Looking for Flexibility in Programs to Manage Resources," *PC Week*, Vol. 3, No. 42 (1986), 83–101; H. Kerzner and H.J. Thamhain, "Commercially Available Project Tracking Systems"; K. Rogers O'Neal, "Second Annual Buyer's Guide Lists Latest Project Management Microcomputer Software," *Industrial Engineering*, Vol. 19, No. 1 (January 1987), 53–63; and *Software Digest*, Vol.4, No. 7 (February 1987).

12. Materials in this section are used with the permission of Primavera Systems, Inc., Bala Cynwyd, PA.

13. Materials in this section are used with the permission of Metier Management Systems, Inc., Houston, TX.

14. Materials in this section is used with the permission of Project Software & Development, Inc., Cambridge, MA.

15. R.W. Palla, "Introduction to Microcomputer Software Tools for Project Information Management," 64.

16. Wasil and Assad, "Project Management on the PC: Software, Applications, and Trends," 76.

chapter 17

Project Evaluation, Reporting, and Termination

We look at it and we do not see it.

Lao-tzu, 6th century B.C.

In project environments the work must be tracked, evaluated, and corrected so that schedules, expenditures, and technical performance can all be kept on target. The project manager oversees the work, assesses progress, and issues instructions for corrective action. As information is received, the project manager judges the status of the project and communicates this to workers, upper management, and the client. Chapters 15 and 16 examined the kinds of information and the measures used for assessing and controlling project performance. The first part of this chapter discusses how that information is reviewed and reported for purposes of evaluation and decision making.

As the project draws to a conclusion, the project manager must ensure that all work is formally closed out, all commitments are met or compensated for, and all remaining "loose ends" are tied up. The second portion of this chapter reviews the project manager's responsibilities in terminating the project and in performing post-project follow-up work and summary evaluation.

17.1 PROJECT EVALUATION

Projects are open systems—they are goal-oriented and utilize feedback information to determine how well they are doing and when they should alter their courses of action. The primary purpose of evaluation in project management is to reveal areas where the project is deviating from goals and to uncover extant or potential problems so they can be corrected. Although it is certain that problems and deviations will occur, it is not known a priori where or when.

Evaluation also serves the purpose of summarizing project status and keeping interested parties informed. Upper management and the customer want to know how the project is progressing, and project personnel need to be kept abreast of project status and work changes. Once the project is completed, the evaluation's purpose is to summarize and assess the outcome.

Two kinds of evaluation occur in projects. One, *formative evaluation*, happens throughout the project life cycle and provides information to guide corrective action. The other, *summary evaluation*, occurs after the project is completed and focuses on the end product or result. Formative evaluation is designed to help pilot the project as it progresses. It asks the questions "What is happening?" and "How is the project proceeding?" Summary evaluation is designed to appraise the project after it is completed. It addresses the questions "What happened?" and "What were the results?"

Project Formative Evaluation

Project formative evaluation must take into account the fact that projects are complex systems: cost, schedule, and work performance criteria are interrelated, and work packages are interdependent and draw from the same pool of limited resources. As a result, well-intended corrective measures that focus exclusively on just one performance criteria are likely to cause problems in others. Similarly, attempts directed solely at improving performance in one work area can have detrimental effects on others. To provide information which realistically portrays the status of the project and enables the project manager to draw accurate conclusions, project evaluation must incorporate three performance criteria simultaneously—cost, schedule, and technical performance—and account for the impact that changes in one work area will have on other related areas. The evaluation process must be able to signal potential trouble spots so action can be initiated before problems are realized. The best kind of evaluation does not just reveal the problems, it points out opportunities to reduce costs, speed up work, or enhance project outcomes in other ways.

Methods and Measures

A variety of methods, measures, and sources should be used to obtain evaluation information. These methods and measures should be specified before the project begins and included in the project plan. Methods and indicators for measuring schedule, cost, and technical performance were described in Chapters 15 and 16.

By relying on a variety of methods and measures (as opposed to just a few) the project manager can more readily spot problems and opportunities. Variety in the sources of information increases the validity of the evaluation, particularly when several sources all lead to the same conclusion.

The four primary ways for obtaining and/or conveying project evaluative information are graphics (charts and tables), reports (oral and written), observations, and review meetings.

Charts and tables are the most expeditious way for displaying cost, schedule, and work performance information. Their advantage is they reduce large amounts of complex information into simple, comprehensible formats. They clarify information on project progress, performance, and future predictions. The charts and tables used in the previous three chapters, particularly the computer generated ones, are good examples. When distributed and prominently displayed they allow everyone to appreciate the current status and direction of the project.

The danger of charts is that they can hide or obscure information and lead to facile and erroneous conclusions. For example, it was noted earlier that since project level charts tend to hide problems at the work package level, conclusions need to be substantiated by more detailed work package level analysis. Also, charts and tables neither reveal the underlying causes of problems nor suggest opportunities. The project manager also has to rely on additional sources of evaluative information, such as personal reports and first hand observation. Charts and tables often require substantial time to prepare and update, and their information value has to be viewed with this tradeoff in mind. Using computerized PMIS's with graphics capability reduces this problem.

Oral reports about project status and performance are another source of evaluative information. These are easy and quick to obtain, but their quality and reliability depends on the interpretative and verbal skills of the presenter. Unless followed by a written report, verbal information easily gets lost or garbled.

Written reports are valuable but their quality and usefulness also varies. Written reports are most effective when they are succinct, summarize information, and make use of ratios and graphics to highlight important points. During the planning phase, the format and timing for all key written evaluation documents should be specified.

The more channels information must pass through to get from sender to receiver, the more distorted the information gets. The project manager can reduce information distortion by increased firsthand observation and on-site contact with supervisors and workers. Not only does this reduce the filtering associated with upward communication, it helps maintain the workers' sense of importance about their contribution to the project. Good project managers do not live in their offices; they are usually on-site. Of course, one person cannot be in all places at all times, and the larger and more geographically disperse the project, the relatively fewer places the project manager can visit, even on an infrequent basis.

All of the above are useful and important ways to obtain and convey evaluative information. Still another way, one of the most important, is the project review meeting.

17.2 PROJECT REVIEW MEETINGS

Purpose of Review Meetings

The main function of *project review meetings* is to identify where the project is deviating from the plan so corrective action can quickly be taken. During these meetings, participants focus on (1) current problems with the work, schedule or costs, and how they should be resolved, (2) problems likely to arise in the future, and (3) opportunities to improve project performance.

Review meetings are the managerial equivalent to the "Quality Circle" groups used in production environments. The purpose of QC groups is to get the people most closely associated with the job—the workers—to (1) identify quality and production related problems and opportunities for work improvement, (2) develop ways to resolve problems and take advantage of opportunities, and (3) implement them. (In larger projects, the use of both managerial review meetings and QC groups helps to identify and resolve problems that either alone would miss.)

To be effective, review meetings should be scheduled both periodically, weekly or monthly, as well as at specific times, as required. Monthly reviews should be scheduled after people have had an opportunity to scrutinize the most recent cost and schedule summary reports. Before meetings, status reports and forecasted cost and time to-complete should be updated. Meetings should be brief and follow an established agenda.

The project manager must make sure that key individuals participate; this includes staff members, functional managers, and, when necessary, senior managers, line supervisors, and technicians. To insure high participation, attendants should be given assignments in advance and be prepared to make presentations.

To encourage maximum honesty and information sharing, the project manager should take on the role of group facilitator. Since the purpose of review meetings is to uncover bad news and problems, conflict and bad news should be expected and openly confronted. Attempts by the project manager to dominate meetings will be met with hostility and withdrawal by team members. Finger pointing, passing the blame, and smoothing over conflict should be avoided since they waste time, discourage attendance, and detract from the purpose of the meetings—to identify problems and reach agreement on which ones require action.

Taking Action

After problems are identified, an action plan is formulated immediately or preparations are made so it can be prepared later. In the latter case, the manager responsible for the action is named and a subsequent meeting is convened with only the affected individuals.

Each action plan includes a statement of the problem, objectives for resolving it, the required course of action, a target date, and who is responsible. Figure 17–1 shows a sample action plan. To assure coordination of work and commitment to the effort, approval should be sought from everyone who will contribute to or be affected by the action plan.

At every review meeting, problems should be documented and an action plan summary prepared. The action plan summary should indicate for each problem the actions to take, the people held responsible, and the target completion date. The status of every problem is evaluated at subsequent meetings with a review of actions taken and progress.

Special Reviews

Besides periodic reviews, special formal reviews are scheduled at critical stages or milestones on the project master schedule. Special reviews are held, for example, following

Problem Area	Objective	Actions	Who	When Completed
I. Planning and Scheduling	1. Establish backup support for each system.	1. (A) Discuss systems with analysts who support them; formulate plan for each system.	Project leaders and analysts	Jan. 1
	2. Review all systems. Eliminate those in nonuse; clean up others.	2. (A) Prepare questionnaire on system status.	Ron Gilmore	Nov. 15
		2. (B) Complete questionnaires.	Analysts and programmers	Dec. 1
		2. (C) Decide on status and specific actions.	PL, analysts and programmers	Jan. 31
	3. Provide information on purposes and uses of new project management system.	3. Prepare seminar on PMS and present to staff.	Joan Gibb	Before March 1

FIGURE 17–1.   Sample action plan.

completion of conceptual design, detailed design, and at the beginning of testing, production, or shipment. Sometimes special reviews are a precondition for work to be continued, such as in the phased project planning approach described earlier. During the review of the most recent phase, the decision is made about if and when the next phase is to begin.

Although the project team is responsible for accumulating information for reviews, an independent auditor should be charged with responsibility for overseeing reviews and making final assessments. To assure that information is accurate and unbiased, auditors should be unassociated with the project organization or prime contractor; they should, nonetheless, be intimately familiar with the workings of both.

Additionally, users should consider conducting their own special formal reviews and visitations to contractor facilities. They should maintain an informal dialogue with project personnel about project progress. The user must take responsibility for being the watchdog over the contractor, regardless of contractual obligations. After all, whenever a project gets into trouble it is the user who ultimately suffers the loss, no matter what the legal agreement says.

Project Meeting Room

Project related meetings and conferences are typically convened in a central meeting place or project office. As described earlier, this place serves as a physical reminder of the project and provides space for storing, preparing, and displaying project information. Gantt charts, project networks, and cost charts comparing planned and actual performance are permanently displayed for easy reference.

17.3 REPORTING

Company management must be kept apprised of the status, progress, and performance of all ongoing and upcoming projects. Problems affecting profits, schedules, or budgets, as well as causes, expected impacts, and recommended actions, should be reported promptly. The customer should also be periodically updated about project status and notified whenever major problems arise. Consideration should also be given to providing status reports to other stakeholders (those who have a perceived or genuine interest in the project), subject to the approval of management and cautions for confidentiality and privacy. These stakeholders include citizen, professional, and activist groups, public agencies, stockholders, and others who have a stake in project outcomes—its end-items, side effects or spin offs.

Reports to Top Management and the Office of Projects

Top management should be sent monthly progress reports summarizing project status. Suggested reports include:[1]

1. A brief statement summarizing the project status.
2. Red flag items where corrective action has or should be taken.
3. Accomplishments to date, changes to schedule, and projections for schedule and cost at completion.
4. Current and potential problem areas, actions required, and possible impacts.
5. Current cost situation and cost performance.
6. Manpower plan and limitations.

When several projects at once are authorized or underway, this information is used by management to maintain monthly summaries of the relative status of all projects. For each project the summary includes:[2] the names of the customer and the project manager; the investment in costs and manpower; scheduled start and finish dates; possible or likely risks, losses, and gains; and other information relating to top management review. The summary enables top management to assess the relative performance of all projects and their combined influence on the company. It also assists the project office in planning, coordination of authorizations, and resource allocation, and reduces the possibility of the firm overlooking key issues or overcommitting itself.

Reports to top management, prepared by the project manager or project staff, summarize the monthly status reports generated by the PCAS or PMIS.

Reports to Project and Program Managers

Reports to the project manager usually cover all second and lower level items on the WBS. They include the value of work completed to date, revised forecasts of costs at completion, and revised calendar schedules for completion (similar to Table 15–1 and Figure 15–7, aggregated up to second or third level items). The same kind of information is accumulated down to the work package level by the project manager or other control personnel in the project office. The project manager also receives monthly financial status reports showing costs incurred and cumulative planned versus actual costs (e.g., the information shown in Figure 16–7). These reports are also sent to the company financial manager or controller.

Reports to Functional Managers

Monthly status reports should be sent to functional managers showing man-hours and costs associated with work packages in their areas. The reports shown in Chapter 14, Figures 14–6 through 14–9, are representative.

Reports to Customers/Users

The project manager should also send monthly status reports to the customer. These reports should include recent changes as requested by the user or changes resulting from unavoidable events, and their impact on work scope, schedule, and cost. The reports should be presented in a format that is clear and understandable to the user. Requests or questions by the user should be quickly followed-up by the project manager.

Although frequently the company marketing or customer relations director is given the job of communicating contract related information to the customer, the project manager should take final responsibility for insuring that the customer is well informed about project status. The project manager is the person ultimately accountable for project performance and must answer to the user for project problems. Keeping the customer well-informed avoids later "surprises"; it helps ensure that claims are quickly settled and snags at termination are minimized.

17.4 TERMINATING THE PROJECT

Projects, by definition, are activities of limited duration; all projects come to an end. When this happens it is the project manager who ensures that all project related work has been completed and formally closed out by a specified date. It is the project manager's responsibility to put an end to the project—sometimes this is a tough requirement, especially when there is no follow-up project.

The Last Step

By the time the end-item has been delivered and installed, many people in the project team will have lost enthusiasm and be anxious to get on with something new. As a result, termination gets little attention as managers eagerly shift emphasis to new, upcoming projects, or scan the environment for leads about potential projects. Yet, as common sense should indicate, terminating a project is no less important than any other project activity. In fact (as Chapter 18 will show), the process of terminating a project is so critical that it can determine whether, ultimately, the project is a success or failure.

Termination occurs in a variety of ways; the best way is by a planned, systematic procedure; the worst is by an abrupt cancellation of work, slow attrition of effort, or higher priority projects siphoning off resources. In the latter cases the project goes sour: it is either terminated before goals are reached, or allowed to "limp along" and just fizzle out before completion. Unless *formally* terminated, projects have a tendency to drag on, sometimes unintentionally because of neglect or insufficient resources, sometimes intentionally for lack of follow-up work. Workers remain on the project payroll for months after their obligations have been met, turning an otherwise successful project into financial failure. As long as the project has not been officially terminated, work orders remain open and labor charges continue to accrue.

Reasons for Termination

Project terminations essentially fall into three categories: project objectives have been achieved, it is more convenient to stop than continue, or default.[3]

Even in the first case—when projects are terminated because contractual objectives have been met—it takes a skilled project manager to orchestrate termination and ensure that no activities or obligations are uncompleted or unfulfilled. The seeds of successful termination are sown early in the project. Since the customer must accept the results of the project, the criteria of acceptance should be clearly defined, agreed upon, and documented at the beginning of the project. Any subsequent changes to criteria during the project should be approved by both contractor and customer. Throughout all phases of the project, the project manager must emphasize achievement of the customer's acceptance criteria.

Some projects never reach fruition because of uncontrollable factors in the environment. They are terminated because changing market conditions, skyrocketing costs, depleted critical resources, or declining priorities make it infeasible or undesirable to complete the job. The decision to abort before completion is made because it appears financially or otherwise more sound than to see it through to completion. The customer may simply change his mind and no longer want the project end-item.

Projects are also halted because of unsatisfactory technical performance, poor quality materials or workmanship, violation of contract, poor planning and control, bad management, or customer dissatisfaction with the contractor. Many of these reasons are the fault of the contractor and project management; they could be avoided if management exercised better project planning and control, showed more respect for the user, or was more ethical. This kind of termination is the worst since it leaves user objectives unfulfilled and casts a shadow over the contractor's technical competence, managerial ability, or moral standing.

17.5 TERMINATION RESPONSIBILITIES

As with earlier stages of work, the project manager is responsible for planning, scheduling, monitoring and controlling activities at project termination. Some of the responsibilities listed by Archibald include:[4]

A. Planning, scheduling, and monitoring completion activities:

- Obtaining and approving termination plans from involved functional managers.
- Preparing and coordinating termination plans and schedules.
- Planning for reassignment of project team personnel and transfer of resources to other projects.
- Monitoring termination activities and completion of all contractual agreements.
- Monitoring the disposition of any surplus materials and special project equipment.

B. Final close out activities:

- Closing out all work orders and approving the completion of all subcontracted work.
- Notifying all departments of project completion.
- Closing the project office and other facilities occupied by project organization.
- Closing project books.
- Insuring delivery of project files and records to the responsible managers.

C. Customer acceptance, obligation, and payment activities:

- Insuring delivery of end-items, side items, and customer acceptance of items.
- Communicating to the customer when all contractual obligations have been fulfilled.
- Assuring that all documentation related to customer acceptance as required by contract is completed.
- Expediting any activities by the customer needed to complete the project.
- Transmitting formal payment request to the customer.
- Monitoring customer payment and collection of payments.
- Obtaining formal customer acknowledgment of completion of contractual obligations and releasing the contractor from further obligations (except warranties and guarantees).

The responsibility for the last group of activities, particularly those relating to payment and contractual obligations, is shared with the contract administrator or whoever is responsible for company-client negotiations and legal contracts. The final activity, obtaining the certificate of customer acknowledgment, may involve claims in addition to the contracted price since the customer may have failed to provide agreed-to data or support, or requested items beyond contract specifications. In these cases the contractor is entitled to compensation. In other cases, described next, it is the client who is to be compensated.

Before the project is considered closed the customer reviews the results or end-item to make sure everything is satisfactory. Items still open, in need of attention, or to be redone, and which the contractor agrees to, are recorded on a list (sometimes called a "punch list"). Items are checked off the list by the contractor as they are rectified.

The importance of doing a good job at termination cannot be understated. Neither can the difficulty. As mentioned, in the rush to finish the project and in the accompanying confusion many of the termination responsibilities listed above are overlooked, mishandled, or botched. To ensure they are handled properly, termination responsibilities should be systematically delegated and checked off as completed. Project termination requires the same high degree of attention and service as other project management responsibilities. A bungled termination can bungle the project.

17.6 CLOSING THE CONTRACT

Delivery, installation, and user acceptance of the main contract end-item (the major hardware, software, or service specified by the project contract) does not necessarily mean that the project is closed. Project completion may be held up pending the contractor's delivery of necessary, ancillary articles—called *side items*—or payment of negotiated compensation for failure to meet contractual agreements.

Side Items

Effective installation, operation, maintenance, and modification of the contract end-item often requires contract side items such as special tools, instruments, spare parts, reports, drawings, courses of instruction, and user operating and maintenance manuals. These are deliverable contract items, the cost of which may cover a substantial percentage of the total project cost. Often the amount of effort required to provide these side items is underestimated. The result is that the project cannot be completed on time even though the main contract end-item is successfully completed. Failure to deliver side items can subject the contractor to penalties or financial loss.

In planning for project termination, the project manager must make certain that the scope of work for side items is well understood and that qualified personnel are assigned with adequate time to fulfill requirements.[5] Side items must be looked upon as part of the scheduled contracted work, not as afterthoughts or project extensions. They must be given full consideration far in advance of the scheduled completion date.

Negotiated Adjustments to Final Contract

In many high cost projects, the contractor receives payment for only a portion of the cost of the project, say 80 to 90 percent, with the remainder conditional on the contractor's performance. Measures of performance may include the performance of the equipment or service provided, the degree of contractor compliance with areas of the contract, or the quality of the working relationship maintained by the contractor.[6]

These final payment contingencies are considered post-acceptance issues since they occur after the major contract items have been accepted by the user. If the delivered equipment is satisfactory but does not perform up to the contracted specifications, if it is found defective after a trial period because of design or production inadequacies, or if the item is delivered late, the contractor may be responsible for paying negotiated compensation to the user.

Contract sign off might also be contingent on how well the product functions after delivery. In that case, the project manager oversees installation, setup, and initial operation at the customer's site. The contractor might also provide on-site user support, at no additional fee, until operating deficiencies have been removed.

Sometimes it is in the best interest of the customer or contractor to negotiate aspects of the contract price or delivery date *after* the project is completed. The U.S. government and other customers retain the right to negotiate overhead rates after the final price on a cost-plus contract is received. Likewise, when an originally scheduled completion date is overrun, contractors want to negotiate to have the contracted delivery date revised to match the actual delivery date so their reputation is not damaged.

17.7 PROJECT EXTENSIONS

When additional work is sought that is related to, but beyond the scope of the original project, a new, smaller project emerges. Such *project extensions* arise from the need or desire to enhance the originally funded system. Extensions occur for two reasons, discretionary or essential.

Discretionary enhancements are requested by the user or proposed by the contractor for the purpose of improving the operation or convenience of the original project end-item. The environment remains the same, but new and better ways are found to improve the item. In contrast, *essential enhancements* are compulsory and without them the item will cease to operate or become obsolete. The environment changes and the end-item as originally planned is no longer adequate; it *must* be enhanced to remain viable.

Enhancements are originated either by a request from the user (e.g., an RFP) or with a proposal from the contractor. They represent the initiation stage for a new project. Project extensions themselves become projects; they follow the stages of a development cycle and are planned, scheduled, and controlled just like the projects out of which they evolved.

17.8 PROJECT SUMMARY EVALUATION

One of the final tasks of the project team, after the project has been terminated and the system is fully operational, is to perform a formal evaluation. This frequently overlooked task is an essential, valuable *learning* component of project management. Without a complete, formal review of the project there is a tendency to mentally suppress problems encountered and to understate the impact of past errors or misjudgments. ("Things weren't really so bad, now were they?")

Summary evaluation is important regardless of the outcome of project termination, even those regrettable cases where the project was ended without achieving its goals. For project and company management to learn from past experience it is as important to review mistakes as it is successes.

Project summary evaluation reviews the performance of the project team and the performance of the system end-item. The purpose of the review is to determine and assess what has been done and what still needs to be done, not to find fault or pass blame. As mentioned earlier, finger pointing and reprimanding are counterproductive because they encourage people to cover up the very problems and mistakes that evaluation seeks to reveal and resolve.

Postcompletion Project Summary

A summary evaluation of the *project effort* should be performed as soon as the project has been completed. The evaluation should:

1. Review initial project objectives in terms of technical performance, schedule, and cost; and review the soundness of the objectives in view of the problem which the system was to resolve.

2. Review the evolution of objectives up to the final objectives and determine how well the project team performed with respect to them; and review the reasons for changes, noting which were avoidable and which were not.

3. Review the activities and relationships of the project team throughout the project life cycle, including review of: the interfaces, performance, and effectiveness of project management; the relationships among top management, the project team, the functional organization, and the client; the cause and process of termination; customer reactions and satisfaction.

4. Identify places where performance was good and note the reasons; review expenditures, sources of costs, and profitability; identify organizational benefits, project extensions, and marketable innovations.

5. Identify problems, mistakes, oversights, and areas of poor performance, and determine the causes.

6. Where policies and procedures are involved, make changes and establish new ones to incorporate what was learned from steps 4 and 5.

Project summary evaluation should incorporate a broad range of criteria and measures. Since a project that is successful to one party may be considered unsuccessful by others, the opinions and assessments of the customer, the project team, and upper management should all be considered. A project that is highly profitable for the contractor might not have effectively solved the client's problem; a project that satisfied the client might have jeopardized the financial stability of the contractor.

To insure fair evaluation, an unbiased evaluator should oversee the collection and compilation of data.

The results of the project review should be documented in a *project summary report*. This becomes the only authoritative document on the project, a learning device that will help later project teams avoid making the same mistakes. The project summary report should describe the project, its evolution, and its eventual outcome. It begins with the project plan, describes how the plan worked, and where it failed. The project summary becomes the reference for project related questions that might arise later. Thoroughness and clarity are essential since people who worked on the project probably will not be available later to answer questions.

Post-installation System Review

Several months after it has been delivered, the fully operational end-item system should be evaluated to assess its performance in the user environment and under ongoing operational conditions. This *post-installation system review* provides data about the end-item system for the project team and the user. It serves a variety of purposes, such as providing maintenance information and operating data for systems designers, and initiating requests for system enhancements. With the original user requirements as the standard of evaluation, the system review attempts to answer the questions: Now that the system is fully operational, is it doing what it was intended to do? Is the user getting the benefits expected by the system? And, what changes are necessary to fulfill the needs or desires of the user?

The project team should make certain that the system being evaluated is *unaltered* from the one delivered. Frequently the user makes system improvements after it has been installed. Although there is nothing wrong with this per se, it changes the system physically or functionally, a fact which must be accounted for in evaluating performance.

During the course of the review the evaluation team might discover parts of the system needing maintenance. Design flaws, operating problems, or necessary enhancements which nobody could have foreseen earlier often become obvious only after the system has been in routine operation.

Results of the review should be *documented*. The system review should describe system performance compared to system objectives, note any maintenance problems, and make suggestions for system enhancements. Both the post-installation system review and the project summary report should be filed and maintained for periodic reference in the planning and conduct of future projects.

17.9 SUMMARY

A variety of sources and measures are used for collecting and communicating formative evaluation information, including graphical presentations, reports, observations, and meetings. Project evaluation utilizes all of these, but the single most important one is the review meeting. Review meetings are scheduled periodically and at special times, such as the attainment of project milestones. During review meetings current progress, problems, solutions, potential problems, and opportunities are identified. When members of the project team and other stakeholders—including the customer, top management, or functional managers—do not participate in review meetings, they should be kept informed with project status reports.

The project is terminated through a series of formal procedures. The project manager oversees the planning, scheduling, and coordination of termination activities and conducts the final close out of the project. The project manager insures delivery of side items and adjustments to the final contract. When a user request or contractor proposal is beyond the scope of the original project, a project extension is initiated.

The final formal activity of the project team is a summary evaluation. Following completion of the project, project performance is assessed and documented in a comprehensive project summary report. This report reviews the project plan, noting work, cost, and schedule performance, as well as outstanding successes and mistakes. After the main contract end-item has been in operation for several months, a post-installation system review is conducted to assess system performance compared to user requirements and to determine maintenance or enhancement needs. The results of the review are documented and combined with the project summary to provide a comprehensive historical document and learning device for future project teams.

The next chapter discusses project failure and success, and identifies prominent factors associated with each. As it turns out, it is an effective way to summarize and tie together the principles of this book.

CHAPTER REVIEW QUESTIONS

1. Describe the difference between formative evaluation and summary evaluation in project management.

2. Why is it better to rely on a variety of information sources for evaluation than just a few? Give some examples of how several sources are used in project evaluation?

3. What are the advantages and disadvantages of the following sources of information: (a) charts and tables, (b) oral and written reports, (c) firsthand observation?

4. What agenda items must participants reach consensus on during review meetings?

5. What is an action plan? What must it include?

6. When are special reviews held? Why should an outside auditor oversee the review? Why would users want their own separate reviews?

7. What should be included in summary status reports to top management? What should be included in comparative summary reports?

8. What reports should the project manager receive? How does the project manager use these reports?

9. What reports are sent to functional managers?

10. When and what kind of reports are sent to the customer? Why is reporting to customers so important?

11. What are the reasons for project termination? How can termination for reasons other than achievement of project goals be avoided?

12. What must the project manager do in planning, scheduling, monitoring, and closing out the project?
13. What is the role of the project manager and contract administrator in receiving customer acceptance of the work and final payment?
14. What are side items? How can they hold up project completion?
15. What kinds of negotiated adjustments are made to the contract, postacceptance? Why would a user or contractor want to specify the terms of a contract after the project is completed?
16. What is a project extension and how do project extensions originate? How is a project extension managed?
17. What are the differences between the two kinds of reviews in project summary evaluation: the postcompletion project summary and the post-installation system review? Describe each of these reviews.

QUESTIONS ABOUT THE STUDY PROJECT

1. How often and what kinds of review meetings were held in the project? Why were they held? Who attended?
2. When and for what reason were special reviews held?
3. How was follow-up insured on decisions made during review meetings?
4. Is there a project meeting room? How often and in what ways is it used?
5. Describe the kinds of project reports sent to top management and the customer. Who issued these reports? What kinds of reports were sent to project and functional managers? Who issued them?
6. How was the project terminated? Describe the activities of the project manager during the final stage of the project and the steps taken to close it out.
7. How was the contract closed out? Were there any side items or negotiated adjustments to the contract?
8. Did any follow-up projects grow out of this one?
9. Describe the project summary report (prepared at the *end* of the project). Who prepared it? Who was it sent to and how was it used? Where is it now? Show an example (or portion of one).
10. Was there a review of the product or project output after it was installed? When? By whom? What did they find? Did the client request the review or was it standard procedure?

ENDNOTES

1. R.D. Archibald, *Managing High-Technology Programs and Projects* (New York: John Wiley & Sons, 1976), 231.
2. Archibald, ibid., 12, refers to this report as the "project register."
3. Much of the discussion in this subsection is based on D.D. Roman, *Managing Projects: A Systems Approach* (New York: Elsevier, 1986), 392–394.

4. See Archibald, *Managing High-Technology Programs and Projects*, 235–236 and 264–270, for a complete checklist of close out activities.

5. V.G. Hajek, *Managing Engineering Projects*, 3rd. ed. (New York: McGraw-Hill, 1984). See 233–240 for a good description of monitoring and support side items for both engineering hardware and computer software projects.

6. Ibid., 241–242.

chapter 18

Project Failure, Success, and Lessons Learned

Fools you are to say you learn by your experience. I prefer to profit by others' mistakes and avoid the price of my own.

Otto van Bismark-Schönhausen

Now that you are familiar with the terminology, concepts, and methodology of project management, it is a good time to review the tenets of this book.

Experienced project managers will tell you that the failure or success of a project has something to do with its management. In this chapter, the principles and practices of project management have been classified, rather broadly, into those contributing to project failure and to project success. The classification is the result of an informal survey of the project management literature over the last twenty years; it includes findings from academic studies as well as the opinions of project managers from various industries—construction, research and development, data processing, and product development. The survey affirms that project failure and success do depend on project management—a great deal, in fact. They also show there is considerable consensus between industries about which aspects of project management influence project outcomes the most.

This chapter is a review of the core issues of this book—the must "don'ts" as well as the must "do's" of project management. We look at project failure (the must don'ts) first.

18.1 PROJECT FAILURE

Why Talk About Failure?

By talking about failure it is not the intent of this chapter to finish off on a sour note; rather, we look at failure for one reason: to learn from past mistakes. Some philosophers (notably Karl Popper) say that knowledge advances not through success, but through failure.[1] In science it is largely in those situations where older theories failed to give reliable and accurate predictions that scientists are forced to advance new and better theories. Newton's theories were supplanted by those of Einstein because they failed to explain certain phenomenon; now Einstein's are being modified. So it happens with common practice. Whenever underlying causes (or theories) are advanced about why a failure occurred, others can try to take actions to prevent similar failures from recurring. Many newsworthy project failures—those spectacular, involving loss of life or investment—are followed by an inquiry or investigation, the results of which are made public. Most failures do not receive full investigation, even when they should. It is in the spirit of learning and improvement that we examine project failure.

What is Project Failure?

No failure occurs in isolation. All failures are *system failures* in the sense that they are actually the *output* of a particular system. That is to say, there are features or defects in the system which *produced* or allowed that failure.[2] Broadly speaking, a system fails if it fulfills either of two criteria:[3]

1. It does not satisfy the requirements of those involved with the system—management, users, or other affected parties. Project failure usually implies not meeting cost, schedule, performance, quality, safety, or related objectives.
2. It produces results that are felt undesirable by those involved with it. A failed project does not meet user or developer expectations or leaves them worse off than before.

The criteria of project failure can be viewed from the two perspectives illustrated in Figure 18–1. As examples:

1. When a fixed price project has a cost overrun the system developer must absorb the excess cost and suffers a loss or reduced profit. From the system developer's perspective, this is a project failure.
2. The project end-item is not accepted or utilized even though it was delivered on schedule, under budget, and according to specifications. This is a project failure experienced by the user or other project recipients.

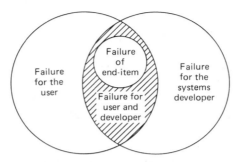

FIGURE 18–1.   Perspectives of project failure.

The two kinds of failure might be mutually exclusive: while one of the parties experiences failure, the other experiences success. For example, even though project cost overruns might drive a developer into bankruptcy, the user may derive considerable benefit from the end-item; in contrast, the developer might earn handsome profits from the project, even though the user is disappointed with or never uses the end-item.

As Figure 18–1 shows, however, the two kinds of failure are sometimes interlinked, as when the project end-item itself fails. For example, the collapse of a building during construction and the personal injury or loss of life it causes represent a "project failure" for everyone—the user, project team, contractor, and others involved. Such a failure adversely influences all parties by increasing project costs and schedules, not to mention the toll of human suffering. Similarly, everyone is affected when rising costs or poor performance force either the system developer or the user to withdraw from the project. The remaining party is then left in the predicament of holding an "unfinished project."

Causes of Failure

Some failures are unavoidable because they are beyond anyone's ability to anticipate, avoid, or influence. Examples are failures caused by weather or labor problems, intractable technical difficulties, or other forces neither foreseeable nor controllable. But, perhaps surprisingly, none of these are the cause of a great number of project failures. Rather, failure is caused by "defects" in (1) the project and user organizations—their attitudes, practices, and structure, or (2) the project end-item—its hardware, software, and component parts. These defects are often interlinked. For example, although hardware failures result from defects in components and procedures, these defects can usually be traced to mistakes in the design, which, in turn, can be traced to defects in the *design and management process* which allowed mistakes to go uncorrected. That is to say, defects in the system that plans and controls the project—the project management system—can result in poor design, poor quality control, inadequate inspection, and, ultimately, failure in the end-item itself ("hardware" or "component" failures).

A case in point is the tragic loss of the space shuttle *Challenger* and its seven astronauts. Although directly, faulty hardware design caused the explosion, the root causes were management ineptitude and flaws in the project organization which permitted design errors to go uncorrected. The Challenger accident was directly attributed to defective O-rings—seals in the booster rocket that allowed hot exhausts to leak out and trigger an explosion in the external fuel tank. But it was known before and well-documented that the seals would perform poorly under certain temperatures and that they constituted a serious risk to flight safety. On the day of the tragedy, several engineers warned of the likelihood that the seals might fail. Earlier decisions to retain the suboptimal seals and the approval to go-ahead for launch, despite warnings, were management judgments that blatantly ignored abundant information to the contrary. It can easily be argued that the accident was the output of a defective management system.

In a similar, more general vein, whenever a user fails to accept or utilize a project end-item (called "implementation failure"), the reason is typically because the end-item did not satisfy the user's requirements or because it was not needed to start with. This is a common failure in computer information projects where systems are installed and then seldom used. Sometimes the problem goes deeper when the *true user* of the system was misidentified. Regardless, blame for failure to meet user needs must rest with project management for allowing such a state of affairs to develop.

The point is that *the root cause of many project failures is not intractable technical problems, nor uncontrollable forces, nor the user, but simply bad project management.* This kind of failure is the output of a defective project management system—organizations, practices, or procedures.

18.2   PROJECT MANAGEMENT CAUSES OF PROJECT FAILURE

Figure 18–2 shows fourteen factors—inadequacies or defects in project management—which are sources of project failure as identified in the survey.[4] Although having any of these factors in a project does not necessarily mean that the project will fail, it is an *inauspicious sign* and should be viewed as increasing the chances of failure. The factors are categorized into three levels: the environment or context of the project, the project management system, and the project planning and control process.

Level I: Failures in the Project Management Context

These are sources of failure traceable to the inappropriate "fit" of the project organization to project objectives, project tasks, top management, and the larger environment. They include the use of a project management model which is incorrect for the project objectives and environment, and lack of top management support for the project.

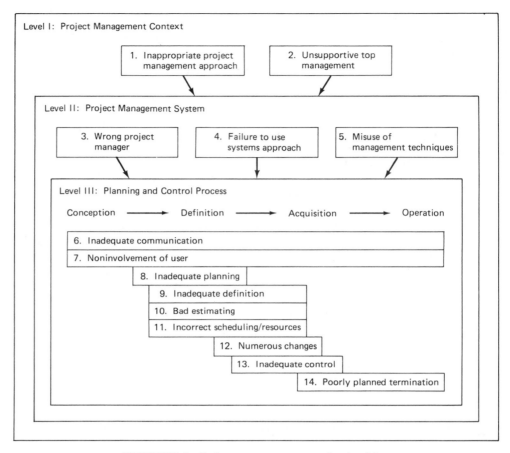

FIGURE 18–2.   Project management causes of project failure.

1. Inadequate Project Management Model.   The project does not have the right organization structure, project manager, or team (in terms of skills, experience, authority, formality, or complexity) to "fit" the project. For example:

a. The project organization structure, planning, and controls are incongruent or incompatible with the project situation, the philosophy of the project manager, or corporate culture and objectives.

b. More emphasis is placed on keeping the team busy than on results. Members of the team are assigned to the project without regard to appropriate skills and experience.

c. Either no one is held accountable for the entire project, or the responsibility, expectations, and authority of the project manager are unclear or undefined.

d. A project team, project manager, or project structure that was successful in the past is "plugged" into a new project without considering the unique requirements of the project or distinguishing characteristics of its environment.

2. Unsupportive Top Management.   Top management does not give the active and continued support necessary to achieve project goals. This is revealed in many ways. For example:

   a.   Top management does not yield adequate responsibility or authority to the project manager, or does not back the project manager's decisions or actions.
   b.   The company does not make the structural and procedural changes (budgeting, planning, and control systems, reporting and authority relationship, etc.) needed to conduct effective project management.
   c.   Top management does not participate in reviewing plans and specifications. Often the result is that it will request frequent changes later on.

Level II: Failures in the Project Management System

These are sources of failure traceable to project management leadership, philosophy, and practice. They include the wrong project manager, neglect or inappropriate use of the systems approach in the project life cycle, and misuse of project management techniques.

3. The Wrong Project Manager.   The person in the role of project manager does not have the background, skills, experience, or personality to lead the project. For example:

   a.   The project manager is unable to confront conflict. She does not ask tough, probing questions, and cannot effectively argue for the best interests of the project.
   b.   The project manager cannot make the adjustment from a traditional work environment to the change and uncertainty of projects. She lacks the ability to function effectively under short time frames and stressful situations.
   c.   The project manager is not well-rounded in technical and managerial skills. Sometimes this arises from a variation of the so-called Peter Principle: putting a good technician into a managerial role about which she knows nothing. In other cases, the project manager has managerial skills, but is so preoccupied with administrative details that she ignores critical technical matters.

4. Ignoring the Systemic Nature of Projects.   The project is not handled as a system. Elements and processes of the project are compartmentalized without regard to their interaction. As a result:

   a.   Hardware, software, resources, and facilities are viewed in isolation without regard to their relation to overall project objectives. Emphasis is placed on optimizing the utilization of inputs rather than on project objectives.
   b.   The evolutionary process of systems development is viewed piecewise, one step at a time, without concern about subsequent or previous stages. This is evident by poor

planning for future stages and inadequate evaluation of past stages. Problems and obstacles are passed from one phase to the next.

5. Inappropriate or Misuse of Management Techniques.   Project management techniques are misunderstood, not accepted, or improperly employed. This problem lies with the project manager, the project team, or the techniques themselves. For example:

a. The project manager fails to distinguish nonproject techniques of planning, coordinating, and control from those necessary for project activities. The project manager or her team do not understand the need for tools such as PERT, WBS, performance analysis, conflict confrontation, and team building; these techniques are used incorrectly or not at all.

b. The techniques used are too sophisticated or otherwise inappropriate for the particular project. Schedules and reports are too detailed or not detailed enough for project decisions. Manual techniques that are simpler, more appropriate, and better suited for small projects are bypassed in favor of sophisticated (but unwieldy or unnecessary) computerized reporting systems.

Level III: Failures in Planning and Control Processes

These sources of project failure rest in the project planning and control process. As shown in Figure 18–2, some, like poor communication and inadequate user participation, can occur at anytime and require continuous attention. Others, such as inadequate definition, inadequate estimation and scheduling, or inadequate control, occur primarily during certain phases of the project.

6. Inadequate Communication in the Project.   These are problems that stem from lack of information quality, accuracy, or timeliness, poor collection and documentation, or inadequate distribution of information to those who need it. For example:

a. Early in the project, information about objectives, responsibilities, and acceptance criteria is not documented. No attempt is made to identify information and sources that will be needed during the project. Parties that "need to know" are not identified or kept informed.

b. During the project there is no posting or reporting of information about project status or about changes to the original system.

c. Meetings and reviews are not fully utilized. Insufficient meetings are convened to collect and disseminate information. Reviews do not delve deeply enough nor ask probing questions. No project log or audit trail of project development is kept.

d. The quality and quantity of information is gradually reduced as the project progresses because "there is not enough time." Communications are not documented so it is difficult to distinguish facts from assumptions.

7. Failure to Involve the User.   The user or customer does not participate in the planning/definition/design/implementation process, and user needs are disregarded. This is one of the most frequently mentioned sources of project failure. Failure to involve the user early in the project usually causes lack of agreement about requirements, numerous change requests later, and conflict between the user and project team during implementation. Even when users do participate in defining requirements, without continued involvement they often cannot visualize the appearance of the final end-item and are disappointed when they get it. Problems are aggravated and more difficult to solve when there are multiple users. Both the user and project management are to blame:

a. The user may feel awkward or uncomfortable and try to minimize his involvement. Some users openly resist participation, even when invited.

b. The behavior of the project team discourages user involvement or does nothing to encourage it. Members of the project team behave arrogantly and make the user feel ignorant or inferior. Such behavior delimits user/project team trust and strains communication.

8. Lack of or Inadequate Project Planning: Analysis of how and when things will be done is inadequate and sloppy; reports and recommendations from previous projects are ignored. Instead of preparing in advance, management reacts to things as they occur.

Although poor project planning by itself is a major reported source of project failure, also cited are particular features of poor planning—the next three factors.

9. Inadequate Project Definition: Vague, wrong, misleading, or no project definition is a frequently mentioned cause of failure. There is no formal definition of technical requirements, tasks, or project scope. Definition problems result from:

a. Lack of, or a poorly prepared proposal, WBS, responsibility matrix, or work role definitions.

b. Lack of user involvement in defining project scope, tasks, and requirements. The project team never becomes familiar with the user's operation and cannot construct a design that relates to user requirements.

10. Bad Estimating of Time and Resources.   Estimates of resource requirements, activity durations, and completion dates are unrealistic. Bad estimating occurs because:

a. Standards or files of similar projects are not used to estimate how long the project should take.

b. Estimates are made without regard to the experience of the workers. It is assumed that all personnel are "experts" and that they will perform the work without a hitch.

c. Estimates are prepared by people unfamiliar with details and problems; those responsible for the work are not involved.

d. Not enough time is allowed for estimating.

e. The user exerts pressures to get the project done quickly; this results in setting unrealistic deadlines and eliminating "unnecessary" tasks like documentation.

11. Incorrect Scheduling and Handling of Resources.   Scheduling and allocation of resources is incorrect; assignments are not anticipated; resource skills and capabilities are unknown; and there is no backup for resources. The problem begins during planning and continues throughout the project:

a.   Resource requirements are not anticipated and scheduled, and resource issues are addressed only as they occur. There is no skills inventory showing who is available for the project, which causes the estimating problems mentioned before.

b.   Project personnel are reassigned or turned over with no schedule adjustments to allow for lost time or the learning curve.

12. Numerous Changes during the Acquisition Phase.   Changes are made to the original estimate without corresponding adjustments to the schedule, budget, or other elements of the plan. This problem is associated with problems of inadequate project communication, poor project definition, lack of user involvement, and inadequate project control.

13. Inadequate Control.   Project management does not anticipate problems but waits until afterward before responding; control is focused on daily issues without looking ahead to potential problem situations; management waits until near the completion date to see if the project is on time. Sources of control problems include:

a.   Planning work tasks which are too long to be effectively controlled, work packages and work groups which are too large to be supervised, and milestones which are too far apart to permit stepwise monitoring of the percentage of project completed.

b.   No adherence to standards or specifications for design, documentation, testing, or evaluation. Auditors do not perform careful, detailed evaluation, and evaluation is not used to determine why problems arise.

c.   No attempt to resolve emerging problems early in the project. Instead of being prospective and preventive, the control process is retrospective and curative.

d.   No forecasting or planning of the funds needed to guarantee completion of project objectives.

e.   The management system takes on greater importance than the people in the system or the project end-item. This strengthens peoples' tendency to resist controls and encourages them to circumvent or sabotage control procedures.

14. Project Termination is Poorly Planned.   It is not known what constitutes project completion or the end-item, what the acceptance criteria are, or who must sign off the project; there is no formal termination procedure addressing objectives, performance, end products, and maintenance issues; the impact on users is not predicted; personnel are not evaluated for performance on the project; there is no post-termination survey addressing system bugs, necessary or already made changes, results, or usefulness.

This problem is often related to poor project definition and lack of user involvement:

a.   When project termination is not clearly defined, the project is allowed to continue even after it has long ceased to make cost-effective progress.

b. When users are not involved in planning, there is greater chance of disagreement over final acceptance. After acceptance, problems with the end-item go unidentified or are permitted to continue despite user dissatisfaction.

Bad project termination has negative consequences beyond failure of the immediate project. When no attempt is made to review project performance, it is unlikely that any knowledge can be gained to transfer to other projects. Recommended enhancements to the system go undocumented and are lost forever. When project personnel are not evaluated at the end of the project, their work performance is forgotten. Records get distorted, and there is no accurate basis upon which to make future work assignments.

Interdependency of Factors

As Figure 18–2 implies, a defect or inadequacy at one level has negative impact on the next lower level. For example, selecting an inappropriate project management approach (Level I) can result in ignoring project systemic features, selecting the wrong project manager, or misusing project management techniques (Level II); these, in turn, lead to poor communication, inadequate definition and scheduling, and other problems in project planning and control (Level III).

Figure 18–2 implies a hierarchy of effects; whenever there are defects or problems at higher levels (I or II), the chance of project failure is increased even when there are no defects at Level III. For example, strong user involvement or good planning (Level III) alone are probably not enough to prevent failure if the project manager is unskilled or does a poor job of managing other aspects of the project (Level II). Similarly, even an exceptional project manager will have trouble preventing failure if top management does not support the project (Level I).

There is good reason for strong emphasis on Levels I and II since, generally, correct action there would help eliminate or mitigate problems at lower levels. For example, using the appropriate project management model and gaining the support of top management tends to encourage (or mitigate the problems of) selecting the right project manager, using the structured systems approach, and appropriate use of project management techniques; these, in turn, tend to mitigate problems and reduce sources of failure further down in the planning and control process.

The caveat is that although eliminating sources of failure at higher levels tends to reduce sources of failure at lower levels, it does not necessarily eliminate them. Given the uncertainty of projects, causes for failure can develop at any level at anytime. Management must continuously monitor for all sources of failure to prevent them from developing.

Does Eliminating Failure Guarantee Success?

Though the 14 factors in Figure 18–2 are frequently cited as sources of project failure, they are not universal verities. Their validity and importance must be uniquely weighed and assessed in each project. They represent a list of potential problem factors to be aware of on a project-by-project basis.

Since in most complex human endeavors absence of failure does not mean success, mere absence of the above factors, itself, will probably not make a project a "success."

Sources of failure are similar to Herzberg's "hygiene" factors—although not having them reduces the chances of failure, it will not guarantee success.[5] For a project to be successful, other factors (similar to Herzberg's "motivators") must also be present in the project.

18.3 PROJECT SUCCESS

What is Project Success?

A project is usually considered successful when it satisfies project objectives. Project objectives, however, commonly involve multiple dimensions or criteria (e.g., the time/cost/performance triad often mentioned in this book), and many "average" projects, though not usually considered failures, do not satisfy objectives in all dimensions. Project management usually makes tradeoffs, and if they are mutually agreed upon by the developer and the user, the project might still be successful even if portions of the objectives were not met. Many firms measure success by considering only the highest priority criteria and give lesser weight to time and cost measures. For example, in aerospace the primary success criteria is engineering performance, while at Walt Disney it is safety.[6]

In a study of "successful" projects, Ashley, Lurie, and Jaselskis asked eight companies to select successful and average projects for purposes of comparison.[7] Based upon interviews with project personnel, "successful" projects were judged to be those doing "better than average" on the criteria of cost, schedules, and the satisfaction of key project participants (client, project manager, project team, and system development organization). Other criteria included follow-up work, end-user satisfaction, end-item quality, and meeting specifications.

Although Ashley, et al. focused on construction projects, their findings are consistent with fields such as R&D and data processing which make similar, frequent reference to budgets, schedules, and developer/user satisfaction as criteria of project success. Other, less frequently mentioned success measures include "within original scope or mutually agreed upon scope changes," and "without disturbing the corporate culture or values."[8]

Perhaps the best overall criterion for project success, regardless of industry, is the satisfaction of the parties involved. By most accounts, if the user, project manager, and system development organization all feel that their expectations were met or exceeded, the project must be considered a success.

18.4 PROJECT MANAGEMENT CAUSES OF PROJECT SUCCESS

The characteristics of project management frequently associated with successful projects are shown in Figure 18–3. (These were identified from a survey of articles that discuss successful projects.)[9] They are broadly classified into three categories: project participants, communication and information sharing and exchange, and the project management/systems development process.

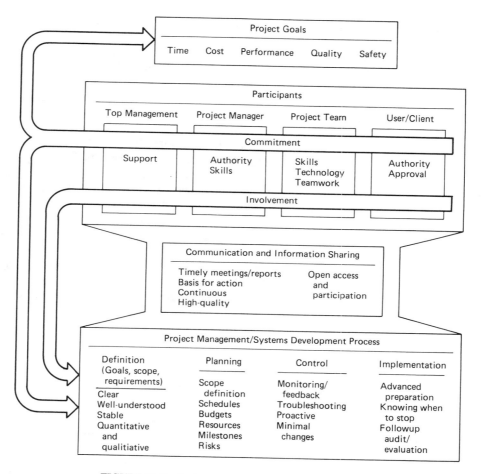

FIGURE 18–3.   Project management causes of project success.

Project Participants

Two ingredients frequently identified as essential for project success revolve around the project *commitment* and *involvement* of key participants such as top management (the developer), the project manager, the project team, and the user.

Earlier it was stated that for a project *not* to fail, it must have goals that are clear and well-defined. But for a project to be successful, it needs more than that: it needs strong *commitment* from all of the participants to maintain and fulfill these goals. Everyone must understand and be motivated to achieve the goals of the project.

Second, besides commitment to project goals, project participants must be committed to the project planning and control process. They must understand the concept of project management, its purpose and goals, and be committed to following steps and procedures for carrying it out.

Additionally, they must be *involved* in the project. They must be given the opportunity and have the desire to provide inputs (e.g., ideas, evaluation, and final approval) at key stages of the project life cycle.

The following sections focus on these and other aspects of project participants' roles in successful projects.

Top Management.   Top management commitment is essential to project success because it affects the level of acceptance or resistance from others to the project. Management shows commitment by supporting the project—allocating necessary resources, giving the project manager enough authority and influence (e.g., to select subcontractors, approve overtime, select team personnel, relax specifications, etc.), and backing the project manager in times of crisis. In successful projects, the project manager is confident about top management's support and is satisfied with the level of responsibility and authority they confer to him.

Often top management shows commitment by appointing a *project sponsor* to champion the project. This person interfaces with users, project and line managers, and top management to expedite responses to potential problems. She is involved from the early planning stages and insures that company and project management values are incorporated into project plans. The program manager in NASA is an example.

Project Manager.   Project managers in successful projects are committed to meeting time, cost, safety, and quality goals. They are deeply involved in the project from beginning to end; they have sufficient authority to oversee development of plans and schedules, make additions or changes, and carry them out.

In successful projects, the project managers are experienced and capable in administration, technology, communication, and human relations. Usually it is more important that they have an understanding of the technology rather than a command of it, but in some high-tech projects they need a command of it, too. They must be both people-oriented and results-oriented, diplomatic and hard driving.

These project managers have leadership styles that allow them to compensate for any "gap" between their authority and responsibility. They are able to utilize styles of leadership appropriate to their workers, even though they may only have a short time to get familiar with workers.

The best project managers get more done by not doing so much. They set up the system of roles, responsibilities, and communication patterns, and then manage it. They trust the skills of their team members and delegate work to them.

They also make vigorous use of management by walking around (MBWA). They are accessible, familiar, and on a friendly basis with people in the project. They keep people talking to each other because they know that in successful projects, "it is usually less necessary to get people to work hard than to get them to work together."[10] The best project managers are intimately familiar with all aspects of the project. They know not only what is going on in the laboratory or shop, but in marketing and manufacturing, too.

Project Team.   As mentioned earlier, in successful projects, the project team is committed both to the goals of the project and to the project management process. The whole team is involved in estimating, setting schedules and budgets, helping solve problems, and making decisions—a process which helps develop positive attitudes about the project, build commitment to project goals, and motivate the team.

Commitment to project management is further enhanced by a corporate culture which understands and supports project management. Kerzner reports that in companies with a "culture of project management," workers are trained to report to multiple bosses; functional managers and project managers maintain a balance of power; both project and functional managers are committed to the job; top managers understand their interface role with project managers; and functional managers are trusted by project managers to get the work done.[11]

In successful projects, the project team is staffed for the necessary expertise and experience. The project team has the requisite skills and knowledge, and is provided adequate resources and technology to perform its function.

In successful projects, there is close teamwork, confidence, trust, and understanding of the roles of others. Team building is employed to define roles and delegate authority and responsibility. To foster good relations that carry through to the work place, team members are encouraged to mix socially.

Users.   In successful projects, there is no question about who the user is. The project team identifies the user before the project begins and understands what the user wants.

In successful projects, the user is strongly committed to project goals and is involved in the project management process. The user is given the authority and influence to share in making decisions, authorizing changes, and helping select subcontractors. Through user involvement in planning and design the project team can better determine what the user wants and can set specific goals and criteria. The user is involved in the implementation process and gives final approval for the installed end-item.

Communication and Information Sharing and Exchange

Successful projects are characterized by good communication and high quality information sharing and exchange. As shown in Figure 18–3, good communication implies a mechanism for effectively integrating the efforts of project participants and for facilitating project management and the systems development process. In successful projects, there is continuous, clear communication between all personnel within the project/user/top management team. Good communication is maintained throughout all stages of the project, from conception through completion.

Good communication partly depends on the quality and quantity of face to face meetings. In successful projects, there are frequent review meetings to exchange information and instructions about project objectives, status, policies, and changes. Access to meetings is open and everyone is encouraged to attend. At meetings it is specified which parties have priority, and leading roles change hands as required. Personnel are committed to addressing problems and resolving them quickly. Frequent "teach-ins" are held so participants at various stages of the project (e.g., planners, designers, and builders) can better understand one another. Meetings are informal, people trust each another, and project managers *listen* to their people.

Project Management and Systems Development

In successful projects, several factors relate to project management functions and to elements of the systems development process. These factors include project definition, planning, control, and implementation.

Definition.   In successful projects, there is complete and clear definition of project scope, objectives, and work to be done. Project responsibilities and requirements are clearly defined and well understood by everyone involved. Clarity of definition produces common expectations among the participants.

Although some flexibility in definition is desirable, goals and requirements need to be relatively stable. It is difficult to proceed when there is persistent change in goals, scope, or requirements; changes require that adjustments be made to plans and communicated to participants; each contributes to confusion and wasted effort.

In successful projects, goals and requirements are quantified wherever possible, but important qualitative aspects of project performance are also included.

Planning.   Major elements of project success include careful, thorough planning, followed by executing the plan with strong management control. In successful projects, plans are related to time, cost, and performance goals. The plans include scope and work definition, schedules and networks, milestones, cost estimates, cash flow analyses, labor and equipment requirements, and risk analysis. They insure that the hard things—things that people want to avoid thinking about—get done first. In successful projects, safety is also an issue, and plans include requirements and means for insuring participants' safety.

Peoples' behavior and attitudes are important, too. People are more likely to perceive success when they are able to meet schedules and plans that they personally helped establish. Good planning takes into consideration those who will be affected by the project and seeks their participation and approval.

In successful projects, the plans provide detailed descriptions of the stages of the project. They include ways to measure performance and arrangements for project control and trouble-shooting.

Control.   Successful projects have good control and reporting systems. These systems provide for monitoring and feedback at all stages and enable comparison of schedules, budgets, and team performance with project goals.

Effective systems of control use checks and balances. They supply information which is timely, meaningful, free of irrelevant details, yet covers everything. They enable ongoing assessment of the effectiveness of the project team, how well objectives are being met, and the likelihood of success.

In successful projects, the control system is proactive and forward-looking. It allows time to anticipate problems, foresee and forestall them, and to react as problems arise. Schedule slippages and cost growth are taken as early warning indicators of problems.

The project manager and project team in successful projects are committed to the process of control. The project manager looks for problems just begun or about to begin and the team takes quick action on its own to resolve problems. The project manager openly discusses problems with the user and the team.

In successful projects, minimal changes are allowed except when essential to safety or to facilitate the job. Most changes are made on paper, early in the job, not later. Pressure is put on planners and designers to produce complete, finished designs before building or fabrication begins.

Implementation.   In successful projects, preparation for implementation is done in advance. It is addressed in the initial plan and throughout the project. There is a strong liaison between the project team and the user about implementation details. Work is paced to minimize downstream adverse impacts on people.

In successful projects, the originally authorized plan spells out how and when the project should be terminated. Without clear criteria for termination, the project may drift from earlier goals, even exceed goals, and the tendency is to do too much or go on for too long.

Even in success there is room for improvement. In successful projects, the team learns from its experience. When the work is finished the team assesses its experience, evaluates its performance, and applies the learnings to subsequent projects.

18.5 A MODEL AND PROCEDURE FOR ANALYZING PROJECT PERFORMANCE

The following sections discuss an approach for using the factors described above to improve project performance.

Project Force Field Analysis

Some years ago, Kurt Lewin proposed a method for analyzing problem situations and determining alternative courses of action.[12] The method organizes information pertaining to organizational improvement into two categories: those "forces" at work which restrain improvement, and those which facilitate it. In theory, the state of affairs of any situation is allowed to persist because the restraining and facilitating forces are in equilibrium (Figure 18–4). If the restraining forces should increase, the state of affairs will be worsened. Conversely, if the facilitating forces are strengthened the state of affairs will improve.

This dichotomy of forces is utilized in a so-called "force field analysis" to determine the best way to improve a situation. Force field analysis begins by identifying all of the restraining and facilitating forces in a situation and the relative strength of each. This makes it possible to then determine which restraining forces must be weakened or which facilitating forces must be strengthened to move the situation toward the ideal state.

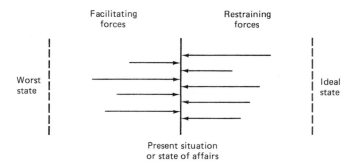

FIGURE 18–4. Force-field analysis.

Although the technique was originally proposed as a means for overcoming resistance to change, it can be used by managers in other applications. In project management, the technique can be used to investigate forces acting on a current project or that might influence an upcoming project, and to determine where emphasis is needed to increase a project's likelihood for success. The factors discussed earlier about project failure and success involve most of the forces which influence a project and are somewhat controllable. A general force field analysis of project management using these factors is shown in Figure 18–5.

Some important features should be noted about the forces in Figure 18–5. First, notice that most of the forces affecting project performance are potentially either facilitating *or* restraining. This means that, for example, "top management support" is a restraining force when it is lacking but a facilitating force when it is present. It does not mean, however, that the forces are "binary." When there is weak or no management support, it restrains project performance. But when support *is* present, its facilitating influence depends on *how* strong and visible it is. When top management provides necessary resources, bestows adequate authority on the project manager, and appoints a sponsor to the project, it is providing a stronger facilitating force than if it only did one of these.

Second, not all forces are equal; some are of general greater importance and influence than others. For example, the commitment and support of top management, the project manager, or the user are potentially greater forces than all of the others combined. Without commitment, involvement, and support, increasing other facilitating forces will be of little help.

Finally, the forces are not independent. Referring back to our discussion of Figure 18–2, some of the forces—such as having top management support or the right project manager—tend to impact other forces. Improving on these facilitating forces has a ripple effect on other facilitating forces.

Implementing the Analysis

A force field analysis can be used in particular cases for determining which forces might hinder a new project, or for analyzing the forces acting on a current project and helping find

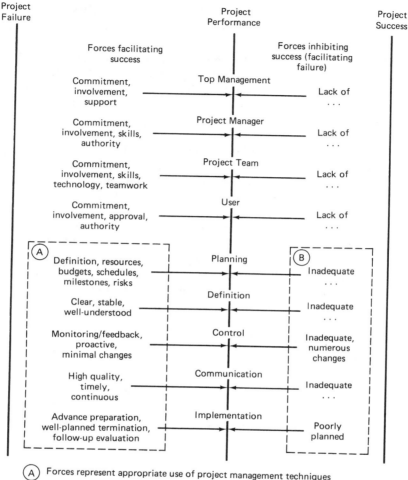

FIGURE 18–5. General force-field analysis of project performance.

solutions. The value of the technique, even if not strictly followed, is that it systematizes thinking and organizes information about project problems and causes.

The analysis begins by gathering information through questionnaires or interviews about the forces facilitating and hindering project performance. The forces shown in Figure 18–5 represent general categories of forces; for individual projects it is necessary to identify *specific* forces—procedures, systems, or behavior and attitudes of individuals and groups that are helping or hindering the project. The survey should include all parties involved in the project or affected by project problems—management, the project team, and users.

The results of the survey are discussed at a meeting where members examine, clarify, and reach agreement about them. Forces which seem to be a complex of multiple issues are broken down as separate forces and listed. The list of forces is posted and arrows are drawn by each force, similar to Figure 18–5. Members are asked to judge the strength of the forces, and the length of each arrow is drawn to represent the average judgment.

The forces are then ranked so that the strongest are given highest priority. They are also rated for solvability. Those rated "unsolvable" (such as imposed by the environment) are noted in order to avoid the pitfall of arguing about unsolvable problems.

The final step is to generate actions for reducing the "solvable" restraining forces with the highest priority, and for increasing the facilitating forces. Plans are prepared showing objectives, actions, target dates, and people responsible for each.

This last step recognizes that actions are tentative and that problem solving is continuous and a part of the project control process. Periodic follow-up meetings are convened to evaluate the status of the forces and to modify actions. The process can be incorporated in the team building efforts described in Chapter 9.

The utility of this analysis process is the systematic framework it provides for viewing problems and trying out solutions with the highest likelihood of success. Many people might resist this procedure as irrelevant or silly, yet the important point is not listing forces and drawing arrows, but identifying key stumbling blocks, prioritizing them, taking action, and evaluating results. Force field analysis is just a convenient way to get the process started.

18.6 EPILOGUE

In a sense, the answer to the issue posed in this chapter—how to avoid failure and get success—has been the subject of this entire book. Although factors like management support and user involvement are crucial for success, it is often the use or misuse of the procedures, methodologies, and systems of project management—tools described in this book—which make the difference between success and failure. And in project management it's only *success* that counts.

But it is not success at all costs. Project management should strive to deliver the end-item to the user's satisfaction, but, as implied elsewhere in this book, it should do so *in an aboveboard and ethical manner*. From the beginning of the project, the contract defines project specifications according to the requirements of (presumably) both the user and the developer. Methods of project management seek to fulfill that contract and provide an end-item that is satisfying to the user and the developer. Ideally, they do it in a way which also rewards and enriches the quality of work life of the participants.

This book has given you the tools of project management and guidelines about how and where to use them. Now comes the hard part—which is up to you: deciding which tools are necessary, desirable, or inappropriate for the goals, resources, constraints, and organization of each particular project. No tool works equally well in all situations, and appropriate use of any tools depends first on selecting the right ones. Many of the tools in this book have more universal application than others, but not every project requires them or would benefit from their usage.

In using project management, you can expect resistance—particularly at first. Project management organization structures, leadership styles, and information, planning and control systems are departures from traditional management. People tend to resist change because they find it risky and threatening. To most people, project management represents a major change, especially if it is implemented all at once.

But seldom is it necessary to implement it all at once. Only in larger projects are all or most of the tools in this book needed. In small projects, only certain ones apply or are necessary. It is better to introduce project management with a small demonstration project and a limited number of project management tools, making sure you include all of the essential ones. A force field kind of analysis will help you decide which tools are essential and which can be left out. A small demonstration project will give you the opportunity to try out certain techniques, to build competence, and to show off the results.

Implementing project management is itself a project. As with all projects, implementing project management should follow a logical sequence of development. To make it work you should have well-defined goals and requirements about what you want to accomplish. You also have to have the commitment and involvement of your top management and the project team. And of course you need a list of tasks, responsibility assignments, a schedule, a budget, a system for reporting and control, and an implementation plan. How you do it is the subject of this book. After that, in the words of the sage Hillel,[13] "All else is commentary."

CHAPTER REVIEW QUESTIONS

1. What are the two criteria of system failure? Describe a recent example for each of a project that failed.

2. Give specific examples (other than those cited in this chapter) of project failures experienced exclusively by either the user or the developer. Give some specific examples of projects where failure was experienced by both.

3. Explain how "defects" in the project end-item are caused by "defects" in the project management system.

4. How can the user's failure to accept or utilize a system (implementation failure) be blamed on project management?

5. Describe each of the following Level I factors and discuss how they contribute to project failure. Cite examples.

   a. Inappropriate project management model

   b. Unsupportive top management

6. Describe each of the following Level II factors and discuss how they contribute to project failure. Cite examples.

   a. Wrong project manager

    b. Ignoring systemic nature of projects

    c. Inappropriate or misuse of management techniques

7. Describe each of the following Level III factors and discuss how they contribute to project failure. Cite examples.

    a. Inadequate communication in the project

    b. Failure to involve the user

    c. Inadequate or lack of planning

    d. Inadequate project definition

    e. Bad estimating of time and resources

    f. Incorrect scheduling and handling of resources

    g. Numerous changes during the acquisition phase

    h. Inadequate control

    i. Project termination is poorly planned

8. Discuss how the factors are interrelated. Which of the factors tend to carry greater weight influencing project failure? Which factors tend to impact other factors?

9. What are the criteria for project success? How do they vary depending on the industry or project?

10. Discuss the importance of commitment and involvement to project success. An important issue not addressed in this chapter is how to build commitment; discuss how it is done.

11. Discuss the role of project participants in achieving project success. Discuss the skills, knowledge, functions, attitudes, behavior, or other factors—where appropriate—necessary from each of the following for projects to succeed:

    a. Top management

    b. Project manager

    c. Project team

    d. Users or customers

12. Discuss the importance of communication and information exchange to project success. What are the crucial features and elements of effective communication and information exchange in successful projects?

13. Discuss the following points of project management and systems development and how they are essential to project success:

    a. Definition

    b. Planning

    c. Control

    d. Implementation

14. What is a force field analysis? Describe a force field analysis procedure for investigating particular projects.

15. Why might you expect resistance to using project management for the first time? Discuss how you might overcome that resistance. (You might find helpful the team building and conflict resolution methods that are described in Chapters 9 and 10.)

QUESTIONS ABOUT THE STUDY PROJECT

1. If the project you are studying is a current project, review the factors of success and failure described in this chapter and, based upon your evaluation of their presence and strength in the project, estimate the project's chances for success or failure. What other unique factors are influencing the project? In your evaluation, you might want to involve the project manager and team members and include their opinions.

   Use a force field kind of analysis to determine which factors or forces (restraining or facilitating) might be altered to improve project performance. Discuss your findings with the project manager.

2. If the project you are studying is completed, was it a success or failure? Did *everyone* consider it a success? To answer this, try to determine how satisfied the developer, the project team, and the user were with the project. Review the factors of project success and failure described in this chapter and determine which were present and how strong they were. How much did they contribute to its success or failure? What other factors were present which influenced project performance?

   Using a force field kind of analysis, determine which factors or forces (restraining or facilitating) might have been altered to improve project performance.

3. Prepare a short, formal proposal describing the results of the analysis, and how to improve the performance of the project you are studying. (If the project is already completed, describe how it could have been improved.) The proposal should indicate the actions, anticipated results, estimated costs, and benefits.

4. If your proposal includes project management techniques that are not currently being used in the organization, consider how they should be implemented. How will you "sell" management on these techniques and convince them that they will be an improvement? How will you ensure that the people to implement or use the techniques will accept them and practice them faithfully? As with any plan, your proposal is a "request for change" and should address the issue of human resistance to change.

ENDNOTES

1. Karl Popper, *The Logic of Scientific Discovery* (New York: Harper & Row, 1968).

2. J. Naughton and G. Peters, *Systems Performance: Human Factors and Failures* (Milton Keynes, Great Britain: The Open University Press, 1976).

3. Ibid., 60.

4. Sources: S. Alter and M. Ginzberg, "Managing Uncertainty in MIS Implementation," *Sloan Management Review* (Fall 1978); Ivars Avots, "Why Does Project Management Fail?" *California Management Review*, Vol. 12, No. 1 (Fall 1969), 77–82; T. Guimaraes, "Understanding Implementation Failure," *Journal of Systems Management* (March 1981), 12–17; L. Holt, "Project Management Principles Succeed at ICI," *Industrial Management and Data Systems*, (March/April, 1983), 4–9; S.P. Keider, "Why Projects Fail," *Datamation*, Vol. 20, No.12 (December 1974), 53–55; M. Lasden, "Effective Project Management," *Computer Decisions* (March 1980), 49–57; J.G. Shanks, "Inflating or Deflating Projects Depends on the 'Big Four'," *Data Management*, (August 1985), 18–22+; W.C. Wall, "Ten Proverbs for Project Control," *Research Management* (March 1982), 26–29.

5. Herzberg's theory considers various factors that impact worker motivation. The theory says that there are some factors—"motivators," the presence of which genuinely serve to increase workers' motivation. There are other factors however, "hygiene" factors, that are needed just to prevent motivation from deteriorating. Although the presence of these does nothing to increase motivation, the absence of them results in decreased motivation. See F. Herzberg, B. Mausner, and B. Snyderman, *The Motivation to Work*, 2nd ed. (New York: Wiley, 1959).

6. H. Kerzner, "In Search of Excellence in Project Management," *Journal of Systems Management* (February 1987), 30–39.

7. D.B. Ashley, C.L. Lurie, and E.J. Jaselskis, "Determinants of Construction Project Success," *Project Management Journal* Vol. 18, No. 2 (June 1987), 69–79. Also see J.K. Pinto and D.P. Slevin, "Project Success: Definitions and Measurement Techniques," *Project Management Journal* (February 1988), 67–71.

8. See Kerzner, "In Search of Excellence in Project Management."

9. Sources: D.B. Ashley, C.L. Lurie, and E.J. Jaselskis, "Determinants of Construction Project Success"; H. Kerzner, "In Search of Excellence in Project Management," 30–39; L. Holt, "Project Principles Succeed at ICI"; M. Lasden, "Effective Project Management"; W.A. Norko, "Steps in Successful Project Management," *Journal of Systems Management* (September 1986), 36–38; J.K. Pinto and D.P. Slevin, "Critical Factors in Successful Project Implementation," *IEEE Transactions on Engineering Management*, Vol. EM–34, No. 1, (February 1987), 22–27; W.A. Randolph and B.Z. Posner, "What Every Manager Needs to Know About Project Management," *Sloan Management Review* (Summer 1988), 65–73; W.C. Wall, "Ten Proverbs for Project Control"; M.F. Wolff, "Rules of Thumb for Project Management," *Research Management*, Vol. 27 (July–August, 1984), 11–13.

10. Wolff, "Rules of Thumb for Project Management."

11. Kerzner, "In Search of Excellence in Project Management," 33.

12. K. Lewin, *Field Theory in Social Science* (New York: Harper & Row, 1951).

13. The words as used here, of course, are in a different context than he intended.

appendix A

Systems Engineering Process

Different industries and organizations use different plans and procedures for conducting systems engineering. However, despite variation in particular stages and terminology, almost all represent the five major stages of concept, analysis, design, implementation, and operation. One particular plan for the application of systems engineering is shown in Figure A–1. This plan has the primary stages of systems concept, definition/preliminary design, detailed design/development, construction/production, and operation, as well as a "pre-stage" of needs identification and a "throughout stage" of evaluation. In addition to addressing the objectives and characteristics of the operating (end-item) system, the plan identifies characteristics of the support system necessary to execute and maintain the operating system.

STAGE 0: IDENTIFICATION OF NEED

Systems engineering is associated with poorly defined problems. The customer may feel that something is wrong or want something new, but might be very unclear about what the problem or need is, what the system should look like, or what it should do. This makes it

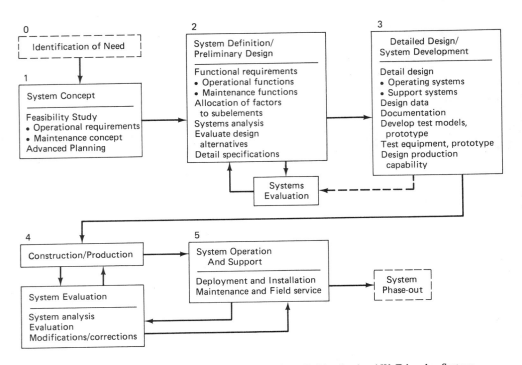

FIGURE A–1. Systems engineering. (Adapted from B. Blanchard and W. Fabrycky, *Systems Engineering and Analysis* (Englewood Cliffs, N.J.: Prentice-Hall, 1981), 238.)

difficult to define the performance requirements of the system and tell the customer what to expect.

Before any work can begin on the system it is necessary to develop a clear conception of the problem and to estimate the value of the desired system. The process begins by asking some basic questions:[1]

1. How did the problem or need arise?
2. Who believes it to be a problem or feels the need?
3. Why is a solution important? How much money (or time, etc.) will it save? What is the value of the system?
4. Is it the right problem or need anyway, or is it a manifestation of some other problem? Would greater benefits accrue if other problems or needs were addressed instead?
5. Does it seem that there would be a reasonable return on effort if resources were applied to this system or would this effort be better applied by tackling another problem or need?

The customer and the systems engineer or contractor answer these questions inter-actively. First the customer states the "felt" need, then the contractor prepares a refined statement of the need and a preliminary description of the system, including performance requirements, cost, and a schedule. The customer reviews the system description and redefines the need; then the contractor redetermines the system descriptions, performance requirements, schedule, and cost. The process continues back and forth until an agreed upon system description is finally reached.

During this stage, the value and need of the system relative to the cost is examined. It must be established that the system will perform a needed or desired function and be justified in comparison to alternative systems or investments. Justifi-cation for the system does not have to be in economic terms: many large-scale military and space systems are justified more on strategic defense or world opinion than on economic grounds.

Once the value and need for the system have been established, the cost and time to produce the system is estimated. Although it is known that the actual cost will seldom be as first quoted, a cost estimate for the given value of the system is necessary to justify proceeding to the next stage. The cost estimate assumes that the system can be produced and operated in a reasonable time period. The time estimate assumes specified performance requirements, reliability, and cost, any of which might be modified depending on the time available to produce the system.

STAGE 1: SYSTEM CONCEPT

During Stage 1, a feasibility study is undertaken to more precisely formulate and define the system. The systems engineering process creates a system to meet a set of requirements; the purpose of the concept stage is to distill a concise set of requirements, concepts, and criteria upon which to base all remaining design and developmental work. Operational requirements for the system are defined for physical parameters, performance factors, effectiveness characteristics, system utilization, and operational environment. At the same time, a system maintenance concept is developed to address issues and policies of operational support, maintenance, repair, and logistics.

The feasibility study is a preliminary systems analysis to develop system goals for hardware, software, support, and other elements of the system. The result of the study is design requirements and criteria for the overall system and a preliminary definition of the functional configuration and physical characteristics of the system; these become the basis for the preliminary system design and serve as reference for comparison with the final, actual system.

The results are reviewed in terms of political, ecological, economical, social, and related issues. This review may indicate that the proposed system is incompatible with the ecological environment or politically or economically infeasible at the present time.

STAGE 2: SYSTEM DEFINITION AND PRELIMINARY DESIGN

The concepts, criteria, and requirements for the overall system are grouped and translated into functions. A function is a specific action required to achieve a specific objective. The list of functions outlines the operations necessary to fulfill system requirements. For example, on most long distance, high volume transport vehicles for humans (airplanes, trains, etc.) there is need for power generation, comfort, food preparation, waste management, and so on. Objectives and requirements are set for each of these, and functions are defined as a general means of attaining them. A function often implies eventual insertion of a piece of equipment with appropriate characteristics, for example, engines, seats, fuel lines, lights, and lavatories.

The process begins by identifying the major functions of the system as laid out by the requirements in Stage 1. Functional flow charts and block diagrams (Figure A–2) are developed to portray system design requirements showing relationships, hierarchy, and interfaces. Analysis is performed (1) on each operational function to reflect the various modes of system operation and utilization, and (2) for each maintenance function to reflect considerations of effectiveness and supportability. To avoid making the system description too complex, the breakdown starts with a simple representation and elaborates where necessary.

Initially, the system description must be sufficiently flexible to permit changes as knowledge and experience is gained during the project. Machine-machine and man-machine interfaces and requirements for subsystems are identified in terms of power, light, temperature, signals, sensing, and so on. Initially, no attempt is made to identify the specific hardware, software, people, or facilities that will comprise the system.

Later in this phase, systems analysis is performed on each block in the flow diagram to determine technical requirements and the most reliable and effective ways to satisfy them. Factors for each level of the system are allocated among subelements to provide guidelines for designers. For example, if a system is to weigh 5000 lbs. and cost $50,000, it must be determined how much each of the subelements should weigh and cost. In turn, the subelements' requirements are subdivided among assemblies, subassemblies, component parts, and so on. Operational requirements are analyzed for hardware, software, people, and facilities, and detailed specifications are laid out. Procedural support needs are also determined wherever people interface with the system (e.g., instructions for installing, operating, troubleshooting, inspecting, and repairing the system). Finally, a schematic block diagram with all items tied together in a system-installed configuration is prepared. This diagram indicates the flows, sequencing, and interface requirements, and specifications with which to evaluate the system design.

A similar procedure is conducted concurrently on the support system: functional flow diagrams are prepared showing all scheduled and unscheduled support functions for correcting malfunctions or performing scheduled maintenance. Each block of the diagram is analyzed in detail to determine the most feasible, reliable, and economic means for supporting the operating system and minimizing downtime. This analysis may lead to

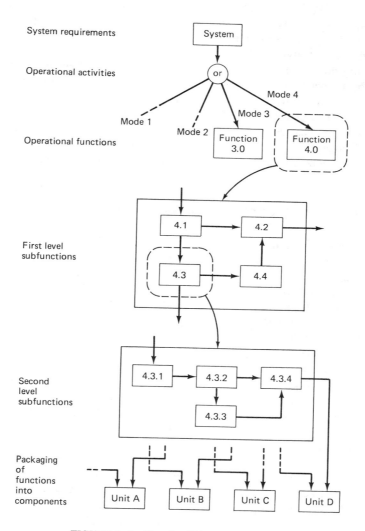

FIGURE A–2. Functional block-flow diagram.

additional operating system features to facilitate testing or parts replacement, or redesigning subsystems and equipment to reduce maintenance.

The functional breakdown and allocation of system requirements establishes boundaries and constraints on each functional block. For each function several satisfactory designs might be identified. Alternative designs are analyzed using mathematical models.

The final proposed operating/support system is synthesized and evaluated. The system synthesis combines the performance, configuration, and arrangement of the system and its subelements along with techniques for test, operation, and life cycle support. A dynamic analysis and evaluation is performed by simulating all units on a computer or subjecting selected units to mathematical analysis. Several iterations may be required before detailed design specifications about the system and input-output requirements of subsystems can satisfactorily be made.

The result of Stage 2 is a list of specifications for system design. The customer review team studies the design recommendations and decides to approve, reject, or request changes. Designing a system in detail can be very expensive, so detailed design usually does not begin until after the system has been authorized and funds allotted.

STAGE 3: DETAILED DESIGN AND SYSTEM DEVELOPMENT

The process of detailed design involves further description of subsystems, units, assemblies, lower level parts, and components of the prime mission operating equipment and support items. Decisions are made about whether subsystems and components will be manual, automatic, or semiautomatic; whether components will be electronic, mechanical, or hydraulic; whether input-output devices will be manual, keyboard, magnetic tape, disks, or other. This detailed description results in design documentation for all elements of the system: specifications, analysis results, study results, detailed drawings, materials and parts lists, and so on. Computer software is also developed at this time.

Everything up to this point has been analytical in nature. The next step is to move from "concepts on paper" to a configuration that is ready for fabrication or production. Component parts which are commercially available are selected on the basis of surveys and comparison testing in a laboratory. Components that must be developed from scratch are tested experimentally using "breadboards." A breadboard is a test model or assembly of components that enables a design to be verified by trial and error. Portions of the system may have to be redesigned pending the outcome of breadboard tests. Breadboards are used to develop individual pieces of equipment which will subsequently be mated and integrated for overall systems development. A nearly complete or "prototype" system, assembled for purposes of developmental testing, may then be used to evaluate the overall system and to ensure that the design satisfies customer requirements.

System development and design testing and evaluation includes:[2]

1. Checking the operation of subsystems when combined in a complete system.
2. Evaluating the validity of assumptions made in the systems analysis.
3. Paying close attention to
   a. "cross talk" among subsystems
   b. power couplings
   c. feedback among subsystems

  d. adjustments and calibrations
  e. serviceability and maintainability.

  The system must be thoroughly checked under a variety of conditions so deficiencies can be corrected. Many problems previously overlooked in the design process will come to light during testing and evaluation. Modifications are often required to correct for oversights, eliminate deficiencies, or simply improve the system.

  When there is insufficient time and money to prepare a prototype for system development, the first few production models manufactured are subjected to developmental testing and design evaluation. Gradually, as minor modifications are made and the design is approved, full scale production begins. Design and development testing is phased out and quality control testing begins. Quality control testing looks at the manufacturing process to ensure it is producing according to design specifications. It continues for as long as the system is manufactured.

  The design of the production capability (facilities and related resources) to make the system also begins during this phase so that by the time the system is fully developed it can be produced (Stage 4). Called "process design," it includes the design of new (or redesign of old) facilities and manufacturing processes, selection of specific materials and pieces of equipment, and preparations for production control, quality testing, manufacturing tooling, product transportation, personnel hiring and training, and data collection and processing.

STAGE 4: SYSTEM CONSTRUCTION AND/OR PRODUCTION

During Stage 4, the system is either (1) mass produced in multiple quantities (i.e., assembly line produced systems), (2) produced in limited quantities with different features (i.e., job-shop produced systems), or (3) built as a single item (e.g., a large ship or other one-of-a-kind item). This stage begins as soon as the design is considered frozen. (In less complex systems, the process may skip the development stage and jump directly here from Stage 2.) Stage 4 involves acquiring materials, maintaining adequate inventory, and controlling production/construction operations to uphold product performance, quality, reliability, safety, and other criteria. Stages 3 and 4 are sometimes referred to as the "acquisition" phase—the phase where the system physically comes into being and system objectives are accomplished.

STAGE 5: SYSTEM OPERATION AND SUPPORT (EXECUTION)

Stage 5 completes the life cycle of the system. Here the customer operates the system until it ultimately wears out or becomes obsolete. The support system is utilized in three ways: assistance in deploying, installing, and checking out the system; field service and maintenance support in assisting day to day operation, and modification and enhancement of the system to ensure continued satisfaction; and support in phasing out or disposing of the system at the end of its life cycle.

THROUGHOUT: SYSTEM EVALUATION

Although system evaluation is the major activity of Stage 3, it is, as well, an ongoing, interative process throughout the entire systems engineering process. The role of system evaluation is summarized in Figure A–3.

During Stages 1 and 2, system evaluation utilizes conceptual, mathematical models to refine system definition and select design alternatives. In Stage 3, evaluation relies upon physical test models and mock-ups to test how well designs satisfy requirements. Prototype

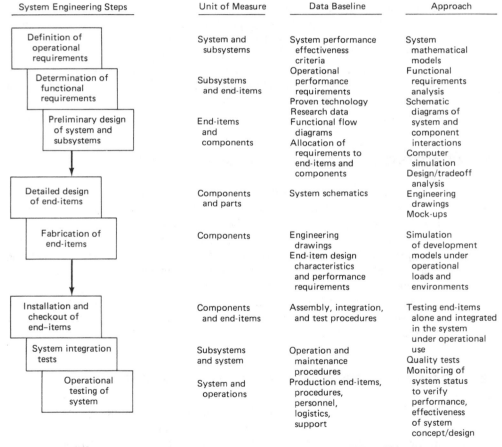

System Engineering Steps	Unit of Measure	Data Baseline	Approach
Definition of operational requirements	System and subsystems	System performance effectiveness criteria	System mathematical models
Determination of functional requirements	Subsystems and end-items	Operational performance requirements	Functional requirements analysis
Preliminary design of system and subsystems	End-items and components	Proven technology Research data Functional flow diagrams Allocation of requirements to end-items and components	Schematic diagrams of system and component interactions Computer simulation Design/tradeoff analysis
Detailed design of end-items	Components and parts	System schematics	Engineering drawings Mock-ups
Fabrication of end-items	Components	Engineering drawings End-item design characteristics and performance requirements	Simulation of development models under operational loads and environments
Installation and checkout of end–items	Components and end-items	Assembly, integration, and test procedures	Testing end-items alone and integrated in the system under operational use
System integration tests	Subsystems and system	Operation and maintenance procedures	Quality tests Monitoring of system status to verify performance, effectiveness of system concept/design
Operational testing of system	System and operations	Production end-items, procedures, personnel, logistics, support	

FIGURE A–3.   System data analysis and evaluation. (Adapted from Wilton Chase, *Management of Systems Engineering* (New York: Wiley, © 1974), 76–77, with permission.)

and production models are evaluated to test total system design assumptions and integration. During Stage 4, production models are evaluated on-site or through sample testing. Finally, during operation in Stage 5, the overall system is evaluated within the operating environment for its ability to satisfy original requirements.

Systems engineering deals with the total system and its complete life cycle. To accomplish overall system objectives, a system must be designed, tested, and supported as a complete entity. The "system" must be seen as including not only prime mission equipment—hardware and software, but everything needed to make it work, including (1) supporting information and equipment for production, control, testing, training, and maintenance; (2) facilities to produce and operate it; (3) selection and training of personnel to produce, operate and maintain it; and (4) management policies and programs to implement, operate, and support it.

No two systems are ever alike, but systems engineering remains a process for making logical systems design decisions regardless of size, purpose, or complexity.

ENDNOTES

1. G.W. Jenkins, "The Systems Approach," in *Systems Behavior,* 2nd ed., John Beishan and Geoff Peter, eds. (London: Harper & Row for the Open University, 1976), 88.
2. Harold Chestnut, *Systems Engineering Methods* (New York: John Wiley, 1967), 33.

Types of Contracts

A contract is an agreement between two parties wherein one party (the contractor) obligates itself to perform a service, and the other party (the client) obligates itself to do something in return—typically make a payment. Both the service requirements and the payment must be clear and unequivocally spelled out in the contract. An ambiguous or inconsistent contract is difficult to understand and enforce.

Different kinds of contracts provide different advantages to the client and the contractor. Depending on the risk of the project and the degree of difficulty in estimating costs, the client and contractor try to negotiate the type of contract that best serves their own interests. In some cases, for example, the client can protect herself by imposing penalty clauses or incorporating incentives into the contract.

The two fundamental kinds of contacts are *fixed price* and *cost reimbursable* contracts. In the fixed price kind, the price is agreed upon and remains fixed as long as there are no changes to the scope or provisions of the agreement. In the cost reimbursable kind, the contractor is reimbursed for all or some of the expenses incurred during the performance of the contract, so as a result, the final price is unknown until the project is completed. Within these two types, several variations exist.

Variables

The variables specified in a contract may include the following:

C_{ex} and C_{ac} — Target (expected) cost and actual cost. "Cost" represent monies expended by the contractor in performing the work. C_{ex} and C_{ac} are the negotiated target cost and the actual cost of the project under normal circumstances.

C_{max} — The maximum cost. This is the negotiated cost ceiling, the highest cost that will be reimbursed by the client.

P_{ex} — The negotiated target profit. "Profit" represents income to the contractor in excess of project costs.

P_{max} and P_{min} — The profit ceiling and profit floor. These are the maximum and minimum negotiated values of the profit. They are usually determined as a percentage of project target costs, actual costs, or the difference between the two.

CSR — The cost sharing ratio. When costs are to be shared by the client and the customer, this is the percentage of the cost that each agrees to share (the sum is 100 percent).

F_{max} and F_{min} — The negotiated maximum and minimum fee. This is the amount, in absolute terms, above costs that the client will pay the contractor.

Price — The price the client pays for the project. Price includes reimbursable costs (or a percentage thereof) incurred by the contractor, plus the contractor's profit or fee.

I. FIXED PRICE TYPES OF CONTRACTS

Fixed Price Contract (FP)

Under an FP or "lump sum" agreement, the contractor agrees to perform all work at a fixed price. Clients are able to get the minimum price by putting out the contract to competitive bidders. The contractor must be very careful in estimating the target cost since, once agreed upon, the price cannot be adjusted. If the contractor overestimates the target cost in the bidding stage, he may lose the contract to a lower priced competitor; if the estimate is too low, he might win the job but make little or no profit.

When a project can readily be specified in detail, an FP contract is preferred by both client and contractor. From the client's point of view, there is less need to supervise the project since she does not have to be concerned with project costs. She need only monitor work progress to see that it meets contractual completion date and performance specifications. Under an FP agreement, clients are less likely to request changes or additions to the contract.

The disadvantage of an FP contract is that it is more difficult and more costly to prepare. Since the contractor can make larger profits by reducing costs, there is some incentive for him to use cheaper quality materials, perform marginal workmanship, or extend the completion to his own gain. The client can counteract these by stipulating rigid end-item specifications, completion dates, and supervising the work. Of course, the contractor also runs the risk of underestimating. If the project gets into trouble, bankrupts the contractor, or is otherwise incompletable, the client may be subject to legal action from other involved parties.

Fixed Price with Redetermination[1]

Contracts with long lead times such as construction and production may have *escalation provisions* which protect the contractor against cost increases in materials, labor rates, or overhead expenses in performing the work. For example, the price may be tied to an inflation index so it can be adjusted in the advent of inflation, or it may be *redetermined* as costs become known. In the latter case, the initial price is negotiated with the stipulation that it will be redetermined at intervals so that the price can be based upon actual cost data. A variety of redetermination contracts are used: some establish a ceiling price for the contract and permit only downward adjustments, others permit upward and downward adjustments; some establish one readjustment period at the end of the project, others use more than one period. Redetermination contracts are appropriate where engineering and design efforts are difficult to estimate, or in long-term quantity production contracts where the final price cannot be estimated for lack of accurate cost data.

The redetermined price may apply to items already produced as well as future items. Since the only requirement to renegotiate the price is substantiating cost data, redetermined contracts tend to induce inefficiencies. After negotiating a low initial price, the contractor can produce a few items and then "discover" that the costs are much higher than expected. The contract thus becomes a "cost plus" kind of contract (described later) and is subject to abuse.

Fixed Price Incentive Fee Contract (FPIF)

A FPIF contract alleviates some of the disadvantages to the client of a fixed price contract because it offers a profit incentive for the contractor to reduce costs and improve efficiency. The contractor negotiates to perform the work for a target price based upon a target cost (C_{ex}) plus a target profit (P_{ex}). A ceiling price (C_{max}) and a ceiling profit (P_{max}) are also negotiated. If the total cost ends up being less than the target cost, the contractor makes a higher profit, up to P_{max}. If there is a cost overrun, the contractor absorbs some of the overrun until a profit floor (P_{min}) is reached.

Profit is determined according to a formula based on a *cost sharing ratio* (CSR). A CSR of 80/20, for example, indicates that for every dollar spent on costs, the client pays 80 cents and the contractor pays 20 cents. It is beneficial to the contractor to keep costs low since he pays 20 cents on every dollar spent above C_{ex} (thus making 20 cents less profit), but earns 20 cents more on every dollar saved below C_{ex}. As further incentive to keep costs down, the ratio might be accelerated at costs above C_{ex} so that the contractor has to pay a higher percentage.

The FPIF applies to long duration or large production projects. It is not applicable to R&D or other projects where the target cost is difficult or impossible to estimate.

FPIF contracts are not true fixed price contracts. They invite contractors to negotiate unrealistically high C_{ex}'s so that extra profits can be made through the incentive features.

II. COST REIMBURSEMENT TYPES OF CONTRACTS

When it is difficult to achieve accurate cost estimates in the early phases of work, such as in R&D or advanced technology projects, a type of contract called cost reimbursement permits work to begin before the costs are fully specified.

Cost Plus Fixed Fee (CPFF)

Under a CPFF contract, the contractor is reimbursed for all direct allowable costs plus an additional, fixed amount to cover overhead and profit. This is justified when costs rise due to increases in the scope of work or escalate because of factors beyond the contractor's control. Regardless of the cost, the fee specified remains the same. Usually the fee is a negotiated percentage of the C_{ex}, though often it is allowed to increase in proportion to actual costs up to a percentage ceiling.

In contrast to the FP contract, a CPFF agreement puts the burden of risk on the client. The contract does not indicate what the project is going to cost until the end of the project, and it provides little incentive for the contractor to control costs, finish on time, or do anything beyond minimum requirements since he gets paid the same fee regardless. The major factor motivating the contractor to control costs and schedules is the effect overruns have on his reputation. The other is the fact that as long as the contractor's work force and facilities are tied up, he cannot work on other projects.

Because of the risks to the client in a CPFF agreement, she must exercise substantial *external* control to insure the project is done efficiently and meets technical, time, and cost targets. She may specify who is to be the project manager or have her own project manager on-site to work with the contractor's project manager. The government has curtailed use of CPFF contracts in favor of incentive type contracts.

Cost Plus Incentive Fee Contract (CPIF)

When the contractor is unwilling to enter into a FP agreement and the client does not want a CPFF contract, an alternative is to use a CPIF arrangement. This has features of both kinds of contacts: it is similar to CPFF in that costs are reimbursed, but instead of the fee being fixed it is based on an incentive formula. Unlike the FPIF where fees are based upon the target cost, C_{ex}, fees in the CPIF contract are based upon a percentage of actual costs, C_{ac}, using a CSR formula. The contract starts with a specified target cost, as in FPIF, and guarantees a maximum or minimum fee which is a percentage of the actual cost. Maximum fees establish the outside limits on a contractor's profit. The minimum fee may be zero or even less.

Multiple Incentive Contracts[2]

Multiple incentive contracts attempt to relate profits to the uncertainties associated with achieving time, cost, and performance goals in large-scale development programs. The intent is to reward contractors that are able to set and achieve realistic targets in *all three* criteria.

Profit weights assigned to the three criteria are used to determine the amount of "profit swing" allocated to each criterion. Consider the example shown below where the cost-fee structure is similar to the CPIF example above. Here the "fee swing" is between 2 percent and 14 percent, or a total of 12 percent.[3]

$$C_{ex} = \$100$$
$$F_{ex} = \$8 \ (8\%)$$
$$F_{max} = \$14 \ (14\%)$$
$$F_{min} = \$2 \ (2\%)$$

The 12 percent fee swing is then divided among the three criteria:

Criteria	Weight	Profit Swing
Performance	0.5	6%
Cost	0.25	3%
Time	0.25	3%
Total	1.00	12%

In engineering contracts, typically the largest weight is given to performance, followed by time and cost. For performance several measures might be used at once, such as accuracy, range, reliability, and speed, in which case a point system is devised so all can be represented as a single performance factor using one curve.

In this example, the performance factor is given a weight of 0.5, which yields a profit swing of 6 percent; time and cost are given weights of 0.25, so each have a profit swing of 3 percent. The profit percentage is computed as a function of all three criteria, as shown in Figure B–1, according to the formula

$$P = (8 + x + y + z)\% \ (C_{ex}).$$

Since all three criteria tend to be interrelated (e.g., performance targets can be surpassed, but at the expense of time and cost, and vice versa), structuring the contract is a complicated issue. The computations and legal terms can be tricky, so this type of contract is seldom used.[4]

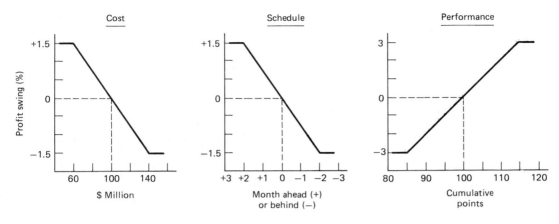

FIGURE B–1. Multiple incentive contract.

Time and Materials Contract (TM)

A TM contract is a simple form of agreement that reimburses the contractor for labor costs and materials as incurred. It provides for payment of direct labor hours at an hourly rate which includes the direct labor cost, indirect costs, and profit. Sometimes a ceiling price is established which may be exceeded, depending on the agreement. Charges for private consultants and other services (electricians, carpenters, etc.) are usually based on time and materials.

ENDNOTES

1. V. G. Hajek, *Management of Engineering Projects,* 3rd ed. (New York, Wiley, 1984), 82–83; D. D. Roman, *Managing Projects: A Systems Approach* (New York: Elsevier, 1986), 297.
2. R.W. Miller, *Schedule, Cost, and Profit Control with PERT* (New York: McGraw-Hill, 1963), 173–184.
3. Example from ibid., 174–175.
4. See Miller, ibid., 183–196, for a more complete discussion of multiple incentive contracts, their usage in PERT systems, and their development and application to program control.

appendix C

Logistical Online System Project Summary Plan

Cover Letter

IV.   Technical Section

   IV.1   Statement of work
   IV.2   Schedule and calendar
   IV.3   Budget and cost
   IV.4   Information requirements
   IV.5   Documentation and maintenance
   IV.6   Work review
   IV.7   Applicable codes and standards
   IV.8   Variations, changes, contingencies
   IV.9   Contract deliverables

Attachments

   Item 1. Robot transporter
   Item 2. MPD site layout
   Item 3. Storage rack assembly
   Item 4. LOGON organization chart
   Item 5. Project responsibilities
   Item 6. Principle subtasks
   Item 7. Project schedule
   Item 8. LOGON project cost estimate

Standard   Memorandum
Industrial
Gadgets

     To: SEE DISTRIBUTION   Ref. Job No.: 390-01

     From: Frank Wesley, Project Manager   Date: 1-1-90

     Subject: Logistical Online System Project,
               Project Summary Plan

The Project Summary Plan for the Logistical Online System
Project for the Midwest Parcel Distribution Company's Chicago distribution center has been modified to include your
suggestions and approved by everyone on Distribution. Copies of this document are herewith sent for use in the performance of contract requirements.

FW:es
Enclosure

Distribution:

     Julia Melissa, Project Engineer
     Sam Block, Fabrication Manager
     Noah Errs, Quality Control Supervisor
     Larry Fine, Software Manager
     Sharry Hyman, Design Manager
     Brian Jennings, Assembly Supervisor
     Frank Nichol, Site Operations Manager
     Emily Nichol, Assembly Supervisor
     Robert Powers, Drawing Supervisor
     Burton Vance, Purchasing Manager

**LOGISTICAL ONLINE SYSTEM
PROJECT SUMMARY PLAN**

I. MANAGEMENT SUMMARY

On September 5, 1989, Standard Industrial Gadgets Company was awarded the contract by the Midwest Parcel Distribution (MPD) Company of New York for the Logistical Online (LOGON) System Project. The system is to be installed at MPD Co.'s main Chicago distribution facility.

The project consists of designing, fabricating, and installing a parcel transport, storage, and data base system, for automatic placement, storage, and retrieval of standardized shipping containers. The system uses an overhead conveyor track system, conveyor-robot transporter units, racks with standard size shipping containers and storage buckets, and a computerized data base for automatic placement and retrieval of parcels and record keeping.

Standard Industrial Gadgets is the prime contractor and is responsible for the design of hardware and software, fabrication of component parts, system installation, and checkout. The major subcontractors are Creative Robotics, Inc. (CRI), Steel Enterprises, Inc. (SEI), United Plastics Co. (UPC), and CompuResearch Corp. (CRC). STING will provide overall project management between CRI, SEI, and UPC Corp. and related contract administration; legal, accounting, insurance, auditing, and counseling services as may be required. The Project Manager is Mr. Frank Wesley, and the Project Engineer is Ms. Julia Melissa.

The project will commence with basic design on or before May 15, 1990; installation at the site will begin on or before January 9, 1991; and final system approval by MPD Co. will be made on or before April 16, 1991. The principle subtasks are shown in the schedule, Item 7.

The price of the contract is $1,452,000, fixed fee with limited escalation, based on a target final approval date of April 16, 1991. Total expenses, tabulated in Item 8, for labor, overhead, materials, subcontracting, and general/administrative are $1,319,518. The agreement provides

for an escalation clause tied to inflation indices for material expenses for the steel conveyor track and rack support
systems. Since the facility will be unusable for MPD Co.
during most of the later part of the project, an agreed to
penalty of $1000 a day will be imposed on STING for target
completion overruns. Contingency arrangements in the agreement allow for reconsideration of the penalty in event of
disruption of work for labor dispute with management.

II. PROJECT DESCRIPTION

On September 5, 1989, Standard Industrial Gadgets Company
was awarded the contract for the Logistical Online System
Project. The award followed a four-month competitive bidding review by the Midwest Parcel Distribution (MPD) Company of New York. The system is to be installed at MPD
Co.'s main Chicago distribution facility.

 The project consists of designing, fabricating, and installing a parcel transport, storage, and data base system, hereafter called LOGON, for automatic placement,
storage, and retrieval of standardized shipping containers. The system will substantially improve the speed of
parcel handling, increase the utilization of storage facility space, enhance record keeping, and reduce labor costs
at the facility. Anticipated ancillary benefits include reduced insurance premium and shrinkage costs.

 The system uses an overhead conveyor track system, conveyor-robot transporter units, racks with standard size
shipping containers and storage buckets, and a computerized data base for automatic placement and retrieval of
parcels and recordkeeping.

 The LOGON system works like this:

 Upon a parcel's arrival at the distribution center receiving dock, it is placed into one of three standard
sized parcel "buckets." The buckets are electronically
coded as to parcel item and shipping destination. This
code is relayed to a master data base from any of four terminal work stations located at the dock. The work stations
are connected via a DEM-LAN network to a CRC Model 4000

computer. The Model 4000 has 180 MB storage with tape backup for retaining information about parcel description, status, storage location, and destination. The system keeps track of available, remaining storage space, and, if need be, reallocates buckets for optimal space utilization. The CRC4000 will also provide reports about system status and performance on request by management.

   The parcel buckets are manually attached to a robot transporter mounted on an overhead track-conveyor system (Item 1). The robot transporter carries the bucket to a "suitable" vacant storage slot within a shipping container located on a rack in the facility. The computer determines which shipping container has a vacant slot of sufficient

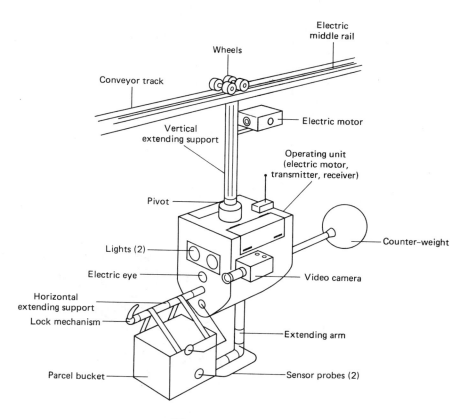

ITEM 1.   Robot transporter.

size and containing parcels going to the same or nearby
destination as parcels in the transporter's parcel bucket.
The robot transporter then conveys the bucket to the appropriate shipping container and unloads it into the vacant
slot. Shipping containers are stacked three high in seven
rows of racks (Items 2 and 3). The storage facility has capacity for 400 shipping containers, each with 150 cubic
feet of storage capacity.

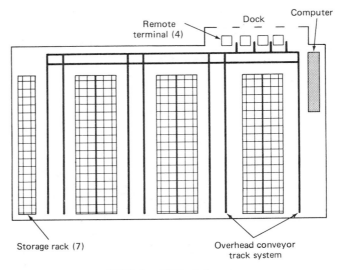

ITEM 2.   MPD site layout.

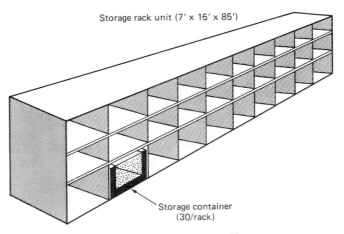

ITEM 3.   Storage rack assembly.

When a truck or rail car going to a specific destination is to be loaded, the destination is keyed in at the dock terminal work station so the data base system can identify all shipping containers having buckets with parcels going to the same or nearby destinations. The system then routes the robot transporters to the appropriate shipping containers for retrieval of parcel buckets. The system has four robot transporters that operate independently and simultaneously. The robot transporters retrieve the buckets and transport them back to the loading dock for placement of parcels into departing truck or rail cars. The longest specified retrieval time in the system is eight minutes.

Standard Industrial Gadgets is the prime contractor and is responsible for the design of hardware and software, fabrication of components parts, system installation, and checkout. The major subcontractors are Creative Robotics, Inc., which will supply the major components for the robot transporters; Steel Enterprises, Inc., which will supply the parts for the overhead track-conveyor system and storage racks; United Plastics Co., which will supply the shipping containers and parcel buckets; and CompuResearch Corp. (CRC) which will supply the terminal work stations, DEM-LAN network, and CRC4000 computer. CRC will also provide support for software development and installation of all computer hardware items.

Structural tests performed by M&M Engineering Corp. indicate that the present ceiling structure of the facility can support additional loads of up to 600 psi. The LOGON system would add a maximum of 325 psi, including parcel weight, and thus can be installed directly to the existing ceiling frame without additional reinforcement. Structural tests performed on walls and floors also indicate sufficient strength to support the system with a safety factor of 2.1. The system can be directly connected to the existing main electrical harness hookup.

During system installation MPD has arranged for alternate, temporary storage at another facility and rerouting of most parcel traffic to its other sites.

As much as possible, design information about existing systems, such as MPD's Tulsa facility, will be utilized to try to initially move the project to an advanced stage. Remaining design work will use as much as possible of work that has been done already, without compromising confidentiality of clients, on previous, similar projects.

III. ORGANIZATION SECTION

III.1 Project Administration

All correspondence on project matters will be between the project manager for STING and the project director for MPD. When specifically authorized, project personnel may correspond directly with the client or subcontractors for information, keeping the project manager and project director informed with copies of all correspondence and memos of telephone conversations.

The account number assigned to the LOGON project is 901-0000. Work packages and tasks will be assigned sub-account numbers at the time when work package instructions and schedules are authorized. A single invoice for the project accounts as a whole is acceptable for billing at monthly intervals.

III.2 Project Organization and Responsibility

The organization of Standard Industrial Gadgets Company for the performance of the project is shown in Item 4. Specific administrative and managerial responsibilities are summarized in the responsibility chart, Item 5.

The Project Manager, Mr. Wesley, is responsible for managing project work, which includes all client contact, reporting of progress, adherence to contractual commitments regarding schedule and technical performance, and monitoring of budgetary expenditures. Changes in scope of contractual services will be recorded in communications with the client. He and his staff will report directly to Mr. Ed Demerest, Vice-President and Project Director for MPD Co.

The Project Engineer, Ms. Melissa, is responsible for establishing specifications and ensuring system delivery to meet technical requirements. She will supervise the preparation of design requirements and drawings depicting

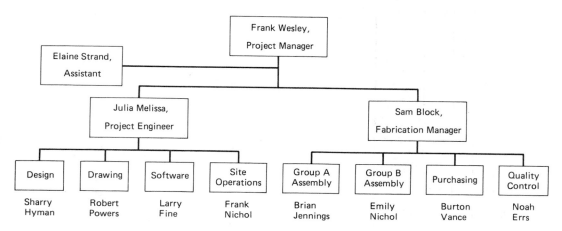

ITEM 4. LOGON organization chart.

system elements, estimate quantities, check drawings and requirements calculations, and ensure that system technical requirements are fulfilled at the site.

The Fabrication Manager, Mr. Block, is responsible for managing procurement, assembly and related work at the STING plant. He will direct procurement and assembly operations, assure the quality of delivered parts from subcontractors meets requirements, coordinate assembly operations of robotic transporters, track conveyor, and storage rack subsystems, and sign off final approval for assemblies prior to shipment to the MPD site.

III.3 <u>Subcontractor Administration</u>

The four primary subcontractors of the project are Creative Robotics, Inc. (CRI), Steel Enterprises, Inc. (SEI), United Plastics Co. (UPC), and CompuResearch Corp. (CRC). Key personnel associated with each are:

Bill Plante	Project Coordinator, CRI
Terry Hemmart	Manager, Manufacturing, SEI
Delbert Dillert	Customer Representation, UPC
Lynn Duthbart	Systems Engineering Representative, CRC
Elmer Hyman	Customer Representative, CRC

Persons Responsible

Responsibility Code

- P Primary responsibility
- S Secondary responsibility
- N Must be notified
- A Must give approval

Project Task or Activity	F.W.	J.M.	S.E.H.	R.L.G.	P.J.	D.V.R.	R.L.P.	O.E.M.	P.V.R.	D.M.N.	R.L.	L.S.F.	L.L.L.	J.R.S.	D.V.Q.	F.W.N.	J.M.W.N.	L.O.T.	A.U.A.	D.A.R.	S.O.B.	E.N.	G.G.F.	R.T.T.	B.V.L.	B.J.	T.T.Y.	H.R.D.	B.V.-Purchasing
Project coordination	P	S																		S								N	
Project development	A	P														A					N								
Project design	A		P				A																						
H Basic design	N		A	P	S	S																							
I Hardware design A			A	A	**P**						N																		
J Hardware design B			A	A	**P**						N																		
K Drawings B			A					A	S	P																			
L Software specs	N		A									A	P	S	S						N							P	
M Parts purchase B	N								S	P										A								P	
N Parts purchase A	N							A	P										A	N									
O Drawings A							A	P											A	N									
P Installation drawings																N			A	N		A						P	
Q Software purchase	N															N				A	N	A							
U Assembly A	N																A	P	S			A	P	S	S		S		
V Assembly B	N																A	P	S	S					A	P	S		
W Test A	N															N				A		A			P				
X Test B	N															N			A	A									
Y Final installation	N															A	A	P	S						P				
Z Final test	N															A	A	P	S	S									

Column groups: Project Manager (F.W., J.M.); Project Engineer — Design (S.E.H., R.L.G., P.J., D.V.R.), Drawing (R.L.P., O.E.M., P.V.R., D.M.N., R.L.), Software (L.S.F., L.L.L., J.R.S., D.V.Q., F.W.N.); Site Operations (J.M.W.N., L.O.T., A.U.A., D.A.R., S.O.B.); Fabrication Manager — Assembly A (E.N., G.G.F., R.T.T., B.V.L., B.J.), Assembly B (T.T.Y., H.R.D.); B.V.-Purchasing.

ITEM 5. Project responsibilities.

Changes or modifications to the respective agreements requested by a subcontractor or by STING will be acted upon by the STING Project Manager, Mr. Wesley, upon receipt of a written proposal from the subcontractor.

Correspondence to subcontractors concerning technical matters will be directed to the above named first four parties or their substitutes. Software specifications related work with CRC will be coordinated by, and communications should be directed to, the CRC customer representative. Project telephone conversations between STING and subcontractors shall be noted in handwritten memos and copies sent to the STING project engineer.

Progress reports shall be prepared by Mr. Plante, CRI project coordinator, Ms. Hemmart, SEI manufacturing manager, Mr. Dillert, UPC customer representative, and Mrs. Duthbart, CRC systems engineering rep. for presentation at weekly meetings to be held at STING Co.'s Chicago office for the duration of scheduled involvement as noted in the respective agreements. Other meetings may require attendance by other individuals as required by the subcontractors or requested by the project manager. The following number of meetings have been included in the respective subcontractor agreement budgets.

CRI	5 meetings
SEI	3 meetings
UPC	2 meetings
CRC	5 meetings (software development)
CRC	8 meetings (site system integration)

The subcontractors will provide information and perform services on the project as follows:

1. CRI will perform all elements of work associated with procurement, manufacturing, and component functional tests of parts and subassemblies according to specifications, plans, and drawings provided by STING. Parts and components for four robotic-transporters will be delivered to STING according to the criteria and dates specified in the agreement.

2. SEI will perform all work associated with procurement, manufacturing, and component functional tests of parts and

subassemblies according to the specifications, plans, and drawings provided by STING. Parts and components for the complete overhead conveyor track system and seven storage racks will be delivered to STING according to the criteria and dates specified in the agreement.

3. UPC will perform all work associated with procurement, manufacturing, and component functional tests of parts and subassemblies according to the specifications, plans, and drawings provided by STING. Plastic containers and parcel buckets will be delivered to the MPD Chicago distribution facility in quantities and according to dates specified in the agreement. One plastic container and one each of three size parcel buckets will be delivered to the STING facility for tests according to the date specified in the agreement.

4. CRC will perform all work associated with development, programming, and tests of LOGON system robotic transporter control software, system data base, and reporting functions according to the specifications provided by STING. Software will be delivered to the STING facility according to dates specified in the agreement.

5. CRC will transport, install, and perform component and integration tests for checkout of four terminal work stations, DEM-LAN network, CRC4000, printer, backup system, and related hardware according to criteria and dates specified in the agreement.

STING will provide overall project management between CRI, SEI, and UPC Corp. and related contract administration, legal, accounting, insurance, auditing, and counseling services as may be required by the project.

III.4 Client Interface

Key personnel associated with the project for MPD Company are:

Ed Demerest	Project Director, Chicago
Lynn Joffrey	Administrative Assistant, Chicago
Cecil Party	Financial Manager, Chicago
Mary Marquart	Operations Manager, New York

Changes or modifications to the agreement requested either by MPD or by STING will be acted upon by the Operations Manager, Mrs. Marquart, upon receipt of a written proposal from STING.

All correspondence with MPD regarding the project will be directed to the project director, Mr. Demerest. If he requests our contacting another person or contractor, he will receive a copy of each item of correspondence between parties. Project telephone conversations between STING and outside parties shall be noted in handwritten memos and copies sent to Ms. Joffrey.

Progress reports shall be prepared by Mr. Wesley, STING Project Manager, for presentation at monthly meetings to be held at MPD Co.'s Chicago office. Other meetings may require attendance by other individuals as required by MPD or requested by Mr. Wesley. Mr. Wesley shall also convene two other meetings, a mid-project review and a project summary, at the New York office of MPD. A total of 15 meetings was included in the agreement budget. MPD Co. will provide information and perform services on the project as follows:

1. MPD will perform all elements of work associated with vacating the site prior to the date in the agreement for commencing of system installation.

2. MPD will provide surveys, design criteria, drawings, and preliminary plans prepared under previous agreements or received through requests for proposals for the LOGON system.

3. MPD will provide design criteria, drawings, and plans prepared for the automated parcel storage and retrieval system at MPD Co.'s Tulsa facility.

4. MPD will obtain all internal, municipal, state, and federal approvals as may be necessary to complete the project.

5. MPD will provide overall project management between MPD, STING, and CRC Corp.; contract administration; legal,

accounting, insurance, auditing, and counseling services as may be required by the project.

The contract administrator is the operations manager. Changes or modifications to the agreement with MPD, requested either by MPD or STING, shall be subject to a written proposal by STING to MPD's contract administrator through Mr. Demerest.

The financial manager, Mr. Party, is responsible for approvals of monthly expense summaries provided by STING and monthly payment to STING. MPD is responsible for securing necessary support from electrical and telephone utilities for system hookup, and for making available to STING all criteria, drawings and studies prepared for the Chicago site facility and the Tulsa facility automated system.

III.5 <u>Manpower and Training</u>

No additional manpower requirements beyond current staffing levels are envisioned to perform services for this project. Five personnel from the design group for this project have been enrolled in and will have completed a robotics seminar at a local university before the project begins.

III.6 <u>User Training</u>

Two systems operations manuals and 16 hours of technical assistance will be provided. Thereafter, ongoing operator training will be the responsibility of MPD Co.

IV. TECHNICAL SECTION

IV.1 <u>Statement of Work</u>

The major tasks to be performed are the design, fabrication, installation, and checkout of the LOGON system for the Chicago distribution center of MPD Co. The work will be executed in accordance with the terms, conditions, and scope as set forth in the applicable drawings and specifications prepared by STING in the written proposal and confirmed in the agreement.

Subtasks required to perform the major tasks noted above are shown on the network in Item 6. The major subtasks are (letters refer to task designations on Item 6):

1. Perform basic design of overall system. (H)

2. Prepare detailed design specifications for robotic transporter, conveyor track, storage rack systems, and shipping and parcel containers to be sent to Creative Robotics, Steel Enterprises, and United Plastics, subcontractors. (J,I,M,N)

3. Prepare specifications for the software system and for DEM-LAN and CRC 4000 system interface. (L)

4. Prepare detailed assembly drawings for robotic transporter units, conveyor track system, and storage rack system. (O,K)

5. Prepare drawings and a master plan for system installation and test at the site. (P)

6. Fabricate robotic transporter units, conveyor track, and rack support subassemblies at STING facility. (U,V)

7. Perform preliminary functionality tests on robotic transporter units at STING facility. (X)

8. Perform structural and functional tests of conveyor track and storage rack systems at STING facility. (W)

9. Perform installation of all subsystems at MPD Chicago facility site. (Y)

10. Perform checkout of subsystems and final checkout of overall system at MPD facility site. (Z)

IV.2 Schedule and Calendar

The project will commence with basic design on or before May 15, 1990; installation at the site will begin on or before January 9, 1991; and final system approval by MPD Co. will be made on or before April 16, 1991. The project master schedule for the most significant portions of the proj-

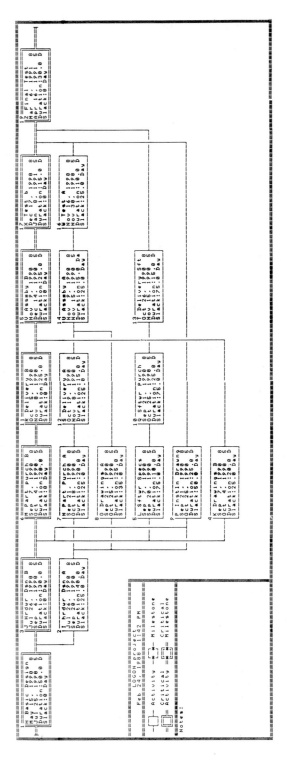

ITEM 6. Principal subtasks.

516

ect is given in Item 7. The significant project milestones indicated are:

1. Commence basic design   May 15, 1990
2. Basic design review   July 20, 1990
3. Transporter and conveyor
   design review   Sept. 1, 1990
4. Computer system specs review   Sept. 19, 1990
5. Hardware Group A&B review   Dec. 10, 1990
6. Begin installation at site   Jan. 9, 1991
7. Final user approval   April 16, 1991

Starting dates for activities dependent on the results of reviews will be adjusted to make allowances for significant changes in the length of predecessor activities, although no adjustments are anticipated.

Work package instructions and a detailed schedule for basic design has been distributed. Subsequent schedule and work package information will be distributed and discussed at review meetings.

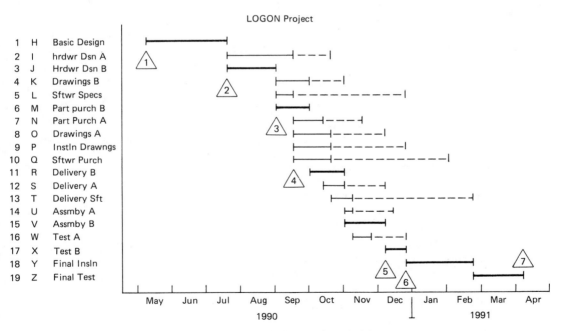

ITEM 7. Project schedule.

The schedule of contract deliverables is given in Section IV.9.

IV.3 Budget and Cost

The price of the contract is $1,452,000, fixed fee with limited escalation, based on a target final approval date of April 16, 1991. Expenses and fees will be billed and are payable monthly as incurred. The agreement provides for an escalation clause tied to inflation indices for material expenses for the steel conveyor track and rack support systems. Since the facility will be otherwise unusable for MPD Co. during the last five months of the project, completion by the contracted date is imperative. An agreed to penalty of $1000 a day will be imposed on STING for target completion overruns. Contingency arrangements in the agreement allow for reconsideration of the penalty in event of disruption of work for labor dispute with management.

Principal tasks, subtasks, man-hours, and dollars to perform them have been estimated. Total expenses, as tabulated in Item 8, for labor, overhead, materials, subcontracting, and general/administrative are $1,319,518.

Expenditures of direct labor, the largest single cost factor, are under immediate control of departments heads in design, fabrication, procurement, and customer service departments since they assign personnel to the project.

Responsibility for expenditures of man-hours and direct expenses belongs to the project manager, who receives biweekly accounting of all expenditures of time and money.

IV.4 Information Requirements

Most of the information required by STING to perform under the terms of the agreement has been supplied by MPD Co. A limited amount of site information will be obtained from additional required surveys performed by a STING survey party. MPD has expressed a willingness to dispatch some of its own personnel for minor survey work to expedite the project.

IV.5 Documentation and Maintenance

Minutes and action plans of review meetings will be formally documented and sent to the project manager. Biweekly

```
==============================
LOGON Project Cost Estimate
==============================
```

Task	Labor Time	Labor Rate	Labor Cost	O/H @ 0.25	Materials	S/C	G/A @ 0.10	Total
Project Coordination	2000.00	28.00	56000.00	14000.00				
	2000.00	12.00	24000.00	6000.00				
		Total	80000.00	20000.00	2,000		10,200	112,200
Project Development	400.00	28.00	11200.00	2800.00				
	400.00	20.00	8000.00	2000.00				
		Total	19200.00	4800.00	4,500		2,850	31,350
Project Design	50.00	28.00	1400.00	350.00				
	150.00	24.00	3600.00	900.00				
	150.00	12.00	1800.00	450.00				
		Total	6800.00	1700.00	6,000		1,450	15,950
H Basic Hardware	300.00	30.00	9000.00	2250.00				
	1600.00	24.00	38400.00	9600.00				
	1400.00	15.00	21000.00	5250.00				
		Total	68400.00	17100.00	5,410		9,091	100,001
I Hardware Design A	180.00	26.00	4680.00	1170.00				
	1100.00	24.00	26400.00	6600.00				
	900.00	15.00	13500.00	3375.00				
		Total	44580.00	11145.00	2,450		5,818	63,993
J Hardware Design B	250.00	26.00	6500.00	1625.00				
	1350.00	24.00	32400.00	8100.00				
	1300.00	20.00	26000.00	6500.00				
		Total	64900.00	16225.00	6,150		8,728	96,003
K Drawings B	160.00	26.00	4160.00	1040.00				
	160.00	18.00	2880.00	720.00				
		Total	7040.00	1760.00	5,740		1,454	15,994
L Software Specs	160.00	28.00	4480.00	1120.00				
	240.00	24.00	5760.00	1440.00				
	240.00	20.00	4800.00	1200.00				
		Total	15040.00	3760.00	2,330	11,600	3,273	36,003
M Parts Purchase B	2.00	28.00	56.00	5.60				
	16.00	24.00	384.00	96.00				
		Total	440.00	101.60	25	75,800	7,637	84,003
N Parts Purchase A	4.00	28.00	112.00	28.00				
	20.00	24.00	480.00	120.00				
		Total	592.00	148.00	35	71,950	7,273	79,998

ITEM 8.   LOGON project cost estimate.

Item 8 (page 2 of 2)

O Drawings A	650.00	26.00	16900.00	4225.00				
	700.00	18.00	12600.00	3150.00				
	Total		29500.00	7375.00	8,580		4,546	50,001
P Installation	450.00	28.00	12600.00	3150.00				
Drawings	600.00	26.00	15600.00	3900.00				
	700.00	18.00	12600.00	3150.00				
	Total		40800.00	10200.00	3,540		5,454	59,994
Q Software	8.00	28.00	224.00	56.00				
Purchase	16.00	24.00	384.00	96.00				
			0.00	0.00				
			608.00	152.00	160	71,800	7,272	79,992
U Assembly A	10.00	28.00	280.00	70.00				
	100.00	24.00	2400.00	600.00				
	120.00	20.00	2400.00	600.00				
	Total		5080.00	1270.00	6,400		1,275	14,025
V Assembly B	100.00	28.00	2800.00	700.00				
	1100.00	24.00	26400.00	6600.00				
	1100.00	20.00	22000.00	5500.00				
	Total		51200.00	12800.00	8,700		7,270	79,970
W Test A	20.00	26.00	520.00	130.00				
	300.00	24.00	7200.00	1800.00				
	300.00	20.00	6000.00	1500.00				
	Total		13720.00	3430.00	4700.00		2,185	24,035
X Test B	30.00	26.00	780.00	195.00				
	450.00	24.00	10800.00	2700.00				
	450.00	20.00	9000.00	2250.00				
	Total		20580.00	5145.00	7000.00		3,273	35,998
Y Final	320.00	28.00	8960.00	2240.00				
Installation	1200.00	24.00	28800.00	7200.00				
	900.00	22.00	19800.00	4950.00				
	Total		57560.00	14390.00	12100.00	10500.00	9,455	104,005
Z Final Test	200.00	28.00	5600.00	1400.00				
	1000.00	24.00	24000.00	6000.00				
	600.00	21.00	12600.00	3150.00				
	Total		42200.00	10550.00	1250.00	6000.00	6,000	66,000
	Total		568,240	140,633	87,070	247,650	104,501	1,319,518

ITEM 8.   LOGON project cost estimate.

expense and progress reports will be sent from functional managers to the project manager. Monthly project summary reports will be sent from the project manager to functional managers and to other managers and supervisors listed on Distribution.

Cost, performance, and progress documentation will be maintained and reported through the company project cost accounting system.

A final summary report will be prepared by the office of the project manager for the company archives.

The project manager is responsible for maintenance of all project files. All copies of project documents sent outside STING will leave only under his direction.

IV.6 Work Review

Internal review of work produced in each of the design, fabrication, procurement, and customer service divisions is a responsibility of the division head for each of the functional disciplines.

IV.7 Applicable Codes and Standards

Track conveyors, storage racks and supporting structures, electrical harnesses, and radio transmitters are to be designed to the applicable standards of AATOP, ASMER, OSHA, the Illinois Building Requirements Board, and the City of Chicago.

IV.8 Variations, Changes, Contingencies

The agreement with MPD defines the conditions for considering a change in compensation or penalties due to a change in the scope of work or cost of steel-fabricated materials, or unanticipated stoppage of work for labor dispute. It describes the procedure whereby authorization for such a change may be obtained from MPD.

The agreement, paragraph 9.2, under prime compensation, states:

"Whenever there is a major change in the scope, character, or
complexity of the work, or if extra work is required, or if
there is an increase in the expense to the CONTRACTOR for
steel-fabricated materials as negotiated in the agreement with
the responsible SUBCONTRACTORS, or if there is a stoppage of
work resulting from a labor dispute with management, the CON-
TRACTOR shall, upon request of the CLIENT, submit a cost estimate of CONSULTANT services and expenses for the change,
whether it shall involve an increase or a decrease in the Lump
Sum. The CLIENT shall request such an estimate using the form
provided herein (Attachment F). Changes for reasons of labor
dispute with management will be reviewed and determined according to the conditions specified (Attachment G)."

During system installation and tests, MPD has made arrangements to reroute about 70 percent of its Chicago parcel business to other distribution centers. The remainder
will be stored at an alternate facility near Chicago. In
the event of an unforeseen schedule overrun, the reroute
plan will remain in effect. MPD requires 30 days notice of
anticipated schedule overrun to extend the agreement with
the alternate Chicago storage facility.

IV.9 Contract Deliverables

All items are to be assembled, installed, and in operation
at the site in accordance with technical specifications in
the agreement.

Transport of components and parts from subcontractors
to the STING plant will be scheduled by subcontractors.
The respective agreements specify the following items as
deliverable to STING:

Item	Date
Parts and components for robot-trans-porters from CRI	Nov. 1, 1990
Parts and components for overhead conveyor track and storage rack systems from SEI	Nov. 4, 1990
One shipping container and one each of three size parcel buckets from UPC	Nov.10, 1990
Robotic-transporter system control software from CRC	Jan. 5, 1991

Transport of Group A and Group B subassemblies from the STING plant to the MPD site will be accomplished in one-half day. Agreement for delivery is with Acme Systems Contractor, Co.

Following are the items identified in the agreement as deliverable to MPD:

Item	Date
Hardware (Group A):	
7 storage racks, 10' x 15' x 6'	
Installed at site	Jan. 31, 1991
Final structural, functional checkout	Feb. 10, 1991
Delivered 400 shipping containers	
Installed at site	March 1, 1991
Delivered 1000 size D43A parcel buckets	March 10, 1991
Delivered 600 size D25B parcel buckets	March 10, 1991
Delivered 600 size D12C parcel buckets	March 10, 1991
Overhead track conveyor system	
(1567' non-contiguous linear section, 18 cross-over points, distribution uniform balance, weld supported at 6" intervals)	
Installed at site	April 1, 1991
Final structural, functional checkout	April 5, 1991
Hardware (Group B):	
4 robot transporter units	
(each 300 lb. max. load capacity compatible with three-size parcel buckets, 380 Mh, retrieval at farthest point 8 min.)	
Installed at site	April 6, 1991
Four unit functional checkout	April 8, 1991
Integration checkout, Groups A and B	March 5, 1991
Software Group:	
Submission of software specifications	
to CompuResearch Corp. (CRC)	Sept. 19, 1990
(Installation of DEM-LAN network, four CRC2950 work station terminals and CRC4000 computer, all performed by CRC)	March 5, 1991
(Software-integration checkout, performed by CRC)	April 6, 1991

Final checkout:

Two copies, system operation/maintenance manuals	March 5, 1991
Robot-transporter/CRC4000 integration	April 9, 1991
Benchmark systems test, with parcels	April 12, 1991
Final system checkout, user	April 14, 1991

NAME INDEX

SUBJECT INDEX